Systematic Theology

A HISTORICIST PERSPECTIVE

Other books by Gordon D. Kaufman

RELATIVISM, KNOWLEDGE AND FAITH

THE CONTEXT OF DECISION

Systematic Theology

A HISTORICIST PERSPECTIVE

by Gordon D. Kaufman

Charles Scribner's Sons / New York

1 3 5 7 9 11 13 15 17 19 M/P 20 18 16 14 12 10 8 6 4 2

Printed in the United States of America
Library of Congress Catalog Card Number 78-50761
ISBN 0-684-15796-9

For Dorothy,
intuitive theologian

Preface*

THE APPEARANCE of a new work in Christian systematic theology calls, perhaps, for some justification on the part of the author. This is particularly the case today—a time of rapid cultural change, of fragmentation, and even of chaos. The proper context for such work, many contend, is a more orderly and stable cultural period, when faith knows itself well and is able to express itself with conviction. In our own time of religious doubt and cultural pluralism the most that we can, or should, attempt, are pieces of occasional theology, tracts for the times, hortatory or critical essays.

My conviction, however, is that—precisely in this time of confusion and doubt—we need not only insightful essays on this or that aspect of Christian tradition or this or that contemporary problem, but new proposals which set forth Christian faith in the round. We need to see whether Christian faith has an integrity and a consistency of its own which make it worthy of our attention, and whether it can sufficiently integrate and illuminate the diverse and often contradictory dimensions of our modern experience, to give our lives some integrity and meaning. We need to see whether it is possible for thinking oriented on the Christ-event to make sense of the great variety of intellectual, cultural and religious currents of our time, or whether such an orientation can no longer properly lay claim upon us. Issues of this sort cannot be addressed in the brief essay or the critical monograph: what is required is exposition of Christian

* The first seven pages of the Preface are derived from the original Preface written in 1968. The second half of the Preface was written in 1977.

faith in its wholeness, enabling us to see how our entire modern existence—political, scientific, cultural, historical, private—looks when grasped in Christian terms. Only systematic theologies, drawing on the vast linguistic and conceptual resources of Christian doctrine which was developed to interpret all sides of human experience, can speak to such needs. It is very much to be hoped that a number of systematic statements of Christian doctrine, each with its distinctive proposal for understanding the significance and import of Christian faith for contemporary life, will appear in the next few years. For only in this way will we be able to see which option or combination of options has relevance and validity for our time. If none do, Christian faith itself may be coming to its end as a significant human reality.

Christian theology—being rooted in and an attempt to explicate Christian faith—seeks to grasp our common human existence in the light of God's revelation in Jesus Christ. It should not be supposed, however, that this implies a deliberate submission to heteronomous authority, whether of church, Bible, or even God. A thinker may never give up his moral and epistemological autonomy and integrity in the search for truth: he can recognize and honestly declare as true only what he himself can perceive to be the truth. However, no man searching out this difficult path cuts an entirely new, untried trail; each is heavily dependent on the work and insights of those who have gone before. Indeed, for the most part, one's intellectual work is the rediscovery of landmarks others have pointed out. Inevitably he thinks and works in terms of some tradition, some point of view, some basic orientation. What distinguishes the Christian theologian from many philosophers is his conscious awareness of the tradition which sustains his thoughts, and his explicit acknowledgment of dependence on the events which created and formed that tradition. His work is rooted in the conviction that it is through an understanding of those events that the real meaning of human existence is grasped. Hence, the concern of theology to relate those decisive events to contemporary existence arises not out of slavish subservience to external authority, but out of the sincere and responsible pursuit of truth itself. In this respect theological claims and contentions are not restricted in import to the community of faith but are of general human significance.

The present work has been composed in the conviction that many of the problems, both of contemporary theology and of the Christian witness to the contemporary world, are rooted in a great fogginess about the theological conceptions of history, historical knowledge, and revelation. Although much is said about the significance of the fact that Christianity is a "historical religion," seldom is the full import of these words carried through consistently into every crevice and corner of the theological interpretation of faith. Moreover, the relationship between the *Heilsgeschichte* with which Christian faith is especially concerned and the ordinary, workaday, secular history in which all of us live every moment of our lives remains almost entirely unspecified. So despite its interest in "history" the Christian faith appears to many moderns to be in fact completely irrelevant to the only history which they know.

The interpretation of the Christian faith found in this work seeks to meet this problem by giving at every point a radically *historicist*[1] view of the Christian perspective and its major doctrines. By this I do not mean to suggest that we shall approach faith from some perspective alien to it, evaluating it by norms drawn from some external source. The theological revolution of the last generation has taught us that such procedures are fatal for theology. Rather, I propose here to take the allegedly "historical" character of Christian faith with absolute seriousness, exploring, as a kind of "experiment in thought" (Kierkegaard), what the various Christian doctrines mean when understood essentially as attempts to grapple with and interpret the nature and meaning of history and man's historicity, and what man's historical existence looks like when its structure is analyzed with the aid of the key concepts found in the Christian tradition. If through this procedure many of the obscurities and supposed absurdi-

---

[1] I am aware, of course, that the term "historicism" has been used in a variety of ways to indicate this or that interpretation of history, including positivism, historical determinism, historical relativism, etc. In using this term I am not seeking to identify my views with any that may previously have been intended. I use the word simply because it suggests a viewpoint that understands the world in historical terms, and man in terms of the radical implications of his historicity; and it is precisely this kind of viewpoint that the present analysis attempts to express.

ties of Christian doctrine become intelligible themselves and illuminative of our existence, we can consider our hypothesis of the radically historical character of Christianity in some measure confirmed. If, however, interpretation of Christian doctrine in this historicist vein appears often forced and misleading, the hypothesis will need reformulation, or perhaps must even be discarded entirely. In any case, no attempt is being made here to impose some alien perspective on faith; rather, we are seeking to uncover and develop a perspective inherent in Christian faith itself.

In order fully to justify the claim that this interpretation of Christian faith within the limits of history alone (to adapt a phrase of Kant) can properly be called *Christian* theology, one would have to show in some detail its continuity with the important statements of Christian faith from the biblical literature to the present. Such a program would require not only learning far greater than mine, but also such a mass of cumbersome historical interpretation and detailed documentation as to defeat my purpose of presenting in relatively compact scope an interpretation of the Christian perspective. Indeed, were such attempted, my desire to set forth clearly the unity and consistency of Christian faith, when seen in historicist terms, would be swallowed up in the proliferation of detailed argumentation. I have, therefore, not presented the kind of full documentation which, in the last analysis, would be required to substantiate this aspect of the present argument, even though this is a rather serious limitation for a position which puts so much emphasis on the historical foundations of life and thought. For the same reasons I have avoided much explicit discussion of principal alternative positions in the contemporary theological scene, although at many points I have referred to those positions.

In evaluating a particular theological point of view like the present one, there are two primary questions that should be considered. (a) What understanding of Christian faith is here being proposed? What positive merit has this understanding and what are its limitations or deficiencies, and by what criteria are such evaluations to be made? (b) How has this understanding of faith expressed itself in theological method? How has theological doctrine been

generated and developed here, and by what criteria is it criticized?
Has the theological method been carried through consistently or only
haphazardly? What strengths do the proposed criteria and procedures
have? What weaknesses? In the course of the present work criteria
for assessing the validity of theological judgments and interpretations
will be defined as carefully as possible. But it must be recognized, of
course, that all such norms and standards are developed from *within*
the perspective itself, and we should never make the mistake of supposing they have finality. The ultimate arbiter of theological validity
is not reason or experience or the Bible or the church, but the movement of history itself—understood theologically: the providence of
God. It is this movement which in actual fact sorts out the valid from
the invalid, the significant from the insignificant. Try as we may we
cannot change this; hence, in this work it will be forthrightly recognized. In so doing, the inevitably tentative character of all our formulations of theological criteria, theological methods, and theological
doctrines will also be acknowledged, however necessary it is that we
seek finality in and through them.

The present work in systematic theology suggests a way to think
about Christian faith, and it tries to show that many theological issues
are resolved if one thinks in this way, but it does not develop the many
important related philosophical questions. It has been possible only
to suggest the directions such investigation might take, namely, toward
a historicist metaphysics of history; in this work I have not been able
to pursue that investigation itself. To do so would have required
working through all the major metaphysical questions (as I have here
tried to work through the major theological issues) from a historicist
point of view. Suffice it to say that such a metaphysics would emphasize process more than structure, would utilize "creativity," "purpose"
and "freedom" as fundamental categories, and would attempt to
develop a cosmology in which the world as a whole was seen as a
"history" and fundamental reality was seen as quasi-personal (i.e.,
as "God"). In chapters 2, 3, 4, 6, 12, 18, 19 and 20 of the present
work will be found the most frequent references to, and thus the most
explicit suggestions regarding, this metaphysics. But its main lines
cannot even be adumbrated here, and the serious (philosophical)

questions which arise from, for example, attempting (as in the present work) to think of God as "purposive" and "personal," or from viewing all thought and value as consistently relative to its historical and psychological context, and the like, can scarcely even be alluded to.[2]

It would not be possible to name and properly acknowledge all who have contributed to the thinking and work which went into this volume. There are some, however, whose help was so direct and specific that they must be mentioned here. The first draft of much of this work was prepared in 1961–62 during a sabbatical leave in Tuebingen, Germany, a leave made possible by a Fulbright Fellowship and a grant from the Howard Foundation. During the years of writing and rewriting I have benefited from criticism and discussion of various portions of this material by Professors Leander Keck of Vanderbilt Divinity School and Warren Groff of Bethany Biblical Seminary, as well as by remarks and suggestions and insights of many of the students who attended my lectures in systematic theology both at Vanderbilt and Harvard; these critics have enabled me to clarify many points that would otherwise be more obscure than they now are, and they have saved me from some serious errors. My wife Dorothy and my children have helped me in innumerable ways with proofreading, checking of references, and the like; Mr. Ralph Lazzaro has helped me with the galleys and with some matters of syntactical and grammatical form, Mr. George Rupp with certain theological and stylistic issues, and Mr. Wayne Proudfoot with proofreading and preparation of the indexes. I am very grateful to Mrs. Arthur Kooman for patiently typing and retyping draft after draft of the manuscript. Finally, I want to thank President Donald Miller and the faculty of the Pittsburgh Theological Seminary for their invitation to deliver the Schaff Lectures in the fall of 1967 and for the cordial reception they accorded me on that occasion; the material for those lectures was drawn from several chapters in Parts Two and Three of this volume.

[2] It should be noted that many of the epistemological, and some of the metaphysical, issues connected with my point of view, particularly in its relativistic aspects, have already been dealt with in my earlier book, *Relativism, Knowledge and Faith* (Chicago: University of Chicago Press, 1960). The reader interested in such questions is referred to that work.

The following publishers have given permission for extensive quotations from works to which they hold the copyright:

Cambridge University Press, for an extract from *Grace and Personality* by John Oman; George Allen & Unwin Ltd., for a quotation from *Symbolism and Belief* by Edwin Bevan; Harper & Row, for excerpts from *Jesus: Lord and Christ* by John Knox and *The Theology of Saint Luke* by Hans Conzelmann; New Directions Publishing Corporation, for an extract from *Suddenly Last Summer* by Tennessee Williams; Oxford University Press, for quotations from *The Epistle to the Romans* by Karl Barth and *Faith and Culture* by B. E. Meland; T. & T. Clark, for excerpts from *Church Dogmatics* by Karl Barth; and The Westminster Press, for quotations from *Christology of the Later Fathers*, LCC, Vol. III, edited by Edward R. Hardy. In addition, Professor Henry N. Wieman has kindly given permission to quote from his book, *The Source of Human Good*.

Unless otherwise indicated, the Bible text in this publication is from the Revised Standard Version of the Bible, copyrighted 1946 and 1952 by the Division of Christian Education of the National Council of Churches, and used by permission.

Where the abbreviation NEB appears, the text has been drawn from *The New English Bible, New Testament.* © The Delegates of the Oxford University Press and The Syndics of the Cambridge University Press 1961, and is reprinted by permission.

G.D.K.
July, 1968

In the ten years or more since I wrote *Systematic Theology: A Historicist Perspective* my understanding of the methods and tasks of theological work has undergone important changes, but my view of the basic meaning and thrust of Christian faith remains substantially the same. I now see much more sharply and clearly how radically *constructive* is theological work. It is true that I already understood theology to be largely constructive when I wrote *Systematic Theology*. I saw that what the theologian must do is present a coherent and full interpretation of life and the world from the Christian point of view

—a kind of Christian world-view—and that this required bringing
the major Christian doctrines into systematic interconnection, showing how they presupposed and implied each other as they each
expressed some feature or aspect of the Christian understanding of
life, criticizing and reinterpreting each in the light of the others to
which it must be systematically related. Furthermore, I was clear that
the only way in which a doctrine of God could be developed was
through systematic imaginative construction. Since God is not directly
available to us simply to describe, as are the objects of this world,
we put together our doctrine of God through the conjunction and
combination of various models and metaphors drawn from ordinary
life, extrapolating and developing them in such a way as to enable
them to represent and express that which faith takes as ultimate
reality.

However, I did not yet understand how far-reaching are the
implications of this constructive activity of the theologian. I took it
for granted that the theologian's task was simply construction of a
Christian world-view and conception of God, largely on the basis of
images and concepts given in and through the Christian tradition.
Theological work had two phases: it began in the appreciation and
appropriation of the main claims of the various Christian doctrines
which have developed historically, and then it sought to put these
pieces together into a coherent and intelligible pattern. Through most
of Christian history theologians have accepted such a traditionalist
orientation as the basis on which they did their work. Whether that
which was regarded as authoritative for the theologian was scripture,
or the creeds or confessions or official dogmas of some church, or a
body of more vaguely defined and articulated beliefs held by the
community to which the theologian belonged, the basic understanding
of theology was the same: the theologian's primary business was to
presuppose the essential truth of what is given in (the accepted)
tradition and, on that presupposition, to occupy himself or herself
with interpreting it.

This understanding of theology is basically authoritarian in
character. That which earlier authorities have declared or revealed
is made the basis of the theologian's work, and theological "proof"

often consists simply in showing that what the theologian is saying today corresponds with or is suggested by the position of some earlier writer (preferably biblical).

To put the matter this baldly makes theological work appear to be simply slavish submission to the past, but few if any theologians have had such a self-understanding. This is because there is a theological interpretation of this authoritarian character of theology which takes away the sting: the doctrine of revelation performs this function. According to this doctrine, theological work is not simply interpretation of mere human tradition. The revelation of God—the One who is Ultimate Reality and the source and foundation of all Truth—underlies the tradition and is its real warrant. For this reason, it is claimed, the authoritarian structure of theology is not really heteronomous and humanly destructive; on the contrary, precisely this structure makes possible the human appropriation of genuine truth—God's Truth—and is thus actually liberating and saving. The traditional claims that the Bible is the "word of God," or that Jesus is the "revelation of God," or that the doctrine of the trinity is a "truth of revelation" are all attempts to legitimize the fundamentally authoritarian character of Christian theology by holding that it is concerned with matters which could not have been discovered by mere human intelligence but which are the indispensable source of true human freedom and salvation.

The authority–structure of faith and theology runs very deep in Christian thinking. Many of the principal traditional symbols directly express this structure—e.g., "Lord," "Kingdom of God," "commandments" of God, "slaves of Christ"—and they are used in such a way as to create an overall pattern which is coherent and mutually reinforcing. According to this picture all created reality (including human beings) has its origin and being in the Creator's purposes and action, and lives now under God's sovereign lordship; to be a creature is to have gained one's very being through the will of another, and it involves continuing to live under the authority of that Other who is the giver of every good and perfect gift. Thus, the fulfilment of human existence and the meaning of human life are to be found in loving and faithful obedience to the divine will. Included within such obedience, of course, and the presupposition which makes it possible, is acceptance of God's revelation as the light of life and the ultimate source of all saving truth. The revelation is vouchsafed to us through scripture and tradition, so it is the Christian tradition which transmits to us and makes available to us the truth about God, humanity and the world. Thus, the authority of the theological tradition rests upon and is believed to be authorized by the ultimate authority of God, and God's authority is in turn expressed and perpetuated through the continued use of the authoritarian symbols of this same tradition. The circle is complete. The position is fully coherent and intelligible, and its authoritarian structure seems legitimately grounded and fully warranted. The business of theology, now, is to formulate and interpret this whole position as clearly and meaningfully as possible. That is the understanding of the theological task which informs the present *Systematic Theology*.

There is, as it seems to me now, a serious flaw in this position: it takes for granted too easily and uncritically that "God's revelation" is a kind of objectively given reality to which the contemporary theologian can or must subject himself or herself. The very images on which symbols like "revelation" are based suggest a kind of interpersonal over-againstness between God and human beings such that God can and does communicate to humans as one person among us communicates to another (see chs. 2 and 3), and we are thus led to think of God's "Word" as objective to us like a spoken word—an uttered noise—of one of our fellows. But that is a fallacy. Divine revelation is never present to us as an objective reality, directly accessible to us and inspectable by us. The only way in which it is ever present to us is in the form of human constructions—human words, symbols, ideas. "God's revelation" is itself an idea by means of which we explain to ourselves how it is possible that One transcendent of the whole human order (this also is a complex idea) becomes known to those of us in that order. But neither what is called "God" nor "God's revelation" are objectively or directly present to us at all. Both are known to us and imagined by us only in and through symbols and images which we ourselves have constructed. "Revelation" and "God" are imaginative constructs created by the human mind as it seeks to give our existence the sort of order and meaning which arises when our consciousness and life are focused on an appropriate and adequate object of devotion and loyalty.

It is now clear to me, therefore, that a properly conceived systematic theology should not begin with simple acceptance of the givenness of "revelation" (as in the present work). This simply perpetuates the authoritarian structure of theology and makes it difficult to see at what points the tradition is to be seriously criticized and reconceived. On the contrary, a theology should begin in a careful analysis of the way in which, and the reasons why, the human mind finds it appropriate, and even necessary, to create and use the concept of God [see my *Essay on Theological Method* (Missoula, Montana: Scholar's Press, 1975)]; and it should seek to define as clearly as possible criteria for the proper construction of this concept and its correct use. Only when this is done, when we understand why we are engaging in "God-talk" at all, are we in a position to grasp what the theological enterprise is all about and how to carry it out correctly. At some point further down the road the question can be raised whether, and in what respects, it is appropriate and necessary not only to speak of "God" but also of "God's revelation." This will depend on how God is conceived: some conceptions of God seem completely incompatible with notions of revelation; others highly consistent. Any talk of "God's revelation" always presupposes a particular and definite concept of God. For this reason, a properly ordered theology must begin with the grounds for constructing the concept of God, and the reasons for constructing it in this way rather than that.

Thus, both the beginning point and the general methodological orientation of this present work are misconceived. The whole authoritarian structure which they presuppose and articulate needs to be replaced by a position which candidly acknowledges the fully constructive character of theology.

These methodological strictures, however, do not invalidate the interpretation of Christian faith found in this book. I am still prepared to argue that the image of the crucified one, spread from its obscure origins in first-century Palestine throughout the world, must remain a highly important normative influence in shaping any adequate modern understanding of what constitutes the genuinely human. I remain persuaded that sin and salvation are best understood as radically historical realities, and that historicity is the very form of human existence. I still want to maintain that the conception of God should be thoroughly reconstructed in terms of the image of the crucified one, and that the atonement can be most adequately understood as a historical process transforming human existence, a process which had its beginnings in the ministry and death of Jesus but which continued and grew through the establishment and spread of the Christian community and is now working very widely in and through the struggles for humanization throughout the world.

But if I were now to rewrite these chapters much would have to be changed. For example, my present understanding of the significance of the fact that the notion of God is our own construct, and not something we receive directly from on high, would require a thorough transformation of the heavily objectivistic talk of God found in this text. God is presented here rather straightforwardly in terms of such anthropomorphic metaphors as "lord," "father," and "creator," and traditional language about God's "faithfulness," "love" and "forgiveness" is not qualified in any serious way. Despite insistence that all these terms are being used only "analogically," their objectivistic form gives the appearance of much more detailed and intimate "knowledge of God" than can properly be claimed: our concepts seem to be providing us with reasonably adequate descriptions of what the divine being really is. This objectivism has a number of unfortunate consequences. The picture of faith to which it can lead, for instance, may give the appearance of a kind of easy familiarity with God; in some passages of the present work this manifests itself in a sort of sentimentality, or even gushiness, of style. Conversely, this same objectivistic imagery encourages an understanding of sinfulness as a kind of straightforward "turning away" from God, and in this book this is then connected much too simplistically with the increasing momentum of secularity in modern culture. A fuller recognition that the idea of God with which we work is always our òwn *imaginative construct*, put together entirely by ourselves out of various anthropomorphic and other images and models drawn from experience, would alert us to linguistic traps of this sort and should help guard us from too easily trivializing in such ways as these the ultimate Mystery within which human life falls.

Breaking free from the authoritarian traditionalist orientation would transform this work in other significant ways. Since the present book assumes the fundamental truth of the Christian position—this, it is held, is a matter to be taken "on faith"—it can be of real interest only to those (mostly Christians) who are attempting to make sense of the more or less traditional faith which they hold. In this respect the work is rather narrow in its vision and parochial in its appeal. A new work, written with the above-mentioned methodological concerns in mind, would have a much broader audience in view. In beginning with the problem why we do and should engage in talk about God, it would be addressing the fundamental question of what human life is really all about. It would thus be raising issues of universal human concern from the outset, and on the basis of these fundamental human questions the interpretation of Christian faith would be approached. Instead of presupposing the essential truth of the Christian perspective, and then trying to show how this perspective interprets various human problems, such a theology would seek to develop a more general anthropological foundation as the basis for elaborating the character and importance of Christian faith; thus, it would deal with distinctively Christian contentions only where these are clearly of more than merely parochial interest. This would not involve giving up a Christocentric orientation in theology, but such an orientation could no longer be simply presupposed as a "given" of "faith"; rather, it would be developed in terms of its basic human significance. Such a theology would not limit its audience to those who are already adherents of, or at least attracted to, the Christian faith, but would be written for anyone with an interest in fundamenal human problems.

This change in orientation would affect the style of presentation and argument in important ways. The present work assumed that the task of the theologian is essentially one of up-dating Christian doctrine, and it is thus heavy with traditional terminology and images, and with biblical references. The felt necessity to use concepts and terms, created in another cultural context for different purposes, sometimes produced an almost allegorical sort of interpretation, as the attempt was made to wring contemporary meaning or illumination out of this or that detail of an ancient myth or traditional doctrinal formulation (see, e.g., what is said about the "pre-existence of Christ" on pp. 204f., or about eating fruit from the tree of "the knowledge of good and evil" on pp. 352ff., or the note on infralapsarianism and supralapsarianism on p. 383). With an understanding of theology as fully constructive in character, such heavy reliance on and use of past images and doctrines would become less necessary, and much of it would quite properly disappear. Moreover, if the criteria guiding theological construction in the present were explicitly set forth, it would become possible to develop more forthright and self-conscious criticism of the theological concepts, terminology and images inherited from the past, including those found in the Bible, and, one hopes, it would be possible to avoid some of their more blatant confusions, prejudices, and distortions. To mention just one example: the present work was written in complete unconsciousness of the sexist language of almost the entire biblical and Christian tradition, and itself expresses that sexism at every point; with clearly formulated criteria of theological criticism and construction, one should be more alert to such matters and thus in a position forthrightly to criticize and thoroughly to reconstruct, or outrightly reject, such traditional formulations.

I have not had the time, nor do I at present have the inclination, to attempt a full revision of this work along these lines, so the text has been allowed to stand as originally printed. Proper revision would have required everything to be rewritten—and yet the interpretation of human historicity and Christian faith would in many important ways remain the same. I hope that these remarks will give readers a clear indication of what in these pages seems to me still worth saying, and what needs thoroughgoing reformulation.

G.D.K.
August, 1977

Contents

Part Two

THE CHRISTIAN UNDERSTANDING OF THE WORLD:
THE DOCTRINES OF CREATION, PROVIDENCE,
AND THE ESCHATON

Part Three

THE CHRISTIAN UNDERSTANDING OF MAN: THE DOCTRINES
OF THE *Imago Dei*, SIN, AND SALVATION

Part Four

**THE CHRISTIAN UNDERSTANDING OF THE
REDEEMED LIFE: THE DOCTRINES OF THE CHURCH
AND SACRAMENTS, DISCIPLESHIP AND FAITH**

Faith must be built upon history.

MARTIN LUTHER

Over against every naturalistic and impersonal understanding of God, Christianity always turns toward personalistic religion, decisively and in principle. . . . The religious valuation of history—above all its center, the personality of Jesus—is therefore the fundamental presupposition. . . .

ERNST TROELTSCH

To discern the ways of God not in supernatural but in all natural and historic events, to respond to his intention present in and beyond and through all finite intentions, that is the way of responsibility to God. H. RICHARD NIEBUHR

Introduction

REVELATION AND THEOLOGICAL

KNOWLEDGE

> *Is an historical point of departure*
> *possible for an eternal consciousness;*
> *. . . is it possible to base an eternal*
> *happiness upon historical knowledge?*
>
> S. KIERKEGAARD

1 / The Theological Enterprise

Before we begin to explore the Christian faith itself, through examining the doctrine of revelation, it is necessary to come to some preliminary understanding of the kind of cognitive enterprise in which we are engaged. It must be recognized, of course, that what can be said at this point about the nature of theology will be at best only provisional and sketchy. Properly speaking, the character of the theological enterprise can be discerned and thus discussed only after we have some understanding of its peculiar foundation, revelation; and an adequate understanding of what is involved will be forthcoming only as we work through the full exposition and interpretation of the Christian faith. Then, in retrospect, we can see more clearly what has been going on. However, to avoid misunderstanding, it is important to make a few preliminary observations.

All learning, it could be argued, is vocabulary study. It begins with words and meanings that in some sense we know and understand; it develops through processes in which we learn to criticize those meanings which we had taken for granted, and through which they become broadened and deepened as we explore levels and depths we had not previously apprehended; it grows as we come to relate these simpler and more primitive notions to new and more complex words and meanings which we had not known before. The increase of learning, thus, can be viewed as increasing mastery of language. Such mastery, of course, is never achieved through mere rote memorizing of words. Our language does not exist in a vacuum, but is the articulation of, and an instrument facilitating, the grasping and control of experience. Thus, a growing sensitivity to certain subtle musical nuances is both accompanied and in part made possible by a growing musical vocabulary, especially developed to facilitate apprehension and expression of these distinctions; a developing skill in the biology laboratory or on the athletic field is both accompanied and facilitated by the acquiring of a vocabulary appropriate to the operations involved. Who could understand the meaning of such a term as "minor chord" without the appropriate musical experience? Can one really understand what the word "chopsticks" means until he tries, and learns, to use them? The genuine mastery of words arises in a deepening and widening experience, and such an enlarging of our world occurs only in connection with a complex linguistic development. To say, then, that increase of learning can be regarded as largely the building of vocabulary is not to claim that knowledge is simply mental and verbal in character; it is to point, rather, to the fact that the mental and verbal dimensions of our experience are inseparably wedded to the rest of life, and to remember how central to our humanness is the fact that we speak.[1]

Each of the several branches of learning can be regarded in this way as a specialized development of the common language in the direction of a precise and technical vocabulary and symbolism especially adapted to the apprehension, interpretation, and control of a particular limited region of experience. In some cases, for example, physics, this development has moved so far from ordinary discourse—as the investigation of experience has led to increasingly general and abstract symbolical formulations—that it has become virtually impossible for the layman to understand the language employed without considerable highly technical training. In other cases, for example, history, which attempts to describe the life of a man or a time more or less concretely, it has been possible and necessary to continue to use ordinary language to a much greater extent; historical writing, therefore, is generally comprehensible to the intelligent layman. Neither the development of a highly technical and esoteric language

[1] For a radical and profound development of this thesis that man's very being is bound up with, and, indeed, grounded in, his speaking, see G. H. Mead, *Mind, Self and Society* (Chicago: University of Chicago Press, 1934). For a fuller statement of my own position on the fundamental role of language for human being, see my *Relativism, Knowledge and Faith* (Chicago: University of Chicago Press, 1960), esp. Pt. II.

in the sciences nor the failure to develop one in some of the humanistic disciplines is to be particularly applauded or deplored; the appropriateness of the language to the task undertaken is the only relevant consideration.

Theology, also, is a study and refinement of the use of certain words, as the etymology of the term itself suggests: *theos-logos*— words or speech about God. The central term to be investigated here, *God*, is drawn from common discourse. This does not mean, of course, that its meaning is either simple or apparent; but it does mean that theology is not concerned with some esoteric or private subject matter, of little or no relation to the experience and concerns of ordinary people. Everyone who speaks English learns the word "God" along with all the other words which go to make up his vocabulary. It may be that for many the most common usage of this word is in oaths, or that they regard it as useful primarily in relatively insignificant contexts such as a church building on a Sunday morning, or as having a largely perfunctory meaning appropriate to inscriptions on coins; but in any case the word "God" is known and used by everyone who speaks English.[2] Despite this fact that the word is never equivalent to a mere "X," its meaning is by no means self-evident and unquestioned, and there are many who believe that it no longer has usefulness or significance and should probably—if that were possible—be eliminated from the vocabulary. Theology, now, is the study devoted particularly to uncovering, exploring, and interpreting the meaning of this word.

This does not mean that our methods here will be primarily philological and historical, although that might be one legitimate way to proceed. Rather than investigate the historical process through which the word came to mean what it does, we shall be concerned

[2] It should be observed here that this fact shows that two familiar and apparently opposed positions rest on the same misconception. (a) The Barthian claim that it is possible to define the meaning of "God" *exhaustively* in terms of the Christ-event overlooks the fact that this term already has a meaning for us when we begin our christological investigations, and it is precisely because of this meaning which *it already has* that we choose to use this term and not some other in speaking of Christ. (b) The secularist's or positivist's claim that the term is "meaningless" or simply "unknown" to him is also false, for as a user of English he has learned *some* meaning for this term which enables him to say it is precisely *this* term and *this* meaning that he does not fully grasp.

here with its logical structure; with the various layers and levels of meaning in it and its connections with and implications for the meanings of other words; with criteria for distinguishing more from less significant dimensions of meaning in the word, more from less valid ways of using and interpreting it. These problems are admittedly all difficult in the extreme, but it should be evident that only a careful treatment of them could possibly establish the real meaning or usefulness of the word, or could justify discarding it.

The *Oxford English Dictionary* gives the primary meaning of "God" in the English language as follows: "A superhuman person . . . who is worshipped as having power over nature and the fortunes of mankind"; since for most English usage this general meaning has become qualified by specifically Christian and monotheistic notions, one must add that "God" is generally conceived as "the One object of supreme adoration; the Creator and Ruler of the Universe."[3]

There are two motifs in these definitions to which we must attend. In the first place, the image which the word "God" calls forth is of a personal being, one who has power to will and to act, and who can and does rule the sphere over which he has sovereignty. But this is no ordinary person; this is a "superhuman person" who has brought into being and who reigns over the entirety of the universe, including both the natural order and mankind. This being must be regarded, therefore, in the second place, not as a part or dimension of the world, or as one "in" the world, but as in some significant way "outside" the world and from this position actively working in and on it; for the world is the object of his creative labors and is subject to his sovereign command, as the clay receives its form from the hand of the potter or the slave his orders from the king. I am of course not arguing at this point that such a world-transcendent super-person exists, but only that it is the image of some such being that the word "God" conjures up in English discourse. Notions of a "man upstairs," or a "cosmic mathematician," or an old man with a long flowing beard keeping careful books on our moral and less-than-moral behavior, are all developments and refinements of this same image; so also is speech about God

---

[3] *A New English Dictionary on Historical Principles*, ed. J. A. H. Murray (Oxford: Clarendon Press, 1901), IV, Pt. 2, 267–268.

as "Father" or "King" or "Judge," and the belief that he "creates" and "redeems," "loves" and "forgives" and "punishes" men: the universal use of the personal pronoun "he" (instead of "it") to refer to God confirms the centrality of the personalistic motif.

We should note some important features of this more or less commonly accepted meaning for the term. The notion appears to be obviously "mythological," since it involves the conception of a being somehow "outside of" or "beyond" the world of our experience yet defined and conceived in terms of images drawn from *within* our experience (God is a "super-person").[4] Because in our time truth and even meaning are increasingly conceived in terms of directly experienced and experienceable realities, such mythological conceptions and ways of thinking have become highly suspect to many, and it may even be claimed that the idea of God can be given no consistent content or meaning.[5] It should be observed, however, that precisely this *transcendent* motif in the idea enhances its theological significance, for it is this which makes possible conceiving God as of universal, and not merely parochial or limited, significance. Standing "outside" the world as its creator, God is significantly related to every dimension, phase, and being "within" the world, and can be reduced to or equated with none. As the one being significant for all other beings, he is the only proper "object of supreme adoration."

At this point we cannot do more than note the fact and importance of these "mythological" notions. Until in the course of our analysis we are able to examine how such notions are to be understood and interpreted, we shall have to proceed tentatively in terms of the quasi-mythological way of speaking about God characteristic of our ordi-

---

[4] Cf. R. Bultmann's definition of mythological language: "Mythology is the use of imagery to express the otherworldly in terms of this world and the divine in terms of human life, the other side in terms of this side" ("New Testament and Mythology," in H. W. Bartsch, ed., *Kerygma and Myth* [New York: Harper & Row, 1961], p. 10, n. 2).

[5] For reference to some of the literature together with some discussion of this problem see my papers on "Two Models of Transcendence" (*The Heritage of Christian Thought, Essays in Honor of Robert L. Calhoun*, ed. R. E. Cushman and E. Grislis [New York: Harper & Row, 1965]) and "On the Meaning of 'God': Transcendence without Mythology" (*Harvard Theological Review* [1966], 59:105–132). In the latter paper I have argued that it is important to distinguish between "mythological" and "analogical" views of God; for, although the former may well be no longer tenable, the latter can be defended. The present work will attempt to develop an *analogical* (not mythological) doctrine of God.

nary language. Although the degree and the respects in which this fundamental conception of a transcendent super-person is adequate or true or even intelligible may be doubted, that some such image is intended in ordinary English usage when the word "God" (or its equivalents in other Western languages) is uttered seems unquestionable, and this is understood by so-called atheists and believers alike. All discourse about God, therefore, in some sense presupposes this underlying meaning and is a development, qualification, or refinement of it; and *our* discourse, until we have had opportunity properly to qualify it, also must begin here.[6] If this underlying meaning were not presupposed, the discourse would not be intelligible either within the church or without. The central problem of theology is to develop and refine criteria or standards in terms of which the adequacy of this underlying meaning can be measured and by means of which it can be modified and reshaped into a more appropriate and intelligible conception, one with some claim to truth.

How shall we proceed with this task? The project is immeasurably simplified by the fact that it is a *Christian* theology we are here seeking to develop. Our question thus becomes that of the sources and bases of *Christian* criteria and standards for developing the conception of God. Even if our interests here were not in this way focussed, there would be some general philosophical and cultural justification for proceeding directly to the question of Christian norms, for the Christian understanding of "God" has so decisively shaped the meaning of the word in all Western languages that a totally "unChristian" or "nonChristian" meaning (whatever that might be) would hardly be recognizable to modern Americans and Europeans. Indeed, it can be argued that precisely the Christian conception lies hidden within the popular notion as its deepest and truest meaning,[7] and that therefore to come to genuine understanding of ordinary usage, we must explore the Christian concept contained within it and presupposed by it. But whatever may be the full historical truth and thus justification of

---

[6] ". . . ordinary language is *not* the last word: in principle it can everywhere be supplemented and improved upon and superseded. Only remember, it *is* the *first* word" (J. L. Austin, *Philosophical Papers* [New York: Oxford University Press, 1961], p. 133).

[7] For elaboration of the way in which the Christian concept has come to shape all Western thinking on this problem, see E. Gilson, *God and Philosophy* (New Haven: Yale University Press, 1941).

our approach, our central concern here is to move from this common notion to a more adequate Christian theological understanding; so we shall turn at once to a consideration of how to proceed toward that objective.

Central to Christian faith is the belief that God has made himself known in some decisive or definitive way in and through the one whom faith calls his "Son," the man Jesus Christ. "No one has ever seen God," says the writer of the Fourth Gospel, "the only Son, who is in the bosom of the Father, he has made him known" (1:18). "In many and various ways," says the writer of the Epistle to the Hebrews, "God spoke of old to our fathers by the prophets; but in these last days he has spoken to us by a Son . . . [who] reflects the glory of God and bears the very stamp of his nature" (1:1–3). ". . . in the face of Christ," says Paul, we are given the very "light of the knowledge of the glory of God" (2 Cor. 4:6); "He is the image of the invisible God" (Col. 1:15). "He who has seen me," says the Johannine Jesus, "has seen the Father" (John 14:9). We cannot at this point consider in detail the Christian understanding of revelation through Jesus Christ; that conception will be explored in the next two chapters. It is necessary to observe at this point, however, that whatever else God's revelation means, it involves at least the contention that somehow at this point in human history God is known and is to be known, that at this place the reality indicated by the word "God" is to be found. If we wish, then, to develop criteria and norms in terms of which an adequate meaning for our term can be elaborated, we will seek to do so by reference to this person-event. Indeed, this is what it means to say we are setting forth a "Christian" understanding of God: that we turn to the Christ-event for the definitive notions with which we carry through our work. It is to be emphasized that this does not mean that systematic theology after all is simply a historical exploration of the ideas of the early Christians, which are then taken to be normative for Christian thought, much as the ideas of Plato might be normative for a Platonist; the way in which the Christ-event plays its decisive role in and for Christian theology is much more complicated than that and will require rather careful analysis. But there is this similarity: the claim that God has in fact revealed himself in Christ means that the proper understanding of the word "God" is not to be derived simply from studies of contemporary or past usage of that word; it is to be in some way derived from and measured by what is given in and through a particular historical event of two thousand years ago.[8]

We are now in a position to state fairly concisely what systematic theology is and what the procedure to be followed in the present work will be. From what has been said it should be clear that theological work involves a double reference: to meanings in the present situation, and to a historical norm. Each must be brought into relation to the other in such a way that, on the one hand, the present meaning becomes decisively informed and transformed by the historical norm, and, on the other hand, the almost forgotten normative meaning becomes once again a living and effective reality in the present.

There are several ways in which this could be accomplished. One could proceed, for example, with a historical methodology. Thus one could (as has been suggested very briefly in this chapter) begin with an analysis of present conceptions of God, exploring their various levels of meaning, their ramifications, and implications; and then attempt to judge, criticize, and reformulate those conceptions by reference to the historical event implicitly referred to by them (because it was most decisively formative of them), the Christ-event. It would also be possible—with somewhat more difficulty, perhaps, in maintaining contemporary relevance—to follow a more traditional type of historical exposition, beginning with an analysis of the Christ-event and then showing both how that event decisively shaped unfolding Western conceptions of God and how it can be the norm in terms of which present conceptions can be measured and redefined.

Though such explicitly historical ways of dealing with the theological problem are both important and necessary, the most they could show would be a vital historical connection between Jesus Christ and the present; it would be difficult for them to show the universal significance for all of life and, indeed, all of being—a significance

---

[8] It may be observed that the conception of a decisive historical norm in terms of which contemporary life and thought are to be measured is rooted in a distinctively protestant understanding of Christian faith. The reformers' criticism of the Roman church by reference to scripture was based on the assumption that God's revelation had a "classical period," so to speak, in terms of which Christian faith and life were forever afterward to be judged; the witnesses through which we come to know that period, of course, are the documents of scripture.

implicit in the word "God" itself, as we noted above—of this God-defined-by-Christ. To carry through this latter task, systematic theology, in the two thousand years of its history, has found it necessary to develop a special conceptuality making it possible to grasp and understand the entire world of our experience as under the sovereign lordship of the God-defined-by-Christ: built into the very logical structure of Christian theological language is reference to the historical Christ as normative.[9] If we explore this language carefully, therefore, we will not only be involved in criticism and reconstruction of our God-concept in terms of the Christ-event (as we would with a more simply historical approach); we will simultaneously be provided with a way of understanding all experience and life in Christian terms, an achievement which is essential if we are really to grasp what is meant by "God" in Christian faith. Each of the basic concepts of Christian theology and Christian faith—notions such as creation, redemption, trinity, church, revelation, sin, etc.—articulates a dimension or feature of experience or reality in relation to God, and all of them taken together give us an understanding of the world as a whole under God. Systematic theology, therefore, as constructive analysis of the structure and terminology of the Christian language, provides us with both a Christian world-view and an understanding of the meaning and significance of "God."

How should we proceed with such analysis? The Christian conception of ultimate reality, in terms of which all other being and beings must be understood, is developed in the doctrine of God. Hence, before it is possible to discuss rightly the world and man, it is necessary to come to an understanding of what is meant by "God," who, in creating the world and man, was (and is) working toward the realization of certain purposes of his own. But who is this God and how are he and his purposes known? As we have noted, Christian faith is rooted in the belief that God himself has acted to reveal himself in and through the man Jesus. This fact provides us with an appropriate starting point for our theological work.

We shall begin by trying to come to some understanding of what

[9] It might be worth noting here in passing (lest my position be confused with Karl Barth's) that my contention is that the Christ-event is "defining" or "normative" for the concept of God, but not the exclusive or exhaustive source of the content or meaning of that concept.

the concept of revelation means and what justification there might be for introducing such a concept in order to throw light on human experience and knowledge. Then we shall try to see what is meant by the claim that God has revealed himself in Jesus Christ. This analysis of the epistemological foundations of the knowledge of God will bring us into a position from which it is possible to develop the Christian understanding of ultimate reality—the doctrine of God. At that point we shall consider how the historical Christ-event, as normative, enables us to redefine and reconstruct the concept of God from the ordinary images noted above to a precise theological conception with a precisely definable meaning and significance. Only then, having sketched the general framework of understanding in terms of which the world and man are to be understood, will it be possible to turn to created being and to show how man and the world, understood as thoroughly historical realities, express the purposes of God. Finally, having sketched this general context—theological, cosmological, and anthropological—in which we exist, we shall be in a position to deal with the problem of contemporary human life and action.

Thus, this systematic theology, when complete, will provide a perspective and a terminology for apprehending and understanding in their interrelationship the ultimate metaphysical reality (God); the phenomenal realities treated by the several arts and sciences (the world and man); and the subjective realities of decision and purpose, value and meaning, with which ethical and existentialistic analyses have been concerned. Systematic theology—the attempt to come to an adequate understanding of the meaning of the word "God"—must finally lead, if its goal is to be achieved, to a new and more profound understanding of all reality experienced and known by man. In order to take a first step on this path, we turn to a consideration of the concept of revelation.

2 / The Concept of Revelation

CHRISTIAN theology claims to be rooted in God's self-revelation. It is not simply a human creation (though it is that too); it is reflection on, and the reflection of, that which breaks into the circle of human culture from beyond: God's act.

This claim has always scandalized thoughtful and sensitive persons, for it appears to be the expression of supreme arrogance: "We have the truth, you are in error; Christian faith is grounded in a special revelation from on high, all other religions are mere works of man's sinful imagination." Moreover, the claim that God has manifested himself in a special way in Jesus Christ appears to imply that God is unjust, being partial to some men while neglecting others. In principle, truth—especially the truth about the ultimate reality with which man has to do—ought to be equally available to all. In any case, a God who plays favorites in this fashion could hardly be regarded as loving; even a human father knows that it is wrong to discriminate without warrant among his children.

Plausible as these common criticisms may seem on their face, closer examination reveals they are grossly misleading. For no one really believes that all men have equal access to truth and reality. The truth we can or will know is very much conditioned by, among other things, historical and psychological factors. Thus, for example, only a minute portion of mankind ever could come to know the truth which Plato made his own. A Chinese or a barbarian of Plato's time had no opportunity to sit at Plato's feet and learn from him; even among the students of Plato, only a few have had the requisite aptitudes, intelligence, and interests to understand him. And yet, sincere

Platonists hold that in Plato's thought as nowhere else the ultimate truth about the world is laid bare. But if that is the case, then the accessibility of truth is far from equal for all men, whatever the rationalists and idealists may allege. The truth that I can know is in many crucial respects relative to the contingencies and peculiarities of historical circumstance. I cannot and shall not come to know the truth about the world that was available to Einstein any more than I have access to the truth known by an African witch doctor. Doubtless certain changes in my historical and psychological circumstances— such as intensive study of modern physics (provided I am blessed with the necessary mathematical aptitude), or sympathetic participation in the life of a primitive community—might eventually enable me to share in the perceptions and knowledge possible from those perspectives. But this fact only confirms the central point: that the truth known and knowable is always relative to the historical situation of the knower.[1]

The Christian claim, therefore, that God has specially revealed himself in and through the historical development of one community, beginning in remote antiquity and ultimately flowering into a universal church, may involve no scandal at all. For all human culture is characterized by a similar kind of development through historical particularity. Man is a thoroughly historical being: all that we experience and understand is shaped by the ideas and language that structure our consciousness, and this speech and thought are themselves in continuous historical process. It should occasion no great surprise, therefore, to discover that Christian faith likewise has emerged in a particular historical development and that its truth can be grasped only by those whose consciousness has been formed in that same history. Indeed, if it is true that here we are dealing with the *ultimately real,* and not merely superficial or peripheral aspects of experience, it might be expected that a long and complex historical development would be required. Before God could reveal himself definitively to man, careful historical preparation was necessary; and after that decisive manifestation, the process of maturation and

---

[1] For a fuller discussion of the epistemological basis and implications of the relativity of all knowledge and truth, see my *Relativism, Knowledge and Faith* (Chicago: University of Chicago Press, 1960), esp. Pts. I and II.

flowering has been equally complicated. Moreover, if this process is at all like other human and cultural developments, one would expect it to be a continuous historical movement—one particular history— not a diffusion of God-consciousness distributed in equal amounts to every community and every individual.

It is the Christian claim that such a history of God's self-revelation to man is found in the Bible. Doubtless in many respects this history is peculiar, differing sharply from our ordinary secular conceptions at just its central point: the claim to be the story of *God's* dealing with men, not merely the sequence of human events. Nonetheless a history it is, and of the utmost significance if true. The Old Testament contains the records of the long development, believed to go back to the very beginning of human affairs, through which God was so relating himself to man as to prepare the way for a decisive event through which he could make himself known. It was no simple matter to bring man into a situation from which he could recognize and acknowledge the ultimate reality with which he has to do, especially since the demands of that reality go counter to much of what man wants for himself. But finally the ground was prepared and the possibility had emerged of perceiving God's true character and purposes in and through the man Jesus. Even so, however, most of those who encountered Jesus—including the bearers of the particular (Jewish) history through which the preparation had occurred—failed to recognize the real meaning of his appearance and rejected him. Only a few apprehended his significance, and they only after the crisis of his death. But with their acknowledgment a new era in human affairs opened up, characterized in a special way by the knowledge and presence of God. It is an era which, in the Christian view, will close only when all the diverse strands of man's history are taken up into this movement in which God is transforming man, and all mankind thus finds its place in one universal community. "Here there cannot be Greek and Jew, circumcised and uncircumcised, barbarian, Scythian, slave, free man, but Christ is all, and in all" (Col. 3:11).

Thus, the historicity of Christianity, regarded by some as scandalous, is in fact precisely appropriate to the actual nature of history and man's historicity. Moreover, the historical particularity of the movement which flowered into Christian history does not really impugn God's justice. For the main contention here is that God, who finally through this long and painful historical process succeeded in making himself known to man, desires to reveal himself to all men, rescuing and saving them from the self-destruction into which they, in their sin, are hurling themselves. The slowness of the process of salvation is not an indication of God's injustice or ineptitude; it is rather (as we shall see later) a measure of his inexhaustible patience: he deals with man in such a way that the fragile and sickly plant of human freedom is healed, not destroyed. It is this active movement of God through history to all mankind that is the ground of the missionary and evangelistic impulse in Christian faith. Hence, it was very unfortunate —and in fact a betrayal of that faith—when men made that impulse serve the purposes of private and cultural imperialism instead of, after the model of God's act, patiently nourishing and ministering to the unique individuality and peculiar freedom which other men and other cultures manifested.

The fact that the "scandal" of the historicity of Christian faith proves to be more misunderstanding than disgrace, however, proves nothing about the actuality or truth of the Christian revelation. We have not even established just what is to be understood by the term, *revelation.* Thus far we have simply tried to see that the decisively historical character of revelation is nothing against it; on the contrary, precisely a historical revelation would be most appropriate to man's historical existence.[2]

What, now, is meant by "revelation"? All our words gain their meanings through their reference to some point or dimension of experience, on the one hand, and through their peculiar connections and

---

[2] I am using the term "history" so as to cut across and ignore the unfortunate, but popular, German distinction between *Historie* and *Geschichte.* The presence in the German language of these two terms has made it too simple for continental theologians to separate what in our actual experience belongs together, thus contributing to the abstractness and seeming irrelevance of much theological work. Perhaps it is providential that we who speak English have only one word, "history," to translate both *Geschichte* and *Historie;* thus we are forced and enabled to grasp historical reality in its oneness rather than artificially dismembering it. It is important, if the present work is to be understood, that my use of "history" not be interpreted in terms of this false disjunction, but instead that the richness and unity of the reality to which our English word points be grasped anew. Only thus will we see how Christian theology in fact provides us with a profound interpretation of our actual historical existence.

relations to other words, controlled by the unique locus of each in the whole fabric of meaning, on the other. To discover genuine content and meaning for the word "revelation," we shall have to uncover these two sorts of connections in which it stands. If we fail to find an adequate experiential root, what is said will remain abstract and verbal —"just words"; if we fail to discover the analogies and connections, as well as dissimilarities, of "revelation" with other more familiar meanings, we will not arrive at any *understanding* of the term. It must not be supposed, of course, that these two dimensions of meaning can be dealt with independently of each other, as if we could first indicate the experiential referent for our term and then show its connections with other words. Any indication and interpretation of experiential roots will necessarily involve a variety of words and their associated meanings; and, in turn, the attempt to show connections with other words and meanings will necessarily involve references to their roots in experience as well. The experiential and the logical dimensions of meaning can never be fully split apart and dealt with independently of each other, and our discussion of this concept will make no such attempt. Instead, we shall look at three quite distinct meaning-experience complexes, which obtain for other perspectives as well as the Christian. These, as we shall see, can provide us with analogues from common experience which assist grasping the meaning of the theological concept of revelation. That technical term—which properly applies to the roots of the Christian perspective—will in turn prove useful in isolating and focusing on certain frequently overlooked dimensions of these other points of view. Thus, the meaning of the theological term will become clear as we discover its utility for interpreting ordinary experience.[3]

[3] This order may seem to some backwards and seriously in error. Does not the autonomy of the biblical revelation require that we begin with it rather than with analogies drawn from common experience? To this the following may be said in reply. (1) There is no biblical concept of "revelation" as such, in the modern sense of that word. After his full survey of the biblical materials relevant to this problem, F. G. Downing concludes: "'Revelation', in any of its modern theological uses, as a major term . . . with which to convey the purpose of the life, death, resurrection of Jesus, does not occur in the New Testament" (*Has Christianity a Revelation?* [Philadelphia: Westminster, 1967], p. 123). The notion of revelation, as W. H. Poteat has pointed out, "is itself the product of philosophic curiosity—albeit one which is directed upon understanding the Bible as the 'Word of God' in contrast with the 'word of man.' To say: 'Thus saith the Lord . . .' is one thing. . . . To talk about what it means to say this is

We shall first seek to orient ourselves properly by considering the order of *significance* to which the term "revelation" points. Then we shall examine certain features of experience and history, seeking to ascertain analogues of the event(s) considered the *locus* of revelation. This will bring us into a position from which we can analyze the type of *structure* implied by "revelation." The isolation of these several features will provide vantage points for grasping the concept of revelation and will also show its usefulness for pointing up certain dimensions of ordinary experience. The whole discussion will then be tied together in concrete terms through a consideration of the peculiar character of the Christian revelation itself. In some respects this analysis can be understood as involving a philosophical generalization of the notion of revelation, as it has developed in specifically Christian thought, for it will provide a conceptual scheme useful for perceiving the otherwise hidden historico-ontological foundations of any perspective. As we shall see, a quasi-revelatory foundation is implicitly claimed in every viewpoint. Our analysis will thus point up both the similarities and the radical differences between Christian and nonChristian points of view.

a. The significance of revelation. By "revelation" is meant the unveiling or the revealing of the fundamental reality with which we

---

quite another: 'doing philosophical analysis.' The category, 'revelation,' is the product of this latter kind of enterprise" ("The Incarnate Word and the Language of Culture," *Christian Scholar* [1956], 39:116). This being the case, our task is not simply to repeat the biblical language, but rather to find a meaningful way to talk about the biblical view in *our* language and with reference to our problems. Hence we must find points in our language and experience from which we can develop our interpretation. (2) Even were the concept an explicitly biblical one, the present procedure would be correct. No words have meaning except as they indicate some dimension or quality of experience. Simply to repeat *noises* because they are found in the Bible assures us not at all of discovering meaning. Biblical language, like all other language, developed in the crucible of the common experience of a community in interaction with other communities. It is because the words referred to something in the experience of the people that they were living and meaningful; if eventually some of these words came to have highly specialized and peculiar meanings, that is not because they severed their relationship to experience. Similarly, these words and concepts will become meaningful to us only as we discover the points in our experience to which they refer and which they illuminate. Failure to do this will result in our parroting empty noises, not in meaningful discourse. Unfortunately, far too much contemporary theology gives one this feeling of emptiness and obscurity about that to which it refers. Thus our procedure, of seeking out analogies in common experience with which we can work, is the only one feasible if the biblical message is to become meaningful for us and not remain mere pious but empty noises.

have to do, that is, God's self-manifestation. Revelation refers, then, to that locus in experience through which men discover themselves in relation to the *ultimately real*, the norm or standard in terms of which all other reality is defined for them, and beside which, therefore, all other realities are necessarily perceived as of lesser significance and meaning. This means that an alleged "revelation" which was, however, of only peripheral or transitory interest to one would not be *revelation* in the theologically proper sense but some pseudo-meaning in connection with which the term has been mistakenly used. For that which is unveiled through revelation is by definition the object of "ultimate concern" (Tillich).

This implies that one can never understand revelation simply by studying others' reports of so-called revelations. Doubtless comrades can serve as helpful and even indispensable guides to the meaningful and the significant, but finally one must perceive significance for himself if it is to be grasped at all. One misuses the term, then, if he designates with it that which others have claimed revelatory but which does not appear of ultimate significance to him. For example, one is not entitled to say, "Revelation is that which happens in and through a 'mystical experience'—but I have never been blessed with such ecstasy." The most that could be said here would be that someone else has reported this to be revelation. Nor may one, without careful qualification, assume the Bible to be God's revelation. The Bible may contain reports of revelation, or others may report that the Bible is revelation for them; but unless and until one perceives the ultimate significance of the biblical witness for himself, it has not become revelation for him. The biblical accounts themselves make clear that what is revelation for one may not be for another. Thus, to take the outstanding case: many witnessed the events of the ministry of Jesus, but only a few saw in them the ultimate disclosure of God's nature and will. One will not discover to what the word "revelation" refers merely by attending to others' views. He must focus carefully on what is of ultimate significance to himself, if he is to find appropriate access to the meaning of this term.

Each of us has some firmly held convictions which order his living and for which he might be willing to die. Perhaps they have

to do with "the American way of life," or with art and beauty or
philosophy and the intellectual life. Perhaps love between persons
seems the one thing worth having, or the struggle for justice and
human rights. Or perhaps one more honest with himself would be less
idealistic in naming his values, and admit that it is power, or money,
or sexual gratification, or even sadistic cruelty that he seeks and
enjoys above all else. Most of us live in terms of some peculiar and
inconsistent complex of all these; but, in any case, there is a center
or hierarchy of value around which one's life is ordered, the focal
point in terms of which he orients himself in his many day-to-day
decisions. Thus, in terms of more or less unquestioned democratic
convictions, one may judge there ought to be more (or less) public
housing, or a more steeply graduated income tax, or desegregated
schools, or less government interference in the lives of individuals,
or a more vigorous war against "international communism." If "democracy" is one's ultimate, what he does in the politico-moral realm
will be interpreted and justified by reference to it as the basic criterion
or standard with which he separates the real from the unreal, the
true from the false, in this arena of human action and intercourse.
It is the "absolute presupposition" (Collingwood) of his thinking
and action here, *assumed* valid and significant but not *proved* so, the
final ground of all proof for him.[4]

Not only politico-moral decisions rest on ultimately unproved
(and unprovable) convictions; all other judgments do as well. Most
of us take for granted, for example, that reality is given us in waking
experience more surely and truly than when we sleep. Yet we know
that in many cultures it has been thought that the gods visit men in
and through dreams, that better clues to the real are given there. It is
not possible, of course, to prove that we are right in this matter and
the others wrong, for all proof which calls into question the validity
of dreams is based upon waking experience and is thus circular.
Despite this circularity, few of us are disposed to question the assumption. Similar problems of circularity arise if one attempts to argue
with a mystic about the reality of the world given in and through the

---

[4] The few examples given in the text in these pages are hardly sufficient to establish
the point being made. For a fuller discussion of these problems see Pts. I and II of my
Relativism, Knowledge and Faith, esp. Chs. VII to IX.

senses. The mystic and the dreamer themselves, of course, are in-volved in similar circles.

One's deepest convictions—those which provide the criteria for all his higher-level judgments and decisions—are rooted in a kind of unquestioned faith, not in logical demonstration. This faith, which is in fact the basic stance or posture of the self, orients all thought and action. The reality (whatever it be) which is object of this faith is not given us like other experiential realities, that is, through the day-by-day processes of question and answer, probing and discovery, insight and reasoning. For every question we frame is already based on it and presupposes it; every discovery we make is discerned and eval-uated in its terms. Because of the unique status of this reality and the unusual mode of its presence to us, it is necessary to frame a con-cept clearly distinguishing it from the other realities of experience. Theological discourse, where the nature and problems of faith have long been analyzed, can provide us with precisely the concept we need. The correlative of faith or the object of faith is one's "god";[5] and the mode through which one's god is given him, or gives himself to him, is called "revelation," thus distinguishing it from ordinary experiential and cognitive processes.

When we use the term "revelation" to designate the process—whatever it may be—through which the objects of one's ultimate con-victions seize and overpower him, we are generalizing the concept from its traditional theological usage, where it is usually reserved to designate the self-manifestation of the One True God. This is not entirely without traditional warrant, however, because it has always been known that the idols and demons also in some sense "revealed" themselves to their devotees. Such generalization is of special value for our purposes, because it enables us to focus on a dimension of experience, common to all men, which can serve as an analogue for understanding the peculiar status and claims of the Christian revela-tion. As a preliminary approximation, therefore, we may use the term

---

[5] Cf. Luther: "What is it to have a god, or what is God? . . . As I have often said, the confidence and faith of the heart alone make both God and an Idol. . . . For the two, faith and God, have inevitable connection. Now, I say, whatever your heart clings to and confides in, that is really your God" (*Large Catechism*, First Part, The First Commandment [Minneapolis: Augsburg, 1935], p. 44).

"revelation" to designate the way—and we have not yet sought to analyze just what that way may be—in which the objects of our deepest-level convictions (whatever they may be) are given us; "revelation" will then refer to that process or event through which the Reality in terms of which we measure and judge all other realities encounters us. Its object will always be grasped as of ultimate significance for us precisely because it is that which determines all significance for us.[6]

Given this analysis, it is clearly not appropriate to request that one *prove* his "revelation" true; such proof would already presuppose the revelation. By "revelation" we are intending to designate the source and ground of the very criteria to which one might appeal in such proof.

These abstract and general formulations can easily be stated in the more concrete terms of Christian faith: the affirmation that God has revealed his true nature and will decisively in Jesus Christ entails the claim that Jesus Christ is somehow the source of the norms which must orient existence; since he is the focal point where ultimate reality gives itself to man, all reality, truth, and meaning (according to the Christian view) must be defined and measured by reference to him. This is clearly a momentous affirmation which few can make without hypocrisy. For the most part we take our effective criteria of the meaningful and the real not from the image of a man dying on a cross but from more obvious and appealing experiences, for example, the effectiveness and reality of power in human relations; though we all live by faith in some "revelation," it is usually that of some more easily worshipped idol. Jesus Christ, for most men most of the time,

---

[6] Cf. Karl Barth: "According to Holy Scripture God's revelation is a ground which has no sort of higher or deeper ground above or behind it, but is simply a ground in itself, and therefore as regards man an authority from which no appeal to a higher authority is possible. Its reality and likewise its truth do not rest upon a superior reality and truth, are under no need of an initial actualization or legitimation as a reality from any other such point, and so are also not measured by reality and truth such as might be found at such another point, are not to be compared with such, nor to be judged and regarded as reality and truth in the light of such. On the contrary, God's revelation has its reality and truth wholly and in every respect—i.e., ontically and noetically—within itself. Only by denying it can we wish to ascribe to it a higher or deeper ground different from itself, or regard, adopt, or reject it from the vantage of such a higher or deeper ground. . . . Revelation is not real and true from the standpoint of anything else, either in itself or for us. It is so in itself, and for us through itself" (*Church Dogmatics*, I, 1 [Edinburgh: T. & T. Clark, 1936], 350).

does not have the significance for existence to which the term "revelation" can properly be applied, however glibly in Christian pulpit and prayer his name is invoked.

In these circumstances, if one wishes to appropriate the Christian revelation as his own, he can do so only by an indirect route. Since one's "revelation" is the source of the very definitions and criteria with which he thinks, he cannot by mere act of will simply shift from one "revelation" to another. One can only begin where he is—experiencing and thinking as he in fact does—and seek to relate what is now of actual significance to that which in Christian faith is claimed to be authentically significant. Learning the Christian vocabulary and seeking to perceive, interpret, and understand existence in its terms would be a step in this direction, for it would provide language and conceptual tools by means of which to perceive, understand, and meaningfully interpret each dimension of the human condition, however pagan or idolatrous, in a Christian way. As one began to think in this way, he would begin to assume the Christian perspective too; that is, he would begin to perceive and understand his existence in terms oriented toward the *Christian* revelation, begin to measure and evaluate the various dimensions of experience by Christ. Thus, he might come to learn the Christian vocabulary and speak the Christian language, not merely as words piously mouthed on "religious" occasions, but as the symbols with which he actually appropriated the profound dimensions of experience.

Christian theology is nothing other than such thinking about existence in the light of God's revelation (see below, pp. 57ff., 72ff.). To theologize, then, it is necessary to begin the movement from habitual orientations and languages—rooted in a variety of secular "revelations"—to discourse enabling perception of the significance of Christ. Our attempt here to generalize the technical concept "revelation," so that we can grasp with its aid the sources and grounds of the actual standards and criteria with which we perceive and evaluate the world, is a first step toward such apprehension of existence theologically.

b. The locus of revelation.[7] "Revelation," we have said, is a concept useful for designating the way in which the objects of our

[7] In my interpretation of the historical character of revelation I am heavily indebted to H. Richard Niebuhr, *The Meaning of Revelation* (New York: Macmillan, 1941).

deepest-level convictions are given us. We must now examine certain features of the structure of the historical process and our historical existence[8] to see if this event or process can be more precisely specified.

It would not be incorrect to say that all that we have—indeed, all that we are—comes from the past. We become selves in the processes of social interaction and communication through which we learn to speak and to play socio-culturally defined roles.[9] Both language and the role-system are created and shaped in the developing history of a society; and they may be regarded as the continuing living presence of that history, providing the context or matrix within which selves emerge. But we must go further than this. Maturing into selfhood, the process of coming to participate actively in a community of selves, is achieved through learning the language and internalizing the roles of that community. The linguistic- and role-systems of the culture— the very reservoirs, as it were, for the values, ideals, ideas, attitudes, and ways of doing things which men have developed over many millennia—thus give structure to the self. Moreover, the language provides categories by means of which the self perceives the world (nouns, verbs); it supplies a ready-made system of possible kinds of relationship between these realities (pronouns, prepositions, conjunctions, verbs); and it furnishes interpretations of significance and value (adjectives, adverbs, interjections). Thus, both the self and its experience are shaped by the cultural system of meanings which we take in with our mothers' milk. And these meanings in turn have become what they are through a particular and unique history, being continuously modified as that history unfolds.

Furthermore, the peculiar attitudes and ways of thinking which define a person's individuality are shaped in his *personal* history. It is in and through one's unique personal experience that the meanings of the cultural-linguistic system are internalized. Each meaning comes to have a peculiar flavor, belonging to and experienced by that in-

[8] Fuller treatment of man's historicity will be found below, Ch. 23, and also in my *Relativism, Knowledge and Faith, op. cit.* (above, n. 1), and *The Context of Decision* (New York: Abingdon, 1961).

[9] See, e.g., G. H. Mead, *Mind, Self and Society* (Chicago: University of Chicago Press, 1934) and H. S. Sullivan, *The Interpersonal Theory of Psychiatry* (New York: Norton, 1953), and many others.

dividual alone. One shares a common cultural history with the others of his community, but he develops into a unique individual. Thus, one comes to have his own private tastes and preferences, standards and values, although his unique self-structure is always analogous in many respects to the other selves in the community, similarly shaped by the basic role- and linguistic-system.

This radically historical character of selfhood means that the ontological foundations of our deepest convictions are in history. Our beliefs and values, our criteria and norms, have come to us out of a social and a personal past in which they first emerged in germ and gradually were formed. Thus, certain crucial *events* (of which we may be completely unaware) are the ontological ground of our values and norms. If these events had not occurred, our convictions and standards would be other than they are, and we would be different persons.[10]

Many examples could be given. The best-known doubtless is the Christian community, which looks back to the events clustering

[10] It would be desirable, if it were possible, to be able to refer at this point to works in which a "metaphysics of history" or a "historico-ontological" position, of the sort alluded to from time to time in the text, is spelled out in detail; but these works do not presently exist. Some of the contentions which might be developed in such a metaphysics can be found in some of the early essays of Tillich (e.g., "Kairos and Logos" and "The Interpretation of History and the Idea of Christ," both published in *The Interpretation of History* [New York: Scribners, 1936]) ; in R. G. Collingwood's *Essay on Metaphysics* (Oxford: Clarendon Press, 1940) and *Idea of Nature* (Oxford: Clarendon Press, 1945) ; and in my own *Relativism, Knowledge and Faith, op. cit.* (above, n. 1) ; but these are very fragmentary. Hegel's attempt to bring together the logical and historical dimensions of thought and culture must be considered as indispensable background for any such position, along with the work of such men as Marx, Freud, and the sociologists of knowledge and culture; and among recent philosophers, Whitehead's metaphysics of process and creativity is quite relevant (though it should be remembered that his basic paradigm was process, not history). The fundamental characteristic of a historicist metaphysics would be its attempt to utilize history, and man's experience of history, as paradigmatic for the understanding and interpretation of all reality. It would, therefore, be founded on a careful analysis of the nature of historical experience and reality and would involve generalization of the basic categories derived from that analysis so as to interpret all reality as "historical." In the present work this section on "the locus of revelation," taken together with Ch. 12, suggests certain of the sorts of distinctions that would have to be made in an analysis of historical experience; Chs. 18 and 19 sketch a "historical" picture of the universe (see also n. 1 and n. 12 of Ch. 3) ; and various materials in the section on the doctrine of God (particularly in Ch. 6) point toward the conception of "ultimate reality" which would be involved. Beyond these and a few other allusions which show the points of connection between this historicist theology and a corresponding metaphysical position, it is impossible to go within the limits of the present work.

around Jesus Christ as the source and ground of authentic knowledge of ultimate reality as well as of the norms in terms of which human existence should be lived. Insofar as this orientation in fact integrates the various strands in the life of Christian individual and community, it is proper to regard that life as having its historico-ontological ground in the person-event Jesus Christ. In order to grasp and interpret these facts and their metaphysical import, the Christian community created its christological language and concepts.

What can quite properly be called "the christological problem" has been in this way openly faced and clearly conceptualized as a metaphysical problem only in Christian thought. However, it is also present, if only implicitly, in all other perspectives. Thus, the orientation of Judaism, for example, is grounded in the peculiar power and significance of the events of Israel's history, particularly those clustering around the exodus and covenant, the great prophets and the exile, while the self-understanding of every American has been drastically shaped by the formative events of this nation—Declaration of Independence, Revolutionary War, creation of the Constitution—as well as by such subsequent crises as the Civil War and the Great Depression. In contrast with both of these, a convinced communist is grounded historico-ontologically in the work of Marx and Engels and the appearance of the revolutionary spirit in history, culminating in the great upheavals of the twentieth century. Again, the rationalist—who more than any of these, perhaps, fails to perceive the significance of the concrete existential and historical grounding of his faith—is oriented by the historical movement which first comes into view in the Greek Enlightenment, later gaining cultural power and significance in the Renaissance, the appearance of modern science, and the eighteenth-century Enlightenment. One could go on. Every perspective has its historico-ontological ground which gave it birth and which continues to sustain and nourish it, without which it would die. This series of events is apprehended as the real core and meaning of history from the given point of view; and it is in relation to this meaningful *Heilsgeschichte* that other movements of history are understood, evaluated, and interpreted.

In accord with our earlier discussion, we can appropriately designate this special series of significant events, through which the basic lines of the perspective were formed, as *revelatory events*. These events can be described as "revelatory" in a special sense not only because their meaning and significance seems self-evident to the adherent of the perspective, needing no further explanation in terms of some other deeper or more intelligible ground, but also because they throw their light on all the rest of experience, "revealing" its meaning.[11] Thus, to return to some of the examples noted above, for most Americans the ideals of the American Revolution, expressed in the phrases that "all men are created equal" and with the right to "life, liberty and the pursuit of happiness," seem so evident as to be taken for granted; and other societies and cultures are perceived and evaluated in terms of their fructification of the values which came into view in this historical locus. In contrast, for those whose orientation is primarily rationalistic, the convictions of the Enlightenment—that experience is to be understood and interpreted by intelligence, and life is to be lived as reason dictates—are assumed. And so forth. Few of us, of course, are sufficiently integrated to avoid being polytheistic in orientation, some areas of our experience having one center, others another. But in all cases there are levels of meaning—ultimate convictions—which are themselves transparent and throw light on all else. The historical events which have created these levels of meaning are analogous to what in Christian faith is called "revelation"; they should be regarded as of an order different from the ordinary happenings and processes of history.

Let us turn now from this examination of "revelatory" events in communal histories to the private experience of the individual self. Our experiences, the different moments of our lives, are of unequal weight of meaning. Some days are times of momentous crisis or decision or of great good fortune, days which shape whole lives; others seem to be of almost no lasting effect. This fact is metaphysically significant. It means that the histories of our lives are not simple continuous realities made up of metaphysically equal moments, proceeding in regular measure day by day and year by year; this image forced upon us by clocks and calendars is radically

[11] Cf. H. Richard Niebuhr, *op. cit.* (above, n. 7), p. 109, *et passim*.

false to actual experience. Our lives consist, rather, of certain high
points around which other events arrange themselves and in which
they focus. It is these moments, filled with special meaning for us
and continuing to live in memory or in the deeper strata of the self,
that have decisively formed us into what we are. These peak moments
tie together the mass of nondescript and almost empty loose ends of
experience, giving existence some unity and consistency.[12] In contrast much of our day-by-day experience is of such slight importance
as scarcely to be noted at all, the question of its meaning or meaninglessness hardly arising. If these remarks are correct, then that
event (or process) which has given the self its fundamental orientation or structure of meaning, and in terms of which all other experience is apprehended and appreciated, will be of *supreme* significance
to the self. This event for some may be a specific dateable point in
time, a "conversion experience"; for most it will probably be a
longer less obvious process.[13] In many cases we may not be explicitly
conscious of this process formative of our very selfhood, but that it
occurred as the decisive event (process) structuring us could hardly
be denied.

It is appropriate to designate this moment as a *revelatory* event
(or process), even though we may not be directly aware of it or its
significance for our existence; for through it such meaning as life

---

[12] These high moments make it possible always to say that life has in fact some
meaning; for, whether negative or positive in value, these moments stand out precisely
because of their special weight of meaning. A genuinely meaningless life would be one
in which all was on such a dead level that the subject could not discriminate at all
between the qualities of meaning of different moments. But such monotony is hardly
even imaginable to us; certainly no one *experiences* it, for experience is characterized
always by differentiations and distinctions.

[13] It may be remarked in passing that, as used here, a "moment" is not a sixty-
second unit of time, nor is an "event" necessarily of some clearly specifiable relatively
short duration. Both of these terms signify a *meaningful unity* of time, whatever the
duration, i.e., a period of time whose limits are determined by the meaning which binds
it into a whole, not by its mere chronological extension. Thus, the fall of Rome is an
event of some centuries; the death of Jesus, of only a few hours. Their event-character
is defined by the unities of meaning binding them into intelligible wholes, not by their
duration. This implies that all of history—if it is to be seen not as a series of dis-
connected events, but as a continuous process and thus in some sense intelligible and
meaningful—must be viewed as one exceedingly complex event. It is a mark of the
philosophical maturity of Hebrew thinking about history that it did not shy away from
this conclusion, seeing all reality as falling within the compass of God's historical
activity, beginning in creation and reaching completion in the eschaton.

has come to have for us has been *revealed* to us.[14] The term "revealed" has been used here deliberately: in no sense can we claim to have discovered or created or produced this meaning through our own initiative. On the contrary, this foundational structure of meaning in our existence *happens* to us; it comes to us from beyond the circle of our private existence; it is "unveiled" to us. However paradoxical it may seem, we may be completely unaware of what thus is the most significant event of our lives, the "revelatory" event or process without which no moment of our existence could be apprehended as meaningful. But the birth in us of genuine self-understanding and self-knowledge—and thus real maturity and freedom —can occur only as we do become aware of this, the real center of our existence. For only then can we begin to bring our consciousness into integral unity with the already established structure of the deeper levels of our selfhood. (These processes, which have been investigated in their own way by the psychoanalysts, will be interpreted later in more specifically theological terms when we deal with the categories of sin and salvation. See especially Chapters 25– 32.)

It is important for us to note that the meaning which comes into our lives in those moments I have termed "revelatory" is not just created *de novo*, appearing inexplicably without ground or reason. On the contrary, such meaning is always rooted in some tradition of the culture into which the self is born. Through such revelatory events the tradition comes to life again in each new self, providing the framework of meaning in terms of which that self appropriates and lives its existence. Thus, we may understand ourselves and grasp our world in terms of American traditions of freedom and equality, or communist traditions, or rationalistic freethinking traditions, or the Christian tradition, or, more likely, with the aid of some combination of all these and others. Jesus—at least as his earliest followers have reported the matter—understood his life in terms of Jewish

---

[14] It may seem paradoxical and inconsistent with the ordinary meaning of "reveal" to say we might not be aware of a "revelatory event"; but this is not so. What we generally attend to when something is revealed to us is that which is revealed, e.g., a significant message or meaning, rather than the *event* in and through which the revelation occurs. The latter may not be particularly noted at all.

traditions about a "suffering servant," a "Son of Man," a "Messiah." The revelatory moment or process in our lives as individuals always involves the appropriation of a *revelatory tradition* lying at hand in one's history.

Such revelatory traditions have themselves emerged from histories structured by earlier traditions. As in the case of individual lives, so also with communal histories, not every moment, every year, or every century can be regarded as of equal significance for the tradition in question. Rather, there have been certain decisive turning points in history through which the tradition was principally formed, and there have appeared at certain times outstanding leaders or creative figures (Hegel's "world-historical individuals") through whose decisions and work the tradition was reshaped and turned in new directions. These moments, these events, these lives gave the tradition the particular form and flavor which it has, just as the decisive moments in a personal life account for its peculiar quality of meaning. Such moments as these may thus be regarded as the "revelatory events" for the tradition, and, indeed, they are the events and the persons to which those born into the tradition repeatedly look back for new light and new meaning. In the Bible the formative events of Israel's history are regarded as "mighty acts of God." This is an appropriate designation because, as the Hebrew writers believed, it was through this special series of outstanding occurrences that the very foundation of their communal existence and meaning— Yahweh—had made himself known and effective in Hebrew life.

With communal history as with the individual we must push our analysis back to that one decisive moment (process) which gave the tradition its unique character. This supreme revelatory event appears from within the tradition as the very "center" of history. For the whole of history prior to it seems to lead up to this moment, preparing the way for it; and the whole of subsequent history appears as the working-out to fulfilment of that which was born here. This central event, then, is apprehended as the ultimate historico-ontological ground for the meaning of the whole tradition. Every tradition is grounded in such a moment, though of course not all are explicitly aware of this. For the Christian tradition—the paradigm for our analysis—the supreme revelatory event is of course Jesus Christ. For Marxism it is the work of Marx—focusing, perhaps, in the publication of the Communist Manifesto in 1848. For the rationalist it may be the Enlightenment of the eighteenth century, or perhaps the beginnings of modern natural science in the work of Copernicus, Galileo, and Newton. For the American patriot this central moment is July 4, 1776; for the Jew, the exodus from Egypt and the covenant with Yahweh. Each of these moments, from within the perspective concerned, appears as the very center of history: every significant historical process or event which preceded it in some way prepared for its advent; all of real significance that has followed has been but the flowering of what was there given birth.

To sum up, our analysis has uncovered in ordinary experience two levels of revelatory moments or processes, in correlation with each other: (a) the personal-individual level, with its moment of conversion or process of formation of the self-structure; (b) the cultural-historical level, with its center of history or process of creation of a meaningful tradition. These are existentially correlated in such a way that a given tradition has ultimate meaning for a person, or is the meaning of history (*Heilsgeschichte*) for him, only as he makes it his own—thus living, experiencing, and thinking from within the framework of meaning provided by that tradition. Conversely, one can find meaning in his existence only through appropriating (consciously or unconsciously) a meaningful tradition, that is, only as one's existence comes into living relationship with, and thus becomes grounded upon, a dynamic center of history.[15]

This brings to a conclusion our consideration of the historical locus of revelation. The analysis can be viewed as an attempt to grasp certain crucial dimensions of human existence with the aid of a concept, revelation, created and refined in theological discourse. The

[15] This correlation of two levels as providing the ontological foundation of the structure of meaning within which the self lives—though useful for understanding any perspective—is of course basically a generalization of the Christian understanding of the self's faith-orientation. For Christian faith understands itself as real only in a living personal act of faith in Jesus Christ as the source of meaning or salvation, i.e., only when there is a vital relation and correlation between one's present existence and the center of history (Jesus Christ) appropriated as the ontological ground of this present —and all other—existence (i.e., as "Son of God").

generalization of the Christian concept has enabled us to bring into view the historico-ontological grounding of selfhood, on the one hand, and of meaning, on the other. If the argument has been successful, we have found an analogue to what Christians call "revelation" in common (as contrasted with exclusively "Christian") experience, thus overcoming the abstractness and emptiness of the term and rendering it more suitable for significant discourse between Christian and nonChristian, as well as within the church.

c. *The form of revelation.* It would be going too far to claim that the only possible way to understand the events creative of the fundamental orientations of communities and selves is through referring them to the revelatory activities of divine beings (as our analysis in the two preceding sections might seem to suggest). All such developments, of course, can be understood in strictly humanistic and naturalistic terms, especially now that we know of the creative powers of the human imagination (cf. Feuerbach, Nietzsche, Freud, Dewey, etc.). Indeed, history is generally written so as to show forth the continuity between so-called creative events and the historical context in which they occurred and out of which they emerged. Nonetheless, it is important, as we have seen, clearly to distinguish such events creative of meaning from the more ordinary moments of day-to-day experience. Since they are the historico-ontological grounds of the meaningfulness of the latter, we have designated them as in a special sense *revelatory* events, events in which meaning is unveiled.

There are a number of models or images with the aid of which such events might be interpreted. It is not our concern here to explore and evaluate each of these, but instead to examine more closely the model implied in the concept of revelation. We shall see, as we seek now to develop a more precise understanding of this concept, that it is not really permissible to employ it as promiscuously as we have thus far, in interpretation of all such creative moments. The concept of revelation has very definite and specific metaphysical implications, and it can be properly employed, therefore, only with reference to such moments as meet the requisite metaphysical specifications. Failure to observe this has often resulted in confused and confusing interpretations of the concept.

The word "revelation" refers to an *act* of disclosure or unveiling;[16] it thus presupposes the activity of another agent over against the subject. It is the mode of our knowledge of persons and should be contrasted with *discovery*, which is the mode of our knowledge of things.[17] A discovery requires no second agent which actively makes something known: it presupposes no more than the accessibility of a fundamentally thing-like object of knowledge, an inert reality lying open to our investigation. Ultimately rooted in and formed by the character of our visual experience,[18] this mode of knowing involves such processes as careful observation and measurement, painstaking efforts to draw the contours of the observed reality with accuracy, and unification of the various fragments of knowledge under increasingly inclusive concepts and formulas, returning again and again to the observed object to check conclusions. Here, although the activity of the *observer* is guided by the intention to gain knowledge, the *object* of the knowledge, however "active" or "living" it may be, is not motivated by such a purpose.

Sharply contrasting with the processes that make up this thing-knowledge is our knowledge of persons. Doubtless here also much is learned by scientific observation and reflection. But the most com-

---

[16] Cf. G. F. Woods: "We are unlikely to gain a plain understanding of the later uses of the word 'revelation', until we have recalled the situation in which the word is primarily used. Its original meaning is the act of removing a 'veil'. In the simplest case, an object is 'veiled' from sight and later 'unveiled'. The second act of removing the 'veil' is an act of revelation" (*Theological Explanation* [Naperville, Ill.: Allenson, 1958], p. 87).

[17] It is to be observed that etymologically there is little difference between the meanings of "revealing" and "discovering," both signifying an uncovering or unveiling. Significant differences of nuance have developed in these words, however. Thus, while I may by my own activity *discover* something of which I was previously ignorant, it would not be correct to say that I *reveal* this to myself. In contrast, when something is *revealed to me*, an act of uncovering performed by some other than myself is implied, a sharp contrast with the implications of the word *discovery*. The categories of "revelation" and "discovery" cannot, of course, be restricted to knowledge of persons and knowledge of things, respectively; for another person may "reveal" a variety of things to me, not only *himself*, and it is possible for me to "discover" something about a person. Nevertheless, insofar as the characteristics of inert objects—"things"—become known, it is because they are in principle open to "discovery" by subjects, not because they "reveal" themselves; in contrast, genuine knowledge of another person, inasmuch as it involves his deliberate speaking or otherwise "revealing" himself, is typically gained through "revelation." Hence, though it is admittedly an oversimplification necessary to make clear a point, the treatment in the text of person-knowledge as primarily "revelation" and thing-knowledge as chiefly "discovery" is by no means arbitrary.

[18] Thorleif Boman, *Hebrew Thought Compared with Greek* (Philadelphia: Westminster Press, 1960), pp. 205–207.

mon and most significant portion of our knowledge of other persons
is gained through their *self-revelation*. It is through speaking together, honestly and straightforwardly, that we make ourselves
known to each other.[19] Knowledge of another person depends quite as
much on the intention of the one known to reveal himself as it does
on the other's intention to know him. Unlike thing-knowledge, which
depends entirely on our ingenuity and industry in the face of what
lies before our gaze, our knowledge of other persons, when profound
and true, is of what would have remained hidden from us had the
other not chosen to reveal it.[20] The depths of the human heart are
unveiled to the view of another only in those rare moments of love
and trust when the activity of each self with respect to the other has
established genuine bonds of community between them. Scientific
knowledge of others, however complete or detailed it may be, never
in this way uncovers another person in his creative and free selfhood;
such knowledge becomes possible only through entering into personal
relation with him.[21]

If we examine the structure of the relationship between knower
and object of knowledge here, we shall find it quite different from
thing-knowledge. Here there is no mere inert object to which we
actively relate ourselves in the hope of discovering more accurately
its nature. This object of knowledge is not accessible to us in that
sense at all but depends on its own act of unveiling. While thing-
knowledge depends on the intentionality only of the knower, personal
knowledge requires a highly complex process of interaction between
agents both of whom are purposive and free. Moreover, the result is
no static map of the reality observed but genuine knowledge of the
other person-in-act, of the other in his freedom, creativity, and pur-

---

[19] It is interesting to note that our term "person" comes from the Latin *persona*
("mask"), and that this probably derives from *per-sonare* (to "sound through"); thus,
a person is a reality that "sounds through" his external mask in speech.

[20] Cf. John Macmurray: ". . . if you refuse to reveal yourself to me, I cannot
know you, however much I may wish to do so. If in your relations with me, you consistently 'put on an act' or 'play a role', you hide yourself from me. I can never know
you as you really are. In that case, generalization from the observed facts will be
positively misleading. . . . For . . . a being who can pretend to be what he is not, to
think what he does not think, and to feel what he does not feel, cannot be known by
generalization from his observed behaviour, but only as he genuinely reveals himself"
(*Persons in Relation* [New York: Humanities, 1961], p. 169).

[21] *Ibid.*, pp. 28ff.

posiveness. In short, in interpersonal relations we come to know another purposive will in its very motion into the future. As that person reveals to us the intentions and goals which motivate his activity, we come to know the hidden and secret inner connection which binds the various moments of his life into a teleologically developing meaningful unity, which is in fact his real being. Despite all the imperfection and deceit in our dealings with each other, in and through personal intercourse a kind of knowledge emerges of a quite different order—and of far greater significance to us—than the best of our thing-knowledge. Through this knowledge comes our awareness of the love and trust of others; and it is this, not the scores made on "objective" intelligence tests or personality profiles, for which we live and which gives our lives meaning.

It is because the active center of the other self transcends my private world completely that his accessibility to me depends finally on his own act of self-disclosure. If he chooses not to reveal himself but to remain a stranger to me, the other—in his innermost being— is simply not accessible in my experience. Even if he offers his friendship, I always remain aware that the inmost depths of his selfhood are hidden from my view. Indeed, it is especially in a close personal relationship that the irreducible transcendence of the other ego is most profoundly realized. For here, precisely because the other reveals his very selfhood, he is known as an active center of freedom and creativity, living in his own world, ultimately escaping my every effort to reduce him to a mere element in mine. Thus, in the intense personal interaction with other selves we come up hard against a reality shrouded in impenetrable mystery, but which through its initiative in intercourse with us unveils itself and enters our world of experience, yet always retaining the transcendent freedom again to withdraw.[22]

The term "revelation," thus, refers not to just any sort of event,

[22] To deny the relevance and meaning of the concept of transcendence here is to deny the realities of personal intercourse in the name of a logic rooted in our thing-knowledge. Such unwarranted imperialism has been so long dominant in philosophy that it may be difficult for us to recognize that our knowledge of persons is more fundamental—genetically, existentially, and ontologically—than our thing-knowledge, the latter being an abstraction from and specification of the former. Thing-knowledge, therefore, should never be allowed to become a decisive norm for judging person-knowledge. Con-

but to an *act*, an act of unveiling through which something is disclosed which had formerly been concealed. It implies a process or series of events with at least (to speak somewhat roughly) three phases: the situation of hiddenness, the moment or process of revelation, the new situation of revealedness. Any new discovery or insight, of course, can be analyzed in terms of a similar three-phase movement, but this should not be confused with the movement we are here considering. With a *discovery* the hiddenness is only factual and temporary, awaiting the appropriate activity and insight of an investigator. But with *revelation* that which is hidden is *in principle inaccessible* to the observation and knowledge of the investigator and might well remain forever concealed and unknown; only a specific act on the part of another over against the investigator can unveil and thus bring into his field of experience that which had been hidden from him. Thus, if the term "revelation" is used to designate the radically creative events in a historical process, an unveiling of that which would otherwise be unknown and would remain unknowable is being asserted. Here, in and through this particular event, something enters the historical process from outside, as it were, something that could not have been produced from within, just as the truly revelatory act of one self to another injects new meaning and understanding into the other's experience, a knowledge and insight which the other could not have created autonomously.

It is important that we recognize clearly that the new situation of revealedness that emerges in phase three was not, properly speaking, available to the man situated in phase one; the moment of revelation (phase two) coming from beyond had to intervene before phase three was possible. If the third phase were understood as a possibility immanent in the first, then the movement here would be only a

---

cepts which are given content and meaning by referents found in experience with persons must be adjudged valid in their own terms. (See *Relativism, Knowledge and Faith, op. cit.* [above, n. 1], Chs. III–V, and "Two Models of Transcendence," *The Heritage of Christian Thought*, Essays in Honor of Robert L. Calhoun, ed. R. E. Cushman and E. Grislis [New York: Harper & Row, 1965]. See also John Macmurray's important two books, *The Self as Agent* [New York: Humanities, 1957] and *Persons in Relation*. Also relevant is Michael Polanyi, *Personal Knowledge* [Chicago: University of Chicago Press, 1958]. For similar claims based on careful analysis of linguistic usage, see Stuart Hampshire, *Thought and Action* [New York: Viking Press, 1960] and A. I. Melden, *Free Action* [New York: Humanities, 1961].)

development—however dialectical—of the original position. Such a dialectical possibility, being immanent within human existence (as Hegel saw when he made it the key to the interpretation of the movement of all history), would mean that the "hidden" was not in fact ontologically hidden, but only temporarily so, due to be uncovered in course of the natural unfolding of the historical process. A much more radical incursion or reversal is claimed when the concept of revelation is invoked, namely, that the ontologically hidden—and thus that which is not naturally available to man or to human history—has become revealed. The concept of revelation thus refers to a movement from *outside the bounds of human history* into man's world, significantly transforming or reversing history through bringing into being new ontological possibilities not previously implicit in human existence.[23] It is this implication of the term "revelation" that makes its use in the analogical or generalized sense of the two previous sections most questionable (however useful such generalization might be for making clear certain dimensions of its meaning); few (the author included) would wish to hold that the "revelatory events" underlying every tradition are due to some sort of "revelatory activity" by extra-human being(s). Such extravagant metaphysical interpretation could be justified at best only for rare and unusual cases. Hence, one should reserve the term "revelation" (in the theological sense) for those situations where he is willing to take seriously its ontological consequences and spell out a doctrine of "God" (i.e., of extra-human agency) as its proper corollary.

The process of personal knowledge, in which one self unveils himself to another, provides us with the fundamental model on which

[23] We can now see that there is a radical and decisive contradiction between the conception of revelation and every form of naturalism, whether idealistic or materialistic. For naturalism always rests on the assumption that all of history is to be understood in and through reference to man's creativity and culture in interaction with natural processes, and that the norms and standards of life are to be interpreted as simply emergent from these processes. In this respect every perspective other than a revelational one makes what might be called the "ontological assumption," though it is only the proponents of the so-called ontological argument who have been sufficiently clear-eyed to see this. Thus it is always assumed in these perspectives that man has open to him in sufficient degree the realities of his world so that through cultural and historical processes of education, political and economic development, scientific method, mystical insight, and the like, he is able adequately to order his individual and communal existence, and perhaps even to succeed in creating the "good life." In contrast, a revelational point of view insists that man must receive *revelation from beyond* before such possibilities can open for him.

the concept of revelation is built. Moreover, only if we keep this model clearly in mind, will we be able to make the concept intelligible. For it is only in the living responsiveness of one self to the actions of another that we have direct experience of an incursion into a history which does not in any way destroy the spontaneity and freedom of the self living in that history but, on the contrary, is an element constitutive of that freedom. When I answer a question directed to me by another, my creativity and spontaneity are not curbed by the invasion of an external power heteronomously forcing me to act; on the contrary, the question put to me is precisely the occasion which calls forth my free response. My freedom is the power to respond meaningfully and creatively (and thus not in some mechanically determined fashion) to the other self with whom I am in dialogue; it is no merely spontaneous action, unrelated and irrelevant to the interpersonal context in which I live.[24] In dialogue, I am continuously in a situation in which the *new* breaks into my field of experience, yet without heteronomously destroying me and my freedom. The concept of revelation, drawn from this root experience, thus makes possible understanding the breaking-in to human history from beyond of new meaning, yet in such a way that the freedom of the men to whom God reveals himself is not disrupted or destroyed. Moreover, just as the disclosure of another's love may be an event of such meaningfulness that it is rehearsed in memory again and again, thus continuously rekindling the love which it first called forth, so God's revelation is an event of decisive significance to those who participate in and remember it: it is at once the original and the continuing ground of any genuine relation to the divine being. Just as the community between persons always grows out of a particular and very specific history of interaction in which those selves reveal themselves to each other, so the relation to and knowledge of God likewise depends on a particular history of interaction with decisive moments or events of revelation.

However, despite the fact that the structural outlines implied by the concept of divine revelation are drawn from finite interpersonal

---

[24] For a discussion of the self as primarily a responsive being, see H. Richard Niebuhr, *The Responsible Self* (New York: Harper & Row, 1963).

knowledge, it is important to recognize certain significant differences. God is not one whom we meet face to face and speak to as another human being; he is the Creator of the world, the Source and Ground of all that is. It is not even possible to conceive the notion of a direct encounter with such a One in a "revelatory moment." When we speak of "God's revelation," therefore, this should not be understood as indicating that the knowledge of God usually comes in some flash of insight or understanding, when we know we have been confronted by the Holy One (though it may come in this way): the term "revelation" is not intended here to suggest certain *psychological characteristics* of the dawning awareness of God. Rather, it is meant to underline the fact that the knowledge of God is rooted in and depends upon God's own self-disclosing action, in this respect being similar to interpersonal knowledge. For Christian faith, as we shall see, this revelatory activity of God extends over a long history, reaching all the way back to man's beginnings; and it was only after many millennia that a dim awareness gradually began to dawn and grow, until finally God could definitively manifest himself in and through Jesus Christ.[25] Thus, the term "revelation" should be understood to refer not so much to certain dramatic and breathtaking moments in individual lives (however important, in certain circumstances, such may be) as to the total historical process—extending over many generations but coming to a decisive focus at a "center"—through which God has been disclosing himself. "Revelation" in the theological sense, like all other terms applied to God (see Chapter 8), is at most analogous to its meaning in interpersonal knowledge, and it will be rightly understood only if this is kept in mind.

Our definition of revelation is now complete: revelation is an image, derived from the reception and creation of meaning in the dialogue between persons, by means of which the Christian community seeks to conceive the event (or process) which is the historico-ontological ground of its meaning-orientation. But is this image actually appropriate for understanding that process? This can be maintained only if the ultimate reality known to that community is

[25] Cf. Paul Tillich's doctrine of "preparatory revelation" (*Systematic Theology,* I [Chicago: University of Chicago Press, 1951], 137–144).

personal,[26] that is, one who has revealed and does reveal himself.
For the most part, the various nonChristian "revelations" which were
discussed in previous sections of this chapter make no such claims
(for reasons which will become clearer in the course of the argument). At best, therefore, they can be considered only analogues to
what is intended by the theological concept, aids to grasping more
easily certain of its ramifications. However, when we turn to explore
the Christian Gospel, we shall discover that the concept of revelation
fits precisely. (It should occasion no surprise, of course, that a concept created and refined in Christian discourse should find its most
appropriate application to the realities of Christian faith.) It is now
necessary to move on from our generalized and preliminary consideration of the concept of revelation—useful for understanding the
historico-ontological grounds of many different perspectives—to its
special and precise usage as the name for a once-and-for-all event
(process) known to Christian faith.

[26] To speak of "revelation" in the case of a reality which is conceived non- or
impersonally would be to misuse the word. Since such a reality cannot be conceived as
moving in free act to reveal itself, discovery or insight is the conception of knowledge
appropriate to it. Hence, if the concept of revelation be used with reference to our
knowledge of ultimate reality, it will be necessary to conceive that reality as analogous
to a free, creative, purposive will, which in his hiddenness transcends our world of
experience but which can act (as can a person) to lift the veil, revealing his nature and
communicating his purposes to us. When the concept is used within the framework of
a nonpersonal ontology, it can be only for the (surreptitious?) purpose of introducing
personalistic meaning and significance into an otherwise impersonal world.

3 / The Christian Revelation

WE have seen that the structures of meaningfulness in human existence are grounded ontologically on particular historical events or processes. It has been suggested that it is useful to distinguish these moments from ordinary events and to consider them quasi-revelatory, since they appear to be analogous in some ways to the historical event (process) known to Christian faith as God's revelation—the history culminating in Jesus Christ. We must now turn directly to this paradigmatic history itself and characterize briefly the Christian revelation.

The central claim of the Christian Gospel is that God comes to man. In and through the ministry, death, and resurrection of the man Jesus of Nazareth, God reveals to man his true condition—sin, rebellion against him—and his need of reconciliation with God; simultaneously he rescues, or begins to rescue, man from that condition. This is expressed in the New Testament through the continuous reference to Jesus as the Christ, or the Son of Man, or the Lord—the one designated and anointed by God as the agent through whom all history would be turned upside down and man released from bondage to the "principalities and powers," to be reconciled once again with the God from whom he had become alienated through his own sin. The New Testament Gospel is the "good news" about an "act of God" performed in history at the appropriate time to "save" man: "when the time had fully come, God sent forth his Son, born of woman, born under the law, to redeem those who were under the law, so that we might receive adoption as sons" (Gal. 4:4–5). Thus, the coming of Christ meant that God's long-standing historical purposes were at last coming to their climax and the work which he had begun with the creation of the world was reaching its fulfilment: "He was destined before the foundation of the world but was made manifest at the end of the times" (1 Pet. 1:20). The beginning of the end of history was at hand, and God's historical work was soon to be accomplished. Jesus himself was apparently convinced that there were among his hearers "some standing here who will not taste death before they see the kingdom of God come with power" (Mk. 9:1). The Christian proclamation was thus epitomized well in Mark's summary of Jesus' preaching: "The time is fulfilled, and the kingdom of God is at hand; repent, and believe in the gospel" (Mk. 1:15).

These words may be so familiar that we fail to see what they imply about the heart of Christian faith. Christian faith does not have as its primary concern the teaching of certain truths, either about God or man; there is no attempt made in the early preaching to prove, for example, that there is a God, or that God is good or wise. Rather, the New Testament presents itself primarily as an *announcement* of something that is happening; it is a proclamation, a newscast. The Gospel is the "good news" of what God is doing in history now, and that is the sum and substance of the matter: despite all appearances to the contrary, the most significant and meaningful of historical events is in process of unfolding. The foundation of Christian faith and Christian theology is this new development in history, together with the proclamation of it.

It is important to note certain peculiarities of this basis. Events in man's history can be known in their particularity and detail only through evidences given by eyewitnesses and inferences based on these evidences. Our knowledge here differs from that of the natural sciences, which have as their objects events of much wider scope.[1]

---

[1] It will be observed that I am not here making the common absolute disjunction between nature and history, scientific and historical knowledge. The historical process, I shall hold throughout, is single and all-encompassing, and "historical" events (in the more ordinary narrow sense, as indicating events falling in the remembered history of mankind) can be distinguished from "natural" events (such as the birth of the solar system, or the occurrence of the ice ages) only within that broader framework of history in which they both fall. The point with which we are presently concerned has to do with the difference in the bases of our knowledge of events of relatively narrow compass and limited extent and concrete character from those much broader and more inclusive and at the same time more abstract. (For a brief note on the elasticity of the concept of

The latter are uncovered through a combination of careful inferences and imaginative leaps which bring together into meaningful unities great varieties of observations often drawn from widely separated tracts of experience. For example, the birth of the solar system, though neither observed nor reported by any human witness, is inferred from the particular geological and astronomical information presently at our disposal. At best such an event is known only abstractly and in its broadest outlines, not in any specificity or concreteness approaching that of our ordinary experience. With the events of human history, however, such concrete knowledge is often possible. Thus, we may be able to discover what Caesar actually did at the Rubicon, what his motives and objectives were, and just what consequences that particular action brought about. In this way we may go considerably beyond general information about how men usually behave in such circumstances as this, to much more detailed, concrete, and particular knowledge of the event itself. Doubtless general knowledge of human behavior is useful here also and may throw some important light on the historical questions at issue through suggesting relevant hypotheses and the like. But by itself it cannot establish any

---

event, see above, Ch. 2, n. 13.) If we wish to speak about the particularity and peculiarity of a specific point in human history, we must have definite evidence (usually in the form of documentary testimony of some sort) on which to base our claims; and our knowledge takes the form usually indicated by the term "historical." If, on the other hand, we are concerned with certain more general movements or features of the historical process, our evidence can be drawn from, and our inferences made to, widely separated events; and our knowledge will take the form usually indicated by the term "scientific." Both types of knowledge are historical in the broad sense, however; i.e., both refer to and attempt to describe certain features of historical events. Thus, to answer the questions about Caesar's crossing the Rubicon requires specific documentation relating to that particular event. But, though such specific documentation of this particular sort is not required, the question whether man is a political animal is no less historical: in this case, of course, we are asking about certain features of the much broader and more inclusive event called "mankind" occurring within the overall history of *life;* or perhaps about that event called "western man" as it has unfolded within human history as a whole. When we see that "scientific" and "historical" knowledge are thus conjunctive within the broader framework of history, we shall not be so apt to pit them against each other as each *sui generis* and completely unconnected. On the contrary, we shall be in a better position to see why "scientific" knowledge, e.g., about the nature of the political process, can throw light on particular historical events such as Caesar's acquiring power in Rome; and, conversely, why the knowledge of such particular historical events can help make possible understanding of broader political movements and tendencies, and, indeed, even of the "power struggle" within and among various living species.

points in question. This can be done only through careful and critical analysis of specific testimony from reliable witnesses.

Thus, the facticity of an event in human history is never established simply by rational argument, experimental evidence, or direct insight. One can never, for example, simply by logical deduction from rational premises, prove a given event *must* have happened—unless one has direct or indirect evidence (i.e., memories and/or documents) from which to infer it. Of course, on the basis of such evidence one can make many ingenious and revealing deductions, but the documentary remains must be there first. Nor is historical facticity demonstrable through experiment. The past is over with and gone; it is not "out there," directly accessible to every inquiring eye. No kind of experiment can either prove or disprove that George Washington chopped down the cherry tree: historical evidence alone is relevant here (though certain scientific tests may be useful for accurate dating of documents, etc.). Finally, historical facticity cannot be established on the basis of direct intuition or immediate insight into the truth, though much sympathetic imagination and insight may be needed successfully to interpret obscure documentary or strange archaeological remains. In short, a particular event in human history can be affirmed to have happened if, and only if, memories, reports, and other documentary remains are available in the present, and careful critical analysis reveals them to be an adequate basis for historical reconstruction.

Therefore, if the Christian Gospel is the announcement or proclamation of a particular act of God in man's history,[2] it is evident that the ultimate epistemological foundation of Christian faith and Christian theology must be the reports of witnesses to that event. Obviously this is a shaky foundation for knowledge, not to say for the fundamental orientation of one's selfhood. The logical reasoning

---

[2] Talk about "a particular act of God" in this fashion, almost without reference to preceding and succeeding historical developments, is oversimplified and somewhat misleading, for it underplays the continuity of the "center" of a history (see above, pp. 30f.) with that historical movement of which it is the center. (See also below, pp. 53ff. and 90f.) Such talk, however, provides a useful way of opening up consideration of the Christian revelation claims, for they come to a sharp focus on a particular event in history. For an explicit analysis of these issues, see my paper, "On the Meaning of 'Act of God.'" *Harvard Theological Review* (1968) 61:175–201.

of rational philosophy, or the carefully controlled observation and theory of experimental science, or the direct intuition into truth of poets and mystics—each of these may seem more adequate and appropriate as a foundation for such weighty structures. For the historical character of the roots of theological knowledge means that this knowledge is radically contingent: if we happened not to have these few and somewhat fragmentary reports of God's action in history, we would have nothing.

Thus, the Christian claim is that the most important thing one can know is not some truths about the nature of God or man or the world—but the truth about certain events. For the Christian belief is that that historical movement which came to a climax two thousand years ago is still swelling and ultimately will engulf all history, gathering up all other historical processes in history's consummation. Even though the true significance of this movement is hidden from our direct vision, it is in fact the central historical stream, all other developments being either contributory to it or mere side-eddies which will ultimately be swept away. This, then, is the central event happening to and for us and our world: whether we know it or not, our history is being turned upside down by God's action in it, and this great transformation will inevitably catch up with us. The situation which obtains here is not substantially different from that of other momentous historical events; in each case we can learn what is happening only through the reports of competent witnesses. Few of us, for example, view at first hand what is occurring in Moscow or Peking, or even Washington. Yet crises in these far places daily affect our lives and may completely destroy our world. Moreover, these events shape our existence whether we know of their importance or not. Our understanding of them must be based on the reports of witnesses and interpreters believed reliable and competent—the local newspaper, *Time* Magazine, or perhaps some "inside dopester." The Christian witnesses claim to be reporting a far more significant historical movement than any of those in contemporary international politics, for this process comprehends all these others—political, cultural, intellectual, and religious—carrying them along with it. If their report is true—and this is obviously an enormous "if"—genuine

orientation in the world is impossible without knowledge of this movement. This vital knowledge is available to us, as with all knowledge
of significant historical movements, only through the reports of these
very same witnesses who insist on its great moment.

It should now be clear why it is peculiarly irrelevant to attempt
to establish or disestablish the Christian faith by means of natural
theologies or arguments for the existence of God, analyses of the
nature of man or scientific theories about the world. Such rationalistic
or naturalistic approaches do not touch its real foundations. The only
decisive question is: Did this event happen or not? Is this historical
movement occurring or not? This kind of question can be answered
only on the basis of the testimony of appropriate witnesses—submitted, of course, to the most rigorous historical and theological examination to which it can be subjected. In such analysis the objective
must be to find out both what the reports declare happened and
whether and in what degree they may be taken as veridical. Christian
theology in general may be defined as just such an attempt to grasp
cognitively and interpret the actual event(s) to which the biblical
documents witness. In this respect it is closely related to ordinary
historical work in both method and objectives.[3]

To what events, now, do our witnesses testify? On what historical
occurrences are they reporting? To any modern mind the claims here
must appear very odd. Unlike our histories, which deal as exclusively
as possible in strictly human actions, here the witnesses claim to be
reporting the revelatory act(s) in history of the Creator of the universe. How are such claims to be evaluated? By what canons can they
be judged? Can such statements be regarded as cognitively meaningful? We shall have to defer consideration of these important questions
until we have considered more fully the express content of the Christian claims. The first step of the historical task must be to *understand*
the documents, not to evaluate them. Indeed, the latter can be carried
out only on the basis of the former. We cannot properly insist that
the premises of the testimony about a God who acts in history be
validated before we give serious attention to the testimony itself, for
we can have no access to the premises of reports apart from understanding what the reports themselves are claiming. However difficult

[3] For a fuller discussion of this matter see Ch. 4 below.

it may be imaginatively to project ourselves into a frame of orientation from which we can grasp what is being said here, precisely this is required by the *historical* nature of the theological starting-point. In this connection, however, we may well remind ourselves that the word "God" as used in ordinary English discourse (cf. Chapter 1) is quite in keeping with the biblical portrayal of him as a historical agent.

In certain respects the Christian claims did not seem so shocking to the men who first made and heard them. They, unlike most of us, had been taught by centuries of Jewish tradition that God acts in history, directing it toward the fulfilment of his purposes. And under the influence of prophetic and apocalyptic writers they had come to expect that the decisive historical act of God was to come in the future, perhaps very soon. Hence, when Jesus came preaching that the time is now, the kingdom of God is approaching and very near—indeed is already breaking into history in Jesus' own ministry (Lk. 11:20, 17:21)— it did not seem incredible. The great event which every faithful Jew expected was finally happening.

The particular form which this event took, however, was difficult to accept, and most who knew anything about the matter were convinced that the early Christian proclamation was false, if not blasphemous. For Judaism, the relationship between God and man was rooted in earlier covenants between God and Noah, God and Abraham, and preeminently between God and the people of Israel under Moses' leadership. In these momentous events God had revealed his Law— the very order and shape of authentic human existence—and it was man's responsibility to govern his life accordingly. If he did so, he would enjoy happiness and well-being; but if he refused or failed, God would punish and might ultimately destroy him. It was also believed, of course, that God was merciful and would forgive the penitent who turn to him in their shortcomings for renewed strength in their efforts to obey. But to the unrighteous and to the disobedient Gentiles, God was a "consuming fire" (Deut. 4:24 KJ). Now came this Jesus preaching that God does not seek to destroy even the most rebellious of sinners; on the contrary, he desires to forgive man's sin and rescue him from bondage to it, and hence he is even now bringing his kingdom into history. Men need only gratefully accept God's

forgiveness and joyously enter the kingdom with its new life of love
to brother and enemy alike. This preaching, threatening as it did religious cultus as well as economic and political interests, resulted in
Jesus' execution. But this only made matters worse. For soon the
disciples of Jesus were preaching the incredible story that in the
ministry, death, and what they now claimed to be the resurrection of
Jesus, the forgiving God himself had come to man in the person of his
"Son," sacrificing himself so that man might be rescued from his
plight and apparently bypassing the Law entirely.

> But now the righteousness of God has been manifested apart from
> law, . . . the righteousness of God through faith in Jesus Christ for
> all who believe. For there is no distinction; since all have sinned
> and fall short of the glory of God, they are justified by his grace
> as a gift, through the redemption which is in Christ Jesus.
>
> ROMANS 3:21–24

This was very strong and very strange language to be uttering
about the God of perfect righteousness and Law, who rightfully exercises his wrathful justice against man's sin. It implied that man's
condition is considerably worse than Judaism imagined. It is so
serious in fact that man himself can do little about it: he is separated
from the real, the good, the true, and he cannot even take the first step
toward healing himself, turning toward God in genuine penitence.
Therefore, there is no possible way for the requirements of the covenant to be realized from the human side even within Judaism, to say
nothing of the Gentiles.[4] Man is in a kind of quicksand such that his
every struggle to escape only mires him deeper.[5] It is also implied

---

[4] "What then? Are we Jews any better off? No, not at all; for I have already
charged that all men, both Jews and Greeks, are under the power of sin, as it is written:
'None is righteous, no, not one; no one understands, no one seeks for God. All have
turned aside, together they have gone wrong; no one does good, not even one'" (Rom.
3:9–12).

[5] ". . . if it had not been for the law, I should not have known sin. I should not
have known what it is to covet if the law had not said, 'You shall not covet.' But sin,
finding opportunity in the commandment, wrought in me all kinds of covetousness.
Apart from the law sin lies dead. I was once alive apart from the law, but when the
commandment came, sin revived and I died; the very commandment which promised
life proved to be death to me. For sin, finding opportunity in the commandment, deceived me and by it killed me" (Rom. 7:7–11).

that God is significantly different from the Jewish conception. Although his wrath against sin is terrible, nevertheless he loves man with such a passion that he is willing to sacrifice even himself in order to restore man's proper relation to him. And precisely this is what he did: he bridged the gap between himself and man by himself becoming a man and participating in all the evils of the human condition.[6] He was even "made . . . to be sin," as Paul put it (2 Cor. 5:21), that is, he suffered in his own being—however paradoxical this may seem—the supreme alienation which man suffers in being lost and alone, separated from God; and the man Jesus died with despairing words on his lips: "My God, my God, why hast thou forsaken me?" (Mk. 15:34).[7]

The impact of the Christian message on many faithful Jews must have been quite negative. Instead of righteously destroying sinful man, God—the Creator of the universe—is willing to be broken within himself, to suffer self-estrangement, in order to rescue man from his terrible plight and win him back. This near-blasphemous proclamation Judaism was not prepared to accept. Even Second Isaiah, in whose prophetic imagination the hard but challenging figure of the "suffering servant" was created, apparently thought in terms of a human sufferer, perhaps the people of Israel or a "faithful remnant." No one had dared suggest that God takes upon himself the whole terrible burden of evil wrought by man's rebelliousness. But the Christian claim was precisely this: that though man had fallen into bondage to "principalities" and "powers," the sinful "rulers of this present darkness" (Eph. 6:12), God had taken decisive action in

[6] "For He, Who had always been God by nature, did not cling to His prerogatives . . . but stripped Himself of all privilege by consenting to be a slave by nature and being born as mortal man. And, having become man, He humbled Himself by living a life of utter obedience, even to the extent of dying, and the death He died was the death of a common criminal" (Phil. 2:5–8 Phillips). "In the beginning was the Word, and the Word was with God, and the Word was God. . . . And the Word became flesh and dwelt among us" (John 1:1, 14).

[7] It is widely held that, since the Markan report of the crucifixion is the earliest and (along with Matthew) knows nothing of the far less harsh words reported in Luke and John, and since, moreover, it is not at all difficult to understand why the early church might have created the latter to replace, or at least supplement, the former, the Markan report is probably historically more reliable. I do not consider here the theological difficulties raised by such an end to Jesus' life, nor the various alternative ways of interpreting these hard words, suggested in the church almost from the beginning.

history in and through Jesus to rescue man from this hopeless condition.

Men might choose to believe or not to believe this message; men might believe God is very different from what is laid bare in this mighty act, or they might believe there is no God at all; men might not even be aware that there was anything seriously wrong with them, and live in relative ease and complacency—none of these various responses would qualify the import or truth of the Christian claim one particle. The only really important thing to know or to say was that because God had acted in human history, the whole character of man's existence had been and was being transformed. Whereas human history and life were formerly separated from their true ground, now, whether men knew it or not, they were being reunited with God, for he had taken this estrangement up into his own being.

Our interpretation thus far has remained on a relatively abstract and mythological level with words about an "act of God" but very little historical or experiential content given that phrase. In consequence we may have before us the image of some momentous lightning-stroke from heaven which, since it seems to stand discontinuous with the ordinary human words and actions which make up the stuff of history, has little positive content or significance. Moreover, since the history we know appears to be made up of just such human actions and words, penetrating and permeating each other so that no events have absolutely sharp and distinct boundaries but all flow into each other in a complex web, it may be questioned whether it is meaningful or appropriate to speak of "God's act" (as thus far sketched) as a *historical* event at all. Has this alleged event actually entered into the on-going historical process and become a factor immanent within human history and existence itself? Until and unless this can be shown, the Christian claim that God has actually acted *in human history* remains empty of meaning.

A moment's reflection will reveal that God's act in Christ, as spoken of in the Christian community, has seldom been understood to be in radical discontinuity with the on-going historical process. It has almost always been held both in the church and in secular culture generally that the event's time of occurrence can be dated with relative precision and the person in and through and around whom it occurred can be described with some accuracy. The event itself was noted in the first place and later remembered, of course, because its impact was sufficient significantly to transform whole lives—and ultimately the whole of Western culture. We must attempt to see, then, how the manward, immanent, historical, experiential side of the event is to be understood.

When it is said that men's lives, and indeed all of human history, have been transformed by God's act, it is clear that some merely physical transformation is not what is meant. Rather, this act was a radical transmutation of the *web of meaning* in which the men to whom it occurred had their existence and their orientation, and it effected a decisive reorientation of their existence and consciousness: fear and distrust were transformed into faith and hope, hate and selfishness into love and self-giving, anthropocentrism into theocentrism. Thus, God's act in Christ was not some event that simply was what it was without regard to human consciousness or response; on the contrary, from the beginning it was conceived as consisting precisely in a decisive reorientation of man's entire conscious and volitional being. The earliest Christians came to apprehend themselves as new men; as Paul put it, "if any one is in Christ, he is a new creation" (2 Cor. 5:17).[8]

How, now, can this "act of God," transforming the very meaning-structure in which men live and thus human being itself, be understood? What kind of action from outside us, transcending the circle of our existence, can break into our world transforming us? Our best analogy here (as we noted in our discussion of the "form of revelation") is interpersonal intercourse. In conversation, for ex-

---

[8] To say this was an event transformative of the "web of meaning" in which men live does not mean "God's act" was a merely "mental" event not affecting the deeper strata of man's being. Man is a psychosomatic unity in which "spiritual" and "physical" interpenetrate each other in such a way that what happens in or to either "side" of man's being has its repercussions in the other. Hence, though events of superficial meaning may be largely "mental," a *radical* change in the structure of meaning in which a man lives affects not only his consciousness, but ultimately penetrates to the core of his being. On the basis of evolutionary theory one might expect that important and relatively permanent changes in the psychological conditions under which life is carried on—e.g., the increasing complexity of modern life, or a changing world-view which so radically transforms self-understanding as to alter the whole sense of the meaning of human existence—over a sufficiently long span of time would, because of the plastic adaptive capacity of life, ultimately have significant effect on man's physical organism, especially its neurological dimensions (cf. Carleton S. Coon, *The Origin of Races* [New York: Knopf, 1962], pp. 106–112, 118).

ample, a word spoken by one is apprehended by another not simply as a noise but as a complex of meaning, thereby qualifying, however slightly, the meaning-structure of his consciousness. Without such appropriation (at least subconsciously) no communication occurs. Upon rare occasions a word may be spoken—for example, "I love you," or "He has betrayed you," or "Your mother was just killed in an accident"—which drastically upsets and reorients the structure of meaning in which a person has been living. The word spoken or deed performed by another, if appropriated by me, may become the agency of my remaking, or, perhaps, my unmaking.

It is significant in this connection that John entitles Jesus the "Word" of God (John 1:1–18). God's act, that is to say, is not a kind of mechanical or physical thrust into the human situation, manipulating it from without. On the contrary, it is like a word spoken between persons, coming from without but working its effect from within as the hearer appropriates its meaning and responds to it. Communication of meaning is never simply a unilateral process; it is completed—and without such completion communication does not in fact occur—only when the hearer's own act of appropriation and response is evoked (at least subconsciously). To say God's act in Christ is revelatory, and Jesus is the Word of God, means that the event Jesus Christ was an occurrence in and through which God spoke and man heard; that is, here God communicated himself with sufficient effectiveness that man was enabled to appropriate the meaning and respond to it, his existence thus being radically transformed. Or, stated less mythologically, one could say that the event Jesus Christ had special significance because in and through it such new and revolutionary meaning was created in human history as decisively to reorient that history. This creation-of-a-new-meaning-orientation is what in this case is denoted (empirically) by the words "God's act."[9]

    [9] Cf. Karl Barth: "[God's] acts are identical with the history, so trivial compared with His eternity, of the people of Israel and of the Christian community which has its centre in the history of Jesus" (Church Dogmatics, III, 2 [Edinburgh: T. & T. Clark, 1960], 524; italics mine). It should not be supposed, of course, that God "acts" only in the realm of "meaning"; according to the Christian view he also created and ordered the (physical) world, guided the evolutionary process, and the like (see Pt. II, below).

It is now possible to understand the relation of this act of God to the *kerygma* and life of the early church. God's act in Christ created a new situation within history itself. Whereas before men had been alienated from the ground of their being and thus broken within themselves, now they were being reconciled with God, and their wounds were healing because of the powerful transformative event within which they knew themselves to be living. In this situation the human task—authentic human existence—became twofold: (a) entering into God's kingdom, living the new life of love to fellows made possible by God's healing man's sin here in his historical existence; and (b) proclaiming this good news of God's act. This preaching and acting were direct expressions in human terms of the radical new meaning (God's act); that is, they were vehicles on the human historical level through which God's meaning-creating act continued. As Paul put it: "God was in Christ reconciling the world to himself . . . and entrusting to us the message of reconciliation. So we are ambassadors for Christ, God making his appeal through us" (2 Cor. 5:19–20). Insofar as this occurred, new hearers came to apprehend and be transformed by the revolutionary meaning; and God's act (being just this meaning) continued to occur in the consciousness, and thus the existence, of wider and wider circles of men.

It is important to recognize that this spreading of the Gospel to new converts was no merely secondary and derivative process, inferior in significance to the event experienced by the original disciples. On the contrary, it was a direct continuation of that act of God (i.e., that transmutation of meaning) first known by those disciples. "He who hears you hears me," Jesus is reported to have said (Lk. 10:16); "He who receives you receives me, and he who receives me receives him who sent me" (Mt. 10:40). The original disciples thus enjoyed no preferential position with respect to God's act. To all who hear the preaching and who appropriate in their lives the meaning of the good news, the event creative of a new meaning-orientation happens anew; and thus all are equally the direct recipients of God's gift of new life.[10] Thus, the same original historical

[10] In the Fourth Gospel this equality of all believers with respect to God's redemptive act is expressed ontologically in the "high-priestly prayer" put in the mouth of Jesus: "I do not pray for these only [i.e., for the disciples who knew Jesus personally],

act of God, carried in preaching and tradition and practices of the church, is transmitted from believer to believer and generation to generation as the meaning of the Gospel is again and again appropriated. Or, to state the same thing now from the other side, God performs his act repeatedly for each new convert (as well as for each new moment of any believer's life)—or better: God is continuously working in and through men's words and deeds in history, making himself known and effective, and thus transforming human existence and history.[11]

God's redemptive act, then, is not an event which happened in some dead past and is now, unfortunately, over with and gone. Indeed, as the central event of history, it is not bounded by Jesus' birth and death: just as all preceding history going back to "before the foundation of the world" must be seen as its preparatory phases, so its fulfilment is not realized until all that ensues is comprehended within it. The selfsame act of God thus continues until all history— and the men living within history—are taken up into its meaning and human historical existence is genuinely transformed.[12]

---

but also for those who are to believe in me through their word, that they may all be one; even as thou, Father, art in me, and I in thee, that they also may be in us, so that the world may believe that thou hast sent me. The glory which thou hast given me I have given to them, that they may be one even as we are one, I in them and thou in me, that they may become perfectly one, so that the world may know that thou hast sent me and hast loved them even as thou hast loved me" (John 17:20–23).

[11] If God's redemptive act is understood in this way as preeminently creative of a revolutionary meaning-complex within human history, the "contemporaneity" of his act in Christ with all believers, and the equality of every generation of disciples with respect to faith, are not the incomprehensible paradoxical mysteries suggested by Kierkegaard (*Philosophical Fragments* [Princeton: Princeton University Press, 1946], Chs. 4–5), and also found in the anti-historical pietism and mysticism characteristic of much traditional Christian thinking about Christ and the atonement. Rather, they are precisely what might be reasonably expected in view of the historical structure of human existence.

[12] It is already apparent that the phrase "act of God" has two meanings, and it is important to distinguish these and keep them clear. As the above paragraph suggests, the phrase refers most comprehensively—and most fundamentally—to the overarching act which encompasses the entire movement of history from creation to eschaton (see Pt. II). But it can also be used (and this is perhaps more in keeping both with biblical and ordinary usage) to designate *a particular phase* of that overarching act, as when one speaks of God's "mighty act" delivering Israel from Egypt, or his sending of a prophet, or his raising Jesus from the dead. In such cases as these it would be technically more exact to speak of "sub-acts" or "subordinate acts," since such events should be understood, finally, as but steps toward the realization of God's ultimate objective(s) and thus as phases of the overarching act in which he is engaged throughout history. However, since these locutions are so cumbersome and since it is much more common to

This can all be true only insofar as this meaning (God's act) can actually be conveyed by human words and deeds. And men's action and language are, at best, even for purposes of ordinary interchange, always imperfect vehicles. Words have a life of their own: we cannot bend them completely to our purposes because they come to us with already formed meanings. There will be connotations and even denotations of which we are unaware, or which we do not desire to communicate, and there is no way for us to cut away these penumbras of meaning. The words used to preach the Gospel already had complex meanings in the cultures from which they were drawn—they could not be created *de novo* for the special purpose of communicating God's redemptive act, or nothing would have been communicated at all—and it was these culturally and historically shaped meanings that were apprehended when words were spoken or deeds performed.

Moreover, it was men, not God, who spoke these words, proclaimed this Gospel. And men—even apostles and prophets—are not above using words for their own ends, commending and exalting themselves rather than God, even though they know they should "Let him who boasts, boast of the Lord."[13] Unfortunately Christians have often been guilty of this perversion, proclaiming the superiority of their faith over other religions, competing in their church programs even with the Rotary Club. It is hardly surprising that the obnoxious self-advertisement of such pious societies has been regarded as "good news" by scarcely anyone. For what was principally conveyed in such activities

---

refer to such particular events as "acts" of God, I have frequently found it convenient to follow this less exact practice. It is important for the reader to understand that whenever such conventional use of the phrase appears in this work, it is not being used in the technically exact sense, but rather to designate what is actually but a phase or stage of the single overarching "act of God," which encompasses the entire movement of (cosmic and human) history. (For further analysis of this problem, see my paper, "On the Meaning of 'Act of God,'" *op. cit.* [above, n. 2].)

[13] Even immediately after making this statement (2 Cor. 10:17), Paul cannot refrain from commending himself: "I think that I am not in the least inferior to these superlative apostles. . . . What I am saying I say not with the Lord's authority but as a fool, in this boastful confidence; since many boast of worldly things I too will boast. . . . But whatever anyone dares to boast of—I am speaking as a fool—I also dare to boast of that. Are they Hebrews? So am I. Are they Israelites? So am I. Are they descendants of Abraham? So am I. Are they servants of Christ? I am a better one—I am talking like a madman—with far greater labors, far more imprisonments, with countless beatings, and often near death. . . . I must boast; there is nothing to be gained by it, but I will go on" (2 Cor. 11:5, 17–18, 21–23; 12:1).

was human arrogance and self-righteousness—even though precisely "correct" biblical or theological words were chosen and properly "religious" attitudes displayed. Genuine Christian preaching and acting occur only in a context of authentic humility before God and fellow man, the humility which knows it is God—not man—who has acted to create a redemptive context of meaning in human history and God alone who can extend this act to new circles of faith. For this reason the church's life and message must always be accompanied not only by prayer—that God's Word and not merely man's will be heard —but also by the most stringent kind of self-criticism, intended to assure that appropriate words are chosen and deeds performed. It is this latter task that is the special province of theological thinking.

4 / The Nature of
Theological Thinking

THE NECESSITY continuously to criticize language and ideas, actions and meanings, by reference to God's act, is the theological basis and justification for Christian theology. Theology is the church's attempt to take her own measure and to improve her language so that she can more adequately respond to and preach the Gospel, that is, become the vehicle of God's saving act. Obviously, Christians are involved in theologizing at every turn. Every attempt to discover and reflect upon the real meaning of the Gospel, of a passage in the Bible, of Jesus Christ, is theologizing; every effort to discover the bearing of the Christian faith or the Christian ethic on the problems of personal and social life is theological. For Christian theology is the critical analysis and creative development of the language utilized in apprehending, understanding, and interpreting God's acts, facilitating their communication in word and deed.

In her attempt adequately to express the Gospel, the church has found it necessary to develop linguistic and conceptual schemes to deal with the many features of the complex interrelationships among God, man, and the world. In time the understanding of the more prominent of these received somewhat standardized and regularized formulations as *doctrines*. Each of the several Christian doctrines— trinity, two natures of Christ, atonement, heaven, sacraments, church, etc.—points toward and interprets an aspect of God's being and action sufficiently important to require that our attention be focused directly on it for a time, if it is to be properly grasped.

Even so, however, the theological subject matter overflows and ultimately escapes being fully comprehended. It should not be surprising, therefore, that there have been rather large differences of emphasis and interpretation within the Christian community. One group grasps more firmly than another the meaning of one side of the Christian faith; accordingly it emphasizes the doctrines or attitudes which most clearly express the crucial importance of this insight. Since none are able to grasp God's activity perfectly in their one-sided human conceptualizations, differing emphases easily develop. Sometimes these have led simply to schools of interpretation existing side by side within the same communion; upon occasion they have resulted in denominational divisions, so characteristic particularly of protestantism. Although these differences in perspective and mode of life have often led to regrettable consequences, they should not be regarded as wholly unfortunate. For the denominations are living witnesses to the importance of the insight into Christian faith which each knows. Within the limits of human finitude such divisions, with the resultant conversations and struggles, may well be the essential sociological expression of the necessity to correct the one-sidedness of every interpretation and every tradition, so that the fullness of the whole Christian faith is not lost.

Whenever any such group officially designates a particular doctrinal formulation as correct, in contrast with other formulations ruled out, *dogma* is created. Through its action the group is seeking to impress upon itself and others the fact that this particular formulation lies at the very foundation of its life. *Heresy*, in contrast, is any doctrinal position explicitly in conflict with, and ruled out by, some dogma(s). It is, of course, a mistake to think that only Roman Catholics or conservative protestants are concerned with dogma; liberals also have means of defining themselves over against others, and even the communities of humanism and agnosticism obviously have their—often rather inflexible—dogmas.[1] Although a doctrinal and dogmatic development is inevitable and necessary in any community-concerned to understand and adequately express the basis of its life, it also has real dangers. The most important of these in the

[1] It is true, of course, that the Roman Catholic church structure is such that the official position of the community can be more readily promulgated than in the case of some of these other groups.

Christian community is the tendency to forget that doctrine has its meaning only insofar as it helps illuminate and enable understanding and expression of God's activity. Doctrines—even dogmas—have no independent meaning or truth: they acquire significance only as they succeed in directing attention away from themselves, back toward God.

Since God is one, not many, simple, not divisible (see Chapter 10), the different doctrines have their proper meaning only when seen in their essential unity, that is, in their interconnection, interrelation, interdependence. *Systematic theology* is the attempt thus to see each doctrine in its relation to the whole Christian faith, and to see the whole with all the fullness and richness which the several doctrines collectively disclose. Such critical systematic study is essential for anyone seriously interested in understanding and appropriating God's action, since we easily fall into extravagant overemphasis and one-sideness, often falling into self-contradiction. Systematic theology, as insight into the unity of the whole Christian faith, is the beginning of genuine theological thinking; as the relating of one doctrine to another in the attempt to see the meaning of each, it is the method of all theologizing; as an overall view which sees the richness and fullness of the Christian Gospel, it is the goal of theological work.

Although the theological task may be neglected by no serious Christian, it also has its dangers. One can become so engrossed in theology as to forget that its end is not itself, but to glorify God and clarify what he has done. This ever-present tendency to revert to anthropocentrism and even egocentrism in theological work—showing itself all too often in nasty and disrespectful disputes among theologians—shows that theology must build into its method a continuous turning-back to the activity of God, which is its source and foundation as well as its true meaning. In the main body of this chapter we must examine how we can do this "turning-back," attempting to see the sources and criteria in terms of which the validity of theology may be judged.

But first we should note the relation of this description of theology, as emergent from and serving the life and work of the church, to our earlier analysis of the theological concept of revelation as a useful tool for understanding the historicity of human existence and

thought in general. Is theology the instrument of a particular historical community, or is it a general philosophical task? If the former,
is it not a kind of ideology or propaganda subordinating the pursuit
of truth to the needs of an insitiution? If the latter, must not the alleged "Christian revelation" be considered but one among many
parochial examples of the historico-ontological grounding of a perspective, hardly an "act of God" in some definitive or decisive sense?
What is the connection between theology as an explication of the
Christian faith and the more general philosophical problems of the
analysis and interpretation of human existence?

Let us begin by acknowledging again the formal analogy between
the Christian faith as rooted in the Christ-event and other perspectives with their historical foundations. Christian convictions and
Christian faith, like any other human stance, are modes of human
existence; they are grounded, like other such modes, in a "revelatory
history," borne by a community (in this case, the church) which apprehends this historical tradition as the very meaning of its life.
There is no reason to dispute this obvious historico-ontological fact:
this was precisely the point of our earlier analysis. But in this case
the *revelatory* character of the events is taken with a seriousness—
indeed, a literalness—not often apparent in other perspectives. For
these events are here interpreted in direct accord with the model of
revelation drawn from interpersonal relations, in which the circle of
experience of a self is "broken into" from "beyond" by the word
of another self addressing him: they are, therefore, events which *properly*—and not merely analogously—are to be conceived as "revelatory." This has very important implications. It means that the Christian community, on the basis of the events inaugurating its existence,
has become persuaded that the decisively constitutive relationship in
which men stand is not to be understood in intrahuman or even intra-
worldly terms, but that our existence and our histories are rooted in
One "transcending" the world as its source and ground. This history,
thus, claims to be more than just another sequence of creative events
which we choose to dub, somewhat overdramatically, as "revelatory";
it claims to be that sequence through which in actual fact the very
Creator of all being has revealed himself.

Since for the Christian community the knowledge of God has been so closely bound up with the actual historical events which produced and shaped Christian existence, in all its determinateness and concreteness, it has not proved possible to conceive him except in terms defined by those events themselves, particularly that person-event which intruded itself upon the church as his definitive self-manifestation. Hence, unlike some of the other perspectives we have described which are scarcely aware how indebted they are to a particular "revelatory" history, Christian faith has been unable to forget its historico-ontological ground, Jesus Christ. Instead of being some unknown historical source of meaning for the Christian perspective—a particular example of a general philosophical category—he has been consciously appropriated as the very norm or criterion of both human and divine being, the standard to which Christian individual and community must continuously deliberately turn. It is thus not as some abstract Ground of Being or Form of the Good—equally relevant, and irrelevant, to every concrete existential situation—that the Christian God is known: a reality like that would hardly have been so definitively encountered in a particular moment of historical existence. He is known, rather, as "the God and Father of . . . Jesus Christ" (Rom. 15:6).

Because of this great weight of meaning inseparably connected with the person-event Jesus Christ, Christian theology has been forced to pay particular attention to the peculiar metaphysical character of historical persons and events and their meanings. In consequence, though theology began as, and in some sense has always remained, essentially a servant of the Christian revelation and church, it generated a metaphysic of human history and man's historicity that is of general philosophical interest and significance. The great characteristic Christian doctrines each interpret some aspect of the realities spoken of in this metaphysic: history, with all its peculiarities of decision, purpose, and more and less meaningful moments, understood as reality; the real, understood as intrinsically historical and personal. This focussing on history is especially evident in the christological doctrines, which analyze and interpret in metaphysical terms the several dimensions of the person-event Jesus Christ, the act of

God transforming the corrupted historical existence of man. The doctrines of the atonement and reconciliation, of the incarnation and the two natures of Christ, are all explications of the metaphysic of this event. But other doctrines are no less involved: the doctrine of the trinity at the heart of the Christian understanding of God; the historical character of all finite being developed in the doctrines of creation, providence, and eschaton; the special character of human history explored in terms of fall and sin, on the one hand, and the new life of faith, hope, and love known in the church, on the other. One could go on until the whole sweep of Christian theology had been compassed and the Christian perspective clearly delineated as an understanding of man's history and historicity in all its subtleties and ramifications. However, since just this is the object of this systematic theology as a whole, no more need be said at this point.

The weight of meaning in the Christ-event—throwing significant light on all reality and brilliant light on human existence—has impressed itself on Christians in such overpowering fashion that metaphysical conceptualization seemed essential. Though all other perspectives have also been born of a "revelatory" history, in none have the events of that history been so sharply delineated, and the vortex of the historical movement been at once so evident and so glorious, as to require such drastic modes of interpretation. This of course proves nothing regarding the validity or truth of the Christian claims, but it does help explain why Christian theology developed a doctrine of revelation. The Christian community knew itself to be living not out of the fullness of its own resources but from beyond itself in the most radical possible way. One could, of course, deny this "absolute dependence" (Schleiermacher) for being and meaning on a reality transcending human existence, history, and even the world. But if this dependence is fact—ontological fact—then doctrines of revelation and creation, expressive as they are of a conception of ultimate reality modelled on the transcendence of the other self over against one in dialogue, are appropriate. Although, as we have seen, such notions can be useful for understanding the historico-ontological grounds of other points of view, it is Christian faith that they fit as glove on hand.

Since theology is the attempt of the Christian community to

understand its rootage in revelatory history, it must be founded upon
the study, analysis, and interpretation of the biblical documents.
"The Bible is the concrete medium by which the Church recalls God's
revelation in the past. . . ."[2] Certain historical events are of central
concern here, and the primary source documents, those nearest the
events and most directly seeking to report and interpret them, are
in the Bible. All subsequent Christian writings are historically,
and thus theologically, derivative from those collected here. The
Bible's authority for theology derives not from its being a magically
"inspired" book whose sentences consist of the very words of God;
it is a human book like any other, written and transcribed by human
hands, translated by human minds, consisting of ink marks on paper
which must be sympathetically and imaginatively interpreted by
human readers to have any meaning. The Bible's authority derives
from the revelatory events of which it contains the primary reports.
Biblical statements, therefore, however significant they may appear
to be, can be of legitimate theological interest only insofar as they
throw light on God's historical acts. How, now, can we apprehend
these with the aid of the biblical documents?

At first sight it may seem that we are confronted here with the
standard historical problem, namely, how does one get behind documents to the events to which they point? How can one reconstruct
events by means of the relevant evidence? But this is a superficial
view. For we are dealing here with a very peculiar event, one apprehended as *revelatory* of ultimate reality and of the meaning of
human existence. Our task as historians here is to uncover and reconstruct this event *in its revelatoriness*, so that we can see it in precisely this peculiar respect.

This presents us with a rather odd historical problem. An event
(or process) can be called "revelatory," we concluded earlier, when
through it the meaning of the existence of a community or individual
has flowed into the historical stream; it is an event because of which
and by means of which a given perspective interprets the rest of
history. Every historian, of course, is himself oriented in terms of
some quasi-revelatory events which give meaning to his work, but
ordinarily a historian may be quite unaware of these theological

2 Karl Barth, *Church Dogmatics*, I, 1 (Edinburgh: T. & T. Clark, 1936), 124.

presuppositions of his own historical existence. Since the crucial
revelatory history is always *presupposed* in his work, there is no
point at which it naturally appears as a special historical problem.
Hence, the ordinary historian may not concern himself at all with
the peculiarities of "revelatory" as distinguished from ordinary
events.

It is not possible to analyze an event in its revelatoriness from any
other perspective than that of the community which apprehends it as
revelation. This may appear a severe and unfortunate restriction, but
it is certainly not unintelligible. The revelatory character of the
event Jesus Christ cannot even be perceived from the standpoints of
rationalists or Marxists, working within different frameworks of
meaning rooted in other historical "revelations." No doubt such
other perspectives can teach us something about this event, but they
cannot enable us to apprehend what it means to take it as God's
revelatory act.[3] Thus, if the event at the root of Christian faith is to
be studied in its revelatoriness of ultimate meaning—and this is just
the task of theology, and, one might add, a legitimate historical
problem—it must be analyzed precisely in its character as the historical source of normative patterns of meaning; it must be uncovered as
the source of the very framework of interpretation in terms of which
it is itself understood.

Despite this peculiarity of our historical problem, many of the
operations to be performed will be similar to those of standard historical work. It is as necessary here as there to engage in word studies,
critical comparison of texts, searching out of inconsistencies and de-
ducing their implications, etc.—all with the object of finally giving
a reasonable historical reconstruction which at once makes sense of
the sequence of events and does justice to all the documentary evidence. But this all must be carried through with very different questions in view: How is this episode in history to be understood as
God's decisive act of revelation and redemption? not (as for the
secular historian), how is it to be understood simply as another epi-

[3] It should be acknowledged, of course, that if the Christian perspective is founded
on an event through which the ultimate source and basis of *all* existence is unveiled,
then these other viewpoints will also be ultimately taken up into, and comprehensible in
terms of, the Christian. This question will be taken up later in the chapter.

sode in man's history? How is this point in human existence to be grasped as the very source of meaning for understanding all experience? not, how is this simply another aspect of human existence, of no significant qualitative or ontological difference from any other? In order to understand and interpret its Gospel, the Christian community must be unsparing in its use of the tools of critical scholarship—for there is simply no other way to get behind historical documents to the events to which they point—but it must not be misled into using these tools only to answer questions posed by other communities. They must be made to serve the purposes and answer the questions which the Christian community cannot avoid asking about its own historico-ontological foundation.

In this search for understanding, the ultimate authority of God's revelatory act over every phase of theological work must not be forgotten. Christian theology is not simply the work of autonomous man thinking whatever he pleases; on the contrary, it is produced when men seek deliberately to subject their thinking to the authority of God's revelation. Since the revelation is apprehended as the right and proper source of the ultimate norms of meaning and truth, to work independently of it could only mean attempting invalid and finally meaningless intellectual activity. We should not suppose this subjection to authority limits the freedom of the theologian in some undesirable way. For everyone, as we observed in our discussion of the concept of revelation, stands under some authority in the sense of more or less spontaneously turning in some *particular direction* to some *particular locus* when he seeks truth: to sense experience or scientific method, to logical or semantic analysis, to psychoanalysis or aesthetic insight.[4] From a Christian point of view, however, if

[4] The basis for selection of one's authority is an interesting question which we cannot go into here. For the most part this choice is not made on strictly rational grounds—i.e., because we see one authority to be more adequate than others—for our very criteria of adequacy are always rooted in the authority before which we have already bowed. The selection takes place at levels of the self below consciousness, doubtless being influenced by cultural and environmental pressures, past experiences, etc. We are confronted here with what is known theologically as the mystery of election (see below, pp. 305f.). On the one hand we wake up one day to discover that our "authority" has chosen us, not we him. On the other, we find ourselves freely consenting to his authority; it is not something imposed on us heteronomously and against our desire.

one's authority is less or other than the very revelation of God, it is idolatrous and enslaving.

This, however, raises as serious a problem for Christian theology as for other perspectives. For how, after all, does one subject himself directly to the authority of God? Every being or reality sufficiently accessible to us that we might submit directly to it is particular and finite, another creature rather than the Creator. Recognizing this, theologians have in practice looked to several proximate but accessible finite authorities for guidance in their work.

1] All forms of catholicism (Anglican, Eastern Orthodox, Roman) have tended to hold the *Christian tradition* as a whole, especially as interpreted by the living church, to be the proper theological authority. In Roman Catholicism this point of view has hardened into the dogma of papal infallibility.

2] The dominant protestant view has regarded the *Bible* as the locus of authority. But the Bible is a somewhat miscellaneous collection of materials written in various times and often from quite different points of view. Whatever some groups may have claimed, therefore, in actual fact the Bible as a whole has never been, and could never be, taken as theologically authoritative; instead, certain portions of the biblical literature have been used as the key by means of which the mystery of the whole was unlocked. Thus, protestant orthodoxy (and neo-orthodoxy) found the point of view expressed in the letters of Paul authoritative; the left-wing Reformation sects looked more directly to the life and teachings of Jesus, particularly in the synoptic gospels; protestant spiritualism found the Johannine tradition most meaningful. In the doctrine of the verbal inspiration and literal inerrancy of the scriptures this protestant conception of authority as biblical was given virtually dogmatic status in some groups. Too often the Bible here was no longer understood as the medium of God's revelation but as identical with the truth itself.

3] Christian mysticism, protestant spiritualism and Quakerism, and much of modern protestantism have sought their authority in the *inner conviction of truth*, the interior witness of the Holy Spirit. This view also has frequently deteriorated and become rigid, not only in the fanaticism of some self-proclaimed prophets and their disciples, but in much modern individualism, according to which *my* opinion, *my* reason or conscience, is regarded as the final truth for me, beyond which there is no authority to whom I am responsible.

Each of these positions can make some legitimate claims to theological authority; but none may be regarded as final and beyond criticism. Such an attitude would be idolatrous, replacing the ultimate independence and mystery of God's revelation with the authority of church dogma or biblical statement or individual conscience. It is important, therefore, that we define rather carefully the legitimate place of these proximate theological authorities, being careful to see that each is kept subject to God's revelatory act.

How, then, can genuine authority for theological work reside in these positions, and yet they be apprehended as derivative and secondary, not ultimate? For the Christian faith, as we have seen, God's revelatory act—the ultimate authority—is a historical event. As with all events in the past, this one is not immediately accessible to us but must be appropriated through imaginative reconstruction on the basis of critical analysis of documentary materials. The ultimate theological authority, thus, is inaccessible in two respects: (a) *as historical event,* God's act cannot be directly experienced but must be mediated to us by means of the appropriate historical evidences and methods; (b) *as revelation* of the One who transcends all history, God's act is not immediately present even in the historical reconstruction of the person-event Jesus Christ, but must be mediated through this event as received by faith. If God in fact reveals himself through this historical event, his revelation becomes appropriated (and thus immediate) to faith only through these two removes of mediation. It is necessary, thus, for us to see how our three proximate authorities function in this double mediation.

It is no accident that these three positions correspond to the three dimensions of authority intrinsic to all historical work.

1] The historian always works within the context of the community of historians. Specifically, he must deal with and is in many respects guided by the commonly accepted interpretations of the events which he is seeking to reconstruct. Even when he departs radically from traditional views at some point, he depends on them to provide the historical context or setting in which he places his re-interpreted event. This is simply to say, the historian cannot avoid giving great weight to his secondary sources, which provide him with indispensable orientation. Secondary sources are thus of proximate authority for him. This authority residing in the community of historians corresponds to the authority of Christian church and tradition in pointing toward God's revelatory act. Here, likewise, indispensable orientation with respect to the event under consideration is provided in liturgy and theology, praxis and ethos. Without such, the historical event would not even be of sufficient interest to warrant investigation; certainly it could not be apprehended as God's revelation.

From the point of view of faith this orienting function of community and tradition should not be understood simply in humanistic terms. Since it is indispensable to the apprehension of God's act of revelation, it must be seen as in a significant sense God's own work, an aspect of his self-revealing activity. Thus, it is usually maintained that God's spirit—that is, God himself—is at work within and through Christian community and tradition, actively orienting men toward his self-revelation in Jesus Christ, and this is the basis for such proximate authority as church and tradition have in theology. The Pauline image of the church as the "body of Christ" and the Roman Catholic concept of the church as "extension of the Incarnation" express this view with great force; but it is not difficult to see how easily they may be corrupted into idolatrously elevating the all-too-human church to the position of ultimate authority. At best the dogmas and doctrines found in tradition and living community should be regarded as only "secondary sources," to be carefully examined and sometimes even contradicted with the aid of the other two proximate authorities through which the ultimate revelatory event is mediated.

2] The second dimension of authority for the historian is his primary sources. It is these that give direct evidence of the event with which he is concerned, and they are thus a court of appeal more authoritative than even unanimous agreement among traditional interpretations. These sources, however, never interpret themselves. For aid in understanding them the historian leans heavily on the work of the community of historians preceding him. Without that linguistic, semantic, and hermeneutical work, he would not even be able to read and comprehend the documents crucial for his reconstruction; nor would he have methods of inquiry enabling accurate evaluation of their value and veracity. Thus, the primary sources also are of only proximate authority for the historian, though they are absolutely indispensable for his work. Similarly the Bible (as we have noted) is the indispensable collection of primary source materials for uncovering God's act in history.

Here, also, a merely humanistic account does not suffice theologically. Although the Bible's special significance derives largely from its containing primary historical source material, in and through these documents we come into relation with a more-than-ordinary person-event—Jesus Christ, the one whom faith grasps as God's revelation. The imaginative act in which this historical image is created, and appropriated by faith as revelation, may thus quite properly be regarded theologically as an act through which God himself is at work. "The Spirit itself beareth witness with our spirit" (Rom. 8:16 KJ).

Since it is Jesus Christ, and not the biblical words, that is God's revelation, it is misleading to refer to the text itself as "inspired." It might be appropriate, however, to designate with that word the image of Jesus Christ that emerges in the act of reading that text with historico-theological understanding, for it is in and throught this *image* —constructed and reconstructed in reading and historical work—that God reveals himself.

3] This has brought us to the third point, the authority of the historian himself. It is sometimes argued that the modern historian does not base his work on external authorities but "is his own authority."[5] Though overstated (for, as we are observing, there are three *proximate* authorities, not one absolute), this points to a crucial dimension of historical work. In any search for truth, historical or otherwise, the individual himself must finally be convinced; he cannot accept at second hand a claim to truth. The historian, then, does not simply take over the picture of the events which he

[5] See R. G. Collingwood, *The Idea of History*, ed. by T. M. Knox (New York: Oxford University Press, 1946), p. 236.

finds in his primary sources, nor does he accept uncritically the prevailing view among his peers. He makes his own evaluation of the
evidence at his disposal, and he develops his own reconstruction of
the events; he assumes personal and full responsibility for the picture he draws. The theologian is in precisely the same situation with
reference to the revelatory events at the center of his interest. In the
last analysis, he neither has the right simply to reproduce the earliest
documentary witnesses (the biblical accounts), nor merely to express
the consensus of the Christian community; he must present his own
understanding of the act of God to which church and Bible also
witness. In this respect the theologian is just as free and just as personally responsible for his work as any other seeker for truth. But
his freedom and responsibility are more akin to the historian's than
the philosopher's, for he is trying to uncover not merely reality as
such (whatever that might be) but the particular reality of a specific
historical event. Hence, the subjective sense of truth cannot be his
final authority: he must also do justice to his "primary" and "secondary" sources.

But, whatever his sources, who is able to perceive *God* acting in
the events of history? And who would take upon himself responsibility for designating the man Jesus Christ as the self-revelation of
God? And who would be foolish enough to accept at face value a
historical reconstruction making such extravagant claims? It is clear
that no one, no matter how great a philosopher or historian, has the
right to speak thus straightforwardly and easily about the ultimate
reality with which we have to do. A good historian can perhaps set
forth the actions of men with insight and clarity, but who can divine
God's acts? ". . . no one comprehends the thoughts of God except the
Spirit of God" (1 Cor. 2:11). Only if God's Spirit be active in the
present, inspiring the theologian-historian to see more than mere
human tragedy in the story he is reconstructing of Jesus Christ, to see
God himself there unveiled before him, could this claim become more
than absurd and extravagant human fancy. Only thus could it become
God's revelation to him, and through him to others.[6]

---

[6] From the beginning, of course, the Christian community has believed in just
such active leading or inspiration by the Holy Spirit. Paul continues the thought above
quoted by saying: "Now we have received not the spirit of the world, but the Spirit

There are, thus, for the theologian as for the historian, three proximate authorities in terms of which he seeks to uncover and reconstruct the event with which he is concerned. None of these can be regarded as ultimate arbiter of the truth: each is only relative and must be played off against and checked by the others. For both historian and theologian *the event itself is the only final authority*. Just as the historian often finds it necessary to correct both his primary and secondary sources, as well as his own prejudgments, in light of the reconstruction which he finally produces, so the theologian frequently needs to reinterpret and amend the portrayal of Jesus Christ which he finds in scripture and tradition, or in his own preconceptions, in terms of the understanding of God's act which is forthcoming in his work. Doubtless his interpretation (like the historian's) must be based upon and rooted in the three proximate authorities to which he is responsible: there is no other ground upon which he can work. But he has no more right than the historian to let any or all of these authorities become more than relative and proximate guides to the reality of the event itself, encountered and known only in the reconstructing "historical imagination"[7] (faith), never simply in the sources.

As we noted above, each of these relative authorities has been allowed upon occasion to usurp the place belonging rightfully only to the historical event(s) in which God has revealed himself. Thus, protestantism has often given the Bible's written word final authority; Roman Catholicism, living tradition especially as expressed in papal pronouncement; spiritualism, the inner conviction of truth. Each of these views, however important, is idolatrous; none takes proper account of the threefold rootage of our knowledge of historical events or of the fact that the event itself transcends all sources which lead to it. The theological task of grasping and interpreting God's decisive

---

which is from God, that we might understand the gifts bestowed on us by God. And we impart this in words not taught by human wisdom but taught by the Spirit, interpreting spiritual truths to those who possess the Spirit. The unspiritual man does not receive the gifts of the Spirit of God, for they are folly to him, and he is not able to understand them because they are spiritually discerned" (1 Cor. 2:12–14).

[7] Cf. Collingwood, *The Idea of History*, pp. 231–249.

self-manifestation must always proceed in terms of this threefold reference: to the Bible (the collection of primary witnesses to the event), to church history and tradition (secondary sources and interpreters), and to our apprehension and conviction of the truth of the doctrine. But even unanimity here would not insure that an interpretation is valid and true. If the ordinary historian can never be certain he has uncovered and represented the motives and actions of his hero, how much more must the theologian acknowledge the inadequacy and incompleteness of his work. Since it is God's hidden purpose for history and God's act in history—indeed, God himself— with which we here have to do, it is finally only the Spirit of God who could give this confirmation.

Our attention thus far has been directed toward the grounding of theological work in historical and biblical studies and to certain peculiarities in the character and methods of that historical work. There can be no responsible Christian theology apart from this continuous historical reference. But our very analysis of the peculiar problems here has brought us up against the other main ground of theology: that it is always rooted in *some particular theologian,* where *he* is, what his *stance and experience* are. Theological work never escapes being based on a particular reconstruction of historical events, a particular interpretation of the evidence, a particular attempt to grasp these events as God's act; and it attempts to make sense of particular lives and experience. Moreover, the ways of grasping and comprehending and interpreting are inevitably very much affected by where men stand in history, in the Catholic Middle Ages, in the protestant Reformation, in the eighteenth-century Enlightenment, or in the middle of the twentieth century. No doubt we can learn much from the work of Christians of other periods, but our efforts and our seeing must finally be our own. We are twentieth-century men, who know modern physics and psychoanalysis, communist tyranny and Hiroshima, Freud and Marx, Einstein and Hitler; and we must seek to grasp God's historical act in Jesus Christ in terms *we* can understand and accept and believe. That is, this event must become revelation to us in the concrete historical determination of our existence if it is to be revelation at all as far as we are con-

cerned. Thus something more than the historical study and reconstruction thus far outlined is required before the Christ-event can be
grasped as the very act of God.

An event is "revelatory," we have said, if it is itself apprehended
as meaningful and throws its light on other dark and obscure aspects
of experience as well. No revelatory event is of ultimate or decisive
significance, however, unless through it comes the meaning that illuminates all our existence, giving us means to understand even the
most elusive corner of ourselves and our world. If the Christ-event
is to be grasped as God's definitive revelatory act, it must be seen as
illumining every dimension of self and world. In its light we should
be able to understand more adequately the problems of personal
existence (guilt, fear, despair, meaninglessness, moral problems,
difficulties of personal decision); the problems of our society (war,
racial tensions, depersonalization, automation); the problems of our
intellectual life (issues raised by "the scientific world-view," by the
social sciences, philosophy, and psychology); the problems of modern
culture (the role of the artist in contemporary society, the significance
of the great historical movements of our time, the meaning of human
history as a whole). Only as these various facets of our actual existence are illumined by God's act in Christ, can we say that it really is
revelation to us and for us. The second great source of materials
with which theology works (the revelatory history being the first)
thus extends to the wide reaches of our world, drawing from every
corner of experience.

Theology must attend to and be prepared to analyze political and
economic developments, scientific and philosophical theory, communal and religious practices, works of art and literature, everyday
personal and social experience—everything that contributes to the
stuff of human existence must be brought under the revelatory light.
Since the Christian Gospel is good news about the human situation as
such, and thus about every dimension of life, no aspect of existence
is too insignificant or too remote to be of theological interest. As these
multifarious materials are exposed to and measured by the standard
of reality and meaning emergent from the revelatory event, the theologian seeks to interpret and evaluate the several dimensions of ex-

perience so as to produce a genuinely Christian perspective on life and the world.[8]

Some theological writers have consciously devoted themselves directly to this sort of theologico-cultural analysis. No theologian can avoid it, at least implicitly, for none works in a vacuum excluding experience. Moreover, seeking to avoid such interpretation of concrete existence can result only in a kind of theological inflation, where traditional terms and doctrines appear in great profusion, but what they refer to or count for in the actual stuff of life is less and less evident—the theological language becoming abstract and empty. Far from keeping the revelation free from all "contamination" by sinful human conceptions and meanings, this sort of theologizing serves only to empty it of revelatory power.

Our conception of the revelation is itself significantly shaped by the actual illumination which it brings to our lives. If it is primarily the ethical problems of personal and social life that appear clarified by God's act, the revelation will be understood in moralistic terms; if it is awareness of the terrors of finitude as experienced in anxiety and despair, guilt and meaninglessness, it will be perceived existentialistically; if it appears as the solution to our profoundest philosophical questions, we will understand it intellectually. It is important— if we are not to suffer from rather serious self-delusion and hypocrisy, not to say fanaticism—that we openly recognize this relativity and make allowance for it in our conception of theology. The interpretation of revelation to which we come can never be more or other than the understanding which *we* have in *our* situation in history with *our* experience of the world as mediated to us through *our* aptitudes and biases and intellect. If and as God should reveal himself to others through our witness, it will be their task (not ours) to grasp their world in terms of the revelatory event, and to see God's act from the

---

[8] What I have here distinguished as two poles of the on-going theological task is sometimes regarded as two different types of theology, "dogmatic" (or "kerygmatic") theology in contrast with "apologetic" theology. This distinction, however, is misleading and destroys the intrinsic unity of theology with the implication that the different kinds of theology draw their norms and content from diverse sources, have differing objectives, and thus stand in a certain tension (perhaps even opposition) to each other. It is essential to regard these two poles as different but inseparable aspects of the single theological task.

vantage point of their situation. If their consequent views and formulations seem to us strange and even wrong, we should remember that we are in no position to render final judgment upon them: this remains to God alone, who judges from beyond all the historical relativities to which we are bound.

Thus theology has a two-pronged task. On the one hand, it must see *all human existence* in the light of God's act. This will involve careful study of contemporary views of the self, society, and the world; understanding of the problems of individual and society; insight into the significant movements in contemporary culture and into other religions and cultures. The theologian seeks illumination of all these dimensions of life by reference to Jesus Christ. On the other hand, it is necessary *to appropriate God's act(s)* from our situation.[9] This requires careful and sometimes complicated historical study, not only of the biblical materials which explicitly record God's activity in history, but of all church history, consisting as it does of the recorded memories of that community which has experienced the growing ramifications of his work.

These two prongs or aspects of the theological task give us two fundamental norms for theological work. On the one hand, there is the *historical* norm: what we take to be God's decisive act should correspond for our time to what the Christian community of other generations has known it to be. We must be able to make sense of Bible and Christian tradition and we may not seriously distort either; we must learn to see with the eyes of Peter and Paul, Augustine and Thomas, Luther and Calvin, Schleiermacher and Ritschl; and we must be able honestly to recognize ourselves as of the same community. This historical work, as we have seen, involves a complex

---

[9] These two perennial dimensions of the theological task Tillich has delineated in terms of his "method of correlation" (*Systematic Theology*, I [Chicago: University of Chicago Press, 1951], 59ff.). This is a somewhat unfortunate designation, it seems to me, because it appears to imply (though Tillich doubtless does not really intend this) a kind of artificial situation in which the theologian is confronted with two "objects" which he must juggle until they are "correlated." But *God's acts* and *our situation* are clearly not objective to us and manipulable by us in this way at all; they are, rather, the two poles of our very being itself, the one illuminative, the other illuminated. Theological work is no manipulating of objects; it is the process through which the interpenetration of these poles of experience comes increasingly into view. In this respect it is essentially a kind of growing self-consciousness and self-understanding. (See also n. 10 below.)

threefold reference to authority. On the other hand, there is the *experiential* norm: our theology must make sense of our own experience, of the world we live in. Wherever there are blank spots, incomprehensible or meaningless experiences—and there always will be such—it is evident that we have not yet successfully carried through the theological task. Theology is thus the continuous attempt to understand our present in terms of the revelatory event in the past, and to appropriate this past from our present situation. The awareness that our interpretation of present by past, and past from present, is incomplete, provides us with norms for adjudging the adequacy of any particular piece of theological work, and is the motivation to push our theologizing ever further.[10]

Although we may quite properly regard both historical event and contemporary experience as "norms" guiding our theological work, it should be clear that they are not on the same level and do not function in the same way. It is with reference to the historical norm that we can adjudge whether a given position or claim is "Christian"; it is with reference to the experiential norm that we adjudge whether it "makes sense." To be a Christian theologian is to believe that a Christian interpretation does justice to the facts of experience and, indeed, illuminates them in ways other views do not. Such a one

[10] It should perhaps be observed that this interrelation is even more complicated than I have thus far suggested. On the one hand, the specifically *historical* work of grasping the Christ-event can be accomplished (as we noted) only in the historical imagination of the contemporary historico-theologian, who of necessity must operate with modern criteria of historical method, conceptions of truth, historical possibility, and the like. Thus, the historical dimension of the theological task is already shaped in many subtle ways by contemporary thinking and experience. Nonetheless, the theologian's *intention* in this aspect of his work is *historical*, to grasp as far as possible what actually happened. On the other hand, the more *existential* task of apprehending himself and his world is never accomplished without the influence everywhere of historically created categories, meanings and norms in terms of which the very experience of the theologian is structured. As a Christian, he will experience his life and himself in terms of such meanings as love and hope, the striving and failure of the self, the assumption of and search for a meaningful history—all heavily colored by the decisive events of the Christian past. However, his *intention* in this dimension of his work will be to grasp, honestly and without distortion, the actual existence of himself and his fellows. These two acts, however complexly interconnected, should not be confused: each must be performed with fidelity to its proper objectives and criteria if Christian theology is to be anything more than mere wishful thinking or parochial opinion. In the last analysis the complex interrelation of each with the other should not disturb us: if there were no such mutual fittingness and rapport, it would not be possible for the past to which Christians look back to have truly revelatory meaning for the present at all.

seeks, therefore, his defining categories in the Christian revelation and attempts to discipline his judgments and his criteria of judgment with reference to that (historical) norm. This norm itself, however, is not simply autonomous and self-standing. If interpretation of experience by reference to it fails to make sense of the facts and problems of life, either new theological interpretations must be attempted, or the revelatory norm itself will be given up as misleading or false. In the latter case a new center of orientation for the self and a new source of defining categories—which more adequately illuminate one's actual experience—is sought (or will already have been found). All conversions away from Christian faith involve just such a movement to a new or different "revelation" because of experienced difficulties with the Christian perspective (whether this be understood relatively superficially or profoundly).

Systematic theology, now, involves this continuous movement of interpretation back and forth between these two poles, and, in addition, involves reflective activity through which the theologian seeks to become aware of and to assess what he is doing at each point. Thus, it is reflexive on itself, always attending to the way in which the actual interrelationship and interpenetration of the revelation and existence are being portrayed and interpreted. If this complex interpenetration is set forth in a naive or confused way, an adequate understanding of neither pole will be achieved; and what is mere cultural or religious tradition, or the direct expression of personal experience, may be mistaken for God's revelation. In this way the theologian may fail, on the one hand, to perceive the actual impingement of the historical act of God upon the present situation; and, on the other, he may give final and divine authority to historically relative norms and values.

Too often the church has blindly and dogmatically imposed supposedly sacred tradition and custom on a social or cultural situation to which they were not relevant, simply because they were thought to be revealed requirements of God. Instead of making certain she was dealing with the actual facts of the world in which she lived and to which she spoke (by carefully analyzing the cultural situation), she projected onto that world ideas drawn from other historical contexts, booming them out as if with God's own voice. Many of the church's temperance materials (at least in America), her too easy criticism of much modern literature as pornographic, her naive pronouncements on political problems, arise simply from failure to understand the real character of the situations to which she is speaking. Sometimes the church has made the opposite mistake of identifying the "highest" or most impressive contemporary cultural traditions with God's purposes. Thus, the revelation has been understood in terms of Kant's stern ethic, or an existential quaking in *Angst,* or the manners of a cultured and cultivated "gentleman"; in every war churchmen on both sides have found it possible to identify God's will with national victory. In such cases as these, the actual significance of God's revelatory act for the historical situation or problem in question has been clouded over or even completely concealed.

It is the task of systematic theology to see that each of these poles is properly distinguished from the other—thus making possible adequate understanding of each—and yet that they are significantly related, so that the genuine impingement of God's historical act on the contemporary world will come clearly into view. To accomplish this the several Christian doctrines, treating of the various features of human existence and the world, must be brought into systematic and coherent relation with each other and with the vision of God's act, or the theological analysis and interpretation will remain fragmentary and highly problematic. This means that to the two norms of theological work mentioned above, the *historical* and the *experiential,* must be added a third, the *systematic*: the various aspects and dimensions, doctrines and dogmas, of Christian faith must be developed and displayed in their interconnection with and implication of each other, with the whole carefully disciplined methodologically.[11]

[11] It would perhaps be appropriate here to say a word about the strengths and weaknesses of the present volume as seen in the light of these norms. Even relative completeness cannot be claimed for any of the three tasks suggested in the text. The most serious deficiency, I think, is the absence of full historical documentation and discussion. I have attempted to suggest some relevant primary source materials, through rather frequent biblical references (though, except for the analysis of the resurrection in Ch. 28, I have seldom taken time to evaluate and interpret these in a historically responsible manner, or to indicate where such discussion can be found in the extensive critical literature). My reference to the secondary materials of church history and tradition has been even more restricted. I can make no claims, therefore, that historical

One final word about the character of theology is necessary. It should be obvious that there is much room for difference of opinion and judgment concerning each of these points. The proper interpretation of Bible and tradition, the powerful personal convictions of truth, the understanding of our contemporary existence, the insight into the meaning of that existence as disclosed in the light of God's revelation, the sense for the systematic interrelationship of all these factors—there will be no unanimity on any of these matters, and on some there will be very sharp divergence and disagreement. We should not be embarrassed about this diversity and clash of theological views. On the contrary, precisely this indicates the fullness of God's revelation, so rich and meaningful that no human interpretation —or synthesis of human interpretations—can hold it. The proper response to the multiplicity of theological positions can only be gratitude that God is not so small and weak that men can domesticate him in their theologizing.

Despite this genuine theological significance of our relativity and diversity, however, each of us must do his own theological thinking in as disciplined and thorough a fashion as possible. There is no excuse for failing to clarify and critically to develop appropriate theological criteria and norms, and for refraining from controversy with those who disagree on theological issues. The three norms of theological thinking outlined here appear to me to be criteria which are operative in various ways in every theologian's thinking: each is seeking to speak with contemporary relevance, in faithfulness to

---

grounding for the positions taken in the present work is here furnished. The volume is somewhat more adequate, I think, with respect to the second theological norm, the interpretation of contemporary experience. Though I can hardly claim to have provided more than sketches and outlines, still the attempt has been made to indicate the bearing of the Christian revelation not only on the usual problems of existence and ethics, but on contemporary scientific and philosophical thinking in such areas as cosmology, anthropology, and history as well. Thus, the broad outline of a Christian view of the world and man, which can be in conversation with astrophysics on the one hand and depth psychology on the other, has been sketched; but of course many issues and problems of all sorts have not been discussed. When the third norm, systematic and methodological thoroughness, is invoked, perhaps a bit more can be claimed for the present work. The understanding of Christian faith that informs it has been kept in view at every point, and the attempt has been made to be rigorously consistent both in developing and applying a methodology and in working through the several doctrines from that perspective.

God's revelation in history, and consistently. If we consciously and explicitly distinguish these dimensions, developing criteria appropriate to each, our theological thinking should more truly apprehend and reflect God's act and more significantly illuminate human existence. But the difficulty of the task should always be kept in view: it will never reach finality or completion; there is always more to be done. Theology remains forever a demand as well as an achievement.

Part One

THE CHRISTIAN UNDERSTANDING

OF ULTIMATE REALITY:

THE DOCTRINE OF GOD

> *God is historical even in Himself.*
>
> KARL BARTH

W<small>E</small> have seen that the Christian revelation is to be understood as a decisive event reorienting men from being centered in themselves, their own needs and desires, to God and his will for them—from anthropocentrism to theocentrism. God is the ultimate reality with which man has to do, for he is the source and foundation of all that is and he is the Lord whose purposes are being worked out in the course of history. Everything is rooted in him and his activity. Thus, if thinking is to be about reality, it must have its anchor in him. Unless we see the world round about us, and ourselves as well, as they are actually grounded in and continuously dependent upon God, we will be dealing in illusions, not actuality. This means that the first and principal Christian doctrine—apart from which the rest of the Christian perspective cannot even be stated, much less made clear —is the doctrine of God.

What we say about the Christian God cannot be based simply on the notion of God found in ordinary discourse, or on vague ideas drawn from general human experience; rather, it must be inferred as carefully and strictly as possible from the revelatory history through which God has made himself known. This is not to deny that ordinary linguistic usage is presupposed in theological work (Chapter 1) or that there are valuable conceptions in other philosophies and religions. In Christian faith, however, revelation is regarded as ultimately definitive of the concept of God and is thus normative for all theological work. Hence, the notion of God must be developed as far as possible out of what is given in the revelatory history, and all denotations and connotations of the term must be examined and corrected in its light. Our exposition of the Christian doctrine of God must begin, then, with a further consideration of the Christian revelation.

The proper definition of the Christian understanding of God will require the entirety of Part One. It would be a serious mistake to regard any introductory statements here as more than rough and preliminary. Nevertheless, it is necessary to have a provisional working conception with which to proceed, if only to rule out certain misconceptions which might confuse the issues to be discussed. In the course of Christian history many different interpretations of God have appeared—some subtle and sophisticated, some crude and coarse—all laying claim to the title "Christian." While it is not possible, of course, entirely to evacuate the word "God" of all these accumulated meanings and start afresh, we must make as explicit as possible the dimensions of meaning which can be regarded as legitimate and with which we will be working, if there is not to be serious misunderstanding. In the following chapter such a preliminary sketch will be presented.

5 / Revelatory History and the Concept of God

ALTHOUGH the definitive revelatory events toward which Christian faith is oriented are recorded in the New Testament, the church has always realized that these events cannot be understood in independence from all others; for they are the climax of a history which they presuppose. It was the Old Testament that was the first scripture of the Christian church, and even after the New Testament documents were written and collected, the church recognized that the Old Testament provided a certain indispensable propaedeutic to them. The important point involved here was the acknowledgment that it was the same God who had begun to make himself known through the critical events of Israel's history—the exodus and covenant, the rise of the kingdom and exile (as interpreted by prophetic spokesmen)—who had now decisively acted in the life, death, and resurrection of Jesus Christ.[1] This event, then, however unusual and unexpected, was no incursion into history of some totally unknown divine being. It was the climactic act of Yahweh, the God long known to the Hebrew people.

The fact that the person-event Jesus Christ thus represented but

---

[1] Cf. Hebrews 1:1-3: "In many and various ways God spoke of old to our fathers by the prophets; but in these last days he has spoken to us by a Son, whom he appointed the heir of all things. . . . He reflects the glory of God and bears the very stamp of his nature. . . ." Also note Stephen's speech in Acts 7; the opening chapters of Matthew and Luke, which attempt to portray the appearance of Jesus as in continuity with and fulfilment of prior Jewish history; Gal. 3-4; etc.

a new qualification of an old and already long history did not make it any the less decisive. For precisely because it was the climax and goal of the preceding history, it alone could make clear the end toward which that previous development was moving, thus making it possible to distinguish and sort out the many false starts and irrelevant occurrences from the actual activity of God. For Christian faith the true movement of Old Testament history could be discerned only from that vantage point which apprehended its outcome as the appearance of Jesus Christ. Nevertheless, for precisely the same reason—namely, that Jesus Christ was apprehended as the climactic moment of just *this history*—it is evident that certain fundamental metaphysical decisions about the character of the ultimate reality with which man has to do were already made long before the Christian era. Thus, it was the God apprehended as active and dynamic will, the Creator of the universe and the Redeemer of Israel, who was known to be decisively manifest here—not some impersonal ground of all being or some logically defined ultimate form or structure. Christian faith inherited from its Jewish background the basic conviction that God was one and was a personal being who could and did engage in interpersonal relationships and covenants with men, a dynamic will who created the world and was sovereign over the continuing course of history.[2] Moreover, he was not known merely vaguely and abstractly as a personal being: to the Hebrew people he was known by his proper name, "Yahweh," and this made possible their calling directly upon him and entering into interpersonal relation with him (cf. Gen. 4:26 and Ex. 3:13–15). In the Christian era the word "God," though originally a common noun, has taken over this highly personalized meaning, and similarly functions largely as a proper name. It is against the background of this unquestioned presupposition about the personal-historical character of God that the Christian claims about his nature and will must be seen.

It should be observed that God's manifestation of himself in a continuous and developing history is thoroughly consistent with his

[2] One could document this obvious point by reference to virtually any page of the Old Testament or New, as well as to much current biblical scholarship. A recent monograph which deals with this matter explicitly is G. Ernest Wright's *God Who Acts* (London: SCM Press, 1952).

being apprehended as personal. For it is precisely through such increasing intercourse that persons become known to each other, that the stranger becomes friend. The knowledge of the other self is mediated and qualified by those moments of revelation which occur in a history commonly shared,[3] some one decisive moment, perhaps, providing the defining image by means of which the one self cognitively grasps the other. Thus, to admit that the Christian understanding of God is emergent from the ancient Jewish history which it presupposes does not mean that Christian doctrine is simply a kind of appendix to the more fundamental Jewish conceptions: rather, this exhibits as clearly and coercively as possible the consistently personalistic-historicistic character of the Christian image of God from beginning to end. This conception finds its definitive form, appropriately enough, in the claim that a particular personal life (Jesus) reveals with finality the ultimate reality with which we have to do.

What follows is a sketch in outline form of the image of this God who begins to make himself known to man in Hebrew history and finally succeeds in revealing definitively his nature and will in Jesus Christ. The first point expresses in the main the Jewish presuppositions of the Christian doctrine (though of course the matters indicated here are not alien to the New Testament, as one or two references will easily show). The succeeding points express more explicitly the Christian qualifications of and limitations of the Jewish understanding (though of course they are not without some historical precedent and preparation in the Old Testament).

1] Whatever or whoever the word "God" indicates, it is clear that he is *one who acts.* Over and over again in the Bible the emphasis is on the *deeds* that God has done. He is, then, to be conceived as a dynamic, living reality, a *will.* Moreover, he is a will of great power:

[3] This position, that our knowledge of God is not direct and face to face, so to speak, but is always mediated through historical words and deeds, can be defended theologically not only on the systematic grounds of the nature of interpersonal knowledge: it is also biblical. Wolfhart Pannenberg has pointed out that contemporary theories of "a direct self-revelation of God" do not in fact find support in the Bible; rather what appears here is "an indirect self-revelation in the mirror of his historical actions. The totality of his speaking and doing, the history effected by Yahweh, shows indirectly who he is" (*Offenbarung als Geschichte* [Göttingen: Vandenhoeck & Ruprecht, 1961], p. 15).

the very universe was called into being by his free decision (Gen. 1, 2; Isa. 45; John 1:3; Heb. 1:3, 10–12; etc.). Thus, all other power in the world is derivative from him and dependent on him. Nor is this power to be regarded as mere abstract might or force, moving blindly and without purpose. From the beginning of the world God has had *purposes* which he has been working out through all history; however, only recently (in the New Testament writers' view), in Jesus Christ, did these become manifest (Eph. 1:4–10; 1 Pet. 1:20; etc.). Hence, this God is not to be conceived as an impersonal *what*. Whoever he is, he is at least personal purposive will, whose creative act lies at the basis of all reality, and who is working in and through history, shaping it in accord with his purposes.

2] It is clearly necessary, however, to say more about this God than simply that he is active will. For the preeminent act through which he has revealed himself has a very specific character: it is an act of love (John 3:16–17; 1 John 4:7–10; Rom. 5:5–11; etc.). This God, then, is one whose purposes are characterized by loving-kindness. His action in Christ is not called forth by the merit or value of man and the world, but simply because he loves. Far from deserving God's goodness, men are "sinners" and his "enemies" who trespass against his will and seek to thwart his purposes (Rom. 1–5; 1 John 1:8; etc.). All that man might conceivably deserve would be punishment and destruction for opposing and seeking to frustrate the very Creator of the heavens and the earth. But this God is no arbitrary tyrant, willing his own purposes without regard to others. His purposes are shaped by love for his creatures. Hence, he does not seek to destroy them, even when they are evil and destructive of his work; his concern is rather for their well-being. The revelatory event in Jesus Christ is an action out of love for man, an action intended to rescue man from the rebellion and enmity into which he has gotten himself, and to reconcile him once more to the Creator and Sustainer of his being. If we take this event as revelatory of the inner nature and will of God, we must regard him as absolutely loving, no matter what is done against him.

3] It is important that we recognize that this love is not merely the charitable "do-gooding" of a sort of cosmic philanthropist who,

having so much that he knows not what to do with it all, showers it
on those whose needs exceed his own. This love is far greater than
that: it willingly and freely sacrifices of itself simply because human
need can be met only by such self-giving. When it is a question of
establishing man in the freedom for which he was created and redeeming him from enslavement to sin, God in his love is willing to
sacrifice even his divine status and absolute power, subjecting himself to the actual evil conditions of history and society in which
man is inextricably involved (John 3:16; 1 John 4:9–10; Phil.
2:6–8) in order to free man and win him back. God's love is not
the kind that stands afar off, offering a lifeline to those sinking in the
"slough of despond," and condolences to those who do not succeed
in grasping it. On the contrary, God moves right into the midst of
the evil situation. This is dramatically expressed in the Christian
claim that he actually became a man (John 1:14; Phil. 2:6–8) and
suffered at the hands of his fellowmen, finally being executed as a
criminal, an outcast from society. God appears here as one who gives
up everything and willingly participates in anything—for man's
sake.

4] Moreover, this self-sacrificial action of the self-giving God
is an action of self-communication to man through which God finally
becomes truly known (John 1:18; Rom. 5:8; Eph. 1:9–10; Heb.
1:2–3), through which the terrifying Mystery in which finite being
is rooted unveils itself as inexhaustible Love. Man is, as it were,
near-sighted. But God comes near enough, through his self-sacrificial
participation in human existence, for man to see who he is, to recognize him as Father. And thus man learns that God loves him absolutely, without reservation. The very Foundation of the Universe
loves man! God is not intending to destroy men (as their sense of
guilt may suggest); God forgives. He is seeking to reconcile men
to himself, enabling them to attain the condition of freedom for
which they were created, a freedom in which they, also, can at last
find it possible to love.

5] Finally, it must be said, this new impingement of God's love
on men—and the correlative awareness in them of the absolute trustworthiness of the Ultimate Mystery at the foundation of their exist-

ence—frees them from doubt and fear, anxiety and despair. No longer is it necessary for men to live in self-centeredness and self-defensiveness, continuously concerned to protect their egos against betrayals and hurts; for now it is known that the very Source and Sustainer of their being may be trusted absolutely. Thus, release from bondage to the self begins, and man is enabled to take the chance of loving God and fellows as God loves him. The transformation in potential is here so great that the biblical writers could describe it only with the most drastic metaphors: we have been born anew, we have become new creatures (John 3:3–8; 1 Pet. 1:3,23; 2 Cor. 5:17; etc.), no longer centered in self but centered in God. Hence the life of man can now come to manifest God's own love; man can be the historical vehicle through which the very love of God flows into human society. The God become manifest in Jesus Christ is one who loves his creatures so much that he enables them also to love.

We can now see more clearly why this decisive revelatory act in and through Jesus Christ should not be viewed as a solitary action of God, a single moment of history isolated from the rest. To suppose that until this moment God was, so to speak, inactive, and that subsequently he has been in retirement, would be to deny both his genuine freedom and his love. To picture his act as a sudden, spur-of-the-moment inspiration would be to view him as an erratic being, subject to happenstance accidents, not as the *free God* who since "before the foundation of the world" (1 Pet. 1:20) had been working out these purposes which only in Jesus Christ have become "manifest" to men. Moreover, such a view would be inconsistent with God's here-revealed *love* for man. For instead of faithfully working with man, caring for him and bearing with him and gradually teaching him, God would appear as one who suddenly and unexpectedly rips into human history and existence, tearing it open and leaving a gaping wound. No, in love and with patience God acts slowly and deliberately, always in accordance with man's receptiveness. This interpretation enables us to see from another side the meaning of the Old Testament: it is the story of God's loving preparation of a people who originally conceived him as warring and

violent like themselves—a tyrant coercing men to do his will[4]—
for the occasion "when the time had fully come" (Gal. 4:4; cf. Mk.
1:15), and he could decisively reveal himself as the love which
evokes and establishes genuinely free beings,[5] the proper citizens
of the kingdom he is bringing into history. The subsequent history
of the church has been the spreading of this message and fact of
God's kingdom of love through all history, to all people. Finally—
if the Christ-event is indeed revelatory of what is really transpiring
in human history—God's purposes will comprehend it all, and man's
alienation from God and from God's love shall be overcome; then
there will no longer be "Greek and Jew, circumcised and uncircumcised, barbarian, Scythian, slave, free man, but Christ [i.e., God's
love come to man, will be] all, and in all" (Col. 3:11).

We started our sketch of the Christian image of God by observing that the God who reveals himself in the history culminating
in Jesus Christ is a God who acts, a being who has power to make
decisions and carry them out. But it is now clear that that statement
by itself is misleading. For, as our further analysis has shown,
when we speak of God's "power," our ordinary conceptions may be
very misleading. In creating and sustaining a material universe, and
in effecting the evolution of life from lower levels through "the survival of the fittest" (cf. Chapter 19), God certainly coerces finite
beings to conform to his will; however, when free beings begin to
emerge in his world, he modulates his power to a mode appropriate
for evoking and sustaining that freedom. As revealed in the cruci-

---

[4] "But if you will not obey the voice of the Lord your God or be careful to do all
his commandments . . . , then all these curses shall come upon you and overtake you. . . .
And as the Lord took delight in doing you good and multiplying you, so the Lord will
take delight in bringing ruin upon you and destroying you" (Deut. 28:15, 63). "For it
was the Lord's doing . . . that they should be utterly destroyed, and should receive no
mercy but be exterminated, as the Lord commanded Moses" (Joshua 11:20). "Thus
says the Lord of hosts, '. . . Now go and smite Amalek, and utterly destroy all that they
have; do not spare them, but kill both man and woman, infant and suckling, ox and
sheep, camel and ass'" (1 Sam. 15:2ff.).

[5] Cf. the Anabaptist, Jacob Hutter (c. 1535) who maintained that wars and fighting
were permitted to the heroes of the Old Testament only "because at that time servitude
was not yet set apart from sonship and the way to glory was not yet revealed. And thus
the law was their taskmaster and they were shackled under externalistic statutes up until
Christ; he released those who were under the law and thus they receive sonship" (Lydia
Müller, ed., Glaubenszeugnisse oberdeutscher Taufgesinnter [Leipzig: M. Heinsius Nach-
folger, 1938], p. 186).

fixion of Christ, God's power does not *compel* men to obedience; God is no tyrant who forces men, against their will, to do his will. Genuine freedom is neither created nor nourished by external compulsion. On the contrary. It is evoked, if at all, as a response to the ministrations of personal love and communion (see below, Chapters 26–29). It is not insignificant, therefore, that the mode of God's power manifest in the cross is his ability and willingness to take upon himself absolute self-sacrifice; it is the power to give, the power to love, the paradoxical power of "weakness" (1 Cor. 1:18–28). Far from beating man into submission, his mercy and forgiveness at length call forth from man's freedom an appropriate response— gratitude, joy, love. God's power is thus much greater than the compelling force of a tyrant who makes others submit against their will, turning them into his slaves; his power is sufficient to transform a willful person from self-centeredness to love, without destroying or even violating the tender plant of freedom. When we speak of God, then—if the event Jesus Christ is to be normative for us—it is the image of *this* Reality, who acts in this manner, that must give content to our concept.[6]

This means that as we develop the various subordinate doctrines that make up the Christian conception of God—for example, the doctrines of omnipotence, eternity, omniscience, justice—we must always make certain that it is to this reality, and not some other, that we are referring. The meaning of none of these doctrinal terms can be taken over without qualification from ordinary discourse, nor for that matter from other theological (or even biblical) writings; before they can be used theologically, they must be subjected to the transformative effect of the revelation. Only then will they facilitate

---

[6] It may be observed in passing that although the Old Testament image of God as the Oriental despot is certainly personalistic in character, it is really not too far removed from the vitalistic will to power that characterizes the struggles of many species of life. Only when the "weakness" of a man dying on a cross is taken as definitive of God's power, is that power interpretable exhaustively as the expression of freedom, i.e., as exclusively personalistic in character; for only freedom—not the vitality which strives for survival and domination—can willingly take suffering and even destruction upon itself out of love for the other (I am of course sharply distinguishing such an act from mere masochism or a covert means of domination [Nietzsche]). In this image, therefore, the personalistic tendencies of the Old Testament drive beyond themselves to a new and radical conception of God's freedom and power, the kind of pure personalism foreshadowed in such rare images as the "suffering servant."

better apprehension of this God-defined-by-Jesus-Christ, through illuminating some aspect of his being which we might otherwise overlook. Too often in Christian history this simple but all-important
rule has been forgotten; and the resultant theological portrait of
the divine being has resembled more a pagan demon, or perhaps an
imperturbable unmoved Stoic wise man, than the God and Father of
Jesus Christ. The doctrine of God's omnipotence, for example, cannot be properly understood merely through the idea of naked power:
it must be seen as the omnipotence of God's love. God's eternity
must not be conceived as some bare and abstract timelessness: it
is the presence in every event of God's love. God's omniscience is
no encyclopedic collection of all possible facts: it is the full and
sympathetic understanding characteristic of God's perfect love. God's
justice is not some abstract, legal, eye-for-an-eye accounting for
every deed: it is a justice that deals with each in accordance with
his individual nature and needs, the justice of perfect love.

It is, then, with the God whose defining revelation was in and
through the person-event Jesus Christ that we must always begin in
our theological work; it is to him that we must return at every point
as we work out our doctrine; it is with him that we must finally end.
Of course, as we shall see in the ensuing pages, the way in which
this reference to Jesus Christ is accomplished in the development of
the doctrine of God is not simple, involving as it does both the presupposed historical development of Hebrew faith in Yahweh and the
question of how a mere *man* can be taken as the defining image or
criterion for the notion of *God*. Despite those difficulties, however,
it is finally this reference, and this alone, which can insure that our
theology is rooted in what Christian faith takes to be God's definitive
revelation. Whenever the term "God" is used in the following pages,
therefore, it will be to this reality that we are seeking to refer and
no other. We must always be on guard lest our preconceived ideas
of God, or feelings about him, prevent us from letting his historical
self-revelation define his nature for us. The reality given in the
events normative for Christian faith is the only proper referent for
our concept; they must thus provide the criteria for our work.

6 / The Trinitarian Structure
of the Doctrine of God

In the previous chapter we looked in a preliminary way at the image of God that emerges from the revelatory history culminating in the event Jesus Christ, and we saw that this must be the criterion for our theological work. We must now try to express more precisely and formally these facts. The *doctrine of the trinity* formulates in technical theological language this rootedness in the divine revelation of all Christian thought about God. It is not possible here to elaborate a full treatment of the several aspects and many problems of this doctrine, but before we turn to the more specific and detailed features of the Christian doctrine of God, it is necessary that we see how and why its basic structure is trinitarian.

For Christian faith "God" is he who revealed himself in Jesus Christ, he who has the freedom and power to love man so fully as to enable man also to love. What, now, has this to do with the doctrine of the trinity? The understanding of God's revelation as historical, which we have been developing, implies a three-point structure in the knowledge of God.[1] Each of the three refers to an essential element in any claim to knowledge of ultimate reality; taken together they represent the minimal structure in terms of which such knowledge can be conceived.

[1] It will be apparent how much I am indebted to Karl Barth's very creative interpretation of trinitarian doctrine (*Church Dogmatics*, I, 1 [Edinburgh: T. & T. Clark, 1936]). However, it is doubtful that Barth would be very pleased with the historicistic use to which I have put his insights.

1] When we speak of God's revelation in Jesus Christ (or else-where, for that matter), we mean to be emphasizing that it is *God* —and not merely some finite reality—with whom we here have to do. That is, the claim is being made that in and through this par-ticular finite event and context is encountered that which transcends every finite being as the ultimate ground and source of all. How-ever necessary it may be to emphasize the importance of the finite locus of the revelation (i.e., Jesus, the man of Nazareth), our atten-tion here is focused on a reality (God) which, though encountered in and through this finite locus, is not to be merely identified with it but utterly transcends it. In this person we are not dealing merely with human history (though that is certainly the case also), but with the divine being; in this event we are not confronted simply with human opinions and imaginings and attitudes (though such are cer-tainly there as well), but with the almighty Creator of the heavens and the earth. God himself is making himself known here.[2]

2] To say God *reveals* himself to us in Jesus Christ is to em-phasize the continuing and *present* effectiveness, meaning, and ac-tuality of this event. This is not merely some interesting report from a dead past, something that happened to a Peter and a Paul centuries ago but died with them. On the contrary, what occurred there and then is living and meaningful here and now: to us in our world God reveals himself through Jesus Christ. Whatever we understand by revelation, it is not something appropriated at second hand. To speak of God's revealing himself in Jesus Christ is to claim that the ulti-mate reality with which *we* have to do is manifest here, that in and through that person-event in the past, *we* encounter God. God is ac-tively revealing himself here and now.

3] God reveals himself *in Jesus Christ*. It is not just everywhere or anywhere in our world—and thus, finally, nowhere—that God definitively makes himself known. According to Christian faith, it is at a particular point in human history, through a very specific

---

[2] It is to be noted that revelation, here, is not of certain truths or *doctrines*, but of *God*. Doctrine and dogma are created in the *human act* of reflection on God's act; they are not what is revealed, but emerge in man's attempt to apprehend, understand, and speak about God's self-manifestation. However indispensable they may be, they are always secondary and derivative, not archetypal or primary.

configuration of events, in a concrete and particular human being. It would be meaningless and empty to speak of God's revelation without being able to say where that revelation is to be found. Reference to such revelation-in-general is really reference to the chaotic sum total of all experience, unordered by specific distinctions or qualifications. But if there are no orders or priorities by means of which we can determine which dimensions of experience or events of history are the more significant, which of lesser importance, then experience reveals nothing to us but the vast undifferentiated givenness of things. Unless we know where to look in that massive lump of givenness for the clue or key to its meaning, nothing whatever is revealed. But the Christian claim is that the *where* is known. The point in human history or existence which is the key to the rest can be specified. It bears the name *Jesus Christ*. In this man, in these events, is to be found God.

In the central Christian claim, then, there are three reference points, none of which can be ignored without undercutting its meaning. If, for example, the first be omitted, that it is *God* with whom we are dealing, the fundamental meaning drops out altogether. The person-event Jesus Christ is no longer viewed as revelatory of the ultimate reality with which we have to do, but is only one more, perhaps interesting, certainly tragic, episode in human history. But its ultimate significance is neither more nor less than that of any other episode. If we eliminate the first point, we thus destroy completely our very purpose in calling special attention to this event, and the notion of revelation collapses.

No more can the second point, that this God is active in our present, that he reveals himself to us, be omitted. If this God, after all, is in no way present to us, if he is not real and active in our world, then how are we to speak of him at all? We can only speak and know of realities which are in some sense present in our own experience, having meaning and reality for us. God, then, must be active and working in our lives, in our world, or he is not God for the world we live in or for us. We then belong to some other who is our actual God, the reality upon which our lives are oriented. We cannot eliminate the second point either, without losing the meaning of the claim of revelation.

But it is just as important that we retain the third. For unless we can select out of the whole range of experience something specific, particular, concrete, to give content to such words as "God" and "God's revelation," they remain simply formal noises in English speech, referring to some vague mythological "super-person" in the skies. In such a case there would certainly be no reason to regard these words as in any significant way "Christian" in meaning. When we say that God reveals himself in *Jesus Christ*, we are indicating that here *in this place*, at this point in history, are to be found the criteria for our word "God." "God" is that reality which comes to man in and through the person Jesus Christ. In this way we can give concrete and definite meaning to what would otherwise be vague, even vacuous. Since the word "God" refers to a reality in some sense transcending all experience, it is difficult to show what content it might have. For this reason it is essential to indicate precisely the point in human experience and history in terms of which the transcendent is understood, if the transcendent is to be discussed at all.[3] We cannot, therefore, eliminate the third point any more than the other two without losing the meaning of the whole. The Christian claim that the ultimate reality with which we have to do is unveiled in Jesus Christ necessitates conceiving our knowledge of God in terms of a three-point structure.

Certain implications of our analysis up to this point may be mentioned here. Although Christian theology is the only perspective which has developed this understanding of the intrinsic threefold-ness in our knowledge of God, every claim to such knowledge involves a similar three-point structure. For example, consider the claim of some to find God (or "Reality") in *reason*. Here once again are our three points: It is *God*—i.e., ultimate reality, not some penultimate or superficial reality—who supposedly manifests himself here; this is the ultimate reality *for us*, for our world and our experience, and is thus present to our existence; he is present and known *at this particular point or level* in existence, namely in reason, not everywhere equally. The same structure will be found in claims

---

[3] It is of course just as necessary to show why language about the transcendent is required in order to deal adequately with this person-event; that is the central problem of christology. Groundwork for understanding that issue has been laid in the earlier chapters on revelation (Chs. 2, 3) and it will be discussed further below in Chs. 11 and 12.

that ultimate reality is to be seen in nature, or beauty, or power, etc. In every case there must be: (a) a concrete and specific point in experience which is the locus of and thus the analogue for our knowledge of the real (e.g., Jesus Christ); (b) an insistence that God is not simply to be *identified* with this point[4] but utterly transcends it (i.e., that we are concerned here with *ultimate*, not merely some penultimate, reality); and (c) the claim that this ultimate reality is here genuinely known to *us*, that this is not mere secondhand report but in some sense firsthand knowledge.[5]

Not only is a certain threefoldness intrinsic to God's self-manifestation: the *oneness* which permeates this threeness must also be emphasized. If we grant that God has in fact revealed himself, then God-in-himself (the transcendent dimension) must be in some sense identical with the God-known-in-Christ. To deny this, holding these two to be radically separate and different, would be denying that

---

[4] Such identification would not only be philosophical naiveté; from a theological point of view it is idolatrous.

[5] The matter can perhaps be diagrammed as follows. Whereas all our knowledge of finite realities (i.e., the ordinary objects of experience) has a two-point structure (however complex be the interrelation of subject and object), our knowledge of God (ultimate reality) must have a three-point character:

All finite knowledge: *Knowledge of God:*

As Barth has noted: "At bottom, knowledge of God in faith is always . . . indirect knowledge of God, knowledge of God in His works, . . . in the determining and using of certain creaturely realities to bear witness to the divine objectivity" (*Church Dogmatics*, II, 1, p. 17). In comparison with the indirect character of our knowledge of the ultimate, all our knowledge of finite being (including that finite which mediates the ultimate) must be regarded as direct and immediate. (Our knowledge of finite reality is of course also mediated on the finite level, especially by language. Indeed, all the relations in these diagrams are very complex, with symbolic mediation involved at every point. I have not shown this here because I am trying to indicate only the peculiar character of the mediation involved in knowledge of God.) Our knowledge as such is always of finite objects of experience. If ultimate reality is known at all, it is by means of clues found in certain paradigmatic experiences or dimensions of experience believed to contain the key to the nature of the real, or, in theological terms, believed to be the locus of God's revelation. Further discussion of these problems will be found in Chs. 11 and 12 below. See also my essay, "On the Meaning of 'God': Transcendence without Mythology" (*Harvard Theological Review* [1966], 59:105–132).

God has in fact made himself known here. Hence, if in Jesus Christ there is true revelation of God, then in this man God himself must be present to man. "I and the Father are one," says the Johannine Jesus (10:30). To take any other position destroys the revelation claim.

Similarly, there can be no essential difference between this trans-cendent God, manifest back at that particular point in history 2000 years ago, and the God presently active in our lives and world. If God does in fact reveal himself to us in Christ, then the ultimate reality of our present existence must be essentially identical with the God-in-Christ, who is in turn identical with the transcendent reality. "When we cry, 'Abba! Father!' it is the Spirit himself bear-ing witness with our spirit" (Rom. 8:15–16).[6]

Thus, God makes himself known as one-in-three, three-in-one. He must be conceived as simultaneously Father (God-as-transcend-ent), Son (having a particular and definite character and being, as seen in the historical person-event Jesus Christ), and Holy Spirit (present in and to and with us in our world). The absence of any of these dimensions to God's being (as we necessarily conceive that being) would mean we were not conceiving of the God who reveals himself in Jesus Christ. Thus, for Christian faith to speak of God as one who loves, or as the one who comes to man in and through Jesus Christ, or as the trinity, is to say essentially the same thing in differ-ent words. The trinitarian doctrine is simply a precise and exact formula that points up the most fundamental presuppositions of the central Christian claim about God's nature and will.

Frequently, however, orthodox formulations of the trinity, though certainly having their origins in such concerns as these, have gone much further in their actual claims and statements. Almost forgetting that the doctrine was a human conceptualization and analysis of the being of God-as-revealed-to-man, it has been maintained that the doctrine itself was directly revealed by God. In this way revelation

[6] Cf. also 1 Cor. 2:9–12: "What no eye has seen, nor ear heard, nor the heart of man conceived, . . . God has revealed to us through the Spirit. . . . no one comprehends the thoughts of God except the Spirit of God. Now we have received not the spirit of the world, but the Spirit which is from God, that we might understand the gifts bestowed on us by God."

was demoted from its status as the unveiling of God himself to being mere impartation of information about him; and, simultaneously, the door was opened to all sorts of speculations about the complexity and character of the internal structure of the divine being. Moreover, very misleading disputes between the "modalists" and the "orthodox," over whether God's threefoldness characterized his inmost essence or merely our way of viewing him, further complicated the matter.

The more earthbound approach to theology developed in these pages enables us to avoid the error common to both modalism and orthodoxy, namely, their tendency to overlook the *relational* character of our knowledge of God. Both presupposed we can know God's inner essence *as it is in itself* or as it is known to himself, not simply as it is known to us. From this common premise they drew opposite conclusions. The orthodox held that God's inner essence is three-in-one; the modalists, that it is simple unity.[7] Neither observed that in distinguishing between God as he is in himself and God as he is known to us, they implied possession of a knowledge which by definition is essentially and forever inaccessible to man.[8] The only knowledge we can have is that open to us by virtue of the relationships in which we stand. The fact that such knowledge is relative to us does not mean that it is any the less true for us. Indeed, knowledge *not* framed in human categories (and thus relative to man's cognitive processes, etc.) would be of no meaning to men;

[7] A favorite illustration of the modalists was taken from our experience of the sun: just as the sun is round and bright and hot, but is actually one sun, not three realities, so we perceive a certain threeness in God, though in actuality he is one being. God thus has three aspects, but his essence is to be distinguished from them all. Modalism is to be rejected not only because of its nonrelational epistemology (discussed in the text), but also because it undercuts the revelation-claim of Christian faith by insisting that in reality God is significantly other than he appears in the alleged revelation. Jesus Christ is hardly the revelation of God's inmost being if he is conceived as simply *one aspect* of that being, as roundness is one aspect of the sun. This view depreciates the significance of revelation doubly, by implying that revelation in fact leads us into error rather than truth, and by suggesting there is some other more adequate source of knowledge of God (by means of which such error is discerned and God is perceived as simple unity) which is to be preferred. However, if we ground our knowledge of God on the revelatory event, a modalistic interpretation of the trinity, with its distinction between God as he appears to us in revelation and God as he really is, must be rejected.

[8] The whole complex discussion of the inner-trinitarian relations rests on the same error. See below, pp. 250ff.

certainly it would be absurd to speak of its "truth" (a human category). Thus, all we can say—and this is all we need to say—is that the understanding of God given in his revelation (i.e., in the actual concrete relationship to him in which we stand) is his *true essence for us.* Since this is *what God really is in his relation to man,* it obviously is all we can ever know or need to know; and it is only confusing and misleading to inquire about some other essence (which by definition we cannot know) which God is in himself and to himself. A relational understanding of the knowledge of God bypasses both the orthodox and the modalistic positions: the only God we know is the God who appears in his self-revelation as three-in-one.

The doctrine of the trinity, then, as developed through analysis of the historical character of revelation, is not an esoteric item of information about the peculiar internal structure of some transcendent being up in the heavens. Rather, it expresses the structure of history (as apprehended in Christian faith) in relation to its ground, and, conversely, the way in which transcendent reality is bound up with history. According to the Christian claim, God decisively manifested himself in Christ. This means that he is known in a special way through the point in history called Jesus Christ (and thus through the particular history of which Christ is the "center"), and that he makes himself known to all the rest of history through that point (and that history). God's being, then, as apprehended in Christian faith, has this threefold structure: it is present in and with every moment of history (including this present), it is in a special way bound up with the historical person-event Jesus Christ, and it utterly transcends these (and all other) finite loci as the ground and basis of them all.

This does not mean that the three persons of the trinity are to be taken as successive manifestations of God, the Father appearing before Christ, the Son in Christ, and the Holy Spirit after Christ (cf. the ancient Sabellians). On the contrary, at every point God's presence in history involves this threefoldness. The first person signifies God's transcendence of the historical process at each point and in its entirety; the second person refers to his special involvement in the person-event Jesus Christ—and this of course also means his involvement in the preceding particular history (Old Testament) leading up to and making possible the life of Jesus of Nazareth, as well as that succeeding particular history brought into being in and through his life, death, and resurrection (church history expanding into world history); the third person designates his being in and with and under all events of history, his presence in every new present. God's being, as apprehended in Christian faith, cannot be conceived apart from this oneness in threeness and threeness in oneness. But this trinitarian structure defines the way God has bound himself to and in human history, and the way in which history is bound to and grounded in God's being; it is not a mysterious and esoteric item of information about the inner structure of some divine reality totally outside of and unconnected with our world and our experience.[9]

Traditionally this three-in-oneness has been expressed in a terminology that can easily be misleading: God is one substance in three persons, *una substantia, tres personae.* Father, Son, and Holy Spirit were each held to be separate and distinct, yet of one essence (*homoousios*). When these traditional formulations are used, it is important that the term "person" not be understood in the sense of "personality." The Godhead is not a cosmic committee of three. The Latin word *persona*, used by the framers of this terminology, had two basic uses. In the theater it designated the *mask* which an actor wore to indicate his character, and in legal parlance it indicated an entity that had legal being and responsibility. In both cases *persona* meant a dynamic acting unity. To speak, then, of one God in three persons is to declare that the one God acts toward us and is present to us—and thus must be conceived by us—in three modes or differ-

---

[9] To take that view would be to mistake the threefoldness of God's bound-up-ness with our world for a threefoldness in his transcendence of our world; it would be to mistake the (external) structure of his relatedness to us (which is certainly a structure of the divine being) for the (internal) structure of his being as such. Certainly, if genuine revelation is affirmed, the character of God's relating himself to his world must express the inmost essence of his being and will; but there is no reason whatsoever to maintain that the *structure* of that external relationship which we perceive in our experience somehow directly mirrors a similar but more primordial threefold structure in the innermost recesses of the divine being. To the internal *structure* of this innermost essence we have no access in history or revelation; and anything said about it is pure speculation. About the trinitarian structure of God's being-in-revelation, however, we can speak with confidence, because this is the only way to conceive what *is* given directly in Christian history and revelation.

entiations or "masks." But in these three, the same one personal
God is acting, not three independent personalities. The latter would
be tritheism, not monotheism.

This unity in the threeness is emphasized for both the being and
the action of God in traditional theology. The oneness of God's being
is developed in the doctrine of *perichoresis* (Greek) or *circum-
incessio* (Latin), according to which the three persons of the Godhead
are in no sense independent but in fact coinhere in each other. Each
interpenetrates the other in such a way that whatever God is as
Father, he also is as Son and Holy Spirit. None of the three is to
be understood as only partly or inadequately God, and none is God
in some fuller or truer sense than the others. Whatever belongs to
one belongs also to the others so that each of the "persons" is to be
understood as the full and adequate presence of the one personal
God. In this respect the holistic implications of the term "person"
(even in the more modern sense) are appropriate to affirm the Christian contention that it is not some truncated God who is encountered
in Son and Holy Spirit, but the one truly personal God.

The unity of God's action is developed in the doctrine of the
"indivisibility of the outward works of the trinity" (*opera trinitatis
ad extra sunt indivisa*): that is, that there is a coinherence in the
works of the trinity as well as in the persons. Thus, we cannot say
that God the Father does one thing (e.g., creation); God the Son,
another (e.g., redemption); and God the Holy Spirit, a third (e.g.,
sanctification). Whatever God does is done by the one whole God.
When this is forgotten, the unity and integrity of the divine being
tends to be lost and he may be pictured as suffering from internal
self-contradictions and conflicts. In certain interpretations of the
atonement, for example, the sacrifice of the Son is required to ap-
pease the vengeful justice of the Father before it is possible for man
to be saved. Such views divide the divine being, destroying the image
of a personal purposive God. Whatever God does, the one whole
God does; whoever God is, the one whole God is.

The trinitarian structure of the Christian understanding of God
provides us with three principal headings under which we can conveniently discuss God's nature as known to us through revelation.

(a) Under "God the Father" we will consider the transcendence of God, his unique deity, his transcendent otherness from the world. Here we will see what it means to say God is the Creator or Source or Ground of all that is, the ultimate limit of everything finite. (b) Under "God the Son" we will consider God in his revealedness to us, his presence to us in comprehensible form. Here we will see God as one who does not stay hidden in his transcendence but comes in love to man and unites himself with man. (c) Under "God the Holy Spirit" we will discuss God as the one continually present and active in every moment of history, within us and among us. These three are, of course, all the same one God who makes himself known through the revelatory person-event Jesus Christ. But to understand that one God better we must think and discuss separately and in serial order what is indivisible in him.

7 / The Transcendence of God

I. Preliminary Considerations

WHEN we speak of God as "Father," we are referring to him as the One who transcends all that is, as its source and ground and origin, and as its ultimate limit; he is not to be confused with any-thing in this world but has his being and comes to us from "beyond" it.[1]

This notion of a reality *beyond* the world which is its origin and limit is very peculiar. Indeed, the problems with the conception of transcendent reality are so profound that numerous writers have questioned whether, strictly speaking, it is meaningful or thinkable;[2] and the idea of a God "up there" or "out there" appears to be in-creasingly unpopular theologically. The roots of the difficulty are not far to seek, though they are, perhaps, not immediately apparent. At first sight the notion of a transcendent source of all that is may seem a legitimate extension of our ordinary knowledge by causes (cf. Aristotle).[3] Thus, we often say that we "know" an object when we know what produced it and how it was produced. For example, we understand what a table is if we know how carpenters working

---

[1] The *content* of the notion of God as Father, here briefly summarized to introduce the more formal considerations to be dealt with in this chapter and the next, will be elaborated in Chs. 9 and 10.

[2] For discussion of some of the literature and some of the problems here, see my two papers, "Two Models of Transcendence" (*The Heritage of Christian Thought*, Essays in Honor of Robert L. Calhoun, ed. R. E. Cushman and E. Grislis [New York: Harper & Row, 1965]) and "On the Meaning of 'God': Transcendence without Mythology" (*Harvard Theological Review* [1966], 59:105–132).

[3] This idea is the basis for the so-called cosmological argument for the existence of God.

with hammers and saws and wood brought this object into being to serve a definite purpose; we know an oak if we know the process through which acorns become saplings and finally great trees which, once again, produce more acorns; we understand another's ideas as we come to see why he thinks that way, what experiences have led him to that position, have formed that attitude, and those experiences in turn are intelligible as we see what led to them, and so forth. Our thinking appears here to be a process of searching out causes and connecting them together in a systematic way.

However, if we try to think the idea of a reality that transcends all that is as its source or origin, we get into difficulty. "Sourceness" or origination is an asymmetrical relation. Thus, the thing caused could not exist without its source or ground, but the latter could exist very well without the former. I could not exist if my father had not existed before me and acted to bring me into being, but my father could and did exist without me; this table could not exist if no carpenter had brought it into being, but the carpenter could and did exist prior to and without the table. To say that Y is the source of Z means that we cannot think out what we mean by Z without referring back to Y, but we can very well think Y without referring to Z. To think Y we would, however, be led to its source X, etc. The notion of sourceness thus indicates a unidirectional movement in both thought and being in which we are driven from the object given in experience to one which lies "behind" or "beyond" it, which "transcends" it.

But now let us try to think the idea of the *source of all that is*. We may symbolize the "all that is" in this phrase by Z. In order to grasp this Z, we seek to see it in relation to its source, Y. That is, every item of experience without exception, every reality in our world, is to be referred to Y in order to grasp its nature; every finite object is to be seen as grounded in and limited by the ultimate Source. This is precisely the theological proposition with which we began.

A brief inspection makes it clear, however, that there is something wrong here, something so serious that it may be doubted whether our theological proposition has cognitive meaning. In the first place, we have no experience of a reality such as this Y. In our

experience each thing always leads us back to its cause, and that
cause in turn to another; there are no objects of experience to which
everything without exception leads. Inasmuch as this Y on which
everything else is grounded is never experienced, it appears to be
merely hypothetical; and suspicions arise as to whether it is only a
figment of the imagination. In the second place, since this source
itself (Y) leads on to nothing beyond itself (it being the source of
all other reality), our thinking is here brought to a standstill. All
lines run to this point, then they stop completely. There is no X
standing behind this Y. But once again, we have no experience of
such a thing, and it is dubious whether we can think it. As we have
seen, in our ordinary experience and thought every reality always
leads back to another. There are no absolute stopping points just
as there are no absolute starting points. When we speak of the source
of all that is, we are speaking of something that implies nothing
other than itself; that depends on nothing other than itself for existence; that has its reality from itself alone. This Y has a kind of
glorious independence and even isolation from all other reality which
it seems not to need in any way, though all the rest of reality needs it.

Clearly this notion is very odd; and it is not difficult to see why
many have held it actually empty and meaningless, a trick played on
us by our language usage. Inasmuch as the reality we are trying to
speak of here—if there is such a reality—is utterly unique and not
subsumable under the concepts applicable to ordinary experience, no
irrefutable defense against such criticisms is possible. But for precisely the same reason it is evident they beg the question. For if there
is such a unique reality, unlike any of the ordinary objects of experience, it could be spoken of only with odd paradoxical language. The
paradox involved is most obvious when we attempt to make the source
of all that is a direct object of our cognition, instead of considering it
in its relation to other reality (i.e., as the source of that reality, where
we can grasp something of what is intended by analogy with other relationships of "sourceness"). When we try thus to think out the meaning of the term itself, our difficulties become even more pronounced.
For apparently this reality, the source of everything else, must have
its origin in itself: God is self-caused, he creates himself. These are

very odd ideas indeed, and it is questionable whether they are sufficiently self-consistent for us to think them. Clearly, when we speak of
God as the source of all that is, we are very near to reducing our
language to meaninglessness.

Nonetheless, it is precisely this risk we must run if we are to
attempt to speak of God at all. For the notion that he is a unique
reality on which all else depends and which is its ultimate limit is
very near the core meaning of the term (cf. Chapter 1). It is not surprising, therefore, that this idea of God's radical independence of all
other being, his dependence only on his own self-originatingness, has
become expressed traditionally as a central doctrine: the *aseity* of
God (*a se*="from himself"). God is the reality who comes from
himself alone, who depends on nothing else for his being. It is God's
aseity which formally defines his *godness*: that which distinguishes
him radically from everything else. He is the self-existent being and
thus "that than which nothing greater can be conceived" (Anselm).
When we speak of God, we are speaking of a being who is not directly
comparable to any other, who is radically unique in such a way that
there are no adequate analogies for grasping his being. For no other
being has this character of utter self-sufficiency. This is why God is
sometimes referred to as the "wholly other."

What justification, now, can be given for such speech about One
who transcends all experience? Sometimes a quasi-empirical basis for
our knowledge of the "wholly other" is sought in the experience of
"the holy" (Otto). For here we apparently sense something utterly
mysterious, uncanny, and awe-ful. Since this is a reality beyond all
human comprehension (cf. "the source of all that is"), it gives rise to
very strong but ambivalent feelings. On the one hand, there is the
feeling of terror and despair at the awareness of one's worthlessness,
even nothingness, before that perceived as holy: "Woe is me! For I
am lost; for I am a man of unclean lips" (Isa. 6:5). On the other
hand, the holy fascinates and attracts us, for it is that which confronts
us as beyond all human goodness and value, as the perfection which is,
in some sense, the goal of the highest human aspiration: "You shall be
holy; for I the Lord your God am holy" (Lev. 19:2; cf. 20:26;-etc.).
The experience of the holy is the experience of the "mysterium tremendum" (Otto), the mystery which gives us tremors, yet fascinates

us. It is the "numinous" before which men quake as they feel their smallness and weakness, their uncleanness and unworthiness. Finitude and sin weigh upon men as they confront this mysterious reality, apparently "wholly other" from themelves.

As far as we know, men of all times and all cultures have, in differing ways and degrees, known the experience of the holy and the concomitant sense of their own finitude and insufficiency; probably every man has at some time or other felt, with a sense of uncanniness and weirdness, his aloneness in a mysterious and alien world. Does this not mean, then, that the very idea of God's godness—his deity, his wholly otherness—is a notion common to all men and thus not specifically rooted in the revelatory history to which Christian faith looks? Theologians have often taken this position, working out a "natural theology" as prolegomenon to their discussion of "revealed theology." Here is set forth what all men "by nature" can know of God. It is here that "arguments for the existence of God" appear together with appeals to the universality of religious experience, both supposedly substantiating the view that genuine knowledge of God is available to man apart from God's special revelation. Awareness of God as Creator, as Father, is given all men as the opposite side of their awareness of their own finitude, their creatureliness. God has left his mark or brand upon us all, and it is the task of the theologian simply to point this out. The authority of Paul is often appealed to in support of this position:

> For what can be known about God is plain to them [that is, to all men], because God has shown it to them. Ever since the creation of the world his invisible nature, namely, his eternal power and deity, has been clearly perceived in the things that have been made.
>
> ROMANS 1:19-20

This whole line of argument rests on a misconception. Beginning with the fact that men universally experience their own finitude, their limitedness, and that this experience of the "boundaries" of human existence upon occasion gives rise to weird and uncanny feelings that may leave one in terror or anxiety, the assumption is made that we experience and come to know *that which limits us*. But the nature of that which limits us ultimately—its inner essence and quality of being—is precisely what we can*not* experience or know directly, any more than a man imprisoned throughout his life in one room could know what lies beyond its boundaries. Even the nature of the walls themselves (i.e., their thickness, the material of which they are made, why they are impenetrable to his touch, etc.) would necessarily remain beyond his ken. He could know only that they restricted and restrained him, that they were the ultimate limits to his movements. Only if it were possible to get beyond the limits sufficiently to determine what there is about these walls that enables them in this way to confine him, could he discover much about their real character, that is, about what they are in themselves and not merely as his limits.

The same must be said about any experiences of the ultimate boundaries within which we live, the experience of finitude. Precisely because we are here brought up against the final *limits* of our awareness and knowledge, we are able to know here only *that* we are limited, not *what it is* that limits us. Of course we may specify to some extent the various ways in which we are limited—for example, that we were "thrown" into existence (Heidegger), that we emerged in *this* particular historical context and not some other, that we have just *these* aptitudes and interests and abilities and are lacking those, that we shall have to die—but such specifications only tell us about ourselves; they teach us nothing about the nature of the reality over against us which does the limiting. Whether this is to be understood finally as simply physical being (materialism), or as some sort of life-force (vitalism) or formal structure (idealism), remains completely undetermined by the experience of ultimate limitation itself. It is the conviction of Christian faith—in this respect belief in God always involves a "leap" to a particular metaphysical interpretation of the ultimate limits of our existence—that the ultimate limiting reality is none of these but is rather personal purposive will; but there is no more direct evidence for this contention in our experience of finitude than for any of the others.[4]

[4] For a discussion of the experiences of limitation and finitude and their importance for understanding the idea of God, see my essay "On the Meaning of 'God': Transcendence without Mythology."

In view of this fundamental difficulty inherent in the program of natural theology, it is not difficult to see why in our own day claims about "proving" God's existence or "experiencing God" directly are viewed with the utmost suspicion. In other times, when Christian traditions more thoroughly permeated and determined the whole culture, and thus the common experience of men, it may have seemed reasonable and credible to argue that some direct "natural" knowledge of God was available, was as much a part of the common stock of knowledge as information and theory about the natural world. In such a setting it was possible to hold in close connection theology and science. But in our day the great advances made by natural science have been on the assumption that the world is autonomous and self-contained, and this has persuaded many that it is possible to come to adequate understanding of the universe without reference to a creative supreme being behind it. Moreover, modern psychological theory has convinced most of us that special feelings of "uncanniness" or "the numinous" prove nothing but that sometimes we have weird feelings. In other societies it was perhaps possible to interpret these as relatively conclusive evidence of confrontation with the divine. Not so in ours. Contemporary culture can be properly described as experiencing an "eclipse of God" (Buber), many apparently living out their lives with scarcely a thought of him, certainly with no awareness of his lordship. Our world is not so much characterized by conscious atheism—indeed, such is rejected with abhorrence in many quarters —or even explicit agnosticism, as it is by the utter irrelevance of God. Claims about transcendent reality can simply be ignored; we have learned to be content with the human world. In view of these facts, apparent on every side, it is not only logically dubious to attempt to speak of God on the basis of a "natural theology"; it seems strangely archaic as well. Such an approach is both irrelevant to the situation of modern man, and theologically misguided. To *this* man, God must reveal himself if he is to be known at all.

But how is this to be understood? What can it mean to say God must reveal himself in order for us even to know whether it is appropriate to use the word "God"? This should not be so difficult to understand in the light of our earlier conclusions that both the notion of God and the concept of revelation are rooted in personalistic experience and thinking. If God is to be understood as active will—as he certainly is in the biblical tradition (Chapter 5)—then he will be known primarily through his historical acts of self-revelation to us, as other personal wills are known. It will be on the basis of an acceptance of a concrete and particular history of revelation that we will be able to speak of him. Only as we grasp certain events as his meaningful and purposive *acts*, that is, as media through which an agent is present to us—in a way similar to our apprehension, for example, of certain noises as meaningful *words*, as media through which another person is speaking to us—are we in a position to speak of a transcendent God at all. Conversely, if we apprehend certain critical events as *revelatory* (in the full meaning of the term), we are certainly entitled, indeed required, to regard the ultimate limit of our experience and world as personal in character, that is, as *God*. Philosophers who wish to speak of "God" but are dubious and embarrassed about particularistic revelation-claims such as those made by Christian faith, are simply inconsistent; they have not thought through clearly the mode in which knowledge of personal beings comes to us. Knowledge of God, of course, also has a root in our experience of finitude, but that in itself is not a sufficient basis for conceiving the ultimate ground and limits of our being in theistic terms. Such faith, involving a personalistic understanding of that which ultimately limits us, presupposes the acceptance of the events of a particular history as the media through which God has made himself known. In this sense all theological statements rest on the acceptance of a positive revelation: so-called natural theology by itself is no adequate basis for making affirmations about God; the self-sufficient One, if known at all, must be known through his own self-manifestation.[5]

[5] It is perhaps important to observe here that I am not following Karl Barth's view that natural theology is completely *irrelevant* to Christian theology. The "natural" experience of finitude is the "hook" in our experience on which any understanding of the ultimate limit of our existence as *God* must be hung, and without which all such talk would be meaningless (see *ibid.*). But one cannot derive from this experience itself anything positive about God, and thus a doctrine of God necessarily has its ground entirely in revelation. (This latter point is the truth which Barth has seen, though he mistakenly understood it to imply the negation of the former. Cf. especially his debate with E. Brunner published in *Natural Theology* [London: Geoffrey Bles, 1946] and *Church Dogmatics*, I, 1 [Edinburgh: T. & T. Clark, 1936] and II. 1.)

Thus, Christian theology may and should be founded directly and entirely on the events taken by faith to be God's revelation. Indeed, if God has in fact revealed himself in some such specific point, the true significance of man's experience of finitude, as well as of the various gods and religions known to cultural anthropology, will become clarified there. As Paul is reported to have stated at Athens: "Whom therefore ye ignorantly worship, him declare I unto you" (Acts 17:23 KJ). If the Christian claim that God has revealed himself is true, we are here given a criterion that can bring order into the confusing welter of man's religious experience, enabling us to distinguish what is valuable and valid from what is superstitious and false. Although a nonChristian theology could hardly accept this claim at face value, this is surely the obvious place for Christian faith to begin any exposition of the doctrine of God. It is true of course that this Christian God is also the Holy One, the Creator, the First Cause, the ultimate Limit of our existence. But only in the light of God's self-manifestation can we come to see what these words properly mean: that it is before *agape* that we should tremble; this is the ultimate mystery, the *"mysterium tremendum"*; the First Cause of the universe is no abstract, empty concept but God's all-powerful love.

It is not to be supposed that the theological rule that we must begin with the Christian revelation requires rejection of every element imbedded in the nonChristian religions. It is well known that, as far back as we can trace historically, Hebrew-Christian faith has been enriched time and again by borrowing from other religious and cultural traditions.[6] Though the fundamental character of the Chris-

---

[6] Cf. Giovanni Miegge: "The theological idea of God in Christianity as a historical religion is a majestic edifice, constructed with a variety of materials, the work of a number of craftsmen of varying techniques and differing inspirations. The foundation consists of the Hebrew idea of God the Creator; not, however, without certain elements derived from the Aristotelian and Stoic development of the ideas of creation and providence. This development was perhaps not carried through without some infiltration of Hebrew influence, at least through Philo, the great middleman between the ancient worlds of biblical and classical thought; however, before its adoption by Christian theology, it had been brought to perfection on pagan soil, and with the techniques of the eclectic philosophy of the first century A.D. The first floor of the edifice is formed by the dogmas of the Person of Christ and of the Trinity, that is, of the idea of the God who reveals Himself and who gives Himself, taking upon Himself the form of a man and sacrificing Himself for the redemption of mankind. But in the elaboration of these dogmas an indispensable contribution was made by the syncretistic idea of the *logos*, and by the philosophical concepts of substance, essence and person. At the summit of

tian idea of God has been shaped (according to the understanding of faith) by God's self-manifestation in and through the events of biblical history—and supremely in Jesus Christ—the myths and concepts necessary to grasp and express God's nature and will were often adopted and adapted from neighboring cultures. There is no revealed theology; there is only the revealed God whom we must seek to apprehend and understand theologically with the aid of whatever human conceptions are at hand. It would be very surprising indeed if it would have been possible to think through the conception of the Creator of the heavens and the earth drawing only upon the resources provided in one somewhat parochial tradition which reflected the experience of only a tiny segment of humanity. Instead of confining themselves within boundaries conceived so narrowly, biblical and Christian writers from the beginning have not hesitated to utilize whatever pagan mythical, liturgical, and philosophical conceptions were available in order to elaborate more adequately the divine revelation.[7]

Furthermore, it is to be expected that the so-called younger churches of Africa and Asia, bringing with them new and different cultural attitudes and traditions, will be able to perceive and understand much that has escaped the best of Western thinkers. Thus, it will become possible and necessary to modify and qualify the Christian conception of God in ways not now foreseeable. God "did not leave himself without witness" among any people (Acts 14:17), and ultimately, the genuine insights into truth and reality in these so-called pagan traditions will have to find their proper place in Christian thought. But this cannot be accomplished simply by examining these religions and traditions in their variety, eclectically choosing a morsel here and a bit of spice there; such a procedure would lead only to a syncretistic mixture of truth and error. God's self-revelation —the person-event Jesus Christ—must be the criterion in terms of

---

the building, the airy gallery open to the sky, is the Neoplatonic mysticism, with its highly developed and hierarchical structure of emanations, and its deeply religious passion for the Infinite and the unutterable" (*Christian Affirmations in a Secular Age* [New York: Oxford University Press, 1958], p. 41).

[7] It is precisely this fact, of course, that is at the root of much of modern man's difficulty with Christian faith, for many of the forms which previous generations found helpful or even essential in speaking of God have become incredible and meaningless "myths" and "superstitions" to us.

which their validity is adjudged and their rightful place discovered.

Thus, the events taken to be revelatory provide not only the basis and justification for all "God-talk" as such (see above, pp. 111f.); they also furnish the criteria for assessing the theological significance of notions drawn from philosophical speculation and the variety of man's religions, the experience of the holy and human experience generally. There is no question that men often seem to "sense the beyond"; that they have significant mystical and religious experiences of various sorts; and that they have developed important and meaningful concepts of God, the holy, the supernatural, etc., in order to interpret these. But for the Christian who believes that the Beyond has come to man and definitively made himself known—thereby judging and transforming but also verifying certain human ideas—the meaning and truth finally to be attributed to all such experiences and concepts must be determined with reference to the historical Jesus Christ.[8]

The experience and thought, both religious and secular, of men of many traditions and viewpoints have always been, and will always provide, indispensable elements in the Christian doctrine of God. It is historical falsehood and anthropological nonsense to insist that Christian theology is a pure distillate from revelation, uncontaminated by human—especially "pagan" or "nonbiblical"—experience and thought. Moreover, such claims can well lead to dogmatic fanaticism

[8] If now we return to a more careful look at Romans 1, we will discover that Paul is not as clear a witness to the independent validity of a "natural" knowledge of God as may first have seemed the case. The passage immediately following the one quoted on p. 109 declares that although in some sense man in general has had knowledge of God available to him, he has refused this knowledge, turning away from it until now he actually knows only idols. "For although they knew God they did not honor him as God or give thanks to him, but they became futile in their thinking, and their senseless minds were darkened. Claiming to be wise, they became fools, and exchanged the glory of the immortal God for images resembling mortal man or birds or animals or reptiles . . . they exchanged the truth about God for a lie and worshiped and served the creature rather than the Creator" (Rom. 1:21–23, 25). Man is not living in a situation, then, in which he possesses "natural" knowledge of God; on the contrary, he has "exchanged the truth about God for a lie" and now he lives in relation to this lie. A theology erected on such a basis can only confirm us in our falsehood and error. However much Paul was convinced that man is responsible for the falsity of his relationship to God, and that it is possible for him to know, as it were, the truth about God, he is even more convinced that man—all men—refuses this truth. In his view, the only possible way for man now to stand in positive relation with God is the way which God himself has provided through coming to man in Jesus Christ. "For all alike have sinned, and are deprived of the divine splendour, and all are justified by God's free grace alone, through his act of liberation in the person of Christ Jesus" (Rom. 3:23–24 NEB).

—a form of self-idolatry—as well as to an ungracious and ungrateful attitude toward those non-Abrahamic children of God who have also made their unique contributions to understanding the divine being. Yet the critical question remains: In the vast panorama of human experience, what is to be regarded as an authentic clue to ultimate reality—to God's nature and will—and what is to be disregarded as misleading or even simply meaningless? How shall we define a criterion by means of which the significant and valid can be sorted out from the trivial and spurious?

We will only be sifting the variety of opinion with no adequate means of discrimination, unless we can believe that at some point Reality has unveiled itself before us, providing us with a criterion. If such genuine revelation be allowed, then we are at liberty to draw from the widest and most various reaches of experience in elaborating our picture of God; without it we are confronted simply with the chaos of human opinion. Said otherwise: if we begin with God's self-revelation and let what is made known there decisively determine the lines of our interpretation, we can draw on common human experience —both religious and secular—to elaborate our theological concepts and doctrines. We can, and doubtless must, speak of God as First Cause and Ground of Being, of his wholly otherness and his absolute self-sufficiency, of his holiness and his aseity. But each of these, and all the other terms we find it necessary to use as well, must be understood and interpreted along the lines defined by God's revelation in Jesus Christ if it is to be the *Christian* doctrine of God that we are expounding. "No one has even seen God; the only Son, who is in the bosom of the Father, he has made him known" (John 1:18).

8 / The Transcendence of God

II. Language about God

To call God "Father," as we have noted, is to speak of him as the source of all that is, as the self-existent being; it is to speak of God's *aseity*. We have already considered some of the peculiarities of this notion, but we have not yet faced directly the problems raised by its implication that God is unique, incomparable with any other. Is it even possible to speak or conceive of such a reality?

Our thinking is a process of *relating* aspects of experience to each other. By comparing, contrasting, and connecting items of experience; by analyzing it into parts which can be related to each other; by synthesizing chunks of experience into larger wholes, we bring the order and structure into our world without which there could be neither experience nor knowledge (Kant). Our concepts, for example, are devices which make it possible for us to relate and compare experiences. Thus, "chair" enables me to hold together simultaneously a wide variety of experiences of things-to-be-sat-upon in such a way that each can be compared and contrasted with the others; "table" functions in a similar way for a different group of experiences; and "furniture" is a concept by means of which both groups are brought into connection with each other. These concepts enable me to bring some order into the everyday world where I constantly deal with chairs and tables. Again, "red" makes possible relating experiences of quite a different sort; and nouns like "pity," "joy," "pain," etc. refer to classes of yet another type. Verbs, adverbs, prepositions, and other parts of speech facilitate a great variety of very complex sorts of interconnection. The point is that each of these terms helps us to relate, compare, and contrast aspects of experiences which are in many and various ways connected with each other.

We come to know and understand a *new* experience through relating it to those features of experience which are already familiar to us, thus seeing how it fits with what we already know. For example, someone tells me of the great sorrow he felt at the death of his mother. Even though both my parents may still be living, it is possible to understand something of what he means by (a) remembering experiences of sorrow I have had, and (b) imagining how I would feel if my mother suddenly dies; that is, by comparing and contrasting this imagined experience with what I already know. It is through the infinite variations of processes like this that we come to know everything that we know. For this reason, as the idealists have always seen, we could never have a totally isolated, individual, unrelated experience: to experience is to see things in relation, and a completely unrelated experience would be a kind of blinding blob of which we could not even be conscious. (It is to be noted that even "blinding blob" suggests certain analogies with particular known experiences.) As long as an item remains isolated from the rest of experience and thus unrelated to our world, our knowledge of it is at best partial and inadequate; if it were totally unrelated (whatever that might mean), we could have no knowledge of it at all. We cannot even imagine what such an experience might be: to *imagine* is to relate by means of an image. Thinking, then, is a process of moving back and forth from one item of experience to another, continuously tightening up the connections between them. In this way we make the network of experience (and thought) ever more secure and certain by gradually working into the weave all the loose ends, until no seams or frayed edges show.[1]

As we have seen, however, *God* must be grasped and spoken of as unique and incomparable, as transcending the ordinary finite order of experience. How, in view of what we have just said about the char-

[1] For a fuller and more precise discussion of the interconnectedness of experience and thought, see my *Relativism, Knowledge and Faith* (Chicago: University of Chicago Press, 1960), Chs. 6-9.

acter of experience and language, is this possible? If all thought and
speech intrinsically involve relation and comparison, how are we to
think or speak of that which is utterly independent and unique? Does
this not imply that "God" is a proper name designating something
which cannot be in any way experienced, thought, or characterized;
about which, therefore, nothing can be said at all? If this were the
case, the term "God" could not even function as a proper name, for
we would not be able to say whether it in any way referred to (a)
reality. It would be indistinguishable from a bare "X" or a meaningless "blah-blah." If we wish to persist in using the term to designate
that transcendent reality "than which nothing greater can be conceived," therefore, it is necessary that we specify the way in which
we are using our terms.[2]

Four observations should be made at this point.

1] It should be clear that we can never use language *literally*
when referring to God. All our words literally refer to some aspect
of experience, relating it to other aspects. Our words are finite vehicles
used by finite men to speak of some finite aspect of experience, thus
bringing it into relation with other finite realities. Even a word like
"holy," which for our linguistic feeling has come to indicate in a special way the divine being in his contrast with our world, refers to an
experience of the "numinous," the "awe-ful," the "uncanny"—that is,
it designates one experience alongside others, thus revealing it as an
experience which can be related to others in various ways, as these
words themselves specifically indicate. But by "God" we do not intend to speak of one human experience beside others: on the contrary,
he is the source and ground and basis of every experience; it is idolatry to identify the ultimately real with one particular dimension of

[2] Some have argued on the basis of these problems that God is simply "ineffable,"
and we should, therefore, not seek to speak of him at all. Long ago Augustine saw the
inconsistency in this view: ". . . God should not be said to be ineffable, for when this
is said something is said. And a contradiction in terms is created, since if that is ineffable
which cannot be spoken, then that is not ineffable which can be called ineffable. . . .
For God . . . has accepted the tribute of the human voice and wished us to take joy in
praising Him with our words" (*On Christian Doctrine*, I, 6). Moreover, as Karl Barth
has noted, there is no reason to suppose that somehow our silence does justice to God
more adequately than our speech. "We must also be silent: but none the less we must
bear in mind that our silence compromises Him no less than our speech. We do the
Spirit no greater service by our silence" (*Epistle to the Romans* [London: Oxford University Press, 1933], p. 273).

the real.[3] "God," then, must not be identified with any one particular experience or aspect of experience—even the experience of the "holy," or of being "strangely warmed" in the heart, not even "mystical" experience.

This means that our words about God should never be regarded as literally true. The literal referent is always some particular (and thus finite) aspect of experience brought into relation and compared with other finite experiences, not God, the radically unique, utterly incomparable Reality. Our language about God involves the employment of terms in some unusual, unliteral way. It is necessary for us to indicate more precisely just what that can be.

2] One way of understanding the peculiarity of theological discourse is to be found in the so-called negative theology, the *via negativa*. The negative way begins with an outright acceptance of the fact that all our words apply literally only to finite experience and hence not to God. From this premise the conclusion is drawn that the only way to speak of God is systematically to *deny* various predicates as applicable to him. Thus God is *in*finite (=not finite), *in*comparable, *im*mortal, *in*conceivable, *ab*solute (=free of every restriction, unlimited, unrelated to anything), wholly other, etc. This kind of negative language is found upon occasion in the Bible,[4] but its real development and usage in Christian theology appeared when the Greek mind sought to speak of God. Thus, the second-century "Preaching of Peter" speaks of "The Unseen who sees all things, the Uncontained who contains all things, the Un-needy whom all things need and by whom they exist—incomprehensible, unending, incorruptible, unmade, who made all things by his word of power."[5] Here an attempt

---

[3] It is not difficult to see why idolatry inevitably becomes polytheistic: other gods must be found to provide the adequate divine grounding for the other aspects of experience.

[4] E.g.: *For my thoughts are not your thoughts,*
neither are your ways my ways, says the Lord.
For as the heavens are higher than the earth,
so are my ways higher than your ways
and my thoughts than your thoughts. (ISAIAH 55:8–9)

"O the depth of the riches and wisdom and knowledge of God! How unsearchable are his judgments and how inscrutable his ways!" (Rom. 11:33). "What no eye has seen, nor ear heard, nor the heart of man conceived, . . . God has prepared for those who love him" (1 Cor. 2:9).

[5] Quoted by R. Bultmann, *Theology of the New Testament* (New York: Charles Scribner's Sons, 1951), p. 72.

is made to say something meaningful about God by denying that this or that characteristic of finite being applies to him. It is no accident that this negative theology, prominent particularly in Hinduism (e.g., the well-known characteristic formula "neti, neti"—not this, not that), became an important element in Christian thought through the religiously similar Greek ethos, especially neoplatonism. Pseudo-Dionysius (c. 500 A.D., a disciple of Plotinus) formulated the *via negativa* as one of the three ways of speaking of God (the *via eminentiae* and *via causalitatis* being the other two members of his *via triplex*) in his work *On the Divine Names*.

It is not necessary here for us to investigate in detail the intricacy and subtlety of the negative theology, or the problems it involves. Its basic claim is certainly correct insofar as it emphasizes that every positive statement about God must immediately be qualified by the admission that it is not intended literally: God is *not* that. The *via negativa*, understood thus as essentially the denial that God is to be identified with anything finite, is necessary to any speech which undertakes to refer to God. It points to the intrinsic limitation of all our speech when applied to the divine being. If this limitation is forgotten, it will be an idol, not God, of whom we are speaking.

3] But the *via negativa* by itself does not enable us to speak of God. On the one hand, pure denials as such tell us nothing of what God *is*. Indeed, they cannot even distinguish him from nothingness, of which everything positive can also be denied. On the other hand, these negative words have acquired their own distinctive positive meaning. This should not be surprising, since they were intended to refer to a positive reality, namely God, who in his uniqueness transcends everything finite. "Infinite," for example, no longer means merely not finite: it points to the limitless superiority of God's being over every finite reality. Similar transformations into positive meaning have occurred with "absolute," "immortal," and many other negative terms. Each has come to indicate some respect in which God's superiority over finite being is to be emphasized. Thus, they represent an effort to raise concepts to the highest power possible when speaking of God; they are attempts to extrapolate beyond everything finite and limited.

This method of *beginning* with the finite (instead of simply negating its limitations) and extrapolating its positive significance and value to an eminent degree or power is called, following Pseudo-Dionysius, the *via eminentiae* ("eminence" = distinction above all others). For example, when we speak of God as "good," we do not mean to use the term in the literal sense of the goods we experience and know; his goodness is something beyond and higher than all human goodness, and yet it is not entirely incorrect to designate its positive value and significance with our word "good." The same must be said of other positive terms applied to God, "just," "wise," "true," for example. "Oh God! thou art not other than Love, but thou art another Love! Thou art not other than Justice, but thou art another Justice!"[6] Certainly if we refer to God as Father, King, Lord, Shepherd, etc., we cannot be intending these words to mean what they do on the human level. At best each is an analogy or symbol for what God is, not a literal description. As with all analogies, it gains its concrete meaning from the actual experience to which it literally applies. If one forgets this, and speaks of the fatherhood of God to one who had a drunken tyrant for his human father, he should not be surprised to be misunderstood.

Since God is unique and incomparable, our language about him will all be symbolical or analogical.[7] No term can be applied to him literally: each must be negated (in its limitations) and extrapolated

---

[6] Henri de Lubac, *De la Connaissance de Dieu* (Paris: Témoignage Chrétien, 1948), p. 111.

[7] Very often terms supposedly especially appropriate to the divine being are in fact metaphors drawn from the most ordinary experience, e.g., that of spatial height. Edwyn Bevan has noted "when man reached a stage of thought in which he came to understand clearly that height was not to be attributed to God in a literal spatial sense, the idea of height, as an essential characteristic of supreme worth, was so interwoven in the very texture of all human languages that it is impossible for us even to-day to give in words a rendering of what was meant by the metaphor. We are inevitably forced, if we try to explain the metaphor, to bring in the very metaphor to be explained. Supposing we say that what it means is that God is superior to all other beings, the word 'superior' is simply a Latin word meaning 'higher.' If we say that it means that God 'excels,' 'celsus' again is a Latin word for 'high.' If we say that it emphasizes God as 'transcendent,' transcendence embodies the metaphor and suggests a visual image of God occupying an otherwise empty space above the space occupied by all the created Universe" (*Symbolism and Belief* [London: Allen and Unwin, 1938], pp. 28–29). Bevan suggests (Ch. 3) that this feeling of the value of height may be connected with our experience of gravity always pulling us downward, on the one hand, and our awareness of the immensity of the heavens above us, on the other.

to an eminent degree (in the positive qualities it is desired to indicate). A consequence of this analogical character of our theological
language is a certain freedom, indeed necessity, to use many symbols
in their variety to indicate the fullness of the divine being. No finite
being can be adequately described in a few terms; how much less is
God—to whom our language applies at best only by a kind of unnatural stretching and pulling, that is, by analogy—so describable.
This means, of course, that no one term or symbol can ever be regarded as adequate simply in itself to refer to the divine being, even
though it has been reserved and hallowed by long years of usage in
this way. The limited meaning of each symbol must be negated and
corrected by others. If we are aware of this symbolic character of
our theological language, we will not be so apt dogmatically to insist
that only *our* symbols, and interpretations of symbols, are appropriate. On the contrary—lest we become idolaters entrapped in our own
language—we will value a certain openness toward symbols to which
we are not accustomed, anticipating new light which they may throw
on God.

It should not be inferred from what has been said here about the
limitations of theological language, and the care with which it must
be used, that its symbolic character is an unfortunate restriction. Paul
Tillich has rightly insisted that only failure to grasp what language
of God involves might lead us to disparage it as "only" symbolic, in
contrast with ordinary language which is literally applicable to finite
realities.[8] Clear realization of the analogical character of theological
language is necessary to help protect against idolatrous confusion of
our ideas and symbols with God's reality.

4] There are, of course, many problems inherent in the symbolic
character of theological language. A certain vagueness or built-in
imprecision in our terms seems inevitable, and the question may arise
whether such language has any definite referent at all. For a symbol
gains its meaning from its finite referent, that dimension of (finite)
experience to which it normally refers; but if precisely this (finite)
content must be qualified seriously (and in ways ultimately unspeci-
fiable) in order to make reference to *God* possible, it becomes

[8] *Systematic Theology,* I (Chicago: University of Chicago Press, 1951), 131

questionable just what, if any, meaning remains to the term in its specifically theological use.[9]

There appear to be two ways to meet this difficulty with the symbolic character of theological terms, while still contending that they refer to some (divine) reality or being.[10] One is to maintain, as Paul Tillich has done, that there is at least one point at which language about God is literal, not merely symbolic; this literal statement is then used as the "hook" on which the symbolic terms are hung and by means of which they are explicated.[11] But to take this course leads one into insoluble difficulties in justifying the selection of the particular term claimed to be literal and in showing that it can in fact apply literally to "God," who (as the discussion above has tried to show) transcends all our categories. An alternative procedure is to regard certain terms as *proper* or *defining* symbols or paradigms for our speech about God, others being given subsidiary roles. It is this procedure that will be followed here.

There are two serious problems with such a procedure. (a) How does one justify the selection of the paradigmatic symbols? (b) How do we know, or how can we ascertain, that these symbols actually tell us something about *God* and not merely about their finite referents, since, presumably, he is known only through the symbols and never directly; and thus we have no way of "checking up" on the symbols' reliability? For a theology the foundations of which are nonrevelational, these questions can hardly be answered. But a perspective which understands that certain historical events and experiences always have preferential position in the formation and formulation of cultural norms and criteria (see above, Chapter 2) is pre-

---

[9] For a discussion of this problem of "death by a thousand qualifications" (Flew), see "Theology and Falsification" in A. Flew and A. Macintyre, eds., *New Essays in Philosophical Theology* (London: SCM Press, 1955), pp. 96–130.

[10] There are of course many other theories of the meaning of theological or religious language, but these generally result in forsaking the referential claims of the language and regarding its meaning as "emotive" or "expressive" (see, e.g., J. J. C. Smart, "The Existence of God," in Flew and Macintyre, pp. 28–46) or hortatory (see, e.g., R. B. Braithwaite, *An Empiricist's View of the Nature of Religious Belief* [Cambridge: Cambridge University Press, 1955]).

[11] In volume I of the *Systematic Theology* Tillich contends that "The statement that God is being-itself is a nonsymbolic statement. . . . However, after this has been said, nothing else can be said about God as God which is not symbolic" (pp. 238–239). But in volume II he backs away from this claim somewhat by suggesting that the only nonsymbolic statement about God is "the statement that everything we say about God is symbolic" (p. 9). This latter claim, however, fails to meet the problem.

pared to deal with them. The paradigmatic symbols for such a perspective, of course, are *already given* in the revelatory event (or process) itself as the historical form in which it is believed God has manifested himself. In the Christian case, the historical person Jesus of Nazareth is definitive here; and we shall see in a moment how this person-event provides criteria for the ordering of our symbols. There is no way to know—independently of this revelation—whether in Jesus Christ we indeed come into relation with God, the ultimate reality with which we have to do. For to regard this person-event as *revelation* is to treat it as the proper source for our criteria, that in terms of which other claims to knowledge must be checked but which cannot itself be justified by reference to some more ultimate ground or norm. Symbols or clusters of symbols rooted here, therefore, may quite properly be taken as paradigmatic and defining.

As maps and models can provide both criteria and content for conceiving or imagining the reality which they represent, even for one who is not himself directly acquainted with that reality and who thus knows it only through these media, so these paradigmatic symbols drawn from the revelatory event(s) are the basis on which the concept of God can be constructed. Unlike most maps, however—the authority of which is grounded upon the direct knowledge which the cartographer has of the territory charted, and the skill with which he depicts it—the authority of the paradigmatic theological symbols derives from the acceptance of the event in which they are rooted as revelatory of ultimate reality (i.e., it derives from a stance of faith with reference to the revelation) and not from anyone's direct or immediate experience or knowledge of God.

It might be helpful to distinguish this proposal to develop our theological construction on an *analogia Christi,* from the more traditional doctrine of the *analogia entis,* particularly characteristic of Roman Catholic thought (but also implicit in much protestant theology).[12] The doctrine of the *analogia entis* involves the claim that there is a genuine "analogy of being" between finite reality and God. Careful analysis of our experience enables us to arrange finite beings

---

[12] A good contemporary statement will be found in E. L. Mascall, *He Who Is* (New York: Longmans, 1943) and *Existence and Analogy* (New York: Longmans, 1949). The very important analysis and restatement of the doctrine by Austin Farrer, *Finite and Infinite* (Westminster: Dacre Press, 1943), should also be noted.

on ascending scales which, when projected to an eminent degree, give us knowledge of the divine being. For example, there is the scale of being itself. Our experience reveals to us different forms of being, beginning with the simplest (inert matter), moving in increasing degrees of complexity through the various levels of plant and animal life, finally reaching the exceedingly complex and highly integrated rational (conscious) life of man. Each of these stages can be regarded as of higher reality than the previous: although the lower levels are heteronomously determined almost in their entirety, the higher become increasingly free and autonomous, and thus independent and self-contained. Intrinsic to finite being as such, then, is a *scale of degrees of reality*. If we extrapolate this line upward in an eminent degree, we will have some idea of the nature of God's absolute self-sufficiency and independence, that is, his reality. Clearly, it will not be a perfectly adequate idea, for we know no being totally self-sufficient, as God's must be when understood in terms of this projection. Even the human mind, the highest level we know, appears dependent on a physical body for its existence, dependent on other minds for the form and content of its ideas, etc. Yet, the growing independence and spirituality suggested in the movement up the scale of being from matter to mind does provide an analogy in terms of which God's absolute independence and spirituality can to some degree be apprehended. Thus, there is a correlation between God's perfect being and (especially certain forms of) finite being. And this *analogy of being* makes possible some knowledge of God.

There are other ways in which finite being may be regarded as inherently analogous to the divine being. For example, scales of value or goodness can be developed on the basis of our distinguishing the better from the worse. When these scales are extrapolated to an eminent degree, they reveal to us something of the nature of God's goodness. On the basis of such scales we can say that God is "good," not "evil"; "just," not "unjust"; "wise," "true," "faithful," etc., each of these terms being given a rather precise meaning. Thus, given our fundamental assumption that there is a genuine analogy between our being and his, we can discover what he is like by examining carefully ourselves and our experience.

The weakness of the doctrine of the *analogia entis* ought to be evident. What justification, after all, is there for asserting a real analogy between finite being and God? What reason can be offered for holding that our symbols refer to him and are not simply projections in the dark to nothing-at-all? The doctrine of the *analogia entis* —that there is a real analogy to God's being *built into* finite being— is an assumption, and a very audacious one at that. It is in fact identical with the assumption underlying every "natural theology," namely, that there is some (rational) way to move from human existence here and now to God, who has his being beyond the limits of our experience. We have already seen how doubtful is that claim (pp. 109ff., above), and the doctrine of the analogy of being inspires no more scientific or philosophical confidence. If it is to be asserted at all, it must be as an article of faith, not knowledge.

Of course, some may have faith that ultimate reality is to be understood on analogy with finite being or experience.[13] This, however, is not the characteristic confession of *Christian* faith. For the latter the clue to the Real is to be found not in finite being *per se*, but in one particular locus within the finite world, Jesus Christ. Here is the point where God has decisively manifested himself, and therefore our understanding of him is to be based on what is found here. In this respect, Christian theology can agree with the skeptical criticism of philosophical arguments for theism, that no amount of direct inspection of finite being in general will produce analogies which can serve as an assured basis for knowledge of God. For there is no more reason to suppose, simply on the basis of finite being as such, that God is good and not an evil demon (for the world from which we are extrapolating is certainly full of evil) ; that he is wise rather than a fool; or even that he is conscious personal will and not blind unconscious power.[14] Finite being betrays a great variety of struc-

[13] Perhaps all philosophies which seek to build a metaphysics simply and directly on the basis of the analysis of finite being or experience, without acknowledging that in fact their conclusions rest on a (somewhat arbitrary) selection of certain dimensions of experience as essentially revelatory of the ultimate (see above, pp. 18ff.), actually rest on just such a faith. (Cf. Ch. 2, n. 23, on the "ontological assumption" made in such philosophies.)

[14] Hume's *Dialogues Concerning Natural Religion* are the *locus classicus* in which this inadequacy of every "natural theology" is clearly exhibited.

tures which may offer some analogy to the ultimate ground of being, and it is not at all clear how one is to select from among them. In view of this problem, if we are to speak of God in a determinate fashion, it cannot be simply on the basis of finite being as such; it must be on the ground of his explicit revelation. That is, in Christian theology the analogies used should be those *which interpret God's revelation meaningfully and with integrity.*

Thus, our speech about God must begin with the historical events —and particularly the definitive person-event Jesus Christ—through which God has made himself known. Our analogies will be initially selected, and must be constantly tested and corrected, with reference to that revelation; any given analogy can be regarded as useful and true only insofar as it enables us better to understand the revelation. Since for Christian faith Christ is the supreme clue to ultimate reality, our point of departure must be the *analogia Christi,* not the *analogia entis.*[15]

In what way does the Christ-event provide a basis for language about God? How can particular symbols be drawn from that event to facilitate discussion of the divine being? The Christian claim is that God revealed himself to man in Jesus the man: that is, that in and through a personal life, a personal being, God makes himself known. As John 1 puts it, God's *Word* (i.e., the vehicle through which he communicates himself to man) is a *person.* This means that it will be preeminently *through personal analogies and symbols that God will become known.* Hence, it must be in personal symbols and analogies that we seek to conceive God, if it is the God of Christian faith with which we are concerned.[16] We can use nonpersonal symbols only in a secondary sense, in order to illuminate some particular

15 My notion of the *analogia Christi* is in some respects similar to, though by no means identical with, Karl Barth's (somewhat imprecise) notion of the *analogia fidei* (see, e.g., *Church Dogmatics,* I, 1 [Edinburgh: T. & T. Clark, 1936], 11ff., 260–283; II, 1 [Edinburgh: T. & T. Clark, 1957], 74–84).

16 If we look at the Bible as a whole, we find a similar emphasis on personal analogies. God is Father, King, Shepherd, Judge, Creator; he is loving, merciful, forgiving, but also wrathful, fearful, and even vengeful. The originality and significance of the biblical idea of God is not that it is nonanalogical or nonsymbolic. It appears rather in the character of the analogies in which that idea is expressed: consistent with the implications of the doctrine of the incarnation, they are most characteristically *personal;* the defining image for God in the Bible is the human person.

aspect of this personal being. (In a similar way nonpersonal symbols are often used to make clear some characteristic of a finite person.) Thus, we may refer to God as "Rock of Ages" to emphasize how unchangeable is his steadfast faithfulness, or "consuming fire" to picture his terrifying wrath, or "being-itself" to underline his universality. But our primary analogue, in terms of which all others must be interpreted, is the human person. This is not because of some anthropocentric predilection for anthropomorphism but because God himself chose this analogy as the vehicle of his revelation to man.

This narrows considerably the field from which we can properly choose our leading symbols. However, it is still too wide. There are many aspects of personal life which might be treated as analogous to the divine being. How are we to decide which are the more appropriate? Three factors serve to narrow the field further, bringing it into manageable proportions.

1] The category "person" is of course drawn from ordinary experience and this shapes in large part the meaning of the term. Moreover, one's own view of what a person really is (e.g., a pleasure-seeker, or a rational animal, or a moral will) will lead him to regard some interpretations as more characteristic and suggestive than others. The sources of these working ontologies of personal existence in terms of which each of us thinks and acts are manifold and obscure, doubtless including experience of self and of others, our acceptance of images from the mass media, our knowledge of psychology, anthropology, etc.

2] However, here as elsewhere in theology ordinary usage and experience cannot be our final criterion. They must be evaluated and disciplined by continuous reference to the person Jesus Christ. For Christian faith believes that it is this person in his particularity— and not just any person, or personhood in general—that is the revelation of God. Hence, our images and concepts for developing the doctrine of God must be qualified in the light of the particular humanness of Jesus. This narrows considerably the field of appropriate personal symbols. For example, in the light of the personhood of Jesus (as historically recoverable), it is clear that the highly personal symbol of hate is not to be applied to the divine being, nor are unconcern and indifference, nor the pursuit of pleasure. On the other hand, certain other characteristics and images come into focus as appropriate for speaking of God.

3] The Bible presents a selection of analogies applied to God in order to mediate his developing historical revelation: for example, father, judge, king, lord, shepherd. Obviously we will want to examine these carefully. We cannot, however, employ all biblical symbols uncritically. It may be that, in the light of the normative revelatory event, some must be judged to be intrinsically inappropriate for grasping the divine being. Language about the "vengeance" of God,[17] for example, may well fall into this class. Other biblical analogies may simply be relatively empty of meaning for concrete modern experience and thus inappropriate for a contemporary exposition of the faith, however valuable they were in other situations. Inasmuch as life is now largely urban and industrial, the symbol "shepherd," for example—very meaningful in a herding economy—has lost much of its usefulness.[18]

We must defer detailed examination of these biblical analogies until later. It is necessary here to point out certain further characteristics of analogical language. Since the finite terms are not being used literally, but rather are the analogical vehicles through which transcendent reality is grasped and known, the proper theological meanings of the analogies or symbols evidently are not completely determined by their finite referents. They must be informed and determined in certain respects from beyond themselves by God's revelation and being, if they are to become instruments for grasping his nature and will instead of the merely finite realities to which they literally refer. It is interesting to observe that such reorienting

[17] Professor G. E. Wright has pointed out to me that the use of the term "vengeance" with reference to God in our English translations is almost always misleading; a more adequate translation of the Hebrew would be "vindication." My doubts about the appropriateness of the former term would of course not apply directly to the latter. However, even though the linguistic problem here devolves largely from faulty translation, it remains an issue for English-language theology and must be so recognized.

[18] The same must be said for the title "Messiah" ("Christ"). Its meaning ("the anointed one"), though very significant in Jewish Christianity, was already so vague for the early Gentile church that by the time Paul was writing his letters (the earliest New Testament documents we have), the erstwhile title or interpretive symbol had become virtually a proper name, interchangeable or conjoined with "Jesus." (See also Ch. 13, n. 2.)

of the original experiential meaning in the light of meaning given in the revelatory events can actually be observed with certain biblical symbols, and doubtless it occurs to some extent whenever a new finite analogy is appropriated for theological purposes. For example, consider the symbol drawn from human fatherhood. It was a profound and creative insight, opening up new possibilities for understanding the nature of God, that enabled someone first to give him the title "Father." This analogy made possible seeing his relation to man in a new light because of the human experience of fatherhood. But with this new use of the word, something happened to the conception of fatherhood as well as to the idea of God. The self-revealing God so overflowed and reshaped the concept "father" that the very character of true fatherhood came to be defined (for faith) by God's dealings with his prodigal children. Beside this, every human father seems but a pale imitation, an imperfect copy; and *God* becomes "the Father from whom every family in heaven or on earth takes its name" (Eph. 3:14–15 Goodspeed); we judge what a human father should be in the light of what our heavenly Father is. In this way the human symbol, "father," has been taken up, as it were, by the revelation and made the vehicle through which knowledge of God—and not simply of human fatherhood—is conveyed.

So also with the other principal analogies used to understand God's nature and will. New meaning accrues to them when they are applied to the divine being. Of course this is precisely what would be expected if our knowledge of God is not merely some speculative and hypothetical extension of our finite knowledge, but in fact derives from his self-revelatory activity. The point is made explicitly in 1 John with regard to the symbol "love": "In this is love, not that we loved God [i.e., we cannot define love simply in terms of our human love] but that he loved us and sent his Son to be the expiation for our sins" (4:10). The meaning of the various dimensions of our humanity—as well as the character of the deity—is thus deepened and illuminated as we seek with a variety of analogies to grasp God's revelation in the man Jesus.

Theological speech about God, therefore, is not grounded chiefly in confidence that finite being in itself can provide appropriate analogies to the divine being (*analogia entis*); rather, it is based on faith that in and through our finite history and existence, and particularly in Jesus Christ, God has revealed himself, and continues to do so. It is his act, manifesting himself through finite images and symbols, that transforms them into analogical vehicles for our theological knowledge. They remain, of course, our images and symbols, created by the human imagination and given their original content and meaning by finite human experience.[19] But it is not this fact that makes them adequate vehicles for the knowledge of God. Only if and because God reveals himself through these symbols are we enabled to know him at all.

Limitations of space make it impossible to discuss in detail the various types of theological symbols,[20] or even all the symbols with

[19] Tillich is certainly right in his contention that it is through symbols created by the human imagination that God is known, and that therefore in a certain sense the imagination is the locus of our encounter with God. Despite this, however, it is misleading to suggest that we should speak of an *analogia imaginis* either alongside of or as a third alternative to the *analogia entis* and the *analogia Christi* (see Tillich, *Systematic Theology*, II, 114f.). For, though the human imagination is the point where finite being transcends itself, this gives us no ground for believing its images are necessarily revelatory of God's being: they may simply reflect the finite order of things, they may be demonic, or they may be simply "imaginary." It is only an imagination controlled by reality that we can trust. The question, then, becomes: in what mode is imagination properly guided by the real? If we postulate a power in imagination itself to fathom the real—perhaps this is what Tillich means to do—we have an interesting theological aestheticism, but no reason to call our view "Christian," for alongside the Christian symbols there will be others of (perhaps even greater) power and meaning. If we reject such aestheticism as leaving us with no criterion to distinguish the images of madness from those of reality, we are confronted with the problem of the criterion: our imagination must be controlled by the structure of finite being as such (*analogia entis*) or by the reality revealed to faith (*analogia Christi*). If the latter is to be the case, the imagination will necessarily be guided and corrected by the historical person-event Jesus Christ. That is, it is in our *historical imagination* (as I suggested above, pp. 67–71), not simply in the imagination *per se*, as Tillich suggests, that God is encountered.

[20] I have made no attempt in the text to set forth explicitly doctrines of myth, saga, legend, etc., but have confined myself largely to a doctrine of analogical symbol, according to which our knowledge of God is built up and expressed in locutions, each of which ordinarily refers to some feature of (finite) experience but which in the theological context is taken to refer by a kind of extrapolation (*via eminentiae*) to God. A theological symbol, thus, has a double reference: to the concrete experiential reality which gives it its content, and to the ultimate or transcendent reality which is taken to be analogous to this. Although in the text thus far our examples have been drawn largely from words or terms, theological symbols should not be thought of as confined to these. Stories, for example, both fictional and historical, may be symbols. When a more or less continuous narrative refers us to the interplay of "God's acts" with the acts of men in such a way as to depict the movement of human history as the locus of transcendent meaning and power, we have a symbol in the form of what is usually called a "myth" (though some would prefer to call this "saga" or "salvation history" or something of

which the *analogia Christi* provides us. I will attempt to deal with
enough of the major ones, however, to sketch a balanced concept of
God. The three fundamental symbols for the present doctrine of
God, providing the major divisions of our discussion, are "Father,"
"Son," and "Spirit." In attempting to interpret these we will find it
necessary to introduce a number of others to enhance the specificity
and concreteness of the interpretation. Of these, three of the most
important may be mentioned here, each epitomizing a central characteristic of the person of the trinity to whom it corresponds. These
are, respectively, "Lord," "Servant," and "Companion."[21]

---

the sort). It should be no surprise that much of the biblical material is of this latter
sort, since for these writers the experiences of the personal and the historical (which
are closely related) seemed to be symbolically the most powerful. Various forms of
activity (ritual), art, and architecture may also be religiously or theologically symbolic,
provided only that the double reference—to the finite and (by analogy) to the transcendent—is present. Naturally for theological work, which is largely conceptual, verbal symbols
—whether these involve the analogical employment of individual terms or the interpretation of complex quasi-historical narratives—will be most helpful.

[21] It may be helpful to point out that in this procedure of selecting and developing
certain analogies to give content to the term "God," we are using "partial descriptions"
to help locate and understand the referent for the word. The referents for many names, of
course, can be indicated *directly* simply by pointing. This holds for present realities. But for
historical or other nonpresent realities, names must be taught with the help of partial
descriptions which more or less adequately help locate the referent. (Cf. John Searle,
"Proper Names," in C. E. Caton, ed., *Philosophy and Ordinary Language* [Urbana:
University of Illinois Press, 1963].) Though one would certainly not wish to contend either
that God is not contemporary with us, or that he is not present, still he cannot be directly
indicated; and thus the proper name "God" is similar in certain respects to the names of
inaccessible finite objects, and its meaning must be taught in a similar manner. The
important theological question, of course, is: which partial descriptions are appropriate
for teaching this name, and how are they to be chosen? I have argued in the text that
for Christian faith, the Christ-event provides the fundamental criteria here.

9 / The Transcendence of God

III. Lord, Father, and Creator

The fatherhood of God, we have said, points to his uniqueness, his aseity, his transcendence, his being the ultimate limit of all finite being. How now can we develop this notion in more positive and concrete terms? We have observed that Christian faith, taking the person-event Jesus Christ to be the definitive criterion for understanding the ultimate reality with which we have to do, seeks to grasp this limit of our being (a) in personalistic language, which is, however, (b) transformed and controlled by the image of the man who died on the cross. It is necessary, therefore, for us to seek out symbols from the realm of the personal and, through appropriate qualification, to attempt to grasp the divine being concretely with their aid. The Bible of course supplies us with many such symbols drawn from common experience; we shall have to confine our considerations to only a few. In each case our concern will be to see how the ordinary usage of the term can and must be qualified so that it can become a vehicle for grasping the ultimate limit of all being and meaning.

It should be remembered that at this point we are developing the conception of God the Father (not the Son), the one whom Jesus also addressed as "Father." This means that what is said here cannot be deduced or developed directly out of the image of Jesus' own historical life and death (as with the conception of God the Son), but rather is its most fundamental theological presupposition. Although, as we shall note in a moment, the application of such symbols as "lord" to Jesus is not at all unusual in the New Testament, for the most part the fundamental meaning of these analogies was developed through the long course of preceding Hebrew history, providing the theological context within which the New Testament understanding of God emerged (see above, pp. 85ff.). Conceptions of God as lord, creator, judge, as omnipotent and holy, etc., are more presupposed than created by early Christian faith. However, they must be significantly qualified and modified with reference to the image of the man dying on the cross, before they become fully appropriate for use in Christian theology. In certain respects those qualifications will be suggested in this chapter and the next, but their full extent will only come clear as we work through the remaining sections of the doctrine of God, and, indeed, of this whole systematic theology.

Let us begin with the conception of God as the Lord. This term is frequently applied to God throughout the Bible (and many translations follow the Septuagint use of it to render the Hebrew YHWH); and in the New Testament it is often applied to Jesus, both "as one who had authority in his own right" (Mt. 7:29; Mk. 1:22), and also in his capacity as God's representative and revelation among men (e.g., Thomas' word: "My Lord and my God" [John 20:28]). The concept of lord is taken from the human relationship of master to slave.[1] The lord is the one who can command, the one with authority to give orders, the one who exercises power, the one who limits the slave in many ways. Moreover, it must be noted, this is not simply abstract power; it is personal power, arising out of and effective in the relationship to other persons and to personal possessions or property. When God, then, is referred to as the "Lord" (or when Christ is called "Lord"), he is being designated as the one with absolute authority over man. He is the one in relation to whom it is proper to conceive of man as only a servant or slave, as one who receives orders. He is the King, the Ruler—and the image here is of an *absolute* monarch, not the figure-head of contemporary constitu-

---

[1] Discussion of the origin, meaning, and usage of many of these symbols in the biblical and cognate languages can be found in Kittel's *Theologisches Wörterbuch zum Neuen Testament* and will not be attempted here at all. The analysis of the term "Lord" (by Werner Foerster and Gottfried Quell) has been translated along with several others in the series of Bible Key Words (London: Adam & Charles Black, 1958).

tional monarchies. That God has absolute power, absolute authority, and especially, absolute rights, over man is the central contention; man is limited and restricted on all sides by God.

personal reader

But in the Bible God is not viewed as merely man's Lord; he is seen as Lord of history and nature as well.[2] This conception we may well regard as an extention of the exclusively personal meaning the term originally held to realms otherwise not necessarily conceived as personal. History, for example, has often been understood in terms of the image of the circle, as the great cycle or gyration of the cosmos following out its ineluctable laws, the movement of historical events being constrained by the turning of the great wheel. Or, as is perhaps truer in our own day, history is seen as a cumulative movement of almost chance or accidental occurrences gradually coming to produce some intelligible pattern (as in certain versions of the theory of evolution). In contrast with both these views, if it is said that history has a "Lord," this means that the course of history is under the authority and purposes of a personal will. Its character and development are not due to the working of abstract power in accordance with immutable and eternal laws, but rather to the personal exercise of personal power as a human lord controls the destinies (i.e., histories) of his slaves, saying, "Go here!" and "Go there!" in order that his own purposes might be realized through their actions. To say, then, that God is the Lord of history is to say (a) that history is *under control*, and is not simply the expression of accident or chance, and (b) that this control is *personal*, not blind fate or immutable law; it is to claim that history is a realm where *purposes* are being worked out. From this perspective, personal values and meanings are not merely some chance flowering of an otherwise mechanical and blind historical process; on the contrary, they are present in the very foundation of history. The historical process, then, has personal significance and a personal character; that is, it has significance for persons because in the first instance it is the expression of the purposes of a Person.

Similar sorts of things must be said if God is regarded as Lord of

[2] In the New Testament lordship over nature and history is attributed also to Jesus, e.g., in the story about his authority over wind and wave (Mk. 4:35–41), and in the belief that he was soon to return as "the Son of man coming in clouds with great power and glory" (Mk. 13:26; cf. 14:62) to inaugurate the kingdom of God (9:1).

nature. Nature is not to be understood as ruled by impersonal deterministic natural law but must be seen within the context of personal
purpose and meaning. From this point of view nature is no closed,
self-explanatory system;[3] it is under God's lordship, his personal
power. The happenings of nature express the purposes of a personal
will who exercises authority over them. It is very difficult, perhaps
impossible, for us of the twentieth century to conceive how this can
be. We think of nature in terms of a scientific world-view according
to which every natural event is to be understood exclusively in relation to other natural events, the concept of teleology being systematically and deliberately excluded. This perspective has become so
dominant in our thinking that we inevitably conceive much of our
concrete experience in materialistic terms. Thus, for example, the experience of flicking a light-switch and seeing the light go on is so
nicely describable mechanistically that even to attempt to think it out
personalistically—for example, as an expression of the faithfulness
of God toward his creatures—seems both absurd and pretentious.
Nevertheless, some such personalistic view is doubtless implied if,
following the Bible, we wish to regard God as Lord of nature.

God, then, for Christian faith, is not only man's Lord: he is absolute Lord of the cosmos. With this conception we have stretched our
analogical use of the notion of lordship almost beyond recognition.
For all human lordship—the experience from which the symbol is
drawn and which gives it concrete meaning—is limited in many respects. Every human lord is restricted by the capacities of the other
men with whom he must deal; he cannot use even those who are his
slaves with absolute arbitrariness. Moreover, whatever be his power
in the community over which he rules, he is limited in many ways by
both nature and history, by such factors as climate, topography, and
physical strength, as well as by the historical and cultural situation
into which he has, quite apart from his own desires, been "thrown."
In all these respects our symbol, "lord," is inadequate to its intended
application to God. For God is conceived as the absolute Lord, limited

---

[3] It may be noted in passing that in these sentences I have followed the common
practice of speaking of nature as "ruled" by "law," being "self-explanatory," etc., i.e., in
quasi-personalistic language; it is perhaps doubtful whether it is possible to conceive the
realities of our world in totally impersonal terms.

by nothing outside himself but himself limiting all else, and thus unique and incomparable in his lordship. The precise nature of God's lordship is not literally conceivable by us, for we know of nothing like it—yet the symbol "lord," as our discussion has attempted to show, gives some content to our notion of the divine being.

There are a number of parallel or ancillary symbols which express the notion of lordship in various other ways, developing it further. The notions of God as King, or as Sovereign, or as Lord of hosts (i.e., military commander), are clearly all parallels to the basic conception which has been explicated here in terms of the symbol "lord." Another related symbol, which develops the image further but in a slightly different way, is that of "judge." In the Old Testament the judges were apparently simply gifted or charismatic military leaders who exercised corresponding lordship. We need say nothing further here about that dimension of meaning in this symbol, but must point to another. The term "judge" early came to mean one who exercises his lordship in determining and implementing the distinction between lawful and unlawful, right and wrong. Lordship *per se*, as we have been considering the notion, may be arbitrary and wicked tyranny; not so for the judge, who must take into account legal and moral considerations. This qualification does not mean that the judge is not really lord in his court, for he is; he is the one who is in control of the situation. But his control must be justifiable; his authority stems from his ability to be impartial, responsible, fair in his judgments. To be in the hands of the supreme Judge, then, is not to be under the control of an arbitrary tyrant. On the contrary, it is to be under the lordship of One whose judgments and actions are absolutely just and equal.

But we must immediately note again how different is this Judge from all human judges, how inadequate is our symbol to express our meaning. In the first place, human judges are themselves always under the law. They must exercise their judgment in accordance with some tradition, some precedent. Moreover the execution of their judgments, and the judgments themselves, are hemmed in by the law on all sides in order to assure fairness and honesty; even so the ideal is seldom attained. But the divine Judge—and here once again our symbol breaks down almost completely—is himself the *source* of law (e.g., Sinai); he is the ultimate arbiter of righteousness and justice. Moreover, the divine Judge is not under the law, nor can he be brought under the judgment of some other jurist, as can a human judge. As the very source of law and justice, he is himself the Judge of all other judges. Throughout history he exercises his judgment, and finally when the "end of history" comes, it will be his decisive judgment which prevails. This means that nothing in the universe is or will be dealt with arbitrarily, but that each will receive its due. The whole course of history and nature, when viewed in the light of this symbol, is developing according to purposes of perfect justice and righteousness, for its Lord is none other than the supreme Judge.

Another symbol, giving the divine lordship a further dimension of meaning, is "father." The father, of course, especially in patriarchal Hebrew society, is also the lord, that is, the one with authority, the one in control in the family; and the father is also the judge who must arbitrate family disputes. But the lordship of the good father is neither tyrannical nor of a legal character. Interpersonal ties of affection bind members of a family together into a special form of community. Within this context the father's lordship, if it is what it ought to be, is of love; and his justice is not that of harsh and inflexible law but is tempered with mercy and forgiveness (cf. the parable of the "prodigal son"). To call God "Father" is to say that he exercises his lordship (which is nonetheless real) in terms of the most intimate personal constraints. Moreover, it is to imply that his lordship is not exercised simply for his sake, or even that the law might be upheld (the judge), but for the welfare of his children. However, in all this concern for his creatures, they never become the *de facto* lords, those with actual power and authority, as rebellious children often do in a human family. Throughout, God remains the Lord—the one with ultimate power, ultimate authority, ultimate rights, the ultimate limiter. He loses none of these characteristics even though he exercises them as a Father. This understanding of God's lordship was specially emphasized by Jesus and has subsequently characterized the faith born of his ministry and death. For the Christian church the Lord of history, the Lord of nature, the Lord of the universe—is the Father of

Jesus Christ, and we also are his children. Of all the symbols of the divine lordship, "Father" has been the most meaningful to Christian faith. It is scarcely surprising, therefore, that it was adopted as the defining symbol for the first person of the trinity.

It is necessary to develop the conception of God's lordship with the help of one more major analogy: God as Creator. In certain respects this symbol sums up and ties together all that we have said thus far about the divine being, for it points to the fact that God is the ultimate *source* of the universe and all that it contains as well as its Lord and Father.

We so often use the symbol "creator" as a direct synonym for "God" that we may forget that it also is an analogy drawn from human experience. Creativity is a power distinguishing man from other finite beings. We can clarify our meaning here most easily, perhaps, by contrasting "creating" with "making" or "building" on the one side and with "generation" on the other. To "create" is not simply to "make" or "build." "Making" (coming from a root meaning to "fit together") or "building" connote a mere assembling of materials which are already available. Moreover, however intricate the structure, the assembling may be accomplished almost unconsciously and by instinct; and it can be repeated many times. Thus, we say that birds build nests and beavers, dams; but we do not say they "create" them. "Creation" suggests a much more radical beginning than making or building. It is not simply a "putting together"; rather it involves a *bringing into existence of something that did not exist before*. In this sense creation is unrepeatable and also unpredictable; it is, therefore, in a certain respect, always awe-inspiring, as with a beautiful work of art.

A creation is something that comes from the depths of the human spirit. Moreover, it requires a conscious, and often difficult, struggle to bring it into being, a kind of labor or giving birth not achieved simply by instinct. The very spirit of the creator flows out into his creation in such a way that it can be identified as the unique expression of just this man—for example, Bach's music, Van Gogh's painting, Shakespeare's plays; the creation comes to "hold" or "contain" the spirit of its creator. In contrast, something "made"—for example, an ordinary bench by a carpenter—precisely because it performs a simple and obvious function and has little that makes it unique, is not rightly called a "creation." It does not have the awe-inspiring mystery and power of the "created" object in which a *new value* and *new meaning,* and not simply a new object, have been brought into existence.[4] An object "made" or even "invented"—for example, an automobile—however important it may be as a technological achievement, becomes obsolete with further technological advance. But a "creation," though it may grow obsolete on its technical side, never does on its creative side; it has a kind of inner life or power of meaning for many situations.[5] It seems to bear the human spirit itself.

We must also distinguish "creation" from "generation," the reproduction of the species. In the latter we give birth to or produce beings which are bearers of our spirits, but these are of the same genus and species as ourselves, that is, they are other persons. But a "creation," though of a different substance from man, nevertheless comes to be infused with his spirit. It is given a kind of life and meaning which are, so to speak, "unnatural" for it; it is given a form and being which it could never have of itself. Creation, then, is a process through which genuinely *new reality* is brought into being from the depths of man's spirit. Animals can make and animals can generate; only man can create. The outstanding example of human creativity, and the one on which all others in many respects depend, is *language.* Here words—mere noises—become the bearers of almost every variation and nuance of the human spirit.

This analogy, referring to the deepest and most mysterious powers of the human spirit, is being employed when God is called "Creator"— not simply *a* creator among others, but *the* Creator of heaven and earth, of all that exists. With this symbol God's lordship is expressed in the most absolute way. Lordship *per se,* after all, always expresses a relationship *between human beings.* However superior is the lord to the slave, the judge to the accused, the father to the child, they are

---

[4] It is just this mystery and depth of meaning which is especially characteristic of a "creation." This is why, as Michael Foster has observed, "The meaning of a painting is not intelligible in the sense in which the purpose of a wheelbarrow is" ("The Christian Doctrine of Creation and the Rise of Modern Natural Science," *Mind* [1934], 43:462).

[5] Cf. Paul Tillich, *Das System der Wissenschaften* (Göttingen: Vandenhoeck & Ruprecht, 1923), pp. 64–65.

still fundamentally equals: they are of the same species, the same kind; all are men. These symbols, then, by themselves, cannot express the radical difference between God and man. This the symbol "creator" does. For that which a creator makes is of an entirely different genus from himself. However beautiful or meaningful a painting or poem may be, no one would confuse it with a person. It is a *thing*, absolutely dependent on its author for existence and to be sharply distinguished from men. When we say, then, that God is the Creator, we are expressing his radical otherness from the world and from man. He has created them, and they must not be confused with him. They could have no being without him; they are absolutely, ontologically, dependent on him for their existence, and thus limited in every respect by him. He, on the other hand, is in no way dependent on them for his being or restricted by them; his resources are entirely within himself. Thus, the symbol "Creator" expresses the intrinsic otherness, the independence, of God from the world, and yet his relatedness to it in its dependence on him and limitation by him. The One who is Lord is in no wise to be confused with his creatures: he is not only of a higher political status; his is a radically different order of being.

We have still not drawn out sufficiently the implications of this symbol. A human creator must always begin his work with materials which are already available to him and which he has not himself made. Thus, the artist has pigments and canvas, traditions regarding aesthetic form, and techniques and methods of work all presented to him by others who have gone before; in this respect he is limited in many ways by other realities. Doubtless he adds something new to all these from the depths of his own spirit, but this is only a tiny achievement in comparison with what he presupposes. God's creativity, however, as understood in Christian faith, is of a radically different order. For God begins with *nothing*; his creation is *ex nihilo*. All that exists —materials, techniques, forms, meanings, and purposes—all are given their being by him.

Thus, the human image of *creator*, even in its emphasis on the utter dependence of the created object, is inadequate to say what is meant by "God." Where a human creator is limited, finite, dependent, unfree in many ways, the Creator God is absolutely free in all re-

spects, dependent on nothing outside his own resources. This absolute
freedom is something we can hardly imagine. The greatest freedom
we know—far superior to that of the lord, who at most can only command slaves—is that of the creator, who can bring into being reality
which did not exist before. But even in the creative act itself—the
very height of human self-transcendence—man's freedom is ambiguous. Who really knows, before writing his poem, what lines will compose it? Who knows, before starting a paper or lecture or sermon,
exactly what he is trying to produce? Indeed, who knows, before the
words have fallen from his lips, just what he is trying to say? In the
creative act we are so far from sovereign that frequently it is only
through the act itself that we discover what we were trying to express.
Though decision and purpose and great effort of will are required to
create, in a certain sense our creativity is blind and what we produce
different from what we had expected and perhaps intended. This is
why we say of great creations that they are inspired by the muses or
gods, not simply deliberately produced by a man who decided in his
freedom to create. Creation is a great mystery; it is no simple product
of the conscious and free purposing of man.

In contrast to all this, to call God "Creator" is to speak of his absolute freedom in every respect. He is dependent on nothing outside
himself for his creativity, neither on materials or training nor on the
inspiration of some muse or blind chance. In his freedom he wills and
purposes what shall be, and in his freedom he produces what he has
willed. It is this incomprehensible majesty and mystery of God's lordship over the world that is expressed in the opening words of Genesis:

> In the beginning God created the heavens and the earth. The
> earth was without form and void, and darkness was upon the face
> of the deep; and the Spirit of God was moving over the face of the
> waters. And God said, "Let there be light"; and there was light.
> GENESIS 1:1-3

God speaks—and it is done! His creation of the world is as free to
him, and as clear an expression of his will, as the uttering of a word to
us. This absolute freedom which has brought the universe into being

is without parallel in our experience. And yet there is an analogy to this freedom in our creativity, especially in our speaking, our uttering words, thus effectively expressing—making external—the purposes deep within our spirits.

We must draw out the implications of God's creativity in one more direction, through one more comparison with human creativity. If I create something—for example, a painting—it comes to have a certain independence from me. Doubtless without me it could not have come to be; but now that it exists I may sell it or give it away, never seeing it again. It needs me no longer in order to exist. I created it; but it is *sustained* otherwise, for example, by the durability of the canvas, the care of its owner, etc. If it changes in time, as it shall, this will not be due to my further creativity, but to the creative or destructive action of other beings. Once again we must sharply contrast God's creativity with ours. There are no agents other than himself to whom he turns over his work: he has created every being. There is no durability of canvas on which he can or must depend: he creates even the canvas he uses, giving it a character in accordance with his will. In short, God's creation is not gone and lost from him after he has created it, left in the hands of some caretaker or purchaser; it is he himself who continues to sustain it in being. To be the absolute Creator is necessarily to be the Sustainer of all that is as well. The deistic conception of God is a contradiction in terms.

To say the same thing in other words: God created the world in time, that is, in a process of change through which it is continuously becoming something other than it now is or ever was; God is still creating his world. He did not finish it in a moment, or in six days; he continues to work on and in his world, shaping it in accordance with his purposes. Every falling drop of rain, every acorn becoming an oak, expresses this continuous creative activity of God, preserving the universe in being and simultaneously transforming it in accord with his purposes. Thus, the absoluteness of the relation between God and the world—expressed in the notion of God's *creatio ex nihilo* at the beginning—applies not only to that moment but to every succeeding one as well. In every hour and every respect we are absolutely dependent on God's creativity to give us our being and to sustain us in our freedom. We would literally (not merely figuratively) *be nothing* without him, for he is the indispensable source and continuing ground of our existence. And he is this in his *absolute freedom*, being in no way coerced either by us or by anything outside his own will.

We must not forget, of course, what the Christ-event makes clear: that as absolute Creator, God is also the Father, the one who loves his children; as absolute Lord, he is also the Servant, the one whose freedom is so great he can sacrifice even himself for his creation. But his love and sacrifice are the greater marvels if we remember that it is the free Creator who is thus to be characterized.

Two further implications of God's lordship over creation can be suggested in preview of later discussion. The first is an existential implication. To speak of God as Creator is to regard him as the foundation on which our beings are grounded. This means we cannot possibly escape from God, or fall away from him, without ceasing to be; so long as we are, we are in relation to him, sustained by his power. Moreover, if the Creator God is loving and trustworthy (as the Gospel claims) and thus is continuously working for *our* good, our anxieties and fears and despair about the meaninglessness of existence become pointless, for we are in the hands of one who loves without reservation. Why then be anxious? What can we fear?

> . . . if God . . . clothes the grass of the field, which today is alive and tomorrow is thrown into the oven, will he not much more clothe you, O men of little faith? Therefore do not be anxious, saying, "What shall we eat?" or "What shall we drink?" or "What shall we wear?" For . . . your heavenly Father knows that you need . . . all [these things]. But seek first his kingdom and his righteousness, and all these things shall be yours as well.
>
> MATTHEW 6:30-33

Our *unfaith* is the root of our anxieties and fears and despairs. If we men had real faith in the Creator, all this would disappear: we would be new men.

A second implication is metaphysical and ethical. Sometimes a kind of competition between God's lordship and human freedom is alleged: if God is really sovereign, we must be puppets; if we are free, then God's power is limited. It should be clear, however, that on the level we are now discussing—God's freedom as Creator—this kind of statement misconceives the issue.[6] For the Creator is the One who gives man his freedom in the first place and who continues to sustain him in freedom even when he abuses it. God could allow us to fall back at any moment into the nonexistence from which he called us, but he chooses to sustain us in existence with his creative power. Our free actions, even our deliberate disobediences of his will, do not and cannot compromise in any respect whatsoever this his absolute freedom over us. Nor is our finite freedom compromised by the fact that it is continuously and freely given by God. His freedom and ours are on different levels: his is that of the Creator; ours is creaturely.[7]

Thus the ethical dilemma sometimes posed in the question, If God does everything, why need we do anything? is false. For the "everything" God does is to create us and sustain us as *free beings,* that is, as beings who can and must decide and act, set themselves purposes, and be creative. In and through his freedom he gives men the possibility of being free creatures in his kingdom; but it is they who must be those free creatures, not God. Thus, God's freedom, precisely because it is absolute, far from destroying or even threatening man's, is its very source and ground. Without it we would not only not be free; we would not be at all.

It will be clear that if God is Creator in this absolute sense, the ultimate limit of our existence, our lives can have meaning and find fulfilment only in doing his will, that is, in being the creatures he created us to be. To attempt something different is absurd, for it is to ignore or deny the very Reality giving us our being and freedom. We thus shatter our potentially free selves, becoming fragmented beings, living in bondage, instead of realizing the full opportunity of obedience to the One "whose service is perfect freedom."[8] If God is really Creator, and if we have been made by him into genuinely

[6] It results from a too literalistic application of the symbol "lord," instead of carefully qualifying it with such other symbols as "creator."

[7] This brief paragraph of course does not dispose of the problem of God's sovereignty and man's freedom completely. Other dimensions of it will be taken up later. See esp. pp. 151ff., and Chs. 13–14, 26–29.

[8] From "A Collect for Peace," in *The Book of Common Prayer* (New York: Church Pension Fund, 1945), p. 17.

free creatures, our freedom must be understood in positive relation to his will, not in competition with it. The first article of the creed, "I believe in God the Father Almighty, Maker of Heaven and Earth," expresses clearly and concisely an image of the ultimate limit of all finite being as personal and thus as the adequate and proper basis of our existence as persons.

10 / The Transcendence of God

IV. The Perfection of

the Divine Freedom

W<small>E</small> have seen that the language about God as Father and Lord and Creator provides concrete images for apprehending the ultimate limit of ourselves and our world as One with absolute and inconceivable freedom. We must now develop this personalistic understanding of the ultimate limit in another way. Instead of searching for further symbols or analogies through which to conceive God's being as a whole, so to speak, we shall now analyze it in terms of certain qualities or characteristics. That is, we shall consider the "attributes" or "perfections"[1] of God which define and clarify further his absoluteness or transcendent deity. At this point we are not ready to examine all the divine perfections, but only those appropriate to that dimension of God's being which we have discussed, the divine "freedom."[2] Later, in the sections on God the Son and God the Holy Spirit, we shall deal with the perfections of the divine love and the divine communing. In none of these sections, of course, is

---

[1] Though the terms "perfections" and "attributes" are interchangeable, I shall, for the most part, use the former expression since it reminds us that we are not dealing with just any being and its various "attributes," but with the unique and unrestricted—and in this sense "perfect"—being. (Cf. Karl Barth, *Church Dogmatics*, II, 1 [Edinburgh: T. & T. Clark, 1957], 322.)

[2] It goes without saying that no claim is made here that this is an exhaustive list, or that God's freedom might not be analyzable in somewhat different terms. What I have attempted to do is provide a characterization (not a complete description) of the divine being with respect to his aseity and freedom.

the language or analysis to be construed in a literal sense. Rather, here as everywhere, we shall be trying to understand the ultimate limit of finite being with the aid of a particular group of analogies and symbols drawn from finite experience.

It is important to emphasize at the outset (a point that will be taken up again in connection with the first perfection) that we are not dealing here with a series of "attributes" to be understood as "accidental" or dispensable characteristics of God's being, as a table's "attribute" of brownness can easily be altered to some other color without substantially changing the table itself. In speaking of God's perfections, we are attempting to express certain characteristics which must belong to the ultimate limit of existence if it is to be conceived in personalistic terms, in accord with the revelatory history culminating in Jesus Christ; we are not dealing with relatively independent qualities each of which can be conceived and discussed as a reality in its own right. What we must speak of separately and successively here (as a series of perfections) exists one and undivided in God. The fullness and richness of the divine being can be apprehended by us only under a variety of words and images though in him it is one. This point is especially emphasized by:

a. The first perfection of the divine freedom: the unity and simplicity of God. If we are to understand the ultimate limit of our existence as personal-active being, we must be careful not to imply that God is either multiple or composite. To do so would be to call into question both his full freedom to act and the adequacy of the Christian revelation. For it would mean either that there is another being beside God, of whom we know nothing since he has not revealed himself, but of whom God must take account and to whom he must relate himself whether he wills or no: in this case God would not be the will that limits all else, but he himself would be limited by another, and Jesus Christ would in fact not be a reliable clue to the ultimate reality with which we have to do. Or it would mean that God is divided within himself and thus potentially or actually at war with himself, and for this reason unable to act freely: the trustworthiness of the Christian revelation would thus be called into question from the other side. God would no longer be the sovereign and free Lord in full control of himself and all other reality. "Hear, O Israel: the Lord our God, the Lord is *one*" (Deut. 6:4, RSV footnote). This is the most fundamental article of Israel's as well as of Christian faith. He who is the foundation of the universe is one and undivided.

Though the conception of God's unity, being the *formal* condition of God's deity, may appear abstract and uninteresting, it is as important for practical day-to-day existence as for theory. Seldom do actual lives express faith in *one* God. On the contrary, for the most part human existence is fragmented and piecemeal and men's aspirations and worship correspondingly promiscuous. In some experiences one thing seems good and becomes normative; in others, something else. Men usually worship and obey different gods for each of the various realms of life—politics, business, art, science, religion, etc. These idolatries in which they conduct their practical lives perpetuate and further the disintegration of their selfhood by orienting them in many and contradictory directions, instead of toward the One in whom existence could find authentic unity and meaning.[3]

God's oneness so far surpasses the partial unities of experience that it is difficult to conceive and express even in theory. On the one hand, we may conceive God's unity in such an abstract "metaphysical" way that it becomes difficult, or even impossible, to apprehend him as a "living" God, one who "decides" and "acts" and "works" through the temporal spread of a historical development to accomplish his "purposes." On the other hand, the necessity to conceptualize God's activity by means of a series of categories such as creation, judgment, redemption, etc. may lead us to forget that he who is acting is one self-identical being, "the same yesterday and today and for ever" (Heb. 13:8). Furthermore, our speaking of God's attributes as several may lead us to forget that in actuality this fullness is one in him; and the doctrine of the trinity, though intended to protect the radically monotheistic character of Christian faith, may all too easily suggest three relatively independent personalities, thus destroying the conception of a single God, one and undivided.[4] For

[3] This problem of polytheism and idolatry will be taken up in more detail below as we discuss sin and bondage (see esp. Ch. 25).

[4] An example of this tendency in contemporary theology will be found in Leonard Hodgson's *The Doctrine of the Trinity* (New York: Charles Scribner's, 1949).

these and other reasons it is difficult to conceive the absolute unity without which God is not God at all but an idol, merely one among many, or one divided and at war within himself, or an abstract unity, hardly the sovereign Lord of all that is.

To understand God as active sovereign will, we must see him as "one" and "indivisible," "immutable" (i.e., not changing in his innermost purposing), and "simple" (i.e., not composite in his fundamental being). Each of these several terms—developed in traditional theology as particular and essential attributes of the divine being—we may consider as expressing in its own way God's profound oneness.[5] It is not necessary to dwell on them further here or to speculate about a "One" or "Unity" underlying all being. Our proper concern is not with such abstractions but with the *one God* who manifests himself and his love in Jesus Christ. The oneness of this divine love, and the oneness of that love with the divine freedom in the one God—this is the ultimate ontological unity to which Christian faith and theology must attend.

b. The second perfection of the divine freedom: the power of God. Whereas the first perfection of the divine freedom defines what is *formally* required for God to be God—that he be absolutely one—we are here concerned with the fundamental *material* requisite, God's absolute power. The uniqueness of God's power is exemplified most decisively in his power to exist. No creature has this power. No creature can bring itself into being or maintain itself through its own efforts; existence is a gift which it receives from beyond itself, from the source of all that is, from God. But God is the self-existent being, the one who, unlike all others, is sufficient unto himself, the one who depends on nothing outside himself in order to be.[6] He is

---

[5] We must be careful, however, lest we follow the lead of traditional theology too far in its development of the notion of God's oneness, thus calling into question his personal and purposive character. In this respect the strictures and proposals of Charles Hartshorne are very suggestive. (See *Man's Vision of God* [New York: Harper, 1941], *The Divine Relativity* [New Haven: Yale University Press, 1948], and *The Logic of Perfection* [La Salle, Illinois: Open Court Publishing Company, 1962].)

[6] It of course goes without saying that when the term "existence" is applied to God, as in the present discussion, it, like every other term applied to the divine being, must be understood in an analogical sense. Cf. Erich Frank: "Existence is a category much too inferior to be applied to the greatness of God. . . . For as the source of all reality, He is so far above the sphere of any determinate being that He cannot be called existent in a

the one whose very nature is to be. In the terms of the scholastic formula: God's essence is existence, that is, to exist.[7] To say the same thing in other words: God is the only reality who is free to exist, who has the power to exist in and of himself. God's power, and his radical otherness from all finite power, is expressed here at the most fundamental level.

However, it is not some abstract existence, barren and empty of content, to which we are referring here, but the self-existence of the One who gives himself in Jesus Christ, the self-existence of almighty love.[8] As soon as the centrality of God's love is recalled, it becomes clear that we cannot rightly speak of God's power simply in terms of his absolute independence and self-sufficiency; we must also speak of his power in relation to his creatures. In this connection it is usually emphasized that God is omnipotent, all-powerful, almighty. What do these words mean? In light of the divine freedom they must mean at least that there is no power that can stand against God and overcome him; he is the one who has power over all others. This must

---

sense similar to the existence of all other beings. . . . Like all other categories, that of existence, if applied to God, can be used only in an analogical sense. Existence of God can be only an analogy of existence. For the existence of God infinitely transcends our thought, our will, and even our belief" (*Philosophical Understanding and Religious Truth* [New York: Oxford University Press, 1945], p. 44).

[7] For an illuminating discussion of this formula, see E. L. Mascall, *He Who Is* (London: Longmans, 1943), Ch. 2. The most succinct and profound classical statement will be found in St. Thomas' *On Being and Essence*, trans. A Maurer (Toronto: Pontifical Institute of Medieval Studies, 1949).

[8] Forgetting the particular concreteness of the self-existent one, as the one who came in Jesus Christ, underlies the development of the so-called arguments for the existence of God. When God's existence *per se* is abstracted from and considered independently of God's concrete being—a conceptual act forbidden by the first perfection of the divine freedom, God's radical unity—we are confronted with the sharp conceptual contrast between God's mode of being and ours, between self-existence and dependent existence. Inasmuch as the latter clearly presupposes the former, and since no finite reality has its being in itself, it is concluded that God must exist. (In the "ontological" argument an adequate ground for finite thought is thus sought; in the "cosmological," for finite *being*; in the "teleological," for finite *value*.) However, all that is really established here is the sharp contrast and the logical relationships between certain abstractions. But since *to those who already believe in God* it is taken for granted that these abstractions refer to reality, the proof seems valid; while to those who do not, who to the best of their knowledge confront in their experience only various forms of finite being and a variety of ways to understand the limits of experience, the proof seems to be pointless playing with words. The awareness of God's self-existence depends not on logical argument, but on standing in faith-relation to the living God. However, given this relation, theological analysis shows God's existence to be certain, i.e., it can be derived analytically from the very notion of God, as Anselm long ago argued.

not be misread to mean, however, that he has all the power. That
would be a denial that there is a created order of being at all; for
creation means that God has given power to agents other than himself—power to exist (in a secondary and derivative sense), power to
act, even power to be free and self-determining within certain limits.
God's omnipotence does not mean that he causes everything; it means
rather that he is omnicompetent, that he can appropriately deal with
any circumstance that arises; nothing can ultimately defeat or destroy him.

Furthermore, this God who loves must not be conceived as possessing merely the kind of power spoken of in deterministic theories,
the power of the puppeteer over his puppets, the power to make
everyone else do his will. God's power is much greater than this: he
is able to create *free agents* who can act with a certain autonomy,
even becoming creators in their own right. Kierkegaard has well
pointed out that the creation of free spirits, far from contradicting
God's omnipotence, presupposes it. For only omnipotence could have
the requisite degree and quality of power for such a project.[9] Moreover, God's power is of such an order and such a character that he
can continue to govern his universe even when the free spirits within
it disobey him and work against his will. Nor is he forced to destroy
their freedom in doing so; on the contrary, he has the requisite power
to win them over from rebellion to obedient love, thus magnifying
in them and fully realizing the freedom that is only nascent and
fragmentary so long as they turn away from him. This is because in
his dealings with men it is the power of love, not naked force, that
is at work. Love is the only power great enough to transform a wicked

[9] "That will sound curious, since of all things omnipotence, so at least it would seem,
should make things dependent. But if we rightly consider omnipotence, then clearly it
must have the quality of so taking itself back in the very manifestation of its all-powerful-
ness that the results of this act of the omnipotent can be independent. That is why one
man cannot make another man quite free, because the one who has the power is imprisoned
in it. . . . Omnipotence alone can take itself back while giving, and this relationship is
nothing else but the independence of the recipient. . . . Omnipotence can not only bring
forth the most imposing of all things, the world in its visible totality, but it can create
the most delicate of all things, a creature independent of it. Omnipotence which can lay
its hand so heavily upon the world can also make its touch so light that the creature
receives independence. It is only a miserable and worldly picture of the dialectic of power
to say that it becomes greater in proportion as it can compel and make things dependent"
(*Journals*, trans. A. Dru [New York: Harper Torchbooks, 1958], p. 113).

heart: no tyranny, however absolute, can accomplish that. As Gregory of Nyssa has said, "God's transcendent power is not so much displayed in the vastness of the heavens, or the luster of the stars, or the orderly arrangement of the universe or his perpetual oversight of it, as in his condescension to our weak nature."[10] God's omnipotence means, then, that although physical power and vital energy shape much in this universe, they are ultimately ordered to and expressive of God's love. In the end self-giving love is all-powerful in the world, and however frequent and frightening may be its historical defeats, ultimate victory belongs to it. For God is the almighty one, the one whom none can overthrow, and "God is love" (1 John 4:7, 16).[11]

[10] *Address on Religious Instruction,* Ch. 24 (*Library of Christian Classics,* III [Philadelphia: Westminster Press, 1954], 301).

[11] Perhaps it will be sufficiently clear by now why I do not discuss, in connection with God's freedom and power where it might be expected, his "wrath." It is not because I regard this symbol as theologically useless and utterly misleading, nor because I intend to develop it elsewhere in my elaboration of the doctrine of God; rather, it is because it is a symbol more appropriate to discussion of the nature (and plight) of *man* than *God.* Such a symbol as the wrath of God—certainly frequently used in contemporary theology, as well as in the Bible and traditional theology—raises interesting methodological questions. If the theological norm for constructing the doctrine of God were the *language* found in the Bible as a whole or in the New Testament, or even in the words of Jesus (a point which liberalism did not very carefully note), then there would be no justification for omitting this symbol from a presentation of the doctrine of God. If the norm were determined by more "practical" considerations, such as the linguistic requirements for powerful preaching, then also the symbol would have to be included here. But in this systematic theology we have taken the position that the norm is the event of God's decisive self-revelation—an event which certainly cannot be apprehended except on the basis of biblical evidence, but an event, nevertheless, which is necessarily apprehended in and through the image produced in our historical reconstruction (see above, pp. 62ff.), and which may thus differ in important particulars from what is implied in certain biblical statements and points of view. *The revelatory event is the norm in terms of which the biblical language and images must themselves be judged.* If this is the case, the proper usage of the symbol of God's wrath comes clear. The man hanging on the cross—for the crucifixion is the definitive moment in terms of which God's revelation must be understood (see below, pp. 193f.; 384ff.; 446ff., esp. n. 9; cf. also pp. 431ff.)—reveals God's nature as long-suffering love, not vengeance or wrath in any sense. "When he was reviled, he did not revile in return; when he suffered, he did not threaten" (1 Pet. 2:23). Hence, in our direct exposition of the doctrine of God such symbols as "wrath" would only be misleading and should be avoided: God reveals himself as love and faithfulness, and this it is that we must seek to grasp here. But this does not mean that such symbols have no place at all. When we are considering the plight of man, we will observe that his being has become so twisted and enslaved by sin that he misapprehends God and God's purposes, even perceiving the One who seeks to save him and give him genuine fulfilment as his enemy, seeing God as filled with terrible wrath, not forgiving mercy (see pp. 311f., 372f.). The symbol of God's "wrath" is appropriate for speaking of the apprehension of God which sinful man, living in despair and guilt and anxiety and hate, possesses; but when, as now, we are concerned not with sinful man's misconceptions, but with God's own revelation of his nature and purposes in and through Jesus Christ, it is hardly appropriate.

The conception of God's omnipotence can be elaborated and developed along several different lines. We must, for example, consider God's omniscience in this connection. To say that God is all-knowing or all-wise is to characterize his power in a special way: it is not blind or unconscious power; on the contrary, it is purposive, an expression of God's free will. God is not ignorant of anything he must know in order to govern his universe and realize his objectives. Ignorance of that sort would be weakness, but God is all-powerful; hence he must be all-knowing as well.

If God is omniscient, it has often been suggested, then his foreknowledge of future events must be complete in every detail; this in turn implies that the character of the entire future is already determinate, and therefore that human freedom is actually illusory, for the resolution of alternatives no longer awaits the actual decisions of men. It is not possible to circumvent the weight of this contention by the sophism that men are really free to decide as they wish in moments of choice, but God knows beforehand what their decision will be—thus saving both man's freedom and God's absolute foreknowledge. The dilemma posed here is a legitimate criticism against traditional views of the divine foreknowledge: namely, that they are based on an impersonal, and thus person-destroying, conception of God's knowledge, the divine omniscience being conceived after the model of a great encyclopedia, as a static, objectivist, pseudo-scientific sum-total of all facts—past, present, and future. But for Christian faith God's omniscience should be understood in terms appropriate to the peculiarities of the knowledge of persons, for the Christian claim is that God has revealed himself as personal and is in interpersonal relation with his creatures. He is not the supreme scientific mind objectively studying a world of objects, but the loving Creator and Father who grants his creatures genuine freedom: that is, a future in some degree contingent on their own decisions, not determinate and closed in every detail from all eternity. In order to see the significance of this point, it will be helpful to consider briefly certain characteristics of finite interpersonal knowledge, as an analogical basis for our discussion.

The wise parent who really loves his child deliberately grants him some privacy, not prying into every detail of the child's life.

Though a certain *factual* knowledge of the child's nature and behavior might be gained by continuous snooping, *real* knowledge of the child-as-person would not. Moreover, since under these conditions the child would not be treated as a free and responsible agent, it is dubious that he could ever become one. Only as the parent honors the child's integrity, grants him freedom to be himself, and does not attempt to destroy the irreducible mystery of individuality and privacy in the child's inmost being, can the child develop into a free person. And only then does the possibility arise that the child may freely *reveal* himself to the parent, so that the parent may come to know him not as a mere collection of facts but as a living personal being with projects and purposes of his own. Of course the parent must have sufficient foreknowledge of the dangers, for example, into which the child may fall, in order to protect him: he needs to know when it is appropriate to grant the child freedom and when to restrict him. But his foreknowledge must never be such as to destroy that freedom.

So also with God: his knowledge must enable him to deal with any contingency that arises in human history, but this does not mean that he needs to know in advance all details of such contingencies. If the Christian claim that God has revealed himself as personal is to be believed, he wills to know men as living persons, who in their love reveal themselves to him, not as mere objective facts which simply are what they are.

This implication about the nature of the cognitive relationship between God and man, which devolves from man's personal character, may appear to make God too passive in relation to man, a circumstance the older theories of absolute foreknowledge were designed specifically to avoid. But when we remember that for Christian faith God as well as man is a personal agent, living, deciding, acting, and interacting, this defect fades away. In the Bible though God's *purposes* remain constant throughout history, *his particular actions* are always fitted to the demands of the specific concrete historical situation in which he is acting. That is, God is pictured as working out his purposes in active intercourse and intercommunion with men, not as rigidly and mechanically determining the whole from the beginning. This does not mean that God is less powerful or wise than the puppeteer who knows not only the outcome but the details of every action in his play; nor does it call into question the fundamental unity in God's being and action. On the contrary, he is more powerful and his unity has external efficacy, for he is able increasingly to realize his purposes within and through a community of free agents. But his power and knowledge and unity are of the character appropriate to a personal-historical agent in living intercommunion with other, albeit finite, personal-historical agents. Doubtless the latter are themselves the expression of God's purposes, and doubtless his purposes for them will ultimately prevail, shaping history in accordance with his intentions. But in the meantime—between the beginning and the end of history—his particular decisions and actions are responsive to the contingencies which arise in history, though still an expression of his ultimate objectives. It is just such constancy of purpose in contingency of action that makes it possible for history to have meaningful structure, even though the agents acting within it have freedom. If we take seriously the Christian claim that the life and death of a *person* are the definitive revelation of God's being, then we must grant the consequence that God's power and knowledge and unity are to be understood in correspondingly personal terms.[12]

If we agree that living history, though contingent and indeterminate, is real, and that the future is genuinely open in certain respects that only concrete personal decisions can close, then it is clear that the traditional conception of God's foreknowledge—implying that God knows every detail of one's life and action even

[12] William Poteat has stated the matter well: ". . . God can be thought of as knowing of his own intentions in a fashion analogous to that in which I can . . . answer questions about my plans and goals. . . . In the case of God, this knowing is not *now* knowing something about the way the world is to (must) be. It is rather a knowing now of what he plans now that the world shall be. . . . It is a knowing *now* what his plans *now* are for what will be. . . . The designs only become actualized when they are no longer known merely as designs, but are known as acts, i.e., enacted designs. . . . In all this, . . . God's foreknowing in no way involves a foreordaining. . . . Therefore . . . we can speak of [God's] *knowing* the creature without being driven to thinking that the foreknowing of his own acts foreordains them. . . . In this sense . . . it is possible to 'embrace both' God's foreknowledge and man's freedom" ("Foreknowledge and Foreordination: A Critique of Models of Knowledge," *Journal of Religion* [1960], 40:24).

before his birth[13]—must be sharply qualified.[14] The inadequacy of
the traditional view is not difficult to understand when it is remembered that it was definitively shaped long before the distinction
between fact-knowledge and person-knowledge had been perceived
and subjected to careful analysis. It is no longer possible to avoid
this refinement, however; nor would it be desirable to do so, inasmuch as the older view led to insoluble antinomies. Some such
restatement as has been attempted here is requisite if the divine
foreknowledge is to be reconciled with the revelation of the divine
love which grants man genuine freedom.

It is important to recognize that the biblical God is never pictured
as a being whose every action has been determined once and for all
at the beginning, his knowledge of every detail of the future being
complete and perfect. On the contrary, he is a living being who acts
in the situation confronting him, sometimes trying one course of
action, then perhaps "repenting himself" (i.e., concluding that it
was a mistake?) and trying something else.[15] These images are often
disparaged as unfortunate anthropomorphisms deriving from the

---

[13] Perhaps the outstanding example of this traditional piety is found in the much-
loved Ps. 139:

> O Lord, thou hast searched me and known me!
> Thou knowest when I sit down and when I rise up;
>   thou discernest my thoughts from afar,
> Thou searchest out my path and my lying down,
>   and art acquainted with all my ways. (1–3)

Up to this point, there is no need to quibble with anything the psalmist has said. But
when he goes on, his declarations become more questionable:

> Even before a word is on my tongue,
>   lo, O Lord, thou knowest it altogether . . . (4)
> Thy eyes beheld my unformed substance;
>   in thy book were written, every one of them,
> the days that were formed for me,
>   when as yet there was none of them. (16)

[14] It can even be argued, as Charles Hartshorne has done, that such views, however
edifying to simple piety, actually imply, when carefully analyzed, that the divine knowledge
is defective. ". . . knowledge is true if, and only if, it corresponds to reality, and things
that have not happened are, in so far, perhaps, not real. To know them would then be
to know falsely, for there is nothing of the sort to know. If the future is indeterminate, if
there is real freedom between alternatives, any one of which *can* happen, then the true
way to know the future is as undetermined, unsettled. To know just what 'is to happen'
is to know falsely if there is in fact no definite thing which is to happen. . . . For if the
future is in fact unsettled, indeterminate, it would not be ignorance to see it as such, but,
rather, true knowledge" (*Man's Vision of God, op. cit.* (above, n. 5), pp. 98–99).

[15] Cf., Gen. 6:6; Ex. 32:14; 1 Sam. 15:35; 2 Sam. 24:16; 1 Chr. 21:15; Jer. 26:19;
Amos 7:3; Jonah 3:10; etc.

philosophical naiveté of the biblical writers. But they are not that. It is only in some such terms that we can conceive God as *living* and as acting with genuine responsiveness to the other living and free beings with whom he is dealing. God does "change his mind" because God is working with free agents; when one course of action proves futile, he must try another. This view involves no derogation of the divine power or the divine knowledge or even the divine unity, but rather an amplification of them: God's power and knowledge are so great that he is able to govern with wisdom even a universe in which other free agents are acting, and his unity is sufficient to draw and hold together an otherwise chaotic and crumbling historical process.

The conception of the divine omnipotence can also be developed with the aid of the doctrines of God's omnipresence and eternity. Without spelling these out in detail, we can see that they deny God's limitedness with reference to two of the fundamental dimensions of our finitude, space and time. Every reality which we know has spatio-temporal location. To say something is *here* and not there, *now* and not then, is to say it has limits or boundaries. Existing side by side with other finite beings and before and after other finite realities, it is finite too. Such power as it has is limited to the particular space and time in which it is found.

To assert this of God would be to regard him as an idol. God is not *one particular thing* that exists alongside others, nor is he found in *one particular time* and not in others.[16] God's being is sovereign

---

[16] As is well known, Paul Tillich has made the most, among contemporary theologians, of the importance of denying that God is a particular being alongside others, holding that he should instead be regarded as "being-itself," this latter conception being the one nonsymbolic term applicable to him (see, e.g., *Systematic Theology*, I [Chicago: University of Chicago Press, 1951], 238ff.; this view was modified slightly in Vol. II, p. 9, however). Tillich is correct in his denial here, it seems to me, wrong in his affirmation. For the former quite properly removes the restrictions of finitude from the divine being—and without this he is not God—but the latter then proceeds to propose a nonpersonal analogy for conceiving him. The matter is complicated even further by Tillich's denial that "being-itself" is analogical or symbolical, thus giving it a significance and status above every other concept or image. To this position one must put the question: Is the *personalistic* character of God's revelation in a *person* normative for the conception of ultimate reality, or is the norm *and thus the really decisive "revelation"* to be found elsewhere? If the former is the case, then—though one agrees with Tillich that God is not *a* being alongside others, and that the predicates of finite being cannot apply (literally) to him—these *negations* are as far as he can go; for the basic conception must be determined by the event of revelation, and that is personalistic. If the latter alternative be affirmed, is the position any longer genuinely "Christian"?

over every space, every time. He is omnipresent and eternal. This does not mean that God *is* all space and time or that all spaces and times are "in" him, as though he were a "container" of the universe with an extra-long life span. Such a being would only be spatial and temporal on a larger scale. Rather, these concepts are intended to suggest that there is no space or time to which God is not present— that is, which is not subject to him, which belongs to some other god —and yet he is in no way subject to them; they are his creation, not he theirs, and as Lord over them he uses them for the fulfilment of his purposes. All the world is bound up in space and time, but God is Lord of the world, even Lord of its basic spatio-temporal structure. Thus the doctrines of omnipresence and eternity express in yet another way the Creator's freedom over his creation.

c. *The third perfection of the divine freedom: the holiness*[17] *and righteousness of God.* God's freedom exists not only on the level of *existence,* what *is,* but also on the level of *right,* what *ought-to-be.* Here again we must contrast his freedom with ours. We have a certain freedom with reference to obligation or moral law: the freedom to disobey it, to violate it. We do not have to do what duty prescribes. But we are not free to choose *what right is.* We are free to decide whether to commit murder or not, but not whether murder is right. Moral obligation impinges on us as something that we ought to do whether we wish or no. It comes to us as a command—thou shalt! thou shalt not!—not as something we can shape as we might like. It is a "categorical imperative" (Kant).

But in just this respect God's freedom must be contrasted with ours. For God is not to be regarded as externally imposed on by the moral law any more than by natural law. When God is said to be Creator of all that is, this includes the realm of values, ideals, goods, as well as of existent objects. These too are given their being by the free action of his will, working out his purposes for the world. To take any other position than this would be to place a god—whether it be called the "moral law" or the "Form of the Good" or the "realm of essences" or values—above God, a god to which even the Lord must be subservient. No, God's creative power and freedom must be

17 See also above discussion of the "holy" (pp. 108ff.).

regarded as the source and ground of all value as well as of all actuality.[18]

This may be put in a less abstract, more existential, way. When we speak of God's holiness and righteousness, we are using the words in a different sense than when we speak of righteous or holy men. The difference can be felt in the word "holy" itself, for it makes us linguistically uneasy to speak of a "holy man" or of "holy people." "Holy" is something we men are not; "holy" is what God, and God alone, is. When men are confronted with the holy, they feel impelled to say with Isaiah: "Woe is me! For I am lost; for I am a man of unclean lips, and I dwell in the midst of a people of unclean lips; for my eyes have seen the King, the Lord of Hosts!" (6:5). The word "holy" points to the contrast between everything human and God; it suggests a certain unhealthiness or diseasedness of man's condition, such that the standard or norm in terms of which human existence is to be judged cannot be found in man but only in the absolute one, the one beyond all human existence, the Holy One. This implies that all of men's moral standards, their notions of truth and falsity and their other valuational criteria, must be regarded as questionable. Since they belong to man with his uncleanness, they can be given no absolute status. Before God, man's loftiest ideals and most cherished values fade away. Even "our righteousnesses are as filthy rags" (Isa. 64:6 KJ); "before God we are always in the wrong" (Kierkegaard). Though men must think and decide and act in terms of their convictions about right and wrong, truth and falsity, they may never suppose these adequate in God's eyes when measured by his standard. All this is felt in and suggested by the word "holy" and our reluctance to apply it to man.

This is consistent with the view that God is Creator even of the world of values. Since they are subject to him and not he to them, they

18 Cf. Luther: "God is He for Whose will no cause or ground may be laid down as its rule and standard; for nothing is on a level with it or above it, but it is itself the rule for all things. If any rule or standard, or cause or ground, existed for it, it could no longer be the will of God. What God wills is not right because He ought, or was bound, so to will; on the contrary, what takes place must be right, because He so wills it. Causes and grounds are laid down for the will of the creature, but not for the will of the Creator —unless you set another Creator over him!" (*Bondage of the Will*, trans. J. I. Packer and O. R. Johnson [Westwood, New Jersey: Revell, 1957], p. 209).

cannot either be applied to him as adequate literal descriptions nor can they be made his measure. We may perhaps speak of a "good" or "righteous" or "just" man, meaning thereby one who fulfills the law of righteousness as humanly understood. But we should never say that God is "good" or "righteous" or "just" in this sense at all; for he is the Creator of the moral law, not its subject—and certainly not subject to it "as humanly understood," as grasped by sinful human minds. If God is said to be righteous or good, it is as the Holy One whose goodness and righteousness are beyond human insight and understanding and capacity for judgment.

From this position it is possible to comment briefly on the problem of theodicy, of the "justification of God."[19] How is it possible for a good God to allow such evil and suffering in his universe? The question posed here presupposes that man is in a position to judge God, that is, that our conceptions of good and evil, right and wrong, are appropriate for measuring him. This exactly reverses the relationship implied by the conception of God's holiness: instead of God and God's standards being our ultimate measure, we supposedly can sit in judgment on him. Clearly this would be possible only if (a) the same standards applied to God as to us (or, at any rate, we knew with what to measure him), and (b) we were in a position to apply them. But both these contentions are false if God's holiness is an expression of his freedom, that is, if he is really the ultimate limit of our experience and being.[20] Nevertheless, God's "holiness" is not simply a word

[19] The discussion of the problem of theodicy in these paragraphs is too incomplete to make clear the bearing of my full position. It should be supplemented by the considerations treated on pp. 212f. and 309ff., below.

[20] Something like this seems to be the conclusion of the poetic portion of Job. After Job had issued all his complaints against God—defined in terms of his conceptions of what should be God's proper reaction to his own good conduct, Job's "friends" all the while insisting that God is in fact true to just those human standards—the voice from the whirlwind speaks, reminding Job how utterly beyond human comprehension are the activities and wisdom and being of God. Before this awe-ful reality of God's majesty and mystery all questions and objections become impertinent, their utter irrelevancy, even blasphemy, now being evident. So Job responds to the Lord:

> I know that thou canst do all things,
>   and that no purpose of thine can be thwarted.....
> Therefore I have uttered what I did not understand,
>   things too wonderful for me, which I did not know. . . .
> I had heard of thee by the hearing of the ear,
>   but now my eye sees thee;
> therefore I despise myself,
>   and repent in dust and ashes. (JOB 42:2-6)

in the "negative theology." For when we apply it to God, we mean to speak positively of his perfection, that he is as he ought to be. Indeed, his perfection is the proper measure of our finite being: we also ought to be "holy," but are not. Thus, the term "holiness" not only points to God's transcendence of our standards of goodness and righteousness, justice and love; it *includes* these conceptions as well, declaring that in fact it is *God* who is the only one genuinely righteous and loving. To speak of God's holiness is to affirm the absolute and final value of God and all his ways. He is the one, the only one, worthy to be worshiped; he alone is truly good, beyond all fractured, partial human goodness. "Why do you call me good?" Jesus asked, "No one is good but God alone" (Mk. 10:18). But his goodness and justice and love are not man's. Though our notions here as everywhere are the only analogues by means of which we can sense something of the glory of the divine being, he utterly transcends them in his brilliance and perfection; though they be indispensable vehicles for analogical knowledge of God, they can never be made his measures.

d. This, God's utter transcendence of everything finite, brings us to *the fourth perfection of the divine freedom: the glory of God.* With this conception all that has been said about the ultimate limit of our being, conceived in personalistic terms as divine freedom, can be drawn together in conclusion. To speak of God's glory is to point to the radiance, the fullness, the beauty, of God as he manifests himself to man. The first perfection discussed was the abstract and almost empty formal notion of God's oneness. This conception was then filled out and given substance through discussion of the divine power, and it was given meaning and worth by consideration of the divine holiness. Now all this is taken up together in the conception of the divine glory. God's reality is glorious!

Paul also makes the point that God is beyond all human standards and judgments: "But, who are you, a man, to answer back to God? Will what is molded say to its molder, 'Why have you made me thus?' Has the potter no right over the clay, to make out of the same lump one vessel for beauty and another for menial use?" (Rom. 9:20–21). These are hard words, but their meaning is clear. God is the Creator—and this means his being has a superiority over man's like a potter over his pot. It is no more appropriate to apply the standards of man to God than to measure the potter by the desires of the pot. What to us might appear injustice or ineptitude in God's actions and will, what we may feel impelled to call God's "wrath" (see n. 11, p. 154, above) gives no adequate standpoint from which to judge the divine being. Here we are up against the absolute limit of our experience and knowledge, and we are in no position to judge at all.

The symbol "glory"—deriving from and pointing to the peculiar feeling evoked by the awareness of very bright and concentrated light[21]—is properly applied to only the most exalted moments of the human spirit. It points to an ecstasy that includes joy and happiness, beauty and the thrill of great power and meaning, an overflowing of all that is cherished and desired. To speak of God's glory is to characterize the final limit of existence with a word which suggests the fullness of all that is good and valuable in human experience.

Yet, once again, the image of glory is but an analogy or symbol. For it is *God's* glory with which we are concerned, and this is much greater than any glory man knows. Man's most glorious moments or achievements are only occasional. Moreover, they are tarnished and crude compared with some of the glories of God's creation: "... even Solomon in all his glory" was nothing beside the common lilies of the field (Mt. 6:29). Man's longing for a glory which he does not possess, moreover, is a clear witness to his finitude, his limitations, his dependency. In contrast, God's glory is manifest in his very self-sufficiency; he depends on nothing outside his own being. His very godness, his aseity, the great fullness to overflowing of his being, is glorious.

But his glory is more than that. For God is not only absolutely sufficient unto himself—and that is glorious indeed!—his power of being overflows and he becomes the Creator of the world. His glorious fullness is such that he can impart reality to beings other than and different from himself. He can create them, order them into a universe, sustain them, work out his purposes through them, finally bring them to a glorious final consummation. In this secondary sense, God's creation enhances his glory. He is not only the God who is God, he is the

21 "If we were called on to explain what we mean . . . by 'brilliant' or 'glorious,' we could only say that the things in question excite in us a feeling which we recognize to be in a certain way analogous to the admiration evoked by bright concentrated light. We could [not] . . . explain to anyone who had never had the feeling in regard to literal light what we mean when we use such terms . . . metaphorically. . . . When we speak of the glory of God . . . we mean . . . that, if we could have a more perfect apprehension of God's being than we can have under earthly conditions, that apprehension would involve something analogous to the feeling now aroused in us by bright concentrated light, something which cannot possibly be described in human language, except by our pointing to that feeling. Thus the light metaphor [is] . . . the most precise way in which the Reality can be expressed in human language. And yet, . . . it is only a figure, not a literal description" (Edwyn Bevan, *Symbolism and Belief* [London: Allen and Unwin, 1938], pp. 148–150).

God who creates the world. "The heavens declare the glory of God" (Ps.19:1 KJ).

But, again, his glory is magnified beyond what has thus far been said. For he not only sustains himself and creates a world: he has willed that this world be no mere mechanical expression of his purposes but that it be the womb in which he could create free spirits, beings who, as pale images of himself, could think with some degree of genuine autonomy, decide with some measure of authentic freedom, act with some real independence of him—and thus themselves become creators in his world, "labourers together with God" (1 Cor. 3:9 KJ). God's sufficiency is such that he can bring into being other free and creative spirits to live in community of love with him and work cooperatively in the realization of his purposes. In this sense lowly man also enhances the glory of God. God is not only sufficient unto himself, nor the mere maker of a world: he is the Creator of spirits into which he has breathed his own spirit.

But this man who is the crown of God's creation, and thus of God's glory, rebels against God. In pride and disobedience he refuses to acknowledge his Creator. And here the real plenitude and beauty of the divine glory become manifest. For God does not react to this offense, as he by all rights might, rejecting man, casting him out, destroying him, declaring him "damned for the glory of God"—though such a display of power and sovereign right might be glorious indeed! Nor does he force man against his own will into obedience. Rather, he comes to man with love and forgiveness, revealing himself to man and redeeming him; he recreates him from within into a new creature; he wins men's hearts with the power of his glorious love. Thus, through his patient and painful work in history, he establishes his kingdom as a community in which love reigns, and he intends the full realization of this community to participate in history's ultimate consummation. This "chosen race, [this] royal priesthood, [this] holy nation, God's own people" (1 Pet. 2:9) who shall ultimately become the inhabitants of a New Jerusalem—this is God's glory!

This vision of the glorious transformation of man's hell into God's perfect kingdom, through the power of his love, is not yet the highest vision of the glory of God to which we can attain. For more marvelous than God's works is the One who works them. That God finally achieves the purposes which he had originally posited despite all opposition and difficulties; that nothing can thwart him in the realization of his goals, neither the immensity and complexity of the universe he has created nor the sin and disobedience of some of his creatures; that he is equal to every task he sets himself—this is his ultimate glory. This brings us back once again to the original apprehension of God's glory in his self-sufficiency. But now that great independence and adequacy is even more enhanced. God is no mere ground of being, a self-establishing but static foundation for himself and all else; God is the one who can *act* with confidence and supreme success, the mighty Agent behind and in and through all history, who "triumphs gloriously" (Ex. 15:1 and *seq.*) in all that he undertakes. "The beams of glory come from God, are something of God, and are refunded back again to their original. . . . The refulgence shines upon and into the creature, and is reflected back to the luminary."[22]

> *From him and through him and to him are all things.*
> *To him be glory forever. Amen.*
>
> ROMANS 11:36

[22] Jonathan Edwards, *A Dissertation Concerning the End for Which God Created the World*, Ch. 2, section 7.

11 / The Incarnation of God

I. God's Coming Into History

UNDER the heading of "God the Father" we have been considering God in his transcendence, his unique and incomparable character distinguishing him absolutely from all finite beings. As we turn now to the second person of the trinity, we must consider a set of different, though related, problems. Before examining these directly, however, it is important to remind ourselves we are not thereby talking about a different God, or even a different task of God. Nor shall we be adding something to God: God is the one who is sufficient unto himself; all things come from him; what then could possibly be added? Rather, we shall now be considering this same God with reference to somewhat different issues. Whereas heretofore we sought to conceive him in his transcendence of history and the world, his lofty independence—so far as this was possible from a perspective within the world—now we shall be viewing him in his act of entering into the world to reveal himself, that is, in his explicit and deliberate relatedness to the world. While before we viewed him primarily as Creator, now we shall seek to see him as Redeemer and Savior. This change should not suggest that we are dealing with something less important in God; it is, rather, a different, but equally indispensable,

---

[1] It should be noted that the christological discussion in this volume is not confined to the present four chapters. Christological materials have already been dealt with in Chs. 2 and 3; and Chs. 27–29 and 33 are almost entirely christological in content. The present four chapters deal only with the implications of the Christ-event for the doctrine of God.

moment of the one God's self-revelation, apart from which we would not know him at all.

We are ready to consider in some detail now a question which has been touched on at various points before (especially in our consideration of revelation), namely, how do we come to know this God, the Creator of the universe? Recall for a moment the difficulties of the problem. God is the utterly self-sufficient being, the One incomparable to all others, absolutely unique, the ultimate limit of man and all other finite reality. How could we possibly come to know such a being? If God transcended us and our world absolutely and in all respects, we could never come to know anything about him at all— even that he is and that he is transcendent. Such a being could come to be and mean something *for us* only through entering into our world, thus becoming a possible object of our knowledge: God would have to take on the form, as it were, of something we could experience and understand, and make himself known to us in that way. This is precisely the Christian claim: God himself has come to man in the very person of a man. In the coming pages we shall examine this claim and its meaning in some detail.

This belief that God has acted to reveal himself is fully consistent with the overall Christian conception of God. If God is really the utterly free Lord who lives beyond the limits of the created world, then he is free to conceal himself from man or to reveal himself to man at his own pleasure. That is, our knowledge of God will necessarily depend, in the first instance, entirely on his will and act. Thus, a radical monotheism, if consistent, implies a doctrine of revelation as the basis for knowledge of God (cf. pp. 111f., above). No other view could maintain the radical *theo*centrism without which genuine monotheism itself dissolves. The important question for any monotheism thus becomes: Where and how is God's revelation found? A "monotheistic" position which does not face up to this question is not really serious.

The Christian claim is that God—who is the ultimate limit of all created being and who does not depend on it in any respect—nevertheless gives himself to man in reconciliation. God is not only the Lord, the absolutely free one; he loves in his freedom and therefore makes

himself into the *servant* of man, ministering to human need through
the ministry of Jesus. As we turn now to consider God as the Servant,
we must be careful not to forget that it is the *Lord* who serves, and he
does not lose his lordship even in his service. Indeed, it is precisely
through his service that he wins sovereignty over men's hearts. Referring to God as "Servant" does not mean he can be viewed as a kind
of slave, subject to our every whim. God is not subject to us: he is
the Lord and we are subject to him. Yet, it is precisely at this point
that God's absoluteness upsets our ordinary human conceptions of
lordship. For, as Jesus in both manner and teaching revealed, the One
who is *truly* Lord has power and freedom enough to forget his dignity
and become the servant of all.

> And Jesus called them to him and said to them, "You know that
> those who are supposed to rule over the Gentiles lord it over them,
> and their great men exercise authority over them. But it shall not
> be so among you; but whoever would be great among you must be
> your servant, and whoever would be first among you must be
> slave of all. For the Son of man also came not to be served but to
> serve, and to give his life as a ransom for many."
>
> MARK 10:42–45

In John's Gospel (Chapter 13) this servant motif is dramatized: Jesus
washes the disciples' feet. Thus, God's lordship is exhibited most decisively, not in earthquake, thunder, and fire—the violent forces of
nature—but, paradoxically, in the self-giving service and sacrifice
of a lowly carpenter and itinerant preacher who was ultimately to
suffer a criminal's execution. Inasmuch as Christian faith takes these
events in the life and death of Jesus as manifesting God's own nature
and will and activity, it is possible to understand and appreciate the
early Christian mythical claim that here God himself had in a significant sense entered into human history and taken upon himself all
the limitations and difficulties of human existence (John 1:1–4, 14;
Phil. 2:6–8),[2] finally suffering a humiliating death; though without

---

[2] What I have here expressed by the somewhat vague phrase, "God himself . . . in
a significant sense," John and Paul of course affirmed more dramatically, but at the same
time in much more strongly mythological language, by referring to a preexistent divine
"Logos," or a heavenly being "in the form of God," who journeyed to earth.

sin, as Paul dramatically put it, he was even made "to be sin" for man's sake (2 Cor. 5:21). Thus, in and through Jesus' absolute self-giving unto death, "God shows his love for us" (Rom. 5:8) and wins mastery over men's sinful hearts. In this way is God's absolute lordship over even his most rebellious creatures at once made manifest and effective.

If the true character of God's freedom and power becomes known to men through the act in-which he wins them to him without destroying their freedom, then it is possible to speak of God's lordship in the Christian sense only from within Christian faith, that is, from within that perspective which has been taken captive by him. When this is overlooked, dangerous and misleading interpretations easily result. On the one hand, it may be forgotten that God is in fact *Lord* in his very serving of men, that in his service he renders men obedient to his will. And so God becomes understood as a kindly but harmless grandfather, a cosmic cornucopia continually overflowing with good things for man but asking nothing in return. This has been the image of much culture-protestantism of recent generations. But God is not the easygoing "man upstairs," available to do whatever men request. He is Lord of the universe! He has purposes for all creation, and his purposes shall be realized, whether men like it or not. He is the one before whom one cannot but stand in fear and awe—the Holy One! "It is a fearful thing to fall into the hands of the living God" (Heb. 10:31) "for our God is a consuming fire" (12:29)! It is the *Lord* whom man comes to know in the form of a servant, and this must never be forgotten.

On the other hand, it will hardly be understood outside Christian faith that God's power and freedom become known precisely in his *service*, that his is a lordship of love. And when this is overlooked, God may be apprehended as a terrible tyrant or demon who arbitrarily and with demonic glee "has mercy upon whomever he wills, and . . . hardens the heart of whomever he wills" (Rom. 9:18). If it is forgotten that the Lord is loving and forgiving toward his children, we may spin out harsh and mechanical doctrines to interpret his activity—for example, so-called double predestination—and the Christian good news becomes instead the evil tidings that the universe is under the control of an inhuman monster. This is just as serious a misunderstanding of God's lordship as the grandfatherly god is a misinterpretation of his love. Each fails to see that the Christian understanding of both God's love and his freedom is rooted in the same event, the same fact: that is, in Jesus Christ, in whom God's power to reconcile the world to himself—realizing his own purposes through becoming servant to the world—becomes known and effective.

It is of first importance, then, that what we say about God be rooted in the historical person-event Jesus Christ. The characteristic images by means of which this event is apprehended historically are to be regarded as defining images for grasping the ultimate reality with which we have to do. What kind of reality, now, is this "Jesus Christ"? The pre-understanding with which we begin our investigation here may have decisive effects on the outcome. As against the nineteenth-century "questers" for the historical Jesus, it has been popular in recent decades to hold that we must begin with the "Christ of faith"—that is, with the biblical picture of Christ—if we are to apprehend God as manifest here. But this demand rests on hermeneutical misunderstanding and leads to serious theological error. First, this is absurd hermeneutically, for it suggests that in coming to understand something, we can begin at a more or less arbitrary position (e.g., the so-called standpoint of the New Testament) rather than *where we are*. But in fact we approach everything we seek to understand, including the New Testament, from our own position; and only if the language used by the New Testament writers is in some measure *already understood by us* are we able to appropriate that which is new in what they are saying. To apprehend what they mean by a technical term like "Christ," we cannot start with that word itself; we must begin rather with their more ordinary terminology, *which we already understand* in some degree, and from there proceed to grasp its meaning. Second, the theological error concealed in the popular but hermeneutically impossible insistence on beginning with the "Christ of faith" is the demand that we perform a specific "work"—namely, believing in the New Testament "Christ of faith," whether it seems absurd or meaningless or not—before God will reveal himself. Thus, instead of faith being the reception of God's free gift, it becomes a task to be performed before God will be gracious; and the profound insights of the Reformation and of the recent theological revival lose out once again to the requirement of a specific kind of "works-righteousness."

If, then, our christological analysis and interpretation cannot begin directly with the "Christ of faith," where do we start? What simpler, less technical and esoteric, more public and ordinary, beginning-point is available? The answer is simple and obvious, though not always explicitly noted. Through what steps did the original disciples come to encounter God in and through Jesus? They first became acquainted with Jesus simply *as a man* to whom, for whatever reasons, they were attracted. Only *after* they knew him in this way and *on this presupposition* did they come to believe that in him God was present to them in some special way.[3] Moreover, it is along this same path that the earliest preachers attempted to lead their hearers and that the New Testament writers carry us. At every point they assume we will understand what they are talking about, because it is not some unknown and esoteric quantity from heaven purveyed through a secret gnosis which is theirs to proclaim, but the *"man* Jesus Christ" (Rom. 5:15). Doubtless he was a special and unusual man —indeed, unique!—but that he was a man and that we will therefore have no difficulty understanding them is always and everywhere presupposed.[4] To come to understanding of what it means to call Jesus

---

[3] Even Paul's overstatement (which might be cited against the position I am defending) that "even though we once regarded Christ from a human point of view, we regard him thus no longer" (2 Cor. 5:16), confesses that his faith in Christ also was preceded by knowledge of him as an ordinary man. Though Paul here seems to be denying that such knowledge is a necessary presupposition for faith, it must be remembered that he nowhere denies that Jesus was a man; and he often affirms it and always seems to presuppose it. It is difficult to see how that presupposition can be understood to involve *nothing at all* of an understanding of Jesus "from a human point of view."

[4] The New Testament throughout insists on Jesus' humanity. In the Gospels he is presented at every point as a man. No doubt he has unusual powers of healing and the like, but then so did other ancient wonder-workers, who also were said to have multiplied bread and walked on water. It was generally believed that such feats were possible to sorcerers and other men whom the gods favored; certainly they did not indicate Jesus was something other than a man. Indeed, Jesus himself recognized that his powers were of the same order as those of certain of the Pharisees' disciples who could also cast out demons (Lk. 11:19). Moreover, he appears to have stated quite openly that there would be no clear proof or evidence given in his lifetime establishing the supernatural truth of his message, or the divine authorization for his work, or the special significance of his person. "Why does this generation seek a sign?" he is reported to have asked (Mk. 8:12); "Truly, I say to you, no sign shall be given to this generation." Further, the Gospels present Jesus

the "Christ" or the "Son of God," we must begin with the realization that it is a particular historical person who is thus entitled.[5] In recognizing this, our inquiry begins in a hermeneutically reasonable way, and it does not lay down the demand to believe even before we know what we are talking about.[6]

---

as one sorely tempted, in a most human manner, to serve his own interests and desires rather than God's. Such temptation appears both at the beginning of Jesus' ministry (in the so-called temptation stories) and at the climax (in the self-struggle in the Garden of Gethsemane), and doubtless was a problem throughout. Finally, Jesus is executed as a common criminal, his mission apparently a total failure. According to the earliest witness still extant, his last word was despairing: "My God, my God, why hast thou forsaken me?" (Mk. 15:34). There is no question that in the Gospels Jesus is portrayed as very human indeed. Doubtless there is a tendency increasingly to overlay his humanity with superhuman powers as we move from earlier interpretations to later ones; and prior to the appearance of critical historical understanding of the New Testament, which uncovered this development, these images were easily confused and blended into a picture of Jesus as virtually a demigod. But historical analysis has made clear how much such harmonizing involved an actual misreading of the biblical documents; without question the earliest portraits of Jesus showed him to be quite human.

The rest of the New Testament is also unanimous on this point. Nowhere is Jesus' humanity denied; in many places it is affirmed. In some places this is done in relatively simple and straightforward form, as in Paul's statement that he was "born in the likeness of men" (Phil. 2:7) and in Hebrews where it is said that he was like us "in every respect" (2:17). In other passages Jesus' participation in human limitations, far from being concealed, is emphasized. Thus, a little later in Hebrews we read that he was "tempted as we are" (4:15) and was "beset with weakness" (5:2); John insists that Jesus was "flesh" (1:14)—i.e., not merely formally human, but participant in the same corrupted nature as we; and Paul makes this same point as explicitly as possible, asserting he was even made "to be *sin*" (2 Cor. 5:21). A more extreme expression for Jesus' full humanity could scarcely be contrived.

This insistence on Jesus' humanness is just as characteristic of orthodox church doctrine as it is of the New Testament. At Chalcedon (451 A.D.) the church—in explicit opposition to every claim that Jesus was only partially or apparently human—officially adopted the position that Jesus (along with his true divinity) was "perfect in manhood, . . . truly man, the same of a reasonable soul and body; . . . consubstantial with us in manhood, like us in all things except sin. . . ." (The present translation will be found in the *Library of Christian Classics*, III [Philadelphia: Westminster Press, 1954], 373.) This judgment, in which the church was only making explicit and precise what was implicit in her other creeds, has never been repudiated. Indeed, it has always been a central affirmation of orthodox Christian faith.

[5] Cf. Luther, commenting on Hebrews: "It is to be noted that he (i.e., the author of the epistle) speaks of the humanity of Christ before he names his deity, and by this approves that rule of knowing God by faith. For his humanity is our holy ladder, by which we ascend to the knowledge of God. . . . Who wishes safely to ascend to the love and knowledge of God, let him leave human and metaphysical rules for knowing the deity, and let him first exercise himself in the humanity of Christ. For it is the most impious of all temerities when God himself has humbled himself in order that he might be knowable, that a man should seek to climb up some other way, through his own ingenious devices." Quoted from Luther's lectures on *Hebrews* in William Hamilton, *The New Essence of Christianity* (New York: Association Press, 1961), p. 92.

[6] Rooting christology thus in Jesus' presupposed humanity of course raises directly the problem of recovering in some degree "the historical Jesus." The best recent discussion of this issue, clarifying many methodological confusions in the decades of debate, is to

Jesus, then, the object of Christian faith, was a man, no demigod or heavenly being concealed behind a human façade. He was born a human being, laughed and cried and played and learned like any child, labored as an ordinary carpenter, finally suffered a violent death at the hands of his fellows. He sorrowed and rejoiced, hoped and feared, like any other man. He experienced the needs which all men know: for food, shelter, emotional response, security, etc.; and he suffered the limitations of his fellows. So far was he from being all-knowing and all-powerful that in his conception of the world and his understanding of himself and his own experience, he shared misconceptions common in his time: he thought, for example, that bodily and mental infirmity and disease were caused by demons, not germs; and he fully expected history to meet its end in the near future. There can be no doubt of Jesus' humanness.

It was in and through this particular man, according to Christian faith, that God definitively manifested himself. Such a position appears paradoxical to the point of sheer nonsense. It seems to say that the One who is the very foundation, source, sustaining ground, and ultimate limit of the entire universe from beginning to end was somehow uniquely present in, and even identical with, a particular human being, a tiny particle within this vast cosmos, who came to be and disappeared again in a few years almost two millennia ago. Can this be credible at all? Or, again, our paradox seems to be claiming that the One whose knowledge and wisdom are infinite and perfect is somehow revealed in an apocalyptic prophet who foolishly and ignorantly thought the world was coming to an end nineteen hundred years ago. It apparently asserts that the supreme power in the universe was definitively expressed in the helplessness of a man hanging

---

be found in Van Harvey, *The Historian and the Believer* (New York: Macmillan, 1966). On pp. 265ff. Harvey shows why and in what respects what he calls "the perspectival image of Jesus" can be regarded as historically reliable. Without here going into the complex methodological issues involved (see n. 9, Ch. 12), suffice it to remark that in the present work every effort has been made to keep the references to and descriptions of Jesus within this compass, which does not extend beyond the circle of fairly well-agreed consensus among New Testament historians. Partly for this reason matters of historical detail and controversy (except on the crucial question of Jesus' resurrection, see Ch. 28) have been avoided as far as possible.

on a cross. How or why should one believe such claims as these? Can they really have significant meaning?

When put in this bald fashion, Christian faith may appear absurd. Yet almost from the beginning Christians have regarded these claims as expressive of the very heart of their faith. We must turn now to an attempt to understand and interpret their meaning.

12 / The Incarnation of God

II. The Formal Meaning of the

Doctrine of the Incarnation

WE have noted a number of times the difficulties involved in justifying any assertion about God. Ultimately, we have contended, there is no final or coercive proof of theological knowledge; it rests, rather, on the decision to believe, on an act of faith. But faith itself is never completely abstract and empty. It is always faith in something; it always has some content. Doubtless one hopes that his faith is in *God*, the transcendent one, and that therefore its content is not drawn simply from human experience. But that way of putting the matter may be misleading. All knowledge of God is analogical or symbolical, and the symbols or analogies in terms of which he is thought and spoken are inevitably drawn from some realm of human experience. They never come, moreover, from just any or every region of experience: they always are found in some *particular* realm. This means that *God is spoken of, even in faith, only on the basis of symbols or analogies drawn from a particular domain within the whole range of experience, that is, one realm of existence is given* preferred status *over others: it is (consciously or unconsciously) re-garded as possessing special power or facility to furnish symbols of the transcendent; it is treated as in some unique way revelatory of the divine being.* One may be completely unaware, when speaking of

God, that he is giving some particular region of experience this preferential status, but he is nevertheless, no matter what his persuasion
or faith. Moreover, the character and content of the faith will be
determined largely by the selection that is here operative.

The Christian community is distinguished by (a) its clear awareness of the region of existence (Jesus Christ) that gives content and
meaning to its language and thought about God, and (b) its open
avowal of this, that is, its frank admission and claim that God has
indeed here revealed himself. In this community the awareness and
knowledge of God are so powerfully associated with the events surrounding the life, death, and resurrection of Jesus of Nazareth that
its members have been unable to minimize or ignore that connection. Doubtless other communities, also, have positively connected
their awareness of God with certain events and persons, but usually
it has been more diffused instead of sharply concentrated at one
point. Thus, Judaism, for example, has known many prophets and
men who covenanted with God; and Hinduism speaks of many incarnations, each of which may teach something important about the
divine. But the belief of the Christian community has been much
more unyielding than this: it has been unable to escape from the
conviction—and it has tried hard over the centuries—that what
really defines and distinguishes its understanding of God is rooted in
Jesus Christ.[1]

This belief had its historical roots in the preaching of Jesus him-

[1] It is interesting to observe that the great humanist and atheist Ludwig Feuerbach—
who was also a profound analyst of Christian faith—was aware of the significance of this
Christian insistence on *Einmaligkeit*. "The incarnations of the Deity with the Orientals—
the Hindoos, for example—have no such intense meaning as the Christian incarnation;
just because they happen often they become indifferent, they lose their value. . . . The
idea which lies at the foundation of the incarnations of God is . . . infinitely better conveyed
by one incarnation, one personality. Where God appears in several persons successively,
these personalities are evanescent. What is required is a permanent, an exclusive personality. Where there are many incarnations, room is given for innumerable others; the
imagination is not restrained; and even those incarnations which are already real pass
into the category of the merely possible and conceivable, into the category of fancies or of
mere appearances. But where one personality is exclusively believed in and contemplated,
this at once impresses with the power of an historical personality; imagination is done away
with, the freedom to imagine others is renounced. This one personality presses on me the
belief in its reality. The characteristic of real personality is precisely exclusiveness. . . .
It presents itself immediately as a real one, and is converted from an object of the
imagination into an object of historical knowledge" (*Essence of Christianity* [London:
Kegan Paul, Trench, Trübner, 1893], pp. 145–146).

self and in the faith of the earliest Jewish-Christian community that the climactic time for which all history had awaited was at last here, and God's kingdom was about to be established with finality (Mk. 1:15). When this conviction led to missionary preaching among Gentiles as well as Jews, the church became increasingly constituted by persons for whom virtually the entire knowledge of and relation to God came through the preaching of the Christian Gospel, their new faith representing a sharp break with their former paganism. Thus, the appearance, death, and resurrection of Jesus was decisive for their orientation toward and beliefs about God. The early Christians could make rather extreme statements expressing their convictions on this point: "there is salvation in no one else, for there is no other name under heaven given among men by which we must be saved" (Acts 4:12); "No one has ever seen God; the only Son, who is in the bosom of the Father, he has made him known" (John 1:18). Despite the reluctance of the Jesus of the synoptic Gospels to make claims concerning the significance of his own person (clearly evident in the fact that to this day historical scholars cannot be sure whether Jesus even claimed to be the Messiah), he at one point is portrayed as saying: "no one knows the Father except the Son and any one to whom the Son chooses to reveal him" (Mt. 11:27; cf. Lk. 10:22). With the Fourth Gospel, of course, Jesus is made to speak frequently and unashamedly of his own unique importance: "I am the way, and the truth, and the life; no one comes to the Father, but by me" (14:6; cf. many other "I"-sayings). The early Christians clearly were overwhelmed by the way in which their relation to God was rooted in the person-event Jesus Christ. And subsequent generations of Christians have confirmed that conviction: whatever is believed or said about God in Christian faith is inseparably connected with these events, this person.

It should be evident that the community's mere believing this is no sufficient ground for holding it true. The question of the events in which faith is rooted is a historical question, and if it can be answered at all, it is only by historical investigation. Such study of the historical origins and development of Christian beliefs is the task of biblical and historical theology. Moreover, even if such investigation should in large part confirm the self-understanding of faith about the events in which it is historically grounded—and it does, at least to a considerable extent—this would not in the slightest degree establish the claim that the God-revealed-in-Christ is the ultimate reality with which man has to do. For Christian faith may be simply a historical continuation of the illusions of a few first-century Jews. The most that could be said historically is that the Christian church is a community which explicitly and openly believes that in some decisive fashion God manifested himself in these particular events, that is, it believes its *historical* ground to be its true *ontological* ground.

This belief about the metaphysical significance of its originating events demands that the Christian community continuously strive to keep historical investigations into the origins of the various dimensions of its life under way. Only thus can it determine the degree to which its actual faith and life are oriented by the events it regards as normative; only thus can these events actually become the effective standards by which the community can measure and reorient its life. The period of the Reformation—as well as the theological awakening of our own time—was just such a historical looking-back to the originating events of the faith, seen as providing criteria for judging every later development. The great historical studies born of nineteenth-century liberalism, and continuing down to the present, should be understood theologically as a continuation of this indispensable work.[2]

The Christian community, then, is distinguished from all others in that it has been seized by the conviction that in those events of two thousand years ago God was present in definitive fashion. Or, to say the same thing in other words, it is that community which inevitably, whether consciously or unconsciously, turns back to those particular events for the fundamental analogies and symbols which give meaning and content to its understanding of ultimate reality.

[2] Indeed, even—nay, especially!—the famous "quest for the historical Jesus," together with the attempt (which we can now, on the basis of further historical work, see to be mistaken) to set the faith *of* Jesus over against the faith *in* Jesus, was theologically proper and necessary in the light of the historical knowledge of the origins of Christianity which was then just emerging. If we take a different—and, as we think, theologically sounder—position on these questions now, it is certainly at least partly because of the refinement in *historical* methods and the continued careful *historical* labors of hundreds of men, which have brought us to somewhat different conclusions about the historical facts.

These matters have been expressed traditionally in the fundamental christological claims of Christian faith: the historico-mythological doctrine of the incarnation, and the ontological claim that
Jesus Christ is truly God and truly man, two natures in one person.
These traditional formulations have led to considerable misunderstanding, for they seem to suggest that the "deity" of Christ is an
objective fact about Jesus' person, and accordingly that any impartial
investigation should be able to marshall evidence for it and draw
the right conclusion. Guided by one's preconceptions about the superhuman powers of deity, one would presumably look for evidence of
Jesus' infallible foreknowledge or unusual powers; and reports, for
example, of his ability to defy the laws of physics by walking on
water, or the laws of chemistry by multiplying loaves of bread,
would be given special importance—even though Jesus himself
clearly rejected similar exhibitions (such as casting himself down
from the temple, turning stones into bread) as temptations of the
devil (Mt. 4; Lk. 4). But such a search for objective evidences involves an implicit rejection of the Christian revelation-claim: that is,
that the criteria for our concept of God are to be *derived* from the
Christ-event. For it is based on the assumption that *we already know
what the marks of deity are*, the only question being whether Jesus
fulfills the requirements. Clearly such a position presupposes another
more fundamental source of knowledge of God (i.e., another "revelation") in terms of which the Christian revelation-claim itself is interpreted and judged.[3] Moreover, this search for and supposed discovery
of quasi-objective historical evidences of the deity of Christ, implying as it does that Jesus had divine powers available to him in his
historical existence, is completely inconsistent with the other central

[3] It might be supposed that it was not until Barth's work that the error in this common inversion of the proper theological order was noticed, but in this as in many other
respects, he was anticipated by some of the much decried "liberals." Cf. E. S. Ames: "It is
common to assume the nature of God, and then to show that Jesus Christ is his son,
but the opposite course may be more historical, more scriptural and more reasonable. The
life of Christ is the given factor in the equation, and from it is to be discovered what
kind of a being God is. To reverse this statement of the problem fills it with all kinds of
impossibilities, for then we demand an explanation of the nature of Christ in terms of the
being of God, when it is the fundamental principle of the Christian religion that the
revelation of God is given through Jesus Christ himself" (*The Divinity of Christ* [Chicago:
Bethany Press, 1911], p. 9).

orthodox claim about Jesus' person, that he was genuinely a man,
participating fully in the situation and plight of his fellows. For no
man has at his disposal legions of angels, and to face life with such
would hardly involve real participation in human trials and suffering.[4]

Since this whole approach, involving the search for and happy
discovery of supposed historical evidences of the "deity" of Christ—
however hallowed it may be for simple piety—is thus destructive of
fundamental tenets of Christian faith, it is theologically untenable.
The claim that here is God incarnate cannot be a statement about
the uniqueness of this man in some observable and obvious sense.
Rather, it should be understood—as it has been when Christian faith
was aware of what it was saying—as a *confession of faith*.[5] To confess the deity of Christ is explicitly and frankly to admit that one's
concept of God is definitively shaped by just these events and not
some others, that this person-event is the norm for the content which
the word "God" has, that here are found the chief analogies and
symbols for understanding ultimate reality. Confession of the deity

---

[4] Much traditional orthodoxy has quite openly, and apparently happily, affirmed this
inconsistent position, thinking it was required by the basic claim that Jesus is to be understood as at once "God" and "man." If my analysis is correct, however, that view is based
on a misunderstanding.

[5] Here I must set myself squarely against a tradition that has been dominant both in
theology and piety until the last century and a half, namely, that Jesus' "mighty works"
make his deity almost visible. Cf., e.g., Athanasius: "For his charging evil spirits, and
their being driven forth, this deed is not of man, but of God. Or who that saw him healing
the diseases to which the human race is subject, can still think him man and not God?
For he cleansed lepers, made lame men to walk, opened the hearing of deaf men, made
blind men to see again, and in a word drove away from men all diseases and infirmities:
from which acts *it was possible even for the most ordinary observer to see his Godhead*"
(*On the Incarnation of the Word*, 18, *Library of Christian Classics*, III [Philadelphia:
Westminster Press, 1954], 72; italics mine). To any historically-conscious modern it must
seem almost incredible that the problems such a position raises for understanding of, e.g.,
the almost universal *rejection* of Jesus by his contemporaries, go almost completely un-
noticed. Indeed, to an increasing number of modern Christians, this traditional christology
badly obscures the central theme of the Gospel, that God is revealed precisely in Jesus' nonresistance to the worldly powers attacking him, in his death, and that Christ's deity, therefore, is to be seen (by faith) precisely in his weakness, not his superhuman powers (see
below, pp. 219ff.). Cf. Bonhoeffer: "Jesus Christ is not in a divine nature, essence, substance or being; thus, he is not in some evident or describable way God, but only so in
faith. Such a divine being does not exist. If Jesus Christ is to be described as God, one
must not speak of this divine being, about his omnipotence and omniscience; on the contrary, one must speak about this weak man among sinners, about his crib and his cross.
When we treat of Jesus' deity, we must speak especially of his weakness" (*Gesammelte
Schriften*, III [München: Kaiser Verlag, 1960], 233).

of Christ, then, is the mark that distinguishes Christian from other faiths; it is not a reference to something perceptible or obvious in Jesus, demonstrable by historical argument or personal experience.

The church has, of course, always in some sense known this, though often her behavior and preaching have belied it. In Matthew's Gospel when Peter first confesses Jesus to be "the Christ, the Son of the living God," Jesus is reported to have said: "flesh and blood has not revealed this to you, but my Father who is in heaven" (16:16–17). That is, the understanding and interpretation of the man Jesus as somehow the presence of God was not an inference based on empirical evidence perceptible during Jesus' career, even as he was known to an intimate friend and disciple like Peter; its source and only possible validation were from beyond everything human, in God himself. What was confessed here was no objective public fact in the ordinary sense. A similar point can be made about the event which in the New Testament is regarded as decisively establishing Jesus as "Son of God in power," namely, "his resurrection from the dead" (Rom. 1:4). The church often seems to think of this as an objective photographable event in which the very power of God became visible to human eyes. Although this is a possible inference from some of the accounts—and is certainly implied in apocryphal stories—the New Testament writers were more sophisticated and careful in what they declared here than is commonly supposed. For example, in Acts it is said that "God raised him on the third day and made him manifest; *not to all the people but to us who were chosen by God as witnesses*" (10:40–41); that is, the resurrection was not a public event at all, but a very peculiar one known only to those within the Christian circle, to faith.[6] Thus, the claim about Christ's deity need not involve paradoxical statements about a man obviously omnipotent and powerless at the same time, one who though omniscient mistakenly supposes the world is soon coming to an end, etc.; the empirical course of human events as viewed by the ordinary objective observer was neither violated nor radically upset by his appearance. Rather, this theological affirmation is an expression of the faith that behind this known man and through him God was (and is) actively at work revealing himself and saving man.

[6] For a full analysis of the problem of the resurrection, see below, Ch. 28.

Perhaps the whole matter can be put like this: *the earliest disciples did not visibly see God in Jesus, thus becoming convinced that Jesus Christ was God; rather, in and through their relations to the man Jesus, they came to a new conviction of the presence and activity of God in their midst, thus becoming convinced that God was somehow present and working in and through this man.* Or, we can put it like this: the doctrines of the incarnation and the deity of Christ are *theories* (as are all doctrines) intended to interpret the central *fact* of which the disciples (and the subsequent church) were convinced, namely, that here *God*—the ultimate limit of our existence and the ultimate reality with which we have to do—is encountered, not merely man. If one were convinced of such a fact, how else might it be interpreted than through such theories as these? From this point of view, given the faith of the church, Christian doctrine about the person of Christ seems both reasonable and appropriate, not absurdly paradoxical. Indeed, to maintain the contrary would be paradox, for it would involve claiming that here God is known to man, yet that which is here is not God.[7]

We must now turn from the problem of the meaning of "deity" in the Christian doctrine of the incarnation to its other focus, that it is just *in this particular man,* Jesus of Nazareth, that God is manifest. This does not mean asserting immediately that in this one person are present two opposite kinds of "nature." Rather, we are simply specifying here the precise point in human history in which the church's faith is rooted. It is important to nail it down so there will be no mistake: just here in the life and death and resurrection of this man Jesus is the basis of the church's convictions about God. This person-event, the climax of a long revelatory history, is to be under-

[7] It seems to me that those, like Kierkegaard, who argue that the incarnation must in the nature of the case be an incomprehensible paradox have failed to grasp the internal consistency of Christian thought, because they have not understood it as a thoroughgoing historicist perspective. If one begins with nonhistoricist Greek assumptions about God as the Absolute, the Unmoved Mover, the impassible One, etc., then of course the Christian claim about God's entrance into history seems nonsense and can be held only as a rationally inconceivable paradox. But if from the beginning the doctrine of God is framed in personal-historical terms and man is seen in his radical historicity—such that the orientation of his very being is understood to be necessarily grounded in a historical event apprehended as the center of history (see above, Ch. 2)—then the christological doctrines are reasonable and indeed rational attempts to think through the ontological implications of Christian faith. Some such doctrines would be indispensable for any ontology that saw reality as ultimately personal-historical.

stood as the historico-ontological ground of the Christian perspective.

We must note what is not asserted here. It is not said that the teachings, or the works, or the ideas of Jesus are God incarnate. That is, God is not identified here with certain particular words or acts or thoughts. Many Christians have made this mistake, understanding Jesus' words and ideas to be God's; then, when it was later discovered that Jesus was mistaken in some of his views, great difficulties were raised for faith. No, the central teaching of the church has been that it is in the historical *personage* Jesus—his total life, death, resurrection—that God's presence is to be found. "The Revelation was the fact of his personal being, rather than the particular acts and words which were always related to the particular circumstances of his acting and speaking."[8] It is the whole man Jesus, so far as historically recoverable, who is the word, that is, the communication of God to man.

What this means concretely we shall consider later. At this point we must note what it implies about the way in which revelation confronts man. Though we always come to know another person through his words and acts, we never understand his particular words and acts simply by themselves but only in the light of what we know of his life and personality as a whole. Words and acts are intentional: they express human purposes. To understand them correctly we must be aware of the intentions they express. But purpose is never directly perceivable; it is always hidden in the heart, and we come to know it only as we come to know the person. Clearly, there is a kind of circle here: we know a person only through his words and acts, but we understand the meanings of his words and acts only by reference to the person. This "hermeneutic circle" (Dilthey) is involved in all interpersonal knowledge. Thus, when one begins to read a book, his understanding of the opening propositions must be held in suspension, as it were, until qualified and confirmed by the fuller grasp of the author's meaning which comes with completing the reading; when one makes a new friend, it is necessary to interpret his words by reference to a tentative image of him, while at the same time one is prepared to reshape that image in light of forthcoming new and es-

---

[8] G. F. Woods, *Theological Explanation* (Welwyn: Nisbet, 1958), p. 150.

pecially revelatory words and acts. We never judge the meaning of particular acts and words without some image of the person as a whole.

With this in mind, let us turn back to the problem of the incarnation. God's self-manifestation, I have suggested, is in the *whole person* Jesus, not simply in his words or acts or ideas. It is true that our records about Jesus are fragmentary, making a biography of him impossible. Yet in and through these reports of particular words and acts a bold outline of the man emerges. It is the historian's task to draw its true features as well as its limits. The claim of the doctrine of the incarnation, now, is that in the *person* revealed in this historical picture God is to be found—or better, in and through this person God reveals himself. It is to this person, this man Jesus, that we must look if we are to come to an understanding of the true God.[9]

[9] It is obvious that the position I am taking here runs head-on into the problem of the relation of the "historical Jesus" to the "Christ of faith" as expressed in the early *kerygma*. For I am contending that the normative revelatory event for Christian faith is *the historical person Jesus*, not simply the image found in the New Testament. However, many biblical scholars claim it is problematic whether much of significance can be reliably recovered about the historical Jesus. Are we then faced with the alternative either of deserting a responsible historical methodology in order to assert by fiat that certain essential facts about Jesus can really be known (the conservative way through the impasse), or of falling back on the New Testament "portrait of Christ" as our standard, eliminating the question whether this portrait has any actual historical referent (the way out suggested by such diverse and weighty thinkers as Barth, Bultmann, and Tillich)? The former way is intellectually irresponsible; the latter, perilously close to gnosticism. I do not think it necessary to accept either alternative. Both rest on a falsely objectivist conception of historical knowledge, according to which the historian is seeking to lay hold of some objective event-in-itself behind all the documents, an event which is what it is quite apart from all interpretations of it. The first alternative says it is possible to do this, therefore we can discover the basic outlines of the person and career of Jesus; the second declares that, in view of the fact that all our reports were written under the transformative impress of the Easter faith, it is not possible to get such an "objective" picture of Jesus. Both views, however—despite the methodological sophistication of some of their advocates—*are determined by a view of historical knowledge as essentially concerned with this recovery of the event-in-itself* as though the latter were waiting somewhere, like a yet undiscovered planet, to be perceived by the eye of the historian.

However (as many of the writers on this difficult problem know), historical reality and historical knowledge are not two distinct types of being, the one simply mirroring the other, as suggested by these images. On the contrary, they interpenetrate each other in a manner and degree unapproached by other forms of knowledge and being. For historical reality never has independent being; an historical object is never out there simply awaiting discovery. *Historical reality exists only in the present, as, on the one hand, vestiges of past events* (which serve as the clues on the basis of which the historian does his work), *and as, on the other hand, living memories and other historical reconstructions in which these fragmentary vestiges are filled out into images and pictures of significance and meaning to living men.* Historical knowledge—indeed, historical reality—more than

We are now in a position to look again at the paradoxical affirmation that Jesus Christ is at once truly God and truly man. Much
criticism of this claim rests on a misunderstanding, perhaps engendered by traditional phrases like "two natures in one person," "God-
man," etc. Confusion arises because we tend to regard such phrases
as expressing (more or less "objective") truths propounded by Christian faith, rather than the fundamental *assumption* of that faith:
that in this man Jesus, *God* has come to man and revealed himself;

---

any other is *relational* in character. There is no such thing as a historical object-in-itself;
there is only the object-in-relation-to-the-historian (as mediated through "historical
evidence"), and it is this object alone that the historian can reconstruct.

We can now see why the dilemma posed above is false. The historian's task can
never be to get back to some Jesus-in-himself, always and forever the same. It can only
be to set forth explicitly and in the round the reality, Jesus, to which the historian is already related through the New Testament documents and images; but precisely because
these documents and images are his *relationship* to the historico-ontological object of
Christian faith, they are not to be confused with that object itself, but must be viewed as
the vehicle through which it is apprehended and reconstructed. This object will never
be the event-in-itself of Jesus, for there is no such reality (and thus the dilemma with
which we began is obviated); it will rather be the historical-event-as-related-to-the-
historian, what Van Harvey has called "the perspectival image of Jesus" (see *The
Historian and the Believer* [New York: Macmillan, 1966], pp. 265ff., for defense of the
historical reliability of this image). If the historian happens to be a believer, this will be
the event through which he believes he has received the very norms of his existence; but
it is quite as much the historical person Jesus with which he is here concerned—to be
uncovered and reconstructed according to the canons and methods of historical knowledge
—whether he is a man of faith or not.

So long as it is possible to say that Jesus existed—and scarcely any responsible
historian would deny this—it is possible in some respects, to some degree, to say *what*
and *who* he was. A bare "that" with no content at all is historically meaningless, and it is
doubtful we can even think it. Only the historian can inform us regarding the precise
limits and character of our knowledge of what and who Jesus was; but, whatever these
may be, that knowledge is the form in which the revelational event is given us, and it is,
therefore, the norm in terms of which even the *kerygmatic* picture of Christ found in the
New Testament records must be judged (cf. Harvey, pp. 275ff.). This does not mean the
historian as such either uncovers or in some way verifies revelation. However, since for
Christian faith God's revelation has come through a particular historical person-event,
the historian's work is required to lay hold of it. Spurning him can lead only to some
construction of gnostic fancy as the focus for faith.

For this reason Christian theology must always have one essential root in historical
knowledge, i.e., knowledge constructed, tested, and refined by the critical methods of the
historian. Any attempt to avoid this implication substitutes a docetic gnosticism for the
radically historical doctrine of the incarnation, and thus destroys the very core of the
Christian Gospel. Paul Althaus has well said: "The historical question must receive a
historical answer. To use the terms of old dogmatic theology, the witness which the Holy
Spirit bears to the truth of the message, cannot extend to a guarantee of its historicity.
To claim the contrary would be fanaticism; it would in fact mean that we were not
holding fast in our theology to the true humanity, the historicity of Jesus, but seeking
to evade the consequent difficulties and distresses to which that humanity exposes us in
our search for certainty" (*Fact and Faith in the Kerygma of Today* [Philadelphia:
Muhlenberg Press, 1959], p. 63).

that in this person-event, then, is not only man but also God. The expression, "Jesus Christ is truly God and truly man," is an articulation of the *faith* that, on the one hand, it is truly God (i.e., ultimate reality) who reveals himself here, and that, on the other hand, it is in this man Jesus (a real historical person) that he makes himself known.[10]

The nonhistorical naturalistic language of Greek philosophy, which was the only precise terminology available to the early Christians (biblical language being dramatic and historical, rather than philosophical, in character), was not fully suited to the problems of the metaphysics of history which arise with such a claim as this. From a modern vantage point where these problems have become clearer, some of the classical formulations (e.g., at Chalcedon) seem much less appropriate than others, since they utilize terminology with such static, nonhistorical implications as only to confuse the already difficult issues. We cannot take space here for full exegesis of the Chalcedonian creed, but the example of two critical passages can be noted.[11] The first is a relatively straightforward statement, the affirmations of which are readily interpretable along the lines suggested in this chapter.

> Following therefore the holy Fathers, we confess one and the same our Lord Jesus Christ, and we all teach harmoniously [that he is] the same perfect in Godhead, the same perfect in manhood, truly God and truly man, the same of a reasonable soul and body; consubstantial with the Father in Godhead, and the same consubstantial with us in manhood, like us in all things except sin . . .

That is, Jesus Christ is the point in history where God is manifest, where, therefore, both God and man are present, and true deity and humanity may be said to coincide.

A few lines beyond this passage, however, an attempt is made to

[10] Cf. Karl Barth: "In distinction from the assertion of the deification of a man or of the humanisation of a divine idea, the statement of the divinity of Christ is to be understood in the sense that Christ reveals . . . God" (*Church Dogmatics*, I, 1 [Edinburgh: T. & T. Clark, 1936], 465).

[11] For the translation followed in both passages, see *Library of Christian Classics*, III, 373.

reinforce this contention and explicate it further with the aid of the technical philosophical notion of "nature." The writers declare Jesus Christ is

> in two natures without confusion, without change, without division, without separation—the difference of the natures being by no means taken away because of the union, but rather the distinctive character of each nature being preserved, and [each] combining in one Person and *hypostasis*—not divided or separated into two Persons, but one and the same Son and only-begotten God, Word, Lord Jesus Christ . . .

Though for the writers this may have seemed clarifying and helpful, it raises many new problems; for now we are presented with the image of two static unchanging realities ("natures") which nevertheless come together and fuse with each other—in itself hardly a consistent, thinkable notion.[12] Moreover, the "two natures" formula tends to obscure the central point, that we are confronted here with two orders of reality so different they must be apprehended through different modes of knowledge or experience; however, when one speaks of two "natures," it sounds as though he were referring to two essentially similar realities, apprehended and confirmed in essentially similar ways. (Thus, one may be led, as noted above, to look for historical evidences of the divine nature as well as of the human.) But, although the humanity of Christ was originally known empirically and directly as with any other human being (and is for us similarly known historically), his "deity" is not apprehensible in this way at all but only in an act of faith. Doubtless, faith takes its object to exist and supposes itself to know something of the character of that object; in this respect the "deity" of Christ is similar to his "humanity." Both are apprehended as objective (i.e., over against the subject) and real. But this should not be expressed as the presence of a divine *nature* alongside a human *nature;* it would be less confusing to speak here of a human nature known empirically (as any other human nature) and *precisely this* being apprehended by

---

12 For a much fuller discussion of these terminological problems, see F. Schleiermacher, *The Christian Faith* (Edinburgh: T. & T. Clark, 1928), §§ 95–97.

faith as vehicle of the divine. For faith the claim about Christ's divinity is ontological and objective: this is really God here. But (as with all metaphysical statements),[13] although objective in reference and taken to be "true," this is a claim which cannot be confirmed outside the community which subscribes to it; it is not an item of empirical knowledge. With the presence of such confusing language, however well-intentioned, in the church's normative christological statement, it is not surprising that subsequent theologies perpetuated and often further confounded the issues so that it became difficult to see the real import of the christological discussions: that here for the first time a serious attempt was being made to grapple with the central problem of the metaphysics of history, the problem of history's "center." We must try to avoid being side-tracked from this issue by the ambiguities of the language in which it was first defined.

In summary of this point: the formal significance for Christian theology of the doctrine of the incarnation is that it specifies the locus in human existence where God's defining revelation and presence are to be found. It is not so much a denial of the validity of other claims to revelation—in the Buddha or Socrates or Gandhi, in Nature or Beauty—as the positive affirmation and confession that the Christian (as distinguished, e.g., from the Buddhist, or the Nature worshiper) looks toward a particular man, Jesus, when he seeks deeper and indeed definitive understanding of God's nature and will. Because the very meaning of existence is thus tied up with this man, he finds it necessary to go beyond the bare statement that here is a man to affirm that in this man God is present to us. I call this the "formal" significance of the doctrine of the incarnation because thus far we have not explored what it implies about the *content* of our conception of God; we have merely noted its significance as a kind of metaphysical pointer to the place in human history where we must look for the answer to that question.

[13] There are similar problems in, e.g., the materialistic claim about the real being matter and the idealistic claim about mind. These are "faith statements" insofar as they make *ontological* claims, empirical statements in the respect in which they refer to that which is open to and known to all (i.e., "matter" or "mind").

13 / The Incarnation of God

III. Servant, Word, and Son

THE doctrine of the incarnation, we have observed, interprets in historico-mythological terms the fact that Christian faith apprehends ultimate reality in terms of the person-event Jesus Christ: God came into history incarnating himself in the man Jesus. The doctrine of the "two natures" of Christ interprets this same claim metaphysically, as the presence in this one person both of God's nature and man's. We need not seek to eliminate or dispense with this mythological and metaphysical language completely, though it might seem a bit quaint or overdramatic; and it will be necessary not to take any of these symbols literally. The advantage of such language, of course, is that it provides us with a wealth of concrete images in terms of which the significance and implications of the Christian claims can impinge upon us with psychological force. In this respect, the abstract language of analysis, though indispensable if we are genuinely to understand what we are talking about, has serious deficiencies. On the one hand, it can never do justice to the concrete reality of a person in the way story-language (whether historical or fictional) can—and Christian faith has a particular person at its center. On the other hand, it does not effectively arouse our specifically human sympathetic and empathetic feelings, as a story can, thus impinging on our emotions and wills with sufficient force to transform our very lives—and Christian faith is concerned with just such capturing of the "whole man" for God. It is necessary, therefore, if we are to come to terms with the Christian faith theologically, that we explore some of the more mythological—and personally concrete—language of the tradition, not to the end of insisting we must "believe" all this to be literally "true" (which it is not), but simply because there is no other way of apprehending the full concrete meaning of the Christian claims.

In our effort to clarify the *transcendence* of God, in the section on God the Father, we saw that it was useful and necessary to analyze and develop the conception with the aid of various concrete human analogies, such as lord, judge, creator, father. These gave some content to the otherwise empty conception of God as radically transcending human experience. How now are we to understand God's definitive presence in a particular locus of human history? What implications for our understanding of God's very being has this central Christian claim? It is clear that symbols or analogies with several special characteristics will be needed here. (a) They will need to be personalistic symbols, in keeping with the personalistic understanding of the ultimate limits of our being (which is central to the Christian claim) and in keeping with the fact that Jesus of Nazareth whom they interpret was a person. (b) They should be drawn from discourse meaningful in our historical situation and to us. (c) They must be symbols with a double reference, illuminating the claim that *the particular man Jesus* is to be understood as the manifestation within history of *the transcendent God*. (d) They must be symbols which allow of an interpretation compatible with the known historical facts of Jesus' career and the origins of Christian faith. Since these analogies are intended to enhance our understanding of the nature of God himself, as seen in the light of the "mighty act" in which he manifested himself definitively in history, they can be regarded as setting forth certain features of the *material* significance of the doctrine of the incarnation.[1]

It is not possible to consider in this connection all the titles applied to Jesus in the New Testament. I shall confine myself to three, all of which have significant meaning in ordinary discourse and in the tradition: Jesus as "servant of God," as "word of God," and as

---

[1] The next chapter, on "The Perfections of the Divine Love," will also be concerned with the material significance of the doctrine of the incarnation for the doctrine of God. Later (esp. Chs. 27-29, 33), we shall consider its material significance for understanding man and history.

"son of God."[2] The first term of this series, "servant of God," clearly affirms Jesus' humanity, though he is a man through whom God's will is done in a special way. Whatever metaphysical conclusions we may finally reach about this person-event, we must not forget that it is the actual historical Jesus, known by other men who lived in Palestine 2000 years ago, of whom we are speaking, not some super-historical—and thus nonhistorical—fantastic being come down from some mythical heaven. It is not surprising that in first-century Palestine, where Jesus was encountered first and preeminently as a man who proclaimed God's word and sought to subject himself to the divine will, the traditional and meaningful notion of God's servant should be appropriated to understand the meaning of his work. The early Christians found, however, that simple titles of this sort were not adequate to say all they felt had to be said. For Jesus was a man through whom, as they were convinced, God himself came to them; and hence they eventually came to speak of him as God's very "word" and even his "son,"[3] not merely his "servant." It is the developing structure of meaning in this series of analogies that we must now explore.[4]

Since in a previous chapter we examined the concept "lord," it

[2] Later we shall have occasion to explicate the titles, "second Adam" (pp. 408f.), and also "prophet," "priest," and "king" (Ch. 33). Perhaps a word of explanation for the omission of what is probably the preeminent title in the New Testament, "Christ" (or "Messiah"), is in order, especially since Paul Tillich has reminded us that the central Christian claim is precisely that Jesus is the Christ (see *Systematic Theology*, esp. Vol. II [Chicago: University of Chicago Press, 1957]). The principal difficulty with this term as a contemporary symbol, of course, is that it is not drawn from discourse directly meaningful to modern men but is a technical term presupposing the Jewish first-century context in which it was first applied to Jesus. The difficulties and inappropriateness of the word outside that context were already apparent to the first-century Christian evangelists to the Gentiles. Thus, in Paul, for example, "Christ" is no longer a special title explicating Jesus' peculiar character and role; it has become a proper name which can be substituted for or used in conjunction with "Jesus" (though it has a somewhat wider connotation than the latter). In our own day, to attempt to use "Christ" as explicatory of the meaning of Jesus, would be, on the one hand, to adopt the position of the "circumcision party" (cf. Gal.) that one must become a Jew in certain respects before one can become a Christian, and, on the other hand, to forget the hermeneutical rule that all interpretation must proceed from the familiar to the unfamiliar, not vice versa (see above, p. 171).

[3] The original meaning of "son" was not very different from "servant"; however, it later came to have much greater metaphysical import (see below, pp. 201ff.).

[4] Although in the present discussion we shall attempt to see a "movement" or "development" of meaning as we proceed from one analogue to the next in the series, this is not meant to suggest that the particular sequential order which has been adopted is that

is not necessary here to give a detailed exposition of the meaning of
"servant"; the latter is drawn from the same human relationship as
the former. A servant or slave is one who obeys the lord's commands.
As one who fulfills the will of another, he is *himself under lordship,*
and he is also the *instrument through which the lordship of the other
is exercised* over other persons and things. It is important to note
that no mere *thing* could be a servant; the term applies properly and
directly only to a human being in a particular kind of relationship
to another. A servant is never simply a puppet manipulated by his
master: in some sense he freely submits to the will of his lord and to
the exercise of lordship over himself. Of course, in most actual
servitude there is a strong element of compulsion involved, usually of
an economic or political or socio-psychological sort. But it is not
compulsion *per se* which defines the servant-lord relationship: it is
rather *submission of will;* for it is also possible *freely* to become the
servant of another.

The disciples remembered Jesus as one who thus freely took up
the role of servant. "I am among you as one who serves" (Lk.
22:27); "the Son of man came not to be served but to serve, and to
give his life as a ransom for many" (Mt. 20:28). For Jesus it was
precisely service that defined greatness in God's kingdom (Mk.
10:35–45). Jesus, then, was remembered as one who freely and
willingly gave up his own wishes and desires to serve God's will; he
was one who sacrificed everything that was Jesus (i.e., finite, individual, particular) to the absolute demands of God upon him (Tillich). And thus, through making himself a servant in the first sense,
through standing under God's lordship, he became also a servant in
the second sense: he became the instrument of the divine will among
men, and *through him* God's will was done. Not only did he proclaim
God's word about the coming kingdom (Mk. 1:15); he acted to re-

---

which actually occurred historically: we do not have the historical evidence necessary to
evaluate or establish such a hypothesis. The order here is a logical movement, beginning
with the simplest notion and that most obviously near to the historical actualities and
moving to the more complex metaphysical-mythological structures of meaning. Our concern here, as with the discussion of the analogies used to explicate the transcendence of
God, will be to see how each of these analogues sets forth something essential to our
knowledge of the meaning of Jesus Christ—and hence of God.

lease men from the power of Satan, casting out demons as though with the very "finger of God" (Lk. 11:20). Thus, he was the agent through whom the kingdom of God itself had "come upon" those around him (Lk. 11:20). To say Jesus was the servant of God in a preeminent sense—and this is what it means to call him the "Messiah" or "Christ," and is also the original sense of the title "son of God"[5]—is to declare that here a piece of finite reality, a man, has become transparent, as it were, so that when we look at him we no longer see simply him and his will; we see the *divine will* and the *divine being* whose will is carried out through his acts.[6] Moreover, this "transparency" is not something foisted upon him from without, God forcing him to become a servant, predestining or determining him in such a way that he has no significant choice in the matter. Rather, Jesus himself freely wills to be God's servant. *He could in fact have decided otherwise*—certainly the temptation stories (Mt. 4:1–11, Lk. 4:1–13) and the final struggle in Gethsemane (Mk. 14:32–42) must signify at least this. But, though it involved a personal struggle to do so, he deliberately chose to align his will with God's. Since it was in the concluding days, and even hours, of Jesus' life that his supreme resolve to subordinate his own wishes and desires to God's will was most clearly apparent to his disciples, the passion story became the center and criterion of their memories of him: here he displayed most clearly who he was; here he was most of all himself.[7] ". . . nevertheless not what I will, but what thou wilt" (Mk. 14:36 KJ). Jesus was freely the servant of God.

[5] See, e.g., C. T. Craig, *The Beginning of Christianity* (New York: Abingdon-Cokesbury, 1943), pp. 205f.

[6] Cf. Tillich, *Systematic Theology*, I, 132–137.

[7] Cf. Hans Frei: "A man . . . *is* what he *does* uniquely, the way no one else does it. It may be that this is action over a lifetime, or at some climactic moment, or both. When we see something of that sort, especially if we see it at some climactic stage which recapitulates a long span in a man's life—when we see the loyalty of a lifetime consummated at one particular point, but even if we see several hitherto ambiguous strands in his character pruned and ordered in a clear and decisive way at that point—then we are apt to say: 'Here he was most of all himself.' . . . Jesus, in this portrayal [in the Gospels], was most of all himself in the short and climactic sequence of his public ministry, rising to this resolve and this entry into the situation of helplessness. We must, above all, not abstract one from the other: as if, in the New Testament, the event of the crucifixion were anything without Jesus' resolve, or the resolve anything without the event in which it took concrete shape! . . . This was his identity. He was what he did and underwent: the crucified human savior" ("Theological Reflections on the Accounts of

This christology has obvious power and appeal, for it appears to make comprehensible the way in which the divine becomes an effective force within human history. Through the subordination of human will to the divine will, God's purposes are carried out within human existence.[8] And since this subordination is a free act of the finite person involved, uncompelled by supernatural power from above, God's immanence and effectiveness within the historical process is achieved without violation of human personality or destruction of man's responsibility for his own action. Moreover, if men are understood as essentially purposive will, as radically historical, as having their very *being* in their *action* (see below, Chapter 23), acts of personal cooperation, in which one person's purpose is carried to completion in another's act, can be regarded as not only harmonious but as in a sense *metaphysically one*. Thus, this analogy of the servant also suggests a way to understand the metaphysical claim about the unity of God and Christ.[9]

The position we are here considering becomes technically developed in the so-called adoptionist christology. According to this view, Jesus was a good man who desired above all to do the divine will, thus making himself plastic to God's purposes for him. Because of this, God "chose" or "adopted" him as his special "servant" ("son")

Jesus' Death and Resurrection," *The Christian Scholar* [1966], 49:273). Helmut Koester has concluded that precisely in using the historical suffering and death of Jesus as the criterion of faith the canonical Gospels are distinguished from the noncanonical early Christian materials, and for just this reason they became normative for Christian faith. "The only point of departure from which the earthly Jesus—at least in the Gospel of Mark—becomes the criterion of faith is his suffering and death. All other traditions of Jesus' words and deeds are legitimate not because they preserve the exact memory of Jesus' life, but because they serve as parts of a theological introduction to the proclamation of Jesus' passion and death. In this way, the church in the canonical Gospel tradition remains subject to an earthly, human, 'real,' and historical revelation which sets the terms for the interpretation of the tradition." ("One Jesus and Four Primitive Gospels," *Harvard Theological Review* [1968], 61:207.)

[8] Cf. Paul: "I worked harder than any of them, though it was not I, but the grace of God which is with me" (1 Cor. 15:10); "work out your own salvation with fear and trembling; for God is at work in you, both to will and to work for his good pleasure" (Phil. 2:12–13); "I live; yet not I, but Christ liveth in me" (Gal. 2:20 KJ).

[9] In certain respects the potential fruitfulness of conducting the christological analysis in terms of the metaphysical significance of will was already discerned during the monothelete controversy in the seventh century. (For discussion, see R. Seeberg, *Textbook of the History of Doctrines* [Grand Rapids, Michigan: Baker Book House, 1952], I, 279ff.).

through whom the kingdom would be inaugurated on earth. It is quite possible that the earliest christology was of this sort, though there is some disagreement in the pertinent texts as to whether the adoption occurred at the beginning or the end of Jesus' public ministry.[10]

If God thus "chose" Jesus as the proper one to carry through his will in definitive fashion, we must ask what this signifies for the understanding of God himself. What is the significance of God's choosing a servant-figure rather than a lord or prince among men? Of what importance is it that precisely a servant-figure becomes viewed as "metaphysically one" with God? If Jesus as *servant* is a paradigmatic image in terms of which God's being is understood, then God also must be characterizable in some sense as servant, indeed as a servant of men. The conception of God as the Lord of the world will need to be qualified and corrected by the understanding that he is simultaneously the world's Servant, One who sacrifices that the needs of others might be met.

But such far-reaching implications do not come fully clear in the motifs of adoptionism and the servant of God, taken simply by themselves. Insofar as the servant is seen merely as the Lord's instrument, it is not at all clear why he should be regarded as simultaneously—and in precisely his role as servant—the revelation of the

---

[10] In Paul's letter to the Romans it is stated that Jesus was "designated Son of God in power" at the resurrection (1:4). Mark, on the other hand, suggests Jesus' baptism was the crucial moment (1:10–11). This is also apparently the view of some manuscripts of Luke in which the voice from heaven says: "Thou art my beloved Son; today I have begotten thee" (3:22 RSV footnote). The whole of the Lukan tradition, in fact, is subordinationist, Jesus being regarded throughout as a man chosen by God to carry out his will and there being no question of metaphysical equality or oneness of God and Christ. "It is taken for granted in the [Lukan] tradition that God the Father has a position of superiority. . . . Only He appears as Creator. . . . There is no mention of the co-operation of a pre-existent 'Son', for the idea of pre-existence is completely lacking— an aspect of Luke's subordinationism. The plan of salvation is exclusively God's plan . . . and Jesus' function within it is that of an instrument. . . . The part played by Jesus in redemptive history and his status have no metaphysical basis, but are entirely the gift of God. God proclaimed or 'anointed' him as Son at the Baptism. . . . All the three principal Christological titles, Christ, Lord and Son, signify in this respect the same facts. Whichever of them is used to express Jesus' position, his office appears as something conferred on him by God. . . . The motif of Jesus at prayer . . . also indicates his subordinate position. . . . The raising of Jesus from the dead is clearly not characterized as a 'resurrection', but as an act of 'being raised'. . . . There is no systematic consideration of the ontological relationship of Father and Son. We find a clear subordinationism. . . . Jesus is the instrument of God, who alone determines the plan of salvation" (Hans Conzelmann, *The Theology of Saint Luke* [New York: Harper & Brothers, 1960], pp. 173–175, 184).

Lord's nature and will: to justify such a claim it is necessary to develop further characterizations of Jesus, for example, that he is God's *word*. Furthermore, to the extent that adoptionism emphasizes Jesus' freely becoming God's servant, it raises serious questions about the reality of God's sovereign power. The very emphasis on human freedom which makes the position attractive and meaningful also implies that everything depends, after all, on Jesus' decisions. Despite all that is said about Jesus doing God's will, and thus God working through him, God's agency here depends so much on man's cooperation that it becomes problematical whether he in fact remains Lord in the situation. The motif of the adopted servant of God portrays too simply and undialectically the way in which God's will is accomplished through Jesus' servanthood. Moreover, it fails to clarify the uniqueness of Jesus as the definitive revelation of God, for many men have been God's servants. Taken by itself, therefore, it does not adequately interpret the central Christian claim.

These difficulties are corrected in another New Testament symbol. Particularly in the Fourth Gospel Jesus is interpreted as the "word" of God. "Word" is a symbol drawn from human communication. A word is the vehicle through which a speaker expresses his meaning both to others and himself; it is an externalization of what is within, a making sensible of what is otherwise hidden. Since through communication we participate in each other's being, coming to understand and know each other, it is language (the word) that in many respects both creates community and holds it together. Even the word of hatred, so far as it is understood, helps reinforce the community of understanding. Only complete silence, the refusal to speak a word, utterly breaks community, and in so doing breaks selves. Words are food without which selves cannot live. The symbol "word" is thus drawn from that which makes existence characteristically human.

When Jesus is called the "word" of God, all these dimensions of meaning are present. Jesus is being proclaimed the vehicle of God's communication to man. As the spoken word is the means through which I make known to you what I am thinking, so Jesus is the means through which God "externalizes" his inward being for us, communicating himself to us and establishing community with us. This symbol, thus, suggests that Jesus is the concrete link between God and man, as the noise made with vocal cords and lips is link between man and man. As the bond which holds God and man in communication and community, he is the life and light which make authentic human existence possible (John 1:4–5).

It is important to realize the far-reaching claims being made here. If calling Jesus "servant of God" focuses too much on the character and decisions of a mere man, claiming he is God's "word" goes to the other extreme. For it emphasizes that what he is and does is an expression not primarily of his personal freedom but rather of God's purpose and act. Indeed, he appears to be not so much a reality in his own right as an externalization of God's inwardness, "the image of the invisible God" (Col. 1:15); he is the link whereby God binds man to himself in community of meaning and being.

We may miss some of the ramifications of the claim that Jesus is the word of God because our English term, "word," does not carry the full complex meaning of the Greek term, *logos*, which it translates. There were two traditions which gave that term its rich content. The one was Greek, where the term had come to comprehend all rationality, order, meaning, wisdom, justice—the very essence of all philosophy.[11] The second was Jewish, which understood God's word as his active power in the world.[12] Both traditions contributed when

[11] Although *logos* apparently originally meant simply the "spoken word" or "noise," and then the "meaning" or "idea" associated with that noise (two dimensions present also in our own term "word"), it very early became important in Greek philosophy, where it came to designate not simply semantic meaning but the universal meaning or structure of reality as such: the *logos* was that in reality which could be grasped by reason and which made being knowable. As early as Heraclitus (c. 500 B.C.) the term was used in this sense to indicate the very structure of the world, the pattern of the great cycle of change which Heraclitus thought characterized the world order. The stoics (last three centuries B.C.) took over Heraclitus' meaning and developed it further, maintaining that the good was also to be understood as comprehended within the *logos*. For those trained in Greek philosophy the term thus had a very broad and weighty meaning, and while not all the technical aspects of this meaning were present in popular usage, it inevitably carried with it such nuances.

[12] In the Septuagint *logos* had been used to translate the Hebrew *dabar*. The latter term designates the spoken word, carrying with it power: in Genesis when God speaks his word, "Let there be light," light is brought into being (1:3). Similarly, when a prophet ·speaking the word of the Lord announces destruction, the evil is bound to come; for the word itself carries power to accomplish its end (cf. Hos. 6:5; Isa. 55:10–11). It is this same conception of the power of the word that makes a curse such a terrible and unalterable thing and a blessing so desirable (cf. Gen. 27). God's word, then, is not only the expression of his "ideas"; it is the active *power of God* at work in the universe.

Jesus was identified with the *logos*. On the one hand, he was seen as the fulfilment of all human aspirations after perfect wisdom and rationality, justice and goodness. This implied, conversely, that whenever and wherever wisdom, justice, and rationality were found, Jesus Christ himself was in some sense present; so all science, philosophy, art—in short all human culture, insofar as it truly was what it ought to be—were expressions of the presence of Christ. On the other hand, as *God's logos*, Jesus was seen as the expression of God's own being, of his inner essence. Thus, he was as universal and powerful as God himself, and wherever God was active—which is everywhere —there also was his *logos*, Jesus Christ. Though perhaps not all these implications were present explicitly to the author of the Fourth Gospel,[13] they were certainly not far from his mind, as the opening words of the prologue make clear:

> In the beginning was the *logos*, and the *logos* was with God, *and the logos was God*. He was in the beginning with God; *all things were made through him*, and without him was not anything made that was made. *In him was life, and the life was the light of men.* . . . And the *logos* became flesh and dwelt among us, full of grace and truth.
>
> JOHN 1:1-4, 14

Very far-reaching claims indeed were being made when Jesus was called the "word of God." No mere human "servant of God," he was here seen as the very link between God and all creation (including

[13] These two traditions giving meaning to *logos*, Jewish and Greek, had already been brought together before John's time by Philo of Alexandria (early first century), who conceived his lifework as relating Greek philosophy and Hebrew prophecy. The great bridge-concept with which he attempted this was precisely *logos*. Thus, for Philo *logos* indicated both the very essence of all philosophy (Greek conceptions) and also the word and wisdom of God—the external expression of the inner essence of God's being, God himself active in the world (Jewish ideas). In this way all man's scientific and philosophic thought, his moral and ethical ideals, his understanding of beauty, truth, and goodness, could be regarded as in varying degrees expressions of the *logos* of God, the mind of God. And the *logos* itself was in a sense God, at any rate the presence of God among men; Philo could call it a "second God"—i.e., secondary in status because still only an expression of God—and yet, as it were, that side of God which we see and experience in all that is meaningful and valuable and rational in human culture. (For discussion, see E. R. Goodenough, *An Introduction to Philo Judaeus* [New Haven: Yale University Press, 1940], pp. 130ff.; H. A. Wolfson, *Philo* [Cambridge: Harvard University Press, 1947], Vol. I, Ch. 4.)

man), that which (from God's side) should be regarded as God's innermost being made external, that which (from man's side) comprehends all that gives life its meaning and worthfulness. This "assertion that the incarnation of the Logos had taken place," as Harnack put it, "gave a metaphysical significance to an historical fact. . . ."[14] Jesus was the point where ultimate reality had become "visible" within human experience and in a special way active in history. If he were not in some real sense the *logos*—with all the richness of meaning that Greek thought had invested in that notion— how could he be the revelation of the universal God, the fullness of whose creation spills over into such multifarious dimensions of nature and culture that only the entirety of history can contain them? How could he be regarded as the definitive manifestation of the actuality which transforms and saves all human existence and history? Only the *word of God* could give life the fulfilment God intended for it.

However, the further one pushes this argument, the more serious become the problems. For how is this "*logos* of God" to be understood as the same as the human "servant of God," Jesus of Nazareth? How can this cosmic reality be identified with a mere human being? How is the meaning of all life and history to be conceived as somehow centered in this one event in an obscure part of the Roman Empire? The Christian claims about Jesus seem suddenly to have become so extravagant as to be incomprehensible and even ludicrous. We can understand in a way the abstract notion of the *logos* of God, in its implication that all that is meaningful and good in human culture is the presence of God's word; but how are we to understand this as identical with the person of Jesus, a man who freely was what he was in a long-gone period of history?

It will be necessary to set out the full historicist interpretation of human existence and history (Parts Three, Four) before it is possible to deal more fully with these questions (the earlier analysis of revelation indicating my basic views on the matter). For now we must note the significance of the juxtaposition of the two titles for Jesus we have examined: the "word of God" (the meaning of life) is not, in the Christian view, to be found in a set of abstract concepts or structure

14 *What is Christianity?* (New York: Harper Torchbooks, 1957), p. 204.

of values (as the Greeks, and all subsequent intellectuals, have tended to think), but in a *personal life*—in that one properly designated as the "servant of God"; or conversely, that one who in his own freedom was the perfectly obedient servant of God is to be regarded the paradigmatic image of ultimate reality and the very meaning of all human existence, God's word.[15]

The title "son of God," the loftiest of all, interprets the Christian claim in the most decisive and consequential terms. It must be recognized, of course, that the original meaning of this title in the Jewish context was little different from "servant of God." David, Solomon, all Israel, were designated sons of God in the Old Testament.[16] Anyone who was obedient to the divine will was a son of God; thus the Messiah, the agent through whom God's kingdom would finally be established, would be the son of God preeminently. However, in early Hellenistic Christian piety and thought the term came to mean much more than this: it designated the unique relationship between Jesus Christ and God, a relationship not shared by anything else.[17]

The christology of the "son of God" is higher than that implied in the title "word of God." For a word, after all, however effective it may be as a vehicle of spirit in communication, is a *creation* of spirit, not identical with it. However indispensable it may be to persons, it remains something *used* by them for extrinsic ends; it has no will or freedom or purposes of its own. To call Jesus the "word of God," then, did not quite express the full meaning of the Christian conviction that *in him God himself is encountered.* Here is not merely the

[15] It will be clear by now that I am in agreement with Tillich's view that "both the incarnational and the adoptionist Christologies have biblical roots and, for this and other reasons, a genuine standing in Christian thought. . . . neither of them can be carried out without the other. Adoptionism, the idea that God through his Spirit adopted the man Jesus as his Messiah, leads to the question: Why just him? And this question leads back to the polarity of freedom and destiny which created the uninterrupted unity between him and God. . . . The incarnational Christology was needed to explain the adoptionist Christology. . . . But it is equally necessary—although not always seen—that incarnational Christology needs adoptionist Christology for its fulfilment. . . . The Incarnation of the Logos is not metamorphosis but his total manifestation in a personal life. But manifestation in a personal life is a dynamic process involving tensions, risks, dangers, and determination by freedom as well as by destiny. This is the adoption side, without which the Incarnation accent would make unreal the living picture of the Christ. He would be deprived of his finite freedom" (*Systematic Theology*, II, 148–149).

[16] Cf Ex. 4:22f; 2 Sam. 7:14; 1 Chr. 17:13, 22:10; Hos. 11:1; etc.

[17] Cf. John 3:16, 18; Heb. 1:2, 8; Mt. 11:27; Rom. 8:3; etc.

externalization of the divine inwardness, God's word; it is God's very being, God's own freedom and love, that is met. Though, as in human conversation, these might be conveyed through words, speech without full personal presence always remains ambiguous and not fully trustworthy. The Christian conviction was that Christ was no mere message from God, but God's own presence among men. To express this meaning the symbol "son of God" seemed most appropriate.

Once more we are confronted with an analogy drawn from ordinary human experience, the parent-child relation grounded in the act of procreation. The special significance of this relation can be seen if we contrast it with creation (or making). Men have two ways of bringing into existence what did not exist before. (a) They can create or make a reality, as the carpenter makes a table or the painter creates a work of art; in this case reality of a different order from man's own being is brought into existence. (As we have noted, this analogy is utilized to interpret the relation of God to the world.) (b) Men can reproduce their own kind through procreating children. Here the spirit of the parents, indeed the human spirit as such, is present in the new reality in a way not true of the things men make. The child is a living and free spirit like the parent, and can eventually become a creator in his own right; no created things can ever be or do this. The parent and the child are thus of the same essence (*homoousia*) in a way that man and his creations can never be. The son is a second instance of the father himself.

In the light of this contrast we can understand what it means to call Jesus the "son of God." Unlike the rest of mankind—which is to be understood as simply God's creation—here God himself is present in human existence in a special and decisive way. This is where the Creator of heaven and earth is to be met and known; here the ultimate limit of our being is encountered as personal and loving.

When Jesus is spoken of as God's son, however, no act of generation like that connected with human sonship is intended: this symbol does not *explain* Jesus' significance; it *expresses* it. There are not two personalities in the Godhead, separate and distinct as human father and son, though related to each other through genes. "Son of God" is an image which expresses concretely the Christian claim that (a) there is *identity of being* between God (the Father) and what is encountered in Jesus ("I and the Father are one," John 10:30); (b) this one being is known, however, in *two loci* (i.e., in history, and transcending all history); and (c) the *manifestation in history is grounded in God's transcendent reality* (i.e., that the son "came from the Father . . . into the world," John 16:28). The symbol "son of God" thus expresses with sharpness and lucidity the central Christian claim that in this historical person the transcendent God is to be encountered, and it provides a vivid and suggestive analogy for grasping the character and possibility of this unique presence.

A symbol of this sort, however, especially when taken too literally, can easily become very misleading. If, for example, it is treated as an *explanation why* Jesus has the significance he does rather than simply an *expression of* that significance, it may spawn and reinforce fantastic mythological notions. When linked with the doctrine of the so-called virgin birth, something of this sort occurs. This latter doctrine also intends to affirm that it is God himself who is here in this man, truly and actually present in his very being. However, it says this crudely, offering a quasi-explanatory account of the matter. Thus, it interprets the relation of Jesus to God as almost literally the same as that of human son and father, namely, as *genetic and physiological*, as a *biological fact* about Jesus' physical being rather than a *spiritual fact* about his person. In so doing (though this is not intended) it turns Jesus into a kind of demigod—half-human, half-divine. Just as the demigod of Greek mythology (well known to first-century men) was conceived when an Olympian had intercourse with a woman, so with Mary: Jesus "is conceived in her . . . of the Holy Spirit" (Mt. 1:20; cf. Lk. 1:35). Thus, instead of expressing the central claim of Christian faith, this sort of imagery actually threatens it. It does not portray Jesus as either truly God or truly man: he is apparently half and half. A kind of pasted-together being, he not unreasonably is taken by many moderns to be simply a piece of fantastic and incredible mythology, rather than the one point within human history which is a genuine clue to ultimate reality, the very *man* who is the revelation of the very *God*. Though one may applaud the intent of the doctrine of the virgin birth to express God's coming into man's history, its crude form should be rejected on both theological and historical grounds.[18] It is important to make this clear lest the meaning of designating Jesus as "son of God"—namely, that in him the very being and love and presence of God are present to man—be grossly misunderstood.

The doctrine of the preexistence of Christ (Jesus), a mythological conception that appears in connection with all three of the titles here

[18] It is not always recognized that the historical evidence in the Bible itself is heavily against the claims of the doctrine. (a) It is nowhere mentioned or even implied by the earliest Christian traditions extant, those found in the writings of Paul and the Gospel of Mark. Paul can even be regarded as giving direct evidence against the claim. In one place he explicitly declares his belief that Jesus "was descended from David according to the flesh" (Rom. 1:3), and since physical descent was always reckoned through the father by first-century Jews, this implies he thought Jesus to have a human father. Mark, apparently holding a proto-adoptionist christology (see above, pp. 195ff.), regards "the beginning of the gospel of Jesus Christ" (1:1) as occurring with Jesus' baptism (Ch. 1), not his birth or conception (as do Matthew and Luke). Moreover, he allows his characters to address Jesus as "son of David" without any correction (e.g., 10:47f.). This is intended christologically, of course, but it rests on a physiological presupposition. (b) Though the doctrine may have been widely accepted by the time the Fourth Gospel was written, John either knew nothing of it or explicitly rejected its crudity; indeed, like Paul, he can be interpreted as rejecting the claim. In 1:45 he makes Philip identify Jesus directly as "the son of Joseph." In 6:42 he portrays "the Jews" as belittling Jesus' ancestry by pointing out he is merely "the son of Joseph," both his "father and mother" being known to all; moreover John in no way seeks to correct this implication by a defensive statement in behalf of Jesus' supernatural lineage, as might be expected in the context. Clearly, he regards Jesus' true character to be more adequately indicated by the conception of the word made flesh (1:14), than by the quasi-biological explanation suggested by the doctrine of the virgin birth. (c) The only two places in the New Testament where the claim is mentioned, the birth stories of Matthew and Luke, are highly unreliable in many other respects where they can be easily checked, giving us little confidence to accept them as veridical on such an extraordinary report. (E.g., the genealogical tables of Matthew and Luke fail to agree at many points; they hold different views of why Jesus was born in Bethlehem but was nevertheless a citizen of Nazareth; 6 A.D., the date of Quirinius' census [Lk. 2:2], cannot be made to square with the view of both Matthew [2:1] and Luke [1:5] that Herod was at that time king of Judea, since he died in 4 B.C.; etc.) Moreover, the very existence of the genealogical tables, both of which trace Jesus' lineage through Joseph, is in direct contradiction with the claim he had no human father; in some of the early Matthean manuscripts Joseph is directly identified as "the father of Jesus who is called Christ" (1:16, RSV footnote). Furthermore, neither Matthew nor Luke mentions or implies the virgin birth in any other place. (d) Mary, the mother of Jesus, is of course the only historical witness who could give evidence on this phenomenon; but the scanty evidence we have of her early attitude toward Jesus hardly suggests she stood in great wonder or awe, occasioned by his miraculous conception: during Jesus' ministry she and the rest of his family appear to have been embarrassed by him, even regarding him as possibly insane (Mk. 3:21, 31ff.). Thus, the preponderance of historical evidence which the Bible itself contains on this question is against the traditional claims, only the birth stories in Matthew and Luke favoring them.

under consideration,[19] may lead to similar sorts of misunderstanding. From the point of view developed here, the real significance of this doctrine is its underlining in yet another way that it is *God* with whom we have to do in Jesus. This is done by emphasizing (somewhat misleadingly) that what is important about this person-event is not simply the peculiarities and uniqueness of this particular human being who appeared in approximately 4 B.C. on the historical scene, but that through him we encounter the everlasting God—the one who existed from all eternity, and thus the one who preexists this Jesus of Nazareth and, indeed, all of creation as its ultimate limit (". . . before Abraham was, I am," John 8:58). However, if this symbol—susceptible of interpretations quite as misleading as the virgin birth, and often, though inconsistently, by the same people— is interpreted to mean that the man Jesus somehow existed from all eternity, thus preexisting his own conception and birth, we are confronted both with logical nonsense[20] and with the theological error of *docetism* (see below).

The symbols "servant of God," "word of God," and "son of God" present three different analogies in terms of which God's presence to man in the historical man Jesus can be expressed. Each contributes a distinct and important element to the conception: "servant" emphasizes that this is a real human being who in his freedom becomes obedient to the divine will; "word" indicates that in and through this free person God himself is active, communicating with man, making himself known as the authentic meaning or *logos* of human existence; "son" concludes that this communication of God is in fact the presence of God himself. Each of these symbols thus points to a different but indispensable side of the central theological claim: that since in Christian faith the man Jesus is apprehended as the definitive clue for understanding the ultimate limit of our being, in his personal

---

[19] Thus, in Philippians "Christ Jesus" is apparently a heavenly being who in the course of time "emptied himself, taking the form of a servant, being born in the likeness of men" (2:7). In the Fourth Gospel "the Word" which was "in the beginning with God" and the very agent of creation (1:1–3) later "became flesh and dwelt among us" (1:14). In Hebrews and elsewhere the "Son, whom he [God] appointed the heir of all things, through whom also he created the world," came to man to speak to him "in these last days" (1:2).

[20] Cf. Barth: ". . . the man Jesus already was even before He was." (*Church Dogmatics*, III, 2 [Edinburgh: T. & T. Clark, 1960], 464.)

being—at once truly free and truly obedient to God—the very being of the transcendent God is present in and to human history.

The claim here being made can be defined in another way through consideration of the two major christological heresies which stand as limiting notions at the boundaries of the orthodox Christian view, ebionitism and docetism.[21] Docetism (from a Greek word meaning "appearance") is any position that holds, explicitly or implicitly, that Jesus is not truly a man but only "appears" to be one. It was a position subscribed to by early gnostic Christians and others. On this view, God, as it were, masqueraded as a man in Jesus—bringing us divine truth but not genuinely suffering the severe limitations of finite human existence. In some of the early gnostic interpretations it was believed that the heavenly Christ descended upon the man Jesus in the form of a dove at his baptism (cf. Lk. 3:22) but departed again just before his crucifixion; in others, Jesus was apparently thought of as a kind of ghost, visible to our senses but not a full-bodied human being.[22]

Few, if any, subscribe explicitly any more to these early docetic doctrines of a walking mirage. Nevertheless, there is still much docetism in Christian circles, few christologies taking with genuine seriousness the proposition that Jesus was a man like others, suffering the same limitations and problems; in subtle and supposedly pious ways, believers nearly always withdraw Jesus from full participation in the human condition. Though supposing they thereby do him homage, in fact they undercut the heart of the Christian claim that God has actually overcome all barriers, coming to men in their misery and disobedience. In addition, in this way they substitute for the one firm point in human experience to which a modern might anchor his faith—the Jesus who lived and died as an actual man in history—a fantastical mythological demigod whose reality must always remain in doubt. But Jesus was no god walking the earth; he

---

[21] F. Schleiermacher proposed utilizing certain of the significant historical heresies as aids to defining the heart of Christian faith, suggesting specifically that ebionitism and docetism are the "natural" christological heresies (see *The Christian Faith* [Edinburgh: T. & T. Clark, 1928], § 22).

[22] For discussion, see R. M. Grant, *Gnosticism and Early Christianity* (New York: Columbia University Press, 1959).

was a man, in many respects a son of his own time, as limited in knowledge and power as are we (cf. above, pp. 172ff.).

The opposite heresy is ebionitism (from the early "Ebionites," who believed Jesus to be simply a great prophet). Much of liberal protestantism and humanism has subscribed to this view: Jesus was doubtless a good man, perhaps the greatest who ever lived; as such he is an inspiring example and his ethical teachings have never been surpassed, but that God was somehow actually present here in definitive fashion must be denied as both absurd and narrow-minded. Ebionitism is of two sorts. It may arise out of theological dullness and ignorance, an unwillingness or failure to realize what is implied about Jesus' relation to ultimate reality if one regards him as the "ideal man," a failure to see that if genuine *healing* comes through Jesus, this can be only because a new relation with the source and ground of our being has been opened up by him. Much liberal ebionitism is due to such failure to think through clearly the christology implicit in the faith of liberal protestantism; it is not seen that from "servant of God" it is necessary and proper to move on to the symbols of "word" and "son." Ebionitism may, however, be more virulent than this and explicitly deny the central Christian claim that the life and death of this man Jesus are the definitive clue to the ultimate limit of our being, thus decisively undercutting the perspective on human existence characteristic of Christian faith. When it takes this form, it is no longer simply a Christian heresy, but has become an outright rejection of the Christian claims.

Such rejection is often due to the crude or archaic way in which the Christian position itself has been presented. The "presence to us of God" in Jesus should not be interpreted as the presence of some special *quality* or *thing*—a divine "nature" in Jesus (or the church); it is rather the presence of a *word* that communicates to man, that is, the presence of the *meaning* of existence, the *logos*. It is, moreover, that meaning it terms of which men become at once free beings and obedient to God's will. The salvation which comes through this historical person (as we shall see in Part Three) is thus no mere memory of some dim and dead irrelevant past; it is the coming to life of man's *true past*—that is, the true origins of his being—and thus it is the possibility and indeed the actuality of authentic existence for man in the present and future. Our analysis to this point leaves these statements mere affirmations; their comprehensibility and credibility cannot be shown until we have had opportunity to explore man's nature and plight.

Since the three titles we have examined in this chapter ("servant," "word," "son") communicate and illuminate the Christian claim that in the man Jesus God himself is present in and to human existence, they also imply more: namely, something about the nature of that God who is here present. Inasmuch as it is in and through a servant, a word, a son, that Christians come to know the transcendent God, this God himself is known to them in terms of precisely these analogies. He is not only the Lord and Creator of the universe and all within it; he is also the Servant, one who gives himself up for others, one who freely sacrifices himself for man. Jesus' servanthood becomes the concrete symbol in terms of which the divine self-giving is apprehended, and God himself becomes understood as one who "did not cling to His prerogatives . . . but stripped Himself of all privilege by consenting to be a slave" (Phil. 2:6–7   Phillips). Thus, Jesus' death on the cross becomes much more than just another human tragedy; it now manifests for all to see the inner disposition of God toward man. God is not only the Creator who has called men into being; he is also the Savior who out of his love sacrifices all to rescue his creatures from their plight. It is in God's act of self-giving to man's need, in his becoming the Servant of men, that men come to know him as Lord and thus become his obedient servants.

We can also now see how misleading it is to think of God as merely the self-sufficient one, the one who is of and from himself alone; for it is quite as important to apprehend him as the Word, the one who communicates himself to all that is, the one who is the source and basis and reality of meaning in existence. However, the meaning of life which here becomes manifest is no easy fulfilment of men's desires and aspirations: the *logos* is the crucified one. The revelation of God's being through the ministry of the man Jesus thus demands a radical transvaluation of all values; for the ultimate reality with which we have to do here shows himself to be preeminently the power to bear suffering inflicted by others, not the power which violently destroys all enemies as it seeks its own way. A cross becomes the symbol of what is authentically good and valuable in human life rather than a crown.

In all this it is no longer possible to think of God as a remote Father in some far-off heaven who speaks his word from a distance and commissions his underlings to bring it to men; such concern to keep himself at a safe remove from the ugly realities of history would be a harsh negation of that very quality of love which the cross displays. This suffering, if it truly manifests the being and disposition of God, must thus be his own, the suffering of God the Son sharing man's plight. The lofty and transcendent God in heaven turns out to be sufferer and patient in human history as much as agent behind it and lord over it: this is the meaning of the orthodox formula which proclaims the Son *homoousios* with the Father.

Here, then, in the midst of human existence, in the reality of human history, is God the Lord of all creation; here in Jesus Christ he shows who he really is, the Servant who gives of himself without limit, that his creatures might find fulfilment. Here the Ground of all being shows his innermost nature to be—*Love*!

14 / The Incarnation of God

IV. The Perfections of

the Divine Love

We have been considering the nature of God viewed as the One who comes to man to establish full sovereignty over him, giving meaning and purpose to human history. That is, we have been trying to see more clearly certain dimensions of the meaning of the words "Jesus Christ," the "second person of the trinity," the "son of God." Each of these phrases points in its own way to the central Christian claim that in the man Jesus ultimate reality is present within history, that God in his mercy and love has condescended from his transcendent position to share man's plight. It is necessary now in this concluding section on the second person of the trinity to summarize briefly what this implies about the nature of God.

Our interpretation of God the Father was summarized and brought to conclusion in terms of four perfections (attributes) of the divine freedom: unity, power, holiness, glory. We are now in a position to speak of four more perfections, this time of the divine love: relativity, grace, mercy, nonresistance. It must be emphasized that these further attributes of God do not add something to the divine nature which was not there before; nor—discussion of them having come somewhat later than the perfections of the divine freedom— should they be regarded as less important, perhaps even peripheral or dispensable. On the contrary, each points to something without which the understanding of God would be severely truncated and inadequate. They belong, then, necessarily to the concept itself.

God's relatedness to man, his entering into history with love in and through the person of Jesus Christ, can be grasped, we have noted, with the aid of such essentially relational notions as servant, word, and son. With the perfections of the divine love this relationality of God will be analyzed into certain essential components. More than the perfections of the divine freedom (which dealt in certain respects with presuppositions about God already largely worked out in Hebrew history), the perfections of the divine love are derived directly from the image of the crucified one and its significance. Thus, motifs implicitly at work in the qualifications it was necessary to introduce when discussing the perfections of the divine freedom will here be made explicit. Although the four perfections now to be discussed are especially perceptible in connection with the second person of the trinity in his dealings with man, like the perfections of the divine freedom they characterize the entire Godhead in relation to all creation. What more, then, must be said about the nature of God in view of the conviction that out of his love he enters into history?

a. The first perfection of the divine love: the relativity of God. God is one who *relates* himself to his creatures. He is not one who stands in the splendid isolation of his glorious holiness as the Unmoved Mover, nor does he remain beyond all essence and existence with the untarnished and perfect unity of Plotinus' *One*.[1] On the contrary, he deliberately enters into relations with his creatures at every point and at all levels, and he has entered into human history. He must be conceived as characterized by relatedness, by a sensitive relativity to all finite being and specifically to man. This attribute is the formal presupposition of the doctrine of the incarnation.

What is implied by this relativity of God's very being? To say that "the word became flesh" (John 1:14) is to claim that God has entered into connection with every dimension of human existence;

[1] Karl Barth goes so far as to suggest that such images refer rather to God's archenemy. ". . . if . . . there 'is' a devil, he is identical with a supreme being which posits and wills itself, which exists in a solitary glory and is therefore 'absolute'" (*Church Dogmatics*, IV, 1 [Edinburgh: T. & T. Clark, 1956], 422).

to say that God in his love deliberately "emptied himself, taking the form of a servant, being born in the likeness of man" (Phil. 2:7) is to claim that he has become involved in the very joys and sorrows, blessedness and despair, of human existence. If God really shares in man's life, his own life gains new color and flavor and meaning as men's joys and anxieties in some sense become his. If and as men become free and creative creatures—as he intends them to be—and thus achieve some genuine satisfaction in the fulfilment of their existence, he too comes to have a certain satisfaction and fulfilment; if men remain enslaved to self, full of misery, frustration, and a sense of incompleteness, he too suffers with them, struggling with them toward the realization of their freedom. God's sharing with his creatures, made possible by the relativity in his being, thus leads to a certain dependence in him on them. As Charles Hartshorne has put it, though God is "supreme," he is "indebted to all" his creatures for the character his own life has.[2] To deny this would be suggesting that man's response of defiance and rebellion makes no difference to him, that man's response of faith and love "means nothing" to him. The traditional notions of God's aloofness and independence and impassibility need radical revision if the divine love is to be taken seriously.

When God's relativity, bringing him into continuous relationship with every dimension of his creatures' lives, is understood, a further long step toward solution of the problem of theodicy has been taken. No longer is it appropriate to infer from the fact that misery and evil continue unabated that God may be standing aloof from his suffering world, self-righteously allowing it to wallow in its self-imposed misery, thus raising the question whether he is even as good as are sinful men. The Christian Gospel is precisely the claim that, far from keeping himself unsullied by the evils of historical existence, God has entered directly into man's world, bearing in full the burden of suffering which sin has cast upon him, so that he might lighten and ultimately remove men's burdens. Though as Creator, God has every "right" to allow his creatures to go to ruin, instead he freely and graciously acts to rescue them from their self-destruction, even though

[2] *The Divine Relativity* (New Haven: Yale University Press, 1948), Ch. 1.

at great cost to himself.[3] The relativity of the Christian God means, then, that his creatures never stand alone in their suffering; the source and ground of all being, in his compassionate love, is always with them.

The doctrine of the divine relativity does not involve denying either that God is absolute Creator or that he is omnipotent. Rather, it describes more precisely the way in which his omnipotence expresses itself: through bringing other free creatures into being, and through entering into their lives with love. God's "relativity" thus shows forth more fully what the perfections of the divine freedom really mean. Charles Hartshorne has put it well:

> God orders the universe . . . by taking into his own life all the currents of feeling in existence. He is the most irresistible of influences precisely because he is himself the most open to influence. In the depths of their hearts all creatures (even those able to 'rebel' against him) defer to God because they sense him as the one who alone is adequately moved by what moves them. He alone not only knows but feels . . . how they feel, and he finds his own joy in sharing their lives, lived according to their own free decisions, not fully anticipated by any detailed plan of his own. Yet the extent to which they can be permitted to work out their own plan depends on the extent to which they can echo or imitate on their own level the divine sensitiveness to the needs and precious freedom of all. . . . This [is a] vision of a deity who is not a supreme autocrat, but a universal agent of 'persuasion,' whose 'power is the worship he inspires'. . . .[4]

[3] "What is our suffering when we recollect that God has Himself felt it so keenly as to give His only begotten Son in order to remove it? Our suffering for sin has not touched us, and cannot touch us, as it touches Him. So we can never take it to our hearts in this way. When we realize the full depth of our sorrow as it is seen and borne and suffered by God Himself, any complaint of ours as to the form in which it confronts and affects us is silenced. . . . It is His heart, not ours, which is suffering when we think that we are the sufferers and that we have a right or obligation to lament. His heart is wounded, and wounded through our heart. How can we reverse the relationship and behave as though we have to suffer, as it were, in the void, divinely, eternally, or on our own account? In the recognition and confession of the mercy of God, what we are accustomed to take so seriously as the tragedy of human existence is dissolved" (Karl Barth, *Church Dogmatics*, II, 1 [Edinburgh: T. & T. Clark, 1957], 374).

[4] *The Divine Relativity*, p. xv.

b. The second perfection of the divine love: the grace of God.
It is clear that the relativity of God presupposes a quality of spontaneous movement outward toward his creatures, even those creatures in active rebellion against him. This quality may be designated as the grace of God. Although the concept of grace is found throughout the New Testament and occasionally in the Old, it is especially a Pauline term. For Paul it points to the heart of God's nature as laid bare in Jesus Christ. Consider a few typical statements:

> Since all have sinned and fall short of the glory of God, they are justified by his grace as a gift.
>
> ROMANS 3:23–24

> . . . where sin increased, grace abounded all the more.
>
> ROMANS 5:20

> For I am the least of the apostles, unfit to be called an apostle, because I persecuted the church of God. But by the grace of God I am what I am, and his grace toward me was not in vain. On the contrary, I worked harder than any of them, though it was not I, but the grace of God which is with me.
>
> 1 CORINTHIANS 15:9–10

> For by grace you have been saved through faith; and this is not your own doing, it is the gift of God.
>
> EPHESIANS 2:8

Grace is God's free movement to man; it is that spontaneity in his nature whereby he comes to his creatures to transform their existence; it is, therefore, that which is shown forth preeminently in and through Jesus Christ, that which evokes from men belief in God and hope for the coming of his kingdom.

God's grace is a qualification of the mystery of his omnipotence and holiness: these are to be characterized as *gracious*; God's grace is his graciousness to creation. On the one hand, since God is absolutely free, his grace in no way depends on his creatures' acts or desert but is totally spontaneous from the divine side.[5] On the other

---

[5] It is this that justifies such statements as Karl Barth's: "Only when grace is recognized to be incomprehensible is it grace" (*Epistle to the Romans* [London: Oxford University Press, 1933], p. 31). "Grace is the majesty, the freedom, the undeservedness,

hand, his graciousness and goodness to creation, since they bring healing and salvation, life and meaning, express at every point God's tempering and conditioning of himself to the being and needs of his creatures.[6] To speak of God's grace is thus to speak of God's freely disposing himself toward his creatures for their well-being. It is God's will for man's best, his will to relate himself to men regardless of how they relate to him.

Since God's grace is the root of his free movement toward man, it can properly be spoken of as *prevenient*, that is, as preceding and underlying and in this way making possible the human response of faith. God seeks out men, tracking them down, refusing to let them escape, no matter how rebellious they have become. This active love of God stretched out to man is the necessary presupposition of his repentance and thus of his redemption. The prevenience of God's grace can conveniently be considered on two levels, cosmic-historical and personal-individual.

By the cosmic-historical aspect of God's prevenient grace we refer to the Christian claim that God was already working toward community with men—not only long before particular individuals responded to him, or even existed—but even before the foundations of the world had been laid. He created the world to serve his personal purposes. Whatever additional meaning the physical universe and plant and animal life have, a central dimension of their significance

---

the unexpectedness, the newness, the arbitrariness, in which the relationship to God and therefore the possibility of knowing Him is opened up to man by God Himself. Grace is really the orientation in which God sets up an order which did not previously exist, to the power and benefit of which man has no claim, which he has no power to set up, which he has no competence even subsequently to justify, which in its singularity—which corresponds exactly to the singularity of the nature and being of God—he can only recognize and acknowledge as it is actually set up, as it is powerful and effective as a benefit that comes to him. Grace is God's good-pleasure" (*Church Dogmatics*, II, 1, p. 74).

[6] ". . . that which was done in the death of Jesus Christ . . . was not a unilateral decision of force or a dictatorial declaration of will or a sovereign overpowering. God did not will to act and He did not act in this way in Jesus Christ. . . . We may think that this would have contributed to His glory or been of great benefit for the world, but it would have been the act of an abstract and godless grace, not His own grace, not the divine grace addressed to man in Jesus Christ, but a faithfulness full of unfaithfulness, just because it is a unilateral decision which over-rides man, eliminating and ignoring him. . . . an act of this kind is unfriendly to man, . . . is at bottom an ungracious act. . . . it is brutal grace—grace as brutal man might conceive it, but not the grace of the true and living God" (Karl Barth, *Church Dogmatics*, IV, 1, p. 737).

is the environment they provide for the development of a community of free spirits in God's own image. This preparation of an appropriate context in which to set man should be regarded as an expression of the prevenience of God's grace toward him. Later, when man sinned and disrupted the community which God had intended, God actively and continuously began to work in man's history, preparing the way for the salvation of his creatures.[7] Thus, God's covenanting with Israel, his sending forth prophetic messengers, his driving Israel into exile—all should be regarded as God's prevenient grace preparing the way for his own coming into history with Jesus Christ. The further movement of history from that time to this—the establishment of the church, the growth of theological understanding and liturgical practices, the spread of the Christian message through many lands and generations—is to be seen as the prevenience of God's grace shaping the course of history so that subsequent generations would be captured by his meaning-creating work. The gracious God always anticipates what needs to be done in history to work out his purposes for creation; and this he has been doing through all time past. Thus, one level of the prevenience of God's grace is his creation and sustenance of the world and his governance of history.

It is appropriate to speak also of the prevenience of God's grace on the personal-individual level, shaping a man's personal response of faith and his decision to give himself to God's service. Every such human response presupposes God's grace on the cosmic-historical level, but it also presupposes a personal graciousness to that man. It is the grace of God—the activity of God relating himself to one— that makes possible his response in faith. What does this mean? Does God's prevenience here imply a restriction of human freedom? Not at all. Consider how a personal relationship is originally established between parent and child, and how reconciliation occurs between estranged persons. Do these begin with the child's move to initiate the relationship, or with the offender's free decision to approach the other and confess his sin? Hardly. Initially the child is incapable

---

[7] For fuller discussion of the history here suggested see below, Pts. II and III. This discussion of God's grace presupposes the historicistic understanding of sin which cannot be presented until later.

of any spontaneous activity; this becomes possible only gradually in response to the parent's almost continuous care and ministration. And one would hardly dare confess his guiltiness to another unless he already sensed something of the other's acceptance and forgiveness. If the other, already offended and estranged, were to learn the full seriousness of the sin against him, the alienation would likely be deepened: every husband (and wife) knows how easily the fragile threads of such partial community as has been established may be further weakened and perhaps even destroyed. But if one can be confident that the other will accept him despite his sin, will not deepen the wound of guilt by outright rejection of his approach, then it may be possible to confess. Such confidence can be had only if the other has in some sense already approached in forgiveness and love, breaching the wall of self-defensiveness and guilt. This does not mean that when the sinner turns in penitence and confession, it is not his own free act: on the contrary, his confession is clearly his own, though an indispensable condition has been provided by the one offended. The latter's "prevenient grace" has freed him from the guilty and unconfessing bondage in which he had been standing. So also with the parent's actions initiating personal relationships with his child: far from competing with the child's freedom, they provide the conditions which make possible its emergence. Unfreedom is precisely one's condition apart from the gracious act of the other; freedom first becomes possible as a response to another's act.

Similar things must be said about the relation of men to their Creator. They are unable freely to give themselves to him in love and service until he shows himself as one who has been giving himself to them, as one whom they can trust. Especially is this true when they become aware of their willful attempts to make themselves centers around which the world revolves, utilizing everything and everyone in God's world for the satisfaction of their own desires: in short, as they become conscious of their full guiltiness before him who created them for love and service and self-giving. It is God's prevenient grace which makes possible even such timid and fearful decisions to trust him and live in faith and love as upon occasion men are able to make. God's grace is the indispensable presupposition of every authentically free act; without it man would only mire deeper in bondage to self.[8] God's initiative in coming to man makes possible his gradual return to his Creator. "For . . . while we were enemies we were reconciled to God by the death of his Son" (Rom. 5:10). Such is God's grace to man. But not only to man, as though we were his favorite: if Jesus Christ is truly revelatory of God's being, such grace must inform his stance toward all his creation.

c. This discussion of God's grace—its freedom and its prevenience—has already implied *the third perfection of the divine love: the mercy of God.* God's graciousness to man in coming into human history must be understood as mercy. For consider to whom his grace comes: to creatures who have been seeking to establish their own self-centered order in life, thus actively defying him who gave them their being; men have made themselves into little gods, running the world in accordance with their own desires, doing as they please; they have entered into rebellion against the very Creator of the universe. Thus they have rent the harmony and beauty of creation—which, as it came from God's hand he could rightly call "very good" (Gen. 1:31)—and have turned it into a chaos of evil and hatred, which finally may culminate in the destruction of mankind and even all life. Man has been rebellious against the divine sovereignty and contemptuous of the divine love; indeed, he has even become uninterested in the divine being. And yet, it is just to man in all his disdain and contempt and pride and unconcern that God in his graciousness has come. Despite repeated offense against his holy will, in spite of continual spurning of his love, he has not destroyed man or forsaken him: he has had mercy on mankind and has come into history with forgiveness. "As a father pities his children" (Ps. 103:13), so the Lord has taken pity on man. God's grace is not only freedom and prevenience and graciousness, but also mercy and steadfast love and forgiveness. God sacrifices on his creatures' behalf. Giving up his transcendent position, he stoops from his lofty place, humbles himself, shows man mercy.

This perfection, God's mercy, expresses a kind of counterpart in the divine love to holiness as a perfection of the divine freedom. God's

---

[8] The justification of all such claims must await further analysis in Pt. III.

attributes of unity and power, we noted, refer to his being source and ground of all that exists, but his holiness depicts him as the ground and ultimate measure of all value. In similar fashion, God's relativity and grace portray him as one who actively and spontaneously relates himself to, and pours himself out upon, his creation; but the attribute of mercy suggests more than this: namely, that he accommodates his divine purpose and plans to the weaknesses and failures of his creatures, that he bends and reshapes even his determinations of value and righteousness in behalf of their needs. God's mercy thus means that his holiness is no inflexible divine standard, oriented on himself alone, a standard which could only fell his creatures when they were measured by it; it means that God's very valuing is oriented toward the well-being of his creation, that it is adjusted and modulated so as to make possible real fulfilment for his creatures, whatever the cost to him.

God's grace, then, expresses itself in mercy toward his creatures, in forbearance with them, in steadfast loving-kindness to them. Thus, the divine holiness, power, unity, and glory become visible in Jesus Christ as the holiness and power of mercy, the unity and glory of graciousness, God come into history to restore human existence to the perfect community which he had purposed in creation.

d. The form in which God's gracious mercy comes to man necessitates speaking of a *fourth perfection of the divine love: the non-resistance of God*.[9] When stated forthrightly in this way, the full scandal of the claim that God loves his creatures is laid bare. For the Christian Gospel is no announcement that God enters into community with men and overcomes their rebellion through *compelling* obedience against their will. Quite the contrary. It is through suffering the cross which men inflict on him that he wins over their hearts in spite of themselves. "God the Creator . . . is powerless to conquer evil by an act of power. It is only the God of sacrifice and love who can triumph

[9] I prefer the term "nonresistance" to, e.g., "submissiveness," here—despite its negativistic implications—because, since this term is biblically based ("But I say to you, Do not resist one who is evil" [Mt. 5:39]), it has become regarded in certain Christian circles (such as the Mennonites) as the term which most appropriately indicates the proper moral stance of the Christian, a stance supposed to reflect precisely that dimension of God's being and action which we are here designating as his "nonresistance."

over evil, the God who took upon himself the sins of the world, God the Son, who became man."[10] God, as it were, "turns the other cheek," and goes "the second mile" (cf. Mt. 5:39, 41); he loves his enemies, and in this way wins them. God does not strike back vengefully or in any other way retaliate; on the contrary, he deigns to suffer whatever wrong his creatures inflict on him, that he might in this way rescue them from the mess they have made of history. The "servant poems" of Second Isaiah well express his stance:

He was oppressed, and he was afflicted,
    yet he opened not his mouth;
like a lamb that is led to the slaughter,
    and like a sheep that before its shearers is dumb,
    so he opened not his mouth.

                        ISAIAH 53:7

But he was wounded for our transgressions,
    he was bruised for our iniquities;
upon him was the chastisement that made us whole,
    and with his stripes we are healed.

                        ISAIAH 53:5

This is what God's power is: *love.* And this is how he wins men's hearts: by *nonresistance.* Through submitting himself to the worst indignities and evils to which rebellious men subject him, without turning again in anger upon them, he finally thaws their frozen hearts. The cross, understood as the profoundest symbol of God's being and action, means that God himself suffers for his creation, allowing himself to be "despised and rejected by men" (Isa. 53:3). The cross shows him to be one who, as Bonhoeffer has said, "is weak and powerless in the world, and that is exactly the way, the only way, in which he can be with us and help us."[11] For that is the only way he

---

[10] N. Berdyaev, *The Beginning and the End* (New York: Harper Torchbooks, 1952), p. 248.

[11] Dietrich Bonhoeffer, *Prisoner for God* (New York: Macmillan, 1953), p. 164. Bonhoeffer is quite right, I think, in holding that in "the world come of age" since the Enlightenment—a world increasingly characterized by the autonomy of science, art, education, economics, and politics, and by the increasing irrelevance of religion—it is no longer possible to conceive God meaningfully as a kind of extension or glorification of

can maintain the full integrity of those creatures to whom he has granted genuine freedom. When men see him, the God of the universe, "bearing our griefs" and "carrying our sorrows" (53:4), suffering "pain" on behalf of his creation,[12] he finally succeeds in communicating his merciful grace, his love; and they are won to his kingdom.

That God can do this, all of this, is his power;[13] that he freely wills to do this for his creatures is his love. The nonresistance of God: this divine perfection takes up in a powerful way all the other perfections thus far discussed. For in it is manifested God's unity and power, his holiness and glory; here it becomes evident how gracious he is to his creatures and how merciful to those who have

the powers of this world, as was too much the case in the traditional Christian view. This God modern man has "killed" (Nietzsche), and therefore modern men find it difficult to be "religious" in the traditional sense. For to be religious meant to be in touch with those supernatural and superhuman and superhistorical powers which directly and purposefully and magically controlled men's destinies—and we know of no powers in that sense any longer. To the extent that the traditional faith in providence conceived things in this way, it has been unfaith—mere wish fulfilment (Freud) or class ideology (Marx). It understood God's dealings with man in terms of the physical force and struggle for survival characteristic of lower forms of finite being. But, though man is certainly emergent from such levels of being and continues to be grounded in them, his distinctively and characteristically human mode of existence is in consciousness, freedom, and history (see Ch. 23); and it is with modes of power appropriate for eliciting freedom and love that God deals with him in history, thus making it a history of salvation from bondage and sin (Ch. 26). Hence, God's activity within and through human history is not primarily as worldly power or force, and he should not be conceived according to such images; the image of a man dying on a cross is here normative for the conception of his power. When this is understood, his absence as (visible physical) power will be seen to be not in fact his absence. For his presence will be—not miraculous signs and wonders displaying power—but the presence of the power to suffer, to bear what is inflicted, to give for others, the supremely and peculiarly *personal* power that can manifest itself only out of genuinely personal freedom (see above, Ch. 5, n. 6). Where this is present, there is God.

[12] "God himself had to enter the world of real sin in order to bear the responsibility of real sin. . . . Only the pain of God can deny fundamentally every sort of docetism. . . . The pain of God could not have existed had not the Redeemer, the personification of God's pain, been a historical figure" (Kazoh Kitamori, *Theology of the Pain of God* [Richmond: John Knox Press, 1965], pp. 34f.).

[13] F. R. Tennant has suggested that the traditional theological rejection of all passibility—and certainly all "nonresistance" or "submissiveness"—in God, on the ground that it implies imperfection and incompleteness, may in fact be hidden anthropomorphism rooted in the "physiological fact, with its psychological consequences, that our limbs and brains become weary through exercise" and continually need restoration and replenishment from beyond themselves if they are going to continue in activity (*Philosophical Theology* [Cambridge: University Press, 1930], II, 61). Certainly if we take seriously the notion that God is *agape*, infinite and inexhaustible loving activity, God's suffering and passibility, his bearing our burdens and submitting to the evil we do to him, cannot rightly be regarded as a "problem" to be somehow cleverly side-stepped: it is of the very essence of the Christian claim.

strayed or offended; here can be seen how fully and profoundly he relates himself to every dimension of existence, even the deepest reaches of personal freedom. But God's nonresistance will not be properly understood unless it is seen in connection with his relativity and mercy and grace, and also his glory and holiness and omnipotence, with his oneness with himself in every time and place in heaven and on earth.

15 / The Presence of God
I. Spirit and Companion

Under the heading, "God the Father," we viewed God as *free Lord* over all creation, the ultimate limit of all finite being; in our discussion of "God the Son" we interpreted him as the *loving Servant* who comes into history in mercy to redeem his creation from its misery. Now we must turn to the third person of the trinity, "God the Holy Spirit," and consider him once more, seen now, however, as the *ever-present Companion*, the one with his creatures in every situation, the one working in and through every moment of history. This "Holy Spirit," of course, is not some God different from the One discussed heretofore. He is the same God with the same attributes, but he must be viewed now with reference to a third indispensable set of considerations.

One might raise the question, What more is to be said? What needs be added to the image of God which has been sketched? In a certain sense it would not be incorrect to answer, Nothing. For when we have understood that God is one who loves perfectly in perfect freedom, the picture is complete; seemingly the whole content of the Christian doctrine of God can be expounded under the heads, "Father" and "Son." Precisely for this reason much early Christian thought was binitarian rather than trinitarian in character. But this position is misleading and even false in certain respects. It implies that "God" for Christians is a *content* to be talked about, a body of statements or propositions to be learned and repeated in classroom or pulpit—but hardly at cocktail party or dinner table—and this misses the essential point of the Christian claim: namely, that *God is a reality in men's lives,* indeed *the* reality for human existence. Whether at afternoon tea or pool hall, at home or school, in church or business or politics, it is *God*—he who is Creator and Redeemer—with whom men most fundamentally have to do. And unless we find a place to say this, everything already said about God remains abstract and verbal and ultimately irrelevant, hence not about God at all. It is necessary, therefore, to take up this third issue and consider what it means for understanding God's nature and action to realize that he is one who is continuously present, who is active in every moment of history.

Considerable confusion has been introduced into Christian thinking by the way in which the presence of the Holy Spirit has often been understood. The church has seldom taken with real seriousness the Johannine words, "And I will pray the Father, and he will give you another Counselor, to be with you *forever*" (John 14:16); or the Matthean phrase, "lo, I am with you *always*" (28:20); or Paul's claim that nothing "*in all creation,* will be able to separate us from the love of God in Christ Jesus our Lord" (Rom. 8:39). Each of these speaks of the presence of God to man in every possible situation in life. However, instead of accepting this radical view, Christians have usually taken the much weaker position that God is present to men principally in particular kinds of experience or in particular situations—for example, in the sacraments or in moments of overt prayer, in semi-mystical experiences when one "feels the presence of God" or in highly emotional moments when one "feels the Spirit." There must be no mistake here: I am not criticizing the affirmation that God is present in these situations. I am suggesting, however, that such focusing on particular experiences or particular kinds of experience, as in some special way the presence of God's Spirit, has led all too often to understanding the doctrine of the Holy Spirit as meaning that Christians have certain kinds of feelings on certain occasions. Such a view involves a great narrowing of meaning. For the "Spirit" is God's presence to man in every situation, "even unto the end of the world" (Mt. 28:20 KJ)—even in the depths of despair, sin, and

emptiness. Psalm 139 expresses the matter far better than interpretations in terms of so-called religious experience:

> *Whither shall I go from thy Spirit?*
> *Or whither shall I flee from thy presence?*
> *If I ascend to heaven, thou art there!*
> *If I make my bed in Sheol, thou art there!*
> *If I take the wings of the morning*
> *and dwell in the uttermost parts of the sea,*
> *even there thy hand shall lead me,*
> *and thy right hand shall hold me.*

> PSALM 139:7–10

The interpretation of the Holy Spirit in terms of particular types
of experience[1] has had unfortunate effects in three ways. In the first
place, it has implied that it is necessary to have certain special types
of experience to be Christian. Instead of acknowledging that God
deals with men as individuals in their individuality, and allowing that
therefore he will be present to different persons in ways most appropriate to their uniqueness, this puts a premium on particular kinds
of experience and temperament; others without the requisite emotional
makeup must either force themselves into experiences not natural to

---

[1] It must be admitted that there is plenty of biblical ground for such interpretation.
In both Old Testament and New the Spirit is often viewed as a kind of divine power
that invades and overpowers a person, manifesting itself in highly irrational emotional
phenomena. However, in keeping with our fundamental theological principle that it is
not biblical statements or views *as such* that are normative for Christian theology, but
God's definitive self-manifestation in the incarnation, it is necessary to interpret the
Spirit—along with all other categories—in a preeminently *personalistic* sense, rejecting
all notions of invasions by impersonal powers except insofar as these illumine some dimension of personal existence. (In this connection it is worth noting that however much
Paul regarded spirit as a kind of power, its really significant expression for him was
its "fruit," certain moral and personal qualities [Gal. 5:22f.] which build up the
community life [1 Cor. 12–14].) Personal life, then, as defined by the historical existence of Jesus of Nazareth, must be normative for the category "spirit," as for all others.
In the present interpretation I have tried to hew this line at every point, even though
this requires ignoring (in such a brief discussion) such additional insights into personal
existence as might be gained through consideration of the notion of the Spirit as primarily a special power. For the same reasons, I have tried consistently to refer to the
Holy Spirit by the personal "he" rather than the impersonal "it." Cf. Joseph Haroutunian:
"If the Spirit is among God's people, then our fellow-men belong with our conception
of the Spirit, and we may not think or imagine the Spirit apart from the human face.
Hence, it is incongruous and profoundly misleading to speak of the Spirit as 'it' and
not as 'he'" (*God with Us* [Philadelphia: Westminster Press, 1965], p. 76).

them or suffer the penalty of feeling condemned by God. Thus, this emphasis easily leads to "works righteousness," salvation being understood in terms of working up the proper feelings instead of as God's free gift.

In the second place, such highlighting of certain types of experience has the countereffect of downgrading the rest of life as religiously unimportant, and faith becomes understood as relevant to but one segment of life rather than the whole. In the worlds of business and politics, in social and intellectual life—in short, in every domain of culture except the specially emphasized realm—men may then live autonomously, free from any significant concrete relation to God. Thus they become polytheists, worshiping Yahweh in their prayers but Mammon in business and Mars in international relations. Such fragmentation of existence is intolerable to any monotheism: the God of Christian faith is Lord of all creation and therefore of every dimension of existence.

The experiential emphasis also tends to forget, in the third place, that belief in the Holy Spirit is, after all, an article of faith, not a matter of the presence of certain empirical evidence. The Christian affirms the presence of the Holy Spirit not because he has had a Damascus-road conversion or a "strange warming of the heart" but because he accepts God's revelation of himself as the loving one who never forsakes man.

The attempt to understand the doctrine of the Holy Spirit in primarily experiential terms, then, must be rejected as inadequate and misleading. Instead, God's Spirit is to be understood as *his actual presence to his creatures* in every situation, whether they consciously "feel" it or not. Much already said about God in these pages has been about the Holy Spirit. Thus, God immanently at work in men's lives, even before they are conscious of him or begin to respond with faith, himself making possible such response (prevenient grace), is the presence of the Holy Spirit; and God immanently at work through all history, providentially leading it according to his purposes until he can bring it completely under his sovereignty, is the activity of the Holy Spirit. The *Heilsgeschichte* recorded in the Bible reports God's special working toward his goals through preparing a community in and to which he could make his continuous presence known. This community developed historically until finally one appeared in its midst through whom his Spirit could enter the ongoing stream of human life with new and decisive effect. When God's "chosen people" thus at last began to become the universal kingdom he intended, a community loving and forgiving enemies as well as neighbors, God's Spirit became immanent in history with new power and effectiveness.

For the presence of God's Spirit in the church is simply his love mediated through the love of finite men. God's Spirit comes to others through those finite spirits in whose midst they exist.[2] To be conscious of God's being with and among us in everyday activities of life is to be aware of the presence of the Holy Spirit.

There is a certain two-sidedness to this consciousness. On the one hand, the confidence that God is really present, in sovereign control of the course of events within which one stands, gives confidence to act and think and feel with the spontaneity and autonomy he has granted men in creating them free. In this way faith makes possible full and hearty secularity, life in *this world* of this autonomous self. ". . . work out your own salvation . . . for God is at work in you" (Phil. 2:12–13). On the other hand, the consciousness of God's continual presence leads toward ordering every decision to accord with his will, taking "every thought captive to obey Christ" (2 Cor. 10:5). The same two-sidedness appears in the intellectual and emotional dimensions of life. The awareness of God's presence everywhere frees one to pursue truth wherever it leads and to savor every subtle dimension of God's creation without fear or inhibition. But at the same time it evokes the search for *God's* truth, not merely man's,

---

[2] Cf. Haroutunian: "To associate the Spirit with a ghostly being in preference to our flesh and bone brother is a confusion of thought. . . . we know no love of God for us without our love for one another, no forgiveness of God without our forgiving one another, no faith or hope from God, except as we have faith toward one another and hope in one another. We hear no good news from God or from his Son, except as we speak it one to another" (*God with Us*, pp. 76, 75). This close interpenetration of divine and human action is suggested in numerous biblical passages. On the one hand, God's activity is in and through finite human activity (e.g.: "He who receives you receives me, and he who receives me receives him who sent me" [Mt. 10:40]; ". . . we are ambassadors for Christ, God making his appeal through us" [2 Cor. 5:20]) ; on the other hand, our human acts have a transcendent meaning: (". . . as you did it to one of the least of these my brethren, you did it to me" [Mt. 25:40; cf. 25:45]).

in one's dialogues with Plato, Einstein, and Freud; and it begets the desire to sense his presence in one's most secular and everyday feelings as well as in moments of ecstasy. The doctrine of the Holy Spirit claims that God is present to man in all these conditions, in every moment of existence, and that men may thus live freely in the created world. ". . . because you are sons, God has sent the Spirit of his Son into our hearts. . . . So through God you are no longer a slave but a son, and if a son then an heir. . . . For freedom Christ has set us free" (Gal. 4:6f., 5:1).[3]

We have seen repeatedly that all our language about God is analogical. Thus, the images of father, lord, and creator give some insight into God's transcendence, while son, word, and servant facilitate grasping the import of his entering human history. There are two principal analogies which help understand God in his continuous presence to man. One is "spirit," as found in the phrase, Holy Spirit; the other is *Paraclete*, used four times in the Fourth Gospel (Chapters 14 to 16) and variously translated as "comforter," "counselor," "helper," etc. Meaning literally "called to be with," the *Paraclete* is one called to be with men, to teach them, to convince them, to comfort them; the root analogy with which we are concerned in this term appears to be "companion" or "friend." Here are two symbols, then, for further explication of the meaning of God's presence to men in every moment, "spirit" and "companion."

When these two analogies are put thus side by side a significant point leaps to the eye: they point to the two sides of the most intimate kind of personal relation we know, that between "I" and "thou" (Buber). In the close interpersonal relation of friend with friend, one discovers his own existence as personal and simultaneously encounters the other before him as a person. Let us examine the two analogies successively to see their implications.

Consider the term "spirit." The original meaning of the word, not only in Hebrew and Greek, but also in English, French, German, and other languages, is "breath" or "wind"; but in all these languages it becomes the designation for the inmost part of man, the very center

---

[3] The sense in which salvation is to be understood as radical freedom from various sorts of bondage will be taken up below in some detail (see Chs. 25–29).

of his being, his heart or soul or mind. This development provides an example of the natural analogical use of language. Breath or wind, the most *im*material of all material substances, came to mean man's inwardness or subjectivity or mind in *contrast* with his body; moreover, since when man's breathing stops, he dies, it is not difficult to understand why primitives associated man's breath with his very essence. But what was thus originally an analogy eventually became the standard meaning of the word; for us "spirit" no longer has materialistic connotations, but stands for all that distinguishes man from mere corporeality. A comprehensive term, it indicates the organic wholeness of man's inwardness or subjectivity (including his powers of will and decision, of intellect and reason, and his feelings of value and meaning),[4] in contrast with what can be known outwardly and objectively, by external observation. To be "spirit" is to live in a world of *meaning*, not simply among things; this term refers to the depths of man's personal being. My awareness of myself as "I"— as a self with secret thoughts and sorrows, pleasures, and desires, over against an "external" world—is my awareness of myself as spirit.

But thus to view man's spirit simply as *ego*, as "I," is inadequate: there is no pure ego as such.[5] Selves come into being only in relation to other selves (especially in the family) and they exist only in such relation; the "I" has being only in confrontation with a "thou." In the encounter with other active centers over against us, yet with whom we can enter into communion, our selfhood is called forth. Above all in the act of speaking—uttering words with meaning to a "thou" who can understand them—one creates and discovers these meanings in himself, and thus discovers himself as an "I"; and in hearing the speech of another—the meanings he expresses—one comes to understand that we both are spiritual beings, beings living in a world of

---

[4] Tillich, *Systematic Theology*, I (Chicago: University of Chicago Press, 1951), 249–250.

[5] In our own time, it is principally the work of Martin Buber (*I and Thou*, 2nd ed. [New York: Charles Scribner's, 1953], *Between Man and Man* [London: Routledge & Kegan Paul, 1947], etc.) and G. H. Mead (esp. *Mind, Self and Society* [Chicago: University of Chicago Press, 1934]) that has established this point. Both, of course, are heavily dependent on the pioneering work of Hegel and his followers for the development of a social conception of selfhood.

meanings. In communication one comes to know the other not simply in his *outwardness* (as body) but in his inwardness, as heart and soul, if he chooses to reveal himself; and likewise, when one trusts the other sufficiently to strip the inward self naked before him, revealing one's deepest feelings to him, one discovers with a new intimacy his own selfhood. Thus, in human love one is granted the profoundest kind of knowledge, of the other spirit and of himself as well.

The term "spirit" refers to this deepest level of selfhood, that which comes into being and is nourished by intercourse with other spirits, that which exists only in relation to spirit. It indicates that which "I" am in the depths of my subjectivity, but also that which the other is—this other whom I know intimately, even as he knows me, in our speaking together as friends who love one another.

When God is spoken of as "spirit," man's relation to him is interpreted in analogy with this most intimate and personal and inward relation in which men stand to each other. His penetration and knowledge of one's being is not from the outside, something external, like the knowledge of material objects: it is from within, as one is known by another spirit to whom he chooses to reveal himself. The interpenetration of his life with man's, his being with ours, is analogous to that between human spirits in community, where we exist as "members one of another" (Rom. 12:5).

It is especially appropriate that there should be two symbols here, "spirit" and "companion" (= "comforter," "counselor," etc.), for this points up the two-sided polarity which this inward relation always involves. On the one hand, my companion is the *other* one, the different one, the one over against me; on the other hand, he is one whom I recognize as (like myself) *spirit*. He is one to whom I give myself in speech and love, that we may become one, that is, animated by the same spirit; and, as my companion, he similarly gives himself to me in love and speech. As my "counselor" he aids and guides me; he is one who is with me (*com*panion), who never fails, with whom I can always be free and open, to whom I can confess my sins, and on whom I can lean for strength. My companion's being interpenetrates my own so that we can be said to share and manifest a common spirit, and yet he is another spirit separate and distinct from me; he is one whose being I interpenetrate while still remaining myself in freedom and individuality. Indeed, I gain myself as a free individual only before some friend, some companion, who will allow me truly to be myself with him.

Thus, to say "God is spirit" and "God is the companion" is not to make two separate statements but to speak of two sides of the same thing. God would be a distant spirit, an alien one, and thus finally, for man, not spirit at all, were he not also the companion, the one with whom men can enter into reciprocal relations to the deepest recesses of their beings. And God would be no genuine companion were he not responsive to the living reality in men's inmost selves, were he not also *spirit,* living reality in *his* innermost being. When the Johannine Jesus says he will send the companion who will "be with you forever," one who "dwells with you, and will be in you" (John 14:16–17), he is expressing John's awareness that at every point in human existence, including man's most inward subjectivity, God is present to and with us.

Having said all this, it is necessary to make some qualifications. This is not just any spirit of which we are speaking; this is the *Holy* Spirit. Though it is necessary to say God is related to man as spirit to spirit, he is still profoundly different from man, radically incomprehensible, utter mystery, "holy."[6] In this respect the phrase "Holy Spirit" expresses the strongest possible paradox, pointing simultaneously to the radical presentness of God to man's spirit and to the profound difference between God and us. "God is *spirit*" (John 4:24), but he is utterly different from human spirits. Much popular Christianity has obscured this tension. In some sentimental hymns, for example, it is suggested that God's presence is felt like another person's;[7] the awareness of God the companion is certainly expressed but that he is the Holy Companion seems almost forgotten. With this analogy, perhaps more than with some others, it is essential to make

---

6 See above, pp. 108ff. and 160ff.
7 Cf. "In the Garden," by C. A. Miles:

I come to the garden alone, while the dew lies fresh on the roses;
  And the voice I hear, falling on my ear; the Son of God discloses.

And He walks with me, and He talks with me, and He tells me I am His own,
  And the joy we share as we tarry there, none other has ever known.

certain the symbols are not taken literally, lest, on the one hand, certain pleasant "warm feelings" or ecstatic emotions be idolatrously worshiped instead of *God*; or, on the other hand, lest the meaning of Christian faith be obscured for those who happen not to have had particular kinds of experience. God is Spirit and God is the Companion; but he is the Holy Companion, the Holy Spirit. Only in this sense are the Johannine words true:

> [When] the "Companion," the Holy Spirit, whom the Father will send in my name [comes], he will teach you all things, and bring to your remembrance all that I have said to you. . . . When the Spirit of truth comes, he will guide you into all the truth.
>
> JOHN 14:26, 16:13

One may be inclined to ask at this point whether this view, that God is present to man in some way merely analogous to the presence of another person, is not an entirely abstract conception. Is it meaningful to speak of his personal presence if visions and voices and other phenomena characteristic of interpersonal intercourse are ruled out?[8] The knowledge of God (I have maintained throughout) never rests primarily on experimental evidence: its foundation is the person-event Jesus Christ, apprehended as God's historical self-revelation. It is because of this event and what it implies that the continuous presence of the Holy Spirit can be and is affirmed.[9] Such an affirmation is empirical, not so much in its reference to the special experience of a peculiar supernatural power as to the creative and living presence of this potent event in memory and culture.[10] For the Chris-

[8] For an analysis of the difficulties here, see R. W. Hepburn, *Christianity and Paradox* (London: Watts, 1958), Chs. 3–4.

[9] This is the significance of the insistence in the Western churches on the so-called *filioque* clause (i.e., that "the Holy Spirit . . . proceeds from the Father *and the Son*") in the Nicene Creed.

[10] Cf. Bernard Meland: ". . . the revelation in Christ became a cultural energy . . . which assumed structure and dynamic power through the symbolisms and organizational witness of repentant and dedicated men and women. . . . Christ is therefore more than a memory in the minds of living Christians. He is the persisting structure of sensitive meaning which works at the level of cultural institutions and creative effort, pointing men to the real energy of grace in their midst" (*Faith and Culture* [New York: Oxford University Press, 1953], pp. 215–216).

tian consciousness this event from the past is the vital center of meaning which orders and gives significance to every corner and cranny of
present, as well as anticipated, existence. Hence, the spirit manifested
in it can quite properly be regarded as present to and with man in
every dimension of life (cf. Gal. 4:4–6). The very experience of the
meaningfulness of the several aspects of existence—a meaningfulness
apprehended in faith as rooted ultimately in an inexhaustible source
of meaning, God—is experience of the Holy Spirit, so far as it is appropriate to speak at all of God's presence as experienceable or experimental. Inasmuch as men are *personal* beings in search of
personal meaning, and since personalistic imagery is dominant in the
notion of God, it is not surprising that peculiarly intense and vivid
experiences of the meaningfulness of existence should sometimes be
felt and interpreted as the personal presence of God's (or Christ's)
spirit—that is, that God's presence is apprehended and understood
as analogous to that of another human being.

The great danger in all such interpretation, of course, is that it
may lead to individualistic and egocentric conceptions of man and
faith, in which, as Augustine put it, one desires "to know God and
the soul. . . . Nothing more,"[11] the relationships to other persons fad-
ing into theological insignificance. It is evident that such views have
little in common with the New Testament conception of the presence
of God's Spirit. For here the Holy Spirit is recognized and distinguished from all imposters by the norm of the historical revelation of
God in Jesus,[12] on the one hand, and by his leading men into lives
of love and self-giving (Gal. 5:16ff.) and the building up of the
Christian community (1 Cor. 14), on the other. The Spirit of Christ
is not known primarily in one's solitude but rather in and with the
others in communion with whom he dwells. "For where two or three
are gathered in my name, there am I in the midst of them" (Mt.

[11] *Soliloquies*, I, 2. (Trans. T. F. Gilligan, *Fathers of the Church*, II [New York:
Cima, 1948], 350.) In more recent times Kierkegaard's radical individualism before
God, in which relations to other persons have little or no significant role to play, is an
example of this aberration (see Martin Buber, *Between Man and Man, op. cit.* [above,
n. 5], pp. 40–82, 157–181).

[12] "Beloved, do not believe every spirit, but test the spirits to see whether they are
of God. . . . By this you know the Spirit of God: every spirit which confesses that Jesus
Christ has come in the flesh is of God, and every spirit which does not confess Jesus
is not of God" (1 John 4:1–3).

18:20).[13] In Paul's view, the Spirit is definitively experienced in and through the community of the faithful; hence, if "you are eager for manifestations of the Spirit, strive to excel in building up the church" (1 Cor. 14:12).[14]

We can now tie together the several threads of this discussion. The concrete experience to which the words "the presence of the Holy Spirit" refer is interpersonal existence-in-the-community-of-love, in which the actual love and forgiveness of other finite persons is apprehended as not merely finite and transitory but, because of God's self-revelation in Jesus Christ, as rooted in, and an outpouring of, the very ground of all being. This interpersonal love is apprehended as bearing all things, believing all things, enduring all things, never ending (1 Cor. 13:7–8), precisely because it is known as "God's love . . . poured into our hearts through the Holy Spirit which has been given to us" (Rom. 5:5).

[13] Cf. the Lukan saying: "the Kingdom of God is in the midst of you" (17:21). (Contemporary scholars agree that the more individualistic King James translation, "within you," is erroneous.)

[14] Paul even suggests that it was because of his predilection for his private religious experiences, in which he "was caught up into Paradise . . . and heard things that cannot be told, which man may not utter" (2 Cor. 12:3–4), that he was punished with his "thorn in the flesh" (12:7).

16 / The Presence of God
II. The Perfections of
the Divine Communing

I⟨T⟩ has been helpful in each of the major divisions of our discussion of the Christian doctrine of God to consider several attributes or perfections of the divine nature. Each of these groups summarizes systematically what was uncovered in connection with one person of the trinity. Thus, the discussion of God the Father was concluded with a consideration of four perfections of the divine freedom; the interpretation of God the Son, with four perfections of the divine love. In a similar way God the Holy Spirit can be viewed in terms of four perfections of the divine communing:[1] faithfulness, responsiveness, understanding, and forgiveness. These are not new elements to be added to God's nature; rather, once again, it is necessary to qualify and modify what was said earlier because of what is revealed about God when he is understood as spirit and companion.

a. The first perfection of the divine communing: the faithfulness

[1] I have chosen the term "communing" rather than the more customary "communion" (e.g., "the communion of the Holy Spirit") because, though it is somewhat awkward and unfamiliar, it emphasizes the fact that the doctrine of the Holy Spirit refers to God's active coming to men here and now, his revealing himself to them, i.e., his communicating himself to them, communing with them, entering into living community with them. The connotations of "communion" are too static, suggesting a more or less stable structure (e.g., we speak of the different denominations as different "communions") rather than the vital reality of speaking and answering and living together, as suggested by "communing."

of God. "Faithfulness," like most of the terms we have found helpful in attempting to understand the divine being, is a concept drawn from interpersonal relations. It denotes the steadfastness in loyalty characteristic of a true friend. A "faithful friend" is one who "keeps faith" regardless of impulses or pressures to the contrary. Faithfulness thus implies difficulties or adversity in maintenance of the friendship; but the difficulties are neutralized and even overcome because the loyal friend wills that these adverse circumstances shall not be sufficient to destroy the personal relation. He binds himself to you in such a way that you can rely on him, can be certain he will not desert or betray you just in that desperate hour when you need him. A faithful friend is one who deliberately sustains community with another, even at severe cost to himself. When one speaks, he will always listen, no matter what the situation; he has sufficient *force* of will, and sufficient *benevolence* of will toward his companion, to sustain the community from his side regardless of the adversities threatening to undermine or destroy it.

Of course, there are no faithful friends in this ideal sense. There is none who might not betray one, or at least let one down, under some circumstances, either deliberately (by failing to will to be faithful) or unavoidably (simply because, as a finite being, he was not strong enough to maintain the relationship under all circumstances—some of the most poignant "betrayals" by friends or loved ones are completely unwilled and unavoidable, e.g., with death). In this context something of the "faithfulness of God" can be understood. God has revealed himself to be both powerful enough and loving enough always to be faithful. It is clear he has the power: the perfections of the divine freedom elaborated the theme of the absoluteness of God's power; nothing can destroy him or his purposes. It is evident, also, that he has the requisite quality of will: the perfections of the divine love exhibit God's unfailing benevolence toward man. God's "faithfulness," then, does not require that we turn to a new theme, not touched on before; rather, it emphasizes and makes unmistakably clear that this power and this love are not mere abstract principles somewhere far off in heaven but concrete realities in actual human lives. But unlike a faithful friend who can, after all, only confront one face to face, God's faithfulness surrounds one, protecting him on all sides.

> *Even though I walk through the valley of the shadow of death,*
>   *I fear no evil;*
> *for thou art with me;*
>   *thy rod and thy staff,*
>   *they comfort me.*

> *Thou preparest a table before me*
>   *in the presence of my enemies;*
> *thou anointest my head with oil,*
>   *my cup overflows.*
> *Surely goodness and mercy shall follow me*
>   *all the days of my life;*
> *and I shall dwell in the house of the Lord*
>   *forever.*

PSALM 23:4-6

This "companion" is not one who may sometime die and thus betray one: "he who keeps you will not slumber" (Ps. 121:3). He is the Creator of all men, and he faithfully sustains them through each day of their lives not only in food and drink but also with the faithfulness of their human friends; he remains faithful to them in trouble and adversity, even patiently bearing with them when they violate his holy will, when in despite and distrust of him they commit treason against his kingdom; he remains faithful even in death, in the loss of all human companions, when all they know and cherish and believe seems gone. Such is "the fellowship of the Holy Spirit."

God's faithfulness, of course, is not restricted only to his dealings with men; his keeping faith with mankind is a symbol of his relations with all his creatures. Each has its role and task within his purposes, and each he faithfully supports and sustains, enabling it to come to the fulfilment he has willed. God's faithfulness, thus, is the presence of his Spirit to and with and for all creation, sustaining it in being, giving it structure, teleologically ordering its processes of evolution and development so they will move toward the realization of his ultimate objectives. The stability and dependability which we find throughout the universe is the expression of God's keeping faith with creation.[2]

b. This discussion of God's faithfulness has brought us naturally to *the second perfection of the divine communing: the responsiveness of God.* Here also is a term drawn primarily from interpersonal relations; indeed, responsiveness might be considered simply one aspect of faithfulness, for how could one be faithful to another without responding to him? However, there is more here than a mere element of what has already been discussed. Among one's faithful friends can be distinguished some who are more responsive than others, and this is no reflection on their faithfulness, that is, on their steadfast willing of personal community. Rather, it points to a sensitivity in their attitude; a certain living receptiveness to the actions, desires, and needs of others; a subtle awareness of every nuance of changing life and consciousness within their friends. Like the dancer who gracefully leaps into the air and then lands on her toes with everything in perfect balance, the responsive friend practices a delicate art, leaping at just the right moments and steadying at others, ever keeping perfect balance with the living reality to which he is responding. It is just such a responsive person that we speak of as especially sympathetic or understanding. Personal relations characterized only by faithfulness, however steady and secure, might well be plodding and dull; it is responsiveness that gives such relations spontaneity, life, vitality. However, a relationship characterized only by responsiveness would not be personal at all, for there would be no firm moral will giving it structure and form through setting enduring purposes to be realized in time; it would be more the mechanical reaction of a ball bouncing off a wall than an authentically personal response. Both faithfulness and responsiveness are necessary for full interpersonal communion between an "I" and a "thou."

It is necessary to speak of God's responsiveness as well as his faithfulness if we are to express adequately his personal presence to

[2] For elaboration of this theme from the side of creation, see below, Pt. II.

creation in the Holy Spirit. Without this, his faithfulness might mean merely that he can be relied on to continue going *his* way. Though this too must certainly be said, it is necessary to add that his way is to *respond to his creatures*, to be in continuous and living relation to their needs and desires and decisions. God's perfect responsiveness is the quality which enables him to deal with every new happening in the created order with freshness and creativity, bending it toward his ultimate objectives without violating its own integrity. On the human level, this responsiveness is the basis for faith's conviction that prayer is significant and meaningful. For prayer is man's conscious and deliberate attempt to focus his being—his gratitude, needs, hopes, fears—before God, in the expectation that he will respond appropriately, as a faithful and responsive friend answers when one speaks.

The relation of all creation to God the Holy Spirit can most adequately be interpreted with the aid of such personal analogies as faithfulness and responsiveness, impersonal analogues hardly conveying what is here involved, and what is actively expressed in the attitude of prayer; in and through the loyalty of friends can be sensed something of that deepest and most responsive loyalty that sustains all that is. But it must also be remembered that these concepts apply symbolically, not literally, to the divine being. They do a serious disservice if they generate expectations that God will reply to man's address almost in human words, as would another man. He is Lord of the universe, ground of all being, not one whom any man meets face to face.[3] Thus, God's responsiveness and faithfulness are never directly *experienced*, except as they are perceived through and in loyal friends, on the one hand, and the creative and sustentive powers and events in nature and history, on the other. Nevertheless, it is proper to characterize him in such terms: there is no better way to speak of his presence as living and personal being.

c. The affirmation that God is responsive to his creatures' every need leads to *the third perfection of the divine communing: the*

---

[3] Already in the Old Testament Moses is warned that he will be allowed to see only God's "back" (Ex. 33:23), for a man cannot see God's face and live (33:20); and in the Johannine writings it is explicitly stated that "no one has ever seen God" (John 1:18; 1 John 4:12).

understanding of God. One reason for imperfect responsiveness on the human level is failure to understand the other and to discern what response would be appropriate and right. But God's response can be perfect because he knows men perfectly, understanding what is needed in order for them to become the beings he intends. To speak of God's "understanding" is not simply to repeat what was said before (above, pp. 155ff.) under the rubric of his omniscience, his grasping how and what all things are. God's all-knowing, as we noted, is an aspect of his power which rules the world. "Understanding" (= to "stand under" or take upon oneself) has a broader and more profound meaning than "knowledge" (which comes from a root meaning "to be able to do something," i.e., to have power over something). Where "knowledge" allows and makes possible external manipulation or control, "understanding" involves an intuitive empathy that perceives and feels from within the situation of the other. To say God deals with his creation with understanding is to imply the rightness, the special appropriateness of his dealings with it: he treats his creatures wisely, not ignorantly or rigidly, not without due consideration of their character and nature. His actions toward and with men and all other creatures are characterized by sympathy (cf. Heb. 2:18, 4:15), and "understanding . . . beyond measure" (Ps. 147: 5).

It requires profound understanding of another to be in every way faithful and responsive to him, thus assisting toward his authentic fulfilment. When our sympathetic understanding of others helps make possible their emergence as free and creative persons in responsible community, it becomes an analogue for grasping the significance of God's understanding of all his creation.

d. The fourth perfection of the divine communing: the forgiveness of God.[4] Thus far this interpretation is still more formal and abstract than appropriate for describing God's concrete relation to men. For one can still ask: How in fact does God show his faithfulness toward man? With what does he respond to him? What stance does his understanding lead him to take? The answer to all three

---

[4] See also some previous remarks on God's forgiveness in the discussion of grace and mercy as perfections of the divine love (Ch. 14).

questions is given with the fourth perfection of the divine communing, which sums up the previous three and in some ways the entire Gospel. The attribute of God's forgiveness preeminently is drawn from interpersonal relations. The experience of estrangement and reconciliation between persons here becomes the symbol for the strained and troubled, yet nutritive and restorative, relation between creature and Creator. Man, created for community with God, now lives in ignorance of and estrangement from him. In his wisdom God understands that he can overcome this alienation and heal the guilt of men through forgiving them. *Tout comprendre, tout pardonner!* And so he does in fact forgive; he accepts men as they are, wiping away their guilt, restoring them to community with him, forgiving their sins as Jesus forgave those who sinned against him (Lk. 23:34) and as he expected his followers to forgive (Mt. 18:21–22).[5]

The forgiveness of God is an expression of the intimacy of his spirit to and with his creatures. There is no such thing as forgiveness at a distance; forgiveness is precisely wiping away the distance that has come between persons because of the sin of one against the other. When one has violated the confidence of another or betrayed him, his guilt clings like the bloody spots on Lady Macbeth's hands. No rationalization can destroy it, nor can the intervention or consolation of friends. A barrier is set up which cannot be overcome—except by the offended one's forgiveness. Only that personal act by the other self can overcome the estrangement and restore the positive relation. Forgiveness of another presupposes, on the one hand, full recognition of the seriousness of the offense—for if one knows the forgiving was in partial ignorance of the offense, his guilt hangs just as heavy —while, on the other hand, the for*giv*ing one "gives" up what he might rightly demand in view of the offense, freely offering to be reconciled. Forgiveness is thus a free act of self-giving, directed toward the guilty one, making possible resumption of communion with him.[6] An act of forgiveness involves not only real love and

5 Cf. 1 John 2:12: "your sins are forgiven for his sake."
6 In this respect, as Ritschl has noted, "forgiveness itself keeps awake the memory of sin and its unworthiness" even while overcoming the estrangement which guilt inevitably brings with it (*Justification and Reconciliation* [Edinburgh: T. & T. Clark, 1900], p. 60).

genuine freedom but profound understanding in the forgiving one as well. Because it is such a delicate act, full and free forgiveness seldom occurs among human beings; our forgivenesses are usually tentative and fearful and half-hearted. God, however, is one whose understanding is perfect, whose love is perfect, whose freedom is without bounds. He, therefore, can deal with his creatures in perfect forgiveness, reconstituting the situation they have corrupted and restoring them to their proper tasks in his kingdom.

Speaking thus of God's forgiveness—as with his faithfulness and responsiveness and understanding—does not add *materially* to the conception of his nature as previously discussed, that is, that he is absolutely free and absolutely loving. Yet, perhaps, all has been transformed. For if one can say, "God forgives!" he is saying that God stands in relation to the most intimate and secret dimensions of his creatures, responding to their inadequacies and failures, to their alienations from self and others and from him, and to that most personal of all possessions, their *guilt.* This is to know him as the *living God,* who is active at every point in existence, the sovereign Creator and Lord of the universe and the "suffering servant" who redeems his creatures. In contrast, to one who cannot really speak of God's forgiveness, he has not yet become Lord over all and savior of men. Not to believe in God's forgiveness of even one's personal guiltiness is not to know the God of Christian faith; but to know God as one who forgives and restores his creatures is implicitly to know the whole Gospel. For its claim is precisely that the reconciling activity of God has been firmly established in man's history with the founding of "the kingdom of his beloved Son, in whom we have redemption, the forgiveness of sins" (Col. 1:13–14). Participation in this reconciling activity and this community is the historical ground of all Christian faith and life.

17 / God as Trinity

It is necessary now to sum up the Christian doctrine of God as we have come to understand it. This can be done most easily by turning again to the doctrine of the trinity. What was said earlier about the trinitarian conception will be remembered: in it we have a concise formula which focuses attention on the three indispensable dimensions of the Christian understanding of God. (1) It is *God,* the transcendent one, the Creator of the heavens and the earth, with whom we are here concerned. (2) The content of the word "God," which would otherwise be abstract and vague, is filled out by reference to the history which comes to a focus in the concrete person-event Jesus Christ, that is, in Jesus Christ is God's self-manifestation. (3) Only because God does not remain transcendent of all human experience or buried in a past event long since gone and dead, but is active here and now making himself known, are we enabled to recognize the Christ-event as more than simply another episode in history, as in fact God's presence among us. All three of these points are presupposed whenever we speak of God; and yet in all we are concerned with the same one God. The Christian doctrine of God is intrinsically trinitarian.

The other chapters of Part One have filled out the meaning of these statements in somewhat more detail, so we are now in a position to examine with fuller understanding the trinitarian structure of the Christian conception of God. The earlier statement of the doctrine portrayed it as dealing essentially with presuppositions of the claim that God reveals himself in Jesus Christ, depending heavily on the analogy between divine revelation and human communication. The latter can be analyzed into three moments: (a) one self (b) reveals himself through media of speech and gestures, and thus (c) becomes internalized in or known by another self; in a similar way God manifests himself through his Word and becomes appropriated within men's spirits. The usefulness of this analogy is apparent; but it is important at this point to note certain limitations of it.

When a man, let us say Plato, reveals himself in this way, he is master (at most) of the first moment, that is, of his deliberate act of speech or writing; but having acted, he loses his mastership. Thus, having once published the dialogues, Plato could no longer retract what he had said; at most he could amend it through further writing. Moreover, Plato is even less master of the *interpretations* of the dialogues which appear within and develop through the work of later students (moment c). Although Plato's original intention carries much weight with interpretation, there is no *living* lordship here: he is subject to the will and understanding of the interpreter.

In contrast, if *God* is revealed, he must remain Lord in all three moments, not merely the first (which would be a kind of deism of revelation). To deny this would be to deny that it is in fact God (i.e., the Lord) who is revealed, because he would not be revealed in his lordship at all but rather as subject to man's disposal. Thus, on the one hand, if one wishes to claim that God is revealed in Jesus, he must be prepared to maintain that he is *present in Jesus* in a more living and vital way than Plato in his dialogues—that is, he actively maintains his lordship; this is the reason for the metaphysical claims about the Christ-event discussed in Chapters 12 and 13. On the other hand, one must also be prepared to hold that God is present and at work through the Holy Spirit in a more active and effective way than Plato in a contemporary platonist: that is, he actively manifests himself to the believer in such a way that the latter submits to him as the Lord. This is why it was contended (in discussing the Holy Spirit) that the Christ-event may not be regarded as dead and buried but is rather a "living presence" (p. 232) which "orders and gives significance" (p. 233) to men's lives. Thus, when it is *God's* self-revelation with which we are dealing, we are involved in metaphysical issues much more far-reaching than with ordinary human communication; the threefoldness of God's being as Lord is unique, and the analogies drawn from human communication and community must be sharply qualified and transcended to grasp it.

One can see from another vantage point the importance of the trinitarian conception by considering the consequence of ignoring or dropping it. Let us examine the implications of *unitarianism*— meaning, of course, not the unity of the one God in three persons, but the unitarianism which rejects the notion of God's threefoldness entirely.

The most common form of unitarianism in Christian history, and the one that seems the simplest, is a unitarianism of the Father.[1] Those who take this position claim to believe in God the Father, Creator of the heavens and the earth, First Cause, Ground of all being; but they are very hesitant to speak about God the Son. The latter conception seems to them to be introducing another God alongside the true God; moreover, in the questionable speculations about the alleged divine nature of the man Jesus, it seems to them to verge on idolatry. Let us, say these unitarians, speak only of God the Father and worship him alone.

When we look a little closer at this position, however, some serious difficulties appear. The unitarianism of the Father is either an implicit trinitarianism, or it is using words with very vague meaning. For consider: Why is God called "Father" here? What justification can be given for thus thinking of him in *personal* terms? This symbol suggests that God is loving and forgiving and merciful to his children, who are viewed as all brothers under the one Father. But how could one ever come to know or believe this? Surely not on the basis of our scientific knowledge of nature. The gods revealed here are of a different sort: if it is the nature known to physics, reality seems to be deterministic order or mechanical law, or perhaps chance spontaneity, hardly the loving care of a father; if it is the nature studied in biology, we are confronted with much seemingly wanton destruction of whole species of life in the unceasing

---

[1] The conception of the three forms of unitarianism and their theological consequences, I have adapted from H. Richard Niebuhr, "The Doctrine of the Trinity and the Unity of the Church," *Theology Today* (1946), 3:371–384.

battle for survival of the fittest, scarcely unambiguous evidence of a father's guiding hand; even the tortuous movements of human history, filled with hatred and greed, bloodshed and warfare, tragedy and destruction, give little evidence of any real brotherhood among men under the universal God. No, knowledge of nature and history, however great and impressive it might be, could hardly be the basis for belief that ultimate reality is fatherly.

If now we seek out the hidden but actual grounds for such belief, the most important will probably be that its adherents were born into a history where God was understood this way. That is, this conception of God was taken over, perhaps unconsciously, from tradition. Most of us in the West have been directly or indirectly immersed from childhood in the Judaeo-Christian tradition; and thus all our thinking about God has been colored by the image of a gracious, personal, forgiving, heavenly Father. The Christ-event had much to do with giving the whole tradition this emphasis (subsequent Judaism also having been powerfully influenced, despite its rejection of Jesus as the Messiah). A unitarianism of the Father, if it is really sincere belief in a loving personal God, in fact thus secretly presupposes the Son to whom he is Father: it is ontologically grounded on that revelatory history for which the appearance of Jesus was decisive. Furthermore, unless this unitarianism is deistic in character, a doctrine of the Spirit is also implied. If God the Creator were simply the Starter of the universe who has now deserted it, he would be irrelevant to our present existence and could and should be forgotten. But if this First Cause is also the living God, active and purposeful in our present—One who genuinely cares for his children and may properly be worshiped by them—then he must be viewed as immanent in history as well as transcendent, Holy Spirit as well as Father. Thus, a unitarianism of the Father usually is in fact an implicit trinitarianism; often it has simply not thought through clearly its own presuppositions.

There is, however, an alternative to this conclusion. Since the actual historico-ontological ground of this faith is unrecognized by its devotees, they may gradually depart from it, with the consequence that the symbol "God" steadily loses its concrete content and meaning. When this happens, ultimate reality should no longer be called "Father" nor even "God," for it is not believed to be personal and living. When unitarianism of the Father loses all trinitarian content, it becomes belief in an abstract first principle of the universe—hardly a sufficient object for religious faith and certainly no adequate basis (in itself) for meaningful personal existence.

Unitarianism of the first person is not the only possibility: if Christian faith is given its content by the person Jesus Christ, why not a unitarianism of the Son? Many Christians have taken this position, the greatest of the early ones being Marcion. Here it may be argued that God the Creator—the foundation of this world in which we find ourselves—is evil, for in his universe power and destruction triumph, and love is crucified; at best he is morally and existentially irrelevant, being simply "omnipotent matter" (Bertrand Russell). But Jesus has shown what meaningful human life consists in. Man must live for and devote himself to love, self-sacrifice, goodness —not cold impersonality. We should become followers of this Jesus who showed men how to live, or, as it is now more fashionable to say, who exemplified authentic existence.[2]

Not all who take this position would openly wish to call Jesus "God." But in actual practice he may function as God: the words of the "sermon on the mount" become viewed as eternal truths or ideals, almost words of God himself; Jesus' actions are apprehended as normative for all human life; his feelings and personality become the object of meditation and devotion. In this way a unitarianism of the second person develops in the Jesus-cults which appear frequently in Christian history: it is Jesus toward whom life is oriented and who is taken as the ultimate reality with which we have to do.[3]

---

[2] The most recent expression of this form of unitarianism is to be found in the so-called God-is-dead theology. See, e.g., William Hamilton, *The New Essence of Christianity* (New York: Association Press, 1961); Paul van Buren, *The Secular Meaning of the Gospel* (New York: Macmillan, 1963); and T. J. J. Altizer, *The Gospel of Christian Atheism* (Philadelphia: Westminster, 1966).

[3] The hymns which these movements produce are instructive in showing how easily divine characteristics and activities can be attributed to the man Jesus by Christians. Consider, for example, Catholic piety with its "Fairest Lord Jesus, Ruler of all nature"; or protestant evangelical pietism, with its "I have found a friend in Jesus, he's everything to me" and "Jesus shall reign where'er the sun does his successive journeys run"; or protestant moralistic liberalism, "O Master-workman of the race, . . . Builder of life divine." The popular piety of Christian faith is full of Jesus-worship in which, for all practical purposes, Jesus is God—the center of devotion and source of meaning and reality in life.

Once more, however, there are difficulties. Either such a position is idolatrous, or it, like the unitarianism of the Father, is also implicitly trinitarian. For consider: By what right is this mere man, Jesus of Nazareth, followed and adored and even worshiped as though he were God himself, the very source of man's being, the Lord of history and nature? Clearly such devotion is justifiable only if it is believed that in some sense he is identical with the transcendent One, the source of all being and meaning; in this person must be present, somehow, the *Logos*, the meaning of existence. This implication is just as true for protestant liberals, who seek to follow the teachings of Jesus as though they were final truth, as for the humblest, most naive converts at a revival meeting. Moreover, since for such second-person unitarians it is the *spirit* of the Galilean which gives life its deepest meaning, some doctrine of the continuing life and presence of that spirit seems presupposed. Thus, our unitarianism of the second person also turns out to be implicit trinitarianism which has not thought out clearly all its implications.

Because it is not theologically self-aware, however, such piety may degenerate into sheer idolatry, worship of the man Jesus. For it may forget that Jesus is significant primarily because in and through him we encounter God the Father, Creator of the heavens and the earth; and only to that extent is any worship or absolute giving of oneself to him justifiable. How often has devotion to Jesus been the idolizing of an attractive human being instead of worship of the true God, Lord of nature and history!

By now no doubt the reader will have discerned the third unitarianism common in Christian circles, unitarianism of the Spirit. "I believe in the God I know in my own religious experience." "It is through my conscience that God speaks to me, and I need nothing more than that." "God deals with each individual in the depths of his own heart." Such remarks represent the tendency to regard the reality known to and in the inner spirit as the true God, to the neglect of the Father and the Son.

However, as with unitarianism of the second person, such views are either implicitly trinitarian or idolatrous. For there are many voices of conscience directing men to do many sorts of things, from head-hunting and murder to loving the neighbor and serving humanity. Are all these then of God? Is there no criterion by which we can and must distinguish among them? The early Quakers, who are sometimes credited with this kind of spiritualism, were actually much more realistic. They knew that the "light within" must in fact be the "Christ within"; if not, it was a false light.[4] That is, true leadings of conscience were to be distinguished from false by a criterion drawn from the historical Jesus Christ. The well-known "varieties of religious experience" (James) gives rise to the same sort of problem. Are Plotinus' mystical experience of union with the One and the ecstatic loss of self-control in the meetings of some pentecostal groups, the sense of awe felt on seeing the Grand Canyon for the first time and the vivid perceptions stimulated by LSD all experiences of the divine? Is there no criterion by means of which to "distinguish between spirits" (1 Cor. 12:10) and to "test the spirits to see whether they are of God" (1 John 4:1)?

Probably no one fully surrenders his faith and life to this sort of chaos: some criterion to test the spirits is always used; and, though this may not be recognized, it is often not as distant from the one suggested in the New Testament as might be supposed. "By this you know the Spirit of God: every spirit which confesses that Jesus Christ has come in the flesh is of God, and every spirit which does not confess Jesus is not of God" (1 John 4:2–3). I suspect that most who subscribe to a unitarianism of the Spirit in fact conceive that Spirit as love, good will, mercy, and the like, that is, they implicitly define it in terms shaped by and ultimately drawn from the history in which Jesus Christ was the defining figure. Moreover, if such persons were to examine their convictions more closely, they might well discover that they are devoted to the spirit of love and mercy precisely because it represents for them what is ultimately Real for man: a doctrine of the first person of the trinity is also suggested. Thus, unitarians of the Spirit also turn out to be implicit trinitarians who have not thought out clearly all the implications of their position. Their avoidance of trinitarianism can only leave them in a

---

[4] See, e.g., Robert Barclay, *An Apology for the True Christian Divinity* (Philadelphia: Friends Book Store, n.d.), Propositions Five to Seven.

chaos of subjective spirits on the one hand (unless they accept some other "revelatory event" as decisive), and in danger of idolatrous worship of their own inner feelings and experience—that is, themselves—on the other.

The fact that these three unitarianisms have appeared and continue to appear within the Christian tradition suggests that each points to a dimension of the Christian doctrine of God which is indispensable. Yet each, when taken by itself, proves one-sided and incomplete. However much Christians try to avoid it—and the repeated appearance of these several unitarianisms is clear evidence that they do—they cannot help speaking of God in terms of all three persons. God is the Father: he is the Creator, the Judge, the Holy One, the Absolute; he is "beyond the limit" of all human being and experience and as such is to be characterized by perfections of unity, power, holiness, and glory. But God also is the Son: he is the Revealer and Redeemer, Servant and Word, Jesus Christ, the One present to man at a particular point in history and properly described by perfections of relativity, grace, mercy, and nonresistance. And God is likewise the Holy Spirit: he is the Comforter and Counselor and Companion, with his creatures everywhere and always, One characterized by perfections of faithfulness and responsiveness, understanding and forgiveness. It is the *one* God who is designated by these three groups of attributes; for Christian faith it is impossible to think him at all without thinking these three simultaneously. Hence we must regard him as trinity if we are to speak thoughtfully and precisely about him.

I have in my exposition of the doctrine of the trinity deliberately avoided the distinction between an "economic" and an "immanent" trinity, a distinction which raises the question whether the Godhead merely *appears* trinitarian in structure *to us* or *is* so *in* himself, *to* himself and *for* himself. The very making of this distinction is misleading and fallacious. It presupposes that we are in a position to say something of what or how God is in himself quite apart from what he is in relation to us, for only thus would we be able to compare and contrast these with each other. But we know only the God we know—that is, God as he is related to us—and hence we have no way of speaking or thinking of God-in-himself as somehow distinct from God-in-his-revelation-to-us.[5] We can, therefore, neither affirm that the doctrine of the trinity is simply our idea of God but not God as he really is ("modalism," or a "merely economic" trinity), nor are we in a position to assert that God in himself is a complex structure of generation and spiration, procreation and procession (the "immanent" trinity with its elaborate internal relations). We can only make the simple affirmation that to speak adequately of the God of Christian faith it is necessary to say three independent, though related, sorts of things; and the doctrine of three irreducible modes or dimensions of the divine being enables and assures this.[6] But we have no warrant to go further and work out an elaborate structure of the relations of the various persons of the trinity to each other. To do so would be to forget that our knowledge of God is always and in all respects in symbols and analogies drawn from finite experience. These provide no basis for detailed deductions about the actual inner structure of the divine being.[7]

[5] See above, pp. 100ff.

[6] The distinction between the "immanent" trinity and the "economic" trinity, though seemingly of great importance, turns out to be a pseudo-distinction, arising from failure to grasp the relational character of our knowledge of God. On the one hand, we cannot but think God as threefold, if we are in fact to be thinking him and not some idol or empty word; and so we must always speak of him as trinitarian if it is truly to be *he* of whom we are speaking. But on the other hand, we are never in a position to go beyond the simple affirmation that for Christian faith God is threefold, and to elaborate doctrines of the so-called inner-trinitarian relations (see n. 7, below).

[7] Only when we forget that our knowledge of God is always symbolical are we tempted to work out elaborate and detailed theories about the interior mysteries of the divine being. Deductions about the so-called inner-trinitarian relations would be possible if God had directly revealed the details of the internal relations in his being, or if we knew our analogies to be sufficiently congruent with God's being to justify inferences from detailed analyses of them to the hidden reality which we know with their aid. But neither of these conditions is met: our analogies, as we have seen, are always loose-fitting, and their precise appropriateness to the divine being always remains somewhat indeterminate (it is just this fact that makes our theological knowledge analogical rather than univocal in character); and God's revelation is not a communication of elaborate metaphysical *theory* and *concepts* accurately describing his being, but is rather the laying bare of his *personal being and will* in and through the personal being and will of Jesus of Nazareth. We must, then, reject any attempt to speak of the inner-trinitarian relations, God as he is in and for himself. God as he has made himself known is the trinitarian God: we cannot know, nor need we know, any more than this. Karl Barth's attempt (*Church Dogmatics*, I, 1 [Edinburgh: T. & T. Clark, 1936], esp. 448–456, 474–512, 533–560) to resurrect medieval trinitarian speculations, appears to me a most unfortunate consequence of his substituting a rationalistic theological *objectivism* for a genuinely revelational relationalism. The speculative reserve (though not the

The real content and meaning of the Christian doctrine of God, as we have observed throughout Part One, is given through the concrete analogies and symbols with which it is elaborated; it is this that people *mean* when they speak of God, and it is this being before whom they bow in worship. But the complex reality suggested by this variety of images is not easily thought. The trinitarian concept provides a form or structure for holding together this fullness of meaning in orderly fashion. When given its proper *formal* role —and not made the *content* of the doctrine of God and the subject of endless speculations—it is indispensable for theological understanding.

---

modalism) expressed in Horace Bushnell's parable would seem to be a much more appropriate attitude toward the mystery of the trinity: "Conceive that a plane, or platitude, is a living conscious being,—conscious, of course, of what it is or what is in it, and of nothing more. It has no categories of thought, save what belong to it as a plane. Given now the problem, to make the plane know or conceive a solid. By the supposition, weight, resistance, color, and other like properties of solids, can not enter into the conception given. Nothing obviously can be done, but to reveal or expose to the plane the inclosing planes of the solid; or to inform it, which is the same thing, that a solid *is* so many planes thus and thus related; for it can not be said that a solid is matter contained or bounded by the planes, because, by the supposition, the inquiring plane has no idea of matter, and no power of conceiving it. But now the instructed plane begins immediately to arrange a speculative science of solids, and lays it down as a certain article of knowledge that so many planes are themselves the essence, or essential properties of a solid. Would it not be wiser in this plane to be more of a disciple and less of a philosopher? to look intently on the planes presented, take them as hints of some profound reality in the solid which it can not definitely think; and then, since it cannot receive into its own plane of intelligence the full conception of a solid, be grateful that it is able to get some very faint impression of this nobler kind of being through so many surfaces? . . . Just so . . . when a human soul meets the revelation of God, who, as the Infinite One, is certainly not within his plane of human thought and conception, and finds Him represented by three persons, which, as forms of thought and conception, are within his plane, would it not be more adequate and wiser to accept these persons rather as surfaces of the Infinite Person . . . ?" (*Christ in Theology* [Hartford: Brown & Parsons, 1851], pp. 138–140).

Part Two

THE CHRISTIAN UNDERSTANDING OF THE WORLD: THE DOCTRINES OF CREATION, PROVIDENCE, AND THE ESCHATON

. . . in order that we may apprehend with true faith what it is necessary to know concerning God, it is of importance to attend to the history of the creation. . . .

JOHN CALVIN

18 / God and the World

For Christian faith, unlike pantheism, God is not all that is real. He has created a world, a second reality, in and through which he is working out his purposes. Within this world he has set man, a creature, in some measure free and creative like himself. We must now turn to the world (Part Two) and man (Parts Three and Four), seeking to understand them theologically.

On the Christian view, God is at once the source and ground of all that is and the fundamental reality with which we have to do. For this perspective, therefore, every object in the world and every phase of experience can be properly apprehended only in relation to him: they must be seen as grounded in and expressive of God's purposes if they are not to be misapprehended and misconceived. "For from him and through him and to him are all things" (Rom. 11:36). For this reason it was necessary to attain some clarity in regard to God's nature and will before we could turn to the interpretation of the world and man. Although the character of the world can no more be deduced directly from the nature of God (Spinoza) or from his revelation (Barth) than can the precise character of a painting from our knowledge of the painter, to gain genuine understanding of the objects of experience, it is necessary to see them, with all their richness of empirical complexity, as expressing the unfolding divine purposes. However, inasmuch as our modern experience and knowledge is so decisively shaped by the canons of science—which require us to interpret and understand every object

of experience only in terms of further experience, never with reference to its ultimate teleological ground—it is problematic whether
it is possible for modern men to grasp themselves and their world
in these theocentric terms. Nevertheless, precisely this is required if
the Christian faith truly has as its object the Creator of all that is,
and not mere verbal abstractions bearing little or no relation to the
concrete realities of life. God is working out his purposes in and
through this world in which we find ourselves; the world's very existence is an expression of his purposive activity in creation. Thus,
both the existence and the character of all finite events and being are
to be understood finally and most fundamentally by reference to
God's purposes.

> *The Lord of hosts has sworn:*
> *"As I have planned,*
> *so shall it be,*
> *and as I have purposed,*
> *so shall it stand."*
>   ISAIAH 14:24[1]

The key symbol in terms of which the relation between God and the
world—and thus the nature of the world itself—can be understood
is the concept *purpose*. We must begin our consideration of the
world, therefore, with a brief analysis of this concept.

Purpose, like the other principal analogies we have found most
helpful, is a concept drawn from the realm of self-conscious personal existence and activity. (It is, therefore, not to be understood
as the Greek concept *telos*, in largely biological and thus impersonal
terms.) It is a concept that refers to man's capacity for and experi-

---

[1] The same theme is continued a verse later:
This is the purpose that is purposed
    concerning the whole earth;
and this is the hand that is stretched out
    over all the nations.
For the Lord of hosts has purposed,
    and who will annul it?
His hand is stretched out,
    and who will turn it back? ISAIAH 14:26–27

ence of "binding time,"[2] his power to connect together successive moments into an organic unity by instituting and carrying through a temporal plan of development. As such, it is closely, perhaps insepatably, connected with our sense of time or history itself, as a developing unity of past, present, and future.[3] The concept of purpose can be conveniently broken down into three (temporal) stages which it binds together in a comprehensive unity: decision, action, realization of the goal. By "decision" we mean that move through which the variety of possibilities before the self is pruned down and one particular objective is defined as the end which the self will pursue; "action" is the deliberate working through the several steps necessary to achieve this end until, finally, the projected goal is realized. The concept of purpose, as used here, implies a *purposer* and *his work*—that is, something other than the purposer which is being created and developed in a temporal process governed by his activity.[4] Thus, the form of purposiveness (including, as it does, both decision and action) may be said to be the metaphysical link or connection between a purposer and his work; and the concrete character of a particular purpose is the actual ground for the particular concrete form and substance eventually to be exhibited in that work. The product of the activity is both (a) brought into its present state of being by the act of the purposer, and (b) brought to completion

2 For further discussion of "time-binding" (Alfred Korzybski's term, see *Manhood of Humanity* [New York: Dutton, 1921]), see my *The Context of Decision* (New York: Abingdon, 1961), pp. 72ff.

3 A. E. Taylor has pointed out: "To introduce *these* distinctions [between past, present, and future] is to make explicit or concealed reference to the individual experient and his interior life of action and purpose, exactly as the same reference is introduced whenever we speak of 'right' and 'left,' 'before' and 'behind,' 'above' and 'below.' In a purely physical world where there were no experients, there might be earlier and later events, but no event would ever be present, past, or future. . . . Now *this* distinction is manifestly based directly on our own experience of ourselves as striving and active beings. The 'future,' the 'not yet,' is the direction taken by a conation in working itself out towards satisfaction (or towards being dropped, because it is persistently thwarted). The 'not yet' is that towards which *I* am endeavoring, or reaching out. Its opposite, the 'no longer,' is that from which *I* am turning away" (*Faith of a Moralist* [London: Macmillan, 1930], I, 73–74).

4 Sometimes, of course, our purposive activity is directed toward ourselves rather than toward external objects (e.g., when we train ourselves to do something in a certain way through repeated practicing). However, since our concern in this section is to utilize the notion of purpose to illuminate the relation of God to the *world* (rather than to his own self-development), we shall ignore such usages and confine ourselves to the meaning in which both an agent and an object for his activity are implied.

through his act. It is dependent on him both for its being and its historical destiny.

This notion of purpose is a helpful analogy for expressing the comprehensive relationship of God and the world. If we speak of the "purposes of God," we are not making pious noises that have no identifiable referent: we are, rather, referring to the metaphysical ground of the actual concrete world roundabout us—the universe as studied by scientists and historians, painted by artists, worked in by all men, the context in which all living creatures exist. We are affirming that precisely this world in which we live has its being only because of God's activity, and that it will eventually be brought through his activity to the goal originally intended by him when "in the beginning God created" (Gen. 1:1). The concreteness of the actual, factual world in which we live out our daily lives can neither be adequately grasped nor understood apart from this metaphysical ground.

There are three fundamental doctrines in terms of which we can conveniently interpret the world as the expression of God's purposes: (1) the doctrine of creation, which deals with all finite being in relation to its origin or source; (2) the doctrine of providence, which refers to the ordering of all finite being in terms of processes of development in history, the working out of God's purposes in successive periods of time; (3) the doctrine of the eschaton or "last thing," which sets forth the end or goal toward which God is moving all history and for which he created the world.

When we conceive the world as thus the expression of purposive activity—as created, as providentially ordered, and as moving toward a final goal—we are grasping it as historical throughout.[5]

---

[5] In this respect history is to be distinguished from mere evolution. The latter includes movement, and even development, through time, but not toward an intended goal; human history, however, is distinguished from mere evolution precisely by the fact that its character and movement is shaped by the conscious decisions and deliberately sought values and goals of purposive beings. Cf. Berdyaev: "The absolutely new arises through creativeness alone, i.e., through freedom. . . . *Creation means transition from non-being to being through a free act.* Evolutionism does not really admit the possibility of creativeness, for it does not recognize freedom and knows only necessity; procreation and redistribution are the only changes it allows" (*The Destiny of Man* [New York: Harper Torchbooks, 1959], pp. 43f.; italics his). The concept of history is thus more comprehensive than that of evolution. All that is meant (scientifically) by evolution can be interpreted in terms of history, but the latter can never be adequately understood simply in terms of the former.

Until about the last hundred years it was not possible to conceive the whole cosmos as in historical development; the immediately preceding centuries viewed it after the image of a machine operating without significant variation through all eternity according to certain immutable "laws of nature." In contemporary physics, geology, and biology, however, this has all been revolutionized, and the concept of development—taken over from man's experience of himself as historical[6]—has become the fundamental category in terms of which the order in nature is grasped. As Teilhard de Chardin has pointed out:

One after the other all the fields of human knowledge have been shaken and carried away by the same under-water current in the direction of the study of some *development*. Is evolution a theory, a system or a hypothesis? It is much more: it is a general condition to which all theories, all hypotheses, all systems must bow and which they must satisfy henceforward if they are to be thinkable and true. Evolution is a light illuminating all facts, a curve that all lines must follow.[7]

Scientific attempts are continuously being made to calculate the age of the universe and the process of development through which it has become what it now is. The appearance of the solar system and the earth, the evolution of life to its highest form, man, the movement of man himself from a primitive animal existence to high levels of culture and civilization: none of these can be understood any longer in terms of the idea of static structure. The concepts of development,

[6] See R. G. Collingwood, *The Idea of Nature*, ed. by T. M. Knox (New York: Oxford University Press, 1945), esp. pp. 9ff. and Part III.

[7] *The Phenomenon of Man* (New York: Harper & Row, 1959), pp. 217–218. ". . . in view of the impossibility of empirically perceiving any entity, animate or inanimate, otherwise than as engaged in the time-space series, evolutionary theory has long since ceased to be a hypothesis, to become a (dimensional) condition which all hypotheses of physics or biology must henceforth satisfy. Biologists and palaeontologists are still arguing today about the way things happen, and above all about the mechanism of life's transformations, and whether there is a preponderance of chance (the Neo-Darwinians) or of invention (the Neo-Lamarckians) in the emergence of new characters. But on the general and fundamental fact that organic evolution exists, applicable equally to life as a whole or to any given living creature in particular, all scientists are today in agreement for the very good reason that they couldn't practise science if they thought otherwise" (p. 140n.).

process, evolution, history, have become the all-prevailing patterns of thought.

It is clear, of course, that this pervasiveness of process-categories by no means necessarily implies or presupposes that modern men characteristically think of the world, or even human history, as the expression of overarching purposes. Indeed, very few scientists would be willing to admit that the category of purpose is relevant to their deliberations. Nature seems wasteful and prodigal, a realm in which new species appear almost by chance and older ones become extinct merely because of their intrinsic inability to survive the rigors life has thrust upon them, a realm in which there are many false starts and failures, much terror and evil—certainly not an order which requires or even suggests the notion of purpose to explain it.[8]

It has not always been clearly understood, however, that this imperceptibility of purposiveness to external observation, and thus to scientific description, is precisely in accord with—even required by— the concept of purpose itself;[9] in no wise does it constitute evidence against the conception of the universe as ultimately the expression of purposive activity. For purpose is the *inner connection* that binds together a succession of temporal moments so they will eventually realize a previously intended goal. Until the objective is reached, however,

[8] In this respect, despite the notable efforts of men like F. R. Tennant (*Philosophical Theology* [Cambridge: University Press, 1930]) and Teilhard de Chardin (*op. cit.*) to revive them, teleological arguments for the existence of God seem, for the foreseeable future, to be quite dead.

[9] Cf., for what follows, Michael Polanyi's contention that "pure" sciences could never uncover the principles ordering machines (i.e., objects constructed for specific *purposes*): "Take a watch to pieces and examine, however carefully, its separate parts in turn, and you will never come across the principles by which a watch keeps time. This may sound trivial, but is actually of decisive significance. For the study of inanimate objects constitutes the science of physics and chemistry and the study of machines forms the sciences of engineering, and we may now conclude, therefore, quite generally, that the subject-matter of engineering cannot be specified in terms of physics and chemistry. Let loose an army of physicists and chemists to analyze and describe in utmost detail an object which you want to identify as a machine, and you will find that their results can never tell you whether the object is a machine and if so, what purpose it serves and how. . . . Textbooks of physics and chemistry do not deal with the purposes served by machines. But the science of engineering speaks at length of these purposes, such as communication, locomotion, heating, lighting, spinning, weaving and hundreds of other manufactures. Hence engineering can deal also with the way in which these purposes are achieved by the aid of machines, while physics and chemistry can form no conception of them . . . [or any other] object or process, the meaning of which consists in serving a purpose" (*The Study of Man* [Chicago: University of Chicago Press, 1958], pp. 47–49).

and the end becomes visible, there is no way to discern the purpose by mere external observation: it is known only to the purposer as the subjective principle with which he is ordering his activity. Only the wood-chopper himself knows whether he is clearing away trees in order to obtain firewood, to provide himself with boards to remodel his house, or to improve the view of the distant hills from his living-room window; the act of cutting wood—that is, that which can be externally observed—does not in itself reveal the purpose of the agent. We should not be surprised, therefore, if we cannot discern whether history has any purpose, or what that purpose might be, since we are not at the end of the process but only somewhere in its intermediate stages. Situated thus in the midst of the historical movement, the most for which we might reasonably hope would be the achievement of some relatively dependable descriptions of the processes in which we are immersed, enabling us to make short-range—in terms of the time-scale of the universe as a whole—predictions, thus gaining some measure of control over our environment. Precisely this is in fact what modern science has succeeded in doing. For this technological and relatively short-range task the conception of overarching purposes shaping the movement of the whole is obviously quite useless.

It should not be thought, however, that simply because the conception of purposive development of the universe is of little significance to science and technology, it is not thinkable or reasonable at all and ought to be eliminated from all cosmological theory. If the concept is introduced and maintained on *other than scientific grounds* —for example, on the basis of faith that God has revealed the purposes he is working out in and with this world—it becomes reasonable and indeed necessary once again to view the events of nature and history as purposive. Although the wood-chopper's purpose could not be discerned by external observation prior to the realization of his goal, if he chose to do so, *he could tell what his objective is;* and we could thus come to know it even before he lifts his axe. Christian faith is grounded in the conviction that God has chosen to reveal himself and his purposes in and through the person-event Jesus Christ.

He has made known to us his hidden purpose—such was his will and pleasure determined beforehand in Christ—to be put into effect when the time was ripe: namely, that the universe, all in heaven and on earth, might be brought into a unity in Christ.

EPHESIANS 1:9-10   NEB[10]

With the shift away from static structural models in cosmology to those rooted in dynamic process, it is at least conceivable that the universe is moving toward some final historical goal, however implausible it might seem that this ultimate objective is "a unity in Christ," that is, the perfect establishment of God's kingdom as a community of love. Christian faith, however, is not grounded on what seems empirically probable but on what is given or implied in the revelatory event. We must, therefore, seek to grasp the world not simply scientifically, as natural process, but theologically, as a purposed history which ultimately shall realize God's original intention.

Thus, every phase of the world-process will be seen as an expression of God's continuing activity, ever moving forward toward his ultimate objective. In every moment and every event God is working in and with his creation, creating his kingdom through time; and we live in the midst of this process. This continuous active presence of God working through time is precisely what is meant by his providence.[11] Providence is not restricted to the happenings of human history; it refers to God's active working toward his ultimate objectives in any and every time and place. During the billions of years before mankind, or even life, had appeared, God was preparing the conditions which would make possible the emergence of free and creative spirits who could enter into community with him; as scientific investigations into the history of the universe show, the course of mere human history has been a relatively short and recent development within God's total work. But all this bespeaks the greatness of God—if one believes in him. The insignificance and relatively late appearance of man from an empirical point of view suggests that we may still be just in the beginning stages of the historical establishment of God's "king-

[10] In Mt. 13:34-35, Jesus is represented as revealing in his parables what had been "hidden since the foundation of the world."

[11] In this respect, as we noted earlier (Ch. 15), providential activity is the work of the Holy Spirit.

dom . . . destined for [man] from the creation of the world" (Mt.
25:34 Goodspeed). When one thinks in terms of this time-scale, the
slow movements of human history—two thousand years having gone
by since the appearance of Christ, and the kingdom not yet come—
are not so discouraging, provided one lives in the confidence that the
providential care of God overarches the whole course of this history
as it moves toward its ultimate goal.[12] It is within this context of a
providentially developing creation—the concrete empirical meaning
of the otherwise abstract phrase, "the purposes of God"—that we
shall later seek to understand man. For human history, and man himself, are to be viewed as significant phases of this overall historical
movement.

A moment's reflection should make clear that the view of the world
suggested here is not alien to the biblical perspective. For the Bible is
essentially a history, "the book of the acts of God."[13] It begins with
the origin of all things in God's creative and purposive activity; it
proceeds to set forth the course of history (as it was understood by
the writers on the basis of tribal legends and Babylonian and other
traditions); it ends with a vision of the ultimate goal of creation, the
appearance of "a new heaven and a new earth" (Rev. 21:1). Some
of the biblical writers, most notably Second Isaiah, directly express
this conception of a God continuously working creatively through history toward the realization of his long established purposes:

> *I am God, and there is none like me,*
> *declaring the end from the beginning . . .*
> *I have spoken, and I will bring it to pass;*
> *I have purposed, and I will do it.*
> ISAIAH 46:9–11

[12] Though modern cosmology provides aid in coming to a recognition of the disparity
between the time-scale of the universe with which God is moving and the time-scale of
our own experience and desires, this conception is not entirely foreign to the Bible. The
delay of the parousia led at least one writer to see "that with the Lord one day is as a
thousand years, and a thousand years as one day" (2 Pet. 3:8). And hundreds of years
earlier a psalmist in wonder and awe could declare that "a thousand years in [God's]
sight are but as yesterday when it is past, or as a watch in the night" (90:4).

[13] See the book of that title by G. E. Wright and R. H. Fuller (Garden City, New
York: Doubleday, 1957).

The former things I declared of old,
  they went forth from my mouth and I made them known;
  then suddenly I did them and they came to pass. . . .
From this time forth I make you hear new things,
  hidden things which you have not known.
They are created now, not long ago;
  before today you have never heard of them.

                                          ISAIAH 48:3, 6–7

The modern conception of the development of the cosmos, when interpreted as the expression of God's historically unfolding purposes, corresponds in overall structure to the biblical view of the world.

It is obvious, however, that there are great differences between biblical and modern views of the history of the cosmos, and these must not be blinked. The need to think out a relationship between these two histories is, of course, a specifically modern problem. Prior to modern historical and scientific work it was taken for granted that the Bible presented an accurate account of the beginnings of the world as well as of the origins and experiences of the Israelites. The historical framework for theological understanding could thus be taken directly from the biblical account: the creation of the world took six days and occurred, perhaps, about 4004 B.C. (according to the calculations of Archbishop Ussher in 1650); shortly afterwards man disobeyed God by eating forbidden fruit in the Garden of Eden and in consequence was banished from that paradise; then came such events as Noah's flood and the building of the Tower of Babel, the call of Abraham and the movement of the Hebrews down into Egypt, the exodus under Moses and the invasion of Canaan, the periods of the judges and the kings, the prophets and the exile—all finally culminating in the appearance of Jesus Christ and the founding of the church. This all could be regarded as a literal and historically accurate account of the general development of human history, and thus as proper context for understanding the nature and problems of man.

It is no longer possible, of course, to accept this view of either human or Hebrew history. We now know that the course of events has not only been vastly more complicated than here suggested but also in many respects quite different. It is necessary, therefore—if the *faith* expressed in the biblical account is to be meaningful to modern men who grasp their history thus differently—to express the modern knowledge of the actual course of events in theological terms, just as the biblical writers interpreted their understanding of the movement of history in terms of their faith in Yahweh as its prime mover. The historical faith characteristic of the Bible can become ours only as we revise thoroughly and rewrite the biblical account of the course of human and Hebrew history in accord with our modern understanding of its actual movement.[14] Such a theological history of the world would provide us with understanding of the relation of God and the world, as well as description of the context within which the existence and problems of men are to be grasped.

[14] This necessity to reinterpret and rewrite received historical traditions in the light of new knowledge and insights was itself felt by the biblical writers. Both Old and New Testaments were produced by a process of writing and editing and rewriting old traditions in accordance with newer perspectives. Thus, in the Old Testament are found the succession of documents by J,E,D,P, the Chronicler and others; and the four Gospels in the New Testament exhibit successive revisions and interpretations of the history crucial for Christian faith. The biblical writers understood that the revelatory history in which they lived must be apprehended anew in terms of the unique problems and attitudes of every new historical situation.

19 / The History of the World

L‌ET us begin our consideration by rehearsing briefly the view of the historical development of the world characteristic of modern educated circles. In this sketch we assume the work of modern geologists, astrophysicists and others to be substantially correct, though of course there is room for discussion at many points and doubtless there will be changes of interpretation, large and small, in the future. The universe itself, as far as we know, appears to be five (possibly ten) billion years old.[1] Life originated perhaps about two billion years ago and the first vertebrates appeared about one and one-half billion years later. Mammals have existed for about two hundred million years, man (in substantially his present physical form) for only about one million. From this point on there was some further evolution of man's biological structure, but this was eventually superseded by his historical development. The latter began at the unknown time when men began to create *symbols* (language), enabling them to relate present experiences to those not present (i.e., to think) and *tools*, with which they could manipulate their world. With the development of language, memory (the symbolic presence of the past) and imagination (the symbolic presence of the nonexistent, including the future) became possible. These in turn enabled men to envision the alternatives con-

[1] The so-called "steady-state" theory, of course, would not allow us in this way to date the age of the universe. I am not concerned here to argue the scientific merits of the several current views (I would not be competent to do so in any case), but rather to show that evolutionary theories (which are apparently at present more widely accepted than the steady-state theory) are meaningfully interpretable from a theological perspective that emphasizes the historical character of Christian faith. Theories which deny genuine development in the cosmos are much more difficult to reconcile with Christian belief in a God who is truly working out purposes in and for the world.

fronting them, evaluating them in terms of past experience; they could thus begin charting their own courses deliberately and executing their plans in personal decisions and actions. Thus, there emerged in the historical process free and responsible moral agents, genuinely historical beings, creators of culture: man proper had appeared on the scene. Finally, about 6000 years ago, writing was invented, and with it came the possibility of keeping records, storing up the experience and learning of each generation with greater accuracy and less loss. And so the great civilizations appeared in the Tigris and Euphrates valleys, along the Nile River and elsewhere.

It is not necessary for our purposes to summarize the course of world history further at this point. The picture obviously becomes much fuller and more complicated.[2] Our interest now must focus on the particular segment of that history which became Israel. Apparently the Hebrews were descended from wild, uncivilized nomads who, between c. 2000 and 1200 B.C., moved in waves into Palestine. Some got down into Egypt where they were eventually enslaved. Then, probably during the thirteenth century, they escaped under a leader by the name of Moses. This Moses convinced the people that a god named Yahweh (of whom he had possibly learned from some Kenites during a period of exile in the desert) had made possible their escape. Hence, they all went to his holy mountain, Sinai, to make a covenant with him: he would be their God; they would be his people.

Later the refugees moved on into Palestine, mixing with the peoples there. There followed a long struggle between the devotees of Yahweh and those of Baal, the agricultural-cult god of the land. Eventually the Yahweh worshipers gained ascendancy and succeeded in establishing a kingdom under his aegis. This had a twofold effect: it meant the coming of civilization and centralized political authority, with the consequent development of the arts, the keeping of records, the concern with culture; but it also meant that interest in and devotion to the king and culture tended to usurp Yahweh's place. In consequence, those loyal to Yahweh became increasingly restless and

[2] An attempt to present a unified sketch of the history of man may be found in W. H. McNeill, *The Rise of the West* (Chicago: University of Chicago Press, 1963).

critical. From their ranks came the great "J" historian(s) of Israel and the major prophets, both emphasizing the binding character of the covenant with Yahweh: he it was who had led Israel in the past, and the people must be obedient to his will; moreover, he was active even now in the events of contemporary history, punishing and seeking to redeem his people. The destruction of the twin Israelite kingdoms and the exile finally brought to an end the political and geographical foundations of the community, but this meant that its religious basis became even more firmly established. When the exiled community was restored to Judah, it was in the hope and expectation that Yahweh's final rule over all history, with the Jewish people his vicegerents, was about to be established.

On this note of hope the Old Testament period closes. The New Testament was written by the Christian community in the conviction that this Jewish hope was realized: God's Messiah—the one who was finally to establish his kingdom over all history—had come, and he would soon return on the clouds of heaven to finish his work. It was not, however, to be a kingdom in which Jews ruled the world. Rather, it was to involve transformation of the chaos in all human existence into a universal community of love—already anticipated in the church— including Jew and Greek, slave and freeman.[3] However, as the years went by without realization of this eschatological hope, the church gradually settled down to becoming simply another religious community, believing that the God of love and self-sacrifice revealed in Jesus Christ rules the world.

We cannot here carry our brief sketch further, nor can we deal with the other very important historical strands (e.g., Greek and Roman) which have contributed to Western civilization. We must turn instead to a consideration of certain theological problems to which the foregoing outline gives rise. This account of how Western man came to believe in the one God Yahweh must be quite unsatisfactory, as it stands, to anyone with serious faith in him. For it suggests that

[3] Cf. Colossians: ". . . the Father . . . has entitled you to share the lot of God's people in the kingdom of light. He has rescued us from the dominion of darkness, and has transferred us into the kingdom of his dear Son, by whom we have been ransomed from captivity through having our sins forgiven. . . . Here, what matters is not 'Greek' and 'Jew,' the circumcised and the uncircumcised, barbarian, Scythian, slave, freeborn, but Christ is everything and in us all" (1:12–14; 3:11 Goodspeed [slightly altered]).

the appearance of this faith was a more or less accidental, and certainly purely immanent, development due to the peculiar contingencies of Hebrew-Christian history. That is, the beliefs about and worship of Yahweh were simply a product of the particular historicocultural process just sketched; given different circumstances and sequences of events, quite different religious patterns would have emerged. "God," thus, far from being Lord of this history, appears to be simply its creation. Doubtless he is a symbol for significant ideals and as such an important historical power. But once he is seen as essentially a product of the human historical process, it is clearly superstitious to "believe in" him as an active agent. Thus, the commonly accepted understanding of how the Jewish and Christian religions arose in history undercuts precisely what faith believes, namely, that *God is in fact the sovereign Lord of the historical process*, the latter being a movement toward his purposed goal. For faith, the history of Israel, and the life, death, and resurrection of Jesus Christ, are "mighty acts of God," not merely the product of human decisions and creativity stimulated by and in interaction with a variety of purely natural powers.

How is this account of the historical process in terms of purely immanent factors—a perspective characteristic of all modern historical writing, implicitly accepted whenever one takes a modern historian's account of an event or development to be substantially correct —to be reconciled with faith in a living Lord of history? Is there any way to harmonize the humanism permeating all modern historical thinking—a humanism few are either willing or able to give up[4]— with biblical faith? Halfway compromises are impossible here. One cannot, for example, adopt modern humanistic historical methods to write the history of Rome and America, but piously exempt the *Heilsgeschichte* of the Bible from the reconstruction to which such techniques leads. There are no sharp boundaries in the historical process making possible such neat discriminations; moreover, such an approach, far from portraying the biblical God as Lord of *all* history, would confine him to a remote and relatively unimpressive segment of the past. Nor is it satisfactory to reconstruct by modern

---

[4] For careful analysis of this point, as well as others in this paragraph, see Van Harvey, *The Historian and the Believer* (New York: Macmillan, 1966).

historical methods the "facts" of biblical history while simultaneously arguing this does not significantly damage the "meaning" of that history as the expression of God's purposes, the latter being the real interest of faith.[5] Historical fact and meaning are not in that way separable; for "fact" is the essential historical anchor-point for "meaning," and a "meaning" is precisely the true or adequate interpretation of a "fact."[6]

It is difficult to see how, in a historical sense, the call of Abraham or the virgin birth can *mean* anything if there never was an Abraham to receive the call or a Mary who conceived without sexual intercourse;

---

[5] For this type of compromise between biblical and modern historical perspectives, the factuality of many biblical reports is openly denied. Thus, the early chapters of Genesis; the stories of Abraham, Isaac, and Jacob; of the plagues in Egypt and the period of the judges; the stories of the virgin birth, the miracles of Jesus, the empty tomb—in all these and many more cases it is granted that the Bible is reporting legend and myth of little historical reliability, and these conclusions are substantiated by the usual historical techniques; the actual history of the Hebrew people was essentially as described by the average secular historian. However, though the Bible's portrayal of the events themselves is inaccurate, its view of their *meaning* is not: in the actual course of Hebrew history God was revealing himself to man, was saving man. Thus, empirical Hebrew history is *Heilsgeschichte*, uniquely different from all other history (which is simply empirical history). And our faith should be in the God of *that* history, as distinguished from the gods of the Babylonian, Greek, or Chinese histories, however arbitrary that might seem to our modern universalistic consciousness.

The biblical perspective itself does not suffer from this kind of arbitrariness. For the Bible does not portray Jewish history as in this way important in its own right. Jewish history is seen within the contexts of cosmic history and human history generally —this is the great importance of the opening chapters of Genesis—and it has its significance only because God is dealing with universal history through the history of the Hebrews. "It is too light a thing that you should be my servant [merely] to raise up the tribes of Jacob and to restore the preserved of Israel; I will give you as a light to the nations, that my salvation may reach to the end of the earth" (Isa. 49:6). This, then, is no mere parochial history; and we are not called to participate in an arbitrary tribal faith. It is the on-going process of the history of the world, and the events—from the exodus from Egypt to the resurrection of Christ—are of special interest only because they contribute decisively to that process of universal history. Biblical history can truly be a history of salvation only insofar as it is in genuine connection with the rest of human history. No mere rewriting of the "facts" of the biblical account by modern historical methods while asserting the truth of the biblical "meaning" can accomplish this end: a theological interpretation of universal history is required.

[6] It is erroneous to regard history either as primarily "fact" (positivism) or "meaning" (idealism and existentialism). Historical fact and meaning are not separable from each other. What in any given case is called a "fact" is always really one dimension of a contemporary scheme of meaningful interpretation, within which the fact is seen to be fact. Facts thus have no existence apart from meanings. However, the demand to "get the facts" is not pointless. It expresses the obligation of the historian to find a *genuine ground in historical actuality* for the meaning he asserts. That is, the term "fact" points to the empirical event which the "meaning" renders comprehensible, if it is a genuinely historical meaning and not merely myth or poetry. Historical meaning is characterized precisely (and distinguished from fiction) by its being rooted in fact.

it is dubious that anything of significance is being added when, after describing the crossing of the Red Sea in purely naturalistic terms, one adds, almost parenthetically, that faith, however, receives this event as peculiarly an "act of God." In such interpretations, "act of God" no longer means a genuine event which decisively and purposefully alters the subsequent course of history—and what else could the word "act" properly mean than this?—but is rather merely a vague phrase which gives a kind of pious comfort to sentimental faith. It has become a *mythical* expression—that is, it expresses in poetic or symbolical fashion some "deep meaning" alleged to underlie every event in history—rather than a *historical statement* about the peculiar character of this particular event.

It is common today openly to dismiss the historical framework of the biblical history—the stories of creation and fall on the one hand, and the visions of a consummation of history on the other—as devoid of any genuine historical value (though perhaps significant as mythical expressions of the meaning of human existence).[7] In such interpretations the degeneration of biblical faith in a God who truly acts in history, into a mythic conception of the depth of meaning in all existence, comes most fully into view. For here, since the "acts of God" have no beginning, effect no real consequences in the historical process, and are not moving toward any genuine historical end, it is

[7] As myths, the stories of creation and fall, of the tower of Babel, and the like, are alleged to portray for us in story form certain of the permanent features of the relation of God and man; but they have little or nothing to do with actual historical developments. They are thus said to provide the "pre-historical" framework for the historical drama which the Bible recounts. The biblical writers, however—who certainly believed these stories to be as "historical" as the others they related—were apparently more acute at this point than their modern critics. For they saw that history unfolds only within a context of prior *history*—genuine decisions, purposes, actions—and that a mythical framework provides no ground for understanding a *historical movement;* the only proper frame for such a movement is prior historical decisions and actions. Hence, they converted the myths they inherited into accounts of actual historical events—just the reverse of our modern writers—and in this way Hebrew history became comprehensible as a segment of universal cosmic history. In doing this the biblical writers were correct. For if timeless myth can provide a proper framework within which the historical process is understood, then the deepest truth about God and man is eternal and structural in character—not established in historical events, in covenants, in acts of faithfulness and acts of disobedience. For such a view the relation between God and man is most fundamentally *non*-historical, instead of, as the Bible continuously insists, rooted in the events of history. An adequate reconciliation between the biblical and modern historical perspectives cannot be achieved by recourse in this way to the category of myth, which really goes counter to both. A thoroughly historical perspective must be maintained throughout.

clear that faith in any actual Lord of history has disappeared. And with it goes the biblical awareness that the events of history in their peculiarity and uniqueness are filled with meaning. But "Israel experienced the reality of its God . . . not in the shadows of a mythical primeval event, but always decisively just in the historical movement itself. . . ."[8] If modern Christian faith is to be in this same living God, a way must be found to understand the actual movement of concrete history as *his particular and purposive activity* moving the historical process toward *his intended goal.*

A first step toward resolution of these difficulties is to cease treating the biblical account as fundamentally a history of the Hebrews, instead of seeking to understand it—as apparently the biblical writers and editors themselves intended—as a history of the *world* in relation to God. The biblical writers' understanding of the actual movement of history, of course, can no longer be accepted, in view of modern historical and scientific knowledge; they were writing in terms of conceptions of the origin and development of the world characteristic of their own time. If one takes them and their work seriously, therefore, his task cannot be simply to "repeat the sagas" (Barth) which they have related; it must rather be to think through for our time and the modern conception of the course of world history the meaning of God's sovereign lordship over it, just as they did for their time. In this work contemporary Christians have a twofold advantage over the Old Testament writers who were most responsible for developing the biblical interpretation of history. (a) The modern understanding of the actual course of the history of the universe is much more accurate than theirs, resting on scientific and historical knowledge and not simply on mythical speculations; it is possible, therefore, to be more adequately in touch with the empirical realities of the historical process than they were. (b) A Christian understanding of the purposes of God being effected through that empirical history can take as its point of departure God's definitive revelation of himself in Jesus Christ, rather than the somewhat confused and confusing images emerging from the decisive events of Israel's history. Just as the Yahwist and other Old

[8] Wolfhart Pannenberg, "Heilsgeschehen und Geschichte," *Kerygma und Dogma* (1959), 5:219.

Testament historical writers projected their understanding of God's nature and will—made known to the Hebrews in exodus and covenant—backwards into the pre-Hebraic past, thus arriving at a picture of the foundations of the world and the early history of mankind as under God's lordship, so contemporary Christians must attempt to interpret pre-biblical and pre-human history as purposive acts of the living God who was definitively revealed in Jesus Christ.

It is not possible here to attempt a theological interpretation of the full course of cosmic history. The most I can do is indicate briefly some of the principal events which would have to be treated in order to sketch the purposive development of which they are significant phases. Where possible I shall indicate connections with the Bible in order that the relationship of this account (both positively and negatively) to the biblical history can be more readily noted.

There are six important stages of historical development in God's cosmic activity—all of them suggested in Genesis—which are prior to and presupposed by that special Hebrew-Christian history often called *Heilsgeschichte*. Each of these may be regarded as of decisive historical importance because it is an event *ontologically transforming the world* (or part of it); that is, in and through it, existent being became in some significant respect qualitatively new and different. This is, then, a metaphysical history, the process of development through which finite being as such has been and is moving. Although what is to be presented here will necessarily be in certain respects hypothetical and speculative, it should not be understood as simply mythical or imaginary pre-history, but rather as suggesting the actual historical development of the world in its theological significance.[9]

[9] It is sometimes argued that one of the principal problems of modern culture arises out of the rationalistic destruction of the "mythical consciousness" in which primitive man lived, a consciousness which expressed and preserved the wholeness of human existence. In contrast, modern culture has broken apart in two directions, toward poetry (which preserves the feeling dimension) and metaphysics (which preserves the cognitive dimension). But neither of these is any longer able to give the sense of direction and meaning which myth provided, precisely because feeling and cognition have here separated and become abstracted from each other (cf. B. E. Meland, *Faith and Culture* [New York: Oxford University Press, 1953], p. 90). The solution advocated is then often a movement toward a modern mythical consciousness. But is there not another alternative? May not *history* be the real successor to myth for modern man? For history, rightly conceived, is the full-bodied representation of the past—out of which we have come and which has produced us—in the present. It can thus both preserve the integrity of the

1] The first event which must here be mentioned, is, of course, the creation of the world. The notion of creation should not be considered, as by many modern writers, to be a mythical expression for the relationship of finite being to the infinite, an anthropomorphic way of expressing the dependence of every particular being on the ground of all being. To convert the notion of creation in this way from a historico-ontological into a static-ontological concept empties it of any possible meaning as the expression of *purposive activity* and makes it designate instead a fundamentally structural relationship. The idea of purpose is time-determined; it implies, as we have seen, the free decision of an active will which then works through time to achieve its objective. If the world is to be understood as the expression of God's purposive activity—as it must, if the heart of the Christian claim is not to be lost—the symbol expressing the fundamental dependence of the world on God, "creation," must not be in any way deprived of its implication of purposive temporal activity.

It must be freely admitted, of course, that the notion of creation here is symbolical. This is not only because it refers to the God who can be thought only by means of analogies (see Chapter 8); it is the origin of all finite being—and thus also the origin of time—which is here indicated, and this cannot be conceived literally. The concept of origin or beginning is itself time-determined, presupposing a tem-

whole man and provide him with an interpretation of his existence. (Cf. Croce: "I compose the history of the situation in which I myself am" [*History as the Story of Liberty* (New York: Meridian Books, 1941), p. 17]; or Hegel: ". . . history is always of great importance for a people; since by means of that it becomes conscious of the path of development taken by its own Spirit, which expresses itself in Laws, Manners, Customs, and Deeds" [*Philosophy of History* (New York: Dover Publications, 1956), p. 163]; or Collingwood: ". . . history is 'for' human self-knowledge" [*Idea of History*, p. 10].) Yet, in sharp contrast with myth, this is accomplished in intellectually critical form. Thus, history can pass beyond myth's naiveté while retaining the union of feeling, will, and intellect. Properly interpreted, it can fulfill the function for modern man which myth did for the ancients, without itself becoming merely mythical. H. Richard Niebuhr rightly contends that "history may function as myth or as symbol when men use it (or are forced by processes in their history itself to employ it) for understanding their present and their future. When we grasp our present, not so much as a product of our past, but more as essentially revealed in that past, then the historical account is necessarily symbolic; it is not merely descriptive of what was once the case. Thus, we observe today how in America the story of the Civil War functions among us symbolically without ceasing to be historic; with its aid we apprehend the structures of our national, historical existence, as North and South, as black and white, as agrarian and industrial; we also discern the tragedy of the judgment that lies on us in past and present and the grandeur of sacrifice and courage that appears in the midst of this guilty existence" (*The Responsible Self* [New York: Harper & Row, 1963], pp. 156-157).

poral continuum as the context within which it has its meaning. This is why one can never avoid asking of every beginning: What happened before that? Our experience is only of *relative* beginnings, and for them such questions make sense and are required; for every "beginning" is in fact always transformation of a prior state of affairs within which something new has now appeared. Hence, when we seek to consider the absolute origin of all that is, we come up against a limit of experience and thought, a limit to which the concept of beginning can be applied only analogically, not literally. It is important, however, that the concept to be used symbolically here be of an *event*, that is, that it be a temporal category; otherwise the God/world relationship could hardly be understood as *purposive*. Precisely this event-character of the relationship between the finite and its ground is suggested by the notion of creation. To assert the creation of the world, therefore, is to deny that the world/God relation is eternal and unchanging and to declare it *historical* down to its deepest ontological roots.

The first event of history, thus, was the beginning of history itself, the world's coming into being. Behind this event we cannot go, and what this event itself was we cannot think. But that it happened one cannot avoid thinking if he supposes, with much modern science, that the cosmos has developed unidirectionally in finite time, and if he believes, with Christian faith, that its very existence is the expression of divine purpose. The alternative to postulating such a beginning would be to conceive the cosmic process in cyclical terms, as in the modern "steady-state" theory and in the conception of the cosmos alternately expanding and contracting forever. Such views cannot, however, be reconciled with an understanding of the cosmic process as itself meaningful or purposive. The contemporary developmental view of the universe makes at least permissible thinking in terms of a beginning of the world, even though what it might have been cannot be imagined. For such a position, the purposive God himself would be the only reality preceding—both temporally (in a symbolic sense) and ontologically—the existence of the world; and he would thus be its ultimate limit. Even the notion of God's active deciding and purposing in that pre-cosmic situation, suggested by the mythical versions in which doctrines of predestination or foreordination are sometimes expressed (cf. John 17:24; Eph. 1:4; 1 Pet. 1:20), is hardly permissible. For this would necessarily involve thinking of a world-coming-into-being, that is, of stages of the world-process *before* the creation of the world.[10] Creation is the first properly historical event of which the Bible speaks and it is the first point where thinking can begin to have concreteness and meaning; it is, thus, at once the extreme limit of human knowledge and its real beginning.

According to modern science the event creating the universe took some billions of years and is in a real sense still going on. In this sense God's creative activity did not occur once and for all and then cease. However, considered as the primary creative act of God which serves as the foundation on which, and the context in which, all subsequent history unfolds, the original creation may be regarded as an act completed with the establishment of the world (cf. Gen. 1). In this respect, this act, itself the expression of God's purpose for the world, was the necessary precondition without which subsequent acts intended to carry out his purpose for men would not have been possible.

2] The first event of history was the movement from nonbeing to being; the second involved ontological development within the world itself, being the appearance of a qualitatively different level of being within the world. It was the creation of life (placed by Gen. 1 on the third day), the emergence of a form of being with nutritive and reproductive powers—that is, the capacity both to organize its environment in certain respects according to its needs, and to adapt itself to its environment so as to perpetuate and increase itself. Undoubtedly the first transitional organisms were exceedingly simple, and would be difficult to distinguish from complex forms of inorganic matter, yet through them the historico-ontological process through which God was working out his purposes moved a further step. Whether life exists

---

[10] From this point of view it is necessary to reject as unintelligible mythology any theological claims about Christ being purposed by God "before the foundation of the world" (John 17:24; 1 Pet. 1:20) except insofar as these are understood to refer to his being grounded directly in the being of God himself (cf. above, pp. 204f.). It is worth observing here that although evolutionary conceptions of the cosmos are by no means committed to the view that the universe began *ex nihilo* in the "big bang," nevertheless for them also it is not possible to project back meaningfully to times and states-of-affairs before that event.

elsewhere than on earth, we do not know, but here it is a second indispensable building block without which the further movements of history would have been impossible. This event, also, has been of extremely long duration, probably some millions of years, and its end is not yet. Through it God's purposes have moved one step closer to realization.

3] The third important event of universal history to which we must attend—regarded by Genesis as the last great creative act of God and placed on the sixth day—was the creation of man, the appearance within history of a being that is himself intrinsically historical. This again was an ontological movement to a qualitatively new level of being, for here appeared a form of reality that is temporal not only in the sense that time determines him (as with nature and life). Since man lives out of his own conscious memories and deliberate decisions in the past, and his life is essentially a continuous creating of the future through his own purposive activity, he determines and shapes (in some degree) what shall be in time. Man is thus *intrinsically historical* in a sense not true of the previous two stages of the historical process. They can be regarded as extrinsically historical, however, since God—a purposive and thus a historical being —shaped and shapes them according to his purposes.[11] With the appearance of man, a "historical being" properly so called first appeared within the created historical order.[12] Man, like God, was able

[11] Since natural science is unable to make this theological assumption, it quite properly holds the category of purpose to be unsuitable for understanding the processes included under our first two events (which comprise most of its subject matter). We are justified in using this category here in the treatment of nature only because the perspective in terms of which this overall cosmology is developed is not rooted in nature alone but is founded rather upon the revelatory event Jesus Christ with its personalistic implications. For these same reasons a "natural theology," which seeks to discern purpose in nature directly and to infer from this the fact or character of a purposive God, is illegitimate, though of course a "theology of nature"—i.e., an interpretation of the natural order in terms of theological categories derived from a revelatory history (as is here attempted)—is indispensable.

[12] Cf. F. Engels: "With man we enter *history*. Animals also have a history, that of their descent and gradual evolution to their present position. This history, however, is made for them, and . . . occurs without their knowledge and desire. On the other hand, the more human beings become removed from animals in the narrower sense of the word, the more they make their history themselves, consciously, the less becomes the influence of unforeseen effects and uncontrolled forces on this history, and the more accurately does the historical result correspond to the aim laid down in advance" (*Dialectics of Nature*, reprinted in Karl Marx and Friedrich Engels, *On Religion* [New York: Schocken Books, 1964], p. 168).

to set purposes for himself, to decide and act and achieve, and thus to transform *even himself* within the historical process.[13] The "priestly" writer was correct when he suggested that man was made in God's "image" (Gen. 1:26–27); for here within God's creation another being, radically historical like God himself, had appeared.[14]

Obviously, this new ontological stage was not achieved simply when biological evolution had proceeded to some point near the present physical structure of man. That evolution itself took some millions of years, but ontologically it remained within the limits of the second event. A further development was necessary: this being had to learn to speak, he had to invent language, before he could become man-the-historical-being;[15] and this essential further creative event took sev-

---

[13] Though Karl Barth argues well that man does not simply *have* a history, but that his being "is itself this history" (*Church Dogmatics*, III, 2 [Edinburgh: T. & T. Clark, 1960], 158), his general conception of the category of the historical is defective in that he defines it principally (as is his wont) in terms of *God's action upon* the historical being and insufficiently in terms of the *self-creative action* of that being. "The concept of history in its true sense as distinct from that of a state is introduced and achieved when something happens to a being in a certain state, i.e., when something new and other than its own nature befalls it. History, therefore, does not occur when the being is involved in changes or different modes of behaviour intrinsic to itself, but when something takes place upon and to the being as it is. The history of a being begins, continues and is completed when something other than itself and transcending its own nature encounters it, approaches it and determines its being in the nature proper to it, so that it is compelled and enabled to transcend itself in response and in relation to this new factor" (*loc. cit.*). This is well and good as far as it goes; but obviously nature also, as we have seen, is historical in this extrinsic sense. Though Barth intends his concept to apply principally, perhaps exclusively, to man as the historical being, it really fails to distinguish between man and nature. Perhaps if Barth did not so disdain the problems of scientific cosmology as theologically unimportant (see, e.g., III, 1, pp. ix–x), his conceptualization of a point like this would be more precise and thus more useful. If man is the finite being who is historical in a distinctive sense, it is because God has created him with *the power to make history and thus to remake himself*, not simply because God acts upon him in history to transform him.

[14] For further discussion of man's historicity as the image of God, see below, Ch. 23, and my "The *Imago Dei* as Man's Historicity," *Journal of Religion* (1956), 36:157–168.

[15] "It appears now that the intellectual superiority of man [over the animals] is due predominantly to an extension of this power [to reorganize memories of experience mentally] by the representation of experience in terms of manageable symbols which he can reorganize, either formally or mentally, for the purpose of yielding new information. This enormously increased power of reinterpretation is of course ultimately based on that relatively slight superiority of the tacit powers which constitute our gift of speech. To speak is to *contrive* signs, to *observe* their fitness, and to *interpret* their alternative relations; though the animal possesses each of these three faculties, he cannot combine them" (Michael Polanyi, *Personal Knowledge* [Chicago: University of Chicago Press, 1958], p. 82). Cf. also G. H. Mead, *Mind, Self and Society* (Chicago: University of Chicago Press, 1934).

eral hundred thousand more years. But with it there appeared within the cosmic historical process of being intrinsically historical, and thus that process was raised once more to a qualitatively new level. God had brought his final objectives one step nearer realization.

4] As might be expected, the picture from this point on becomes exceedingly complicated. No longer is there merely one being, the Creator, working out his intentions; now there are many finite creators also acting to realize their purposes. It is evident that so long as these finite purposes coincide with the overall divine plan—and what that is has not yet come clear within the historical process itself—there will be no particular problems; the course of history will continue to move on as an expression of the divine will. However, if and when in their freedom they deviate from the divine purpose, tensions will appear within the historical process; and forces, at odds with each other and at cross-purposes with the divine, will begin to transform the previously harmonious movement into one increasingly chaotic, into a struggle and warfare of purposes. This development, again an ontological movement into a qualitatively different historical situation —but not, this time, forward toward the realization of the divine plan —was the fourth great historical event to which we must attend. It is the event generally referred to theologically as the "fall" (cf. Gen. 3).

We shall deal with the precise character of the fall in more detail below (Chapter 24). It is necessary here, however, to make clear that the fall is not to be regarded, in accordance with the prevailing contemporary theological opinion, simply as a myth describing pictorially the relation of each man to God, a quaint old story to be interpreted according to the view (found already in Kant)[16] that "every man is his own Adam."[17] While this is doubtless suggestive and helpful, in a more important sense the fall was historical (as it was understood both by the biblical writers and in traditional Christian theology). It is the name for that point in world history when, with human freedom already becoming a reality (i.e., man had been

---

16 See *Religion within the Limits of Reason Alone*, Bk. I, sec. IV.

17 That Karl Barth's category, "saga"—which he somewhat pretentiously substitutes for "myth" on the ground that it is not nonhistorical like the latter (*Church Dogmatics*, III, 1, pp. 81 ff.)—is really just as abstract and nonhistorical as myth, can be seen in the fact that he, also, can find no genuine historical meaning in the fall (see *ibid.*, IV, 1, pp. 500f., 507ff.).

created), man began to act in a way disruptive of the historical process, working against God's purposes for him and for the world and thus acting in a manner destructive of his own being and welfare; it refers to the point in human history where man, no longer simply an animal determined by drives and instincts, disrupted the harmonious development of God's purposes through deliberate and self-conscious *self*-seeking and *self*-centeredness, thus raising (or lowering) the natural struggle for survival to the *moral* level of bitter hatred and jealous conflict and warfare; it was that event in which historical forces were loosed which have not yet been stopped—indeed, which in our own generation threaten to destroy all mankind—forces at whose mercy we now find ouselves. The fall was thus an actual historical event—though not one that happened in a moment to some solitary couple in paradise. It was an event of many generations' duration that happened to the species *homo sapiens* in its historical development; and its consequences are still with us. As the Bible suggests, the fall antedated all civilization, determining its idolatrous character.

Only if the fall is understood *historically*—and not merely as myth, however profound—will its full significance and meaning be perceived. Moreover, only thus will it become evident why man's salvation also can come—indeed, if there is to be salvation, must come —through further developments in the historical process, through a salvation-history. The Christian faith is eminently historical not only because it sees man's being as radically immersed in history; but because it understands that the evil from which man must be saved is a diseasedness and contamination of this historical process and historical being, which man himself has effected through his historical action; and because it believes in a salvation not *from* history but precisely *of* this history and the man inextricably bound up with it. When understood as the expression of a thoroughly historical perspective, Christian theology is a consistent and profound interpretation of human existence. To regard the fall as myth rather than in some sense genuine history shatters both the consistency and the meaning of Christian faith.

5] We know little of the many critical turning points in human history which occurred before relatively well organized societies and civilizations appeared on the scene. The next important event which may be noted here is the process which culminated in the appearance of civilization. It is symbolized in the Bible by the story of the building of the tower of Babel (Gen. 11), where men are portrayed as seeking to resolve the difficulties and problems of human existence not through obedience to God but through cooperatively trying to storm heaven; in consequence they find themselves mired deeper in difficulty. This is in many ways a parable of the ambiguity of man's culture-creating efforts: glorious and proud, yet infected by poisons of destructiveness and mortality. Human activity was now no longer restricted to the immediate problems of survival and propagation; it had moved to the qualitatively new level where man's efforts were directed primarily toward re-creating the world in which he lived. No longer was man simply adapting himself to his environment: he was now refashioning that environment into the home which he would henceforth occupy; and in so doing he was transforming himself into a being who would live by civilized patterns and social norms. History was moving to a new ontological level through man's creation of a hitherto nonexistent form of reality, the artificial world of complex culture with its civilized and socialized men, more at home among their own creations than in nature.

It is significant that the Bible places the building of the tower of Babel—the beginnings of high culture or civilization—as the last great event before the call of Abraham. This suggests that human history generally was fully established as the history of civilization—it had reached the ontological level on which man even today still finds himself—when the history of salvation began. But it had come to this position as an ambiguous history, partly as the expression of God's purposes, partly the work of fallen man now working at cross-purposes with God. Thus, the event in which civilization was born and lives was already full of tensions and strife, even though it was also a step forward. Moreover, the rise of civilization complicated matters further, for it made possible cumulation and growth of the destructive powers in history so that ultimately they would have the potential to annihilate both civilization and the man who created it—unless new and redemptive currents were to enter the historical process.

6] It is at this point in the biblical account that the history of sal-

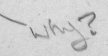

vation begins with the "call of Abraham." One can no longer suppose that this was simply a remarkable event in the life of a single man; it is not even certain that "Abraham" ever existed. Yet this ancient account (as in the case of the earlier events sketched) symbolizes an event which must not be neglected. It would be impossible to understand the important occurrences through which Israel's religion was to be defined—the exodus and covenant—unless there had been preparation of a people whose modes of life and thought were such that they could receive those events as genuine acts of the savior-god Yahweh. The development of nomadic social organization with its many covenants, and of Near Eastern religion with its myths about the gods, its blood-sacrifice cults and the like, was indispensable to the appearance of the "chosen people" in covenant with Yahweh. The whole development of primitive religion—especially in Babylon, Canaan, and Egypt—should be conceived as under God's providential guidance, working now toward rectifying the chaotic historical currents man had created.

This historical development involved a somewhat more particularized activity of God in his dealings with man. Up to this point the whole of mankind has been at the center of our attention; now the focus is narrowing toward a particular group and a special history. This does not imply that God has lost interest in or concern for the rest of mankind. Though Yahweh was soon to "bring up Israel from the land of Egypt," he would also bring "the Philistines from Caphtor and the Syrians from Kir" (Amos 9:7); in short, he would care for each people within its particular place in history. But each would have its own unique role. Israel was to receive and transmit God's revelation to mankind, thus serving as an important vehicle through which human history would come to its intended consummation. Precisely this understanding of those ancient historical roots of Hebrew faith and life is expressed in the biblical writer's portrayal of Abraham's call:

Now the Lord said to Abram, "Go from your country and your kindred and your father's house to the land that I will show you. And I will make of you a great nation, and I will bless you, and make your name great, so that you will be a blessing. I will bless those who bless you, and him who curses you I will curse; and *in you all the families of the earth will be blessed.*"

GENESIS 12:1-3 [RSV footnote for italicized clause]

The particular history which was here beginning to emerge would be characterized by a special responsiveness to God's will: Abraham obeyed the divine summons. Not that Israel as a people would remain loyal in all circumstances to the covenant with Yahweh; precisely the reverse was true. But within the context of Israelite history and culture the possibility of rightly understanding and responding to the divine will began to emerge; and this possibility became in some degree actualized in the great Yahwistic prophets and priests, historical writers and political leaders, in short, in the men who put the stamp of their faith on the pages of the Bible. Thus, ancient Near Eastern culture and religion served as the womb within which a new possibility for man was created—the possibility of salvation, of man once again moving into right relationship with the source and ground of his being. And thus, again, an ontological change occurred within the historical process.

It must be emphasized, however, that without the several major preceding events or stages of history, each transforming the historico-cosmic order qualitatively, the universal significance and profound consistency and thus the very meaning of this salvation-history would be dissolved away. There was good reason, then, for "J" and the other Hebrew writers to project their exodus-rooted faith backward to the beginnings of the world; this was the only way it could make sense. And only if modern men similarly interpret cosmic origins and history theologically will their faith be lifted from abstractness and arbitrariness to authentic meaningfulness.

7] Since full attention will later be devoted to the history of salvation itself (Chapters 26–30), this brief sketch can be brought to conclusion with the barest outline of the further course of the historical movement. In the exodus and covenant (13th century B.C.) the Hebrews bound themselves to Yahweh and his service in the consciousness that they were his "chosen people." The real significance of their peculiar relation to God did not become clear, however, until "J" published his history (c. 950 B.C.), displaying Israel's place within world history under Yahweh's lordship.[18] This emerging Hebrew consciousness that man's many cultures—indeed, all the powers of the cosmos—are but parts of a unified historical movement proceeding toward its goal under a single Lord was an important step toward overcoming the fragmentation of human life begun with the fall; it was a step which only in modern times has come to some fruition in the steady dissolution of the separate individual cultures and histories of mankind and the emergence of "one world." This whole development was decisively informed by the event bearing the name Jesus Christ, in which the history of salvation reached its climax. Here at last God's work to rectify the alienation (dating back to the fall) between man and the ground of his being, and between man and man, resulted in the successful establishment of a historical community of reconciliation among men.

It should not be supposed that history (seen from a theological point of view) has been standing still for the last two thousand years, that there has been no further movement bringing it more fully under its Lord. Only a few of these developments can be mentioned here. The Christian church's appropriation and baptizing of the Greek spirit in the first generations of her existence, however ambiguous its consequences, was an important long stride toward the universalization of the particularistic Jewish history which had given her birth; her growing sense of responsibility for the socio-political order, though leading into serious compromises during and after the Constantinian period, was another important step if the God and Father of Jesus Christ was to become Lord over every segment of existence. In more recent times the Reformation, the rise of natural science,[19] and the

[18] The historical consciousness here emerging is the ultimate source of the modern sense of history and of the modern belief that all particular histories are ultimately one. Through its development man became conscious of himself as historical and even of history as the form of all reality (cf. Wolfhart Pannenberg, "Heilsgeschehen und Geschichte," *Kerygma und Dogma* [1959], 5:219–222), thus making possible also the conception of nature in quasi-historical evolutionary categories.

[19] Not to be forgotten in this connection is the metaphysical and historical rootedness of modern natural science in the Christian world-view. See especially the articles by Michael Foster, "The Christian Doctrine of Creation and the Rise of Modern Natural Science," *Mind* (1934), 43:446–468; and "Christian Theology and Modern Science of Nature," *Mind* (1935), 44:439–466, and (1936), 45:1–27. Also, R. G. Collingwood, *An Essay on Metaphysics* (New York: Oxford University Press, 1940), Pt. IIIA; and T. F. Torrance, *Theology in Reconstruction* (Grand Rapids, Michigan: Eerdmans, 1965), Ch. 4.

a positive thing?

secularization of the West have all contributed to freeing man from superstition (i.e., bondage to the "demons"), thus helping to clarify the nature of faith as well as facilitate the rise of modern culture. Finally, the emerging fact and consciousness that all human histories are one, that human kind is single and that we live in "one world," is of great theological importance. Christian faith has always understood itself in universalistic terms, and in ancient and modern missionary movements it has given direct expression to this conviction; but it is only in recent times that this belief and hope has sufficiently taken on the flesh and bone of concrete historical fact to be visible almost to all.[20]

We do?

In sketching this movement of salvation-history, I do not mean to suggest a simple progressive pattern in the historical process. Each step has been ambiguous, productive of evil as well as good. Though the nineteenth century could believe that the evil in history was gradually being overcome, in our own time this has become very dubious; and many wonder anxiously if human history may not soon come to a catastrophic end, the Frankensteinian powers which man has loosed having gotten completely out of control. Confidence in real historical progress must thus be grounded beyond empirical history, on faith in the capacity of history's Lord to achieve his ends. Though the actual movement of empirical history may make such belief, rooted in revelation, seem not entirely implausible (as I have been suggesting here), it certainly does not provide clear and unambiguous evidence of it.

8] Christian faith, I have been arguing throughout, believes God is accomplishing something in history and that therefore the em-

---

[20] Cf. Lesslie Newbigin's observation: ". . . What is happening now . . . is that the peoples who have no history are being drawn into the history of which the centre is Jesus Christ; and that is the only history. In other words, that which has been static, or at least cyclical, in which the only movement was round and round, life and death, rise and fall—that is being drawn into a movement which is linear and dynamic, which is moving irreversibly and can never be back where it was before. The ferment of change which arises from the impact upon ancient cultures of the Gospel, or at least of that kind of life which has its origin within Christendom, is the force which is giving an irreversible direction to that which was static or merely cyclical. When I say the impact of the Gospel or of that kind of life which has its origin within Christendom, I include technology, western political ideas, Communism—all those things which have come into the eastern world from the West and have their roots in the Christian tradition" (Quoted in A. Th. van Leeuwen, *Christianity in World History* [New York: Charles Scribner's Sons, 1964], p. 17).

pirical history in which we are immersed is moving toward a goal.[21] Doubtless there must be many further developments before that goal will or can be reached, but we are in no position to speculate on these. It is necessary, however, to round out this sketch of the Christian understanding of the world as historical by touching briefly on the climactic final event for which Christian faith hopes.[22] This event—which like creation is at the very limit of man's thinking and can be conceived only symbolically, by analogy with the partial fulfilments realized within history—is the consummation and fulfilment of the historical process. As the *telos* toward which all else is moving, it is the ground without which the various segments of life would remain mere fragments and pieces, and thus finally meaningless. As the objective of God's cosmic striving, even he must be viewed as finding a kind of fulfilment here. When or how or what this event can be, no

[21] Some might object that the analysis of purpose in this work, as involving a definite goal, is too narrowly conceived: with certain purposes it is never expected that a goal will be achieved, e.g., one's purpose to become a good man, or one's intention always to help others maximize the good available to them, or one's pursuit of beauty or truth. Such purposes have a real place in human life, and it could be contended that they provide a better model for developing the conception of God's purposes; this would allow him to do everything necessary for him to do, yet it would not require positing some inconceivable "end" to history. One might raise several questions with such a proposal. (1) Although this model of purpose may be useful for interpreting some aspects of the behavior of men, is it really satisfactory to hold that God never achieves his objectives? or, to hold that God does not have as an objective the actual overcoming and ending of the opposition to him of the powers of evil in the universe? Does not such a view seriously undercut and ultimately destroy the symbol of God's lordship over the world? (2) Is not this open-ended sort of purpose in fact secondary to and derivative from the kind of purpose that seeks to achieve a specific goal? Is it not simply a variation of this latter model, based on the notion of an asymptotic approach to the goal rather than its direct realization? Its derivative character, of course, would not disqualify this conception from serving as a theological model; however, one could not help but wonder whether there is not also for God—as there is for man—a more fundamental sort of purpose, namely, one in which he actually realizes his objectives. This would give rise not only to the difficult question whether there are two sorts of purposes in God, how they are to be related, etc., but would also raise again the issue of God's sovereign power. (3) Is not the three-phase model of decision/action/goal much closer to the biblical picture of history, as well as to that suggested by the theological concepts of creation/providence/eschaton?

In view of these sorts of issues it has seemed preferable to the present writer to develop the notion of God's purposes in terms of a model in which the goal is ultimately achieved. That there are serious difficulties involved in going this way—not the least of which is the problem of making (at least symbolical) sense of the notions of a beginning and end to history—I am quite prepared to admit; but they have seemed to me less intractable than with the alternatives.

[22] For further discussion, see Chs. 22 and 30, below.

one is in a position to say,[23] but for Christian faith the revelatory person-event Jesus Christ is the clue to this final consummation also. The Christian hope is that the goal toward which history is moving is the transformation of the present world into God's perfect kingdom, love and freedom and creativity thus finding ultimate vindication. Toward this end, therefore, men's struggles must be directed; confidence that God's purposes will one day be achieved gives those struggles meaning.

The basic claims of Christian faith and theology—that in and through our actual existence lived out in this world God is working his purposes—are consistent and meaningful if the universe is seen in thoroughgoing historical terms such as these. A historicist perspective makes possible conceiving the entire cosmic movement as in fact the expression of the purposes of a living personal being, of God.[24]

[23] "But of that day or that hour no one knows, not even the angels in heaven, nor the Son, but only the Father" (Mk. 13:32).

[24] It might not be amiss to point out here that, with the exception of the greater attention I have devoted to the period between creation and the beginnings of Hebrew history (in keeping with the greater knowledge of that period now available, as well as with the course of history sketched in Genesis), a theological interpretation of history similar in many of its bearings to the present one is already to be found in the New Testament writer most concerned to see the Christian movement within its historical context, Luke: "Although Luke gives no explicit description of the structure [of history], his whole account is based on a definite conception. . . . The basis is the idea of God's plan. Its beginning is marked by the Creation, which, however, is not thought of as an 'epoch,' but represents the limit of reflection concerning redemptive history. . . . The corresponding limit at the other extreme is the Parousia. Again speculation is strictly avoided, more strictly than in the rest of the New Testament—including Paul. No account is given of the Parousia itself, and no statement is made as to what follows it. Only the course of events up to it is described.

"Between these limits history runs its course in three phases:

The period of Israel, of the Law and the Prophets.

The period of Jesus, which gives a foretaste of future salvation.

The period between the coming of Jesus and his Parousia, in other words, the period of the Church and of the Spirit. This is the last age. We are not told that it will be short.

"There is a continuity linking the three periods, and the essence of the one is carried through into the next" (Hans Conzelmann, *The Theology of Saint Luke*, tr. by Geoffrey Buswell [New York: Harper & Row, 1961], p. 150).

20 / The Creation of the World

KEEPING in view the overall picture of the history of the cosmos as the progressive realization of the purposes of God, we must turn now to a more detailed examination of the three principal moments within which this whole movement is enclosed: creation, providence, the eschaton. Then, with this conception of God's dealings with the world as a whole in mind, we shall turn to the problem of man.

To understand what is implied in the claim that God created the world, let us first recall the earlier discussion of God as Creator. A fundamental emphasis of this analogy, we saw, is God's radical otherness from the world: God is the absolutely self-sufficient one; the world, in contrast, is absolutely dependent. We must examine this analogy from the other side now to see what it tells us about the world. The first thing to be noted is the dependence of the world on God. Everything other than God owes its existence to him; no being could exist without his willing it. This conception is usually expressed in the formula that God created the world out of nothing, *creatio ex nihilo*. Though not a strictly scriptural formula,[1] it expresses the biblical understanding through its emphasis that the heavens and the

---

[1] The formula itself is found nowhere in the Bible, and the opening chapters of Genesis even seem to deny it, suggesting that perhaps God worked with preexistent primeval waters, though "the earth was without form and void" (1:2), or with a preexistent barren wilderness-earth "when no plant of the field was yet in the earth and no herb of the field had yet sprung up—for the Lord God had not caused it to rain upon the earth" (2:5). In Second Isaiah there are passages which come close in their meaning to the formula, however, e.g.: "I am the Lord, and there is no other, besides me there is no God; . . . I form light and create darkness, I make weal and create woe. I am the Lord, who do all these things" (Isa. 45:5, 7); "I am the Lord, who made all things, who stretched out the heavens alone, who spread out the earth—Who was with me?" (44:24). The earliest explicit statement of the idea is found in 2 Macc.: "I beseech you, my child, to look at the heaven and the earth and see everything that is in them, and recognize that God made them out of things that did not exist" (7:28, RSV footnote).

earth, and all that is in them—the totality of all reality not God—
were not developed or made out of some already existent being alongside or other than God. On the contrary, apart from God's creative
act, there was and would be nothing. God required no independently
existing material to produce his world; he created it out of nothing.[2]
Moreover, without the continuous sustenance of God it would fall
back into the nothingness whence it came. Thus, all that is depends
absolutely on God.

This contention about the ultimate dependence and contingency of
all finite being is the basis of the Christian understanding of the world.
The world cannot even be thought as a unity, that is, a "universe," in
itself—in itself it is "nothing." Such unity as the world has, making
it a cosmos rather than chaos, is from God. Because he has brought it
into being to realize certain purposes of his own, it has the particular
order and structure which characterizes it. We have come to take this
all-pervasive orderliness so much for granted, and have built such an
impressive science on it, that we easily forget that it is an *assumption*;
but it can be argued that this "assumption of cosmic unity and singularity *follows* from—before anything else—the assumption of a single
creator-god."[3] This does not mean that one can move, in the manner

---

The earliest extant expression of the formula itself is in Theophilus of Antioch (c. 170–
190): "they [the prophets] taught us with one consent that God made all things out of
nothing; for nothing was coaeval with God: but He being His own place, and wanting
nothing, and existing before the ages, willed to make man by whom He might be
known; for him, therefore, He prepared the world. . . . matter from which God made and
fashioned the world, was in some manner created, being produced by God." (Quoted by
Jaroslav Pelikan, "Creation and Causality in the History of Christian Thought," *Journal
of Religion* [1960], 40:250.)

[2] It is important not to misunderstand this formula as meaning that "nothing" was a
kind of preexistent primal stuff (or chaos) out of which God ordered and shaped the
world, for this would transform the radical monotheism of Christian faith into a form
of dualism.

[3] Max Scheler, *On the Eternal in Man* (New York: Harper, 1960), p. 111. "The
world is world (not chaos), and the world is one world, only if and *because* it is God's
world—if and because *one and the same* infinite will and spirit is latent and active in
every entity. . . . Pantheism, which begins by postulating the world-character of sub-
sistent being and the unity of the world, both independently of God, is only guilty—
in a more blatant way—of the error committed by those who conclude the existence of
God from a presupposed oneness and unity of a world-reality. From this we understand
that wherever pantheism has made an appearance in history it has been always an
end, never a beginning, never the dawning red of a sunrise of belief but always a sunset
glow. It invariably rests on the fact that, in their outlook on the world, men cling to some
of the consequences of a positive religious attitude, though its root and basis be forgotten" (p. 112).

of the cosmological argument, from the order observed in the world to the existence of God. On the contrary, it implies that one cannot understand, or even apprehend, the real structure of the universe simply by examining it. Its structure and meaning are not intrinsic; they are extrinsic, having been given by God and being continuously given by him as he shapes and reshapes the world through history in accordance with his purposes.

There can be, then, no successful natural theology, that is, knowledge of God derived simply from the study of nature. Since it is not even possible to come to a true knowledge of nature without reference to the God who gives her her character, how much less is it legitimate to make inferences from nature as empirically known (i.e., as known without reference to God) to the being and character of God. The understanding of the finite order as *created* is an inference based on belief that ultimate reality is purposive and loving personal will; its ground is thus the history culminating in the person-event Jesus Christ accepted as the revelation of God,[4] not an objective scientific or philosophical inspection (if such were even possible) of the bare finite

---

[4] From this fact that knowledge of God as Creator is rooted in the revelation in Christ, Karl Barth draws the erroneous conclusion that Jesus Christ exhausts the meaning of the entire creation, i.e., that creation was solely for redemption, for the covenant. But there is no need to go this christomonistic (and ultimately anthropocentric) way. In and through the Christ-event one does not learn all God's secret purposes (as Barth seems to imply); rather he learns the *clue* to the mystery of ultimate reality, that it (he) is purposive and redemptive. Though one learns this principally with respect to man here, it must be remembered that it is the infinite and mysterious God who is here encountered. One should not conclude that God's whole purpose is exhausted in his covenant with man; rather he should conclude that his covenant with man is a symbol of God's way of dealing with all creation. As with man, he has brought other realities into being for purposes of his own (doubtless unknown to us); and as with man, it is to be assumed that these purposes are *good* and *redemptive* for the creature involved, i.e., that they involve a kind of realization and fulfillment of the creature for his own sake. Thus, every creature of God's should be understood as in some sense for-itself, to be cherished in its own right. Beginning thus with a christocentrism of faith, one need not end with an anthropocentric cosmology which makes the end of all creation to be God's covenant with man (Barth); on the contrary, precisely because a properly understood christocentrism must lead to theocentrism, it becomes possible to see that every dimension of creation, in addition to such instrumental purposes which it might serve, also exists in its own right. For it was created by the God who pours himself out in love for his creatures and does not merely *use* them for extrinsic purposes. (For a full analysis of the anthropocentric character of Barth's doctrine of creation, see the unpublished dissertation by Paul Santmire, *Creation and Nature: A Study of the Doctrine of Nature with Special Attention to Karl Barth's Doctrine of Creation* [1966], deposited in the Andover-Harvard library of Harvard Divinity School.)

order as such.[5] *Creation* is the event (or process) in which world history has its origin and continuing ground.[6]

The meaning of the Christian claim that creation was *ex nihilo* can be better understood if it is contrasted with two alternative views which stand at its outside limits: pantheism and dualism (or pluralism). Every interpretation of the world deals in some way with the problem of the one and the many, an issue pervasive of every realm of being and knowledge. One alternative is to hold that the world (or "being") and all in it is a unified structural system—that is, it is *one* reality. But it is not an abstract and empty one; rather it contains within itself all the fullness of being and hence expresses itself in the great diversity and variety of the world. This is the general perspective of pantheism (e.g., Plotinus, Spinoza) as well as every other position which holds the world to be a relatively tight and unified structure of determinate form, all parts fitting together in a systematic whole. Every contention that man can know the real character of the world (or God) simply by direct examination of nature and history presupposes such a unified structure of relations, the character of the whole being inferrable from the characteristics of the parts. On this view "God" may be regarded as the essence of, or principle of unity of, the world or being, and the "world" simply God's fullness appre-

---

[5] It is this fact—that all creation must be understood as grounded in the reality manifest in Jesus Christ—that makes comprehensible the otherwise extravagant claim of certain biblical writers that Christ was the very agent of creation (cf., e.g., John 1:3; 1 Cor. 8:6; Col. 1:16).

[6] Thus to root the understanding of the foundations of history in the revelatory event at its center is to proceed in a fashion parallel to those Old Testament writers who first proclaimed Yahweh the Creator of the heavens and the earth. "The idea that God created the world . . . is not an axiom of the Old Testament but a conclusion drawn from it. The creation . . . is thought of as the inauguration of history. If we would understand the biblical faith in creation, we must discover the centre of the Old Testament revelation out of which the belief in creation arose as its final conclusion. That centre is God's mighty and merciful leading of the people out of Egypt through Moses" (Thorleif Boman, *Hebrew Thought Compared with Greek* [Philadelphia: Westminster Press, 1960], p. 172). In this connection it might well be remembered that the oldest account of creation, "J," uses the name of Yahweh as the Creator, i.e., it describes the world as made by the one who had made a covenant with Israel. The covenant comes first, and out of it comes the understanding of creation. It is only the generalized and stylized "P" account that refers the creation to "God." This development may be regarded as symbolic of the way in which the implications of God's creative activity become understood. First it is grasped as the work of "our God," and then by reflection and analysis (i.e., metaphysics) believers come to understand that God's universality implies he is Lord of all the earth and the heavens.

hended in its plurality. The world is quite as necessary to God—it being simply the opposite face of God—as God to the world. The world is no product of the free decision and purposive act of God, no expression of his *will*; it simply *is*, and it is whatever it is, and all that occurs is a necessary expression of its (God's) fundamental nature (cf. Spinoza). God and the world are conceived as mutually inter-dependent—or better: God is understood as one aspect (the unity) of the cosmos, the latter being the more fundamental and all-embracing concept.

This interpretation of reality has the merit of providing an apparently secure foundation for our cognitive endeavors—science, for example—in that it portrays all that exists in terms of *structure*, which from the Greek period has been understood to be the proper object of knowledge. Unfortunately it purchases this advantage by undercutting another significant dimension of existence, value. For everything here—evil as well as good, falsehood as well as truth—is understood as a necessary expression of God's nature. Spinoza rightly saw that for this perspective "good" and "evil" must be regarded as terms relative to our finite and human strivings; they do not properly apply to the universe as a whole (to God). Thus, both in its subordination of God to the all-inclusive concept of the world (instead of seeing the world as expressive of God's purposive act), and in its undermining the metaphysical significance of value, pantheism presents an understanding of the world sharply different from the Christian doctrine of creation.

At the other extreme from pantheism is pluralism, in its most common form, dualism. On this view there are several fundamental metaphysical principles (or assortments of gods and other powers) which, in their interaction with each other, have produced the present world. We may think we have outgrown such perspectives, since cosmogonic myths no longer seem credible. But when translated into more familiar religious language as the struggle between God and Satan; or into more abstract metaphysical language as the conflict between good and evil; or the interaction of mind and matter; or of form, life and matter, pluralism seems more plausible. In each of these perspectives the character of the present world and the course of history are understood by reference to a diversity of ultimate principles or divine powers. In this way the multiplicity in nature, as well as distinctions in value, is given a metaphysical foundation and explanation. Unlike pantheism with its undercutting of the moral struggle, here we are required to take sides, to decide for the good God (or the good principle, e.g., spirit, rationality) and against Satan (or body). Since both powers have shaped the world and us who are in it, each has some sway over us; hence we must struggle. Moreover, this moral struggle is of no merely human significance: the entire cosmos is involved.

Despite the dramatic appeal of such a view, it has serious weaknesses. It is especially difficult, for example, to account for the structurally unified character of the world, making it a possible object of knowledge. The universe is always on the verge of breaking apart into the various principles which make it up, there being no all-embracing unity which holds it together. But clearly the world as we know it—for example, in our science—does not suffer from this defect. Here the Christian doctrine of creation (as well as pantheism) can give a much more satisfactory interpretation. For the Christian conception there are no independent realities or metaphysical first principles alongside God, having their being of themselves and not from him. He is the creator of all, and he is thus sovereign over all; none could exist apart from his willing. (In the Christian mythology even God's arch-enemy Satan is understood as a fallen angel, i.e., as God's creature, and thus radically dependent upon him.)

From a theological standpoint each of these perspectives (pantheism and pluralism) is an expression of the same error: it denies God's sovereignty over the world. Each maintains in its own way that the world is not God's deliberate creation, the purposive and meaningful expression of his will. Instead it is understood as a necessary expression of the eternal nature of things (uncontrolled by purposeful volition), or an accidental (necessary?) outcome of the struggles between gods or the interaction of prime principles.

However, certain metaphysical implications of the doctrine of creation are similar to some emphases of these other viewpoints. On the one hand, the Christian doctrine agrees with pantheism that the world is unified; it is a structural whole. Moreover, it gains this structural character through God's immanence in it (the Holy Spirit). However, this immanence of ultimate reality is not understood as simply the opposite face of the world itself but as the sovereign presence of the transcendent and free God, shaping and ordering the world, his creature. On the other hand, the Christian doctrine agrees with pluralism that there exist other realities than God—namely those making up the world—which are not to be identified with him, indeed which are of a radically different nature. Moreover, some of these realities—for example, men—have sufficient power and freedom to oppose, and in some measure frustrate, God's will. Inasmuch as these have entered into struggle with him, the *present* character of the world, and the course of history which has produced it, are to be referred to a plurality of principles or powers. But on the Christian view these diverse principles, though they have a certain autonomy, are not radically independent of God. Indeed, they have been created by him and are now sustained by him, and they are gradually being brought in spite of themselves to the realization he intends. Without the Creator's continuous sustenance they could neither be nor engage in struggle with him; without his continuously working toward the realization of his purposes, the world would have no order. As at once *orderly* (thus knowable) and *contingent* (thus knowable only *a posteriori*, through observation and experiment), the cosmos as theologically described corresponds precisely to the world apprehended in our experience and known in our sciences.[7]

We can sum up these contentions by noting that the significance

[7] Cf. E. L. Mascall: "All that we are concerned with here is the question what sort of a world will the God of Christian theism create if in fact he creates one; and the point . . . is that it will be both contingent and orderly, since it is the work of a God who is both free and rational. It will embody regularities and patterns, since its Creator is rational, but the particular regularities and patterns which it embodies cannot be predicted *a priori*, since he is free; they can only be discovered by examination. The world of Christian theism will thus be one whose investigation requires the empirical method, that is to say the method of modern natural science, with its twin techniques of observation and experiment. . . . The scientific method makes a double assumption: first, that there are *regularities* in the world, otherwise there would be nothing for science to discover; secondly, that these regularities are *contingent* and so need to be looked for; they cannot be predicted *a priori*" (*Christian Theology and Natural Science* [New York: Ronald Press, 1956], pp. 94–95). See also Michael Foster, "Christian Theology and Modern Science of Nature," *Mind* (1935), 44:439–466, and (1936), 45:1–27.

of each aspect of creation will be found in its fulfilment of the purposes of God. For it is its place within his purposes that gives each
being the reason for its existence. Hence, if any part of the created
order should get "misplaced"—that is, should move into other situations and relationships than those God intended for it—the meaning
of its (now transformed) existence would be undercut and dissipated;
it would be a square peg in a round hole, its existence would be distorted and placed under strain, tensions would arise which might even
lead to its destruction. As we shall see later, just this has happened to
man. In consequence, man's being has become crippled and is threatened with ruin, and his existence is lived under the continuous threat
of loss of meaning. Inasmuch as man was created for freedom, this
loss of his proper place is really a movement into bondage, unfreedom. Rescue from this condition and restoration of man's rightful
freedom is possible only if he can be brought back into the place
allotted him by the purposes of God. There—and only there—can he
find genuine fulfilment, profound meaning in his existence, true liberty. But of all this, more later.

The radical dependence of the world on God is not the only important conclusion to be drawn from the claim it is his creation; several other things must also be said. First, and perhaps most important,
the world is *good*. It has been created by a good God in order to carry
out his purposes: hence, it is good that the world exists and has the
particular character it does. In Genesis 1 after every creative act it
is said that God looked upon his handiwork, "and behold it was
good." This has important implications, both for understanding the
world and for ethics (i.e., man's activity in the world in response to
God). It means that nothing in all existence, so far as it *is*, should
be regarded as evil; *qua* its existence, everything without exception
is good.[8] To regard anything as *evil by nature* is the Manichaean
heresy, involving finally an ultimate dualism.

There are clear implications here for Christian ethics. Albert
Schweitzer has suggested that the fundamental ethical principle
should be "reverence for life"; Christian ethics must go beyond this
and express a reverence for all being. "True virtue most essentially

[8] See Augustine, *The Nature of the Good*.

consists in benevolence to being in general."[9] The inanimate as well as the organic world is God's creation and has its place within his purposes; as such it also is to be honored and respected, neither wantonly exploited nor deliberately defaced or destroyed. One who acknowledges God as Creator of the finite order must seek to live with a certain awe and respect toward all creation, giving every creature its due, reviling none.

A second implication about the world which follows from God's having created it—and a kind of further specification of its goodness —is its *order*: God created a cosmos. ". . . the Lord, who created the heavens . . . who formed the earth and made it . . . did not create it a chaos, he formed it to be inhabited!" (Isa. 45:18). The world has structure; its various parts are each there for a reason. Each object, each event, is in some way an expression of God's purposes; each has its place within the overall historical development of the universe, a movement itself characterized by logic, reason, order. Though existence in history may often seem chaotic, faith believes there is an underlying structure sustained by the God of order. Moreover, this structure of the world is not to be thought of as suppressive or destructive of free personal existence—for example, it is no strictly mechanical order. On the contrary, the world was "formed . . . to be inhabited"; it is an order through which personal purposes are being realized.

Ethical implications also follow from the orderliness of creation. Our response of reverence for the goodness of being must include appreciation of its order. It is with our minds that we grasp structure: man's reason (*logos*) enables him to grasp the structure (*logos*) in things. Thus, the affirmation that creation is orderly entails the ethical demand that men use their minds in intellectual work, that they may comprehend and appreciate the magnificence of God's world. History, philosophy, science—especially insofar as they are "pure" sciences, seeking to know simply for the sake of knowing—thus have important places as dimensions of man's response to the order of creation; they belong to man's reverence for being. The church has often denied her doctrine of creation through attempting to hamper and censor intel-

9 Jonathan Edwards, *The Nature of True Virtue*, Ch. 1

lectual inquiry into certain realms of experience. This is a refusal to grasp and appreciate the order of God's creation in the only way open to man, namely, with his reason. Open, objective, impartial, uninhibited intellectual work is a duty laid by God on man in placing him in the created world.

A third implication about the world, also an expression of its goodness, is its *beauty*. "He has made everything beautiful in its time" (Eccl. 3:11). In its proper place within the created order everything has its own distinctive beauty, a unique splendor that belongs to nothing else. The goodness of the world may be more apparent through its beauty than in any other respect. When overwhelmed by the stately majesty of an old oak tree, or the vast and intricate sculpturing by wind and water of a Bryce Canyon, or the brilliant colors of a Kansas sunset at harvest time, one may feel directly the goodness of the creation in which God has placed him. A God of "grace" (elegance, harmony, beauty, glory) might be expected to create a beautiful world as expressive of his goodness, and so he has.

Once more, there are ethical implications to be drawn. It is through man's aesthetic sensibility that he apprehends beauty. One must simply "stand still and look" to see the beautiful; one cannot do so in the hurried, utilitarian, everyday busy-ness that turns men into machines and the beauties of nature into the ugliness of much industrial life. But the beauty of creation does not only require that men learn to look; it also lays on them the demand to become artists, to share in the production of the beautiful as they share in God's creative and re-creative work. To produce ugliness, as man all too often has, is to deny—indeed, to disdain—the grace and glory of God, defacing and spoiling the beauty of his world. The church has been mistaken when she has been fearful of great art, instead of appreciating and encouraging it as the appropriate response of a creative creature to the beauty of God's world.

God, however, did not create man only as an intellect who could apprehend the order of the world or as an aesthete and artist appreciating its beauty. He created men to *work* in his world as "labourers together with God" (1 Cor. 3:9 KJ), as co-creators within the his-

*i debut this is
denyed of Babel !*

torical process through which he is creating his kingdom. The Yahwist expresses this by declaring that man was put in the garden "to till
it and keep it" (Gen. 2:15); the Priestly version goes even further:
man is to "subdue" the earth "and have dominion over the fish of the
sea and over the birds of the air and over every living thing" (1:28).
In this world of order and beauty a being has been created who, like
God, is himself historical, who can shape world history through his
own creative activity as he works in freedom. God created man to
work along with him in further creativity; the creation of culture and
civilization, the human world of art and artifacts, is his special task
within the created order, his unique contribution to the cosmic historical process. "A creative act is therefore a continuation of world-
creation," as Berdyaev has said, "and means participation in the
work of God, man's answer to God's call."[10] The appropriate response
to God's goodness—as manifested in his creation of the world and
man—is not merely gratitude: it is further creation of new goodness
by man. The proper response to the order of God's creation is not
merely intellectual appropriation: it is creation of original order
by man. The fitting response to the beauty of God's world is not simply appreciation: it is further creation of fresh forms of the beautiful. In this way the human community makes its unique contribution
to God's kingdom. For this goal of all history includes the community
of free and creative spirits, living in loving relation to each other
and to the holy God, jointly creating a world of order and beauty as
well as goodness. Unfortunately, however, as we shall see when we
consider the fall and human sin, man has failed to respond thus in
his freedom and creativity. Along with some goodness he has produced much evil; along with new order, chaos; along with beauty,
ugliness.

[10] *The Destiny of Man* (New York: Harper & Row, 1959), p. 86.

21 / The Providential Ordering
of the World

THE doctrine of creation, we have noted, means, on the one hand, that all that is has its source and ground in the purpose(s) and act(s) of God; on the other, that the meaning and significance of the various aspects of finite reality can be understood only in relation to God's purposes. We must now consider briefly the way in which God has been guiding and directing the world so that his purposes will gradually be realized. This is the province of the doctrine of providence.

The word "providence" comes from a root meaning to "foresee" or "provide." Divine providence, then, made possible by God's "foresight" in dealing with the world as it moves through the various phases of historical development, is his provision for the needs of each of those stages, so that the events of history proceed in accordance with his purposes and the historical process as a whole moves toward the end he has intended. This doctrine deals with the *middle stages* of the historico-temporal development, rather than beginning or end. All that is said here will again be symbolical in character, with human purposive activity naturally the principal analogy. Hence, a brief look at the "middle stages" in the realization of human purpose will facilitate understanding providence.

Almost any example of relatively long-range purposes could serve; let us consider a vocational decision and its consequences. In high school a boy decides to become a physician. The act which carries through this decision will contain many successive steps, each involving decisions and problems of its own. He will have to obtain the right education, choosing an appropriate college, and electing and passing courses which will properly prepare him; he will need to develop new skills and interests, uncover adequate financial resources, discipline himself through long years of preparation. Every step of his program will bring forth new problems and unexpected emergencies which must be dealt with in terms of the needs of the moment. Yet at each point he will be working out the overarching purpose to become a doctor. There may be many bypasses and delays: each must be handled with respect both to its own demands and his long-range goal. Frequently the young man's progress will be tortuous, and it might be impossible for an outsider to see how his decisions lead to the ultimate goal. For example, it may be necessary at some point to drop out of school to earn money; perhaps he will be drafted into the army; perhaps he will elect many courses in music simply because he enjoys and has an aptitude for it. These detours and side-roads may be so frequent and bewildering that if one were to isolate some twelve-month period within his eight years of preparation, analyzing it strictly in terms of the empirical evidence available within that period, it might be difficult for an external observer to ascertain what purpose, if any, unified the whole and gave it meaning. The ultimate objective would be known only to the young man who made the decision and was carrying it through—and to those to whom he chose to communicate it. Only he would be able to see how each twist and turn in the road was actually a step toward the goal. Others, not knowing either the beginning (the original decision) or the end (the goal posited in that decision), nor understanding the relation of the particular problems encountered to the boy's purpose, would be unable to discern the pattern unifying and giving meaning to each of the individual acts; they might conclude that our hard-working young student was in fact spineless and irresolute, with no goals in life.

The point of this parable is twofold: first, if "providence" designates the way God is working out his purposes in the on-going historical movement, then his providential activity may not often be visible to external observers (e.g., men) examining some particular segment of history. The segment they are observing may be one of the "twists" or "turns" in which the ultimate objective remains hidden and obscure. Hence, they could never induce or deduce with certainty what purpose was being realized in the historical movement —*until the end or goal had been reached or became clearly visible.* The most such observers could hope would be that some occasional events in history might provide insight, giving some clue to the meaning of the whole (as when our student applies for admission to medical school); but even these would remain problematic and dubious unless in one or more of them *the purposer himself chose to communicate what he was seeking to do* (as when our medical student explains he is not dropping out of school because of laziness, but because he must earn money to complete his education). Such a moment of self-disclosure by the purposer, of course, would never compel credence; we all know well the deceits and conceits with which agents often clothe their activities. One could choose either to believe or disbelieve that the true character of the history had been disclosed.

Even if one chose to believe, many things would remain dark and unclear. This is because—and this is the second point of the parable—not only the purpose but also the way in which it is being realized is known only to the purposer. Only he sees how he is adapting himself to each new moment so that its demands are met even while his ultimate objective is advanced. This hiddenness of the realization of purpose in the activity of the agent we take for granted daily: when we place ourselves in the hands of an "expert" (e.g., an architect or a physician), we often are unable to see how his every action—including those that seem to us unimportant or ridiculous—contributes to the desired end, but we trust that *he* knows what he is doing.

One should, of course, not take this finite analogy to God's providence as an allegory, supposing, for example, that God takes time off to develop purposes peripheral to his main goal (as the medical student taking music lessons), or that he must meet problems essentially irrelevant to his objectives (as the student must earn money). Finite beings are often involved in activities only distantly related to each other, for no finite purpose can comprehend all dimensions of existence. But every existent reality and event owes its being to God's decision and act, and finds its authentic meaning and significance within his purposes. Hence, even the "twists" and "turns" in history must be viewed as not imposed on God from without, but as developing from within as an expression of his purposes: God's decision, for example, to create free and creative beings is the ultimate metaphysical ground of the historical struggles between himself and men; and the true significance of those struggles can be understood only with reference to that decision. Moreover, God may well be working out a variety of purposes in and through his creation, most of which are completely unknown to us; belief that God has revealed his intentions for human history does not entail the conclusion that we know everything he is doing with his world.

With these qualifications in mind the specific point of the analogy can now be indicated. (a) We will not be able to perceive God's purpose for human affairs—that is, the meaning of human history—except in such moments as he chooses to reveal it. (b) Even then the way in which God is realizing his purpose in the tortuous course of world history will never be fully clear to us. Though one can trust that he understands the significance and rightness of every step, the most that will come into view through his revelation will be rudimentary outlines; the being and work of this purposer far exceed human imagination and understanding. "For as the heavens are higher than the earth, so are my ways higher than your ways and my thoughts than your thoughts" (Isa. 55:9).

In the light of these considerations let us examine the distinction often made between "general" and "special" providence. The former supposedly refers to God's general governance of nature and history with a view to realizing his ends; the latter indicates particular acts—perhaps interrupting the general order—in which God does something of special significance for a particular group or individual, for example, parting of the Red Sea, or sending sea gulls to a shipwrecked sailor for food. A distinction made in this fashion, however, raises difficult theological problems. In the first place, this conception of special providence clearly suggests that God's general ordering of things is not particularly competent since he must intervene with alterations and corrections from time to time. Secondly, it implies that instead of dealing in impartiality and justice with all his children, God plays favorites.

In the light of our parable about purposive behavior, however, it is possible to develop a somewhat different distinction between general and special providence. I have suggested that the conception of providence refers to God's governance of all history so that it will realize his purposes. This governance is not an act performed once and for all at the beginning of the historical process, like winding up a clock and then letting it run; it is, rather, the continuous activity of a living agent, and it necessarily involves God's responding in particular and unique ways (in the light of his final objectives) to each new historical situation as it arises out of interaction with his creatures. Thus, general providence includes what is usually called "special providence" (i.e., God's special treatment of particular situations); we do not need an extra category to speak of a Red Sea or of a pious sailor's sea gulls. These events should be understood like all others, as grounded in God's particularized acting in accordance with the unique needs of each new situation, moving it along toward his ultimate historical goal. The conception of general providence covers everything which needs saying here.

This does not mean, however, that the distinction between general and special providence should be dropped. For though we may be hesitant about claiming such far-reaching ontological differences in God's relationship to events, it is obvious that not all events are equal with respect to their impact on man's relation to God, and hence their significance for the realization of certain aspects of his purposes. We noted above (in the parable drawn from finite purposive activity) that there are some moments in which the otherwise hidden purpose binding together a succession of actions becomes relatively clear (e.g., when the purposer himself tells what he is doing, or performs actions which are especially revealing). If obscure activity is to be judged purposeful by someone other than the purposer, it will have to be in terms of such revelatory occasions. The concept of special providence is useful for distinguishing from the ordinary flow of events such moments or processes when God's otherwise hidden purposes for history become visible, thus making possible a new or changed relation between man and God. These are events when faith in the over-arching purposes of God is *created in men* and sustained through adversity, when *from man's side* it becomes clear that God truly acts in care of his creatures. Obviously the occurrence of such events does not *prove* that God acts purposively with and for his creation (nor do similar moments in the intercourse between finite agents certainly establish purpose); but they are the principal, if not the only, ground for belief in his purposeful activity.

The acceptance of such events as authentic expressions of divine activity—and thus a proper ground for believing in "general providence"—is called faith; unfaith, in contrast, is that attitude which views such moments as mere chance or coincidence and of no special significance. Though these events are of first importance to faith, they should not, as we have seen, be viewed as acts in which God discontinues or sharply alters his ordinary patterns of action. Rather, their peculiar significance derives from their providing the indispensable historico-psychological grounding for the appearance and continuance of faith in the purposive and living God,[1] in this way serving as "break-throughs" advancing the historical realization of his purposes. It is hardly surprising that moments of such importance were grasped as sharply different from other events and given the

[1] It is fashionable among some contemporary theologians to speak as though authentic faith had no empirical or psychological grounding, it being an immediate creation of God in the soul of the believer. Apart from the question whether such a view has any content or meaning—when one has abstracted from *all* psychological or other experiential content, what, after all, is left?—it is theologically vulnerable in that: (1) it so separates God's redemptive activity from his creative as to call into question the doctrine of creation; (2) it involves an implicit denial of the doctrine of the incarnation which claims that God comes to man precisely in this empirical and historical existence; (3) it makes the notion of faith itself unintelligible since its relationship to the concrete, living, empirical self enmeshed in psychological and historical processes—which is the actual self that I am and the only self I know—remains completely unspecified: the "decision of faith" thus becomes an empty abstraction unrelated to all the concrete decisions through which one orders his life, and the God of that faith is precisely opposite from sovereign Lord of the self. If these consequences are to be rejected, and faith is understood as the vital orientation of the concrete self toward the living God, then theology can no longer avoid attempting to specify as clearly as possible the precise interrelation, and mutual interpenetration, of Christian faith and the ordinary empirico-psychological processes of the self. It is meaningless to speak of "acts of God" unless we can see what those acts are in the actual experiential world in which we live, and why it is important and proper to designate events in this way. Interpretation of "special providence" in terms of the concrete historico-psychological events which in fact provide empirical grounding for the faith of particular individuals or groups is intended to be a step in this direction.

title "special providences." This understanding, though untenable in its crude form, is correct in its suggestion that these moments do in fact relate man to God in a way decisively different from the ordinary events of history—namely, through giving birth to faith—and in this sense they may be regarded as ontologically distinctive, as "special acts" of God.

Special providence, as we are here defining it, refers, on the one hand, to the *special history*—that is, the revelatory history—through which God's character and action have become clear; on the other hand, it refers to the particular luminous events within that history (or any other) in which God's providence has been especially manifest. The special history here will of course always be that history which the particular believer accepts as manifesting the real meaning of all history. For the Christian this *Heilsgeschichte* is the history of the Hebrews, filled with many events both prophetic and miraculous (see below), understood as preparing the way for and leading to that culminating prophetic-miraculous event: God's coming into history in Jesus Christ.[2] To know oneself as standing in this history

[2] Since in and through this history and this event God reveals what he is doing in all history and all events, "Jesus Christ" is for Christian faith the name for the center of all history (not merely for the climax of the Hebrew history which was the immediate and direct preparation for his appearance): all preceding events, therefore, are to be understood as the actual preparation for his coming, and all subsequent events as the working out of its consequences. In the sketch of the "history of the world" in Ch. 19, above, I have tried to indicate something of what is involved in such a view. A fuller treatment, of course, would have to deal in detail with such matters as the way in which non-Hebrew culture and religion contributed to the preparation for the coming of Christ— e.g., Babylonian mythology, Persian eschatology, Greek philosophy, Roman political organization, etc.—and also participates in the subsequent movement toward the consummation. The special contributions which non-Western peoples can and do and will make as mankind grows into one historical people should be remembered here, as well as the special preparation for faith in the God of all history which each of these peoples has received in its own cultural development. If the Father of Jesus Christ is indeed that God, it is inconceivable that all this cultural creativity and value in societies not so immediately connected with the rise and development of Christianity should be to no purpose. Henri de Lubac has made the point beautifully: "There is no comparison between [the role of 'unbelievers'] and that of the scaffolding which, necessary as it is in the construction of a building, is discarded once the building is complete without further thought of what will become of it. For if the heavenly Jerusalem is built of living stones, it is also living beings that go to make its scaffolding. . . . As 'unbelievers' are . . . indispensable for building the Body of Christ, they must in their own way profit from their vital connexion with this same Body. . . . Though they themselves are not in the normal way of salvation, they will be able nevertheless to obtain this salvation by virtue of those mysterious bonds which unite them to the faithful. In short, . . . they are an integral part of that humanity which is to be saved" (*Catholicism* [London: Burns, Oates & Washbourne, 1950], p. 116).

as part of this community is to know oneself as elect of God.[3] The doctrine of election expresses awareness of God's sovereignty over the whole course of history, and thus over the particular history in which one stands, such that it is necessary to say: *he chose us*—and only because of this could we choose him. For those conscious of election, history is not a chaos of conflicting human decisions but rather has a prevailing order shaped by the purpose—that is, decision, election—of God. There is no basis in this consciousness for a doctrine of reprobation. To be aware of being chosen by God as instrumentality of his transformation of the chaos of human history into his kingdom has nothing to do with being aware that he has rejected others; on the contrary, it is to be conscious of a *mission* to precisely those others. "God . . . through Christ reconciled us to himself and gave us the ministry of reconciliation. . . . So we are ambassadors for Christ" (2 Cor. 5:18, 20).

In this discussion of the *special history* to which the term "special providence" refers, we have already invoked the other level of meaning to which it points—that is, those *special events*—"miracles," "prophecies"—which lay bare God's activity in all events. The concept of miracle is often confounded by a tendency to interpret the biblical writers in terms of modern notions and problems instead of their own. We may forget, for example, that there is no conception of "natural law," or even of "nature," in the Bible, and that to view miracle as an event which goes "counter to natural law" is anachronistic.[4] To understand the conception of miracle, one should not try to imagine how he would account for a "burning bush" if he happened to stumble across one. Rather, he must first grasp what the

[3] It is worth noting in this connection that this priority of God's plan for and action in the overall course of history, over his choosing particular individuals, the latter being simply a specific expression of the former, is in keeping with Luke's view: "God's plan [in Luke] is primarily concerned with the saving events as a whole, not with the individual man and his destiny. According to it redemptive history leads up to Christ, and then on to the Last Judgment. The predestination of the individual has not yet come to expression in the conception of the plan. . . . Luke is not familiar with the idea of a fixed number of elect. . . . So far as Luke is concerned the saving events as a whole are more important than the individual aspect of election" (Hans Conzelmann, *The Theology of Saint Luke*, pp. 154–155).

[4] See H. W. Robinson, *Inspiration and Revelation in the Old Testament* (New York: Oxford University Press, 1946), Pt. I, for full discussion and documentation of much of what follows.

biblical writers were attempting to express with such stories. The original meaning of the word "miracle" was simply *wonder*—but not just any striking event, a wonder appropriated as a *sign* of God's activity.[5] That is, it was an event whose primary significance was not its reference to the matrix of natural causes through which it occurred but rather *its peculiar transparency to the ultimate cause,* to the purpose of God. *Any event which one finds himself led to interpret by reference to God's act rather than finite acts or causes* (though not necessarily denying that such finite agency is also involved) *is a miracle.* In this sense, as Schleiermacher said, "Miracle is simply the religious name for event."[6] Moses' burning bush was miraculous, not because of the peculiar character of the burning—that is a scientific and historical problem—but because through the experience of it Moses came to new convictions about God's purposes for himself and the Israelite people. Even the transformation of coarse green grass into nourishing milk by the humble cow, if perceived as a "wonder" which turns men in awe to the mystery of God's purposes, is a miracle; for it is then a sign-event, a "special providence," through which trust in "general providence" is created and strengthened.

A similar sort of analysis may be given to "prophecy." The prophet is one who speaks for God; he is God's mouthpiece. Hence,

[5] On the one hand, something as "natural" as a rainbow could be viewed as a "sign" of God's grace (Gen. 9:12–17); on the other, when Pharaoh's magicians perform such wonders as turning their rods into snakes (Ex. 7:11f.), or water into blood (7:22), this is no sign because it is not particularly indicative of God's activity. Similarly in the New Testament: the healings of Jesus are interpreted by him and his disciples as signs of God's presence but by his enemies as evidences of the devil (Lk. 11:15ff.). The important thing in the conception of miracle was not simply its wondrous and unusual character but that it was an event understood as especially signifying God's activity. ". . . to say that God reveals his power in a miracle is apt to deceive, for we are prone to define the term 'miracle' by categories drawn from an alien thought world, by reference to a system of natural laws defined by contemporary scientific knowledge of cause and effect. That the Biblical perspective resists reduction to these categories should be obvious. For over and over again, the prophets and apostles protest that incidents that appear to be miraculous, as judged by objective standards, are not miraculous at all; they do not truly disclose God's purpose but are the stock in trade of false prophets and magicians. And repeatedly the Scriptures present as wholly miraculous incidents that are neither extraordinary nor inexplicable by natural and rational means. . . . The prophets did not proceed logically from the observation of an inexplicable phenomenon to the question concerning its cause; rather, a fresh apprehension of God's activity led them to a radically new understanding of the hidden purport of an incident" (Paul Minear, *Eyes of Faith* [Philadelphia: Westminster, 1946], p. 144).

[6] *On Religion: Speeches to Its Cultured Despisers* (New York: Harper Torchbooks, 1958), p. 88.

any human words apprehended as not merely human but as the *word of God*—that is, as referring one to and laying him under obligation to God's purposes—are prophecy. Words become prophetic, not because a so-called prophet, or the Bible, makes special claims for them, but when they seize one with the conviction that this is the truth, *God's truth.* Unlike miracle—an event in the natural order, and thus apprehended as meaningful only in terms of a context or framework of interpretation—prophecy is an event in the order of meaning (language). As such it is fitted by its very nature, so to speak, to be the vehicle through which ultimate meaning—God's purpose—is communicated and the historico-cultural process correspondingly affected. For this reason, though both are vehicles of the knowledge of God, prophecy has epistemological priority over miracle; or rather, an event can be grasped as miraculous only on the basis of (implicit or explicit) prophetic or theological interpretation.

This does not mean, however, that prophecy is the really important category here, miracle being dispensable. Such a valuation would lead to the idealism or gnosticism all too prevalent in contemporary theology—that is, to the view that faith and theology are concerned only with *interpretation*, not *fact*. The concept of miracle involves the claim that the factual order of nature itself is subject to and expressive of God's purposes, and upon occasion is so experienced. If this claim cannot be made, theological concepts are at best only poetry, at worst empty words signifying nothing. Thus, the two concepts are polar, each being required if God's genuine sovereignty over a unified world of nature and history is to be maintained.

Neither miracle nor prophecy need be understood as involving violations of natural law or disruptions of the historical process, God's supernatural act of "special providence" invading and overturning the orders of nature and history shaped by his "general providence." They are, rather, theological conceptions which designate those events *within* the natural order and historical process through which men come to see and believe that nature and history are not autonomous and self-contained orders but are the direct expression of purposes which transcend them. In thus reshaping human consciousness, they facilitate the advancement of God's ultimate objectives.

These considerations may not be concluded without taking up again the so-called problem of evil, a title referring to those experiences which seem to call in question the fundamental claims of the doctrine of providence.[7] How is it possible to believe in providence in face of so much evil in the world? Is it really possible to justify God (theodicy)? The concept of "natural evil"—that certain events and powers in the world are themselves "evil," thus raising serious questions about the Creator's goodness or power or both—rests on a failure to recognize what our parable about purposive behavior has already made clear: the purpose inspiring and connecting a series of events is often not visible to anyone but the agent himself. Thus, there will inevitably be dark and obscure periods *between* the moments of miracle and prophecy in which God's purposes are revealed, events or periods which man cannot easily see as expressive of the good purposes of a good God—terrifying earthquakes, "nature red in tooth and claw," incurable and apparently meaningless diseases. By definition, these events are occurrences in which God's providential care is not visible. Such moments and periods will inevitably impress themselves on the eye of the observer, precisely because purpose is an *inner* connection of events, created by the teleological activity of the agent.

I say then, that though all things are ordered by the counsel and certain arrangement of God, to us, however, they are fortuitous,—not because we imagine that Fortune rules the world and mankind, and turns all things upside down at random (far be such a heartless thought from every Christian breast); but as the order, method, end, and necessity of events, are, for the most part, hidden in the counsel of God, though it is certain that they are produced by the will of God, they have the appearance of being fortuitous, such being the form under which they present

---

[7] It should be recalled that other dimensions of the problem have been discussed on two previous occasions, pp. 162f., 212f. Though certain further aspects of this problem can now be clarified, the discussion must remain provisional, for it is not yet possible to consider human sin. The blindness and perversity given birth by sin affect the way man sees and experiences nature—particularly the supposedly threatening powers in nature—and thus contribute to what is taken as "naturally" evil. These complications, however, cannot be discussed until a clear conception of man's historical nature and his involvement in sin is before us (Chs. 23–25).

themselves to us, whether considered in their own nature, or estimated according to our knowledge and judgment.[8]

There will always be events which stand in apparent contrast with—and even contradiction to—the events of "special providence," that is, the miracles in which God's purposes are evident. These events may lead men to lose faith or to rebel against God; they thus may give rise to temporary or even serious set-backs to his historical purposes. "Natural evil" is a somewhat inaccurate way of referring to this fact that God's hand cannot always be seen—that men often are, indeed, engulfed in what appears to be the very denial of loving purpose.

Faith is the stance that interprets such moments of experience, and periods of history, in the light of those other moments called revelation. Faith, thus, is able to believe that God is working providentially in and through earthquake and disease—even though men cannot directly observe this. Unfaith reverses this, interpreting faith's "miracles" and "moments of revelation" in the light of other events taken as paradigmatic, for example, events of so-called natural evil; with such paradigms one may well conclude that no God exists at all, or that he is a demon.[9] It is not possible to prove the truth of either po-

[8] John Calvin, *Institutes of the Christian Religion*, Bk. I, xvi, 9.

[9] A remarkable explicit example of this is to be found in the recent play, *Suddenly Last Summer*, by Tennessee Williams, Act I, Scene I. Mrs. Venable relates to a psychologist how she and her son, Sebastian, visited the desolate Encantadas Islands one summer. "We saw the Encantadas, but on the Encantadas we saw something Melville *hadn't* written about. We saw the great sea-turtles crawl up out of the sea for their annual egg-laying. . . . Once a year the female of the sea-turtle crawls up out of the equatorial sea onto the blazing sand-beach of a volcanic island to dig a pit in the sand and deposit her eggs there. It's a long and dreadful thing, the depositing of the eggs in the sand-pits, and when it's finished the exhausted female turtle crawls back to the sea half-dead. She never sees her offspring, but we did. Sebastian knew exactly when the sea-turtle eggs would be hatched out and we returned in time for it. . . . The narrow beach, the color of caviar, was all in motion! But the sky was in motion, too. . . . Full of flesh-eating birds and the noise of the birds, the horrible savage cries. . . . Over the narrow black beach of the Encantadas as the just hatched sea-turtles scrambled out of the sand-pits and started their race to the sea. . . . To escape the flesh-eating birds that made the sky almost as black as the beach! And the sand all alive, all alive, as the hatched sea-turtles made their dash for the sea, while the birds hovered and swooped to attack. . . . They were diving down on the hatched sea-turtles, turning them over to expose their soft undersides, tearing and eating their flesh. Sebastian guessed that possibly only a hundredth of one percent of their number would escape to the sea. . . ." The doctor inquires why Sebastian was so fascinated by this sight, and Mrs. Venable replies: ". . . my son was looking for God, I mean for a clear image of him. He spent that whole

sition here: each selects from the whole range of experience a particular portion viewed as the clue to ultimate reality, to the meaning of the whole, and there is no way to establish the rightness of the choice. But the choice may have rather considerable historical consequences for the self or community making it, since it determines the stance taken toward the meaning and character of the history in which they are immersed.

If we understand the nature of purposive activity—its inherent hiddenness to others than the purposer—and if we remember the feebleness of man's imagination and knowledge as he reaches after the majesty and glory of God, we will not be surprised that much in nature and history remain dark and incomprehensible. Faith, thus, can understand—and accept—its lack of full understanding; it will not need to speak of "natural evil." For on the basis of its paradigmatic moments of revelation, it knows that nothing evil comes from the hands of the good God. From the vantage point of the supreme revelatory moment, Jesus Christ, it can believe that all history is working out God's loving purposes, and that "all things work together for good to them that love God" (Rom. 8:28 KJ).

Since sin and unfaith are closely bound together (as we shall see below), man's experiencing of events and features of his world as "naturally evil" is directly connected with his fallen condition. This is not to deny that we in fact so experience our world; rather, it is to claim that such experience, insofar as it is regarded as seriously calling into question God's providential care, is the mark of disbelief that the world is really governed by divine purposive activity and/or distrust that this activity is beneficent. It is only when we no longer believe in our dentist's competence or trust his good intentions that the pain inflicted by his drill becomes evidence against him. To the degree that man's alienation from God prevents him from either believing that God ordains what occurs, or trusting that his purposes are good for his creatures, men will experience much in life as evil, threatening to destroy them and all they hold dear.[10] Only as they are "saved" from this condition and granted the gift of faith in God's providential care does the problem of "natural evil" dissolve into awareness that even though men are not privy to all God's purposes nor to the way he is working them out, they can trust him through the darkest and most obscure moments.

Genuine faith in God's providence has important existential and ethical significance. If one believed his entire existence to be rooted and to have its meaning in God's loving purposes, his anxieties about self and world, about life and death, would be dissipated, and he would be free to exist as a creative and loving self in community with others. Self-centered striving for certain forever elusive goods and values which he had hoped would so enhance his situation that the evils in existence would be more bearable would no longer be regarded as the good life; nor would it consist in unswerving conformity or obedience to an unbending moral law from which guilty conscience allowed no escape. It would, rather, simply be living the spontaneous life of freedom and creativity and love for which men were created, neither in bondage to self or other finite goods, nor in enslavement to sin or law: a *person* in the midst of other persons. Real self-fulfilment and the discovery of authentic meaning in life would appear as one came to know the new freedom of an existence within the context of God's providential care.

For faith to have this existential and ethical import, it is clear that "providence" should not be conceived simply as a concept playing an important role in a "Christian philosophy of history." It must, rather, pervade the *actual concrete reality* of human existence, enabling men to face confidently the most severe trials of life and death: providence is the fundamental historical reality with reference to which day-by-day life is lived. Faith in providence thus has to do with the concreteness of historical existence, not the abstractions of a philosophy of history: it is openness to what God is doing in his world and what he requires of men in each new moment, not a concern with generalities, whether rationalistic, existentialistic, or moralistic. The

---

[10] It is not difficult to understand why doctrines of the "wrath of God" could rather easily develop out of such stances of partial unfaith (cf. below, pp. 372f.).

doctrine of providence, however, is the attempt to understand and interpret this dimension of faith; it is, thus, part of a philosophy or theology of history. Learning the doctrine can never, of itself, give rise to the faith or be a substitute for it; given the faith, however, theological interpretation can illuminate its meaning and significance. For that being who lives in consciousness of self and existential situation—for man—it can, like the other theological doctrines, enhance and strengthen faith.

22 / The Consummation of History

In the Christian view, as we have seen, the universe expresses the purposes of God: the doctrine of creation asserts that the world's source and ground are in God; the doctrine of providence maintains that every phase of history is under God's guidance. Moreover, both creation and history are steps toward the realization of God's ultimate purposes, and it is in virtue of this that they gain their deepest meaning. To a consideration of the final end or goal which brings order and significance to the rest of history we must now turn.

Eschatology has often been regarded as the most questionable and speculative of all Christian doctrines since it deals with that which is completely inaccessible to man's observation and experience, namely, the future—not the immediate future about which some reasonable prognostications can be made, but the final future, beyond death, the end of history. Would it not be wiser in such dubious matters simply to maintain a discreet silence? Who knows, or possibly could know, what comes after the termination of existence here on earth? How could one possibly obtain any evidence justifying speculations about the end of the world? Perhaps such notions as these are simply verbal and empty and careful examination will reveal internal logical inconsistencies which render them meaningless.[1] When it was believed that God whispered secrets to prophets who carefully

[1] The logical problems connected with conceiving a final *end* to history—like the problem of conceiving history's beginning—have already been noted (see above, pp. 285ff., 274f.). Our knowledge here is at most symbolic and analogical. Similar problems arise with the conception of the termination of one's own individual existence, one's death. If death is defined as the genuine termination of my existence, it is clearly very odd to speak, then, of an existence which I will have after my existence has ended, or to wonder what things will be like—i.e., how they might be experienced by me—after I am dead.

recorded them in books eventually to become our Bible, eschatology may have seemed reasonable. But few today can regard the Bible as the book of God's secrets about the future; it appears to us a very fallible expression of the behavior and beliefs of an all-too-human people—a people, moreover, of two thousand and more years ago, with far less knowledge of the world and of history than we. Are we now to regard these ancient texts as adequate basis for speculations about the future of the universe?

If our notion of a historical understanding of the world is by now clear, it will be evident that such an attitude toward the eschatological problem misunderstands the issues. Eschatology is not primarily a collection of deductions made from biblical "prophecies": it is an indispensable dimension of any perspective that seeks to understand man and the world as historical—that is, as coming from a past, moving through the present and into the future. A coherent and consistent conception of the world as dynamic—as a unified process of development through time—is not possible without some view of the future into which the process is moving.[2] Attempting to confine oneself to past and present is like trying to discover the true unity and structure of a living body from a specimen with the upper half missing: much could be learned about the structure of feet and legs; but that, taken together with the cross section of raw flesh and broken bones, the maze of blood vessels, muscles, and nerves, would hardly be sufficient to discover the true structural unity of the mutilated organism—unless, by image or analogy, some conception of the missing half could be supplied. No more can the structure of the living historical process—cut in twain by the ever-moving present—be seriously studied or meaningfully interpreted without some, perhaps implicit, image of the yet-to-be interrelations and connections of those living fibers in the future. To halt our understanding of the

[2] ". . . if you want universal history, you must have some notion of the future and its goal; for only in the light of such a notion can the record of man be drawn together into a unity. . . . The attitude towards history which is merely specialist, or for that matter merely contemplative, has to be transcended: the image of Clio has to be made to face, once more, towards the great and universal problems of the future. The rigour, the width of equipment, and the devotion of research into what has happened, must be combined with the will that acts and shapes the future . . ." (Ernst Troeltsch, "The Ideas of Natural Law and Humanity in World Politics," in Otto Gierke, *Natural Law and the Theory of Society* [Boston: Beacon Press, 1934], p. 218).

historical process with the present is to see its components hacked off, as it were, in the middle of their various stages of development, presenting us with the spectacle of mangled, raw, and bleeding flesh. Our view of the future may be optimistic (as with the hoped for Good Society of liberal democratic humanism and Marxism) or pessimistic (e.g., naturalism's expectation of the ultimate destruction of man and society as matter rolls on relentlessly), but some sort of image will always be there, affecting every judgment.[3] Men are acting beings, always having to decide in the present what course of action to undertake in the future; it is impossible, therefore, for them to avoid conceiving the future under some image. No perspective which faces up to the dynamic and historical character of reality can avoid an eschatology.[4]

If we ask, now, On what foundation can eschatological convictions be based? the answer will have to be: the past. Meaningful past events and experiences serve as keys or clues with which men seek to anticipate the future and grasp experience as a whole. For the Christian, as we have seen, Jesus Christ is the decisive event revealing the character of ultimate reality: it is the loving and faithful God —Creator of the world and Purposer of history—with whom men have finally to do. Christian eschatology is the attempt (on the basis of the revelatory event) to state explicitly what those purposes for history are and to conceptualize the future as their realization. Unless such specification of the future is in some degree possible, it is empty euphemism to speak of God as, for example, a loving Father; and the theological understanding of self, world, and ultimate reality is threatened. Eschatological doctrine, far from being superfluous and dispensable speculation, deals with the very foundations of Christian faith.

The understanding that what is said about the future must be based on the revelatory event Jesus Christ—the formal ground of

---

[3] For further analysis, see my *Relativism, Knowledge and Faith* (Chicago: University of Chicago Press, 1960), Ch. 10.

[4] Every interpretation of human motivation, apart from that psychological hedonism which claims man always seeks only immediate pleasures, has an eschatological element. Whenever one endures present pain for expected future pleasure, he is interpreting the meaning of present events in the light of a hoped-for future which will explain and justify the present painful experience. Such an interpretation is formally eschatological.

theological eschatology—is expressed in the doctrine of the so-called second coming of Christ. In this doctrine the metaphysical presupposition of all specifically Christian thought about the future is made explicit: what was manifest in Christ is significantly valid for all the future, including even the "end" of history. Doubtless this conviction seems highly questionable. There is simply too much evidence that suggests the absurdity of believing that the real meaning of history has been revealed and rooted in Jesus Christ. In Mark's Gospel the expectation that the course of events will in this way strongly militate against faith is attributed to Jesus himself:

> For nation will rise against nation, and kingdom against kingdom; there will be earthquakes in various places, there will be famines; this is but the beginning of the sufferings. . . . for they will deliver you up to councils; and you will be beaten in synagogues. . . . And brother will deliver up brother to death, and the father his child, and children will rise against parents and have them put to death; and you will be hated by all for my name's sake. . . . False Christs and false prophets will arise and show signs and wonders, to lead astray, if possible, the elect.
>
> MARK 13:8–9, 12–13, 22[5]

Thus, times are to be expected when it will seem ridiculous to believe that the real meaning of history is to be found in the purposes of the loving God manifest in Christ. The doctrine of the second coming is the affirmation in the face of all this that in the last analysis—that is, at the end—such conclusions will prove wrong, that ultimately the purposes of the Father of Jesus Christ will prevail.

> But in those days, after that tribulation, the sun will be darkened, and the moon will not give its light, and the stars will be falling

---

[5] Cf. also Paul, who suggested that the days of "rebellion" will come when the "man of lawlessness is revealed, the son of perdition, who opposes and exalts himself against every so-called god or object of worship, so that he takes his seat in the temple of God, proclaiming himself to be God. . . . The coming of the lawless one by the activity of Satan will be with all power and with pretended signs and wonders" (2 Thess. 2:3–4, 9).

from heaven, and the powers in the heavens will be shaken. And then they will see the Son of man coming in clouds with great power and glory. And then he will send out the angels, and gather his elect from the four winds, from the ends of the earth to the ends of heaven.

MARK 13:24-27 .

Or, as Paul put it:

For the Lord himself will descend from heaven with a cry of command, with the archangel's call, and with the sound of the trumpet of God. . . . For God has not destined us for wrath, but to obtain salvation through our Lord Jesus.

1 THESSALONIANS 4:16, 5:9

Thus, the God present to man in the historical person Jesus will be the same God present to man at the end. The doctrine of the second coming expresses the conviction that in the face of Jesus Christ is seen the one who shall also appear at the end, when he has finally brought all history under his sway and thus to its consummation. This doctrine makes explicit in dramatic mythological language an indispensable dimension of Christian faith: that the entirety of the future—as well as the present and past—is to be understood in terms of the reality manifest in the person-event Jesus Christ.

What, now, can be said about the goal or end of history? Where is history going? The answer can be given in only the most general symbolic terms: the world is becoming the kingdom of God. Jesus came preaching, "The time is fulfilled, and the kingdom of God is at hand" (Mk. 1:15). In his ministry, death, and resurrection, God's reign among men was becoming concrete historical reality "in the midst" of Jesus' followers (Lk. 17:21).[6] To be sure, God's dominion over all history was not yet fully evident, but the seed—tiny and inauspicious as a mustard seed (Mt. 13:31-32)—had been planted, and it was certain that God's full reign over history was being established. God

---

[6] "This, then, is the good news which the New Testament with unanimous voice proclaims: that Jesus is indeed the promised Messiah, fulfillment of all the hope of Israel, who has come to set up the Kingdom of God among men" (John Bright, *The Kingdom of God* [New York: Abingdon, 1953], p. 190).

had sent his Messiah to accomplish just this task; and the end of history will be precisely that time when he delivers "the kingdom to God the Father after destroying every rule and every authority and power" (1 Cor. 15:24). The meaning and purpose of all history is the full establishment of God's reign over all creation, including especially the community of free spirits for whom he had intended a place "from the foundation of the world" (Mt. 25:34; cf. Eph. 1:4). History itself is nothing else than creation in the process of becoming God's kingdom, and that process has found a climactic new beginning in the historical appearance of Jesus Christ.

As we saw in our christological discussion, Jesus, a human being making free decisions like all men, was one who, particularly in the concluding hours of his life, fully sacrificed his own desires and human possibilities in obedience to God. "Father . . . remove this cup from me; yet not what I will, but what thou wilt" (Mk. 14:36). Jesus was one in whom God's purposes and will became present actualities in his own decisions and actions. He can be described, therefore, not only with such traditional metaphysical formulas as "God-man," "two natures in one person," etc., but perhaps more appropriately and meaningfully as the one in whom God's reign became real *within*—and not merely over—the historical process. Thus, the goal of all history, the full establishment of God's reign over creation, reached a significant new level in the Christ-event, through which a community of persons freely and lovingly obedient to the divine will was created (see Chapters 27–29, below). Christian faith, of course, does not and cannot know all that this implies about ultimate human fulfilment, but from the beginning it has expected it would involve the realization and completion of the fragmentary personal existence now known by the children of the truly personal One.[7] "Beloved, we are God's children now; it does not yet appear what we shall be, but we know that when he appears we shall be like him, for we shall see him as he is" (1 John 3:2).

In many respects it seems incredible that the purpose of the whole cosmic historical process should include the creation of a community

[7] The fulfilment for which man may properly hope will be dealt with in more detail below, Ch. 30.

of persons responsible to the divine will, a community of free persons who love. How can the meaning of a universe hundreds of millions of light years in diameter be understood in this way? Can it be believed that this universe exists for, and has its goal in, personal purposes? There is no way to answer this question empirically: any answer given will not be based simply on an impartial inspection of all being—that would be impossible—but will be rooted in a decision to take some particular event or segment of experience as the clue to the whole. Christian faith—grounded as it is on the revelatory event Jesus Christ—is distinguished from (many) other perspectives precisely in the claim that ultimate reality is personal (i.e., is *God*) and that the universe, therefore, is to be understood in terms of purposive activity. If God created the world for his (personal) purposes and is working in it providentially to carry these out, the final goal of history when God is "everything to every one" (1 Cor. 15:28) must also be understood personalistically. From this point of view it is conceivable that the end would involve the creation and sustenance of personal community. It would be the realization of that situation when, on the one hand, the forces destructive of personal existence within the human situation—sin, guilt, hate, and the like— are overcome, and when, on the other hand, the apparent irrelevance and even destructiveness of what now seems a vast impersonal universe is neutralized and even rendered of positive significance.

The biblical writers do not neglect the implication that a kind of transformation, not only of man's being and sin (which we shall discuss in Part Three), but of the whole cosmos, is required before it can thus be conceived as the proper context for personal community. Nature also is in history and must be brought to her goal if man, immersed as he is in nature, is to be brought to his. Accordingly, it is not surprising to hear that God is actively engaged in transforming the natural order:

> *Behold, I am doing a new thing. . . .*
> *I will make a way in the wilderness*
> *   and rivers in the desert*
> *. . . to give drink to my chosen people.*
>   ISAIAH 43:19-20

In the vision of some biblical writers, moreover, God is not merely altering details within the cosmos; the very framework of the impersonal universe we know is undergoing transformation in history: "For behold, I create new heavens and a new earth; and the former things shall not be remembered" (Isa. 65:17). Such a transformation from its present condition is required in order that the cosmos finally realize God's original intention that it provide an appropriate context for truly personal existence.[8] In his vision which brings the Bible to its conclusion, John the prophet sees precisely this culmination to be the glorious conclusion to which God is bringing his work:

> Then I saw a new heaven and a new earth; for the first heaven and the first earth had passed away, and the sea was no more. And I saw the holy city, new Jerusalem, coming down out of heaven from God, prepared as a bride adorned for her husband; and I heard a great voice from the throne saying, "Behold, the dwelling of God is with men. He will dwell with them, and they shall be his people, and God himself will be with them; he will wipe away every tear from their eyes, and death shall be no more, neither shall there be mourning nor crying nor pain any more, for the former things have passed away."
>
> And he who sat upon the throne said, "Behold, I make all things new."
>
> REVELATION 21:1–5

The "holy city, new Jerusalem,"—the realization of the kingdom of God—portrayed as the time when the "dwelling of God is with men" (i.e., when the estrangement of God and man is finally overcome) and all suffering has been wiped away, occurs within the context of "a new heaven and a new earth." Only when the present patterns of cosmic order have been transcended in the movement of history, and the cosmos has thus been transformed, will the purposes of God to dwell in community with men be realized.

This awareness that the whole creation—not only man—must

---

[8] The poet goes on to declare that it is within this altered cosmic context that God will "create Jerusalem a rejoicing" in which there shall "no more . . . be heard in it the sound of weeping and the cry of distress" (65:18-19), and all injustice and meaninglessness in life will be overcome (65:22-23). In short, this new cosmos will be the context of genuine human fulfilment. (Cf. also 66:22-23 and discussion of Rev. 21, below.)

participate in the process of historical change if the kingdom of God is to come is also suggested in other ways. In one of his visions, Isaiah of Jerusalem sees the animal kingdom as governed no longer by the struggle for survival but at last living together as a virtual community of love;[9] and in Romans, Paul suggests that all creation is in a kind of bondage from which it awaits liberation at the end-time. Although the present order of nature does not yet properly sustain the personal community which is God's kingdom, it is "groaning in travail" to give birth to that order in which the whole of "creation itself will be set free from its bondage."[10]

It is not possible to state concretely what kind of transformation is involved here: if we could, we would no longer be living in "the first heaven and the first earth." But this much must be said: these visions imply recognition that the present order of nature is provisional and is in the process of becoming what God intends. Great, perhaps unimaginable, changes will be required ("a *new* heaven and a *new* earth") before the cosmos expresses fully the personal will which created it, and becomes the proper setting within which a community of persons can find authentic fulfilment. Our awareness of the impersonal destructiveness of nature certainly confirms all this to be true: until and unless a radical transformation of the natural order occurs, personal existence will be lived under threat of destruction by the nature which gave it birth. However, those who believe the universe to be originally the creation of a purposive God may also believe he is still working to make it into a more appropriate home for the personal beings he has placed within it. The hope for a new heaven and a new earth is thus an inference from the funda-

9 "The wolf shall dwell with the lamb, and the leopard shall lie down with the kid, and the calf and the lion and the fatling together, and a little child shall lead them. The cow and the bear shall feed; their young shall lie down together; and the lion shall eat straw like the ox. The sucking child shall play over the hole of the asp, and the weaned child shall put his hand on the adder's den. They shall not hurt or destroy in all my holy mountain; for the earth shall be full of the knowledge of the Lord as the waters cover the sea" (Isa. 11:6–9). It is significant that Second Isaiah restates this vision within the context of the "new heavens and the new earth" (65:17, 25).

10 "For the creation waits with eager longing for the revealing of the sons of God; for the creation was subjected to futility, not of its own will but by the will of him who subjected it in hope; because the creation itself will be set free from its bondage to decay and obtain the glorious liberty of the children of God. We know that the whole creation has been groaning in travail together until now" (Rom. 8:19–22).

mental Christian conviction that it is God who is Creator of the world; and it is an essential dimension of the hope that his kingdom will ultimately come.

This is not the proper place to discuss in detail the other symbols of the consummation of history (the "last judgment," "heaven" and "hell," the "resurrection of the body," etc.). Each of them refers to a different side of the conviction that the consummation of history is to be understood in personal terms. Since they delineate different aspects of that consummation as it applies to man and his ultimate destiny, they can more appropriately be discussed in connection with the problem of human existence (see Chapter 30, below).

It is necessary to say one concluding word about the problem of eschatology in general. There is a debate in theological circles over whether Christian eschatology should be thought of as "realized" or futuristic, and there appears to be fairly general consensus that it must have both dimensions. We are now in a position to see how this is possible and what it means. In any teleological development the end or goal is present in a certain sense in the beginning and in all intermediary stages of the process, though it is not *fully present* until its completion. Thus, to return to our earlier example (from Chapter 21): in respect to his motivation and desires the high school student begins to become a physician in the very moment he makes a definite decision; even before that moment there are many forces within him working toward this end. As he proceeds through premedical studies in college, the goal becomes increasingly present and effective, until, when he finally completes medical school and receives his degree, the end is in a significant sense here. And yet he is not really a doctor in the profoundest sense of the word until he has devoted most of his life to medicine, and this has become the very form of his existence. We may speak in a similar way about the history of the world. If it was God's purpose from creation onwards to establish a community of free beings who love each other and him, this end was present implicitly within the historical process during all the billions of years of cosmic evolution. When man finally appeared on the scene, the ultimate goal was nearer realization and in fact began to be actualized in the historical process. Man, however, sinned, distorting and disrupting and threatening with destruction the very communal existence for which he was created, so the end remained hidden and invisible even though human culture developed to an advanced level. At last, with the self-sacrifice of Jesus and the appearance of the church as a community whose members loved one another, this goal of the historical movement became clear for the first time. The end had become visible within history itself: in a real sense it had become present and actual within history. In comparison with the billions of years of cosmic evolution, and the millennia of human history which preceded, it would not be incorrect to say that at last the end was really here. But if one looked ahead to see what still needed to be done to transform all creation into this kingdom, it was clear that the appearance of Christ brought history only to the threshold: the end will not be fully here until the transformation is complete.

We live in this period after Christ and before the final consummation. Looking backward from our existential situation through human history to the luminous revelatory event, one may say that the great reversal of human sin has begun and the goal of history become manifest: the kingdom of God is here. But as we look at ourselves, at human society and human nature, we cannot but see that man is a long way from perfect obedience to God's rule; the end when God shall finally bring in his kingdom must be in some distant future. It should not surprise us that the first Christians, in their enthusiasm over the revelation and new life vouchsafed them, supposed the final consummation to be very near, coming within their own time,[11] even though they recognized that "of that day or that hour no one knows, not even the angels in heaven, nor the Son, but

[11] For this conviction they had the apparent authority of Jesus' own words, e.g., "Truly, I say to you, there are some standing here who will not taste death before they see the kingdom of God come with power" (Mk. 9:1) ; "Truly, I say to you, this generation will not pass away before all these things take place" (13:30). Paul, also, apparently expected to be among those who would be "alive . . . until the coming of the Lord" (1 Thess. 4:15) ; accordingly, he does not hesitate to make recommendations to the Corinthian church about matters of social order on the basis of the conviction that "the appointed time has grown very short. . . . For the form of this world is passing away" (1 Cor. 7:29, 31). Similar views are found among otherwise very different writers, e.g., James ("Establish your hearts, for the coming of the Lord is at hand" [5:8]), and 1 John ("Children, it is the last hour; and as you have heard that antichrist is coming, so now many antichrists have come; therefore we know that it is the last hour" [2:18]).

only the Father" (Mk. 13:32; cf. 1 Thess. 5:1ff.). It was not long, however, before the church discovered its error, adjusting in a variety of ways to the delay of the *parousia*. Historical development conceived (as in the present volume) as a slow and painful process was not, of course, among the explicit New Testament solutions to this problem. However, as I have tried to show, this view is rooted in the Old Testament sense and conception of history and is not inconsistent with the fundamental New Testament claims. Moreover, it provides a basis for interpreting Christian faith in such a way that its meaning and truth can be appropriated by modern man with his all-pervasive historical orientation. Suggestions pointing toward this way of understanding history were soon being made in the early church,[12] culminating finally in Augustine, who could say in his great theology of history: "The education of the human race, represented by the people of God, has advanced, like that of an individual, through certain epochs, or, as it were, ages, so that it might gradually rise from earthly to heavenly things, and from the visible to the invisible."[13] From this point of view, it is not some incomprehensible mystery, but a strictly intelligible interpretation of the historical situation in which we find ourselves, to declare that the kingdom of God is here, and yet not here, that God always has ruled the world, and yet the world has not yet come fully under his reign.

If one could not hope for the actual transformation of creation into God's kingdom, faith would be empty and meaningless, a fraud; it is not possible to dispense with the eschatological expectations of Christian faith. And yet one must also recognize that these are simply *hopes* not yet realized, hopes with a foundation outside themselves.

---

[12] Cf., e.g., Irenaeus: ". . . He who makes is always the same; but that which is made must receive both beginning, and middle, and addition, and increase. . . . Thus, therefore, has the one and the same Lord granted, by means of His advent, a greater gift of grace to those of a later period, than what He had granted to those under the Old Testament dispensation. . . . God formed man at the first, because of His munificence; . . . and prepared a people beforehand, teaching the headstrong to follow God; and raised up prophets upon earth, accustoming man to bear His Spirit [within him], and to hold communion with God. . . . Thus, in a variety of ways, He adjusted the human race to an agreement with salvation. . . . God thus [determined] all things beforehand for the bringing of man to perfection . . . that man may finally be brought to maturity at some future time, becoming ripe . . . to see and comprehend God" (*Against Heresies*, Bk. IV, xi, 2, 3; xiv, 2; xxxvii, 7). See also the quotation from Gregory of Nazianzus on pp. 378f.

[13] *City of God*, Bk. X, Ch. 14.

That foundation is the faith that "in Christ God was reconciling the world to himself" (2 Cor. 5:19, RSV footnote). This gives solid ground for a hope that enables endurance of the unhappiness, sorrow, and despair of present human existence; for it gives confidence that men are in process of being transformed into "sons of God" (Rom. 8:12–24). Human life, thus, gains its meaning by reference to the two decisive points in history between which we live, each being essential to the other: Jesus Christ, and the eschaton. In terms of these two bench marks, the process transforming man and history is appropriated as *salvation*, not only for Christians, but for all the world. For the whole "creation . . . will be set free from its bondage to decay and obtain the glorious liberty of the children of God . . . in this hope we were saved" (Rom. 8:21, 24).

Part Three

THE CHRISTIAN UNDERSTANDING

OF MAN: THE DOCTRINES OF THE

IMAGO DEI, SIN, AND SALVATION

What man is, only his history can tell him.

WILHELM DILTHEY

23 / The *Imago Dei* as Man's Historicity[1]

Wᴇ have observed that the overall perspective in terms of which the Bible understands reality and the world is historical or historicist: God is a being who acts historically to produce the world, and he subsequently continues to develop it in history; human history and within it the history of salvation are segments—in some ways a culmination—of this cosmic historical process. Human history has this special significance because in it another historical being in addition to God appears and begins to work out his own purposes, thus creating further history. Being intrinsically historical like God himself, man is capable of entering into community with him, responding to him creatively and freely. This fact, that man, though on the finite level, is in certain respects like God, is expressed theologically in the doctrine of the *imago Dei*. "God created man in his own image, in the image of God he created him" (Gen. 1:27; cf. 9:6).

Numerous attempts have been made in the history of Christian thought to define and describe the *imago Dei*: it has been viewed as the gift of reason or the power of will, as man's religiousness or the supposed immortality of his soul. These definitions all have some value, but they also suffer from serious difficulties. Each tends to be unduly one-sided and narrow in defining man's being in terms of one dominant characteristic. Moreover, when this unique property is viewed as God's image, it is implied that man's uniqueness derives

[1] For an earlier version of some of the ideas found in this chapter, see my article with the same title, *Journal of Religion* (1956), 36:157–168.

[handwritten margin note: could it not be that there is a divine spark in humanity?]

from his possessing a special "divine spark" and that he is thus, at least in this respect, himself divine, no merely finite created being. Furthermore, none of these various attempts at definition stand particularly close to the biblical understanding of man.

These difficulties can all be overcome, however, if the *imago Dei* is conceived in terms of man's historicalness, his historicity. The totality of human existence is immersed in history and is history: the conception of historicity, therefore, involving man's whole being, takes the partial insights of these other views up into itself. Furthermore, it does not involve a claim that man is in some respect divine, that he possesses powers lifting him above the relativities of finite existence. Moreover, the emphasis on man's historicalness is simply a summary statement for what is disclosed in the biblical portrayal of man's being and existence through recounting his history. Indeed, as we shall see, only on the presupposition of man's radical historicity is it possible to make clear sense of the biblical picture and the derivative theological claims that the fall, original sin, salvation, and so forth, are all historical events or processes.[2]

Viewing man as fundamentally historical is in keeping with tendencies of much contemporary thought. While ancient thinkers regarded man as the rational animal or the political being, moderns find such definitions both narrow and abstract in contrast with the full-blooded "man of flesh and bone" (Unamuno). Man is apprehended in his concreteness, as the living existing man, only when he is perceived as *history*: as coming from this particular concrete past, living in the tensions of this existential present, moving into this particular, yet undetermined and unknown, future. "To say man is to say history," Barth has observed. "On a false understanding no less than a true we are forced to put the statement 'I am' in the form of a little history, describing it as that self-positing. Similarly, the statement 'Thou art' denotes a history."[3] Defining man's very being,

---

[2] It might be noted here that the not infrequent claim in contemporary theology that it is unintelligible or meaningless to attempt to understand these theological realities as historical events or processes derives precisely from the failure to understand man's being in radically historical terms.

[3] *Church Dogmatics*, III, 2 [Edinburgh: T. & T. Clark, 1960], 248. Cf. Paul Schubert: "There can be no more convincing argument for the all-pervasiveness of our modern historical consciousness than that we cannot define the meaning of our existence

then, in terms of his historicity, is no arbitrary imposition of an abstract and irrelevant biblical conception on concrete experience: it is
to grasp human existence in the very form we experience it.

A theological concept should link meaningful contemporary language with the revelatory center of meaning, enabling understanding not only of our existence but also of the way it is illuminated by
revelation. Precisely such linkage is provided by the concept of historicity. The concept itself is neither found in the Bible nor has it
been constructed on the basis of direct inspection of the definitive
revelatory event, the man Jesus. This event presents paradigmatic
images and definitive norms for grasping ultimate reality, God, but
it is not an unlimited resource, a kind of magician's hat, from which
the clever theologian can haul out definitions and concepts covering
every aspect of finite being.[4] Revelation is the light in terms of which
genuine understanding of the experienced finite world is gained—
but that world itself is grasped in and through experience, not by
direct revelation (see above, Chapters 2–4). Of course, the character,
significance, and meaning of man's role in the finite order cannot be
properly apprehended or understood in abstraction from the revelatory history—and in this sense the true nature of man cannot be so
grasped. Yet it still remains that man—I, as acting subject; you,
as the one to whom I am speaking—is a reality known in interpersonal experience and grasped only in the living moment of experience. Thus, though the image of the man Jesus is to be regarded as

---

except in terms of the past, present, and future. Aristotle, this relatively late Greek
representative of Near Eastern culture, could be satisfied with defining man as a *being
in society* (*zoon politikon*). In Aristotle's thought history played no leading role, for
community (*polis*) is for him but an actualization of a timeless form. . . . Modern man
can only define himself as a *being in history* (*zoon historikon*), a being with a past, a
present, and a future, however difficult it may be to say what past, present, and future
are or mean in this connection. It suffices to add here that all schools of contemporary
thought share the realization that truth, understanding, and reality have the character
of events rather than of things" ("The Twentieth Century West and the Ancient Near
East," in R. C. Dentan, ed., *The Idea of History in the Ancient Near East* [New Haven:
Yale University Press, 1955], pp. 314–315).

4 All too often Karl Barth gives the impression that this is how he conceives revelation. Thus, he supposes he can say almost everything necessary about finite being by
speaking of man, and that "As the man Jesus is Himself the revealing Word of God,
He is the source of our knowledge of the nature of man" (*Church Dogmatics*, III, 2, p.
3). Although Barth attempts to work out the whole of his doctrine of creation in these
terms, it is obvious that he has drawn insight and understanding from a great many other
(unfortunately unacknowledged) sources than the biblical picture of "the man Jesus."

normative for human existence,[5] it does not of itself make clear the *nature* of man's being. Not only is the record too fragmentary to make possible such speculations: to engage in them would be to debase revelation from the *light of meaning* with which experience is appropriated to the mere impartation of items of information about the world.

How, then, is the nature of man to be defined theologically? In Part Two the decisive steps have already been taken. There it was seen that all finite reality—the entirety of the world and what is in it— falls within the historical purposes of God. Within this overall context man also has his place and proper meaning. He has been created in the on-going movement of history (as has all other finite reality) and been shaped into a being intrinsically historical, one whose distinguishing characteristic is his historicity, one who therefore can create culture and further history.[6] Man, thus, is capable of free and creative responsiveness to the primordial historical being, God. It is in terms of this conception of man's place within the comprehensive historical movement that we shall seek to understand him. The doctrine of man—though of especial importance to us because we are its subject-matter—is no relatively independent conception whose insights and definitive notions can be appropriated without regard to the rest of Christian theology. It is, on the contrary, an integral part of the Christian understanding of finite being as created and governed

---

[5] See above, Chs. 2–3, and below, Chs. 27, 29, 31–33.

[6] We may observe at this point that many so-called historical interpretations of man which speak glibly of man's "historicity" are not that at all, but simply modern versions of the old Greek-naturalistic view that man has a permanent form or essence— only now that nature of man is said to be his "historicity," the structure whereby man, unlike the lower animals, creates history. Such interpretations—failing to see that man and his historicity themselves arose in the historical process, and, therefore, cannot be its ground—do not express a genuinely historical view but are destructive of the very conception of history, and thus also of man's historicity. "Heidegger [holds] . . . that the origin of all history is to be sought in the historicity of man. . . . One should ask however if the opposite is not much more the case, that historicity is grounded in the experience of reality as history, as it was disclosed in the historical process bound together by God's promises to Israel long before the fulfillment in Jesus Christ. . , . The emancipation of historicity from history, the reversing of the relationship between these two so as to ground history in the historicity of man, appears to be the last step of the road that began when in the modern era man was made the bearer of history in the place of God. . . . With the loss of this fundamental source and basis man's experience of reality as history today again threatens to disappear" (Wolfhart Pannenberg, "Heilsgeschehen und Geschichte," *Kerygma und Dogma* (1959), 5:232–233, 231).

by God; and it can neither be apprehended nor understood except within this overall theological context.

What, now, does it mean to say that man's defining characteristic is his historicity? Man is preeminently a historical being because he is both made by his history[7] and he himself makes history: thus man makes and remakes himself. All of nature is created in the historical process; man alone takes an active part in his own creation in history.[8]

In what sense is it true that man makes himself? We can conveniently consider this conception on three levels:

1] *I create myself.* It is obvious, of course, that I do not create myself *ex nihilo;* but I do transform myself in time. This is what it means to say that I *make decisions.* To decide is to determine within certain limits (often unpredictable) what the shape of my future will be. Thus, if in high school I decide to become a physician, this will determine much about my future: I will go to college and medical school, I will elect certain courses and reject others, I will develop certain interests while letting others atrophy—the friends I meet, the books I read, the values I cherish will all in significant measure be determined by this choice. In short, in many respects this decision will affect the sort of person I become; my very selfhood will be shaped by the decisive moment of vocational choice. In similar ways, every other decision we make, large or small, shapes our being. It is obvious, of course, that we have no absolute power here to make ourselves what we will: it may turn out that I do not have the proper aptitudes to become a doctor, or I may not be able to obtain the necessary funds, or I may simply lose interest; there are many sorts of unpredictable limiting conditions. Yet, if there is

---

[7] On the way we are products of history, see in addition to the present Chs.: the Introduction, esp. pp. 23ff.; also Ch. 19.

[8] In many respects Augustine anticipated the conception of man's historicity as involving his power to create himself. For example: "The soul was not . . . given all that it had power to become. . . . It has received the power to seek diligently and piqusly if it will . . . the power with the aid of the Creator to cultivate itself. . . . he [the soul] had something that would enable him to attain what he did not have, provided he was willing to make a good use of it" (*On Free Will,* Bk. III, 65, 56, 72; trans. from *Library of Christian Classics,* VI [Philadelphia: Westminster Press, 1954], 210, 204, 213–214). The notion was even more explicitly stated by Hegel: "Spirit is only what it makes itself become" (*Lectures on the Philosophy of Religion* [London: Routledge & Kegan Paul, 1895], I, 275).

any meaning at all to the word "decision," in some very real sense *I make myself* when I plot the future course of history in which I shall be involved. This is one level, then, on which man makes himself.

2] *Men create each other.* In many respects I am created by my contemporaries: the decisions and actions of others affect me, shaping and developing me. This occurs first and most obviously in the relationship between parents and children. Parental decisions affect children in almost every dimension of their existence: the food they eat, the values they cherish, the prejudices they have, the friends they associate with. Initially the parent makes nearly all the child's decisions for him; gradually the child begins to decide for himself, but never without reference (either positive or negative) to the parent's prior and accompanying decisions and actions. Thus, in a real sense the child is created into what he becomes by the parent. Of course, once again, there are important limits. The parent cannot make the child as a sculptor his statue, deliberately chipping a little here, shaping a little there: the child is in some measure free (in contrast to the marble); so his action is often unpredictable and unaccountable. Nevertheless, in many significant ways the parent creates the very form of the child's selfhood. In a similar manner in all our relations with others, they create us and we them. Every word spoken affects those who hear it; every act performed shapes those to whom it is directed, and often many others as well. This is especially obvious in the more intimate relationships between husband and wife, parent and child, friend and friend; but it is true of all interpersonal relations. Thus, we not only make ourselves; we also make others and they us. Selves are not independent and isolated atoms, "windowless monads" (Leibniz), which are what they are without regard to the others roundabout. They are *relational realities* gaining the form and substance of their being through the relations in which they stand. We are what we are largely because of the communities in which we participate.

3] All this makes sense only if we can say more generally that *man is created by his history.* The decision our high school student makes to become a physician, once it is made, is *history,* and it is as history that it determines his course of action; the decisions and actions of parents and friends also continue to have their effects on us as living history. Even the spoken word, in the very moment it is pronounced, is past and is kept alive and effective in the present in the memory of the hearer, where he holds it before himself, considers it, thinks about it, eventually replies to it. Man's history-preserving memory together with his history-creating will makes him a radically historical being, one who can create himself.

But when all this has been said, a good deal more has been implied: we are what we are because of the unnumbered decisions of the entire human past which are stored up in the vast reservoirs not only of individual memory but in social structures and institutions, customs and habits, mores and ideologies, artifacts and written records. If I am what I am because of my father's decisions, it is equally true that his father's actions shaped his being—and thus I am what I am because of my grandfather. Though my grandfather is dead and gone, his decisions and actions have been stored up, as it were, in the character and memory of his children; and thus they continue to live, affecting and shaping the present. Moreover, this series goes all the way back through human history to the beginning. Every decision and act which affected others, every word spoken and heard, has in its own, perhaps almost infinitesimal, way influenced the course of history and thus shaped, in some measure, the structure of the present. We have been created by the whole human past.

This should be easily understood by Americans, the children of immigrants. For it is clear that our speech, ideals, beliefs—our way of life in all respects—has been profoundly affected by our fathers' decisions to come to America, perhaps hundreds of years ago, perhaps only recently. If they had stayed in Russia or Germany, in England or Italy, we would have developed into very different persons—indeed, *we* would very likely not be at all. This example, of course, can be multiplied in many ways and directions for the entire past. To say man is historical is to emphasize that he makes himself, as a species, through his long history, as individuals and communities interact with each other.

It is helpful to relate this analysis of man's historicity to two traditional interpretations of the *imago Dei*, as man's will and as his reason. Both of these are involved in the conception of human nature we have been sketching, but rather as dimensions than essence. Thus, it is because man is dynamic active will that he can make history, for by "will" is meant just this power of man to project himself and his purposes into the future, to "bind time." But again, this is possible only because man is "rational," a *symbolizer* living in a symbolic world, one who is able to create canons of truth and meaning and to judge and evaluate various aspects of experience in terms of them. Moreover, this can all occur only because men have a *history* which has bequeathed elaborate and complex systems of symbols and meanings (i.e., language) to them. Human rationality and will express dimensions of man's historicity but not the wholeness of man. The conception of the "rational man" is, after all, an abstraction, just as the view that man is essentially "will to power." Consequently, the ideals which have grown out of these one-sided views of man's nature are also abstract. The conception of "truth" as the power and the need to know reality "as it really is" and that of "free will" as the power and need to determine one's own course of action and ultimately one's destiny, though certainly very important, can be misleading if not seen as expressions of man's historicity. Perhaps no one claims that man can have "absolute" truth or freedom (whatever these might be). Yet the way in which his limited truth and limited freedom are to be understood is seldom clearly worked out. These conceptions and problems can be clarified by reference to man's historicity.

First, then, what is free will for historical man?[9] It must be emphasized immediately that "freedom" and "predetermination" are not to be viewed as mutually exclusive terms; they are, rather, mutually inclusive, each involving the other. On the one hand, freedom involves predetermination: by *decision* we mean precisely a movement in the present moment through which the future course of events will be determined. If such predetermination were not possible, the

---

[9] For what follows, compare also my *The Context of Decision* (New York: Abingdon, 1961), Ch. 4; and below, pp. 438ff.

concept of decision would be meaningless and man would have no freedom. Moreover, men's decisions in some respects determine the future of others. If a father's decision did not significantly shape the future of his son, in what sense would he be *free* with reference to his son? There can be freedom in a meaningful sense only if when "The fathers have eaten sour grapes, . . . the children's teeth are set on edge" (Jer. 31:29; Ezek. 18:2). On the other hand, predetermination involves freedom. To "determine" (cf. "terminate") means to set limits; to *pre*determine is to set limits prior to the event. Predetermination thus presupposes the power to anticipate an event and to set certain bounds within which it will occur. But such power significantly to bind the future is precisely what is meant by freedom.

Thus, freedom and predetermination presuppose each other, each expressing a different side of the same historical process. They are terms indicating the two opposing directions which a living self faces. On the one hand, the self is aware of having grown out of the past, of being shaped by (its own and others') past decisions and actions, of being "predetermined"; on the other hand, the self knows it is always moving into an open future which will be shaped by the decisions—and thus the freedom—of the present (as well as the past). This two-sided stance is involved in every concrete decision, every act. Thus, the self deciding about the vocation of medicine will be a concrete "I"—with particular interests (developed in the experiences of childhood and adolescence), particular ideas about the medical profession (gained in contacts with doctors, books, movies, etc.), particular friends and influential advisers. That is, the person one has become as the result of *past* decisions and actions (of himself and others) will decide in this present. This present decision will in turn shape future choices, determining future personal contacts and experiences, significantly shaping the person into which he is developing. It is important to note here that it was not his *past* decisions that determined whether he would go to medical school; they only determined what he *now is*. Rather, it is his *present* decision, the present act of this living historical self, which determines whether he will prepare for a medical career or not. To deny the freedom of the self in this present moment with regard to the significant choices facing it, on the ground that past decisions and actions have already determined what the present choice will be, would be inconsistent and absurd. For it would involve a similar denial of any such freedom in the past, and this would mean that those past choices really did not predetermine this present at all. If there is genuine predetermination of the present by the past, then the self has genuine freedom: it can act now to determine the future just as truly as it acted in the past to predetermine this present. The historical process, we can now say in summary, is a complex of acting and interacting persons (themselves being shaped through the process) which is characterized by a peculiar combination of structure and creativity precisely because at every point it is constituted by these twin moments of freedom and predetermination.

With this historical character of selfhood in mind, we are in a position to look briefly at the doctrine of predestination. It is often alleged that the claim that God is working out his overarching purposes in the historical process, and is thus determining beforehand man's ultimate destiny, contradicts human freedom. It should be clear from the above that this is not necessarily true, however; for, with one important qualification, the same considerations hold for the relation of freedom to predestination as to predetermination. The qualification: divine predestination means that the structural context in which present existence is lived should not be conceived as predetermined exclusively by interacting and conflicting *human* purposes, a chaos with no definite direction or ultimate goal; on the contrary, human history is seen here as itself having a context, the flexible but all-comprehensive purposes of God, which give it both meaningful structure and direction. Since these purposes were prior to any man's, they have been effectively shaping the entire process of history, as God brings the whole toward the realization of his objectives. My great-grandfather's decision to come to America did not destroy my freedom, though it predetermined me to be an American—that is, it meant that America would be the context in which my freedom would develop, and that my historical destiny would be bound up with America's. No more did God's predestining man—and thus the course of human history—for his kingdom destroy human freedom; rather, it set the context in which man's freedom would appear and mature, and what its ultimate destiny would be. ". . . before the foundation of the world . . . he destined us in love to be his sons through Jesus Christ, according to the purpose of his will" (Eph. 1:4–5).[10] God's predestination does not conflict with human freedom; on the contrary, it provides the prior condition for finite freedom, namely, a meaningful historical process, which can be an appropriate context for finite decisions and purposes but which the chaotic forces set in motion by the finite agents cannot undermine and finally destroy. It will be clear, of course, that both predestination and the meaningful historical process that follows from it will be known only to faith.

We must turn now to the problem of truth as seen in the light of a historical view of the self. On the one hand, if the self is truly historical, truth (and all other values)—indeed, everything about the self—will be relative; they will have the character they do because of the self's place in history.[11] What one believes true, the values he cherishes and seeks to live by, will differ widely for a thirteenth-century European, an eighth-century B.C. Hebrew, and a twentieth-century American. They will think differently, they will pursue diverse goals, their experience will be significantly different both in detail and in its main lines. A historical being simply does not have available some "absolute" truth, self-identical for all time and eternity; the most he can know is the truth for his time, the goods and values relevant and meaningful in his situation. On the other hand, this does not mean there can be no truth at all for a historical being. The fact that I do not have final truth does not mean I can make no distinctions between truth and error; the fact that a primary school child does not grasp the nature of numbers as adequately as a mathematician does not mean he cannot add $2+2$. The distinction between "true" and "false" is indispensable to man in the continuous assessment and interpretation of experience, evaluation of memories, and

10 Cf. Romans 8:28–30: "We know that in everything God works for good with those who love him, who are called according to his purpose. For those whom he foreknew he also predestined to be conformed to the image of his Son, in order that he might be the firstborn among many brethren. And those whom he predestined he also called; and those whom he called he also justified; and those whom he justified he also glorified."

11 For a full examination of the problem of the relativity of truth, together with certain philosophical and theological presuppositions and implications, see my *Relativism, Knowledge and Faith* (Chicago: University of Chicago Press, 1960).

planning for the future. Without this distinction human action—that which distinguishes human behavior from mere biological process—would be impossible. But the "truth" we discover—indeed, the very meaning of the concept "truth" (like all our concepts)—will only be what is available within our particular historical situation, not some final truth for all time. The corollary of this, of course, is that the precise concrete truth-for-this-time accessible to us can be discovered in no other time. In each new present men are faced with the task of finding the truth; they can never take over without question or qualification the truth from some past, however venerable. This, in fact, is the mistake of every wooden orthodoxy; and at precisely this point such orthodoxy stands in sharp contrast with a living faith which freely and openly faces each new present and future, seeking to live not by ancient law but by the ever-present guidance of the Holy Spirit, "the spirit of truth [who when he] comes . . . will guide you into all the truth" (John 16:13).

The conception of truth as radically historical is fully consistent with the Christian belief in God's sovereign presence over and in history, leading and guiding man in his cognitive endeavors as in all others, "speaking" his "word" in each new historical situation. If there really is a *living God*, one would expect him to manifest himself at appropriate moments. What he revealed on such occasions, however, would not be "eternal truths" about God and man expected to remain the same forever, to be handed down from generation to generation unchanged.[12] In the living human act of communication, the experience from which our analogical concept of God's "word" is drawn, a word is always concrete and specific, relevant to—and thus relative to—the particular situation in which it is spoken. It is a moment of a living conversation, and it is just *at that moment* that it has both its meaning and its truth.[13] So also with God's word to a

---

[12] In this respect some of the later and lesser writings of the New Testament, with their conception of a "faith which was once for all delivered to the saints" (Jude 3), represent, as is widely agreed, a serious deterioration of the dynamic views of a Paul or a John.

[13] The symbol "word" has a meaning sharply contrasting with the idea of abstract and eternal truth holding for all situations. Here the primitive meaning of the term, which is still the primary meaning in English (as well as in Hebrew), is to be preferred over the philosophical meanings associated with the Greek *logos*.

particular situation, as spoken through prophet (or preacher) living
in that situation: it should be understood as the truth-for-that-situa-
tion. Since it is a living word, however, pregnant with relevance and
power for the occasion on which it is spoken, it may be of significance
to other times and places as well—as what a friend said on an
earlier occasion may suggest what he might say now were he here—
but that truth itself must always come in some new formulation
relevant to the concrete actualities of this new present. Thus, the
word of God is always a fresh and living revelation, to be grasped
anew in each new situation. In this respect the notion of revelation
and the conception of truth as radically historical belong together.
That God's living revelation can be expected is the meaning of faith's
claim to be led by the Holy Spirit.

A word must be added here about the implications of this relativity of truth for the Christian claim that Jesus Christ is God's
definitive revelation. This central Christian notion might appear
jeopardized: though Christ may have been the truth for some past,
by now he is surely outmoded and must be surpassed. This, however,
is not the case. We have seen that it is *history* which makes men what
they are, their orientation toward truth being shaped by their particular past. Moreover, not all moments of the past have the same weight
in this shaping. For the Christian community the one decisive moment (historical process) in and through which it became apparent
that *God* is Lord of history—that is, that the historical process has
meaning because through it God's loving purposes are being realized—bears the name "Jesus Christ." Without the faith sprung from
this event, the whole Christian conception of God, man, and the world
would fall to pieces, and there would be no reason to expect, for
example, the "leading of the Holy Spirit." It is the conviction that
God has made himself known (as personal), engendered by this
historical event (and all that led up to and succeeded it) that is
basis for the confidence that he does and will continue to reveal himself and his purposes in history. It is too simple, therefore, either to
identify revelation exclusively with Jesus Christ or to think of it
only as God's fresh word for each new situation. As the trinitarian
analysis has shown, revelation involves both that definitive event (or

history) through which God became known to man as the living and personal God (Jesus Christ), and the continuing address of this same God to every new situation (Holy Spirit). Because knowledge of the latter presupposes the former as its foundation, the Christ-event has a unique place in the Christian metaphysics of history. Jesus Christ is understood as the "center of history" or the source and foundation of faith, not merely one divine revelation among others; and christology deals with the metaphysical uniqueness of this event, not merely its epistemological significance (see above, Chapters 11–13). For Christian faith, therefore, it is inconceivable that this event in its full meaning and significance might be surpassed (though of course it must be continually reinterpreted), for it is the basis and key in terms of which all else is grasped as meaningful. The movement of history subsequent to the Christ-event is to be understood as the process through which ever new perspectives are brought under its influence.

We have been seeking here to explore the notion that man's being is radically historical. But the concept thus far has been developed largely as a useful way to understand the peculiar character of human existence. Why regard this historicity of man as the "image of God"? What reasons can be given for conceiving the theological notion of the *imago Dei* in terms of the anthropological concept of historicity? I shall propose five points in answer to these questions. The first two deal explicitly with the way in which God's nature is reflected in man's historicalness; the next two point out the distinctive character of man's nature as found in this reflection; the last relates the concept directly to biblical history.

1] God's radical difference from the entire created order is expressed in the idea of his *aseity* (see above, esp. Chapters 7 and 10). God is *a se* ("from himself"); he depends on nothing outside himself in order to be—or, as we might say paradoxically, he creates himself. Man, of course, is not *a se* in this decisive sense; on the contrary, he is finite and dependent at every point. And yet, in a certain respect man is an image of God's aseity. For man does create himself. Through decision and action he makes and remakes himself and others into realities different from what they would otherwise be, and through the whole course of human history he has been creating himself into what he now is. In a real sense—though certainly only in a derivative and secondary sense—man *comes from himself*, creates himself, as no other creature does. As Thomas Aquinas suggested, "we may observe in man a certain imitation of God, consisting in the fact that man proceeds from man, as God from God. . . ."[14] God's being grounded in himself alone, his absolute self-sufficiency, finds an image in man's historical development of himself, his relative self-creativity.

When the *imago Dei* is defined in terms of man's creating himself through history, the old question whether sin merely defaces or effectively destroys God's image—a question that could have no satisfactory resolution in the terms it was framed[15]—is bypassed. As long as man exists, he will be continuously creating himself and will thus bear the image of God, his historicity. However, this image, this historicalness, may become corrupted, corrupted so seriously in fact that the history man creates becomes destructive. Sin (as we shall see below) is just such a historical process of cumulating corruption through which man, like a blind Samson, is, in the very strength of his historicity, pulling down the temple in which he stands, destroying his historicity and thus destroying himself through his own creative power.

2] Everything other than God is radically dependent on him. He

---

[14] *Summa Theologica*, I, Q. 93, art. 3.

[15] On the one hand, if the image was only marred in some degree (however serious this defacing be conceived) by the fall, man's nature and his relation to God remain *essentially* intact. The disease of sin thus is not necessarily fatal: man may be able to heal himself, thus rendering God's decisive act of salvation in Jesus Christ dispensable— at least for those who are not weaklings. On the other hand, if, in order to protect the indispensability and wonder and glory of God's mighty act, it is contended that the image has been damaged beyond all possible human repair, and that thus, in effect, it has been destroyed, then "man" (whose unique being had been defined precisely in terms of the *imago*) is apparently no longer man but some other species of being, and salvation cannot be the salvation of *this* existence but must instead involve replacing these beings now walking the earth by others of another species. Both these views reflect the same error. They attempt to understand and interpret the peculiar structure of continuity and discontinuity characteristic of a historical process—the self—in terms of the static naturalistic categories of substance and attribute, essence and accident. As early as Zeno it became apparent that process and change could not be understood in this way; but it was not until relatively recent times—with the discovery of historical modes of conceptualization (see R. G. Collingwood, *The Idea of Nature* [Oxford: Clarendon Press, 1945], pp. 9ff.)—that a satisfactory way of dealing with this problem became available.

is the Creator, the self-existent being, and all other beings gain their existence from him. Here, once again, though man is as dependent on God as any other creature, he is an image of the divine being. For man is also a creator: the whole world of culture has been brought into being by him. Every artifact is the product of an act of freedom and must be regarded as in some measure created *ex nihilo*.[16] Thus the creation of culture, itself intrinsic to man's historicity, images in its own way God's creation of the world (though of course only on a finite and relative level, for God is not dependent on the world for his being as man is reciprocally dependent on culture).

Once again the *imago* viewed in this way as man's historicity is not some attribute or feature of man's nature which sin destroys, though leaving man a historical and cultural being; rather, the *imago* is itself precisely this immersion in and creation of the living historical process. However, if this man and this process have become seriously diseased, man's creativity will produce a history of cumulating evil, a history continuously accelerating toward final self-destruction.

3] It is important to recognize that it is man as such, his historical nature, the totality of his being, that is made in God's image, not some attribute or aspect of his being, a kind of divine element that has been added to his otherwise animal nature. History is the form of everything human. Every feature of man's existence is in history and is shaped by its position in the historical process. From the loftiest thought and most spiritual inspiration (given form as they always are by the mythological and ideological heritage of philosopher and saint) to the most elemental drives and immoral behavior (always given their peculiar shape by the particular customs and institutions of the society, in which even the crudest and most wicked of men are found), everything human bears the inex-

16 Cf. Berdyaev: ". . . people . . . believe that human creation never is out of nothing. But the creative conception itself, the original creative act, does not depend upon any material. It presupposes freedom and arises out of freedom. It is not marble that gives rise to the sculptor's conception, nor is that conception entirely determined by the statues or human bodies which the sculptor has observed and studied. An original creative work always includes an element of freedom and that is the 'nothing' out of which the new, the not yet existent, is created" (*The Destiny of Man* [London: Geoffrey Bles, 1937], p. 85).

pungeable hallmark of man's immersion in culture. In this sense, contrary to Rousseau and all his disciples, one must maintain that our very humanity is bound inseparably to existence in culture; to go "back to nature" would be to return to a pre-human form of existence.[17] Thus, to regard man's historicity as God's image is to maintain that the very form of human existence is a reflection of the divine being. The *imago* is not some attribute of man (e.g., his religiousness), which may be regarded as dispensable and even irrelevant to human life if one chooses to take up a "non-theological" point of view: it points directly to the heart of our humanity, to considerations which (in their own way) are acknowledged by naturalism and materialism as well as by romanticism and idealism. Since the doctrine of the *imago Dei* is an interpretation of man's actual existence, it can provide a basis for fruitful conversation with non-Christian points of view.

4] It is man's historicity that most sharply distinguishes him from the lower animals, indeed, from all other forms of finite being. Nothing else has history in the sense man does: no other being can *deliberately shape history* as well as be shaped by it. Since it points to the distinguishing mark of this particular form of finite being, the concept of historicity has philosophical and scientific usefulness (as well as theological adequacy). It thus makes possible theological interpretation of scientific and humanistic studies of man's nature, while simultaneously facilitating understanding by secular students of the significance and meaning of the theological viewpoint. Bypassing the old mind-body problem in favor of a holistic conception of human nature, it encourages fresh thinking about both man's dif-

---

[17] Cf. Leslie Paul: "If there is food, [the animal] will eat: if not, it cannot. If it is on heat, it will mate, if there is a partner: if not, it cannot. If food is available, or if a mate is available, and anything seeks to restrain it, it will fight. Man alone chooses another way. Only man, while establishing control over natural things, unnaturally surrenders rights over his life and liberties to the society into which he is born . . . how this potentially sovereign natural being . . . is able to turn upon the nature with which he is endowed and subdue it or crush it . . . is indeed an enigma. . . . Man has to give his allegiance to something other than his natural gifts and impulses. He must step outside nature into another frame of reference, a frame which in contrast with nature is going to be artificial—for this other frame is not a birthright, but in a sense is at first completely unknown, and grasped at with difficulty and constructed and maintained with infinite pain and endless labour" (*Nature into History* [London: Faber and Faber, 1957], pp. 82–83).

ference from the lower animals and his relationship to them—and these matters can be discussed in their *theological* significance as well as their scientific and philosophical ramifications.

5] The notion of man's historical nature provides precisely the anthropological conception necessary to understand the biblical picture of man and his destiny. Not only does it facilitate thinking in monistic and holistic anthropological categories (the Bible has little place for such fundamentally Greek dualisms as body-mind [or -soul], spirit-nature, etc.[18]). Even more important, when man is conceived as thus radically historical—as both shaping and being shaped by the movement of history—it is possible to understand the biblical drama in the Bible's own terms, that is, as a genuine historical movement: creation—fall—God's calling a particular people out of the totality of mankind—his repeated covenanting with them—finally, the appearance of the "new creation" within history, salvation wrought through a historical person-event—the entire process moving toward a final consummation. Unless man's being is conceived as so interwoven with the historical process that both his "nature" and the relationship to his source and ground change with the movement of history, these events, even though thought to signify something "very profound," as Hegel put it, will always be translated from the "kind of accidental history" found in the Bible into symbols of an "everlasting necessary history of mankind."[19] That is, unless the theological conception of man's nature—the *imago Dei*—is radically historical (i.e., understood as man's historicity), it will not be possible to conceive the other principal theological notions as referring to actual historical events and persons; and the historical point of view of Bible and Christian faith will be forsaken for some form of idealism or gnosticism.

Let us turn now to examine more closely the ramifications of man's historicity for his actual existence. Man is a being-in-process,

[18] For discussion, see H. W. Robinson, *The Christian Doctrine of Man* (Edinburgh: T. & T. Clark, 1911), Ch. 1; J. Pederson, *Israel: Its Life and Culture* (London: Geoffrey Cumberlege, 1926), pp. 99–181.

[19] G. W. F. Hegel, *Lectures on the Philosophy of Religion*, I, 276. It is ironical that Hegel, who more than anyone else since Augustine taught Western man to think historically, himself finally deserted in this way to idealism.

coming from a distant past, moving toward a hidden future. What he now is has been shaped by that past; his own present decisions and purposes are shaping that future. Being at once dynamic and conscious, man can find meaning in existence only if he apprehends his present as having a significant twofold reference: *backward* to those decisions and actions which have created his self and world and which thus make them intelligible; *forward* to that future where present tendencies and actions will find completion and fulfilment. For a dynamic being, for one whose very existence is purposive activity, meaning can never be found, as the hedonists (and the mystics?) have supposed, in mere intense pleasure of the present moment with no reference to past or future; it emerges only out of awareness of significant participation in a meaningful—that is, *purposive*[20]—historical process, a process therefore believed to have originated in personal decision (or an analogue of it) and to be moving toward the realization of personal purpose. To deny meaningful historical movement is to present a picture of hopelessness and futility, as, for example, in the book of Ecclesiastes.[21] In sharp contrast with such a picture, meaningful existence arises from the sense of standing within a dynamic development, a movement *from* a significant past, *through* this creative present, *into* a meaningful future.

[20] "Meaning" = that which is *meant*, i.e., intended or purposed.
[21] *Vanity of vanities, says the Preacher,*
  vanity of vanities! All is vanity.
What does man gain by all the toil
  at which he toils under the sun?
A generation goes, and a generation comes,
  but the earth remains for ever.
The sun rises and the sun goes down,
  and hastens to the place where it rises.
The wind blows to the south,
  and goes round to the north;
round and round goes the wind,
  and on its circuits the wind returns. . . .
What has been is what will be,
  and what has been done is what will be done;
  and there is nothing new under the sun. . . .
There is no remembrance of former things,
  nor will there be any remembrance
of later things yet to happen
  among those who come after. ECCLESIASTES 1:2–6, 9, 11

There is no development here, nothing new; and hence there is neither remembrance of a significant past nor expectation of a meaningful future. Everything is on the same level, and in consequence it is a dead level.

In short, for a historical being *history* must have meaning if existence is to be meaningful.

But just this fact raises terrifying problems for the finite historical being, man. For, although he knows himself to be in process, in history, he does not know whether this history has meaning. He has no certain knowledge of the beginning from which he sprang; and thus he knows nothing of a significant intention or purpose underlying the historical process within which he has emerged into being. It may be, as many contemporary evolutionists teach, that his appearance was a more or less accidental occurrence. Man seems to have been "thrown" (Heidegger) into a historical process already going on, to be at the mercy of events and decisions in some distant past of which he knows nothing. Since his decisions and actions occur in this larger historical context not of his own making and unknown to him in its full significance, his purposes are always set largely in ignorance of what is in fact going on round about him.

Moreover, the future is, if anything, even darker to man than past and present. The end toward which the historical process is inexorably moving is completely hidden from view. Even the immediate consequences of his own carefully considered actions are often quite other than had been intended; and their effects in the distant future he cannot hope to see or participate in, for between him and them stands the impenetrable barrier of death. Thus, men are never able to make decisions with any real confidence that they know what they are doing, why they are doing it, or what the results will be. Yet they never escape from this present with its inexorable demand that they *decide*, that they set themselves with determinate purpose toward some *particular* future; as historical beings they live continuously in the moment of decision and action, impelled willy-nilly into a future which their actions will shape and for which they are in significant measure responsible.

Caught between finitude and historicity, it is no wonder that man's life is filled with anxiety. Indeed, anxiousness—about himself and his actions, his past and his destiny, his friends and his world—seems the very form of man's inner life. "Anxiety is finitude, experienced as one's own finitude."[22] If men were historical but not finite—like

22 Paul Tillich, *The Courage to Be* (New Haven: Yale University Press, 1952), p. 33.

God—they would not be anxious. For then they would know whence they had come, would know their own decisions had brought them to the present juncture, and would know the ultimate goal of their efforts. History would not be a process to which they were subjected, the externally imposed context of their activity; it would be their own creation: *their activity* would be the context in which history occurred. Though they would be responsible for history's outcome, they would also know themselves equal to the demands thereby laid on them. Anxiety is not a character belonging to historicity as such—God is not anxious: it is the mark of finite historicity. Again, if men were finite but not historical—that is, mere animals—they would not be anxious. For then they would not be forever called upon to *decide* and to bear *responsibility* for their decisions. Animal existence is not characterized by continuous deliberate setting of purposes and acting toward their realization; it does not involve conscious shaping of the future, together with the self-knowledge and guilt which accompanies the ability to act as responsible agents. Hence, animal life, finite but not intrinsically historical, does not know the ever-present undertone of anxiety and guilt characteristic of human existence.

But for man, whose being is at the juncture of finitude and historicity, who is limited and yet simultaneously free and creative, there seems no escape from guilt and anxiety. Thus, the very characteristic that makes man unique among finite beings, lifting him above all others—his historicity, his being created in the "image of God"—also and inevitably poses a terrible threat for him. For it means that his existence is intrinsically precarious and that he knows it. In this situation it is always possible that the tremors of anxiety will shake him to pieces; or that, in Promethean defiance and rejection of his anxiety, he will destroy himself. The nearer he comes to great creation—of self, of culture, of history—the closer he seems to approach destruction of self and world. Human existence appears a tragic web which man must endure heroically but from which there can be no escape so long as he is man.

Though this fearful position midway between the gods and joyous unself-conscious nature may rightly describe man's present self-awareness as a finite and sinful creature swept onward by the current of history, we have oversimplified the matter. In the first place, no account has been taken of the birth of anxiety and guilt and the significance of these historical beginnings for understanding the human condition; to those questions we must turn in the next chapter. Second, the tragic view of human life just sketched, rooting all human problems in man's precarious finite historicity—that is, in his nature as such—fails to observe that given a proper context, there might be other alternatives than simply anxiety and guilt, despair and Promethean defiance. If man could believe that the historical context into which he has been thrown were meaningful, if he could believe it to be the expression of the loving personal decision and purpose of a compassionate Father who is moving all history toward a significant goal, then anxiety would be dissolved. If he could believe his existence and decisions and actions had an indispensable place within larger purposes shaping the overall movement of history, and that even his stupid blunders and wilful perversities could be rectified and redeemed, his anxiousness and guilt could give place to confidence, creativeness, hope. This, of course, is precisely the claim of the Christian Gospel: the overall movement of cosmic history is in the hands of the God and Father of Jesus Christ. God loves man, God gives himself to man in Jesus Christ, God continuously seeks to bring man into his community of love and freedom and creativity.

> Therefore I tell you, do not be anxious about your life, what you shall eat or what you shall drink, nor about your body, what you shall put on. . . . Look at the birds of the air: they neither sow nor reap nor gather into barns, and yet your heavenly Father feeds them. . . . Consider the lilies of the field, how they grow; they neither toil nor spin. . . . But if God so clothes the grass of the field, which today is alive and tomorrow is thrown into the oven, will he not much more clothe you, O men of little faith?
>
> MATTHEW 6:25-30

If men could really believe this, they would suffer no anxiety; for they would experience their freedom and responsibility within a context rendering even their slips and falls and deliberate perversity meaningful. Such a context could provide the peculiar combination of security and plasticity necessary for the growth of authentic freedom, creativity, and love. Such immersion in the love and care of God would render the existence of the finite historical being something other than tragic: "the glorious liberty of the children of God" (Rom. 8:21).

The Christian Gospel, thus, brings us to a vantage point from which can be seen something of what authentic human life might be. It would be existence in finite freedom yet without fear, with full responsibility but without irremovable guilt, in genuine creativity yet unaccompanied by the threat of loosing powers of destruction and evil which could not again be leashed. To live such a life, oriented always toward the creative personal source of all being, would be to become at last a fully historical being, a *free man*. Our own historical existence, lived as it is in anxiety, guilt, and despair, is but the faintest shadow of this vision of human fulfilment. Although we are intrinsically historical, we have not yet realized our historicity. Such fulfilment can and does occur only as the chains of our present choked-up existence, introverted and narcissistic as it is, are broken; and we are drawn out into the cool fresh air of the world in which the loving God is lord and savior. Man truly *is* only insofar as he emerges from his present being into faith, the context in which genuinely free and creative personal existence is possible.

For man to be authentically and fully and intrinsically historical is thus more the goal of human history than present actuality. Man's problem is that he does not and seemingly cannot believe that the context of his existence is essentially defined by the purposes of the all-loving God. Instead, he believes he has been thrown into a cruel and cold and alien world, hostile to his fulfilment, ultimately destructive of human values. And so he lives in self-centered and self-enclosed defensiveness instead of open freedom and creativity. This situation in which man now finds himself has itself come about through a historical movement, and salvation from it is a further historical development. To those movements we must now turn.

24 / The Fall

THE *imago Dei* interpreted as man's historicity provides a way to understand theologically the distinctiveness of man, on the one hand, and to grasp the intrinsic precariousness of human existence without faith—expressing itself in anxiety—on the other. It should not be supposed that this interpretation sets forth the "nature" of the historical being conceived as a permanent and unchanging form which characterizes man always and everywhere; for a historicist perspective there are no such "natures." Rather, we have been examining what are actually two stages of the on-going movement of history: the emergence of a finite being who is intrinsically historical, and his later precarious situation apart from faith in his Creator. The original creation of man—that is, the emergence of the finite historical being in the process of the development of language—probably consumed some hundreds of thousands of years. Moreover, as we noted at the end of the last chapter, though this enabled man to become intrinsically historical and thus a new form of finite being, the process of man's creation has not yet reached completion because of the interference of certain unfortunate events and processes. We must now turn to an examination of this interruption and reversal of man's creation, that is, to the historical event (or process) through which he became alienated from his Creator and human existence became filled with anxiety and guilt: the fall.

The biblical account of the matter is found in Genesis 2 and 3. There are many dimensions of meaning in this story, and we shall make no attempt to exhaust them. Our interest here will be directed to seeing what light the story throws on the historical beginnings of human rebellion, distrust, and warfare. "Historical beginnings" is not used to suggest that we will be able to uncover some datable event—in the Garden of Eden or elsewhere—with the aid of this ancient account. Rather, we shall seek light on the historical process through which man—now on the scene as the historical being, the creature who can speak—developed into a *sinful* being in rebellion against his Creator and at war with his fellows. Obviously, what is to be said cannot be based on historical evidence in the usual sense, documents dealing explicitly or implicitly with the actual event in question; we are concerned here with a corruption common to all known human history, and therefore with an event that antedates all records and artifacts. (It is significant in this connection that the biblical account places the fall immediately after the creation of man.) Despite the lack of direct historical documentation, however, the fall should be regarded as a genuinely historical event or process; for *we cannot understand the continuing historical processes, filled as they are with hatred and disharmony, guilt and distrust, without presupposing an earlier one through which these came to be what they are.*[1] It is to this historical *prius* of the historical processes we know that we must direct out attention with the aid of the early chapters of Genesis.

It is significant that it was fruit of the "tree of the knowledge of good and evil" (2:17) which man was instructed not to eat, and that when he ate of this particular tree he became a sinner. This implies that man's moral knowledge, his ethics, his awareness of the distinction between good and evil, is the result of the fall and to be understood as a feature of man's fallen state, a conception directly counter to the moralistic and idealistic tendencies in much protestant thought. Men often suppose that God's will for them is to seek the "good"; but here the very distinction between good and evil in man's consciousness and culture, and thus good as well as evil, is a product of

---

[1] It will not do to consider these characteristics of human history to be simply man's heritage from the animal nature out of which he evolved; for the problem is precisely the *self-conscious* hatred, distrust, and perversity with which man acts, something quite different from anything known on the animal level. (Cf. F. R. Tennant, *The Origin and Propagation of Sin*, second ed. [Cambridge: University Press, 1908].) These are characteristics, moreover, which do not necessarily follow from man's historicity as such, as I shall seek to show below. Rather, this burden peculiar to man's existence and history is to be understood as having come into existence through a particular event or series of events.

man's disobedience. Why so? An answer is not too hard to suggest: it is in terms of the good/evil distinction that man's moral autonomy— and thus his freedom *from* God—becomes possible. The good/evil dichotomy serves as a kind of internal compass enabling men to chart their course, to decide and act and set purposes without reference beyond ourselves to the transcendent Lord of history. So they become their own masters, and the question of God's purposes for them drops out as superfluous. It is on the basis of "knowledge of good and evil" that every autonomous and humanistic culture is created. Through this knowledge, as the serpent had claimed, man becomes his own lord: ". . . when you eat of it your eyes will be opened, and you will be like God, knowing good and evil" (3:5). Man's conscience makes him autonomous; because he is an ethical being God is no longer necessary to him.

These facts lie at the root of the theological necessity to reject every legalism and moralism as undercutting faith in God. Whenever men have immediately in hand the means for distinguishing right from wrong—whether this be expressed in terms of ecclesiastical rules and customs, codes of law such as the ten commandments, so-called moral or spiritual ideals (of Jesus or anyone else), or the dictates of their own consciences—a barrier has come between them and God. They become their own gods instead of responding continuously to the living God, and thus they live as *fallen* men, no matter how "good" their moral ideals and behavior.

We can now see to just what primeval historical event, lying at the root of man's problems, this ancient account of man's fall away from God refers us: it is the *rise of morality* within human history, the appearance within consciousness and culture of the distinction between good and evil, the development of autonomous norms of action.[2]

___

[2] Cf. Karl Barth: "I am already choosing wrong when I think that I know and ought to decide what is right, and I am doing wrong when I try to accomplish that which I have chosen as right. I am already putting myself in the wrong with others, and doing them wrong, when—it makes no odds how gently or vigorously I do it—I confront them as the one who is right, wanting to break over them as the great crisis. For when I do this I divide myself and I break the fellowship between myself and others. I can only live at unity with myself, and we can only live in fellowship with one another, when I and we subject ourselves to the right which does not dwell in us and is not manifested by us, but which is over me and us as the right of God above. . . . When man thinks that his eyes are opened, and therefore that he knows what is good and evil, when man sets

To understand this occurrence—certainly a genuine historical event—as having such decisive significance for all subsequent human history, it is necessary to push backward behind it to see more clearly how and why it occurred, and forward to see why and how the corruption of the subsequent course of history flows from it. First, then, how is the rise of morality to be understood historico-theologically? Why did it happen? This is the problem of the so-called original sin, in the sense of the *first* sin. Why and how did it occur? Let us return again to our Genesis story. We are presented here, with a picture of man created by God and living in immediate personal relationship to him. This is symbolized by God and man speaking virtually face to face. However, despite this reciprocity, God is clearly in authority, his commands unquestioned by Adam and his wife. As long as this immediate and responsive relation between man and his Creator remains, there are no problems, either between man and God or between man and man. The open and unhibited character of human existence is symbolized here by the nakedness of Adam and Eve: though exposed in their full being both to each other and to God, they "were not ashamed" (2:25).

The problems arise when an event occurs which breaks the immediacy of these personal relations and raises questions about their fidelity and honesty. "Did God say such and so?" asks the serpent; "but the whole matter is really quite doubtful—you won't die at all" (3:1–4). It is significant that another creature than man first raises this question leading to man's critical reflection on his own being and his relation to the reality in which he is grounded. This reflective movement did not arise directly out of the immediate relation between God and man: that would be incomprehensible. Rather, the question about the relation to his Creator arose for man because there was also a third thing to which he was related—namely *nature*, the finite world round about him, the context in which he had been placed. The fall occurred when man began to orient himself by and toward dumb,

himself on the seat of judgment, or even imagines that he can do so, war cannot be prevented but comes irresistibly. When the Law and its commandments and prohibitions and promises and threatenings is taken out of the hands of God and put in those of man, when it is enforced and expounded and applied by man, then it can only bring wrath" (*Church Dogmatics*, IV, 1 [Edinburgh: T. & T. Clark, 1956], p. 451).

impersonal nature, thus turning away from God. In this movement, questions arose about the reality grounding his existence. Does this natural order in which he was placed really have the meaning God declared it to have? Must he refrain from eating the fruit of the forbidden tree? To demythologize: Cannot nature be dealt with intramurally, so to speak, in terms of what one aspect of nature (the snake) implies about another (the tree) without reference to God at all? Cannot this tree be understood in terms of the finite, created order alone, in terms, that is, of what is available and directly accessible to man? To do so would give man new power over himself and his world. He could live autonomously in terms of his growing world- and self-knowledge without raising questions about subjection to the authority of his Maker. Thus, the power and knowledge of God himself seems at hand.

This sort of development would be inconceivable for any other than a free, historical being, a being who could symbolically create new possibilities and seek to actualize them; but given such a being, it is quite plausible, perhaps almost inevitable.[3] As man became man in the historical process, he increasingly became conscious of the natural order round about him as a distinctive and important reality in his life; and he created language to make it possible to differentiate, classify, and remember the various features of his world. It is significant that in Genesis 2:19–20, *before the fall*, Adam gives names to the finite creatures in his world; linguistic activity, and with it a certain measure of consciousness of and control over the world, is portrayed as present before man began to break with his Creator. With

---

[3] In his book, *The Rhetoric of Religion* (Boston: Beacon Press, 1961), Kenneth Burke presents a dialogue in which the Lord and Satan discuss the way in which both man's freedom and his sin are rooted in his ability to speak. The Lord: "When I introduce their kind of words into my Creation, I shall really have let something loose. In dealing with ideas one at a time (or, as they will put it, 'discursively') they can do many things which can't be done when, like us, all ideas are seen at once, and thus necessarily corrected by one another." Satan: "I see it! I see the paradox! Splendid! By their symbolicity, they *will* be able to deviate! A pebble can't make a mistake; it merely exemplifies the laws of motion and position; but an Earth-Man can give a *wrong* answer. At least in their *mistakes*, then, they will be 'creative'; and to that extent they will be really free." The Lord: "Yes, and all sorts of new routes can be found, when you start putting things together piecemeal, rather than having everything there in its proper place, all at once, before you begin. Discursive terminologies will allow for a constant succession of permutations and combinations" (p. 282).

this emergence of language, however, the possibility arose of conceiving nature, in Tillich's words, either "autonomously" (as having its order and meaning in and from itself) or "theonomously" (as receiving its significance and being from Reality transcending both itself and man).[4] Either direction in interpretation was possible. We should not suppose that the choice was made at one particular moment in history by one man or woman. It was a choice which became decisive over many generations and centuries through which, instead of coming to regard all finite being as ordered by a transcendent purposive will, man increasingly came to view certain spheres of nature and culture as *secular*, as profane and autonomous, as having their meaning in and from themselves.

It is not necessary to suppose (as seems implied in the ancient biblical story) that before the fall there was a historical period of "original innocence" when man knew God perfectly. Indeed, if we take modern views of the historical origins of human existence seriously, such is hardly conceivable. The notion of the original innocence of man—with its implication that man, as he came from the hand of his Creator, was a perfectly mature and responsible being—was intended to insure that man rather than God would be held responsible for the fall. There are good theological reasons for such attribution of responsibility; and it may be that, before full emergence of historical understanding of human existence, this was the only way to protect the goodness of God from a most incriminating blemish. But a historicist interpretation can achieve this same end without the difficulties of the more traditional view.[5] According to the view we have been sketching man was already well on his way to becoming intrinsically historical—that is, man—before the fall occurred:

[4] See, e.g., *The Protestant Era* (Chicago: University of Chicago Press, 1948), pp. 44ff.; *Systematic Theology*, I (Chicago: University of Chicago Press, 1951), 83ff., 147ff.; III, 249ff.

[5] In addition to the incomprehensibility (in terms of the contemporary understanding of the historico-evolutionary origins of man's being) of the notion of a period of original innocence, the conception actually makes impossible any understanding of how sin could have entered the created order. For how or why would a perfect being (whatever that might be) in perfect relations to its source and ground ever disrupt and corrupt those relations, especially since God himself was supposedly doing all in his power to sustain them? This theory, far from illuminating the fact of sin and the character of the relation between man and God, simply renders them incomprehensible. It fails, therefore, as a theological conception.

such complicated modes of discrimination and reflection as are involved in the distinctions between good and evil, truth and falsehood,
right and wrong, sacred and profane, presuppose a relatively advanced and self-conscious stage of socio-cultural and linguistic
development. Thus, inasmuch as man's being is essentially linguistic-
historical, he had already in large part emerged into his peculiar
mode of existence—he had already been created by God—when the
fall (the emergence of moral consciousness) occurred.[6] Only because man had already in significant measure become a free and
creative being—and thus one who could *act*—could distinctions between proper and improper modes of action (right and wrong) be
meaningful, significant, and necessary, and thus be created.

I do not mean to suggest that these conceptions appeared only
recently in human history; on the contrary, they antedate every
cultural and historical epoch we have been able to investigate directly. The point to be emphasized here, however, is that these normative distinctions in culture and consciousness are man's invention,
not God's. Hence, it is man who is responsible for their existence and
employment as well as for the consequences they have wrought.
While it would have been possible in the historical development of
human culture for man to have moved toward a growing awareness
of the theonomous purpose of all things, and of the nature and will of
that God who created and sustains them, instead men came increasingly to regard certain spheres of existence as secular and autonomous, to be apprehended and used without reference to the divine,
however primitively this was all understood.[7] With this development
the question which increasingly required answering when men acted
was not: What is *God's will* here? but rather: What values can *we
realize* here? The secular realm or dimension of existence became
understood and interpreted primarily in anthropocentric and utili-

---

[6] It is striking in this connection (as noted above) that the biblical story portrays
man's invention and use of language (Adam naming the animals, Gen. 2:19-20) as
occurring before man's disobedience of God (Gen. 3).

[7] In this connection B. Malinowski's contention that even in the most primitive
cultures there is always a region of nonreligious or secular activity and being, is very
significant as against those who argue that primitive man was "naturally" religious in
every domain of his life. (See *Magic, Science and Religion* [Boston: Beacon
Press, 1948], Ch. 1.)

tarian terms, focusing always on the human values to be gained. It is interesting to note in this connection that Eve observes that eating the forbidden fruit will enrich man with all three of the traditional classical values: "So when the woman saw that the tree was *good* for food, and that it was a delight to the eyes [i.e., was *beautiful*], and that the tree was to be desired to make one wise [to acquire *truth*], she took of its fruit and ate" (3:6). In this moment (or epoch) when man began to seek his own ends or values autonomously, without reference to the will of God, occurred the *fall*. In this moment there was a transition to a new historical situation in which man began to live with reference principally to his own standards of good and evil, the anthropocentric standards which he created and came to possess in his very movement into autonomy.

It is important to note here that man's fall was not a necessary and inescapable consequence of his historical nature. As primitive man emerged from a pre-human level of existence, he may at first have lived in a kind of carefree thoughtlessness similar to the innocent spontaneity and playfulness of the young child.[8] This increasingly

[8] This "childlike innocence," however, which may have been a historical stage through which mankind passed, is not to be confused with the "original innocence" of traditional doctrine (see above, p. 357). The latter notion seems to imply that it was as a mature and fully responsible self that Adam fell, and this is inconceivable both historically and psychologically (see n. 5, p. 357). Childlike innocence, on the other hand, does provide an analogy in terms of which the historical emergence of the complexities of maturity and freedom, responsibility and guilt, can be grasped; for it refers to the preliminary stages of a similar emergence in the empirical development of selves. In this development we see a movement from moral unawareness ("innocence") to a genuine freedom, and we do not hesitate (except in extreme cases) to hold the self both morally and legally responsible for the kind of being it thus becomes. It is important to note here that we do not regard the spontaneous and morally unconscious child as *nonhuman* nor even as *pre-human;* childhood is a stage of genuinely human life. Similarly, we need not regard the pre-moral, primitive, speaking-being as less than human: this was a stage of *human* history from which later morally-conscious stages gradually emerged and for which man himself was "responsible." Like "original innocence," the notion of childlike innocence thus lays responsibility for sin on man himself; unlike original innocence, however, it grasps this fact as an intelligible historical development. Cf. Augustine: "No one is so foolish as to call an infant foolish, though it would be even more absurd to call it wise. An infant can be called neither foolish nor wise though it is already a human being. So it appears that human nature receives an intermediate condition which cannot be rightly called either folly or wisdom. . . . There is a transitional state between sleeping and waking as between folly and wisdom. But there is this difference. In the former case there is no intervention of will; in the latter the transition never takes place except by the action of the will. That is why the consequence is just retribution" (*On Free Will,* Bk. III, 71, 73; trans. from *Library of Christian Classics,* VI [Philadelphia: Westminster Press, 1953], 213, 215). Irenaeus' view, that when man was first created he was an

free and creative man might have developed in the direction of seeing all creation in relation to the transcendent will in which it is grounded. But with genuine freedom emerging it was also possible—perhaps even likely—for the movement toward self-centered autonomy to occur. And this was in fact the direction taken by actual human history. This is not said simply on the basis of the authority of the biblical story we have been examining; an old legend of this sort in itself can establish nothing historically. However, in this case the story illuminates a historical fact characteristic of every culture of which we know: that in it there always appears a secular and autonomous realm.

In our own culture this sphere has expanded and grown in power to the point of dominating our experience and our orientation in life. This is doubtless partly due to the increasing capacity of man to manipulate nature for his own ends, made possible by a science which assumes the realm of nature to be autonomous and self-contained. However, inasmuch as the accelerating movement in this direction—over the last four or five centuries—of scientific perspectives and knowledge is itself rooted in Western man's growing anthropocentrism and secularity, the whole development must be thought of as a cumulating spiral centered ever more certainly in the completely secular and autonomous man. In this respect the increasing scientism and technocracy of Western culture can be regarded as a kind of end-product (and *cul-de-sac?*) of that movement of human history dating back to the fall.

Thus, the fall was that primeval historical event when man through the growing exercise of his freedom began to become *secular* man—and simultaneously, of course, since they are polar, *religious* man—creating and then living by his own standards of good and evil. It was the event or process in which man lost the childlike innocence which had characterized his prior existence (cf. Gen. 3:7);

"infant" who could not be given perfection immediately but had to learn and develop through experience (*Against Heresies*, Bk. IV, xxxviii), may also be compared with mine. (In some respects my concept of childlike innocence is similar to Tillich's notion of "dreaming innocence" [see *Systematic Theology*, II, 33ff.], though unfortunately Tillich, in keeping with his nonhistoricistic ontologism fails to show the relevance of his notion to man's actual historical development, so its empirical meaning remains unclear.)

hereafter man would live in a certain separation from God (symbolized in the biblical account by Adam and Eve hiding from God, God having to seek them) and from his fellows (symbolized by their covering their nakedness and openness to each other with fig leaves). Through this process-event in which man began to create his own norms, new powers—alienation and estrangement—entered human history; thereafter they would be significant elements of the historical context in which mankind lived.

We must turn now from the attempt to understand the historical origins and meaning of the fall to an examination of its consequences. The first point to be noted has already been suggested. On the one hand, man increasingly lived and worked with a certain new autonomy: he could decide and act in terms of his own conceptions of good and evil. On the other hand, precisely because of his new self-centered autonomy, man was alienated from God and his fellows, and as his autonomy increased, so did his alienation. Human existence was thus rising (or falling) to a new level: it was becoming *existence in anxiety*, for in his decisions man had to rely on himself in new and terrifying ways. Being conscious of himself but not knowing the source or end of his being, he became uncertain whether his existence had meaning in the ultimate scheme of things. Thus, all the dimensions of anxiety came into being,[9] and guilt toward God and fellowmen was given birth by the awareness that the ruptured existence in which man lived was his own doing. Both anxiety and guilt deepened as the awareness of good and evil became more pronounced in human history and man's conviction of his own unavoidable responsibility and freedom grew.

The Genesis story also depicts these developments as direct consequences of the fall: "And they heard the sound of the Lord God walking in the garden in the cool of the day, and the man and his wife hid themselves from the presence of the Lord God" (3:8). But the full terror of their meaning is symbolized by the account of man's being banned from the garden. No longer would human existence be

---

[9] It is interesting to note that the psychoanalyst Erich Fromm, in his secular-humanistic interpretation of human existence, also sees this historical movement as the root of human disequilibrium and anxiety. (See *The Sane Society* [New York: Rinehart, 1955], Ch. 3.)

in paradise; hereafter life would be filled with conscious struggle and difficulty. Even—nay, especially!—in the most characteristic tasks of man and woman—daily work and the bearing of children—there would be pain and misery and sorrow, and human life would finally come to its end in hopeless and apparently meaningless disintegration, in death: ". . . you are dust, and to dust you shall return" (3:19).

I have been suggesting that this story of the fall illuminates an actual historical development, though not in some Garden of Eden with a couple named Adam and Eve. It refers rather to the process through which, as man invented language and became man, he also became autonomous and self-seeking, thus developing his own standards of morality, becoming anxious, fearful of death, and guilty. There is, of course, no way to date this process; it has already occurred and is presupposed in every culture of which we know (though expressing itself in very different ways and degrees in the great variety of human cultures). But it nonetheless was an actual historical process, a development within the culture which man himself freely created. Man, not God, invented morality and religion; the act of man in his freedom was thus the source of human anxiety and guilt, and man, not God, must bear responsibility for this historical deterioration in human existence. God created man a free being—in the ultimate sense God also bears responsibility for the subsequent course of history—but it was man who in his freedom fell. The fall itself, as a matter of fact, is the strongest possible evidence that God created man genuinely free: an unfree being would merely be able to carry out God's will as a puppet dances for the puppeteer; only a free being could violate the will of its Creator.[10]

It is perhaps almost unnecessary to remark here how the fall, a primeval event lost in man's historical origins, has continued to affect decisively man's history all the way down to the present. Earlier it was argued that the distinctive characteristic of man is his

[10] Thomas Mann points out that this implies that God, in his own primordial decision to create man, evidently placed a higher value on freedom than on sinless conformity to his purposes (see *Doctor Faustus* [New York: Knopf, 1948], pp. 100f.). Or, to put it in somewhat more precise language theologically, sin and the fall mean that God's purposes may not be narrowly understood as inflexible blueprints laying out every detail of history long in advance; they are, rather, purposes for beings themselves genuinely free and creative and who thus have real power significantly to shape the course of history.

historicity—that in history he can and does shape his own nature through decision and action. The relevance of that conception to this problem should be obvious. The emergence of autonomy and secularism, anxiety and guilt, within human history meant that these would inevitably become dynamic factors in the historical process. Each generation passes on to the next—explicitly through formal educational procedures, implicitly through all that is acquired "at mother's knee"—the attitudes, values, beliefs, hopes, fears important to its own existence. Views of life and the world—and the understanding of their meaning—are transmitted through myths and stories, moral and legal codes, social institutions and customs. Hence, a new generation never approaches a world which is naked and exposed; it is always the world as interpreted in the culture of the preceding generation. Because no generation need ever learn completely afresh what its forebears experienced, cumulative development of human culture becomes possible and man's very being becomes historical. But for the same reason, each new generation is imprisoned in the ideas and attitudes of its predecessor; though these can be built upon and sometimes creatively altered, they can never be entirely escaped. Thus, the anxious and guilty father, however much he desires, can never deal with his son in perfect openness and freedom and spontaneity but must always in some measure cover his nakedness; and consequently the son in his formative years never knows a fully free and spontaneous relationship of love with another human being but himself becomes anxious, fearful, guilty. When he in turn has a son, this corrupted stance will once more be passed along, whether wittingly or not. So the sins of the fathers are passed on to the third and fourth generations, *ad infinitum.* "Therefore . . . sin came into the world through one man and death through sin, and so death spread to all men because all men sinned" (Rom. 5:12).

In this way the estrangement and anxiety born at the dawn of human history became a structural feature of human existence in all periods of history. Separation from God—call it disobedience, idolatry, secularity, what you will—was the root sin, the "original sin," from which sprang the other significant historical evils (as we shall see in the next chapter). Man's autonomous attempt to overcome his anxiety and guilt only mired him deeper in difficulties—giving birth to selfishness, pride, warfare, idolatry—bceause it was precisely man's autonomy, and the correlative anxiety, which needed to be overcome.[11] And so history became corrupted by all manner of evils, each transmitted from generation to generation.

Clearly the appropriate solution to this problem would be the entrance into history of a new impulse, a community of reconciliation and love which could provide a context for freedom without anxiety. Such a community, itself working within the historical process, might possibly overcome the evils loosed in the fall. This, of course, is precisely the Christian claim: that God broke into history in Jesus Christ, loosing an impulse of reconcilation and thus creating a community of love which finally will overcome man's estrangement and warfare, taking all men up into itself. In this way God is working toward ultimate realization of his purposes in creating man.

---

[11] ". . . what good works could a lost soul do except as he had been rescued from his lostness? Could he do this by the determination of his free will? Of course not! For it was in the evil use of his free will that man destroyed himself and his will at the same time. For as a man who kills himself is still alive when he kills himself, but having killed himself is then no longer alive and cannot resuscitate himself after he has destroyed his own life—so also sin which arises from the action of the free will turns out to be victor over the will and the free will is destroyed." (Augustine, *Enchiridion*, Ch. 9, 30; trans. from *Library of Christian Classics*, VII, 356.)

25 / Sin, Idolatry, and Bondage

THE fall brought man into a situation of moral autonomy, on the one hand, and estrangement and anxiety, on the other. But this was by no means the end of the matter. Man was now in a condition of unstable equilibrium which would set in motion a cycle of cumulative degeneration with disastrous historical consequences. It is not difficult to see how the tensions, complexities, and evils of the empirical history which we know flowed directly from the chaotic historical forces loosed by the fall. As a matter of fact, we are justified in regarding the fall and the cycle of consequences following in its train as genuinely historical event-processes, even though we have no direct historical documentation for them, only because they provide presuppositions for understanding the character of human history as we know it. Although the ordinary historian is entitled to avoid such "speculations" about the "pre-historical" period —and the problems with which we are here concerned certainly lie outside the domain of the biological analysis of human evolution— the theologian and philosopher, whose business is to *understand* man's historical existence and not merely to describe it, must provide an intelligible interpretation of "how we got this way." Genuine understanding of a historical being—a being constituted by its past —can be gained only through apprehending the decisive events which shaped that being into its present structure. Therefore, even though some of these events and processes are not open to inspection through the usual historical procedures, it is necessary to reconstruct and analyze them as best we can, if the actual course and character of human history are to be understood. The present interpretation of the fall and its consequences is an attempt to provide such a conception of certain critical events decisively determinative for human existence. An interpretation of the fall itself has already been set forth here. In order to justify the claim that this was an actual historical event-process and is not mere speculation, it is necessary to show that certain dimensions of our existence do indeed become comprehensible when seen as consequences flowing directly from it.[1]

The first thing to observe is that the twofold consequence of the fall—autonomy and anxiety—is itself intolerable and thus unstable. For in this condition men grow to consciousness of themselves as alienated from their true good, the ground of their being, and estranged from their fellows. They know themselves to be somehow incomplete and inadequate. As though physically hungry, they have a gnawing need, but this is emptiness of their whole beings, not merely their bodies: they are *ontologically* hungry, filled with a painful void. What do they need? They know themselves to be free and responsible, forced to decide and act, but they do not know the real meaning of their existence. From whence did they come? They were "thrown" into existence. Where are they going? Toward death —nonbeing. They do not know, then, the real context of their action

---

[1] The discussion of such events as the fall and its consequences does not represent such a radical departure from strict historical methodology to "mere speculation" as might be imagined. All historical work proceeds by a kind of presuppositional or "transcendental" (Kant) method. The historian has certain "evidences" in the present with which he begins—documents, archaeological remains, institutions, oral and written traditions, etc.—and his task is to reconstruct the history *presupposed by these evidences*, i.e., to create a reconstruction which will provide an intelligible interpretation of the evidences at his disposal. Sometimes the critical events for his reconstruction are explicitly discussed in the documents, but frequently they are not. In any case the historian's sketch of the events he supposes decisive—based on his own careful analysis and imaginative inference—will never coincide precisely with what he has found in the documents, and in many cases it may diverge sharply. His task is not to reproduce the documents but to reconstruct the events *presupposed* by them and in the light of which they must be understood, and it is the convincingness of his demonstration that just *this* reconstruction of the events is presupposed that is the measure of the *historical truth* in his account. (Cf. Collingwood, *Idea of History* [London: Oxford University Press, 1946], pp. 231–282.) It will be observed that this presuppositional methodology is also being followed in the present reconstruction of the primeval events of the fall and its consequences, only here we are concerned not with the events presupposed by certain specific documents—i.e., with a tiny segment of history—but with the events presupposed by certain characteristics of the entire known historical process—i.e., with those events presupposed, so to speak, by *all* historical documents. To perform this historical task is quite as important as more traditional historical work, however problematic it may appear. From a philosophical or theological point of view, it is more important, since it is concerned with man *per se* and his history, and not merely with this or that particular man or group of men.

—the meaning of their history—and its significance for their decisions. If they could believe that the context in which they are living
and acting were the outworking of loving purposes of a God who wills
that they act in freedom, and who will therefore sustain them in
their freedom, not permitting them to destroy themselves or their
loved ones, they could act freely. But they are characterized precisely
by estrangement from this God: they do not know him and they
cannot believe this about him. What then are they to do? Despite
their ontological lostness they still must decide and act and thus
create history: for historical beings there is no escaping historicity,
however terrifying it might be.

To make this unbearable situation somewhat more tolerable men
either attempt to treat something they know, something which lies at
hand, as the true and proper satisfaction of the ontological hunger,
or they seek to deaden their very sensibility and consciousness. The
majority of the traditional "seven deadly sins"—for example, pride,
covetousness, lust, gluttony—express the first alternative: they describe conditions of inordinate attachment to some finite reality (sex,
self, property, etc.), ultimately devoting one's whole being to that
reality and thus making it one's *god*.[2] "Sloth," however, refers to
the alternative course: withdrawing from the struggles of existence,
increasingly retreating from life itself.

If one takes the first alternative in face of the anxiety about his
finitude and the unknown future, he must find a guarantee for existence and action, however feeble it might be. Since in man's estrangement God—the true source of his being and ground of his security
—is not immediately present but is invisible to him, he has no choice
but to make tangible, visible, present realities his gods; there is
nothing else to which he can turn. So he may seek meaning for
existence through regarding the *self* as worthy of all devotion, thus
becoming utterly self-interested, self-centered, filled with pride. Or
he may give himself to certain particular experiential *pleasures* (as
in lust or gluttony). Or he may attempt to exert dominating *power*
over others in order to demonstrate both to himself and them his
self-sufficiency and strength, thus becoming a martinet or tyrant, or

---

[2] ". . . whatever your heart clings to and confides in, that is really your God"
(Martin Luther, *Large Catechism*, Part I, The First Commandment).

simply surly and brutal. He may gain meaning through identifying with a larger social reality which he treats as god—for example, the "good family man" who is, however, unconcerned about others; the super-patriot, who becomes chauvinist and war-monger; the racist, with his Nazi concentration camps and his White Citizens' Councils; the ecclesiasticist, putting the church and her programs above all else. The finite gods to which desperate men give themselves are endless. Each case involves seizing some accessible finite reality and convincing oneself, perhaps almost unconsciously, that if he gives himself to it the emptiness and anxiety and guilt in life will be taken away.

If, on the other hand, one takes the second alternative, seeking to withdraw from tension and responsibility, he increasingly loses the very power to act, retiring finally, in extreme cases, into a kind of catatonic stupor.

We need not examine in detail here the way in which the ontological hunger given birth by the fall works itself out in the great variety of particular sins which have appeared in the course of history. The point I want to emphasize is that this movement into sin, once given the fall and man's consequent ontological instability, was unavoidable. A being conscious of himself and his responsibility in action needs a framework of orientation and interpretation to apprehend the meaning of his existence and work; if he has been cut off from true understanding, he needs to find a substitute in the finite reality at hand. Or else he must withdraw from action, thus attempting to forsake his very historicity. Inasmuch as the fall into autonomy and anxiety antedates every period or society of which we have direct historical knowledge, all known human institutions, ideologies, and activities are contaminated with such sinful idolatries and withdrawals, and in turn become further transmitters of them. All are involved in the movement into sin simply because they have emerged out of and continue to participate in the human history which bears it. Thus, there is real truth in the old couplet expressing the orthodox doctrine of original sin:

In Adam's fall,
we sinned all.

The whole historical process has become corrupted and in consequence corrupts whatever emerges within it. The actual form which sin takes in different societies and individuals is of course not determined by the fall, though the general structure of sinfulness to which we have been attending is an irreversible cycle of development underlying each of the manifold forms of sin.

Since the sinful movement toward withdrawal from life and history leads rather directly and simply into stagnation and ultimately death, we need not expand on it further here. Instead we shall focus on the highly complex and dynamic movement into idolatry. In this movement, as we have seen, one gives oneself to some finite reality. But the immediate consequence of this step is the very opposite of what was intended: instead of salvation from meaninglessness one is enslaved to a merciless master. This can be most easily seen with the passions. The more one seeks meaning through satisfaction of, for example, drives for food or sex, the more he becomes enslaved to gluttony and lust and thus plunged deeper into the search for genuine meaning and satisfaction. The reason, as Augustine long ago saw, is quite simple: no finite object can satisfy man's craving for God. "Our hearts are restless till they find their rest in thee."[3] Seeking gratification in the finite object only increases the craving, thus plunging one deeper in enslavement to the passion. Moreover, such meaning as he originally found in eating and sexual activity begins to grow flat and cloy upon him as he becomes satiated but still unsatisfied, and it becomes obvious that this was in fact not what was needed. But this only makes him more desperate in the search for meaning and salvation, and so he plunges yet more blindly into deeper bondage.

A similar development could be described in the lust for money and property, in the desire for power and prestige, indeed in all forms of self-indulgence. It is not only in vices such as alcoholism or dope addiction that one becomes increasingly the slave of this or that finite reality, finally losing completely, in extreme cases, all freedom to decide and act. In every idolatrous movement one gradually but increasingly is dominated by the passion (= the power before which one is *passive*) to which he has given himself.

---

[3] *Confessions*, Bk. I, Ch. 1.

Usually, however, men are unable to give themselves completely to one finite reality, one dimension of experience, as does, perhaps, a Don Juan or a miser or a Hitler, becoming thereby completely demonic: most men do not find it possible to be idolaters and monotheists simultaneously. Hence they become polytheists, worshiping and serving many gods. One may be a "good family man" and at the same time a sharp operator in business, a faithful churchman and a super-patriot and racist. What is meaningful and valuable in one domain of life seems irrelevant elsewhere, so with part of their lives and energies they give themselves to one goal, with another fraction to something else, perhaps inconsistent with the first. In this way they are saved from demonic one-sidedness and fanaticism, but fall instead into a situation where their personalities are threatened with disintegration. Life breaks down into many separate compartments, each with its own little meaning, but unrelated or only tenuously related to the others. This pluralism or polytheism pushed to the extreme results in breakdown of the self into split or multiple personalities, different fragments of the self becoming so enslaved to different gods that they lose contact with and even awareness of each other. Thus, idolatrous polytheism also leads ultimately to the destruction of the effective freedom of the self, to a slavery in which the self no longer is able to decide or act as a unified whole.

The important thing to note here is that in both these forms of idolatry—demonic monotheism and polytheism—the self becomes involved in a historical process of its own making but which progressively destroys its freedom. Thus the very power which distinguishes man from other finite beings—the power to make history —becomes the means of the self's undoing and destruction, for one enters here into a historical process which can end only in the destruction of his very historicity. The movement in which the self is involved remains a historical movement, a process which the self has created, but now the self no longer is involved in a history moving toward increasing freedom and creativity—the history which had created man; on the contrary, it is now a history of increasing enslavement. Though certain features of Augustine's doctrine of original sin certainly need modification, he saw clearly that it was the self's power to make and remake itself in history—its historicity—which made possible its self-enslavement.

> . . . I was rather an unwilling sufferer than a willing actor. And yet it was through me that habit had become an armed enemy against me, because I had willingly come to be what I unwillingly found myself to be. . . . Thus with the baggage of the world I was sweetly burdened, as one in slumber. . . . *For the law of sin is the tyranny of habit,* by which the mind is drawn and held, even against its will. Yet it deserves to be so held because it so willingly falls into the habit.[4]

Throughout this destructive movement the self is acting to create further history and thus remains a historical being—the *imago Dei,* man's historicity, continues to define man's being so long as the self exists at all—but now this is a history destroying the self, a history in which the self is moving away from freedom into slavery and thus into no-history. As history unfolds in sin, the *imago* moves forward through a continuous process of self-destruction.

Man's estrangement from God leads to a lack of fulfilment in the social dimensions of existence quite as much as the individual, the same sort of historical processes being set in motion by alienation and anxiety in society, with the same two-sided possibilities appearing. On the one hand, the community in search of meaning to sustain and fulfill its existence may fall into a demonic one-sidedness through the elevation of certain finite values to a position of ultimacy, all else being subordinated to the demands of this one god. Thus, with Naziism, or in an unrestricted *laissez-faire* economy, or in an ecclesiastically dominated social order, demonic powers are loosed in history which often destroy not only the particular people which first bowed before them in worship but many other more or less innocent communities as well. On the other hand, when a pluralistic and polytheistic solution is attempted, as in the medieval "two swords" theory of the relations between church and state, or in the

---

4 *Confessions,* Bk. 8, Ch. 5; trans. from *Library of Christian Classics,* VII (Philadelphia: Westminster Press, 1955), 164–165. Italics mine.

contemporary chaos of conflicting national sovereignties in international relations, the order is unstable; and society is always in
danger of disintegrating into fragments at war with each other. As
with the progressive self-enslavement of the individual, the movement of the community in one or the other of these directions is obviously always movement through a history of its own making. Here,
also, the *imago* as man's historicity is not immediately destroyed by
sin; but, once again, this is a history of progressive destruction of
communal existence. Instead of creating a history which will further
the development of communal freedom and creativity—and thus of
man's historicity and man himself—demonic powers are raised up
which threaten to overwhelm and destroy the human community completely.

This inevitable historical movement of selves and communities
suffering from the ontological hunger produced by the fall further
intensifies the estrangement already present in self and society. As
enslavement to false gods grows, it becomes increasingly impossible
to turn back to the true God: alienation from him intensifies, and
so far as he is perceived or believed in at all, he may be blamed for
the plight into which man has gotten himself. As the Creator of
both man and the world, is he not responsible for the frustration and
suffering in existence? Indeed, he may even have willed it so. Perhaps he is an evil demon, a God of wrath and hatred. Men's guilty
awareness that they themselves are in some significant measure responsible for the mess that existence is in, and thus that they deserve
punishment, even destruction, from him who created them for quite
different ends, only enhances the sense of God's wrath and drives
the wedge of alienation and despair deeper.[5] And so their concern

---

[5] Cf. Barth: "Man cannot alter by anything that he does what God is and wills in
Himself. But it is inevitable that to the man who has become guilty before God, but
who has not fallen from Him and cannot escape Him, God should *appear as an enemy*
when He encounters him, that everything that God is for him should now be directed
against him, that his whole being, the order of life which God has established and
appointed, the good things which God has done and still does for him, should all
openly or secretly become to him a burden and grief and embarrassment. It belongs to
the freedom in which God is gracious to man that *He cannot appear to man and encounter him as the One He is*, when on the side of man the freedom to confess Him as
the One He is has been senselessly abandoned and lost. *In these circumstances God necessarily appears to him and encounters him in the alien form of a wrathful God*" (*Church
Dogmatics*, IV, 1 [Edinburgh: T. & T. Clark, 1956], 489–490; italics mine).

for God and his will decreases as they openly rebel against his tyranny, or as they deliberately ignore and eventually come to forget him entirely. The vicious cycle moves ever deeper.

The continuously increasing secularism of the modern world, where even the question about God has become uninteresting and irrelevant, may be understood as one of the final historical consequences of the movement into autonomy beginning with the fall. Man has certainly achieved in our time astonishing scientific and technical mastery over his environment; but this has been purchased at the price of such exclusive attention to a world of objects become detached from any final purposes of a creator God, that it is hardly possible any longer for him seriously to concern himself with, or give himself to, that which transcends the finite order absolutely. He has become modern secular man who can be adequately described, as Camus noted, in one brief sentence: "he fornicated and read the papers."[6] It is ironical, but perhaps not surprising if our interpretation of the historical cumulation of the destructive powers of evil is correct, that precisely at this juncture in history where man has finally almost achieved his goal of autonomy—where his life is characterized by scientific and technical mastery over the powers of nature, as well as freedom from the authority of God in his pervasively secular culture—man's instruments of destruction have for the first time made it possible for him to annihilate himself in an act of race-suicide, and under the threat of such an event we all now daily live.[7]

Further new dimensions of alienation and other new evils are introduced into man's existential situation by the very decision to serve an idol. One finds it no longer possible to be honest with himself or others. On the contrary, it becomes necessary to deceive both self and associates with the lie that this idol is what is really wanted and needed to give life meaning. To convince himself that devotion to this false god is proper and right, one rationalizes (Freud) one's action and existence, attempting to prove them good and honest and

---

[6] *The Fall* (New York: Knopf, 1957), pp. 6–7.

[7] Is this the beginning of the reign of anti-Christ, which the early Christians thought was to precede the consummation of history (cf., e.g., 2 Thess. 2:3ff.)?

true. But such self-deceit is only a further step in destruction of the self. On the one hand, the self is doing the deceiving; on the other, it is this same self that is deceived. In rationalization the self splits even further, standing over against itself, knowing its deceitfulness yet refusing to acknowledge it—a living self-contradiction always in tension and always threatened with further disintegration. A similar movement into further alienation occurs in the idolatrous community. To justify itself and its relations to other social groups, the community creates ideologies (Marx). The most brutal kind of enslavement and murder of other peoples seems not so evil if Germans are a "master race"; the continuing subordination of Negroes to whites is appropriate if the former are "inferior"; imperialism cloaked as the "white man's burden" justifies exploitation of "backward nations"; the "righteous" battle against "atheistic communism" makes right the wanton destruction of enemies and innocents alike; and the church, being a "divine institution," ought to be honored as the veritable representative of God on earth. The ideologies with which communities justify their behavior involve the same sort of internal self-contradiction as rationalization in the individual. Moreover, both rationalization and ideology set man against man and community against community in such a way that social strife can only increase, thus multiplying the estrangement among men without limit.

Human existence has been further complicated by the unnumbered historical evils spawned by the developments we have just been considering: strife, murder, dishonesty, terror, despair, and further guilt; nationalism and racism, imperialism and war, radical economic and social inequalities—each adds its burden of evil to the relentless historical movement. Thus the principal tensions and problems of historical existence arise out of the cumulative unfolding of the consequences of the fall, the movement of man— begun in pre-history but not yet come to its terminus—into autonomy and secularity.[8]

[8] It will be remembered that Paul also described the cumulation of historical evils as consequent upon man's estrangement from his Creator: "[Men] bartered away the true God for a false one, and have offered reverence and worship to created things instead of to the Creator. . . . Thus, because they have not seen fit to acknowledge God,

Three points should be underlined in conclusion. First, this whole movement into sinfulness is to be understood as an actual historical development that followed inexorably on an actual historical fall. Because of his alienation from God and resultant anxiety, man in history became an idolater worshiping a multitude of false gods. In consequence, he became enslaved to demonic powers which, as they worked themselves out in history, brought chaos and doom. The course of history, instead of developing into a context within which genuinely free beings could emerge and be nurtured in communities of love and trust, became increasingly destructive of authentic freedom, with human communities able to exist only on a fragmentary and tenuous basis. Thus, the tensions, disharmony, warfare, and destructiveness with which history is filled—powers always threatening to overcome the forces of creativity, freedom, and constructiveness working within history from its beginning—are to be understood both historically and theologically as the direct and inevitable consequence of the fall.

Second, it is clear that all recorded history, including our own time, is deep in the midst of this morass of sin and evil. This is the context within which selves emerge, communities are shaped, ideals and ideas are created. It should not be surprising, then, that these all are corrupted in the very process of their creation and in turn become further corrupting powers. Into this kind of existence all men have been born, and since they are part and parcel of this history their very selves are distorted, corrupted, self-centered, and sinful. In this sense original sin is *inherited* by all—not biologically, as Augustine argued, but historically[9]—and there is no possible way to

---

he has given them up to their own depraved reason. This leads them to break all rules of conduct. They are filled with every kind of injustice, mischief, rapacity, and malice; they are one mass of envy, murder, rivalry, treachery, and malevolence; whisperers and scandal-mongers, hateful to God, insolent, arrogant, and boastful; they invent new kinds of mischief, they show no loyalty to parents, no conscience, no fidelity to their plighted word; they are without natural affection and without pity" (Rom. 1:25, 28–31 NEB).

[9] Though he did not make a great deal of this, Augustine also could suggest that sin is transmitted through the historico-cultural process, which in turn infects those selves which emerge within it: ". . . the soul so far excelled in dignity every corporeal creature that one soul could start from the position to which another had fallen. . . ." "It is not to be wondered at that man . . . cannot see what he ought to do or fulfil it when he will, *in face of carnal custom* which, in a sense, has grown as strong, almost, as nature . . ." (*On Free Will,* Bk. III, 56, 52; trans. from *Library of Christian Classics,* VI, 204, 201–202;

avoid it. One can quite properly cry with the writer of Psalm 51:5:

Behold, I was brought forth in iniquity,
   and in sin did my mother conceive me

or with Paul: "None is righteous, no, not one" (Rom. 3:10; cf. Ps. 14). Man was created in the image of God, and thus he is a historical being. But he has transformed himself into a being continually in the process of destroying his historicity and thus annihilating his selfhood. As long as this process has not run to its fatal end, man will continue to exist as historical, stamped with God's image, one who though formed by his past cannot evade responsibility for his present existence and future. Although he might like to escape his guilt by arguing that, as victim of a past he cannot avoid, he ought not be held responsible for present and future, he cannot. His awareness in action that it is he—not someone else—who is acting, will not permit him to fail holding himself responsible, however much he seeks to rationalize this away with such high-sounding slogans as "ought implies can." It is not impossible that the long process of sinful history, through which—beginning with the fall—man has been progressively destroying himself even while building profound cultures and magnificent civilizations, may finally come to its end with his complete obliteration. This at any rate is conceivable in our day for the first time in history. Man may have brought himself and his history into a *cul-de-sac* from which he cannot extricate himself; for the selves which are required to do the extricating have themselves been corrupted in and by the history in which they live, and so their every action only has further lethal effects.

This brings us to the third and last observation. There could be hope for man in this situation only if a power of love and reconciliation were to break into this sick history, gradually healing it of its

---

italics mine). It is significant that Augustine continued to hold these views long after his notion of biological inheritance of sin had become dominant. In the anti-Pelagian writing, *On Nature and Grace* (Ch. 81), he explicitly cites the second of these quoted passages with approval. It was Schleiermacher, of course, who most fully developed the notion of sin as corporate evil transmitted socially (see *The Christian Faith* [Edinburgh: T. & T. Clark, 1928], § 71), though he was not prepared to regard the fall as historical, as I have done (*ibid.*, § 72).

ills. Such a power could not arise immanently from the diseased and dying body itself. It would have to break into the historical order from beyond its bounds—from the God who created not only man and his history but all the world. The Christian faith, of course, holds that from the time of the fall, when human history began its accelerating descent into perdition, God has been working to enter history with love and reconciliation, that finally after long historical preparation this became possible and actual in and with Jesus Christ, that the community born through his ministry became the historical center from which reconciliation is gradually taming the wild and destructive powers at loose in existence, and that finally—at the end time—this rebellious history will thus be transformed into the kingdom of love which God had created it to be.

26 / The History of Salvation

W<small>E</small> have seen that man's central problem is that his history, created to become God's kingdom, has become corrupted and demonic. Instead of men living together as a community of love, their existence is colored by chaos, war, guilt, misery, despair. How, then, are God's purposes for them to be realized? How is fallen man to be rescued from the plight into which he has gotten himself? How is human history to be so transformed that it can become the kingdom God had intended it to be?

Inasmuch as the problem here is *man*—the historical being—and *history*, salvation must itself be *historical*, i.e., it must come through *events* which further transform history, thus finally healing man himself. Were salvation anything other than a historical process—for example, were God to act directly upon man, lifting him with supernatural power out of the morass of historical evil in which he is immersed, cleansing him of it all, then placing him in some perfect heaven to praise and adore him forever—far from healing and saving this creature whose very being is his historicity, it would simply destroy him. For it would rip him apart from his historically-formed selfhood, replacing this free and self-creative historical agent made in God's image with a being entirely externally determined, a mere thing. As Gregory of Nazianzus long ago asserted, the change could not be

made on a sudden, nor at the first movement of the endeavor. Why not . . . ? That no violence might be done to us, but that we might be moved by persuasion. . . . And therefore, like a

tutor or physician, he partly removes and partly condones an-
cestral habits, conceding some little of what tended to pleasure,
just as medical men do with their patients, that their medicine
may be taken, being artfully blended with what is nice. For it is
no very easy matter to change from those habits which custom
and use have made honorable. . . . Then, when once men had
submitted to the curtailment, they also yielded that which had
been conceded to them . . . , being beguiled into the gospel by
gradual changes. . . . For this reason it was, I think, that he
gradually came to dwell in the disciples, measuring himself out
to them according to their capacity to receive him. . . .[1]

If the being whose very nature is historicity is to be saved, it will be
necessary to work in and through history itself, turning it from the
sinful process it has become to one increasingly responsive to God's
will. Moreover, since human history and human creativity have
themselves become corrupted, this transformation cannot be effected
by purely immanent historical powers, that is, man cannot himself
overcome his alienation from the origin and ground of his being;
there must be a movement from God's side through which powers of
reconciliation and renewal are brought into history to work immanently within the historical process, gradually transforming it
so that it can ultimately become his kingdom. The "history of salvation" is the special activity of God directed toward this end.

It is not possible to trace the course of salvation-history in detail
here. But several of the most important stages should be mentioned
(cf. Chapter 19, above). The *first*, symbolized in Genesis by the
"call of Abraham," was the preparation of a certain receptiveness
in man to the fact that God's requirements are distinct from man's
(autonomous) desires. Until it was possible for men to distinguish
between divine will and human will, obedience to God—and hence
the "kingdom of God"—could not come. The beginnings of this
distinction between divine and human purposes and wills appeared
with the rise in history of the primitive religious cultus, making

[1] *Fifth Theological Oration—On the Spirit*, 25, 26; trans. from *Library of Christian
Classics*, III (Philadelphia: Westminster Press, 1954), 208-210.

claims on man in the name of the supernatural authority of the gods.[2]
As men discovered that the special requirements or commandments of
the gods demanded special acts of obedience, the possibility of transcending a purely anthropocentric religion arose; they might even,
upon occasion, obey the divine commands for their own sake. The
biblical story of God summoning Abraham to leave family and homeland—that is, normal human security and fulfilment of his personal
desires—to go out "not knowing where he was to go" (Heb. 11:8),
and *his obedient response* symbolizes an awareness of this distinction between human desires and One whose will is of ultimate importance; even more striking in this respect, as Kierkegaard has made
dramatically clear,[3] is the story of Abraham's acceptance of the
obligation to sacrifice his son Isaac at God's command. The important historical fact to which the Abrahamic legends point is the rise
in Near Eastern religious cultus of the awareness of obligation to
the will of the gods. For Christian faith, believing that God had long
been working to break into history, this development may be understood as a critical first stage through which God began to make himself known. These beginnings were crude, of course, and if one could
not see the goal to which they would ultimately lead, their importance would hardly be apparent. Yet they provide the historically
essential presupposition without which the subsequent history of
salvation could not unfold.

The *second* stage or event of salvation-history which we must
note is the exodus-covenant complex through which the people of
Israel bound themselves in a historical compact to the God Yahweh.
Here the totalitarian character of the loyalty claimed by God began
to become apparent, together with the genuinely personal character
of the relation between man and God. It was in personal freedom that
the covenant was made by both parties and it would be sustained
only through personal loyalty and faithfulness, a continuous determination to fulfil the covenantal obligations and strengthen the bond.
The relation between man and God here did not depend primarily
on natural structural connections between finite existence and the

---

[2] This, of course, is the opposite side of the growing prominence of a "secular"
sphere of life and culture, which had its origins in the fall.

[3] See *Fear and Trembling* (Princeton: Princeton University Press, 1945).

ground of being—a permanent unchanging order of relationships grounded in the structure of reality itself—as expressed in cosmological mythologies and philosophical conceptions of cosmic order. Nor was it dependent on the vagaries of experience, neither the emotional ecstasy of a "mystery" cult nor the rigid disciplines of mysticism. The relationship instead was grounded in the contingency of historical acts—not the happenstance contingency of mere process, but the moral contingency of the historical fabric in which free personal decisions lead to binding moral obligations and new structures of communal interrelationship. Thus, in the covenanting act the relation between God and man became defined primarily in historico-personal terms; it was a relation depending on the historicity of both parties—on their ability to bind themselves to each other in time and through time. Of course, Moses and his associates scarcely realized, in just these terms, the significance of what was happening.

The real significance of the covenant, in fact, did not become evident until three or four hundred years later when "J" and the prophets found it possible to interpret all Hebrew history—and their present existence and expectations about the future as well—with reference to it. With this development we are into the *third* stage or event of salvation-history. Yahweh, it now became evident, is the absolute Lord of all history; the whole course of history, therefore, must be understood as working out his personal purposes. It was not yet fully clear just what those purposes were or what Yahweh's real nature was, but it had become evident that he is just and righteous and merciful and requires the same of his people. Moreover, there was no question that his righteous kingdom would be established when history was finally brought to its climax in judgment and salvation. Thus, all history was moving toward the kingdom of God, and Israel's history would be in a special way the vehicle of its inauguration. A savior, a Messiah, a son of David, who would overthrow God's enemies and establish through Israel his rule over the nations, would surely come; or perhaps, as those later influenced by Persian religious traditions came to believe, one like a "son of man" would come on the clouds of heaven with hosts of angels to inaugurate the kingdom. In any case, it would soon come to pass.

This understanding that all history was under the dominion of one God, together with the expectation that he was about to establish his kingdom, was the indispensable historical presupposition for God's finally making himself known in the fourth great event or stage. In this sense, as Paul has it, "The law was our schoolmaster to bring us unto Christ" (Gal. 3:24 KJ). Before we move on to that, however, it is important to recognize the significance of the fact that each stage thus far described emerged out of previous developments as an *immanent* historical movement. At no point in this history did God impose himself on man in such a way as to violate human freedom, creativity, and personality—thus destroying man's historicity. Rather, at every point God worked out his purposes within and through free human decisions and purposes and creativity, gradually developing within a people a certain responsiveness to him and receptivity for him in the expectation of his final act. The historian of the Joseph-story in Genesis makes precisely this point about the way God works through human freedom. When Joseph, now lord over Egypt, identifies himself to his brothers who had sold him into slavery, he says:

> I am your brother, Joseph, whom you sold into Egypt. And now do not be distressed, or angry with yourselves, because you sold me here; for God sent me before you to preserve life. . . . So it was not you who sent me here, but God; and he has made me a father to Pharaoh, and lord of all his house and ruler over all the land of Egypt.
>
> GENESIS 45:4–5, 8

In God's governance of history, man's freedom is not destroyed nor even momentarily overpowered; rather, it is utilized by God. In this way God gradually accomplishes his purpose to overcome the alienation between man and himself in reconciliation. Indeed, man's freedom and creativity are so respected by God at every point that it is possible to interpret the whole development of Hebrew history as *nothing more* than a free historical movement within a peculiar human culture—and every humanistic writer does precisely this with Israel's past. Faith, however, sees that behind and within this free and creative human cultural movement, the purposes of the holy God, Creator of the universe and Lord of history, are gradually coming to expression and fulfilment.

The *fourth* stage or event of this historical movement toward man's salvation bears the name Jesus Christ. We have already devoted considerable attention to this in considering revelation and the doctrine of God, and it shall be analyzed in more detail in succeeding chapters; here we can only indicate briefly its position and meaning within the overall movement of salvation-history. This event includes the actual "bridging of the gap" between God and man, and the broadening out once again of what had seemed to be the particular history of an obscure nation into universal history, with the emergence of a community destined to include all nations.

The claim that God was incarnated in Jesus Christ is the claim that the estrangement or separation between man and God was overcome in the person of Jesus Christ (see above, Part One, "God the Son," and below, Chapters 27–29, 33). Here a point in history was finally reached where God's will was perfectly done in and through the free response of a human being. Thus, the kingdom of God—God's full sovereignty over a history of free spirits—actually began to break into human history here and could now become an effective force *within* history. That is, at *this* point, in and through *this* obedience, God was able to enter history and work within it in a way not possible before.

It is necessary to interpret this event, the effective historical beginning of the kingdom of God, from two sides. On the one hand, it must be seen as beginning the fulfilment of God's purposes for man in creation. In creating the world and sustaining it throughout history God had been working to bring into being free spirits who could and would respond to his love in obedient love and freedom. Here, then, was not only the beginning of the end of man's rebellion; it was simultaneously the beginning of the ultimate fulfilment of God's original purposes for man.[4] From this point of view the appearance

---

[4] One can see in this twofold significance of the appearance of Christ that there is important truth in both so-called *infralapsarianism* (the view that salvation in Christ was determined by God consequent upon man's fall) and *supralapsarianism* (the view that this salvation is a realization of God's purposes antedating the fall and even creation).

of Jesus Christ may be interpreted as intended by God from the beginning of history. (All doctrines of the "preexistence of Christ"
make this point.) Moreover, inasmuch as this is at last a situation
in which God's will is done as he intends, here God himself is present
in history in a new way. For an agent is present in his act: this is
precisely what distinguishes an agent or person from a thing.[5]
Whereas the latter is contained within its (spatial) boundaries, the
very being of the former is precisely this "reaching out" in action,
touching and transforming that which is beyond the seeming bounds
of the self.[6] Since in the self-giving action of Jesus, particularly on
the cross, God's purpose and action interpenetrate human history as
nowhere before—man's disobedience of and alienation from God
being overcome—it is appropriate to say that here God himself is
present as reality within man. (All doctrines emphasizing Jesus'
radical uniqueness and his oneness with God—that he is Son of God,
Word of God, God Incarnate, etc.—make this point.) Immanuel!—
here God is actually with man in history! The kingship of God has
come in the action and thus the person of Jesus.

On the other hand, this presence of the kingdom must be seen as
an act of human freedom. (All doctrines of the humanity of Christ
stress this point.) It was not something compelled from without, the
omnipotent God overpowering man. That would not, in fact, have
been the establishment of God's sovereignty over free spirits at all.
It was a free but obedient response from within man. In this respect
recognition of the genuineness of Jesus' temptations and his struggle
in the Garden of Gethsemane is crucial for Christian theology. God's
kingship, his actual sovereignty over man, is precisely man's free
and obedient response to God's loving will. Therefore, it comes into

[5] Cf. Hegel: "The true being of a man is . . . his act; individuality is real in the
deed. . . . The individual human being is what the act is. In the simple fact that the act is,
the individual is for others what he really is . . . , and ceases to be merely something
that is 'meant' or 'presumed' to be this or that" (Phenomenology of Mind [London:
Allen & Unwin, 1910], pp. 349-350).

[6] It is this self-transcending movement of the self in action—another way of speaking
of that dimension of historicity through which the self projects itself beyond itself and
creates the future—which makes it quite proper for Paul to speak of Christians being
"members one of another" (Rom. 12:5; Eph. 4:25), i.e., they literally interpenetrate each
other; or for Paul (e.g., Gal. 2:20) and John (e.g., John 17:21ff.) to speak of Christ
being "in" us.

history only when and where this response occurs. For Christian faith this happens first and in a most radically creative way in Jesus of Nazareth.

The truth of this claim is, of course, by no means obvious: Jesus was *destroyed* in history; his work was opposed by both the civil and the religious authorities of his time; his movement was brought to a dead halt. Only the occurrence of an extraordinary event after his death—his "resurrection" (see below, Chapter 28)—in fact finally established, as an effective historical force, the faith and love which had broken into history in his life and death. The significance of the resurrection (as we shall see) was this: it disclosed that just this kind of nonresistant laying down one's life (crucifixion) in love to God and fellows *is* the presence of the kingdom of God in human history; God was uniquely present in Jesus' act of self-giving precisely because he is *not* one who overpowers free spirits but one who loves, not one who violently stamps out sin but one who bears it meekly. "When he was reviled, he did not revile in return; when he suffered, he did not threaten" (1 Pet. 2:23). Just this "weakness of God is stronger than men" (1 Cor. 1:25). The resurrection, then, meant that what seemed the worst sort of unfreedom from the point of view of human wisdom—Jesus' crucifixion—was in fact authentic freedom.[7] Moreover, this supreme act of human freedom, which was this just because it was voluntary obedience to God's will, was by the same token the long-awaited triumph of God's purpose(s) over man's rebellion and hence the effective inauguration of God's kingdom. Jesus had preached that "the reign of God is near" (Mk. 1:15 Goodspeed): with his crucifixion it arrived in history, and with his resurrection the disciples realized what the kingdom was and how it had come upon them. The long historical process through which God had been preparing a people to receive him had finally culminated in the self-sacrificing obedience of one man, Jesus of Nazareth, on a cross. And with that act, and in it, God finally actually

---

[7] Cf. Paul: "For the word of the cross is folly to those who are perishing, but to us who are being saved it is the power of God. . . . For Jews demand signs and Greeks seek wisdom, but we preach Christ crucified, a stumbling-block to Jews and folly to Gentiles, but to those who are called, both Jews and Greeks, Christ the power of God and the wisdom of God. For the foolishness of God is wiser than men, and the weakness of God is stronger than men" (1 Cor. 1:18, 22–25).

overcame man's estrangement, entering directly into the historical process as an active and effective force.

But of course this is a peculiar kind of historical force. The power of love is not like other modes of power: it expresses itself through ability to win men's hearts in freedom, not through the compulsion characteristic of other historical forces; it is a power that achieves its purposes through sacrificing self for the enemy (Rom. 5:10; Lk. 6:27–36); it is the power to give without reservation, to take all the abuse which enemies heap upon one, and thus, through bearing the chastisement of others, to make them whole (Isa. 53:5). It was the presence of this power of God—the Holy Spirit —which the first Christians knew in their midst at Pentecost; it was this power which was the foundation of the new community of reconciliation—the church—whose doors would be open to men of all nations, whose task was to bring reconciliation of men with God and each other, overcoming all estrangement. ". . . if God so loved us, we also ought to love one another" (1 John 4:11). Insofar as the obedience to God manifest in the self-giving of Jesus on the cross was present in the church, the church was the continuing presence of God's kingdom in history, and the mission of Christ had had concrete historical effects. Thus, with the establishment of a community of authentic freedom and love among men, alienation from God was being overcome. ". . . if we love one another, God abides in us" (1 John 4:12). The purpose and thus (one could say in hope) the ultimate destiny of the church was to become God's kingdom— that community in which God's will-to-love is really performed; that community, therefore, in which men are truly free; that community which would finally take up into itself all nations, freeing all men to become that for which God had created them.

We ourselves live in this historical period in which the community of reconciliation has been established but has not yet overcome the world. The long slow struggle of God's love to free man from the self-enslavement introduced into history by the fall is still, so far as one can see, far from finished. But awareness of the historical origins and growing complexity of sin and evil on the one hand, and of the historical emergence and development of God's

act of salvation on the other, provides one with a basis for understanding the character and meaning of this situation. Man is a historical being. This means that his present condition was defined
and created, given its peculiar structure and character, by the past
from which he came. He can be adequately understood, therefore,
only in concrete relation to that past, even though, since men are
beings-in-act, they are pointed forever forward, toward the open
future. Christian faith sees in this past the emergence of sin and bondage, but it also finds revealed there the action of God rescuing man
from enslavement to destructive powers. Christian faith lives in the
hope that the God manifest in Jesus Christ is indeed the Lord of all
history, and that therefore to give oneself to him, his will and his
way, is the ultimate realism; for it is to step in the direction of the
future toward which history is in fact moving, however dubious that
might seem in this present. To unfold the meaning of these claims
more fully it is necessary to turn once again to the Christ-event,
attending particularly now to its form and effects as a decisive
turning point in history. But before that can be done in the next
chapters, it will be helpful to summarize briefly the understanding
of sin and salvation to which our historical point of view has brought
us.

Sin is nothing else than life lived in independence of God, life
lived as a turning away from him. Though sin has its moral dimensions, it is not properly defined as violation of the moral law but
goes far deeper: it is living out one's existence as though God were
not the Lord, as if God were not at all. God "was in the world,
and the world was made through him, yet the world knew him not.
He came to his own home, and his own people received him not"
(John 1:10–11). Sin is most fundamentally the kind of *secular*
existence that most men lead most of the time. The attempt to live
independently of God, to regard the world as autonomous and free
of his lordship, is sin. Violations of the "moral law"—adultery,
murder, war, racial discrimination, and the like—are, as was observed in our consideration of the fall, expressions of this more
fundamental evil: man's attempt to be free of God. However evil
these violations may be in themselves, making it of great human

importance continually to struggle against them, in their deepest meaning they are signs: they point to man's inability to live the autonomous existence he has staked out for himself.

The Christian claim is that God has acted, and is acting, historically to rescue man from this plight, through restoring his lordship. This means that salvation in the Christian view is simply life under God; it does not involve the exchange of human existence for some other kind of life. It is human existence lived under God's sovereignty, as creature in relationship to, and thus fulfilling the purposes of, the Creator. Or, to use the comprehensive biblical symbol: it is life in the kingdom of God, existence in the community over which God in fact —not merely in name—rules.

In order to grasp more adequately the way in which God establishes his sovereignty in as well as over human history, and to see the full meaning and nature of his rule, we must look with special care at the decisive turning point of history, the Christ-event. Its larger significance will become clear if we attend carefully to two particular problems. (1) How serious are the complications introduced into history by man's sinfulness? What peculiar difficulties for "bridging the gap" between God and man do they raise, and how does God's act in Jesus Christ overcome these difficulties? The doctrine of the atonement is directed toward these issues. (2) How can this "bridging the gap" in and through one man, Jesus, be effective for all? It will be necessary to reconceive the atonement in order to meet this question, since nominalistic moderns can no longer think meaningfully in terms either of a platonistic human "nature" assumed and redeemed by Christ or of a concept of Jesus as the "representative man"— presuppositions on which the older interpretations were founded. Such a restatement is possible, however, for a historicistic perspective.

27 / The Christ-Event

I. The Atonement

Salvation in the Christian view is nothing else than living as free though finite creatures under God; or, to say the same thing in other words, it is loving God and fellows; or, in yet another image, it is living in the kingdom of God. This at-one-ment with God and fellows is made possible through the incarnation, in which God became one with man in Jesus Christ.[1] When put thus verbally, the matter may seem almost uninteresting. This is because we have considered but the barest outline of the Christian view of salvation, setting it

[1] Perhaps we do not often enough note how many of the most central theological terms have as their root meaning this at-oneness between God and man. Thus, for example, "atonement" (which is sometimes supposed to involve a kind of propitiation of God the Father by the Son) means literally at-one-ment, a bringing together of parties at two's and three's with each other and thus divided against each other. It is important to observe that the meaning is not simply "one-ment," i.e., identity, between God and man; there are indeed two parties, but now they are at-one with each other, in harmony, in communication. The meaning is thus basically the same as another important theological term dealing with Christian salvation, "reconciliation." Reconciliation is the bringing together of parties who had become alienated and reuniting them; relations which had become strained and distorted are brought back to the harmony and peace and fulfilment of friendship and love. The word "salvation" has a similar meaning. It indicates a making whole or making well, a bringing to health; that which had been distorted and incomplete and wounded is now healed and brought to its proper fulfilment. Thus, man's salvation is his reconciliation, his atonement, with God. Instead of separation from his Creator—experienced as alienation and estrangement (feelings); disobedience and rebellion (will); ignorance, error, and dishonesty (intellect), these all being dimensions of man's secular, i.e., "this-worldly" existence—men have at-one-ment with him. The doctrine of the incarnation involves a similar claim: that God is with man (Immanuel)—not merely for man, but *among* men—because *in* a man he has come into the very midst of human existence; the gap between God and man has been bridged by God. All these terms, thus, refer to the historical event-process through which God has been (re)establishing sovereignty over men.

forth in intellectual terms—that is, in idea—but not yet existentially, so that one is grasped to the roots of his being. Until this latter occurs, what has been said will remain empty and unimportant words, formulas to which one might give verbal assent but which would have little to do with the actual existence in which he lives. The word "atonement" in the Christian vocabulary has pointed to the more poignant, moving, existential dimensions of the Gospel. This is because the various theories of atonement have been devoted to the analysis and interpretation of the obstructions and blocks in the way of accomplishing salvation; and this focusing on the difficulties overcome has drawn attention to how great a thing, how impressive and freighted with meaning for man, is this salvation which the Gospel announces.

The central problem of salvation, as we have noted, is that man has turned away from God and toward himself; instead of pursuing God's will, he seeks his own selfish interests. In consequence, man has exchanged the possibility of a harmonious and creative community of love on earth, in which each self could find freedom and fulfilment —the kingdom of God—for a war of all against all; and the life of man has become, as Hobbes put it in a classic phrase, "solitary, poor, nasty, brutish, and short."[2] The problem, now, is how this condition can be rectified. How is this collection of self-centered men, warring against each other, each pursuing chiefly his own goals, to be transformed into the kingdom of God, the community in which God is acknowledged as sovereign and men love each other?

Clearly, there are two dimensions to the problem. (a) God's sovereignty itself must be fully confirmed and established; it must in no way be weakened or threatened by the solution. (b) Genuine love and self-giving among men must become the characteristic actualities of human intercourse. The several theories of atonement each deal with both these dimensions, though their respective emphases differ considerably. Sometimes these theories are classified into two groups (corresponding roughly to the above two dimensions), regarded as "objective" and "subjective" views, according to whether the changed relation between man and God is understood to depend principally on a change in *God* or in *man*. The so-called orthodox doctrine of propi-

2 *Leviathan*, Ch. 13.

tiation is said to be the outstanding example of the former; the "moral influence" view, of the latter. For the purposes of the present analysis such classifications must be disregarded as more misleading than helpful, and my suggestion that there are two *dimensions* involved in the atonement should not be understood to refer to this ordinary twofold classification of theories. These dimensions are not alternatives between which we may choose: both are required if there is to be genuine atonement, and it would only make misunderstanding inevitable were they to be tied in some way to the "objective" and "subjective" theories. We shall, then, view the doctrine of atonement as interpretation of the way in which the disharmony and chaos into which human existence has fallen is restored into the kingdom of God.

From the earliest period Christians were confident that the church was living in the midst of this process of transformation. In the New Testament the appearance of Christ was understood as the beginning of the great change: "in Christ God was reconciling the world to himself" (2 Cor. 5:19, RSV footnote). Though the change was thus well under way, it had not yet reached completion: "For as in Adam all die, so also in Christ shall all be made alive. But each in his own order: Christ the first fruits, then at his coming those who belong to Christ. . . . he must reign until he has put all his enemies under his feet" (1 Cor. 15:22–23, 25).[3] This process of at-one-ment through which Christ was overcoming his enemies will soon reach its climax: "When all things are subjected to him, then the Son himself will also be subjected to him who put all things under him, that God may be everything to every one" (1 Cor. 15:28). Thus, the early church was conscious of living through the turning point of the battle between God and his enemies; all existence was shortly to be brought under God's sovereignty.

It is not difficult to understand why the earliest church frequently interpreted this great transformation in terms of images drawn from the human experience of warfare. It was not uncommon in the ancient world for the cosmos to be visualized as a great battleground

[3] Upon occasion the early Christians were not averse to spelling out in some detail the several stages of the historical process in which they were living (cf. 2 Thess. 2; Mk. 13; etc.).

between God with his forces of light, and the demons and principalities and powers—the forces of darkness. In terms of this conception, man, who had for long been in bondage to these evil powers, was now being freed; in a great battle Christ is overcoming—has already overcome!—the power of the devil. The magnitude of the battle required to accomplish this work is made dramatically clear by the fact that God's mighty warrior, his own Son Jesus Christ, was himself killed in the fray.

. . . you were ransomed from the futile ways inherited from your fathers, not with perishable things such as silver or gold, but with the precious blood of Christ.

1 PETER 1:18–19

For in Christ our release is secured and our sins are forgiven through the shedding of his blood.

EPHESIANS 1:7 NEB

The children of a family share the same flesh and blood; and so he too shared ours, so that through death he might break the power of him who had death at his command, that is, the devil; and might liberate those who, through fear of death, had all their lifetime been in servitude.

HEBREWS 2:14–15 NEB

For the Son of man . . . came not to be served but to serve, and to give his life as a ransom for many.

MARK 10:45

Though the battle was fierce and the price tremendous, in the end the tragedy of Christ's death was itself a victory over the evil powers that held man in bondage. Because Christ paid this supreme price for man's sake

and became obedient unto death, even death on a cross . . . God has highly exalted him and bestowed on him the name which is above every name, that at the name of Jesus every knee should bow, in heaven and on earth and under the earth, and every tongue confess that Jesus Christ is Lord, to the glory of God the Father.

PHILIPPIANS 2:8–11

Thus, the death which had seemed to be supreme tragedy turned out eventually (i.e., in Christ's resurrection from the dead) to be total victory. And it could be said that though he was "delivered to death for our misdeeds," he was "raised to life to justify us" (Rom. 4:25 NEB).

The consequences of Christ's sacrificial victory were twofold. (a) The sovereignty of the evil powers to whom men had been subject was broken, and they could now become obedient servants in God's kingdom. "He has delivered us from the dominion of darkness and transferred us to the kingdom of his beloved Son" (Col. 1:13). No longer need men fear that any power "in all creation, will be able to separate [them] from the love of God" (Rom. 8:39). God's kingdom is well on the way to being established. (b) Men no longer are in bondage to self and sin, but are now free beings who can live in genuine community with love for their fellows. "For freedom Christ has set us free; . . . only do not use your freedom as an opportunity for the flesh, but through love be servants of one another" (Gal. 5:1, 13). A new life has thus opened up for man, an "abundant" life (John 10:10) of authentic freedom and creativity and love; man has become veritably a "new creation" (2 Cor. 5:17). Thus, with the victory over the demons won through Christ's death, God's full sovereignty over his world was being reestablished even while the possibilities of a life of genuine fulfilment and meaning were opening once again for man. In the near future, when "the Lord himself will descend from heaven with a cry of command, with the archangel's call, and with the sound of the trumpet of God" (1 Thess. 4:16), the forces of evil will be completely wiped out and the great battle will be brought to its end with victory for God and his mighty warrior, Christ.

For those who thought man's situation and problems resulted from his being caught in the middle of a cosmic battle, the Christian proclamation must have been exciting news indeed. For according to this message God does not stand aloof from man's terrifying situation. Rather, he girds on his mighty sword and enters into the dangers of the battle in man's behalf. The powers that hold man in slavery are sufficiently strong that salvation is a difficult work even for the Creator of the universe: he must finally sacrifice his own Son in order to achieve the victory. But he manages at last to outwit and overpower the devil and to free man. And so now man, also, can join battle against the demons, suffering as Christ suffered to help release other captives (cf. 2 Cor. 5:19–6:13). Inasmuch as man was himself responsible for his plight and thus the world's chaos—since his guilty disobedience of God had brought him into bondage to the powers of darkness (Rom. 1:18–3:20; Eph. 2:1–5, 6:12; etc.)— how joyously could he now enter the fray, for God himself, before whom he was guilty, had forgiven him and acted to free him from bondage (2 Cor. 5:18–19; Eph. 1:3–8, 2:4–8; Col. 1:12–14, 2:13– 15; etc.). These images have had great significance to those who accepted the mythology of the cosmic battle and thought they saw it finally drawing to a close in God's victory. This was a meaningful way to understand both the present disorder, terror, and bondage—for what is more chaotic than a bloody battlefield?—and the means through which it was at last being transformed into the kingdom in which God would be fully sovereign. Since this view of salvation is the one most prominent in the New Testament and the church fathers, we may well refer to it, with Aulén, as the "classic" theory of the atonement.[4]

The classic view has some very obvious limitations, two of which we may consider here. First, it is heavily dependent on the mythology of the great battle between light and darkness. As long as men subscribed to this world-picture, the conception was potentially relevant and meaningful. But if the mythology changes, and men can no longer think in these terms, what then? In the middle of the twentieth century—indeed, long before—it has seemed simply absurd to speak of literal demons and powers which hold man and the world in bondage and which God must overcome in a mighty battle. Unless it is possible to demythologize this understanding of God's mighty act so that it can be grasped also by those who no longer think in such

---

[4] Gustaf Aulén, *Christus Victor* (London: S.P.C.K., 1953). Aulén, however, would not accept my designation of the classic view as a "theory," because—in accordance with his anti-theoretical anti-philosophical bias—he regards this view less contaminated by human speculation than the other interpretations of the atonement; it is therefore to be regarded as an "idea" or a "motif" while the others are mere theories and doctrines (see pp. 174f.). One cannot help but wonder what kind of perverseness or anti-cultural admiration for the primitive leads some theologians to regard man's attempts at disciplined thought to be somehow wrongheadedly "speculative" in a way that his creation of fantastic mythologies is not.

terms, the whole Christian message appears a fantastic, if somewhat fascinating, product of man's all too fertile imagination.

Second, the classic view is time-bound not only in the sense of being informed by prescientific conceptions of the world and human bondage. For its meaning depends not only on the conviction that there is a cosmic battle in process, but that that battle is now rapidly coming to its end, thus establishing once and for all God's full sovereignty. Only if it can be believed that the fight is nearly over and God's victory won does God's act in Christ retain its overwhelming significance. But if the end of the world does not come and seems never to come, what then? God's kingdom apparently is not established after all; the victory was not complete; the final stages of the battle drag on and on, and one wonders whether God has failed to defeat the devil in the moment of decisive encounter. Thus, this mythology, instead of proclaiming God's final sovereignty, only succeeds in making it appear problematic once again. Are the faithful in God's kingdom or not? Have they been freed from bondage to sin and the devil or not? As these questions arise and become increasingly insistent, the classic theory appears less and less adequate, for it no longer is an expression of the central conviction of Christian faith: that the kingdom of God is really breaking into history, and the church lives in the midst of the process of its establishment.[5]

[5] Anselm as early as the eleventh century sought a new interpretation of the atonement partly because he realized that the "classic" view of God's act, with its outmoded and somewhat crude mythology, gave far too much power to the devil and the other powers of evil, thus calling into question God's sovereignty in an intolerable way (*Cur Deus Homo*, Book I, Chs. 6–7). Moreover, the image of God engaging in conflicts and transactions of various sorts with the powers of the underworld was unseemly. (In some versions of the classic view, for instance, God was portrayed as paying a ransom [the death of his Son] to the devil; or it was even suggested that God defeated the devil by deceitfully outwitting him: the devil, seizing on the bait of Christ's human nature "as it is with greedy fish," swallowed the fishhook of his divinity, and thus was destroyed [Gregory of Nyssa].) Such images, Anselm argued, violated God's proper dignity in the most offensive manner. The mythology of the cosmic battle was thus inadequate and it was essential to find another analogy to understand the salvation which God had provided. But what was to be substituted for it?

The problem, as Anselm formulated it, was essentially that of the stained and strained relationship between lowly man and the Lord of the universe (rather than God in mortal conflict with the powers of evil). What analogy could be more fitting for this new formulation than the relationship between lord and serf as found in the contemporary social structure? Lowly man has violated God's holy will—a mere serf has defied the Lord of the universe—and this creates an intolerable situation (see, e.g., Bk. I, Chs. 11–15, 20–24; Bk. II, Ch. 5). God must assert his righteous lordship over the cosmos through

must not require this chaos

people the chaos

✓

What sort of restatement of the atonement is possible and necessary in order for men in the twentieth century to grasp how the chaos
of history is being transformed into the kingdom of God? Let us
recall the two dimensions necessary to any adequate Christian view
of salvation, both included under the comprehensive biblical symbol,
the *kingdom of God*. On the one hand, it must be *God's* kingdom, his
authentic and full sovereignty over his world, which is being established; on the other hand, this kingdom must be seen not simply in

---

punishing, even destroying, the evildoer. However, God is merciful and wishes to forgive
man, reestablishing community with him. How, now, can God's righteousness and proper
honor be maintained, on the one side, while man is forgiven and restored to fellowship
with God, on the other? Obviously, the problem is completely beyond solution from the
human side. God is the infinite and absolute being, and this means that even the slightest
peccadillo is of immeasurable weight (Bk. I, Ch. 21; here of course the feudal conception
that the measure of guilt increases in proportion with the status of the one whose honor is
violated is clearly at work). It is, then, impossible for man ever to make reparation for
his disobedience to God, for it is necessary that such a reparation be infinite. Here, then,
is the answer to the question, why God became man: though perfectly innocent of any
sin, by offering himself up for sacrifice on the cross, the God-man Jesus was able to
offer an infinite reparation, at once satisfying God's honor and making it possible for
God, for Jesus' sake, to remit to other men as reward what Jesus had won and wished
to bestow upon them (Bk. II, Ch. 18). Thus, through an ingenious chain of reasoning,
Anselm resolved one of the principal problems of the classic view of the atonement
through proposing a theory in which God's sovereignty and initiative is clearly
maintained throughout; and at the same time he explained the necessity of the orthodox
paradoxical beliefs about the Incarnation.

However, there are problems with Anselm's view of man's at-one-ment with God
quite as serious as those of the classic view. Not the least of these is its contrived and
artificial appearance. While to a medieval mind who took for granted the truth of the
Christian dogmas Anselm's explanation might appear rational and clear, to a modern,
dubious in any case about the Christian claims, it seems an outrageous play of concepts
and words. What is a "God-man"? Is God so divided that one "part" of him (the Son) can
be conceived as doing something for another (the Father)? How can such a transaction
within the Godhead have anything to do with my load of guilt and sin, which is a
personal burden I must bear? What can it possibly mean to say that the righteousness of
another man is somehow transferred to me or my account? Moreover, even so far as it is
comprehensible, Anselm's formulation has misleading implications. Guilt and sin appear
not so much as qualities of a personal relationship between God and man which require
to be removed by personal forgiveness, as "things" which can be transferred away from
man through a complex transaction within the Godhead. In an interpersonal situation, how,
after all, can another make reparation for my guilt? Even God's sovereignty, though
central to Anselm's concern, is hardly given its due in his theory. For God's love and
honor are so set over against each other that it appears impossible for him to act in
genuine and straightforward personal forgiveness of man. Instead of proposing an interpretation of the way in which the death of Christ altered the interpersonal relation between
God and man and made it possible for man to find the personal and communal fulfilment
God had intended for him—thus simultaneously realizing God's objectives and man's
—Anselm developed an intricate theory explicating a dubious dogma about two metaphysical natures in the one person Christ. And God's *personal* sovereignty over the *personal*
subjects in his kingdom tended to be forgotten.

transcendental or supernaturalistic or symbolical terms, but as the actual empirical establishment of a community of authentic love among men.[6] The doctrine of atonement is the interpretation of how this two-dimensional kingdom of God actually is coming to be. We can best develop the conception by beginning with the classic view of atonement, demythologizing and elaborating it in certain respects.

It goes without saying that demythologizing is required here. Few moderns could accept the mythology of the cosmic battle even if they wished to. No doubt some in our time (e.g., Jehovah's Witnesses) still claim to think in terms of a great struggle, soon to come to an end, between forces of light and darkness, but most find such a view utterly fanciful; the notions of demonic and angelic hosts seem to have no warrant. Even less credible is the claim that Jesus of Nazareth will soon return with these heavenly hosts to vanquish the foe. However, the problematic character of these mythological conceptions does not mean that the classic view is to be regarded as fallacious and outmoded in every respect.

Two points in the imagery of the cosmic battle must be noted. In the first place, the reality of human bondage or enslavement is taken seriously. In the conception of men being in the hands of God's enemies—the devil and other evil powers—is expressed awareness that human history has gotten into the grip of evils from which man cannot escape. Every attempt fails; men are unable effectively to grapple with the situation. This bondage involves suffering and continual frustration for man, and salvation from it can be purchased only at the cost of further suffering. The notion of the cosmic battlefield, with its gruesome images of chaos and destruction and frightful struggles culminating in bloodshed and death, expresses well the horror and evil of this situation: man is now suffering as prisoner of evil powers; later, when he is freed, it will only be to become a warrior in the battle against them. Thus man's suffering will continue until victory

---

[6] With respect to this second emphasis in particular, the interpretation of the coming of God's kingdom in the next pages (and in this work as a whole) is similar to that of the sixteenth-century Anabaptists (cf., e.g., Robert Friedmann, "The Doctrine of the Two Worlds," in *The Recovery of the Anabaptist Vision*, ed. G. F. Hershberger [Scottdale, Pennsylvania: Herald Press, 1957], pp. 105–118). The full significance of the views of these men of the "radical reformation" for our contemporary "post-Christian" situation is only very belatedly becoming realized.

is finally won and God's kingdom comes. God himself must sacrifice much—his only Son!—to achieve victory; not even the almighty God can bring man's bondage to an end simply by a word.

In our own time we have once again become aware of the reality of human bondage. The course of history seems out of control. We do not know but what we may destroy not only ourselves but all civilization and possibly all mankind. It is not, of course, that anyone desires this. Rather, somehow we have gotten into the grip of powers which we cannot handle, which control us. The great wars of our century have shown that political processes are not directly subject to man's will; the persistence of poverty in wealthy America shows that economic processes cannot easily be managed, nor are they benevolent when left uncontrolled; the rise of urban industrial society, with the consequent appearance of "mass man" and all the related social, moral, and cultural problems, has created new fears that just in his "progress" man may be destroying the possibility of authentic personal existence. All of these, taken together with an exploding technological advance, mean that human existence has become more precarious than ever before (though, of course, it is also true that many middle-class individuals now lead lives with few physical hazards). Brainwashing and the H-bomb have become veritable apocalyptic symbols. In our time once again we know bondage to "principalities and powers" which seem to determine almost every facet of existence, tending it toward evil. And this is a bondage from which there seems no escape. The Anselmic doctrine of a substitutionary atonement[7] appears irrelevant to the problem; Abailard's hope for a mere changing of the hearts of men[8] seems pale and weak.

---

[7] See above, n. 5.

[8] For Abailard (a younger contemporary of Anselm) the important problem was not so much the threat to God's sovereignty raised by man's sin (Anselm) as the actual fact of lovelessness in human existence. Men were in bondage to themselves. How could they be freed to love God and neighbor? We should note here certain affinities with the classic view of the atonement. Once more the problem is thought of as human bondage, though this is no longer conceived in the mythological terms of the earlier view, but rather psychologically. How now does God's act in Christ free man from this self-slavery and make it possible for him to love? Abailard's answer is at once simple and profound. Somehow genuine love must break into the circle of man's lovelessness, for only this can evoke from man the response of love which he otherwise could not generate. And this in-breaking of God's love is precisely what is proclaimed in the Gospel. It is through a "unique act of grace manifest to us" that "we have been justified by the blood

Somehow, men must be enabled to believe there can be and is occurring an actual historical process through which this present chaos is being brought into order. They must be able to hope that, despite all evidence to the contrary, *God is winning the battle proceeding in the very historical existence in which they are living.*

This brings us, in the second place, to the central contention of the classic view, that victory is assured, God is indeed overcoming the powers of darkness. Even though much misery and evil remains in human existence, "the sufferings of this present time are not worth comparing with the glory that is to be revealed . . . because the creation itself will be set free from its bondage to decay and obtain the glorious liberty of the children of God" (Rom. 8:18, 21). That is, it is not on the basis of the present empirical evidence in history—"the sufferings of this present time"—that Christians believe God

---

of Christ and reconciled to God." This is an act which "frees us from slavery to sin . . . [and] wins for us the true liberty of sons of God" by evoking from us a "deeper affection . . . so that we do all things out of love rather than fear—love to him who has shown us such grace that no greater can be found." (*Exposition of the Epistle to the Romans* [Second Book], commentary on Rom. 3:19–26; trans. from *Library of Christian Classics*, X [Philadelphia: Westminster Press, 1956], 283–284.) In Abailard's view, God transforms man, not in any mechanical or heteronomous or impersonal way, but by so dramatically manifesting his own love to man that man's heart of stone is thawed and replaced by a heart of flesh (Ezek. 36:26). The magnitude of God's love has become visible in the sending of his Son, and in his death on the cross at men's hands. When this fact is appropriated, that the King of the universe gives himself for men, suffers for them, their self-centered shells are broken through and a response of gratitude and love to God is evoked, along with the desire really to serve him through loving their fellows and sacrificing for them as Jesus did. Thus, in Abailard's view what is necessary is that men become genuinely aware of God's great love for them, for "if they . . . see the glory prepared for them by God's mercy, at that moment, along with discernment, the love of God is born in them" (*ibid.*, p. 287). In this way, through Christ's teaching and death, God's "express purpose of spreading this true liberty of love amongst men" (p. 284) is accomplished.

Abailard's theory is strong where Anselm's is weak, for atonement remains an abstract and empty conception unless one can see how human existence is actually changed concretely and empirically by God's act in Christ; and Abailard tried to show how precisely that act makes possible the appearance of genuine love among men. But his view is also weak where Anselm's is strong, for it focuses attention so much on man's need and man's redemption that it tends to overlook the other evil wrought by sin, namely, that God's sovereignty is threatened. With this anthropocentric emphasis it is but a short step to a view of God as nothing but man's servant, a kindly old gentleman who pulls men out of difficult situations but has little other function or meaning. If this humanistic tendency is carried to an extreme, God as a genuinely active agent may drop out of the picture entirely, the unbreakable bondage to sin and self may be forgotten, and the Gospel interpreted largely as an exhortation to follow Jesus' moral example of self-sacrifice. Certainly this was not Abailard's intention, but developments along this line occurred in the liberal protestantism which found his view preferable to either the classic or the Anselmic view.

will achieve victory. Such evidence appears to suggest all is going wrong; man's bondage is far from overcome. If one surveys the whole of history "objectively," there seems little evidence that God is winning the battle and the day of bondage is past; indeed, all of creation "has been groaning in travail together until now" (8:22). Nevertheless, "in this hope"[9] that God is in fact accomplishing his mighty redemptive act "we were saved" (8:24). What is the ground for such faith in God's sovereignty and deliverance?

As throughout the biblical record, it is *memory*. Remembrance of what God has done in the past gives rise to hopes for what he yet shall do to deliver his people. Just as Old Testament experience and faith grew out of reflection on memories of the exodus and covenant when God's mighty arm delivered his people from bondage to Egypt, so here God's great gift of himself and his forgiveness in Christ is the sufficient ground for confidence about what is really happening in present and future. "He who did not spare his own Son but gave him up for us all, will he not also give us all things with him?" (8:32). On the basis of this glorious memory anything the future might bring can surely be faced in the full confidence that nothing "in all creation, will be able to separate us from the love of God in Christ Jesus our Lord" (8:39). Paul's claim here, thus, is that he and his fellow Christians are living "between the times"—between the mighty act of God in Christ which is the foundation for their faith, and the fulfilment and completion of that act in the full release of creation from the bondage in which it labors. Faith is grounded in memory but lives in hope. The victory has not yet been fully won: but it shall be won in the near future! And the church is living in the midst of this process of transformation of chaos into God's kingdom. Even though present existence is filled with suffering and evil, a more exciting or meaningful moment in all history could scarcely be imagined. This is not so much due to the intrinsic meaning of this present, as to that glorious future to which this present will certainly

---

[9] It should be noted that Paul makes very clear that what he is affirming here does not have the kind of certainty characteristic of empirical knowledge, but is rather a matter of hope, the self's venture or stance of confidence in face of an open (and unknown) future: "Now hope that is seen is not hope. For who hopes for what he sees? But if we hope for what we do not see, then, in waiting for it, we show our endurance" (Rom. 8:24-25; vs. 25 adapted from NEB).

lead. As with all moments within an on-going teleological process, the significance of the present depends on its relationship to the past from which it comes and its connection to the meaningful goal toward which it is moving.

All this makes good sense in our contemporary historical situation. We live in a period characterized by the "eclipse of God" (Buber). What God is doing—indeed, whether there is a God—is not evident to modern man. As we look at the world round about us, we do not see signs of One without whose care no sparrow falls to the ground (Mt. 10:29), but rather we see a universe governed by impersonal natural law. The history in which we exist does not seem to express the purposes of a benevolent God so much as the dysteleology of blind chance or fate. The selves we know and the selves we are scarcely seem on the road to new freedom and fulfilment; on the contrary we know ourselves to be enslaved—to self and to others, to passions and idols of every sort. There appears little reason for believing in the sovereignty of a personal God whose will is love, little basis for hoping this present chaos is being transfigured into God's kingdom.

An existence like this, seemingly cut off from any adequate ground of personal meaning in the immediate present, can find genuine significance and thus fulfilment only through apprehending itself as one of the intermediate moments in a teleological process expected to flower into authentic historical fulfilment. The teleological form of human activity makes comprehensible the way in which moments not intrinsically meaningful themselves are given positive significance and value by their position in a historical process leading to an expected fulfilment. The pain of surgery, for example, endured with the expectation of consequent better health, the tedium of long hours practicing scales in the hope of finally being able to play Chopin—indeed, almost every purposive process in which man engages leads through stages in themselves empty or boring or even highly disagreeable or painful, all accepted and endured for the sake of the desired end. If this teleological form of experience were taken as the model or analogue in terms of which one sought to understand the emptiness and negativity of historical existence generally—that is, if present bondage and meaninglessness were apprehended as but an intermediary stage in a process to culminate in freedom and fulfilment—one would be able to live creatively and productively even in the midst of severe difficulties. But this would be possible only if something akin to the classic mythology of the cosmic battle were true. Only if one could believe he were in the midst of an actual transition into the kingdom of God, that the historical process into which he had been "thrown" had both purposive form and a goal of genuine significance to personal beings, would he be able to make sense of the present confusion and evil in which he lived and even of the apparent eclipse of God.

If the overall context of man's existence is not a purposive movement and his history is not actually going anywhere, if there is no ontologically significant change occurring in the historical world, then that event of two thousand years ago can have little meaning today. It is but another tragic fact of human life, so distant from us as to remain largely abstract and irrelevant. However, *if that event can be understood as beginning a historical process which is transforming human existence into God's kingdom, then it has significance for all time and direct relevance to the contemporary situation.*

In certain respects the position suggested here resembles the hope of liberal protestantism that God is guiding present history into the historical realization of his kingdom.[10] If men could really

---

[10] It could be argued that liberalism, a perspective often supposed to have ignored such matters as the atonement altogether, in fact subscribed to what we might call a "progress view" of God's act. The atonement is concerned with the becoming at-one of God and man, with the conversion of the chaos of human affairs into the kingdom of God; every theory has developed this theme in its own way. Only the earliest or classic view, however, portrayed the kingdom as actually to be established on earth with the imminent coming of the end of the world. As this mythology became increasingly unbelievable, it dropped out of succeeding interpretations, which portrayed the atonement as occurring in God himself (Anselm) or in the individual soul (Abailard), rather than in the movement of history. To the nineteenth-century progress theologians, however, the notion of the kingdom of God on earth once again seemed somewhat tenable; so for them the expectation of the establishment of a real community of love among men in history reappeared also. However, though in this respect there was a return to certain emphases of the classic view, the old mythology had now disappeared entirely. No longer was there belief in Christ's imminent conquest of the demons from below; rather, now God's (or Christ's) conquest of the self-centeredness of the human heart (cf. Abailard) was proclaimed, and with it the kingdom would really be established among men.

Above all, the progress theologians insisted that the atonement must have genuine relevance to the actual social structures and institutions of human history, and not simply

believe this—as the liberals did—then they could endure such suffering as they might have to undergo, as well as the most discouraging reversals, because in the light of their hope all such would be
apprehended as but temporary and bound ultimately to fail. The
meaninglessness and absurdity in present existence could be tolerated
"while we wait for God to make us his sons and set our whole body
free" (Rom. 8:23   NEB). Unfortunately, the faith of liberal protestantism did not have a foundation adequate to withstand all reversals; for it was rooted, at least in part, in what seemed to be clear
empirical evidence of the imminence of God's kingdom: the supposed
continuous progress upwards of Western civilization. When that conclusion had to be revised and even reversed because of new data
coming to light in the twentieth century, the faith and hope based on
it foundered also. Liberalism should be criticized not so much for
the content of its hope—that the kingdom of God is indeed coming
—as for its grounding of that hope more on supposed empirical
evidence than on God's revelation, and for its somewhat superficial
belief that this coming could occur without great suffering and struggle and even terrible reversals. The classic view did not suffer these
limitations. It recognized that the battle in which God and men were
engaged was nothing less than cosmic in scope; and it saw clearly,
therefore, that its hope had to be rooted in God, and him alone, if
it were to be securely grounded. But from such a position it was
possible also to say, "If God be for us, who can be against us?"
(Rom. 8:31   KJ). The earliest Christians were thus able to place

---

to individual souls isolated from the community. They saw the atonement as a process
now going on, a process in which men participate in the present but which will not be
completed until God's kingdom is the context in which human life is actually lived. And
they were able to hope, therefore, that God was actually guiding the movement of
empirical history toward the ultimate goal of his kingdom. Unfortunately, however, the
technological progress of the nineteenth and twentieth centuries was so impressive to
the men who thought in these terms that they obscured the very real strengths of their
position by certain additional convictions. Not only did they somewhat naively believe
the kingdom's full establishment in history to be imminent (here also their view can be
compared with the earliest Christians), but they often failed to recognize the depth of
hard suffering (classic view, Anselm, Abailard) required to usher it in. It thus became
possible—and this was theologically most disastrous of all—for them to believe that
perhaps man himself, through his own efforts, was really the one bringing in the new
community of love. And thus the kingdom of God became watered down to a humanistic
utopia, and the necessary ontological foundation for this hope for history—the loving
purposes of the Creator of the heavens and the earth—tended to drop out of view.

their faith in the very Foundation of the universe, who had revealed
to them, as they believed, himself and his purposes for history. This
meant they could also believe—experiential evidence to the contrary
notwithstanding—that God's kingdom was in fact coming; and they
could live and act on that belief in the historical interim in which
they found themselves, regardless of the suffering they had to bear.

Let us now tie together some of these points. It makes little sense
to speak of a substitutionary atonement (Anselm) as an event which
occurred two thousand years ago but somehow effects men's redemption today, or to preach of God's love manifest two thousand years
ago but somehow piercing men's hearts today (Abailard). Such
events are so historically and metaphysically remote, both from the
contemporary sense of existential meaning and value and from the
form in which the human problem impinges on contemporary man,
as to appear absurd abstractions or sentimental and irrelevant ways
of escaping the harsh historical realities of existence. However, one
can make significant sense of that event of two thousand years ago
if it is seen as the *creative beginning of a redemptive process that is
actually going on in history*, reshaping man's rebellion and consequent enslavement into obedience to the Lord of creation and consequent freedom. Through this process—beginning with Jesus of
Nazareth and expanding outward (with many reversals of course)
through the centuries of church history—God is penetrating human
history with his spirit, converting men's continuous "war of each
against all" into a community of love. Of course, the belief that this
is the real significance of the church's history is scarcely to be inferred directly from the somewhat sordid empirical facts of that
history itself; for the church has hardly been such a community.
Rather, the Christian hope and expectation is that the church shall
finally become this community—not because the historical facts of
her life give warrant for such belief—but because this is God's ultimate will.

Those who know themselves to be living in this still not clearly
visible, yet genuinely expected, transformation of human existence
into God's kingdom, are in a position to understand the significance
of Jesus Christ. He is the very center of history, for through him

this otherwise mere dream became a real *historical possibility*. Jesus' death and resurrection did in fact create a new community conscious of and responsive to God's sovereignty and whose members "loved one another." In this way those events began the process of breaking man's bondage to the demons—an enslavement we can best understand, perhaps, as man's bondage to himself (Abailard) and to evil social structures and patterns (liberalism). God's redemptive love, come to man through Jesus' act of self-giving on the cross and appropriated by man through the resurrection (see Chapter 28), evoked new possibilties of human love not known before, even the capacity to love and forgive enemies. Thus, here was born a community in which God's spirit (love) was uniquely present and active. For it Jesus' crucifixion, besides being history's decisive turning point, was the paradigmatic event which definitively unveiled God's true will and nature (cf. Chapter 3). The crucified one thus provided the normative image in terms of which authentic human existence was henceforth to be judged[11] and increasingly became the center of interest and devotion in the church. Thus, the death of Christ has continued to sustain and nourish the Christian community as well as provide the principal norms for judgment and reform. (For further discussion of this continuing significance of Jesus' crucifixion in the life of the church, see especially Part Four.)

The earliest Christians, orienting themselves toward the reality laid bare in the cross, knew themselves to be living in an alien age or foreign environment; they were "strangers and exiles on the earth . . . [who were] seeking a homeland . . . a better country, that is, a heavenly one" (Heb. 11:13–16).[12] But the Spirit of God—authentic self-giving love—was already known to them; the kingdom of God, to be fully realized only at the eschaton, was already present in "foretaste" (Rom. 8:23 Goodspeed). In the church the old bar-

11 Cf., e.g., Phil. 2:5–7; 1 Pet. 2:21–23; 1 John 4:7–11.

12 For this reason the earliest community could regard itself as a kind of "colony of heaven" (Phil. 3:20 Moffatt). The metaphor is suggestive: a colony is found perhaps thousands of miles from the mother country in a land of different climate and topography, strange customs, and social institutions. Although the members of the colony must participate in this foreign environment, they remain in the deepest sense closely related to the homeland. The colony is in fact a kind of transplanted homeland, where the spirit of the mother country truly lives and flourishes. In a similar way God's Spirit was already present and active in human history in the life of the church. (Cf. p. 479.)

riers which had separated men from each other were beginning to break down, and a truly universal community was being established. "There is neither Jew nor Greek, there is neither slave nor free, there is neither male nor female; for you are all one in Christ Jesus" (Gal. 3:28; cf. Rom. 10:12; Col. 3:11).

That spirit of love known in the earliest community has been passed on from generation to generation all the way down to the twentieth century, modern Christians also having "consciousness of adoption as sons" of God (Rom. 8:15 Goodspeed).[13] Through participating in the community which lives by this memory (tradition) of God's self-giving love as its origin, and this hope of gathering up all human history as he finally establishes his kingdom, they find themselves captured by God's love—providing they "really share his sufferings" (8:17 Goodspeed). But for them also, awareness of this spirit is at best only a "foretaste" of what shall yet appear. Nevertheless, it is a sufficiently powerful foretaste to give confidence that *by* this and *for* this they should live. Even though much empirical evidence (e.g., of the powerlessness of love in human history) appears to point in a contrary direction, their existence is oriented in confidence that the reality of God's love will ultimately prevail and his kingdom finally come. "For in this hope we were saved" (8:24).

For those who live by such faith, there can be no easy optimism that the kingdom is about to be established. In this respect it is no longer possible to share the view either of the early church or of protestant liberalism. With Buchenwald and Hiroshima as living memories, and the present racial and international situations a clear vision, our generation can realize as perhaps not many before how hard it is for God to change the hearts and communities of men. Believers, desiring to be vehicles through which God can transform this world, can properly anticipate only suffering for themselves. There is no place for ease or comfort in this view of the atonement: it involves God's suffering and sacrifice, and man's, if the troubled world we know is really to become his kingdom; and there is no

13 "The Spirit [alive in this community] itself testifies with our spirits that we are God's children, and if children, heirs also; heirs of God, and fellow-heirs with Christ, if we really share his sufferings" (8:16–17 Goodspeed).

reason to suppose that either we or our great-grandchildren will see the end. But at the same time such suffering or sacrifice as one is called to undergo is given new meaning, for he is able to apprehend it as a living symbol of—and thus historical participation in—that suffering through which God is redeeming the world.[14]

Clearly, this fantastic hope is justified only if God has in fact established a beachhead in human history with the appearance of Jesus Christ, only if history is in fact being transformed into his kingdom. The anthropological presupposition of such a claim is a historicist view of man in which it is held that we are "members one of another" (Rom. 12:5; Eph. 4:25) in such a way that what happened with Jesus happened not to him and his contemporaries alone, but through them to those others with whom they stood in community, and through them to still others, reaching finally even to the present. Such a conception makes it possible to understand meaningfully how an event of two thousand years ago can still be of significance in the middle of the twentieth century; and the words attributed to Jesus in Matthew 10:40—"He who receives you receives me, and he who receives me receives him who sent me"—are grasped as truly descriptive of his historical impact. Thus, Jesus' obedience to God *was* the actual breaking into human history of God's sovereign rule. As the beginning of the establishment of God's kingdom in man's existence, it was the beginning of the transformation of *all mankind*, the historical turning point from which shall ultimately flower God's perfect reign.[15]

14 Cf. the remarks of Kazoh Kitamori: "By serving as witness to the pain of God, our pain is transformed into light; it becomes meaningful and fruitful. By the pain of God which overcomes his wrath, our pain, which had hitherto been the reality of the wrath of God, ends in salvation from this wrath. By serving the pain of God which is the glad news of salvation, our pain ends in sharing the salvation. By serving him through our pain, the pain of God rather saves and heals our own pain. When the pain of God heals our pain, it already has changed into love which has broken through the bounds of pain—'the love rooted in the pain of God.' By this love, whoever follows the Lord, bearing his own cross and losing his life for Christ's sake, will find life. Through our service in the pain of God, the wounds of our Lord in turn heal *our* wounds, thus our pain can actually be relieved by serving the pain of God. All kinds of pain experienced in this world remain meaningless and fruitless as long as they do not serve the pain of God. We must take care not to suffer human pain in vain" (*Theology of the Pain of God* [Richmond: John Knox Press, 1965], pp. 52, 53).

15 In the Gospels, with their portrayal of Jesus' life and death, it is clear that the events of salvation occur within the on-going movement of history. Moreover (though

In this historically realistic and meaningful sense Christ was the "second Adam" (1 Cor. 15:45–49; Rom. 5:12–21). This suggestive title need not be understood in some esoteric or mystical sense as meaning that Christ stands before God in place of other men, or that he becomes the "representative man" before God.[16] It can be understood in a fully intelligible historical sense: he was the actual historical beginning of the new humanity, the new community destined to become God's very kingdom, as "Adam" stands for the actual historical beginning of the old.[17] In him atonement—the at-one-ment of God and man—really began; in his death and resurrection God's love succeeded in breaking into human history, becoming a new element in the on-going historical process. And thus without him, men could not become at-one with God, reconciled with him. But the

---

perhaps this is not so immediately apparent), the Gospels portray that transformation of history which those events are effecting as culminating in the establishment of a new people within history. Thus, for example, "Mark presents Jesus' passion as an essential element in a series of eschatological events rather than as the ground of a doctrine of the atonement. . . . the passion of Jesus was a necessary event in the outworking of the divinely determined apocalyptic scheme of 'history,' both past and future. . . . What is at stake . . . is the founding of a New People, an eschatological community. In rejecting Jesus as God's final Word, the Jewish nation is unwittingly laying the foundation for the new community. This seems to be the fundamental meaning given by Mark, and/or the tradition on which he drew, to the death of Jesus. . . . the cross is presented as prelude to the reconstitution of the circle of followers: 'Do not be amazed; you seek Jesus of Nazareth, who was crucified. He has risen, he is not here. . . . But go, tell his disciples and Peter that he is going before you to Galilee; there you will see him, as he told you.' [16:6–7]. . . . Mark regards history as the chain of events by which the divine purpose is worked out, through struggle and seeming defeat. . . . The basic function of Jesus as Son of God in Mark is as bringer of the eschatological salvation. . . ." (Quoted from the forthcoming book by Howard Clark Kee, *Jesus in History*, to be published by Harcourt, Brace and World, 1969.)

16 In the past this term has often been understood in quasi-platonistic terms. Jesus was held to be no mere individual but the *form of man* as such, or he was regarded as the "representative man," so that whatever affected him necessarily affects all, his actual relationship to God becoming the possibility of a new relationship for every man. But for most moderns, with their conviction of the reality of the individual person, such conceptions are no longer intelligible. Even were they able to think in these terms, there would remain serious problems—e.g., how can one particular man be at once the form of man and still a particular exemplification of that form? To questions of this sort platonistic orthodoxy has never been able to give a clear and convincing answer. The historicist interpretation of Christ has the advantage of preserving a genuine metaphysical primacy and uniqueness for Jesus in terms intelligible to historically oriented moderns while avoiding the metaphysical difficulties into which platonistic interpretations fall.

17 Cf. Schleiermacher: "The appearance of the first man constituted at the same time the physical life of the human race; the appearance of the Second Adam constituted for this nature a new spiritual life, which communicates and develops itself by spiritual fecundation" (*The Christian Faith* [Edinburgh: T. & T. Clark, 1928], § 94).

atonement was not completed in this death and resurrection of a man
of two thousand years ago, and it shall not be completed until the
divisions which keep men from being at-one with God and with each
other are overcome in the perfect community which is God's kingdom. It will not be completed, then, until the present course of history has run to its end, thus fulfilling God's purposes for it. It is in
this hope that the church lives, and it is for the establishment of this
kingdom that Christians struggle. The word "atonement" points to
this on-going struggle in which Christians, under God's sovereignty,
are participating.

At the beginning of the present chapter it was suggested that the
popular distinction between "objective" and "subjective" theories of
atonement must be discarded to reconstruct the doctrine meaningfully. In summing up now, we shall return to that point. A meaningful interpretation of the way in which reconciliation with God is
effected can confine itself neither to an act by God accompanied by
a change in his disposition toward man, nor to a transformation in
man. On the one hand, since man's estrangement from the ground of
his being is the problem, genuine reconciliation with God will necessarily change man: a kind of personal and communal fulfilment,
unknown before, will become possible. Unless we can speak of such
empirical historical consequences, the atonement will be abstract and
ultimately meaningless. On the other hand, precisely because man's
estrangement from the ground of his being—and thus man himself
—is the problem, no purely immanent solution is possible: God must
act decisively to restore man, breaking into the circle of human existence from beyond it. Atonement thus cannot occur without (a)
God's act breaking into the circle of human lovelessness, making love
and self-giving once again possible, and (b) man's act of appropriation through which love and human fulfilment become actualities in
human history. But (c) if this is true, more must be said as well.
As reconciliation occurs between man and God, a certain "healing"
occurs in God also. For man's alienation from God has meant that
God is also, in a certain sense, inwardly frustrated and divided
against himself: his love for man was hurt by man's rejection, and
man's sin (as Anselm clearly saw) has meant that God's purposes

I think this may need a bit more explication

were not finding realization. God's act to reconcile man to himself thus means that God also will ultimately realize a certain at-one-ment within his own being. This should not be understood as an "eternal moment" in some "eternal process" we call God, but as the culminating phase of that actual historical movement through which God and man are reconciled with each other. If the relation between God and man is in fact personal-historical and living, no event that occurs between them can fail to have its effects on both.[18]

Since the mythological framework underlying the classic view of atonement is scarcely credible any longer to modern man, in the present chapter I have suggested a personal-historical conception. Use of such a model preserves the integrity both of God and man, and enables understanding how the act of God actually frees man from bondage to stultifying guilt and sin. We must turn now to an examination of the empirical historical occurrences which gave rise to the conviction that God was acting in this decisive fashion in and through the man Jesus. Without an anchor in actual empirical history for this claim, it remains simply an interesting speculative idea about ultimate reality. The anchor to which Christian faith clings as its historico-ontological foundation is twofold. On the one hand there is the complex of events which gave birth to faith: the "resurrection of Jesus" and the founding of the church. On the other hand there is the historical object of faith: the man Jesus, especially the culmination of his life in death, apprehended as God's atoning act and thus the beginning of a new historical life for man. In the next chapter we shall turn to the first of these, the historical birth of *faith*; in the succeeding one, to the second, the beginning of a new empirico-historical *life* for man through the paradigmatic event of Jesus' death and its appropriation as the form of a new communal life.

[18] As P. T. Forsyth has noted: "When two friends fall out and are reconciled, it does not simply mean that one adjusts himself to the other. That is a very one-sided arrangement. There must be a mutuality. . . . Our reconciliation is between person and person. It is not between an order or a process on the one hand and a person on the other. Therefore a real and deep change of the relation between the two means a change on both sides" (*The Work of Christ* [London: Independent Press, Ltd., 1910], pp. 73, 75).

II. The Resurrection

WE are ready to consider a question now that has been lurking behind much of the discussion of revelation and christology and theology in these pages: Why and how did it happen that Christians came to regard a fellow human being as the very center of human history, the ultimate norm of existence and a proper object of devotion? I do not mean here to be restating a question we have already dwelt on sufficiently, namely: Is such an attitude to a mere man not idolatrous? The answer to this latter question, as we have seen, is simply that it misrepresents the issue; for it is believed that present to men in this man is the One High God. I am here suggesting that we push back to a prior question which anyone contemplating Christian faith must doubtless ask: Why, after all, do Christians believe such a thing? Are there reasonable grounds for taking this position? Or is it simply due to an emotional need for security in a cruel world, or to cultural conditioning from early childhood? Why would anyone regard a man who had died two thousand years before as having such great continuing significance?

We must be clear, before trying to answer these questions, about what we are looking for, what would constitute adequate answers to them. There are two quite different levels on which the answers can be given, and they are usually confused, giving rise to many of the supposed difficulties in the problem. On the one hand, by an "answer" to a question of this sort we generally mean *an explanation or in-*

terpretation *which we can understand* or make sense of; an answer
is an explanation (= "making plain") in humanly comprehensible
or "reasonable" terms. On this level of understanding, we are seeking a convincing reason for believing Christ to be the manifestation
in history of the Lord of the universe. And this itself appears to be
a legitimate demand of faith: one ought to be able to give a good
"reason of the hope that is in" him (1 Pet. 3:15   KJ). On the other
hand, Christian faith is aware that the only adequate justification
for such a claim about Christ would be that God himself had "made
him both Lord and Christ, this Jesus whom you crucified" (Acts
2:36)—that is, that his significance *is not explicable in human terms,
not justifiable by mere human reasons, but interpretable only by
reference to the self-revealing act of the God who is beyond the limits
of human experience and understanding.*

Clearly these two levels conflict. If the true answer to our question
is that God has revealed the movement of history to be ordered
toward Christ as its center, then no fully satisfactory answer in
strictly human terms is possible; conversely, if a humanly reasonable
and verifiable answer can be given, this implies that everything of
importance here can be adequately understood in terms of what is
accessible in and to human experience, reference to the transcendent
God being superfluous. We cannot have it both ways: we cannot have
an answer which is both reasonable and verifiable by ordinary epistemological procedures and yet which makes the ultimate ground of
Christian faith God's revelatory act, for acts in which a self discloses
the true character and movement of a purposive historical process,
as we have seen (above, Chapter 21), are not verifiable "objectively"
until the end of the process has been reached; prior to that such dis-
closures can only be believed or disbelieved.

With these two levels of answers distinguished, we are now in a
position to clarify the problem further. There will be two types of
answers to our question. One will remain at all points within the
circle of humanly comprehensible interpretation: it will seek to make
sense of the Christian faith in strictly human terms, as a this-worldly
phenomenon. This answer, however illuminating it may prove, will
of course never be fully satisfactory to faith, since faith does not

believe "God's act" to be merely an odd and somewhat archaic way
of speaking of purely immanent historical realities. The other type
of answer, more satisfactory to faith but less convincing to the demand for intelligible explanation, is the claim that faith is actually
rooted in God's acts of self-manifestation, not simply in human psychological or cultural causation. Both types or levels of interpretation
of theologically significant historical events are possible and necessary. For if this is really the *act of God* in and through *finite human
acts*—the *appearing of God* in a *real man*—it is both possible and
necessary to define and clarify every aspect of the event as finite and
historical, within the context of other finite historical events, as well
as to perceive and indicate its peculiar reference to and embodiment
of the transcendent. Inasmuch as neither dimension of the event is
dispensable theologically, both emerging from the very heart of the
Christian claim, both types or levels of interpretation are required.
(Here the significance of Chalcedon's "two natures" formula again
becomes apparent.) In order to avoid serious confusion and misunderstanding, it is essential to recognize clearly the level on which
one is speaking in order to discern what is, and what is not, appropriate to or required by the particular point under consideration.[1]

Unfortunately the church has not always been as careful about
this matter as necessary, and she is therefore responsible for many
confused and even absurd opinions on christological questions. We
earlier (pp. 203f.) noted one of the earliest, and most unfortunate,
of these confusions: the doctrine of the virgin birth is an attempt to
understand the theological fact that for faith Jesus Christ is Son of
God, in humanly comprehensible quasi-biological terms, confusing
the two levels of interpretation rather seriously. It is not necessary
to repeat here again the analysis of that problem. Instead, we shall
turn now to the other prime "miracle" of the Christian tradition, the
resurrection of Jesus, for in this event is to be found such answer as
can be had to the problem of the actual historical foundation of
Christian faith.

It is well known that Christian faith as such had its beginning

---

[1] We noted earlier (pp. 187ff.) certain difficulties in this regard with the "two
natures" formula.

with Easter, with the unexpected appearance of the conviction that
the one crucified on the cross was not dead but risen. This in itself
shows how much more crucial for Christian faith is the resurrection-
event than the alleged virgin birth. Whereas the latter was a theologically crude attempt to explain something already believed in—that
Jesus was the Son of God—*the resurrection was the event in which
this belief itself was born.* As Paul put it: Jesus, a descendant of
"David according to the flesh" was "designated Son of God in power
. . . by his resurrection from the dead" (Rom. 1:3–4). The term
"resurrection of Jesus" thus points to the historical event which gave
birth to Christian faith. The answer to our question, Why did Christians come to believe that in Jesus Christ God himself is encountered?
was the occurrence of the resurrection-event. Thus, only through careful analysis of that event will we be able to grasp the historico-
epistemological foundations of Christian faith. What was this event?
What happened? Was this in any intelligible sense an event at all?
How can we in the twentieth century understand it?[2]

It is important to be clear first of all that when I say the resurrection of Jesus is the answer to our question, I mean that in the

---

[2] I am well aware that at least since the beginning of the theological renaissance, with
the publication of Barth's *Epistle to the Romans* in 1918 (E. T.: London: Oxford University Press, 1933), it has been fashionable to take the paradoxical (and possibly non-
sensical?) position that the fundamental basis of Christian faith is nothing less than
Jesus' resurrection, and yet the latter "is not a 'historical' (*historisches*) event beside the
other events of history (*Geschichte*), but the 'unhistorical' (*unhistorische*) event, by which
these other events are bounded and to which the events before and on and after Easter
Day point. Were this event itself 'historical' (*historisches*), that is, a psychical, or super-
physical event, it would have taken place on a plane which would . . . render legitimate
the putting forward and discussion of hypotheses such as apparent but not real death,
deception practised by the disciples or by Jesus Himself, objective or subjective visions,
and many other . . . theories. Common to all these hypotheses is the opinion that it is
not God Himself and God alone who here enters upon the scene" (p. 203; translation
slightly altered). I trust my analysis makes sufficiently clear the theological and other
difficulties with which such positions as this bristle. Barth himself would no longer
accept such a statement, insisting now that the Easter event is "in the sphere of history
(*Geschichte*) and time no less than . . . the words and acts and even the death of Jesus"
(*Church Dogmatics*, III, 2 [Edinburgh: T. & T. Clark, 1960], 442), a statement which
on the face of it would be quite acceptable to the present writer. The difficulty arises
when it develops that the history to which Barth is here referring is that preserved in
"saga" and "legend" and is not open to our ordinary methods of historical knowledge
(*ibid.*, 446ff.), so that one wonders if we have not really to do with a kind of non-
history anyhow, despite all his claims to the contrary. For a discussion and summary of
opinions on the theological problems surrounding the concept of Jesus' resurrection, see
R. R. Niebuhr, *Resurrection and Historical Reason* (New York: Scribners, 1957).

occurrence of this event we are presented, first, with the *historical* answer to the problem, and, second and consequently, with the *theological* answer. *There would have been no Christian faith had this event not happened.* Historians are agreed that Jesus' crucifixion brought disillusionment and despair to the hearts of his disciples, and it appears probable that they fled back to Galilee (cf. Mt. 28:16; also Mk. 16:7, Mt. 28:7)[3] in fear for their lives. As far as they could see, all they had worked and hoped for was over. Their hopes "that he was the one to redeem Israel" (Lk. 24:21) were now dashed, and it was evident that Jesus' tremendous expectation that "the kingdom of God is at hand" (Mk. 1:15) was naive and false. Then an event happened which convinced them that God himself had vindicated Jesus, that the kingdom which Jesus had proclaimed was in fact being inaugurated, that the great transformation of history, for which every Jew hoped and which Jesus had taught was imminent, was really occurring. This event, whatever it was, created a new hope out of their despair—"we have been born anew to a living hope through the resurrection of Jesus Christ from the dead" (1 Pet. 1:3)—and a bold resumption and continuation of Jesus' work out of their defection and defeat. It was in the conviction of Jesus' resurrection that the church was founded and the Gospel preached to all nations. It was because of this event, therefore, that Christian faith became a powerful force in Western culture and ultimately the whole world, and to this day is a significant and powerful reality in human lives.

Thus, the resurrection has been, together with the crucifixion which it completes, of supreme importance for Christian faith. It means that *God is Lord* despite all that men believe and do to the contrary. Even though men rejected Jesus of Nazareth and destroyed him as effectively as they could, apparently removing all possibility of his further historical effectiveness, God "raised him up" (Acts 2:24) and made him *after his death* the mighty transformer of history. In a very special sense, then, the resurrection of Christ is the concrete meaning and evidence of the claim that though men are free

[3] As is well known, this Markan-Matthean tradition, which seems historically most probable, is not shared by Luke, who emphasizes the centrality of Jerusalem in the post-crucifixion period. See n. 19, below.

in history to do as they will, God is Lord. If this event in its power
and meaning were to dissolve, much of the basis of the Christian
claims would be destroyed. For then the end of the revelatory event
would be Jesus' crucifixion, and the meaning of human existence
revealed in that occurrence taken simply by itself is bleak tragedy
and death. Unlike the "virgin birth" which is a peripheral and dispensable symbol, "resurrection" points to the heart of Christian faith.
In Paul's words:

> . . . if Christ has not been raised, then our preaching is in
> vain and your faith is in vain. We are even found to be misrep-
> resenting God, because we testified of God that he raised Christ.
> . . . If Christ has not been raised, your faith is futile and you are
> still in your sins.
>
> 1 CORINTHIANS 15:14–15, 17

What now are we to make of Jesus' "resurrection"? What actually
happened?

This is not the place to attempt a detailed analysis of the historical evidence, full as it is of conflicts and inconsistencies, but we
must look briefly at it.[4] Unlike the passion narratives, in which the
four Gospel accounts are substantially the same, there are wide differences in view here;[5] furthermore, the narratives in the Gospels

---

[4] A good historical analysis of the evidence and current discussion of the problem
will be found in Hans Grass, *Ostergeschehen und Osterberichte* (Göttingen: Vandenhoeck
& Ruprecht, 1956; 2nd ed., 1962).

[5] To give a few examples: in Matthew the tomb of Jesus is guarded (27:62–66), but
in Mark and Luke there is no indication of anyone around who might be strong enough to
roll away the stone for the women who visited it (Mk. 16:3–4); according to John only
Mary Magdalene came to the tomb on Easter morning (20:1), but Matthew suggests
that two women, both named Mary, came (28:1), and Mark has a report of the visit of
three (16:1); Matthew (28:7) and Mark (16:7) suggest that the disciples are to go to
Galilee and there they will see Jesus again, but Luke has no such report at all and places,
on the contrary, all of the resurrection appearances in the Jerusalem vicinity; according
to Luke the first appearance was to two disciples(?) on the road to Emmaus (24:13–35),
but Matthew (28:9–10) and John (20:14–16) believe Jesus appeared first to some women,
while Paul suggests Peter was the first witness (1 Cor. 15:5); in Mark the women upon
discovering the empty tomb are fearful and tell no one (16:8), but in Matthew they
run immediately to bring the disciples the news (28:8); finally, according to Luke the
resurrection appearances are terminated apparently in a few hours with Jesus' ascension
into heaven (24:13, 33, 36, 50–52), while in Acts it is reported they continued intermit-
tently for forty days, the ascension not occurring until then (1:3, 9); etc. It is
evident there are many difficulties in the reports.

differ significantly from Paul's report. All agree only in the central contention: Jesus is risen. It is not possible to determine what historico-theological meaning the term "resurrection" can have without first reaching some conclusions about what is historically reliable here. If the *resurrection event* (and not simply reports about it) was in fact the decisive culmination of God's self-manifestation in human history, enabling man to become at-one with him, then it is theologically of the highest importance to determine as precisely as possible what that event was; otherwise our theology, not being founded on historical actuality, will be a gnosticism of speculations and opinions. Only the barest outline of an appropriate procedure is possible here. We shall begin with the earliest reports to see what they suggest about the character of the event. Then, with this clue, I shall state as straightforwardly as possible what seems most probably to have occurred[6] (with a few suggestions on how contrary reports and interpretations in the New Testament may have arisen), concluding with an analysis of the theological issues involved and conclusions to be drawn.

As we noted above, for Paul, our earliest writer, the resurrection of Christ was central to Christian faith. But what kind of event was it? Apparently Paul thinks of resurrected existence as radically different from our present physical life in a body of flesh and blood.[7]

---

[6] It may be remarked here that on the historical questions about the resurrection of Jesus there has been less candor and more obscurity among theologians than on almost any other issue. For an analysis of the biased historical argumentation characteristic of many Christians, see Van Harvey, *The Historian and the Believer* (New York: Macmillan, 1966); for his analysis of such interpretations of the resurrection, see esp. pp. 107ff., 154ff., 218ff.

[7] Whatever resurrection means for Paul, it is evident that it does not mean resuscitation of a dead physical body: "But some one will ask, 'How are the dead risen? With what kind of body do they come?' You foolish man! . . . There are celestial bodies and there are terrestrial bodies; but the glory of the celestial is one, and the glory of the terrestrial is another. . . . So is it with the resurrection of the dead. What is sown is perishable, what is raised is imperishable. It is sown in dishonor, it is raised in glory. It is sown in weakness, it is raised in power. *It is sown a physical body, it is raised a spiritual body. . . . I tell you this, brethren: flesh and blood cannot inherit the kingdom of God, nor does the perishable inherit the imperishable*" (1 Cor. 15:35ff., 50). Kendrick Grobel has pointed out to me that in the Greek the sharp distinction between the physical and the spiritual in this passage is even more pronounced, because it is not at all clear that the impersonal "it" refers to some continuing "body" at all. Hence he translates: "There is sown in corruption . . . , dishonor . . . , weakness a body (once) animate; there is raised in incorruption . . . , glory . . . , power . . . a body spiritual"—the two "bodies" thus being quite distinct realities.

He finds it necessary, therefore, to invent the highly paradoxical concept of "spiritual body" (1 Cor. 15:44) to denote this state. Paul's claim that resurrected existence is no mere resuscitation of physical existence implies he could hardly have regarded Jesus' resurrection as consisting simply in the raising of his physical body.[8] It should not be surprising, then, that—in contrast with the Gospels, which make much of the story of the empty tomb—Paul nowhere shows any interest in or even knowledge of such a legend. This does not mean he doubted it was really Jesus of Nazareth who was raised from the dead—that is, that he doubted the genuine continuity of the resurrected with the historical Jesus. Nor does it mean that a bodiless Jesus (whatever that might be) was what appeared. Rather, it was a radically transformed Jesus, clothed now in a "spiritual body," something to be sharply contrasted with his flesh-and-blood existence. Paul believed Jesus was alive again but in some nonphysical mode of being.[9]

In order to reconstruct the event of Jesus' resurrection, we must know something of this mode of existence, and here the evidence is slim indeed. The concept of "spiritual body," however, taken together with Paul's statement that the resurrection became known to the disciples through a series of "appearances" of Jesus to himself and others,[10] suggests that for Paul (the earliest writer on this matter

[8] Paul apparently thinks of Jesus' resurrected existence as similar to that which he expects all men of faith will enjoy, because he can argue from the expectation of a general resurrection to the fact that Christ was raised (1 Cor. 15:13, 15–16), as well as from the fact of Christ's resurrection to the hope for all (15:12, 14, 17–18, 20–23). For Paul, Christ is to be regarded, then, as "the first fruits of those who have fallen asleep" (15:20). The concept of resurrection here involved is univocal.

[9] Paul's highly paradoxical concept of "spiritual body" really helps little in understanding what this nonphysical mode was, since it is not clear with what analogies in our experience we should interpret it; until we find such analogies it remains a bare word. He evidently intends to affirm personal continuity while denying *physical* continuity, but there is little more we can say.

[10] "For I delivered to you as of first importance what I also received, that Christ died for our sins in accordance with the scriptures, that he was buried, that he was raised on the third day in accordance with the scriptures, and that he appeared to Cephas, then to the twelve. Then he appeared to more than five hundred brethren at one time, most of whom are still alive, though some have fallen asleep. Then he appeared to James, then to all the apostles. Last of all, as to one untimely born, he appeared also to me" (15:3–8). It is important to note that Paul uses the same word for the "appearance" to himself as for the others, and apparently regards them as on the same footing. He believed his was as genuine an encounter with the resurrected lord as any other.

still extant) the risen lord had manifested himself in what we would call "visions,"[11] which convinced the disciples Jesus was again alive.[12] This conclusion is also consistent with the summaries of early Christian preaching found in Acts.[13]

It is obvious, however, that the testimony of the earliest preaching and of Paul is in conflict with the accounts in the Gospels.[14] When we turn to these records and compare them with Paul, we are immediately struck with the fact that he has told us nothing about their central emphasis, the discovery of an empty tomb, nor about Jesus' ascension into heaven.[15] The story of the empty tomb, already in Mark the very heart of the Gospels' dramatic picture of Easter, may have been relatively late in appearing[16]—an extrapolation from, and

[11] See Grass, *op. cit.* (above, n. 4), pp. 186–249.

[12] This interpretation is also consistent with the reports in Acts of Paul's conversion, assuming this was the occasion on which he had "seen Jesus our Lord" (1 Cor. 9:1). Though these reports differ from each other in significant details, in all of them Paul is represented as seeing a vision and hearing the voice of the risen Lord (9:3ff., 22:6ff., 26:12ff.).

[13] See C. H. Dodd, *The Apostolic Preaching and Its Development* (New York: Harper, 1936), pp. 21ff.

[14] Paul himself believed that on this matter he was transmitting earlier Christian tradition, not inventing a novel interpretation of his own (see n. 10, above). Moreover, he believed his experience and understanding of the matter to be on a par with the other apostles—and this was one of the cornerstones of his claim to the title (cf. 1 Cor. 9:1, 15:8ff.; Gal. 1:1, 11ff.). Even though recognizing that Acts—with its view that the resurrection-appearances were terminated in forty days with Jesus' ascension (1:3,9), and that therefore Paul's experience was of a different order—sharply disagrees with Paul's claims in this respect, the present analysis will take the Pauline testimony as its fundamental reference point. Paul's general reliability is greater than Acts and his testimony is firsthand (while Acts is second- or thirdhand); he represents a stage of the rapidly developing early Christian tradition some thirty or forty years closer to the events reported. (For a convenient analysis of the relative historical reliability of Paul and Acts, see John Knox, *Chapters in a Life of Paul* [New York: Abingdon, 1950], esp. Chs. 1, 2.)

[15] Apparently these reports were either unknown to Paul—for he would hardly have omitted mentioning such remarkable evidences of the resurrection—or else he did not accept them as true, since they implied the resurrection of a *physical* body.

[16] There are good reasons for holding this account to be late. For example, Mark regards his story of the empty tomb as a secret known only to certain obscure women who were said to have discovered the tomb empty but who "said nothing to anyone, for they were afraid" (16:8). But it seems likely that Peter and James and John and others of the well-known disciples had preached Jesus' resurrection first, and they had spoken only of appearances, not an empty tomb (1 Cor. 15:3ff.; Acts 2, 3, etc.). Perhaps even at the time Mark was writing, the story was known to so few that it seemed a secret to him. This conjecture is supported by the fact that by the time Matthew was written, about twenty years later, the story was apparently well known (having been circulated by Mark), for now it was no longer believed to have been first kept secret: Matthew reports that the women immediately "ran to tell his disciples" of their discovery (28:8).

objectification in physicalist terms of, the original reports of appearances. The resurrection faith probably did not begin with such a
discovery; in any case, this would have proved nothing important,
since there are many possible reasons why a body might be missing.
Rather, it began with a series of appearances or visions[17] of the risen
Christ, probably first of all to Peter[18] and then to others in Galilee,
possibly continuing later in Jerusalem.[19] Apparently these appear-

When one takes such special peculiarities of the stories together with the fact that the
versions in the later Gospels (especially Matthew and John) have considerably elaborated
the account of the discovery of the empty tomb as reported in Mark, it is clear that a
considerable development of this tradition was occurring. Furthermore, the very appearance of this story can be quite easily explained as a relatively easy and natural extrapolation from and elaboration of the earliest preaching about the appearances of the
risen Lord. The latter, as we have seen, are susceptible of sophisticated interpretations
(such as Paul's concept of the "spiritual body"), but it was only natural that most of
the unsophisticated early Christians understood the resurrection to have been of Jesus'
physical body—and the obvious conclusion to be drawn from this was that the tomb
where that body had been laid was now empty. Thus, it is relatively easy to account for
the appearance of stories of an empty tomb if we suppose the original events to have
been appearances (visions). However, if we attempt to reverse this order of interpretation, giving priority to the accounts of the empty tomb, it is not only much more
difficult to give any historically intelligible account of what may have happened, but the
evolution of the tradition which we have noted is also rendered incomprehensible. Therefore, while recognizing there are important theological insights and historical evidences
in the empty tomb traditions, the present analysis takes as its primary clue to the event
the Pauline evidence.

[17] In addition to the evidence already cited for the vision-character of the originative
events, it should be noted there are also many suggestions in this direction in the
Gospel accounts. For example, the sudden and inexplicable appearance and disappearance
of the resurrected Jesus (e.g., Luke 24:31,36), his apparent going through locked doors
at will (e.g., John 20:19,26), and the fact that the disciples doubted they were really
seeing the dead Jesus alive again (note here not only Thomas' well-known doubt
[John 20:24–27], but also reports in Matthew [28:17] and Luke [24:21–31, 41]) all
suggest the nonphysical character of the appearances. It must be admitted, of course,
that the evangelists themselves would hardly have accepted this interpretation of the
meaning of their stories; in Luke 24:39, for example, it is explicitly denied that the
resurrected Jesus is a spirit, "for a spirit has not flesh and bones" as the resurrected
one has.

[18] Not only is this explicitly stated in 1 Cor. 15:5; it is also suggested by the
repeated primacy given to Peter both in many of the other traditions which fail to report
directly that he was the first witness (e.g., Lk. 24:34; John 20:6, 21:15ff.; and also Lk.
22:32; the confession at Caesarea Philippi [Mk. 8:29]), and in the early church itself,
as seen, for example, in the first twelve chapters of Acts.

[19] The tradition in Mark (14:28, 16:7) and Matthew (28:10, 16–20) that the first
appearances were in Galilee seems more probable than Luke's view that they were in
Jerusalem. With Jesus' death the disciples had no reason to stay and every reason to
leave Jerusalem and return home. If they then saw the risen Lord, they may well have
returned immediately to Jerusalem, where more appearances occurred (accounting for the
Lukan tradition). If the appearances began while they were still in the Jerusalem area,
however, it is not at all clear where the stories about Galilean appearances came from.
(Cf. Grass, op. cit. [above, n. 4], pp. 113–127.)

ances were not simply private visions, but were publicly experienced,[20] though only within the group of Jesus' erstwhile followers. Eventually, a good many years later, the original account had been sufficiently elaborated to include the discovery of the empty tomb, and thus it came to have the familiar form still found in the Gospels. However homiletically useful these stories may be, and however valuable certain emphases found in them, our theological understanding of the actual historical event in which Christian faith decisively arose must be determined primarily by the significance of the appearances.[21]

What now are we to make of these appearances? What kind of answer does "Jesus' resurrection" give to our problem: Why do Christians believe God was uniquely present to man in Jesus Christ? The brief historical analysis just completed makes it possible to see more easily what this question means, for now it is clearer what is designated by the word "resurrection." *It does not refer to anything directly experienced by the disciples;* what was experienced were "appearances" (and possibly an "empty tomb"). When the early Christians spoke of the "resurrection of Jesus," they were presenting *their explanation* of these experiences. That is, on the basis of events directly known to them in which, as they believed, they encountered Jesus after his death, *they inferred* that another event had occurred after his death which they had not witnessed: Jesus' being awakened from the dead. (Nowhere in the canon is the claim made that someone directly witnessed the reawakening of Jesus.) Thus, the early church's conviction about Jesus' resurrection was

[20] Most of the reports, both in Paul's list of appearances and in the Gospels, involve more than one witness, suggesting that it was when the disciples reassembled as close friends and particularly in the intimate fellowship of a common meal (note, e.g., Lk. 24:30–31, 33–43; John 21:12–14; etc.) with its undoubted rehearsal of warm but painful memories, especially of the last supper with Jesus, that Jesus was known to them again as raised from the dead. It should not be thought that this quasi-public character of the resurrection-appearances distinguished them decisively from what we commonly think of as visions. There are numerous recorded contemporary instances of several persons experiencing the same vision or apparition at the same time, just as they share ordinary "objective" experiences. (See G.N.M. Tyrrell, *Apparitions* [London: Gerald Duckworth & Co., 1943], pp. 36–37, 51, for some examples.)

[21] For a quite different estimation of the significance of the empty tomb stories, see Wolfhart Pannenberg, *Grundzüge der Christologie* (Gütersloher Verlagshaus Gerd Mohn, 1964), pp. 85–103.

belief in the truth of a historical hypothesis[22] necessary (as they believed) to account for certain experiences which remade their lives. This conviction was so effectively induced by the appearances that the erstwhile despair of the disciples was transformed into a powerful hope, turning upside down not only their own lives but ultimately the whole course of human history.[23] Christian faith was born in the experience of the appearances, interpreted as made possible by God's mighty act of raising Jesus from the dead.

If we recognize that the phrase, "resurrection of Jesus," does not refer to an experienced event but to a hypothetical one, we are in a position to evaluate more adequately the traditional Christian view. It should be evident that interpretation here can be and always has been given on each of the two levels earlier discussed. Thus, on one level we can say that these alleged appearances were in fact a series of hallucinations produced by the wishful thinking of Jesus' former disciples who had so strongly hoped and believed "that he was the one to redeem Israel" (Luke 24:21). The disciples interpreted these experiences as made possible by the actual coming-back-to-life of their crucified master. If one is seeking an explanation "comprehensible" in human terms, this is a reasonable conjecture about what happened.[24]

[22] It should be noted here that Paul, our earliest witness on the matter, was himself aware that the announcement that Jesus had risen from the dead was no bare report of some positivistic "fact" but was rather an *interpretation* of what had recently occurred. When he admits that if there is no such thing as resurrection of the dead, then Christ also was not raised (1 Cor. 15:13,16), he is making clear that the Easter-event was regarded by the early Christians as a "resurrection" because it was interpreted in terms of certain Jewish apocalyptic conceptions, not simply because of its own self-evident character. Paul is admitting that if there were to be no general resurrection—if the Jewish belief here were untrue—then it would be false to suppose that Jesus had been raised from the dead. The Easter-event in and of itself, then, did not give rise to the belief Jesus was risen: it was susceptible of a variety of interpretations. However, because the disciples apprehended and interpreted that event in terms of the Jewish apocalyptic faith, they took it to mean their master was again alive. If, now, we bring a different framework of interpretation from Jewish apocalypticism to this critical event in which Christian faith was born—as we must—we should not be overly surprised or dismayed when we find it necessary to understand the character of the event somewhat differently from the first Christians.

[23] If it be thought that mere "visions" or "appearances" could hardly be "real enough" to convince the early Christians that Jesus had actually been raised from the dead, I suggest the dubious reader examine some accounts of the powerful conviction to which some contemporary "mere visions" have given rise (see, for example, the already-cited work by Tyrrell, n. 21, above.)

[24] It may be objected that "hallucinations" could hardly have had the positive creative

However, the early Christians claimed more than this: that through these events—however understood on the human level—God himself was acting. Thus, to faith the description of the events as mere human history does not tell the whole story or even give its most significant dimensions. In order to grasp the full theological significance of the appearances, it is necessary to move to what was described above (pp. 411ff.) as the second level of interpretation. On this level faith will say that through these appearances ("hallucinations") the almighty God was making himself known,[25] through them he was designating Jesus Christ the "Son of God in power" (Rom. 1:4), and thus through these events he was continuing what he had brought to a climax in the earthly ministry and death of Jesus of Nazareth: the radical transformation of human existence into his own kingdom. Why would faith say this? Simply because, as matter of actual historical fact (so far as we know), it *was* the experience of these appearances that gave birth to the faith that in and through the crucified Jesus God was acting decisively in human history.[26]

---

consequences which the resurrection appearances had. But such objection arises largely because of the negative connotations of the term "hallucination" in popular speech, and because it is not well-known that hallucinatory phenomena of various kinds and degrees are a frequent accompaniment of genuine creativity and insight. In a series of three articles (reprinted from *Psychiatry* in *A Study of Interpersonal Relations*, ed. Patrick Mullahy [New York: Hermitage Press, 1949]) on the nature and conditions of insight, Eliot Dale Hutchinson cites relevant evidence in this regard. He concludes: "Sensory experiences—non-recurrent visual and auditory hallucinations—in extreme cases are common. Men *see* a sketch of a completed picture, they see music written in scoresheets, and *hear* themes in inner hearing. Moreover the seizure of the motor pathways, causing trembling, walking, pacing, jumping, vocalizing, is likewise frequent. Men shout for joy, stand surprised at the hallucinatory vividness of their insights, rush to tell their friends of their successes. And in addition the emotional life quickens indefinitely. In short learning is instantaneous, and the experience opens the way for new volitional possibilities which are a most important consideration in education and ethics. . . . If one had the least vestige of superstition, it is easy to see how he might suppose himself to be merely the incarnation, merely the mouthpiece, merely the medium of higher forces. It is the impersonality and automatic production of such moments of inspiration that has led to endless theories of extra-personal revelation. . . . Like lightning—and the hallucinatory components of many a historical insight are no mere accident—an idea flashes out, appearing as inevitable, necessary, without hesitation as to form. One never has a choice. And he not only produces something; he becomes something [new] as well" (pp. 440, 445).

[25] Cf. Bultmann: ". . . if it is possible for the historian to see nothing more [in Jesus' resurrection] than visionary experiences of fanatical persons, then we are simply asked whether we believe that God acts in such things, as they themselves believed and as the proclamation maintains" (review of E. Hirsch, *Die Auferstehungsgeschichten und der christliche Glaube*, in *Theologische Literaturzeitung* (1940), col. 246).

[26] Cf. Pannenberg: "The Easter appearances are not to be explained as produced

The appearances were thus the climactic moment within human history of God's self-manifestation.[27]

These two levels of interpretation of the radical transformation through which the earliest disciples knew themselves to be going—the event as humanly intelligible, the event as divine act—were already necessary for the earliest disciples,[28] and neither can be avoided by contemporary Christian faith. For they point to the two inseparable dimensions of the event through which man is called to faith by God's act in Christ. Can it be believed that through these "hallucinations"[29] God was acting to bring his kingdom powerfully

---

by the Easter faith of the disciples; rather, the other way around: the Easter faith of the disciples was produced by the appearances" (*Grundzüge der Christologie*, p. 93).

[27] Cf. Ulrich Wilckens: "Revelation . . . according to the united judgment of all of the otherwise so various witnesses of primitive Christianity is found only in the occurrence of the reawakening of the crucified Jesus of Nazareth from the dead, in which God has allowed the New Aeon to break in. This . . . common fundamental knowledge has bound together Jew and heathen into the one community of God's salvation" ("Das Offenbarungsverständnis in der Geschichte des Urchristentums," in Wolfhart Pannenberg, ed., *Offenbarung als Geschichte*, p. 87). Already in *The Epistle to the Romans* Karl Barth had taken a similar position: "The Resurrection is the revelation: the disclosing of Jesus as the Christ, the appearing of God, and the apprehending of God in Jesus" (p. 30).

[28] If it be supposed that the early disciples did not utilize the humanly intelligible level of explanation, but resorted only to appeal to divine miracle, it should be remembered that the claim that Jesus was no longer dead but was alive again was itself such an interpretation (to the disciples intelligible and meaningful, for stories of the dead being raised were by no means unknown or totally incredible to first-century man) of their experience of the "appearances." Moreover, for the early church this bare explanation of the experiences was not enough: they required further explanation, interpretation, even proof. So the elaborate and dramatic stories of the discovery of the empty tomb, of the inspection of the holes in Jesus' hand and side (John 20:24–27), of Jesus' eventually rising to heaven before the very eyes of the disciples (Acts 1:9–10; Luke 24:51, RSV footnote), etc., became prominent parts of the resurrection tradition. All of this was explanation and interpretation in "human terms" intelligible and significant to the earliest Christians, however incredible or absurd it may seem to our scientifically conditioned minds.

[29] Most Christians, I suppose, feel a definite repugnance toward referring to the resurrection-appearances as "hallucinations," for this seems to imply (and for this reason nonChristians have freely used the term) that they were false delusions believed to be veridical because of the abnormal character of the experience. About this feeling several comments may be made. In the first place, why should one expect that the decisive act, through which God made known the real meaning of the ministry and death of Jesus of Nazareth, would be apprehended by men in a relatively normal, everyday experience? The word "hallucination" points to the fact that what occurred here was very much outside the normal and the ordinary, and this would seem to be an advantage rather than a disadvantage. In the second place, the term "hallucination" indicates that the appearances were not objective and public but occurred only to a few, and this is clearly in keeping with the biblical testimony. "God raised him on the third day and made him manifest; not to all the people but to us who were chosen by God as witnesses" (Acts

into human history? To this faith will still answer, Yes; unfaith, No. Since in this answer twentieth-century faith affirms in its own terms the essentials of what traditional Christianity has meant by the "resurrection of Jesus," when that phrase is used in this work as expressive of contemporary faith, it should be understood to designate *the appearances theologically interpreted*.[30]

The negative connotations to our modern ears of words like "vision" or "hallucination" should not be allowed to call into question the ultimate validity of what was communicated in and what occurred through these events. Or can God not speak and act through visions and voices? If one took such a position, he would, in his modernity, be discrediting *a priori* much testimony both in the Bible and out; moreover, he would be putting very questionable restrictions on God himself. Such an attitude requires God to make himself known exclusively in man's somewhat dull and unimaginative waking experience. In this respect, perhaps the naive superstition of a group of first-century Galilean fishermen had a real advantage over modern naive skepticism, and one might consider it providential that God's

---

10:40–41). "Hallucination" is a term that points to just such a nonpublic but privately extremely significant experience; it is a type of experience, moreover, which not infrequently accompanies genuine creativity (see n. 24, above). Apart from its negative connotations, what modern category could be more appropriate? As a matter of fact, in the third place, precisely these negative connotations can serve to remind Christians today, as almost nothing else could, that their faith is, after all, both an absurdity and a scandal (1 Cor. 1:18ff.)—something they always try hard to conceal and forget.

[30] It will probably appear doubtful at this point that "the appearances theologically interpreted" contain the essentials of the traditional meaning ascribed to "Jesus' resurrection." Justification for this claim will be given below, pp. 427ff. Perhaps a word here is in order, however, about the linguistic propriety of using this term to designate the experienced *appearances* of the disciples when they themselves designated by it the *prior event of Jesus' raising*, which they believed made possible the appearances. Obviously my usage is somewhat out of accord with the literal meaning of the word as well as traditional usage. Here one must make a choice: he either should use the historically more precise word "appearances" ("hallucinations") and dispense with the term "resurrection" altogether (so that, for example, one might use a formula such as "life, death, and appearances of Jesus"); or, if one wishes to retain the ancient symbol, "resurrection," which carries within it (as "appearances" does not) the full theological import of the event that gave birth to Christian faith, he will have to remember that modern understanding of that event is somewhat different from the first-century view, as well as from what "resurrection" literally suggests. It is this second alternative that I prefer, since a word like "appearances" could hardly be made to bear the symbolic freight which "resurrection" has come to carry in Christian faith. Moreover, though the literal referent for the term is changed in my interpretation, its theological meaning is not essentially altered (see below): it still refers to the event making possible the birth of Christian faith, i.e., to God's decisive act, and that is what is crucial.

definitive act occurred two thousand years ago instead of today. For at that time it was possible for hallucinations to convince men that Jesus was really raised from the dead; and thus a church could be founded and a tradition well enough established to enable even men of the modern skeptical age to believe. Contemporary belief, of course, will not necessarily involve the conviction that the crucified Jesus became personally alive again; rather, it will see the events of Jesus' ministry and death—especially as appropriated through that strange event called the "resurrection"—as the actual establishment of the kingdom of God (see Chapter 27, and below), the founding of a new community of love in which the purposes of God for human history are being realized and the anarchy of human history is being overcome through God's power and love. Perhaps this conception of the historical dependence of modern Christians on thought-forms now outgrown, however hard to accept, is implied in Paul's profound phrase, that it was only "when the proper time came, [that] God sent his Son" (Gal. 4:4 Goodspeed): in contrast with the first century, modern times would hardly be propitious for such a momentous event.

It will doubtless be objected that the interpretation of the resurrection I am proposing here is too subjectivistic to be theologically acceptable. For it implies that the resurrection was nothing but (a) a series of hallucinations (b) interpreted by faith as God's act, both dimensions having their locus in the disciples' minds. Moreover, the Bible does not portray the matter in this way at all (despite the current existentialist tendency to argue that it does). With the disciples everything rested on the conviction that it was *this same Jesus* whom they knew before who was alive again. If anyone had convinced them they suffered hallucinations, and Jesus himself had not in fact been raised from the dead, their faith would have been destroyed; for it was just this that convinced them that God had vindicated Jesus. "The two facts—he was known still and he was remembered—constitute together the miracle of the Resurrection; and neither is more important than the other."[31] On this view, if the

---

[31] John Knox, *The Early Church and the Coming Great Church* (New York: Abingdon, 1955), pp. 52-53.

faith is not delusory, there must be genuine continuity between the one who appeared and the one they had formerly known. To interpret the resurrection appearances as hallucinations appears to deny this objective continuity, thus destroying the meaning of the event and with it Christian faith.

There is no denying the weight of this criticism nor the fact that my treatment thus far has not adequately handled the point at issue. But is the historical continuity between Jesus of Nazareth and the appearances—in the precise form affirmed by the earliest Christians —the only, or even the most adequate, statement of the issue, or should that continuity be understood somewhat differently? I am not suggesting that the continuity between the historical Jesus and the resurrection appearances can be neglected or eliminated; it cannot without destroying Christian faith. But I am suggesting that there remains an important question as to what in fact is necessarily continuous here; and I will try to show that my interpretation of the matter, instead of eliminating that essential continuity, points more precisely to it.

According to the traditional view, the continuity was, so to speak, the personality of Jesus: it was the same Jesus they had known before who was now risen from the dead. However, it was recognized that he was also very different—he went through closed doors, he had a "spiritual body," and so on. Nevertheless, the man who had died was again alive. And therefore, all that he had formerly meant to the disciples—that the hopes and expectations of Judaism were at last to be fulfilled, that the kingdom of God was at hand and was already beginning to appear—all this which in their minds had died with him was now also again alive: the end-time was really here! Indeed, the disciples now had the best possible evidence of this, far more dramatic and convincing than the mere preaching of Jesus: the resurrection of the dead, which everyone knew was to happen at the end of history, had already begun! And they were direct witnesses of it. "Christ has been raised from the dead, the first fruits of those who have fallen asleep" (1 Cor. 15:20)! Surely, "it is the last hour" (1 John 2:18)!

The interpretation of the resurrection that I am here proposing

contends that it was really *what Jesus' resurrection signified* for the
disciples that was the crucial dimension of that event. That is, more
important than Jesus' being reawakened was that which was revealed
to the disciples through their belief: that God really *had* broken into
history through Jesus of Nazareth, and *still was* breaking into history
in the community of the church, that *God's presence in history in
Jesus of Nazareth was continuous with his presence subsequently,*
that Jesus' death—far from bringing to an end what had begun during his ministry—was instead the focal point of God's revelatory
and redemptive act. Something really new broke in then and still
lived—*and this new reality was historical fact.* They were new men,
and the community of love and forgiveness, of creativity and freedom, which they had known before in Jesus' presence was known
among them again when they gathered together. Doubtless the disciples became conscious of this continuing presence of God's redemptive act through the medium of their experiencing the reappearance
of the man Jesus in their midst, resulting, as it apparently did, in
the reestablishment of the community of love and forgiveness which
they had begun to know during his ministry.[32] But the theologically
important element in their new-found communal faith was their

[32] On this whole analysis compare H. N. Wieman's (a bit too speculative but
provocative) interpretation of the relation of the experience of Jesus' earthly ministry to
the resurrection appearances. During his ministry "Jesus engaged in intercommunication
with a little group of disciples with such depth and potency that the organization of their
several personalities was broken down and they were remade. They became new men,
and the thought and feeling of each got across to the others. It was not merely the
thought and feeling of Jesus that got across. That was not the most important thing.
The important thing was that the thought and feeling of the least and lowliest got across
to the others and the others to him. Not something handed down to them from Jesus
but something rising up out of their midst in creative power was the important thing.
It was not something Jesus did. It was something that happened when he was present
like a catalytic agent. . . . Something about this man Jesus broke the atomic exclusiveness
of those individuals so that they were deeply and freely receptive and responsive each to
the other. . . . When Jesus was crucified, his followers saw that he could never carry to
fulfilment the mission of the Jewish people as they conceived it. . . . They reached that
depth of despair which comes when all that seems to give hope to human existence is
seen to be an illusion. . . . After about the third day, however, when the numbness of
the shock had worn away, something happened. The life-transforming creativity previously
known only in fellowship with Jesus began again to work in the fellowship of the
disciples. It was risen from the dead. Since they had never experienced it except in
association with Jesus, it seemed to them that the man Jesus himself was actually
present, walking and talking with them. Some thought they saw him and touched him in
physical presence. But what rose from the dead was not the man Jesus; it was creative
power. It was the living God that works in time. It was the Second Person of the Trinity.
It was Christ the God, not Jesus the man" (*The Source of Human Good* [Chicago:
University of Chicago Press, 1946], pp. 39–40, 44).

consciousness of the *continuing activity of "the God and Father of . . . Jesus Christ"* (Rom. 15:6) *in their historical existence,* not the resuscitation of their former friend and leader.[33] It can hardly be questioned that they apprehended this theologically significant historical continuity through and by means of the series of hallucinations. Moreover, it would perhaps have been psychologically impossible for them to experience again and recognize the reality of God's forgiveness and love, which they had known first in the presence of the man Jesus, had they not believed him to be once again in their midst. Hence, both their hallucinations and their interpretation of them as the real presence of Jesus may well have been epistemological pre-conditions for the birth of Christian faith; and in God's providence these conditions were met.

But it does not follow that these historically relative necessities are relevant also to us, who, in the providence of God, live under radically different historical and epistemological conditions.[34] The theologically important fact both for the first Christians and for us, as we have been noting, was not that this *finite man* as such lives again, but that *God's act begun in him* was a *genuine historical act* which *still continues,* that the love, mercy, and forgiveness present in their midst with Jesus, and brought to a burning focus with his self-sacrificial death, was still present with them, and was thus becoming an effective force in human history; in this sense, as the biblical writers claimed, Christ himself was raised from the dead.[35] It is this continuity of God's act in the midst of finite historical reality, an act that is in fact working a genuine transformation of

---

[33] Thus Acts, for example, depicts virtually every important decision and action of the disciples as a movement of the Holy Spirit.

[34] Kant anticipated this suggestion that certain miraculous events, though no longer credible to us, may nonetheless have considerable historical significance: "it is wholly conformable to man's ordinary ways of thought, though not strictly necessary, for the historical introduction of [a religion based on the spirit and the truth] to be accompanied and, as it were, adorned by miracles. . . . [But] the true religion, which in its time needed to be introduced through such expedients, is now here, and from now on is able to maintain itself on rational grounds" (*Religion within the Limits of Reason Alone,* trans. T. Greene and H. Hudson [New York: Harper Torchbooks, 1934], p. 79).

[35] John Knox has especially emphasized the fact that the New Testament writers do not restrict the term "Christ" to the particular *person Jesus* (alive, crucified, risen), but also use it more broadly as the name of *God's act* through this Jesus, as well as for the *new community* that emerges in consequence of his ministry. "But what is Jesus Christ? . . . I believe, that the reality with which we are concerned appears under no fewer than three aspects: (1) as the event or closely knit series of events in and through which

human existence,[36] that is essential to Christian faith, without which
Christian faith would be destroyed; and this continuity is clearly
affirmed in the interpretation of the resurrection given in these pages.
*The question whether Jesus was alive again or not does not bear
directly on this issue.*[37] Therefore, the difference between the present
interpretation of the resurrection appearances and that found in the
Bible is not theologically important.[38]

God made Himself known; (2) as the person who was the center of that event or complex
of events; and (3) as the community which both came into existence with the event and
provided the locus of it. . . . The empirical reality, Jesus Christ, always involves all three;
but one or another category may be dominant at a given moment or in a given context. . . .
    "When Paul says, 'I live, yet not I, but Christ liveth in me' (Gal. 2:20), or 'My
desire is to depart and be with Christ' (Phil. 1:23)—in these statements he is clearly
speaking primarily of a person. . . .
    "But when Paul writes, 'In Christ God was reconciling the world unto himself'
(II Cor. 5:19), he is thinking primarily not of the person simply as such, but of the
event which happened around and in connection with that person. . . . His great statement,
just quoted, is not an answer to the question, 'Who was Jesus?' but to the question, 'What
was God doing in and through the event of which Jesus was the center?' . . . .
    "But when the same Apostle asserts, 'As in Adam all die, so in Christ shall all be
made alive' (I Cor. 15:22), he is making a somewhat different use again of the name.
'Christ' here stands for the new order of relationships between men and God and
among men, the new and divine community, which is pre-eminently heavenly and
eschatological but which in a real though partial sense has come into historical existence"
(*Jesus: Lord and Christ* [New York: Harper & Brothers, 1958], pp. 205–208).
    [36] It will be noted from this discussion that I am not resting my position on the
currently popular theological opinion that faith is rooted somehow directly and immediately in God's act and thus that there are no finite historical conditions or causes
through which it arises, that it is sheer miracle, unknown to and unknowable by the
mere historian. On the contrary, I would agree with the critics of this abstract and
docetic position that the biblical claim that this is Jesus of Nazareth again risen, is a
claim that, though faith arises ultimately through God's act, its immediate occasion is
always *an objective reality on the finite level* (in this case the resurrected lord). In
my interpretation I have argued that the finite objective historical reality correlative to
faith was not in fact the reawakened Jesus of Nazareth but *the new community of love
and forgiveness* (cf. Wieman, n. 32 above, and Knox, n. 35), recreated and recognized
under the impact of the resurrection appearances. Because of this actually present historical reality the disciples' interpretation of the hallucinations as in fact the very act of God
was not sheer subjective fancy; it was rooted in the experienced new quality of community, a quality they could attribute only to God's creativity, not to themselves. ("In
this is love, not that we loved God but that he loved us and sent his Son to be the
expiation for our sins" [1 John 4:10].) In support of this emphasis that the historical objectivity present in the resurrection was really the new community, note the frequent
suggestions that the resurrected one was made "known to them in the breaking of
bread" (Lk. 24:35)—i.e., in the midst of the experienced community in the present—
and that he "opened to [them] the scriptures" (24:32; cf. 24:45–47)—i.e., showed
them the true meaning of their communal history.
    [37] It does bear, of course, on the question of the specific character of the Christian
hope for man, and will have to be taken up again in that context (see below, Ch. 30).
    [38] Although it cannot be denied that the view I am taking here is different from that
of any of the biblical writers, my interpretation has not departed very far from Paul's view,

We may now return to the problem with which this consideration of the resurrection was begun. Why do Christians believe that God is uniquely present in Jesus Christ? The historico-theological answer, I have claimed, is "the resurrection of Jesus." That is, it is because an event occurred—comprehensible on the *human* level as a series of "appearances" or "hallucinations" creative of and in the context of a new community of love and forgiveness—through which the earliest disciples came to discern a new and deeper meaning in the life and death of Jesus: that here was the definitive manifestation of the unfailing love of almighty God toward man. "God shows his love for us in that while we were yet sinners Christ died for us" (Rom. 5:8). Thus was born a new awareness of the authentic meaning of human existence and a new hope for the future movement of human history; thus was born the church as the community in which that meaning was already experienced in foretaste and in which that hope would finally be realized; thus entered a new meaning and reality into the empirical historical process. Understood on the *theological* level, the resurrection was that event through which the real meaning of Jesus' career and death—and thus of all human history—broke into history.[39] That is, it was that event when God's

---

with which, it will be remembered, the analysis began. For Paul is so uninterested in the historical Jesus and so exclusively interested in the resurrected Christ as to make clear that for him there is a radical discontinuity between them, probably considerably greater than the one proposed here. The resurrected Christ is really the reigning sovereign love of God present to man, which broke into history with the crucifixion of Jesus and was confirmed in the resurrection appearances and the activity of the Holy Spirit in the church. But Paul has little more than this to say about the continuity between historical Jesus and resurrected Lord. *This* continuity is also affirmed in the present exposition. Moreover, I have insisted to a much greater extent than Paul on the importance (which of course he had never experienced) of the concrete presence of God's love and forgiveness in the historical love and forgiveness of Jesus of Nazareth in life and death (see Chs. 13 and 27 above). Thus, in these pages there is a greater emphasis on the continuity between historical Jesus and risen lord than in Paul, though this continuity is not expressed in terms of the continuation of the man Jesus, as Paul, perhaps, would wish to do.

39 Cf. Barth: "In contrast to everything which went before . . . the resurrection and ascension [were] the definitive and comprehensive, the decisive and unequivocal event of revelation. . . . What was to be revealed—the being of Jesus Christ as very God and very man . . . was indeed virtual and potential from the very beginning of His history and existence, but it was only in His death on the cross that it was actually and effectively accomplished and completed. . . . In the earlier sequence He was moving towards this fulfilment—but only moving towards it. How could that which had not yet been completed be revealed as completed? . . . The fulfilment comes in the passion. . . . The resurrection and ascension of Jesus Christ are the revelation which corresponds to *this*

real purposes for human history, which from the beginning he had
been working out in and through that history, came to the surface,
becoming visible to men; for it was the event through which it became
clear that Jesus' crucifixion was not simply the tragic death of another good man but was the definitive expression of God's being and
will. Bultmann rightly queries: "Can talk about the resurrection of
Christ be anything other than the expression of the cross' significance?"[40]

This discovery that ultimate reality was disclosed in the suffering
and death of Christ on the cross involved, as Nietzsche saw, a complete overturning of ordinary human conceptions of value.

> Modern men, with their obtuseness as regards all Christian
> nomenclature, have no longer the sense for the terribly superla-
> tive conception which was implied to an antique taste by the
> paradox of the formula, "God on the Cross." Hitherto there had
> never and nowhere been such boldness in inversion, nor anything
> at once so dreadful, questioning, and questionable as this for-
> mula: it promised a transvaluation of all ancient values.[41]

Man could now see for the first time that ultimate reality is not to
be understood simply in terms of the all-too-human conceptions of
worldly power, the ability to achieve what one wants regardless of
obstructions or handicaps thrown in the way. The cross could never
be made to symbolize that. On the contrary, in the cross were found
meekness and submission, nonresistance to evil, self-sacrifice: and
the resurrection meant that just this cross was the very revelation of
God's innermost nature and his mode of action with the free spirits
he had created in history. The resurrection was a vindication of
Jesus and his work, not in the sense that God now gave him power
to compel "every knee [to] . . . bow, in heaven and on earth and
under the earth" (Phil. 2:10); rather, it meant that precisely that

---

completion of His work, manifesting it as such, declaring its meaning and basis. There is
disclosed in them that which took place definitively and decisively in His death on the
cross . . ." (*Church Dogmatics*, IV, 2, pp. 140–141).

[40] "Neues Testament und Mythologie," in H. W. Bartsch, *Kerygma und Mythus*, I
(Hamburg: Evangelischer Verlag, 1951), 44.

[41] *Beyond Good and Evil* (Chicago: Regnery, n.d.), sec. 46.

vicarious suffering for others which brought Jesus to his cross *is* the ultimate reality in this universe before which every knee finally will bow—that is, that "God is love" (1 John 4:8,16), and that this love which he is "bears all things, . . . endures all things . . . never ends" (1 Cor. 13:7-8). John Oman has stated the matter well:

By many the doctrine of the Resurrection has been cherished chiefly for the reason that it seems to end [Jesus'] humility of appeal. He who humbled Himself was exalted. He who came as a country workman in mean garments, comes as the Son of Man with glory on the clouds of Heaven. What can that mean if not the close of the rule of meekness and the opening of the rule of might? . . . Thus the life of Christ becomes a temporary episode in God's dealing, and ceases to be an eternal revelation of His mind concerning what is truly coming from above with power. . . . The joyous spirit of His followers, so downcast before, shows that in some sense they took the Resurrection to mean that all power was given to their Lord in Heaven and in Earth, but it was because His method had been vindicated, and not because it had been changed. To Peter it meant that He was a man approved of God, His method, which seemed to be defeat, being shown to be God's way of victory. To Paul it declares Him to be the Son of God with power according to the spirit of holiness, the spirit He manifested in meekness and lowliness. For both the Resurrection merely made plain the meaning of the life and death of Jesus, that the moral order of love is the will of God, the last, the Divinest issue of all experience, the natural, the all-prevailing, the irresistable dominion, such as is given to no overriding might; and it called them to like service in the assurance of like victory, not because God had substituted power for love, but because He had shown them that love in the end alone is power.[42]

The resurrection, thus, was not primarily an odd physical event that happened two thousand years ago; there have been other alleged reawakenings from the dead without these consequences. The resurrection was preeminently an event in the *history of meaning*; indeed,

[42] *Grace and Personality* (London: Fontana Library, 1917), pp. 217f.

it was the indispensable conclusion to the central event in that history. For it was the event through which the real meaning of human existence first became sharp and clear and certain to men, thus becoming the center of a human tradition and an effective power within history. In consequence of this transformation of the actually experienced meaning of human life, and this creation of a new community living out of this meaning and in hope of its consummation, for Christians the "resurrection of Jesus" is an event of unparalleled importance. Because of this event and all it involves, Christ—the ultimate reality manifest in and through the event—is acknowledged by Christians to be Lord of all creation. Questions about the physical and psychological dimensions of the resurrection-event pale finally into insignificance when one sees its centrality in the history of human meaning and thus its significance for the meaning of all existence.[43]

[43] To regard the resurrection as in this way primarily an event in the history of meaning rather than in the history of physical fact does not involve a final victory for the docetic heresy, as some might suppose. This can be clearly seen with the help of an illustration. Suppose I become estranged from a friend, but do not really understand what has happened between us. We grow apart and eventually have nothing to do with each other. Then, some years later, I receive a letter from a mutual friend that explains how this alienation between my friend and myself has developed. This throws the "fact" of the alienation into an entirely new light, and so now my friend and I become reconciled. Now it is clear that the receipt of this letter can be regarded as the most important event in the history between me and my friend. But its importance is not in its own right, but rather because it illuminates the *actual historical facts* about our previous estrangement, i.e., the latter bears the real *meaning* (and thus communicates the real *facts*) of the earlier historical event. It has, therefore, a twofold reference to historical fact: (a) it is itself an event (receipt of paper with writing on it); (b) it refers to an earlier event (of estrangement). Its importance is of course (b), not (a). That is, the mode of communication is not important (e.g., it could just as well have been a dream), the matter is. Nonetheless, the receipt of the letter is itself a real event, and it refers to another real event.

Similarly with the resurrection. Its importance is not its own character (a), but the historical event to which it refers (b): the real meaning (i.e., the real facts) of Jesus' life and death. Nonetheless, it is genuinely historical itself and its referent is actual history; this is, then, not docetism, nor simply a concern with "meaning" apart from "facts." However, the "facts" here are the facts about Jesus, not the facts about a resuscitated body, etc., just as in the letter the facts are about the alienation, not about paper and ink. Thus, the contention that it is theologically unimportant whether the resurrection was a *body* or a *hallucination* does not involve docetism.

This distinguishing of the character of the resurrection event (as having its significance in that to which it refers) from, e.g., the crucifixion (which has its significance in its own specific character) is justified by the New Testament itself. For it is made clear there that the resurrection was *not* a public event (like the crucifixion) accessible to all, but a private event known only to those on the "inside." This is precisely the character of all events that have their meaning primarily in their reference to some other event (as the above example of the receipt of the letter illustrates).

29 / The Christ-Event

III. The Community of

Love and Freedom

In the discussion of the Christ-event thus far[1] I have attempted to sketch an interpretation which would be in accord with contemporary understanding of the historical facts about Jesus and the beginnings of Christian faith, as well as provide a theological conception of God's actual establishment of his kingdom in and through those historical events. This historical act of God has had three great moments, none of which is dispensable, and these remain the foundations of Christian existence. The first, roughly corresponding to the ministry of Jesus and culminating in his death, was the actual and effective breaking into history of the divine action, will, and life through human action; the second, making possible apprehension of the true significance of Jesus' life and death, was his "resurrection"; the third was the historical reception of these acts of God by a body of believers whose lives were thereby transformed —that is, the establishment of the church, and its continuance through the long history of Christian faith. All three moments were (and are) essential to the historical establishment of God's kingdom. Without the first there would be no normative point or standard in history

[1] One should include as part of or relevant to this discussion much of the material on revelation in the Introduction, and on "God the Son" in Pt. I, as well as the previous three chapters. The concluding Ch. 33 also is largely christological.

to serve as the definition and measure of authentic human existence; there would be nothing concrete and historically actual to which men could respond when and as they sought to live in response to God's action toward them. Without the second, no one would have perceived the cross, and received it in faith, as having such revelatory and normative significance. Without the third, no men's lives, in their consciousness and freedom, would actually be ordered and reordered according to God's will, and God's act would have had no objective effects in history; that is to say, it would not have been a genuine *act* at all, and speaking about "what God has done for man" would be mockery. In discussing the Christ-event thus far we have attended for the most part to the problems of conceiving God's atoning act (Chapter 27) and understanding the historical birth of faith with the resurrection-event (Chapter 28). We must turn now to the new empirico-historical life itself, given its paradigmatic form by Jesus' life and death, and eventuating in the establishment of a new community of freedom and faith as the act of God initiated in and through Jesus moved beyond him into a community of men which was to become its bearer in history. Discussion of the Christ-event can come to completion only as we succeed in characterizing the new human existence in the community which was (and still is) its historical culmination and consequence.

We move in analysis here from a consideration of the *past* to the *present*. This does not mean we are now going to shift from the first century to the twentieth. For the present with which we are here concerned had its beginning already in the first century and will continue, presumably, considerably beyond our time. This is the present which was created and informed by the acts of God culminating in the death and resurrection of Christ. As a historical being, man always lives *out of* a specific past which has given his existence the particular shape it has and which provides him with the symbolical structures of meaning in terms of which he interprets his existence (see above, Chapter 2) and *toward* a future for which he hopes and works (see Chapters 22 and 30). Historicity is characterized precisely by this dynamic movement from a concrete past into this present, and from this present into that (expected) future. A Christian would scarcely want to deny the momentous importance of many of the events of the past 2000 years; but the decisive past event, in the Christian view, which reoriented all human existence and in terms of which the meaning of all human life must henceforth be interpreted, was the Christ-event. New actualities and new possibilities entered into the human situation with that event, and, accordingly, human existence now has a different structure than previously.[2] It must be admitted, of course, that great historical event-processes like the merging of Hebraic and Hellenic cultures, the Renaissance, the rise of modern science, the growth of technologically oriented society, the entrance into the atomic age, and the like, have each had decisive impact on the present within which we live. History has not been standing still since Christ; and we are very much in need of a theological analysis and interpretation of this movement which could be put alongside the more usual humanistic interpretations. However, no matter what weight one might give to these more recent occurrences, they have all taken place *after* God's definitive historical act, and *before* the consummation of his historical work. Thus, from a theological point of view they are to be understood as developments within what is fundamentally the same present historical era. The *foundational* structure of our present existence, that is to say, was formed by the events of salvation-history, though doubtless important superstructural modifications and qualifications have been effected by these other events.

It should perhaps be noted here that this particular ranking of past event-processes represents a decision of faith. It would also be possible to see the present as shaped by a past defined primarily in terms of the growth of science, or democracy, or socialism, etc., and moving toward a future as grasped and anticipated from these various perspectives. Each of these would lead to a different periodization of history into past, present, and future, as well as to a different interpretation of the foundational structure of existence in the pres-

---

2 "The revelation of God in Christ . . . became concrete, dynamic, formative, and impelling within the human structure and in a living community. This was a world event as truly as the atomic bomb. . . . As a novel advance within the human structure, this emergent life of grace and redemptive power has effected *a permanent revolution*. . . . The culture of the West has never been the same since its innovation" (B. E. Meland, *Faith and Culture* [New York: Oxford University Press, 1953], p. 215).

ent. Any such analysis, of course, involves abstraction and even over-simplification: many events and processes of history, and many levels and dimensions of structure, must be overlooked or eliminated in order to enable that which is thought fundamental to stand out clearly for all to see. The dynamic movement of history is much more complex than any breakdown into three stages of past, present, and future could possibly suggest. And yet, the only way for conscious beings living in this dynamic process to orient themselves is by reference to points in past and future which make it possible to apprehend something of the present direction of movement. Hence, an analysis of the present structure of existence with reference to the events of salvation-history and the eschatological hopes of faith is essential. In the next chapter we shall complete this skeletal picture by an explicit consideration of the third point of reference for a historical being, the future, as illuminated by certain critical eschatological doctrines.

The most comprehensive term with which to characterize the present existence of man made possible through God's act in Christ is *freedom*. "For freedom Christ has set us free," declared Paul in a climactic sentence, "stand fast therefore, and do not submit again to a yoke of slavery" (Gal. 5:1). In an earlier chapter it was suggested that men and events in their historical connectedness and mutual determination of each other could be best understood if man were defined as the *historical* being, the one who is not only made by history but who himself makes history. A piece of human existence never is an isolated atom but always has intrinsic connections with men and events both preceding and succeeding it; it is a phase of historical process. But each piece of human existence has an internal character or nature as well as connections to that beyond it. It is to this that one points when he speaks of man's "freedom." Human existence seen as a *process* of development is history; human existence seen as *moments* of historical process is freedom. Either perspective taken by itself would give a misleading view of man. For precisely that which distinguishes historical processes from organic developments or mechanical movements is the inner working of freedom and purpose; without freedom there could be no history.[3] Conversely, the only matrix within which free decision and purposive action can occur, so far as we know, is (human) history, and their exercise in turn eventuates in further history. Thus, to say, "Christ has set men free," is to declare that he has opened up the inner condition of man's historicity, making it possible for the corruption and damming up of human history to be cut away so it can once more move forward toward the goal which God originally posited for it, and man can realize his potentialities.

We have already seen that freedom and pre-determination are not mutually contradictory as often supposed but reciprocally presuppose each other in the structure of historical process (pp. 336ff.). Each is a distinct dimension of man's power to bind time, to shape the future. Indeed by freedom we mean precisely this power of man to plot his own course in some measure. It would take us too far afield here to develop a metaphysical argument proving that man has "free will." Freedom is one of a number of words, such as "intention," "action," "purpose," etc.[4] without which it is doubtful we could carry on ordinary discourse about ourselves and our behavior; and that fact will have to serve as sufficient justification for its introduction here. We speak of *deciding* to do this or that, of its being our *intention* or *purpose* to perform some task or accomplish some objective in the future. It would be virtually impossible to conceive of human existence or to conduct the ordinary business of life without some conception of man's power or ability to make plans and carry them through, to determine his own course of action. In contrast with "imprisonment" or "restraint" or "inhibition," *freedom* is the situation which obtains when men have the power to decide and act without unusual or frustrating conditions which cancel or significantly reduce their effectiveness.[5] Free behavior is thus not some sort of uncaused or spontaneous behavior: that would be as little

---

[3] "There would be no history without freedom. It is the metaphysical basis of history" (N. Berdyaev, *The Meaning of History* [London: Geoffrey Bles, 1936], p. 58).

[4] For illuminating analyses of these words dealing with personal action, see Stuart Hampshire, *Thought and Action* (New York: Viking Press, 1960), and A. I. Melden, *Free Action* (London: Routledge & Kegan Paul, 1961).

[5] Cf. J. L. Austin, *Philosophical Papers* (London: Oxford University Press, 1961), p. 128.

under one's deliberate control as motions mechanically determined. It is rather that which one *does*, and which he does deliberately and purposefully to achieve some end which he had previously posited.

When I say that freedom in this sense is the inner condition of (human) history, I am considering history as that complex network of action, in which men are pursuing goals and objectives. Doubtless history includes many other factors also, but that which most decisively distinguishes historical from organic or other natural processes is the intentional or purposeful action of men which is everywhere effective, positing objectives, creating culture, effecting social change. Any historian knows, of course, that there are unforeseen events and unobserved contingencies that sometimes change the course of history, and any psychologist knows there are unconscious processes and hidden desires which affect and sometimes seem to determine the conscious and deliberate activity of men. Indeed, to some these factors have seemed so powerful that they thought it necessary to regard men as really pawns in the hands of other powers, man's alleged self-determination being illusory. But such interpretations go too far. For they obliterate the distinction between historical and other processes, the distinction between action and other forms of behavior, and thus they explain away their subject matter rather than explain it. Human history is a process in which deliberate and purposive action as well as other powers and forces are effective; and human decision is affected by conscious deliberation as well as secret drives and unconscious impulses.

Thus, in his action and history man is both free and unfree, and sometimes (as seen in hindsight) he is most unfree just in those moments when he thought himself powerful and free. The maniacal drive for and exercise of power characteristic of a Hitler is at once the expression of uncontrollable psychological and sociological forces and an instrument which destroys wholesale the freedom of both individuals and communities, whatever Hitler himself may have supposed about his own self-determination. We noticed earlier (Chapter 25) that the problem of man's historical existence—sin—is his enslavement to powers and institutions and practices which control and ultimately work to destroy him, rather than enable him to exercise and increase his freedom, thus genuinely realizing himself as the historical being. Man's most fundamental problem is thus to gain the conditions of true freedom. If this could be achieved, man would come into his own. For then he could build the good society and the good life and find genuine fulfilment. What, then, makes possible freedom, and how can man become free?

"For freedom Christ has set us free; stand fast therefore, and do not submit again to a yoke of slavery" (Gal. 5:1). It is the Christian claim that man's true freedom becomes a live possibility through Christ. How is this to be understood? Let us observe first that the contrast underlying the Pauline statement is not that of freedom vs. mechanical determinism but rather freedom vs. slavery. Man has become enslaved; Christ sets him free. Man has been inhibited or prevented from coming into his own; Christ breaks the bonds. There is no question here of Christ creating man's freedom in some metaphysical sense: man as the historical being has whatever abstract or metaphysical freedom is required for him to make history. But in his history man's freedom has become restricted and man himself enslaved; and he needs a release that will make it possible to exercise again his history-making power. We need not dwell here again on the cumulative corruption that has entered the historical process through man's increasing turning away from God, turning history into a cauldron of destructive powers. Man's potentially suicidal enslavement is evident for all to see. In what way, now, has the Christ-event turned this tide?

The treatment, of course, must be appropriate to the disease. If man's problem has been (a) that he has turned away from God's lordship to anthropocentric autonomy, and—since he is finite and thus not capable of being fully his own master—(b) this has transformed his existence into anxiety, so that (c) he readily becomes enslaved to a variety of demons of his own creation; then clearly the remedy must consist in restoring God's proper lordship over human existence. It is important that we underline the word *proper* here. Not just any and every kind of divine sovereignty would in fact return to man his freedom,[6] his power of real self-determination in the

[6] Luther, for example, in his essay on *The Bondage of the Will* misleadingly suggested that God's sovereignty is exercised in the same way as the devil's, and it is simply a matter of being enslaved to one or the other. E.g.: "So man's will is like a beast stand-

historical process. Certainly the traditional picture of God as the king who gives direct orders or commandments which men then are to obey is at best a crude conception of the proper relationship. This image suggests too easily a despot concerned only to realize his own desires, utilizing his subjects as mere instruments for his objectives. If we qualify the image to that of the "benevolent despot," we will be moving a bit closer; but we have also learned in our time something of the insidious effects of paternalism, which prevents men from exercising their full freedom and responsibilities and keeps them perennial children. The New Testament symbol "father" is by far the best for expressing that aspect of the divine lordship over human freedom with which we are here concerned. The advantage of this image is that it combines the notion of the authority and independent purpose proper to God's sovereignty with an emphasis on his genuine concern for the well-being and independent freedom of man. A true father's objective is to enable his child to become an independent and self-reliant mature human being who can make his own decisions with responsibility and concern for others, and his authority over the child is exercised precisely with that end in view. The process through which this is achieved—when it is achieved—involves the most delicate and sensitive treatment of the growing child, sensing just when he can be given a bit more rope and thereby learn to exercise his freedom, when to draw the reins tighter to protect him from dangers and difficulties of which he is unaware. Even the best human father fails many times in this endeavor due to ignorance, impatience, and even malice; and thus such freedom as the child acquires is knotted and obstructed with compulsions and inhibitions of various sorts. Of course this image has its dangers and distortions too: on the one hand, there is the tyrannical authoritarian father; on the other, the weak, sentimental purposeless father, ruled by his own child. The proper conception of God's lordship must combine independent purposefulness for the universe and man with loving concern for creation, expressed in the intention and capacity to give man freedom.

It is now possible to grasp a bit better, perhaps, the force of the

---

ing between two riders. If God rides, it wills and goes where God wills. . . . If Satan rides, it wills and goes where Satan wills" (Pt. II, viii).

Christian claim that man's difficulties arose out of his turning away from God. The only context we know in which responsible and free selves can emerge and grow to maturity is the human family (or some similarly intimate interpersonal situation). "Wolf children" or other isolated children never become speaking and thinking beings, capable of free and responsible decision. Moreover, a mere environment of persons is not enough: the child needs to experience the love and concern of his parents, needs to know he can rely on them to care for his needs, forgive his failures, correct his mistakes. In short, the home must provide the kind of emotional security that encourages the child to exercise his own initiative at levels of which he is capable and that supports the child in his efforts to become a mature self. Warped and stunted antisocial selves are the consequence, in considerable measure, of failure in the home to provide the context of love and purposeful order needed by the growing child. No child can create himself into a free human being; he can emerge as such only within the proper context. Freedom is not, then, a quality belonging to the atomic individual, simply to be generated from within as the individual matures. It is more a response evoked within the appropriate interpersonal context than an inherent quality. Its creation and nourishment requires the presence and love of a "thou" quite as much as the independence and agency of the "I." Freedom is relationship, not autonomy. It is no accident that the word "freedom" comes from the same root as "friend," a root meaning "to love."

If this quasi-psychological account of the emergence and maturation of free and responsible selfhood is at all correct, we are in a better position to understand the significance of the Christian claim that man's freedom must have as its context God's purposes and love. The development of free selfhood within human history as a whole is here being interpreted by analogy with the growth of the individual self. Just as in the individual man freedom is no mere spontaneous eruption from within but emerges in interpersonal relationships, so with the species man freedom should not be thought of as something that simply developed out of man's animal nature, a product of evolving *homo sapiens* in relation to a totally impersonal environment; here too it is to be understood as a responsive emergent within an interpersonal situation. The early millennia of human history were the childhood of the race when under the loving care of God humanity was gradually being evoked from man's prior animality. Slowly, under God's fatherly tutelage man emerged as the historical being.

> I led them with cords of compassion,
>   with the bands of love,
> and I became to them as one
>   who eases the yoke on their jaws,
>   and I bent down to them and fed them. . . .
> I took them up in my arms;
>   but they did not know that I healed them.
>   HOSEA 11:4,3

Man's freedom as a historical being, then, as one who is able in some measure to determine his own course in history, to shape his own destiny, has its source and continuing sustenance in interpersonal relation to God. A delicate and sensitive reciprocity between mankind and Father God is just as requisite here for the emergence of true freedom and responsibility as between child and human parent; and serious upsetting of the balance or disordering of the relation results in stunted growth, disorder, bondage.

This inner connection between divine lordship and human freedom is the presupposition for understanding God's act in Christ, to which we now return. The fall and man's subsequently cumulating historical bondage, like the child's rebellion against parental authority, may have seemed at first to lead to a desirable autonomy in which man was his own master. But such autonomy was spurious freedom. As with the undisciplined child who falls into habits which enslave him and can ultimately destroy the very possibility of ordering his life, so man's supposed autonomy called forth historical powers and patterns which he cannot control and which may ultimately wipe him off the earth. In both cases the parental context of love and purposeful order must somehow be maintained despite the disruption and disorder effected by the rebel. If that can be done, the wounds may be healed, the process of maturation into freedom can be resumed, and man may gradually "come of age" (Bonhoeffer) as the free and responsible agent God intended him to be. The Christ-event is God's decisive act directed toward reorienting man's autonomy into genuine freedom.

I shall not rehearse here again the account of God's historical preparation for this event (see above, Chapters 19 and 26 for brief outlines). It was necessary for God to establish within mankind an awareness of and responsiveness to not only his lordship *per se* over the world and man (this he began to achieve in the history of Israel); he also had to show mankind that his was a lordship of love, not tyranny, that he was working to establish men's freedom, not merely to break their autonomy. That is, he had to win back the hearts of rebellious men. This could hardly be accomplished through a merely abstract or intellectual change in men's *beliefs* about God; the problems of disorder in selves and communities penetrate far below the levels of conscious awareness and control. It was necessary for the divine parent to establish within human existence and history a "family" or "home," as it were, which could provide the proper context of security and love essential for the remaking of rebellious mankind; it was necessary to provide a situation of acceptance[7] and freedom where even the guiltiest could find peace and a renewed confidence and trust in the Lord of the world; it was necessary to establish a universal community in which the walls and bounds separating men from each other would be cancelled and the love which makes possible both friendship and freedom would become a power of increasing effect within history. The only way to reverse the flow of history toward increasing autonomy and self-destruction was to set forces loose in that same history working toward community and genuine freedom. The events of atonement and resurrection as appropriated by the earliest Christians eventuated in the establishment within history of a new and (potentially) universal community of love. The founding of the Christian community was in this way the

---

[7] Cf. Paul Tillich's interpretation of justification by faith as acceptance (*Systematic Theology*, II [Chicago: University of Chicago Press, 1957], 177ff.; *The Shaking of the Foundations* [New York: Charles Scribner's, 1952], Ch. 19).

culmination of the Christ-event[8] and the beginning of the reversal of those historical powers enslaving and threatening to destroy man.

The three sub-events—atonement, resurrection, establishment of the new community—were each indispensable to the historical effectiveness of God's act. The atonement, as we have seen, was the event in which the actual at-one-ment of God and man within the historical order occurred—that is, it was the event in which God's transcendent purposes and activity successfully entered the historical order as an effective force. The long preparation through Hebrew history in which God was gradually making himself known and making his will effective within history culminated in the ministry, and especially the death,[9] of Christ, where in Jesus' self-sacrifice his will was done with decisive effect. Jesus' act of self-giving could become the definitive symbol—and thus the decisive historical vehicle—of God's nature and will because God himself "is love" (1 John 4:8); and love is able to manifest itself definitively as such only through self-sacrifice for the beloved. But all this would have been to no avail if the disciples had apprehended Jesus' passion as merely the death of the man who was their friend and leader. It had to be appropriated as symbolic of and the vehicle of God's own attitude and act, as the movement of God himself toward man in love and mercy and forgiveness.

---

[8] "It is this reality of the *koinonia*, whatever the word for it may be, which denotes the concrete result of God's specifically purposed activity in the world in Jesus Christ" (Paul Lehmann, *Ethics in a Christian Context* [New York: Harper & Row, 1963], p. 47).

[9] Van Harvey, in his study of the way Christian faith is founded on historical knowledge, has pointed out that the historical image of Jesus, so far as we are able to recover it reliably, involves three interrelated elements: "the content and pattern of his teaching and preaching, the form of his actions, and his crucifixion. These three motifs reinforce and condition one another. The teaching provides the context for interpreting his actions, and his actions are symbolic exemplifications of the teachings. Both of them acquire a peculiar power by virtue of the crucifixion. So much is this the case that the crucifixion can itself become a selective emblem representing the entire ministry" (*The Historian and the Believer* [New York: Macmillan, 1966], p. 270). Cf. also Karl Barth: "Now, the life of Christ is His oboedientia passiva, His death on the Cross. It is completely and solely and exclusively His death on the Cross. . . . Neither the personality of Jesus, nor the 'Christ idea', nor the Sermon on the Mount, nor His miracles of healing, nor His trust in God, nor His love of His brethren, nor His demand for repentance, nor His message of forgiveness, nor His attack on tradition, nor His call to poverty and discipleship; neither the implications of His Gospel for social life or for the life of the individual, nor the eschatological or the immediate aspects of His teaching concerning the Kingdom of God—none of these things exist in their own right. Everything shines in the light of His death, and is illuminated by it" (*The Epistle to the Romans* [London: Oxford University Press, 1933], p. 159).

Precisely this, of course, was made possible, as we have seen, through the event after Jesus' death which is traditionally referred to as his resurrection.

For when "God raised up" this Jesus (Acts 2:32) he thereby designated him "Son of God in power" (Rom. 1:4; cf. Acts 13:33, etc.)—that is, the special agent of his own divine action, and Jesus' passion and death were seen as the manifestation of God's inner intention. So it became possible to say, with Paul, that "God shows his love for us in that while we were yet sinners Christ died for us" (Rom. 5:8), or with John, that "God so loved the world that he gave his only Son . . . that the world might be saved through him" (John 3:16–17). Through the resurrection, the ministry and death of Jesus were grasped as saving historical actions of God himself,[10] bringing to man a veritable new existence.

But for this existence truly to become man's, it had to be appropriated and lived. The establishment of the new community was thus the indispensable conclusion to God's act of atonement. In this community life was governed by, and was a manifestation of, the same spirit expressed in Jesus' death and resurrection (Rom. 8:11);[11] and therefore participants in this community became, like Jesus, sons and heirs of God himself (8:14–17). This was true, of course, only "provided we suffer with him" (8:17), that is, only insofar as the actual existence of the community manifested the form of suffering and service evident in Jesus' passion. Jesus' death was thus at once the source and definition of the new life, and its norm and measure as well.[12] The

---

[10] "The faith of the days after Easter knows itself to be nothing else but the right understanding of the Jesus of the days before Easter" (Gerhard Ebeling, *Word and Faith* [London: SCM Press, 1960], p. 302).

[11] "The Body of Christ is Christ himself; the Church is Christ as he is present with us and meets us here on earth after his resurrection" (Anders Nygren, *Christ and his Church* [Philadelphia: Westminster Press, 1956], p. 10).

[12] In this context we can understand something of why the church came to declare that Christ was "sinless." As the one through whom sin was conquered, as well as the one whose action was taken as the very norm for human life, how else should he be regarded? The concept of sinlessness, however, is a very ambiguous one, subject to serious misunderstandings. It seems to suggest, for example, that Jesus was a "perfect" man in some empirical or observable sense. But according to the record Jesus did not, e.g., in a moralistic way, refrain from all peccadillos or always hold his temper (cf. cleansing of the temple, Mk. 11:15ff.), nor did he always speak kindly and without sarcasm (cf. the denunciation of the Pharisees, Mt. 23). Neither was he perfect in more existentialist terms: never anxious or worried about himself or his fate (cf. the Gethsemane scene,

very "mind" of Christ, manifest in his "taking the form of a servant"
and humbling "himself . . . unto . . . death on a cross," was to become
the mind and inform the life of Christians (Phil. 2:5–8). ". . . if
God so loved us . . . [that he] sent his Son to be the expiation for our
sins . . . , we also ought to love one another" (1 John 4:11, 10). Indeed, the manifestation of this new life of love and service was the
mark or criterion of God's historical presence and action. ". . . he
who abides in love abides in God, and God abides in him. . . . [But]
if any one says, 'I love God,' and hates his brother, he is a liar; for he

---

Mk. 14:32ff.), never tempted—and thus never tending—to seek fulfilment of his own
desires instead of God's (cf. the temptation stories, Mt. 4:1ff., Lk. 4:1ff.; and the
Gethsemane scene), never so frustrated and despairing as to doubt whether God was
with him at all (cf. Mark's report of the last word uttered from the cross, "My God,
my God, why hast thou forsaken me?" 15:34). "Judged by the record of what He
did and omitted to do, His sinlessness can be as easily denied as ours can, more easily,
in fact, than can the sinlessness of those good and pure and pious people who move
about in our midst. And, indeed, His matter-of-fact contemporaries—who did not know
what we think(!) we know—quite openly denied it" (Karl Barth, *Epistle to the Romans*,
p. 279).

A more important theological difficulty with the notion that Jesus was "sinless" is its
apparent implication that he was really a different sort of being from other men, one who
did not suffer all the difficulties of historical existence—for is sin not the very epitome
of man's problems? The crucial passages in Hebrews unfortunately lend themselves to
just such an interpretation: on the one hand the writer wishes to maintain (rightly)
that Jesus was "made like his brethren in every respect" (2:17), "one who in every
respect has been tempted as we are" (4:15); on the other, he finds it necessary to qualify
this full humanity of Jesus by declaring he was all this "yet without sinning" (4:15). It
is clear that the writer is seeking to maintain two points: (a) that Christ was *like other
men*, yet (b) that he is the one *in whom sin is overcome*. Obviously, if man's problem
is really separation from God, the latter is not possible unless the former is also true;
for in that case the separation from God would not be overcome in its actual locus, namely,
in the concrete empirical human history in which men live. Insofar, then, as the formula
"sinlessness of Christ" suggests that Jesus did *not* participate in the actual temptations,
frustrations, and misery of human existence, it borders on the docetic heresy and undercuts
the very salvation it seeks to proclaim.

In light of these considerations, Paul's formulation of the matter is more satisfactory
than that of Hebrews, for it is not so easily subject to docetic misinterpretation. Paul
does not hesitate to say that though Christ "knew no sin," he was made "to be sin . . .
so that in him we might become the righteousness of God" (2 Cor. 5:21). That is (whatever this difficult passage might mean in detail), Paul is maintaining that Christ
definitely participated in sinful humanity. To deny this, or to suggest he was somehow
not really involved in human sinfulness, would be to deny that the historico-ontological
gulf created by man's sinful rebellion was overcome through the Christ-event.

It is this fact that in Christ the chasm between man and God is really bridged
even in the terrifying depths of despair, and the power of sin as the ultimate breaking
away from God is thus in fact—whatever may be the appearances—broken, that the traditional doctrine of the sinlessness of Christ (somewhat inaccurately) designates. But it
formulates this insight too much in static terms, as though the victory over sin were a
state of Christ's being ("sinlessness") rather than a climactic event. This is because the
older theology tended to see Jesus more as a structure (nature) in which sin was simply

who does not love his brother whom he has seen, cannot love God whom he has not seen" (4:16, 20).[13] Here, then, in a communal existence ordered by God's love and service to one's fellows, true freedom—authentic human existence—was to be found. The new order of life experienced here represented such a profound transformation of what these early Christians had known before, that they found it necessary to characterize it with such images as "new creation" (2 Cor. 5:17), and "rebirth" (John 3:3; 1 Pet. 1:3, 23, etc.), suggesting that the most appropriate analogies to this transformation were the original creation and the genesis of the self. Here was fulfilment for human existence, authentic and abundant life (John 10:10).

We can summarize what is involved here by reference to a more traditional doctrinal distinction, that between justification and sanctification. According to a frequently affirmed protestant position,[14] the sinner is justified—that is, pronounced righteous—by God because of and in the work accomplished by the death of Christ. This is an act of God's forgiveness performed in a certain sense independently

---

not present than as the climax of *God's developing act* overcoming sin. Or, to make the same point from the other side, since Jesus was seen as eternal son of God—and thus just as much God's son in life and death as in resurrection—he must necessarily have had all the qualities of God's son (including "sinlessness" or unity with God) throughout his life. As we have noted above, this static or structural thinking raises serious problems. But these are bypassed with the more dynamic view developed in the present volume; for the focus here is not on a supposedly unchanging man Jesus but on the unfolding of God's act of salvation, which comes to its climax in the crucifixion/resurrection of the man Jesus. Since it is only here at the end of Jesus' life that sin is finally overcome, it is not necessary to develop a doctrine of "sinlessness" as a perpetual characteristic of Jesus; the contention that the power of sin is broken at this climactic point is sufficient. Thus, though the emphasis of the older theology on Jesus' "sinlessness" is understandable, this conception is no longer necessary for a dynamic or historicistic view of salvation.

13 Cf. Paul: "But I say, walk by the Spirit, and do not gratify the desires of the flesh. . . . Now the works of the flesh are plain: immorality, impurity, licentiousness, idolatry, sorcery, enmity, strife, jealousy, anger, selfishness, dissension, party spirit, envy, drunkenness, carousing, and the like. . . . But the fruit of the Spirit is love, joy, peace, patience, kindness, goodness, faithfulness, gentleness, self-control. . . . And those who belong to Christ Jesus have crucified the flesh with its passions and desires" (Gal. 5:16–24).

14 For discussion see, e.g., Luther, *Freedom of the Christian Man, Lectures on Galatians;* Calvin, *Institutes,* Bk. III, Chs. 11–18; Ritschl, *Justification and Reconciliation* (Edinburgh: T. & T. Clark, 1900), Chs. 7–8. The position developed in the text, which denies the propriety of the sharp distinction between justification and sanctification characteristic of the main-line reformers, has Anabaptist roots (cf. G. H. Williams, "Sanctification in the Testimony of Several So-called *Schwärmer,*" *Mennonite Quarterly Review* [1968], 42:5–25).

of any actual change in man or history. Though one is unrighteous
and sinful, God pronounces him just: despite his unacceptability, God
accepts him.[15] No prior work or achievement on man's part is required; indeed, it would be impossible to perform a work adequate to
justify him in the eyes of God. Out of his mercy alone, God forgives
and enables man to stand. God's act of justification, thus, is really
God's act of salvation. Sanctification, the actual transformation of
the sinner, is a process that follows along behind, as in gratitude to
God for his wondrous grace man responds increasingly in obedience
and love.

According to the analysis developed here, this view of the matter
is abstract and misleading. We can see the abstraction both on the
strictly doctrinal level and on the more existential level as well. To
begin with the latter: if God's act of justification were *wholly* independent of any human consequences or effects, an act that takes
place entirely in heaven, as it were, then men could not even know
of it; for knowledge involves an alteration of man's consciousness, and
this in turn would involve an alteration in man's action and being.
If men are able to speak of God's act of justification at all, it already
is having certain effects within the human cultural sphere: certain
patterns of speech—and doubtless other behavior as well—are being
altered; men are beginning to appropriate the meaning of their existence, and specifically their guilt and sin, in different ways; and thus
the transformation of human existence—that is sanctification—is
already under way. A doctrine of justification which makes it totally
God's act, involving no kind of human responsiveness, cannot even
be stated in a logically consistent way and is thus, in the strict sense of
the word, meaningless. It is, therefore, spurious and misleading
abstraction to attempt to separate justification entirely from sanctification, as though these were two independent acts of God not presupposing each other. At the very best, these concepts are analytical
abstractions from God's one act of salvation by means of which we
focus our attention first on its beginnings within the divine being,
beginnings entirely independent of man's response (justification),
and then on its external expression and completion as it works trans-

---

15 Tillich, "You Are Accepted," in *Shaking of the Foundations*, pp. 153-163.

formative effects in human existence (sanctification). But if it is this distinction that is indicated by these terms, it would probably be clearer to utilize the ordinary language of intention and action. The beginnings of God's movement toward man lie in his *intention*, that is, in the spontaneous movement of his personal inwardness or transcendence which is—if God be God—quite independent of human stimulus or empowering. But intention is nothing if it is not the beginning of action; hence, only as God begins effectively to free actual historical men from the enslaving powers to which they have become subjected, transforming them once again into his obedient children (sanctification), is his action of salvation occurring. To speak of God's justification of man (intention) as though it were a separate act independent of his sanctification of man (his transformative action) is false abstraction.

When we are rid of the abstractness resulting from artificial separation and hypostatization of justification and sanctification, certain dilemmas dissolve. There is, for example, the ambiguity, already present in the protestant slogan "justification by faith." Does this mean one must *believe* in God's justifying act in order to be saved? If so, apparently salvation is contingent on a "work" performed by the sinner and is not really the result of God's free grace. If not, apparently the state of one's consciousness and beliefs is just as irrelevant to salvation as his moral works,[16] and the distinctions between believer and unbeliever, Christian and pagan, lose all meaning.

[16] Paul Tillich has rightly shown that the traditional protestant doctrine should imply that the doubter is justified by God in his doubt quite as much as the believer in his faith. ". . . the principle of justification through faith refers not only to the religious-ethical but also to the religious-intellectual life. Not only he who is in sin but also he who is in doubt is justified through faith. The situation of doubt, even of doubt about God, need not separate us from God. There is faith in every serious doubt, namely, the faith in the truth as such, even if the only truth we can express is our lack of truth. But if this is experienced in its depth and as an ultimate concern, the divine is present; and he who doubts in such an attitude is 'justified' in his thinking. . . . You cannot reach God by the work of right thinking or by a sacrifice of the intellect or by a submission to strange authorities, such as the doctrines of the church and the Bible. You cannot, and you are not even asked to try it. Neither works of piety nor works of morality nor works of the intellect establish unity with God. . . . But just as you are justified as a *sinner* (though unjust, you are just), so in the status of *doubt* you are in the status of truth" (*The Protestant Era* [Chicago: University of Chicago Press, 1948], pp. xiv–xv). But is Tillich suggesting that only the man who experiences his doubt "in its depth and as an ultimate concern" is justified? Is the superficial man with his trivial concerns not also justified? Is "ultimate concern" a work which we must perform in order to acquire God's favor?

The difficulties here arise from the methodological error of beginning with the word "justification," which like all other human terms has its original significance in relation to other words and to experience, and then attempting to use that term so that it discriminates nothing at all in human experience but refers only to "God's act" somewhere in heaven. With such misuse of language we pay the price of strange confusions and even insoluble antinomies. Man's words are *his* words, and always gain their meaning in reference to *his* experience. It is false abstraction to suppose *he* can speak words whose referent and meaning has no locus or direct connection with experience. If man is to speak of "justification" or of "God's act," he can do so only as these actually impinge on him through some real effect in the world of human history and experience.[17] Since the traditional language of justification and sanctification lends itself so easily to these errors (whatever the intention of the reformers themselves), I have preferred to develop my analysis more or less independently of these terms. God's act to save man, as we have seen, can be conveniently broken into three phases, each of which has concrete historical content: Jesus' ministry and death (the actual at-one-ment of God and man); the resurrection (the event through which that at-one-ment was recognized as such and God's new presence in history perceived); pentecost (the establishment of the new community governed by the spirit of self-giving and love broken into history with Jesus' death).

These terms refer to events or processes remembered by or going on in the Christian church. That is, within this historical community the participants apprehend themselves as justified and accepted by God, forgiven of their sins and granted new peace and joy and freedom. In this community human existence is experienced as being transformed; men are being "sanctified." It is important to emphasize that these events occur and are known, however, only insofar as there is actual forgiveness and love practiced in the community, only as neighbor serves neighbor, only as enemies are actually reconciled and men are freed from bondage to the various demons and powers which enslave them. Insofar as this community is thus the concrete historical

---

[17] Similar methodological errors are involved in the controversy over whether justification is simply "forensic."

context in which selves actually gain a new life, it is appropriate to speak of the mercy and forgiveness of God present and known here. If, however, in this respect there were no specifiable phenomenological or empirical difference between this community and others, to speak of "God's act" saving man would be an empty abstraction, better dispensed with entirely. "Without true fellowship the blood of Christ can cleanse nobody from his sin."[18]

This, of course, is not to say that by "God's act" I mean *nothing more* than a certain mode of human existence or a particular historical community. That would be a completely misleading form of reductionism. For this community understands itself to have arisen within a history of interaction between men and the ultimate reality which is the source and ground of all that is, God. To live as a member of this community is to appropriate one's life as emergent from this process of interaction, a process which cannot be reduced to the merely human pole. That is, it is to experience human love and forgiveness as an expression of one's relation to the cosmic origin and ground of things; it is to understand the human and historical meanings of events as symbols of and analogies for their ultimate meaning. These events and experiences have their peculiar and significant meaning and transformative power precisely because they are appropriated as the vehicle of one's relation to the ultimate source of all that is. In this way the knowledge of acceptance and at-homeness in the community of faith comes to mean that one is actually at-home in the world and accepted by God himself, and thus the partial freedom made possible through the love and forgiveness of others becomes in fact the vehicle for an ultimate freedom of man in the world.

In short, the church as the beloved community is a spurious and temporary sanctuary from the real world, a shield hiding the real character of life, "the opiate of the people"—unless its life and character are in fact genuinely analogous to, and thus revelatory of, the actual nature of the real world in which man lives. It is this point that the metaphysical claims about God's acting in and through men's historical actions are intended to express. Without these claims

---

[18] Quoted of the Hutterite, Andreas Ehrenpreis (1650), in Robert Friedmann. "The Essence of Anabaptist Faith: an Essay in Interpretation," *Mennonite Quarterly Review* (1967), 41:15.

Christian faith and Christian community are nothing more than another variety of human existence. But with them Christian faith has
the possibility of making available an unparalleled freedom and
fulfilment of personal existence, for—in a way no mere naturalism or
humanism can—it grasps the widest and most comprehensive context
of human existence, the natural world from which we have emerged
and within which we live, as the expression of personal purposive
activity and thus infused with personal meaning.

For Christian faith in this way to make sense of the whole of life
and grant genuine freedom to believers, it must have this double-
sidedness: it must have a real historical locus in a community where
love and forgiveness and freedom are truly known and received and
given, and it must involve an appropriation of these finite historical
actions and events as the vehicle of an ultimate love and forgiveness
and freedom at the foundation of the universe. Without the first the
Christian claims are abstract and ultimately empty; without the
second, they are delusory and simply one more expression of man's
tragic fate as a personal being in an impersonal world. Together,
however, they give the Christian faith both historical concreteness and
cosmic significance, and the Christian community becomes in fact the
point in human existence where one is enabled to be at home in the
world, a free man.

The world, however, as we have seen (Part Two, above), can be
understood as the continuing expression of purposive activity only if
it is moving toward some goal or end; and the Christian church
similarly could not be the dynamic center of God's continuing activity
if it lived merely with an eye on the past, on what God has done. The
dynamic of personal existence is always forward, toward the future,
toward goals unrealized but presently being striven for. If the Christian community is to be the proper historical home and continuing
context for purposive beings, it may not be conceived merely stati-
cally but must be moving toward a future fulfilment or consummation.
To the hope for the completion of God's act begun with the creation
of the world and reestablished with the Christ-event—a fulfilment
without which that act must always remain unfinished and thus not an
act at all—we shall turn in the next chapter.

30 / The Hope for Man

We have already seen in an earlier chapter (Chapter 22) why any historical understanding of existence and the world must have a doctrine of the future, an eschatology. Without some conception of that toward which the historical process is moving, both the significance of developments in the past and the meaningfulness of present events are undercut. The concrete images or notions in terms of which the future is apprehended and interpreted are always derived from meaningful past events and present experiences which, precisely in their meaningfulness, are taken as clues to what the future will bring. Every doctrine of the future, therefore, however "open" it may supposedly be, presupposes continuity with known past structures which are extrapolated into or projected upon the unknown. In a Christian understanding of the cosmic historical process, the Christ-event is taken as revelatory of the ultimate reality underlying all history. Hence, the God and Father of Jesus Christ is regarded as Lord of all history and sovereign over every possible future. This claim is symbolized in the mythical notion of the "second coming" of Christ at the "end" of history, which means simply that when history has finally exhausted all its possibilities, it will be evident that the reality made known in the historical appearance of Jesus Christ is history's sovereign Lord. Thus, the foundation of all Christian interpretation of the future is the conviction that the Christ-event is the clue for its proper understanding.

With the previous discussion of the problem of the future, within the context of a historical understanding of the world in general, as background, let us turn to the more specific problem of man's destiny as understood within Christian faith. Our analysis of man's historicity (Chapter 23) was intended to show that man's uniqueness lies in his power to make history, to determine in some measure the future. Our consideration of the fall and sin, however, indicated that although man's power over himself and his history expanded greatly in certain respects during the human past, he has corrupted this power in such a way that the history which he is making is threatening to destroy his historicity; we have even reached the point where race suicide is possible and may not be avoidable. The development within history of countervailing forces to counteract the destructive powers loosed by man's autonomy was necessary in order to begin freeing him from enslavement and to restore him to his rightful position as an obedient and loving creature under God. God's activity in history, culminating finally in the Christ-event, created such a redemptive historical thrust by (a) revealing the absolutely self-sacrificial character of the God who loves, and (b) making God's love an effective power within history through establishing an intrahistorical community within which this spirit of God was known by men, was effective in transforming their lives, and became manifest in their relations to others. Thus, at work within that same historical process in which man is transforming himself through the creation and development of culture and high civilization are redemptive powers aiming to overcome man's self-destructive autonomy and to establish him in the freedom which God had intended for him.

The importance of the Christ-event and the community created through it does not derive from the claim that all that is good and valuable—or even all that is liberating—is rooted therein. Clearly man's own creation of language and the arts, civilization and culture, science and technology, through the course of history, has enabled him to gain a most impressive control over his natural environment, his life, and in some measure, himself and his historical destiny. All this was a proper growth of man's historicity and freedom, in and through the historical process in whose shaping man has increasingly participated. But his great growth in power and effectiveness has been accompanied, as we have observed, by a corresponding increase in the ability to, and danger that he may, destroy both himself and his history because of the cancer at work in his very creativity. To neutralize and eventually overcome this disease, thus freeing man at all levels of his being to develop and enjoy his culture and history, is the special work of the redemptive love loosed through the Christ-event and become historically effective through the community created by and responsive to that event, the church. Man's ultimate destiny is to become man, that is, the free being who can create himself through making history; but this freedom can be truly his only as the demonic powers to which he has enslaved himself in his striving for autonomy can be disarmed. Ultimate human destiny must thus be seen as the conjoint product of three factors, none of which is dispensable: (a) God's creative work, through which man, the historical being, was brought on the scene and is sustained there; (b) man's own historical work, in which, through his creation and transformation of culture, he has been creating and recreating himself, enhancing and transforming his own freedom and historicity; (c) God's redemptive work, through which the self-destructive powers loosed by man are rendered innocuous and he at last becomes a truly free—though still finite—being, able to participate in the kingdom of God as his child and heir (Rom. 8:17).

Thus, the goal of human history is the completion of God's original creative intention to produce a free and responsive historical being through the historical process, but its realization requires turning aside such obstacles to that end as have arisen along the way: it is the bringing to fulfilment (with respect to man) of both God's creative and redemptive work. The entire movement of human history is toward that end.

This somewhat abstract and general formulation quite properly underscores the point that the meaning and goal of history is to be understood in terms of God's original and ultimate purpose, not man's desires or objectives. But God has made man into a historical and self-conscious being who himself orders his activity and life teleologically and who cannot but ask how the movement of history will contribute to the realization of his own goals. Moreover, in Jesus Christ God has revealed himself as one who seeks man's own good out of love for him, one who would be Father to man, not his tyrannical

lord, indeed, one who himself suffers and becomes "poor, so that by
his poverty [man] might become rich" (2 Cor. 8:9). It is quite
appropriate, then, to move beyond formulations of the goal of history
which are framed entirely in terms of God's purposes—thus remaining abstract from the human point of view—to a consideration of the
relevance of this end to human desires and hopes. What fulfilment
of human aspirations is promised to Christian hope?

The beginning of an answer can be discerned immediately in the
central theological symbol designating the goal of history, the kingdom of God.[1] This symbol emphasizes that the significance of historical creatures and movements is to be discovered ultimately by
reference to the divine king; but it also suggests that the order within
which these creatures will find their fulfilment is analogous to that
of a community of loyal subjects. Thus the goal toward which human
history labors is a communal order of peace and justice and productivity under the rule of God, shared in by all peoples and nations.

> . . . and many nations shall come, and say:
> "Come, let us go up to the mountain of the Lord, . . .
> that he may teach us his ways . . ."
> and they shall beat their swords into plowshares,
>   and their spears into pruning hooks;
> nation shall not lift up sword against nation,
>   neither shall they learn war any more;
> but they shall sit every man under his vine and under his fig tree,
>   and none shall make them afraid.
>
> MICAH 4:2-4

The diverse histories of mankind will become one history and the
warring societies will become one community, and all will live together in peace as one people under the God who has made himself

[1] Creation already *is*, and always has been, the kingdom of God in the sense that
it is a realm under God's sovereignty in which his purposes are being worked out; but it
is only *becoming* God's kingdom to the degree that his purpose includes as yet unrealized
objectives, such as the creation of a community of genuinely free historical agents,
responsive and loving toward each other and to him. To the extent that there still remain
serious obstacles to the realization of God's purposes for his world, it is appropriate to
speak of the kingdom as the goal of history. (See discussion of the problem of "realized"
and unfulfilled eschatology in Ch. 22.)

known in Israel's history and preeminently through Jesus Christ. "The kingdoms of this world [will] become the kingdoms of our Lord and of his Christ; and he shall reign for ever and ever" (Rev. 11:15 KJ).[2]

How is this hope to be understood? Is it to be interpreted as the expectation of some other-wordly social order beyond history and

---

[2] This passage is a New Testament paraphrase of an Old Testament vision about the coming of "one like a son of man":

> And to him was given dominion and glory and kingdom,
> that all peoples, nations, and languages should serve him;
> his dominion is an everlasting dominion,
>   which shall not pass away,
> and his kingdom one
>   that shall not be destroyed. DANIEL 7:14.

Paul, it should be noted, places the emphasis at a slightly different point in order to make clear that the ultimate Lord is God himself to whom Christ also is subject: "Then comes the end, when he delivers the kingdom to God the Father after destroying every rule and every authority and power. . . . When all things are subjected to him, then the Son himself will also be subjected to him who put all things under him, that God may be ever̄ g to every one" (1 Cor. 15:24,28).

       this expectation of the ultimate triumph of God's redemptive love as manifest in C   hat is, of course, the basis for the recurrent Christian speculations about universal salvation of all mankind at the end of man's history of disobedience. "Then as one man's trespass led to condemnation for all men, so one man's act of righteousness leads to acquittal and life for all men. . . . For God has consigned all men to disobedience, that he may have mercy upon all. . . . For from him and through him and to him are all things" (Rom. 5:18; 11:32,36). The insistence of universalism that God's ultimate triumph over all powers that oppose him must be understood as the triumph of his redemptive purposes, rather than his punitive vengeance, must certainly be regarded as theologically correct, if Jesus' life and death is taken to be the definitive revelation of the nature and will of God. One cannot but agree with the judgment of John Stuart Mill (and many others) that the traditional conception of hell reflects disastrously on the character of God: "[Consider this] recognition . . . of the object of highest worship in a being who could make a Hell, and who could create countless generations of human beings with the certain foreknowledge that he was creating them for this fate. Is there any moral enormity which might not be justified by imitation of such a Deity? And is it possible to adore such a one without a frightful distortion of the standard of right and wrong? Any other of the outrages to the most ordinary justice and humanity involved in the common Christian conception of the moral character of God sinks into insignificance beside this dreadful idealization of wickedness" (J. S. Mill, *Utility of Religion* [New York: Liberal Arts Press, 1958], p. 74). If one finds it necessary on methodological grounds (i.e., by appeal to the definitiveness of the Christ-event for the understanding of God) to question seriously the traditional view of hell, it does not necessarily follow that one is committed to universalism, at least in any traditional form. The expectation that all men will be saved into some blissful heaven depended upon the acceptance of the traditional somewhat naive myth about individual life beyond the grave. However (as we shall see below, pp. 464ff.), since precisely this myth, in its traditional form at least, must be seriously questioned, the major point of the universalists about individual destiny—as well as the major contention of their opponents—dissolves away, and we are left finally with the simpler, though more abstract, Pauline expectation that ultimately "God [will] be all in all" (1 Cor. 15:28 KJ).

death? Or should the Christian anticipate that "the Lord himself
will descend from heaven with a cry of command" (1 Thess. 4:16)
to inaugurate the new kingdom here on earth? Each of these views
has been held by Christians in the past, often simultaneously. Both,
however, depend heavily on literal acceptance of mythological pictures of the present rule of God (or Christ) and of future existence
beyond death and history. If one's theological point of departure
and ultimate standard of truth were the mythological or metaphysical
conceptions of the Bible, then of course it would be necessary to explain the Christian hope by direct interpretation of these myths, on
the assumption that they give secret *gnosis* of the future as revealed
by the God who knows it already in detail.[3] My approach has
been quite different, however. Instead of claiming that revelation
gives specific information about matters of fact—for example, what
is going to happen at some particular time in the future—I have interpreted it as showing us God himself, who he is, and what his nature
and will are. The significance of Jesus Christ was not that he disclosed new factual data about what God is going to do but that in his
person as a man he became the supreme symbol, and thus the revelation, of God's nature; and in his act of self-giving on the cross he
manifested God's disposition and activity of self-sacrificial love
toward mankind. Though the Christ-event thus provides criteria for
apprehending, analyzing, and evaluating experience, it is not the
fundamental source of the data to be assessed: such data are supplied
by the whole wide range of experience.

If, then, one is to speak of the future theologically, he will do so
with a double reference: to factual knowledge (scientific and historical) of the processes and forces at work in history, and to belief about
the ultimate ordering power working itself out through the whole
course of history. If his concern is with the more or less immediate

---

[3] The problems this traditional view of God's (and consequently man's) foreknowledge raises for any genuine conception of the openness of the future, the reality of
decision in the present, etc., need not be rehearsed again here (see above, Ch. 10). One
should also note that all such views depend, on the one hand, on highly questionable
conceptions of revelation as the transmission of certain true divine ideas from God to
man, and, on the other, on more or less uncritical acceptance of the ideas, myths, and
world-views of one rather small segment of mankind two or three millennia ago, as
containing in some special way "absolute" or "final" truth.

outcome of particular movements of history, his conception of the precise character of the future will be heavily dependent on factual knowledge (though not uninfluenced by the belief, for instance, that the ultimate power in history is working toward reconciliation and community, not warfare and destruction). In contrast, if his interest is in the ultimate outcome of the historical process, there is little to be said of a strictly factual sort—for who can prophesy all the way to the end of history on the basis of what he *knows*? His conception, therefore, will be essentially an imaginative elaboration of the outcome of the purposes he thinks God is accomplishing in and through history as a whole. Images of the goal of history, such as the "kingdom of God," provide a way to imagine or picture the ultimate end toward which the whole process is moving; but they do not give precise data about that outcome.

This is the only way the future can be conceived or imagined so as still to remain genuinely *future*: it must be thought as determinate, as having some particular character, but not as determined or closed in advance; it will always be seen as in some way the development of what has been at work in present and past—and never thus completely blank and open—and yet its precise form and character remain a matter of unpredictable creativity. No matter what one's concrete interpretation of the future, it will utilize mythical or imaginative conceptions drawn out of the past and projected loosely forward in such a way as to guide action and to provide a focus for hope (or for despair, if the images be negative in implication). The Christian eschatological images sketch out a picture of what can be expected for man in the unknown future, and they put this in sufficiently concrete terms to have some import for his present life. If these images, however, are made into objective bits of information, literally or allegorically true descriptions of a coming state-of-affairs, their proper function and meaning is destroyed, and they become the basis of superstition and sometimes fanaticism.

The governing symbol of the Christian hope for the outcome of history, as we noted, is the "kingdom of God," a community of love and peace and productivity under God's sovereignty. How or when this kingdom will "come," or what its specific character will be, no

one is in a position to say.[4] The symbol means, however, that (if the
Christian understanding of God is correct) there will ultimately be
genuine fulfilment of human communal life, that the warfare and
destructiveness and chaos of man's present existence will be overcome by powers of reconciliation and justice which build up human
community. It is not expected that this communal fulfilment will
come merely as the result of human effort, or through the outworking
of some iron laws of history, or by chance; it will come only in and
through God's sovereignty. As the human community is transformed
from a merely autonomous and secular society into God's realm, with
men his loyal and responsive subjects, the new order of communal
life will become possible. The kingdom of God will thus be the completion of God's original work of creation, the fulfilment of the human
historical process through which man is creating culture and recreating himself, and the overcoming of the negative and destructive
powers presently at loose in history (cf. above, p. 457).

Insofar as the church is a human community which is in a special
way responsive to God's sovereign love, and is thus the vehicle of his
spirit in history, believers have a kind of "foretaste of the future"
(Rom. 8:23 Goodspeed) kingdom. The meaning and power of the
spirit of love and self-giving known here provide a sufficient "earnest"
or "guarantee" (2 Cor. 1:22; 5:5) of what is ultimately real in history, and thus of what will finally come, to enable believers to act and
live toward that end rather than some other. To participate in the
church is thus to participate in the new humanity, in the human-com-
munity-being-transformed-into-God's-kingdom, because it is participation in a principal agency through which that transformation is
being historically wrought. There is, of course, little direct evidence
that the church is becoming God's kingdom. Much of church history is filled with the evil of superstition and the terror of fanaticism; if judgment about the ultimate meaning of the church's life
had to be based on empirical evidence to date, it could hardly be so
optimistic. But faith's judgment is based primarily not on historical
evidences but on acceptance of God's self-declaration in Christ. If

---

[4] "But of that day or that hour no one knows, not even the angels in heaven, nor the
Son, but only the Father" (Mk. 13:32).

that event means what faith takes it to mean, namely, that "in Christ God was reconciling the world to himself" (2 Cor. 5:19, RSV footnote), then the community created by that event has more than ordinary historical significance; it is, in fact, the continuing historical agency through which "God [is] making his appeal" (5:20) to men and thus transforming them.

This conviction about the eschatological significance of the church's life and history lies at the basis of the missionary impulse in Christian faith. The Christian community is not a society of God's favorites whose principal characteristic is that they have been granted a "foretaste" of future bliss denied others; it is rather a historical beachhead through which God is advancing his purposes to convert men into his loyal subjects. It exists therefore only for its task of mediating God's love throughout human society; its life consists entirely in mission to others; its only purpose is to be the vehicle through which that history derivative from and centering in God's decisive act in Jesus Christ envelops and encompasses all the parochial histories of mankind, thus enabling each to find its proper place within the divine kingdom. Insofar as this occurs through the church, she is a foretaste in the here and now of the anticipated kingdom.

Thus, the eschatological hope for human-kind is a projection or extrapolation into the future of certain features of present existence discerned by faith as especially expressive of the will and work of the Lord of all history; conversely, the full significance of the life of self-sacrifice and love known in the church and required of its members comes into view when we see that only this mode of human existence ultimately has a future, that all human history is moving toward this end, that the kingdom of God is the goal of man's history.

Because societies and nations survive their members, what is sown by one generation often not being reaped until much later, it is possible and meaningful to project images of ideal communal existence into an indefinitely long future. Thus, to think of the work of a whole community not being realized until some unforeseeable time is not unreasonable. But men are individuals as well as members of communities, with aspirations for self-fulfilment as well as for society. What hope is there for them in this respect? Here the problem of the

future becomes more difficult. The church after all has already sur-
vived 2000 years and gone through many changes. However incredible it may seem to regard her final historical destiny as
somehow the kingdom of God, who can say, in the long centuries and
millennia of the open future, what she may become? She is already in
some sense a universal community, transcending boundaries of race,
nationality, and sex; perhaps in the future she will be able finally to
take all mankind into her bosom. However much traditional Christian
faith may have regarded the eschatological symbols as referring to
some post-historical life in "heaven," a historical fulfilment of the
meaning of those symbols is not entirely inconceivable.

But with an individual person this nonmythological mode of interpretation is closed to us. For individuals die in a matter of a few
years!—and we have no reason to suppose their life continues beyond
the grave. Human consciousness and self-consciousness, in the only
way we know them, are intimately tied up with bodily existence; and
with death the body falls into decay and dissolution. Men of other
ages and cultures, subscribing to different psychologies, could develop doctrines of the "immortality of the soul" according to which
man's true essence is divine and survives bodily death; to modern
psychology and medicine, man appears a psychosomatic unity whose
spiritual life is inseparably bound to its physical base.[5] The end of
the body, therefore, is the end of the man, except to the degree his
ideas and attitudes and actions continue to affect the communities
and cultures within which he lived and worked. To many moderns,
the Old Testament dictum, "dust thou art, and unto dust shalt thou
return" (Gen. 3:19 KJ), seems more likely true than the Greek
hopes of immortality that informed many centuries of Christian
belief.

There is, of course, considerably stronger emphasis on a life
beyond the grave in the New Testament than in the Old.[6] This is

[5] For a full philosophical discussion of the inseparability of man's very being from
his bodiliness, see M. Merleau-Ponty, *The Phenomenology of Perception* (London:
Routledge & Kegan Paul, 1962).

[6] For a brief summary and analysis of Old Testament conceptions of afterlife, see
H. W. Robinson, *Inspiration and Revelation in the Old Testament* (London: Oxford
University Press, 1946), Ch. 7; convenient analyses of New Testament views (as well as
those of the church fathers) will be found in K. Stendahl, ed., *Immortality and Resur-*

rooted in part in the fact that during the centuries immediately preceding the Christian era a growing confidence that God would raise the dead—the faithful to a reward, the unfaithful to eternal punishment—was emerging in some Jewish circles (e.g., the Pharisees in contrast with the Sadduccees); and Jesus himself clearly shared that view (cf., e.g., Mk. 12:18–27).[7] Of even more importance here was the impact of the Easter event: Christian faith was born in the conviction that Jesus came to life again after his death, the "first fruits" (1 Cor. 15:20,23) of the general resurrection expected at the end of history. The decisive experience underlying Christian faith thus "proved" that the hope for a life beyond death was valid (for Jesus' resurrection could not have occurred if the dead were not in fact to be raised) and at the same time presupposed its validity (if there were to be no resurrection of the dead, then of course it was a delusion to believe Jesus had been raised).[8] There was thus a direct and seemingly unbreakable connection between the founding event of Christian faith as understood in the early church and the hope for a life in glory: to believe in Christ necessarily meant to expect "eternal

---

rection (New York: Macmillan, 1965). Only in two places in the Old Testament—and those both from late writings—is an afterlife definitely expected and promised. In a small apocalypse found in Isaiah 24–27, and dating from about 300 B.C., it is stated of those faithful to the Lord: "thy dead shall live, their bodies shall rise" (Isa. 26:19); but this is not expected for the unrighteous (26:14). By the time Daniel was written, perhaps 100 years later, it was thought that many, although apparently not all, of both righteous and unrighteous would be raised: "And many of those who sleep in the dust of the earth shall awake, some to everlasting life, and some to shame and everlasting contempt" (Daniel 12:2). For the most part, however, the Old Testament regards the place of the dead as beyond even God's rule, the sentiment in Isaiah 38:18, e.g., being typical: "For Sheol cannot thank thee, death cannot praise thee; those who go down to the pit cannot hope for thy faithfulness."

[7] It is worth noting, however, as Henry Cadbury has observed, that "the more sure we are that Jesus in fact accepted the perspective of those who believe in future existence, the more evident it seems that it was not the center of his interest. . . . For him and for us it was part of the morrow about which neither he nor we need be anxious. If death of the body is not to be feared, if one is to go his way today and tomorrow whatever the third day has in store, there is no need for the comforting thoughts of an afterlife to banish the fear of death" ("Intimations of Immortality in the Thought of Jesus," in Stendahl, p. 140).

[8] Paul put the matter in precisely these interconnected terms. "Now if Christ is preached as raised from the dead, how can some of you say that there is no resurrection of the dead? But if there is no resurrection of the dead, then Christ has not been raised. . . . For if the dead are not raised, then Christ has not been raised. If Christ has not been raised, your faith is futile and you are still in your sins. . . . But in fact Christ has been raised from the dead, the first fruits of those who have fallen asleep" (1 Cor. 15:12–20).

life" in a "heaven" beyond the grave. As the Jesus of John's Gospel put it: "because I live, you will live also" (14:19).

It is important to note that the basis of this Christian expectation was quite different from that of the Greek hope for immortality. The latter was founded on the conviction that man's innermost essence was a divine, and thus undying, principle;[9] that is, it was rooted in a conception of man's nature and possibilities. In contrast, the Christian view clearly recognized man's inherent mortality, but believed that God would raise him from the dead, granting him the gift of immortality;[10] and this expectation was itself founded on belief about what God had already done for the dead Jesus. Thus, the ground of the Christian hope was belief about *God's past and expected actions*, not man's inherently divine nature; what *God does*, rather than what *man is*, was the basis of the Christian expectation. This meant that the early Christians did not need to conceive life after death as involving only a "part" of the earthly man, the naturally immortal soul freed from the prison-house of the body. In his glorious miracle God would raise again the whole person, including his body— whether this body be thought of as "spiritual" with Paul (1 Cor. 15:44), or more crassly as "flesh and blood," as in the Gospel accounts of Jesus' resurrection and in the later creeds—for had he not already raised Jesus, body and all? In its emphasis that life after death involves the "whole man," not a mere disembodied soul, as well as its realistic understanding that no part of man can naturally survive death, the Christian conception of "resurrection of the body"

[9] Cf., e.g., Plato: ". . . the soul is in the very likeness of the divine, and immortal, and intellectual, and uniform, and indissoluble, and unchangeable. . . . That soul, I say, herself invisible, departs to the invisible world—to the divine and immortal and rational; thither arriving, she is secure of bliss and . . . for ever dwells . . . in company with the gods" (*Phaedo*, 80–81 [Jowett trans.]). Also Pindar: "There is one self-same race of men and gods; and from one mother have we both the breath of life; only faculties altogether diverse distinguish us; since man is a thing of nought, and those have brazen heaven for a sure abiding home. And yet we have some likeness, either by greatness of soul or by fashion of body, to the Deathless Ones" (quoted in Edwyn Bevan, *Symbolism and Unbelief* [London: Allen and Unwin, 1938], p. 72).

[10] Cf. Paul: "For this perishable nature must put on the imperishable, and this mortal nature must put on immortality. [Paul clearly thinks this is an event which is yet to occur rather than a possession already owned.] When the perishable puts on the imperishable, and the mortal puts on immortality, *then* shall come to pass the saying that is written: 'Death is swallowed up in victory'" (1 Cor. 15:53–54).

is more nearly consonant with modern views of the psychosomatic unity of the self than is the doctrine of man's immortal soul.

This remote similarity, however, is hardly adequate ground for commending the doctrine as somehow more credible to the modern mind:[11] indeed, to make such a claim is inconsistent with the fundamental bearing of the doctrine itself. For the claim of the doctrine of resurrection is that only because of what God does have men reason to believe in a life after death, not because of what man is. That is, only *theological* expectations, not a plausible *anthropology*, can provide adequate basis for understanding man's ultimate destiny. This theological rule—implicit in the doctrine of resurrection in contrast with the notion of immortality—which refers all discussion of the ultimate meaning of finite existence to the doctrine of God, is surely correct. Just as in the early church, contemporary theologians should ground their views of man's destiny on what God has done and may be expected to do, rather than on a conception of man's nature, whether as mortal or immortal.

A brief review of what was said earlier about the resurrection of Jesus (Chapter 28) will make clear why a contemporary understanding of individual human destiny can hardly be identical with that found either in the New Testament or in much of the tradition. There I took the position, it will be remembered, that although the earliest Christians certainly thought the man Jesus, who had died on the cross, had again come alive, a historical reconstruction of the evidence in the Bible hardly supports that interpretation. No doubt the early Christians experienced "appearances" or visions and auditions of Jesus; but these are adequately explicable historically in psychological terms, and there is no need to resort to the extraordinary hypothesis accepted by the early church. Moreover, as we saw, that hypothesis is not intrinsically connected with the central claim the church wished to make in proclaiming Jesus' resurrection, namely,

---

[11] See, for example, such varied writers as Reinhold Niebuhr (*The Nature and Destiny of Man* [New York: Scribners, 1949], II, 311f.; *The Self and the Dramas of History* [New York: Scribners, 1955], pp. 237ff.), and Wolfhart Pannenberg (*Was ist der Mensch?* [Goettingen: Vandenhoeck & Ruprecht, 1962], pp. 34ff.; *Grundzüge der Christologie* [Gütersloher Verlagshaus Gerd Mohn, 1964], pp. 82ff.), who seem to think resurrection of the body is more intelligible to the modern than immortality of the soul.

that the God who had been acting through Jesus' ministry and especially in his death was still actively at work in the community of believers. The breaking into history and continuous effectiveness of *God's action* was the theologically important point, not the resuscitation of their dead master. Although the earliest disciples were enabled to believe in and grasp the former in and through their conviction about the latter, these are, as we noted, logically and psychologically independent notions. Since Christian faith depends on belief in the continuity of God's act before, in, and after the death of Jesus, not the continuation of Jesus' personality, I argued that contemporary historical reinterpretation of the reports about Jesus' resurrection, far from being fatal to Christian faith, actually clarifies its real import. For the meaning of the historical event in which faith was born, which is traditionally designated as "Jesus' resurrection," is that God's work redeeming mankind is effectively continuing, not that there were certain peculiar happenings to a man named Jesus.

Although contemporary reconstruction of Jesus' resurrection clarifies the ultimate convictions of Christian faith about God's nature, will, and activity, it completely undermines the traditional basis of hope for individual life after death. As we noted above, this was grounded on the belief that Jesus had been raised from the dead as "the first fruits of those who have fallen asleep" (1 Cor. 15:20), and that "those who belong to Christ" would be similarly raised upon his imminent return to earth (15:23). If, however, the man Jesus was not restored to life as traditionally believed, "the appearances" being events of quite another order, then the special basis on which the Christian hope for immortality was founded is completely gone. This does not mean, of course, that Christians no longer can have hopes for personal fulfilment; it means rather that these hopes now must be based directly and simply on Christian faith in God—as is all other Christian understanding of the future—rather than on a supposed special connection between our individual destinies and Jesus'.[12]

[12] This puts the Christian understanding of the destiny of the individual very properly on the same basis as other Christian doctrines dealing with the meaning of created reality: it must be grounded in the convictions about God's nature and purposes and nowhere else. The traditional understanding of Jesus' resurrection had made it possible to develop a doctrine of Christian life after death on a basis relatively independent of the doctrine of God, viz., the alleged occurrence of a particular historical event.

We start, then, from the Christian conviction that God is Lord of history and life, the loving and merciful Father of mankind, made known in Christ as one who willingly gives of himself for man's sake. What does this conviction enable one to hope about his individual future, specifically with regard to death? Can he still shout with Paul, "Death is swallowed up in victory" (1 Cor. 15:54)? I think he can. If Christian belief is true, and the ultimate reality with whom man has to do is really a loving Father, then one could not possibly do better than put his entire destiny in God's hands. To believe in God is to trust he will care for one as he ought to be cared for—in every contingency, in every future. In respect to his well-being and destiny, therefore, it involves, as Jesus put it, taking "no thought for the morrow" (Mt. 6:34   KJ); for one's heavenly Father knows his every need and will provide for it properly. To have faith in God is precisely to give one's eternal destiny over into his hands, to do with however he sees fit (including being damned for his glory, as some of the old Calvinists put it, if that be his will). Any specification which man lays down regarding *how* God is to deal with him, or in what *mode* his future existence shall be, represents an unwillingness to rest in God's wisdom and love and mercy on this matter. To insist, for example, that God will surely grant man some sort of self-aware life in "heaven" after his death on earth is to demand an assurance which finite man can never have and about which, if he truly trusted God, he would not concern himself. "Though he slay me, yet will I trust in him" (Job 13:15   KJ) is a more appropriate expression of the radical stance of faith. Men's unwillingness fully to trust God *unless they know what he will do with them* is an expres-

---

Thus, the principal importance of the Easter event, that it was the historical epistemological basis of Christian faith generally, tended to be forgotten in the emphasis on its importance as the foundation of Christian hopes for resurrection and/or immortality. In view of this, it is little wonder that Christian faith has often been understood as largely an "other-worldly" hope for "heaven," with a correlative lack of interest in life here on earth; and that critics could regard Christian ideology as largely built up out of selfish desire for and expectation of personal rewards in a hereafter, rather than as radical theocentrism. The destruction of the peculiar basis for this preferential treatment of doctrines of immortality occasioned by historical reinterpretation of Jesus' resurrection undercuts this lingering anthropo- or even egocentrism; and makes it possible for the entirety of Christian doctrine to be built up on a radically theocentric basis.

sion of the lingering desire to establish and preserve themselves, to be their own masters; it is a manifestation of unfaith.

Whatever may have been true in the Christian past, then, the symbol "resurrection of the body" should not be too easily and simply identified with some personal existence beyond the grave. God created man as a finite being. Each man has his own beginning and end, and his own particular place within the on-going movement of history. Each has the particular finite tasks to perform which God gives him in this place. His proper life as God's creature is the acceptance of his role and tasks in gratitude and love, not demanding to be some other being with some other—perhaps immortal—nature. In thus living as creature under the Creator he is granted the fulfilment appropriate to his mode of existence.[13] There is no reason whatsoever to suppose that an everlasting extension of his finite existence would somehow be a great and glorious consummation for human life; indeed, as Paul Tillich has suggested, such "an infinity of the finite could be a symbol for hell."[14] The proper and adequate consummation for human existence is not something known to us at all; it is known only by God. Through the revelation in Jesus Christ, Christian faith has learned

[13] On this whole interpretation of the implications of finitude, cf. Karl Barth: "Man as such . . . has no beyond. Nor does he need one, for God is his beyond. Man's beyond is that God as his Creator, Covenant-partner, Judge and Saviour, was and is and will be his true Counterpart in life, and finally and exclusively and totally in death. Man as such, however, belongs to this world. He is thus finite and mortal. One day he will only have been, as once he was not. His divinely given promise and hope and confidence in this confrontation with God is that even as this one who has been he will share the eternal life of God Himself. Its content is not, therefore, his liberation from his this-sidedness, from his end and dying, but positively the glorification by the eternal God of his natural and lawful this-sided, finite and mortal being. He does not look and move towards the fact that this being of his in his time will one day be forgotten and extinguished and left behind, and in some degree replaced by a new, other-sided, infinite and immortal being after his time. More positively, he looks and moves towards the fact that this being of his in his time, and therewith with its beginning and end before the eyes of the gracious God, and therefore before his own eyes and those of others, will be revealed in all its merited shame but also its unmerited glory, and may thus be eternal life from and in God. He does not hope for redemption from the this-sidedness, finitude and mortality of his existence. He hopes positively for the . . . redemption of his this-sided, finite and mortal existence. This psycho-physical being in its time is he himself. . . . And he himself as this being knows that already in the totality of his own this-sided existence, above and beyond which there is no other, he is claimed by and belongs and is committed and thankful here and now to the God who as his gracious Judge and therefore his Saviour from death is his true beyond" (*Church Dogmatics*, III, 2 [Edinburgh: T. & T. Clark, 1960], 632–633).

[14] "Frontiers," *Journal of Bible and Religion* (1965), 33:22.

that God can be trusted to bring about that proper consummation, whatever it might be. And so death, the great symbol of the unknown, is robbed of its power to destroy creativity and freedom in despair and nihilism;[15] and it is no longer necessary for Christians to concern themselves with old myths purporting to give special *gnosis* in regard to life beyond the grave. That which is beyond all human knowledge, experience, and power belongs properly to God and not man, and to him it can be entrusted. The symbol "resurrection of the body," though originating in mythological speculations, quite properly emphasizes that the ultimate future is beyond all human powers and ken; and the fulfilment it will bring—a proper consummation for the existence of the "whole man" (body)—depends exclusively on God's act. Understood in this way, as affirming such confidence about the future as is made possible by faith in the God manifest in Jesus Christ, this symbol is an appropriate expression of the Christian hope for the individual. For "this is eternal life, that they know thee the only true God, and Jesus Christ whom thou has sent" (John 17:3).[16]

We are now in a position to dispose rather quickly of such symbols as the "last judgment," "heaven," and "hell." None of these, any more than those symbols with which we have already dealt, should be interpreted as providing secret *gnosis* of future events or circumstances. All should be seen as expressions in mythological form of the confidence that God will ultimately succeed in realizing his purposes for history and for mankind. The "last judgment" speaks of God's ultimately overcoming and destroying the historical powers which now oppose and frustrate him; history will at last be set to rights. Moreover, this ultimate success of God will not be simply the arbitrary victory of the overpowering might of a tyrant; it will be

---

[15] Heb. 2:15 suggests it is not so much death itself as the "fear of death" which subjects men "to lifelong bondage." It is this fear which faith quite properly overcomes.

[16] Without claiming that John had no expectations of life beyond death, it should be observed that he very explicitly reinterprets the expectation of the resurrection of the dead so that it emphasizes no longer what will happen to a man after his death but rather the present "eternal life" made possible by God's coming into the world in Christ: "Jesus said to her, 'Your brother will rise again.' Martha said to him, 'I know that he will rise again in the resurrection at the last day.' Jesus said to her, 'I am the resurrection and the life; he who believes in me, though he die, yet shall he live, and whoever lives and believes in me shall never die. Do you believe this?'" (John 11:23–27)

right and just, like the impartial judgment of a righteous judge. Each
will receive what is appropriate to and due him. In this respect the
symbols of "heaven" and "hell"—including their elaborations into
the New Jerusalem with streets paved of gold (Rev. 21:21), on the
one hand, and the torment of "unquenchable fire" (Mk. 9:43), on
the other—are simply somewhat colorful expressions of the notion
that in the end God's justice will prevail and set right all the wrongs
of history.[17] Thus, in their positive emphasis on God's ultimate success, these symbols make much the same theological point (with
somewhat different emphases in detail) as the expectation of the
resurrection of the body or the coming of the kingdom of God.[18] In
their suggestion of a certain discrimination at the end of history
between those powers cooperating with God's will and those opposing
him, with final destruction of the latter and ultimate vindication and
establishment of the former, these symbols point to the lasting impact
and permanent significance of every historical decision and action:
what occurs in history, particularly the decisions and actions of men
with respect to God's revelation and will, is not of mere ephemeral or
passing import; its consequences will be felt through the entire future, indeed, through all eternity. God's ultimate sovereignty over
history, therefore, does not mean that human actions are finally
meaningless. On the contrary, in the last judgment God finally
realizes his objectives through redeeming and completing the historical work which man has done. God had originally created man as
a creaturely creator to work with him in building his world; at the
end it is quite appropriate, therefore, that each man's work, and that
man himself, should find proper place in God's kingdom.

The Christian hope for man's future—both collective and in-

---

[17] For brief discussion of the traditional view of "hell" (and also the problem of
"universalism"), see n. 2 above.
[18] Cf. Karl Barth: "Divine judgment in the biblical sense means that God vindicates
himself against man, but that in so doing he vindicates man against all that is alien and
hostile to him. It means that God does what is right for himself and therefore for man.
Hence it is not a No for its own sake, but a No for the sake of the Yes. . . . Thus as
an act of divine sovereignty over man it spells his emancipation. It protects man by being
so relentless towards him. . . . Thus God's reaction to man's sin—his powerful and
effectual opposition which man must bear in consequence of his rebellion against God
and betrayal of himself—is the expression of his grace, a corollary of this primary fact"
(*Church Dogmatics*, III, 2, pp. 32–33).

dividual—is an indispensable dimension of Christian faith. Without it we would be unable to interpret theologicallv the fact that as dynamic, historical beings, men are always forward-running toward goals and hopes presently unrealized. Since the future is never present to man directly in experience but is known only in imaginative projections of various possibilities discernible in the present, it should not trouble one overmuch that the Christian hope is spun out through mythical extrapolation of concepts and images drawn from ordinary life. How else, after all, could the last goal of all man's striving and the last outcome of all his decisions and actions be expressed? The end of all history, like its beginning, cannot be literally or precisely conceived or imagined. When we attempt so to do, we inevitably wonder what happens "after" the end: our investigation falls into antinomy and absurdity. Despite this difficulty, however, one cannot dispense with the notion of an ultimate end to cosmic and human history. For man's individual and collective historical striving is finally rendered of no account and thus ultimately meaningless, if it is not consonant with and part of a similar purposive movement in history as a whole. Precisely this is the point of the Christian claim that history is governed by a sovereign Lord whose objectives will finally be achieved. It is doubtful whether the conception of a genuinely purposive history can be sustained metaphysically in any other way than by such reference to an agent who is its Creator and Lord.

The proper function of these images of the end-time is to sketch out to a kind of fullness the picture of man's future as seen by faith; if they are taken as providing bits of revealed information about certain coming events, they can only be misleading and even the basis of fanaticism. This is not to say that these time-determined notions should be interpreted as simply crude expressions of a supposedly unchanging relation between God and man. To attempt in this way to extract "eternal" truth from these mythical symbols is to miss the point entirely. "Purpose" is itself a time-determined notion; if time is abstracted from it, it loses its meaning. Similarly, recognition that these symbols are mythical must not lead one to de-emphasize the importance of their temporal character. It should, rather, free him from any literalizing interpretations, with all the misleading conclusions that can result, and enable him to appropriate them as genuinely illuminative of the meaning of human history and existence as understood in faith. In this way they will, in turn, enhance that faith and its meaning.

Part Four

THE CHRISTIAN UNDERSTANDING

OF THE REDEEMED LIFE:

THE DOCTRINES OF THE CHURCH AND

SACRAMENTS, DISCIPLESHIP AND FAITH

For a Christian, life is no child's play . . .

HANS SCHLAFFER (c. 1527)

THUS far I have attempted to sketch an interpretation of revelation and God, the world and man, which would be in accord with contemporary understanding of the facts of history as well as an appropriate development of traditional Christian doctrine. We must now turn from this attempt to grasp systematically the Christian *Weltanschauung* to a consideration of the Christian life. Some may suppose so much of traditional belief has been cut away by the agnostic knife of modern historical criticism and secular unbelief in the preceding pages that the significance of Christian faith and life is destroyed; others will argue that so much remains here of traditional superstition and myth that no truly "modern man" could possibly accept and live by it. The proof of the pudding is in the eating, of course; and theology is nothing but speculative foolishness if it is not understanding and interpretation of, and thus contributive to a deepening and enhancing of, the actual lives of men and women. I have tried to show throughout that the Christian perspective is unified and consistent, focusing on the conviction that the God revealed in Jesus Christ is both the source of all existence and actively at work in empirical history, overcoming destructive powers at work there; I have suggested, moreover, that the radicalness of the transvaluation of all human values and conceptions involved in this view that the image of a helpless man dying on a cross is revelatory of the ultimate reality with which we have to do is exposed in all its starkness only when much of the confusing mythology of traditional belief, together with the consequent welter of inconsistent and incredible doctrine, is cut away (as has been attempted in the present work), exposing a powerful unity of fundamental perspective and import. In order to see now what this actually means for human existence, it

remains to sketch briefly a picture of the Christian life. Such an outline, of course, is no substitute for actually ordering one's existence
in this way and thus experimentally testing the meaning of Christian
doctrine. "Whoever has the will to do the will of God shall know
whether my teaching comes from him or is merely my own" (John
7:17   NEB). A description such as this, however, can at least provide for the imagination a view of what such living might involve.
In this way it can serve as a fitting elaboration and conclusion of the
foregoing interpretation of Christian doctrine.

31 / The People of God

CHRISTIAN existence can be characterized formally as life under the lordship of Christ. Informed by his prophetic teaching, its deepest levels of meaning mediated by his death, it is oriented toward and ordered by the will of the self-giving God come to man through him. Christian existence remains life in this world, participating in ordinary creaturely work, but to the end that the Creator's will be done and his kingdom come (Mt. 6:10). It is not a pining or longing for another world or another life or another place in history: such attitudes would represent ungracious refusal to accept, or at least displeasure in, the place and task in his world which God has given one.[1] It would thus involve faithless rejection of his lordship and sinful distrust of his loving care, as well as a foolish exchange of the actual life and work with which one is confronted for mythological pie in the sky of which he knows nothing. It is precisely in their creaturely tasks in this life that men are called to be loyal subjects of the divine King.[2]

This means that at its deepest level Christian life is simply human life. Mankind was placed on this earth "to till it and keep it" (Gen. 2:15), that is, to cultivate and domesticate the wildness of nature by and in human culture. Through subordinating the other creatures

---

[1] From this point of view one must use only with considerable care biblical texts which suggest Christians are "strangers and exiles on the earth" who are seeking as a "homeland" a "better country, that is, a heavenly one" (Heb. 11:13–16). Certainly such hopes are no justification for giving up ordinary daily work and responsibilities (cf. 2 Thess. 3:6–13).

[2] ". . . let every one lead the life which the Lord has assigned to him, and in which God has called him. . . . Every one should remain in the state in which he was called" (1 Cor. 7:17,20).

to his own needs and ends, man gains a certain mastery over them (Gen. 1:26,28), while participating in God's work of transforming natural order into a more explicitly teleological order informed directly by purposive activity. The building of culture and civilization is, thus, man's proper responsibility and work, that for which God created him.[3] Participation in the redemptive community involves no release from this common human task but must rather be seen as serving it. One is a man before he is a Christian, and his Christian status is not an overturning but rather a qualification of his humanity. If it is true that human history has become snarled and diseased through sin, it is equally true that it is precisely man that God is seeking to release from this bondage. Whatever else the existence of the church and of Christian faith might mean, its primary objective is helping to make and keep human life genuinely human.[4]

From this we may conclude that the principal tasks of the world's work are quite properly Christian tasks as well. Christian faith does not (except in unusual cases) require that one refrain from participation in the various levels and tasks of the economic order through which the physical needs of men are supplied, or the politics through which a community plans for the general well-being of its citizens and keeps order among them. Science, through which man seeks better to grasp the world in his knowledge; and art, through which he is actively re-creating it; as well as philosophy, in which he strives for the most comprehensive sort of understanding of himself and his world, are all appropriate tasks for the Christian. Christian life can be neither anti-cultural nor anti-humane, for it must always be service of the God who made man a culture-creating being.

Nevertheless, Christian existence is not simply an indistinguishable double of other human life. Far from being "incognito" (Kierkegaard), it is a transformed existence within a new community

---

[3] Though there are anti-agriculture and anti-civilization passages in the Bible, the widely accepted romantic notion that life in the wilderness or desert was a kind of Old Testament ideal in contrast with the more orderly agricultural or urban existence has been shown to be definitely false. See Paul Riemann, *Desert and Return to Desert in the Pre-exilic Prophets* (unpublished dissertation in the Andover-Harvard Library of Harvard Divinity School, 1964).

[4] Paul Lehmann, *Ethics in a Christian Context* (New York: Harper & Row, 1963), pp. 14, 66, 85, etc.

which serves to express and draw attention to, and thus be the further vehicle of, God's "mighty deeds" transforming history. This does not mean Christian existence is distinguished from other modes of human life by its inclusion of certain additional "religious" duties, such as praying, supporting the church, meditating on "spiritual" themes. If such activities are involved at all, they are secondary and derivative, not primary. The business of the redemptive community is not the promotion of a special (and somewhat archaic) style of life called piety nor is it ministering to men's "religious needs." Its role is universal-historical: to be an agency through which God can overcome man's bondage to the various powers which have enslaved him, enabling him to become the free and creative historical being originally intended.[5] The character of the people of God, therefore, should not be drawn with reference to certain more or less external "religious" marks. It must be defined exclusively in terms of the historical task which it is called to perform. ". . . you are a chosen race, a royal priesthood, a holy nation, God's own people, *that you may declare* the wonderful deeds of him who called you out of darkness into his marvelous light" (1 Pet. 2:9).[6]

[5] Cf. B. E. Meland: "The importance of the Christian community within the culture . . . consists in this, that it bears witness to the message of persuasive love that was released into culture by the events of Christ's life. This Christian community within the cultural community serves to keep the social stream of meaning impregnated with the redemptive force of those events which persists from age to age. . . . Such a view would represent the church, not simply as an institutional witness to an inherited faith or as the custodian of a tradition; but as the actual bearer of the seminal meanings which can reawaken people again and again to what is deepest in their natures and in their history by reason of these revelatory events that characterize the Christ. To the degree that the church can render these seminal meanings vivid, significant, compelling, through the sensitively spoken word, through dramatic art, through the great musical epics such as Bach's *B-Minor Mass*, Mozart's *Requiem*, Brahm's *Requiem*, Handel's *Messiah*, the numerous chorales, significant hymns, through whatever medium that is consonant with the message of these events; to that degree the church provides resources within the culture upon which symbolization can feed, as it were; or, to change the figure, such that symbolization in the culture can, by reason of these resources, reach the depth of creaturehood" (*Faith and Culture* [New York: Oxford University Press, 1953], pp. 145–146).

[6] Cf. Paul: "God . . . through Christ reconciled us to himself and gave us the ministry of reconciliation. . . . So we are ambassadors for Christ, God making his appeal through us" (2 Cor. 5:18, 20); and John: "God sent the Son into the world, not to condemn the world, but that the world might be saved through him. . . . As thou didst send me into the world, so I have sent them into the world. . . . The glory which thou hast given me I have given to them . . . so that the world may know that thou hast sent me and hast loved them even as thou hast loved me" (John 3:17; 17:18, 22–23).

It is, then, as a witnessing community that the church must be understood. Its witness emerges from its special awareness that the chaos in human history which has rendered man homeless and alone is being overcome as the Lord of history calls men back from their rebellion and autonomy to freedom and fulfilment under his care. "Once you were no people but now you are God's people" (1 Pet. 2:10): this is the tremendous awareness out of which the church lives, the only basis for its continuing work in the world. The life of the church, therefore, has a double reference: backward to the acts through which God has been overcoming man's autonomy and secularity, establishing a community within history which knows him as Father and Lord; and outward to the world still unaware of God's love and care, to whose wounds, suffering, and death she must minister in the hope and expectation that ultimately all those who presently are "no people" will come to be explicitly, and to know themselves as, "God's people."

The internal structure of the church's life can be justified only insofar as it serves this dual focus and thus enables the church actually to be a historical agency through which God is remaking the human world.[7] It is not possible here, of course, to discuss and evaluate the claims of the various forms of polity and institutional organization, the emergent new forms of the church's life and the new types of ministry associated with them, sacramental vs. prophetic conceptions of the church, church vs. sect, etc. At most I can indicate briefly certain fundamental conditions which must be met if the church is to do her proper work: (a) she must order her existence in such a way as deliberately to keep in view the basis of her life and her task in history; (b) she must order her existence in such a way that she can be an effective agent within the wider human society, through whom God's redemption of that society proceeds. I am not

---

[7] This may be implicit in the traditional four historic marks of the church—unity, holiness, catholicity, and apostolicity (Niceno-Constantinopolitan Creed, A.D. 381)— and in the Reformation teaching that the church is wherever the word is truly preached and the sacraments rightly administered (see, e.g., *Augsburg Confession*, art. 7; Luther, *On the Councils and the Church*, Pt. III; Calvin, *Institutes*, Bk. IV, i, 8–12) ; but it was surely not made explicit enough. Accordingly, in modern times the church has become simply one more institution in society, characterized, doubtless, by these marks, but having little real relevance to the life of the world and the on-going movement of history.

claiming here, of course, that the future prospects of God's kingdom among men depend entirely on what men in the church do; that would be to forget that history, and especially the church, are under a sovereign Lord. But insofar as God is accomplishing his objectives through the church, he is working with human beings who must make their decisions and carry out their work according to their best understanding of what is required. It is necessary for Christians to make clear to themselves, then, what is fundamentally required of them (by God) that his work may be carried on by and through them.

What does and must the church do so as to keep clearly before herself her true basis and task? The source of the church's life, I have argued throughout these pages, is double. The ultimate foundation of her existence is the God who is creator of the world and its lord; the empirical ground of her existence is the historical movement, tracing back to Moses and before, which culminated in the ministry and death of Jesus and the birth of the Christian community. Though these two must be distinguished from each other, they are not really separable. For the church comes to know her God through precisely this history and he is identified to her as the God and Father of Jesus Christ; conversely, the special significance of this history to the church is not merely that it is *her* history, but rather that it is the story of the "mighty acts" of God. If the church is to discern correctly her work in the world as a present historical agent of God's purposes, she will continuously and repeatedly have to remember this history from whence she came and attend to this ultimate Agent who is working through it. Should she lose sight of either, she will lose both. But she dare not confuse the finite course of history with its sovereign Lord, lest she fall into a mere henotheistic idolatry of her own past and fail to serve the Lord who is transforming that past into a new and unforeseen future.

It is in her "religious" functions, for the most part—in such activities as worship and prayer, meditation and Bible study—that the attempt is made most straightforwardly and directly to focus on these foundations of the church's life. Worship, with its confession of sin before God, its praise of and gratitude to God, its listening for God's word spoken in the present moment, is a disciplined attempt to draw attention away from everything created and finite and focus it on the Creator and Lord.

It should be obvious why some such frequent discipline is essential if the church is to be the church. Men are beings filled with finite desires of all sorts and their lives are immersed in a world of finite objects. The Creator of the world never directly confronts them, or is seen or experienced by them.[8] One can easily devote his whole life to the pursuit of finite goods and values and forget entirely that his true being and freedom are found only in relation to the ultimate source of all that is—this is the essence of all secular humanisms or naturalisms, whose pull upon men is admittedly strong. Or he can mistakenly devote himself to some particularly meaningful reality or value which he finds in experience or tradition, supposing it to be in fact the One High God—this is the essence of idolatry, and very easily leads to fanaticism. Of course there can be no guarantee that one will not fall into one or another of these forms of sinful bondage, but worship is an act in which the intention is to distinguish sharply between all things finite and God, thus making it possible to attend more certainly to him and his will. Such an activity is indispensable for that finite historical community which understands its mission to be the fulfilment of God's purposes among men.[9]

All worship, of course, consists of merely finite acts with finite images and objects in view and utilizing finite symbols. For this reason the activity of worship may, and frequently does, become perverted to an idolatrous devotion to some traditional meaning or liturgical form. Indeed, worship is perhaps more susceptible to such perversion than any other human activity precisely because of its religious intention and language: one may all too easily suppose

[8] "No one has ever seen God" (John 1:18).
[9] In this respect the position of those who advocate a "religionless" or "a-theological" Christianity is hardly intelligible. Christian faith without God is but one more—perhaps interesting, probably merely sentimental and foolish—form of humanism. If one believes man really to be alone in the universe, then he ought to say so openly and build his world-view accordingly. Doubtless some elements from the Christian tradition might be incorporated into such a perspective, and, if one busied himself particularly with those elements, he might convince himself that his position was "Christian." But the fundamental Christian claim—which is about God—would not, and necessarily could not, be included. In such a case to persist in calling one's position "Christian" would be at worst dishonest, at best very misleading, English usage.

that merely because he uses these religious forms he is in fact attending to God, and thus his very religiousness can shut off the possibility of perceiving his idolatry. One of the most significant features of the history of salvation from which Christian faith emerges has been the appearance again and again of prophetic protest against such false religiousness, calling men back to the ethically relevant worship of the true God.[10] In our own day the task of critically warning the church of her perennial tendency to slip into idolatry has fallen, in part, to the theologians, whose work involves continuous reassessment of the church's language and praxis.[11] But since the theologian can perform his task only if he, also, distinguishes carefully between God and everything finite, worship and theology can be said to complement and require each other.

The Christian community has not, however, understood God simply negatively, as one who transcends everything man can intend or utter, conceive or believe; it has believed in a God actively at work in the very history in which men live, directing its course in accordance with his purposes and revealing his nature and will within it. The basis of the church's existence, therefore, is not simply *God*, in some unmediated or direct sense; it is, rather, as with all

---

[10] *I hate, I despise your feasts,*
   and I take no delight in your solemn assemblies.
Even though you offer me your burnt offerings and cereal offerings,
   I will not accept them. . . .
But let justice roll down like waters,
   and righteousness like an everflowing stream. AMOS 5:21-24

Bring no more vain offerings;
   incense is an abomination to me. . . .
I cannot endure iniquity and solemn assembly.
Your new moons and your appointed feasts my soul hates;
they have become a burden to me,
I am weary of bearing them. ISAIAH 1:13-14

"Woe to you, scribes and Pharisees, hypocrites! for you tithe mint and dill and cummin, and have neglected the weightier matters of the law, justice and mercy and faith. . . . Woe to you, scribes and Pharisees, hypocrites! for you are like whitewashed tombs, which outwardly appear beautiful, but within they are full of dead men's bones and all uncleanness. So you also outwardly appear righteous to men, but within you are full of hypocrisy and iniquity" (Mt. 23:23, 27–28).

[11] Karl Barth, from his furious and prophetic *Römerbrief* onwards, has emphasized the sharp distinction between God and all else; similarly Paul Tillich, from his early essay on "Die Ueberwindung des Religionsbegriff in der Religionsphilosophie" (*Kantstudien* [1922], 27:446–469) to the more recent talk about the "God above God" in, *inter alia, The Courage To Be* (New Haven: Yale University Press, 1952), pp. 172ff.

other historical communities and institutions, the particular history through which she came to be, a history apprehended as the sequence of events through which God is remaking the entire human community. God, thus, is not known to faith merely abstractly as the transcendent one who can be characterized properly only by negative attributes; he is known, rather, as the God who is doing this particular redeeming and reconciling work in history, the Father of Jesus Christ. It is this dimension of historical concreteness and particularity in the church's life which prevents her worship from becoming abstract and empty, and which provides criteria for making particular historical discriminations and decisions. The church knows that she must be a reconciling rather than a dividing community, because she was established in and by a historical event in which God was reconciling the world (2 Cor. 5:19–20); she knows she must bind up men's wounds and forgive rather than hurt or destroy, since her master was a healer and one who forgave; she knows she should be willing to suffer and give up all claims on others, rather than strive for power and glory, "because Christ also suffered for [her], leaving [her] an example" (1 Pet. 2:21); she knows she ought even to love and serve her enemies (Mt. 5:44) rather than seek their punishment or destruction, for she is founded on an event in which God himself manifested forgiveness to his enemies (Rom. 5:10) through Jesus' forgiveness of those who were destroying him (Lk. 23:34). It is the particular history from which she comes, and especially the Christ-event culminating in the cross, that provides the church with the concrete knowledge of who God is and what he requires. If her life and work is to be the continuing vehicle of the will and work of *this* God, she will have to immerse herself continuously and repeatedly in this history and its climactic revelatory event. For here is where he has shown himself to man as he truly is, the Lord and Father who loves and forgives; and here he has shown man how he works to reconcile those alienated, through allowing himself to be wounded for their transgressions and bruised for their iniquities, so that through his own suffering and chastisement they are made whole (Isa. 53:5; 1 Pet. 2:21–25). Here and here alone is where the church learns over and over again that man's all-too-human and worldly desires and methods and goals are not God's, that God has turned upside down man's every conception of what he ought to do, and that men must participate in and accept this overwhelming transvaluation of values if they would worship and serve him.

This essential immersion in the events which are her concrete historical basis is ordinarily accomplished in the church in three ways, through reading and reflecting on scripture, through participation in a sacramental act, and through actual commitment and service.[12] Scripture, as we have seen, is the record of God's dealings with man and of man's gradually growing awareness of God. Through study of the Old Testament men learn how God has been working with them from the time of man's earliest memories and records, finally making possible his decisive self-manifestation in Christ; and also how badly men have misunderstood, how much they have resisted, and yet how they have gradually come to apprehend who God is. The Old Testament is indispensable for proper understanding of God's revelation in Christ because it contains the account of the long and painful historical preparation necessary before God's final act of self-manifestation was possible. Without the Old Testament Christian faith would hardly be understood as thoroughly historical and thus genuinely relevant to contemporary existence; faith would be condemned to some form of docetism or supernaturalism. Despite this, however, it is not until the New Testament that the report of God's definitive self-manifestation is given. Here, and here alone, are the documents through which the historical Jesus is encountered and in which is recorded the earliest interpretation of that encounter as revelatory of God. Without the New Testament, therefore, Christians would lack criteria for discriminating what is of real significance in the Old, and what is misleading or false; for it is only in the culmination or completion of a historical process that one can discern its real direction and meaning. New Testament and Old, thus, each interpret the other, though in quite different ways; and the church has rightly insisted that both belong in her canon.

12 It will be observed that whereas the first two of these are largely retrospective, being the concrete form in which the church keeps in view "the basis of her life and her task in history" (a, p. 482), the third has to do with the church's actual stance and work in the world (b, p. 482).

The Bible is used in many ways in the church but the justification of them all is the same: it is the medium through which the church is able to apprehend again and again, and to reconstruct, the history which has produced her and the events which provide her with norms by which to order her life. To this end Christians have always engaged in private devotional reading and study of the Bible; and the reading and interpretation of scripture have been built into communal worship. For protestantism, with its strong emphasis on the need of a historical norm to stand over against the church as a basis for criticism and correction of her life, scripture has been apprehended as indispensable to faith. When, however, this emphasis was carried to irrational extreme, and the very words of the Bible were made into absolute law for men's minds and actions, the authority of God was displaced by scripture in idolatrous perversion; it is little wonder that during the rise of liberalism and historical criticism this idol was found out and dethroned.

The loss of an adequate hermeneutical principle for discriminating between the significant and the unimportant or misleading in scripture made theological appropriation of the new historical methods and discoveries difficult for a time, although they were making available to the nineteenth and twentieth centuries an understanding of biblical history far more accurate and complete than previously possible. For a genuinely historical understanding of Christian faith, every such increase in knowledge of the history through which God was specially working is a gain. It is in large measure because of historical analysis and reconstruction that the biblical story can now be seen to be reporting an actual historical movement coming to decisive culmination in the appearance of Jesus of Nazareth.[13] Thus, historical criticism has become an indispensable aid to the use and proper understanding of the Bible in the modern church.

The Bible probably cannot, and undoubtedly should not, again

[13] I am not claiming here that this is the only way to read Hebrew history; there are of course Jewish and Moslem interpretations as well as various secular ones. What one takes to be the culmination or climax of a historical movement always depends in considerable measure on his point of view, since there are a variety of strands in every historical process, often working themselves out in diverse directions. But surely no one will deny that one such strand in Hebrew history reaches its zenith with Christ: that is the historical basis of the Christian theological claim.

become simply and directly the "word of God" for contemporary Christians as it was for many earlier generations; such language about scripture too easily identifies it uncritically with God's revelation. But as long as there is Christian faith, the Bible will be the indispensable medium through which his historical Word to man— Jesus Christ (John 1:1–18)—is appropriated. Unfortunately, in much uninformed private Bible study or meditation, as well as in the public exposition and interpretation of scripture by preachers and teachers who know better, the attitude toward the Bible is still determined too much by the traditional (and often bibliolatrous) protestant conception that in itself it is God's word. This leads, in believers, to misunderstanding of the meaning of the text as well as misapprehension of God's revelation; to knowledgeable unbelievers it appears to be sheer superstition or idolatry and is an artificial barrier often preventing their seeing the import of Jesus Christ. For Christian faith it is Jesus who is "the image of the invisible God" (Col. 1:15), not the Bible, and the significance of the latter is to be found only insofar as it mediates the former. If scripture is to perform effectively this indispensable mediatorial role—a function without which the church cannot retain sight and awareness of her true and proper basis and commission, and will thus cease being the church of Christ—in worship and meditation, preaching and teaching, churchmen must read it with proper historical understanding. When they do, its relevance for contemporary life, so often lost on modern Christians and nonChristians alike, may become evident.

The Bible is the *intellectual* medium through which the church's relation to her historical basis and foundation is repeatedly renewed; it is through the (primarily intellectual) acts of reading and reflecting and interpreting that the Bible is appropriated. But there are deeper levels of the self than consciousness, and Christian faith is not a mere appropriation of ideas; it involves a reorientation of the whole person. To effect this change the dramatic impact of a more direct participation in the climactic events of God's self-manifestation is necessary.

The sacrament of the Lord's Supper has this function of stirring the emotions and moving the will at deeper levels. This sacrament is, first of all, a reenactment of Jesus' last meal with his disciples (Mk. 14:12–26), done deliberately in remembrance of those last hours before his death and of his death itself (1 Cor. 11:23–26). It calls up, therefore, the intimate group in which Jesus was known best and of which he was master and teacher, and it invites the participation of each communicant in that group. The moment dramatized is not one of happy fellowship or even hopeful prospect; it is the moment of darkest self-consciousness in the group, occasioned by the expected imminence of Jesus' arrest and possible death. Jesus himself had intimated this would be his last meal: "I shall not drink again of the fruit of the vine until that day when I drink it new in the kingdom of God" (Mk. 14:25). And either he himself suggested, or the church in retrospect came to interpret, this last breaking of bread and drinking of wine as symbolic of his coming death. The participation with him, then, in this ordinary act providing bodily sustenance came to mean a participation in his very existence and fate. After his death and resurrection this ritual reenactment naturally was reinforced and loaded with memories of the crucifixion itself, so that the breaking of bread and drinking of wine no longer referred simply to that last meal, but to the actual body broken on the cross and blood shed there. "The cup of blessing which we bless, is it not a participation in the [shed] blood of Christ? The bread which we break, is it not a participation in the [broken] body of Christ?" (1 Cor. 10:16). Thus, the supper in which succeeding generations of Christians have participated has not signified merely the last moment of unity between Jesus and his friends; it has been a witnessing of and participation in the suffering and death of the man hanging helplessly on the cross. Through eating that supper together Christians have found a new and positive relation to God the Father[14] and a new unity with each other,[15] as well as a new hope for their future and that of all mankind, which at last will know the lordship of the One manifest in the crucified Jesus.[16] The sacramental enactment of the

[14] "This cup is the new covenant" (1 Cor. 11:25).
[15] "Because there is one loaf, we who are many are one body, for we all partake of the same loaf" (1 Cor. 10:17).
[16] "For as often as you eat this bread and drink the cup, you proclaim the Lord's death until he comes" (1 Cor. 11:26).

Lord's Supper has thus become a dramatic reenactment of the events on which the church is founded, in which each new generation of Christians may repeatedly participate.[17]

The sacrament of the Lord's Supper provides a necessary complement to biblical study. While the Bible supplies an interpretive framework of historical understanding without which the sacrament would be unintelligible and meaningless, the supper enables participation in the foundational events of Christian faith below the verbal and intellectual levels of the self. Together, word and sacrament may move and transform the whole man.

The interpretation of the Lord's Supper sketched here throws some light on the controversy between those who wish to speak of a special "real presence" of Christ in the sacrament and those who regard the supper as simply a "memorial" to his death, the elements being mere "symbols." Each party has seized one essential in the matter and exaggerated it to the point of seeming to exclude the other. Those who speak of Christ's "real presence" in the sacrament, or even of the "transubstantiation" of the elements, are surely correct in holding that the Lord's Supper is no mere commemorative exercise performed by Christians simply because of an arbitrary biblical command. On the contrary, in a very real sense the community here comes into renewed relationship with its ultimate foundation, and that not in some merely intellectualistic or doctrinal way (as the symbolic view suggests) but so as to affect the participants at levels of their being below consciousness. The very power and being of God the Father which came into human history through Christ is effective *ex opere operato* in the community in and through the sacrament. These elements hardly seem like everyday bread and wine,

[17] Cf. Teilhard de Chardin: "Christ died once in agony. Peter and Paul receive communion on such and such a day at a particular hour. But these different acts are only the diversely central points in which the continuity of a unique act is split up and fixed, in space and time, for our experience. In fact, from the beginning of the Messianic preparation, up till the Parousia, passing through the historic manifestation of Jesus and the phases of growth of His Church, a single event has been developing in the world: the Incarnation, realised, in each individual, through the Eucharist.

"All the communions of a life-time are one communion.

"All the communions of all men now living are one communion.

"All the communions of all men, present, past and future, are one communion" (*The Divine Milieu* [New York: Harper, 1960], p. 102).

then; since they feed the soul with the "bread of life," Jesus (John 6:35, 48), it seems quite proper to speak of his "real presence" in and through them, their mundane substance being transformed into his divine. As long as such expressions are understood to be poetic or mythical ways of speaking about the supper's effective re-presentation to faith of God's love and power, which was first definitively manifest on the cross, one should have little objection. But the terms used—"presence of Christ," "transubstantiation," "*ex opere operato*"—when taken literally, presuppose supernaturalistic notions of Jesus' resurrection and present life in the church which we have already found it necessary to reject, not to say a near magical view of the alleged special connection between the resurrected lord and the elements of bread and wine.

At this point we may profitably consider that interpretation which holds the supper to be principally a "memorial" to Jesus' death, made specially vivid and meaningful through the "symbols" of bread and wine. To the extent this terminology suggests that the sacrament is really no different from any other act of commemoration, its elements having a purely arbitrary connection with its meaning, it is clearly inadequate. For this commemoration is of the foundational events of a community's life, and participation in it renews once again the living effectiveness of that past in this present. In vividly confronting the church with the historical basis and purpose of her existence, it establishes her afresh in her proper life, so she can take up again the work assigned her. Through this "memorial," then, what might otherwise have fallen back into the dead past is kept effectively at work as living memory, and the symbols carrying this meaning of the past become channels of life for the community. Understood in this way, however, "memorial" and "symbol" are seen to be vehicles of the "real presence" of the One who is at once source and lord of the church, the God and Father of Jesus Christ. The language of "memorial" and the language of "real presence" thus complement and correct each other. A historicist theology can utilize and interpret both in its attempt to grasp the way in which the present church lives out of the saving events of her past, as she moves into an unknown future.

Word and sacrament ministering to intellect and feeling provide in complementary ways for the church's repeated reappropriation of her foundation and purpose. But man is more than mind and heart; he is also active will. And the church is not in history merely to understand and enjoy; she has a task to perform. The repeated reappropriation of her basis and life is not complete, therefore, until she enters again upon her proper work in the world as the historical agent through which God is transforming human society into his kingdom. Too often the church has wanted to savor the Gospel of God's forgiveness and the comfort of the sacrament without taking up the burden of her ministry, involving, as it must, self-sacrifice and suffering. "If any man would come after me, let him deny himself and take up his cross and follow me" (Mk. 8:34). The task which the church has been given is nothing less than the continuing mediation of God's reconciling love among men in order that his kingdom finally come. What this means can be seen from the historical paradigm which is the church's final norm, the death of Jesus. God's method of overcoming evil and hatred is not primarily through retaliation nor even the establishment of justice through legal order: it involves, rather, bearing the evil inflicted by others in hope that the offenders, overwhelmed by forgiveness and love, might finally respond in kind.[18] To take up one's cross means to make the pattern of life manifest in Jesus' march to the cross his own, so that the reconciling power working through Jesus might also work through him. "Have this mind among yourselves, which you have in Christ Jesus, who . . . emptied himself, taking the form of a servant, . . . and became obedient unto death" (Phil. 2:5–8).

The church has not often found it easy to shape the form of her

---

[18] "For one is approved if, mindful of God, he endures pain while suffering unjustly. For what credit is it, if when you do wrong and are beaten for it you take it patiently? But if when you do right and suffer for it you take it patiently, you have God's approval. For to this you have been called, because Christ also suffered for you, leaving you an example, that you should follow in his steps" (1 Pet. 2:19–21). Cf. also Jesus' word: "If you love those who love you, what credit is that to you? For even sinners love those who love them. And if you do good to those who do good to you, what credit is that to you? For even sinners do the same. And if you lend to those from whom you hope to receive, what credit is that to you? Even sinners lend to sinners, to receive as much again. But love your enemies, and do good, and lend, expecting nothing in return; and your reward will be great, and you will be sons of the Most High; for he is kind to the ungrateful and the selfish" (Lk. 6:32–35).

existence in the world after this image. She has succumbed again and again to the desire for human approbation and glory, wealth and power; and she has succeeded often in winning these—to her shame! Even when her motives have been higher, and her concern has been the well-being of the underprivileged or the suffering of the oppressed, she has seldom been content to model her attack against these evils on the strategy of her professed Lord. Worldly methods of power and pressure always seem more likely to bring results than the naiveté of a love that "bears all things, believes all things, hopes all things, endures all things" (1 Cor. 13:7), even though one may declare his belief that such love "never ends" (13:8) since it is the very nature of God himself (1 John 4:7–12, 16). And so the church repeatedly thinks it necessary and proper to find what she supposes are better ways for carrying on God's work of reconciliation in the world than the way he himself revealed to be his own. Thus, her action proves her claimed appropriation and reappropriation of the historical foundations of her life in word and sacrament to be truncated and spurious; it is clear she has not really grasped in faith what God has manifested and done in her history, because she is herself unwilling to be the agency of further action according to his mode. But to think she can be a "hearer" of the word only, and not a "doer," is to deceive herself (Jas. 1:22).

This is not the place to spell out in detail what the church's non-resistant[19] stance in the world would involve. Obviously, there can and will be great differences here in judgment about specific problems and programs of action, tactical and strategic details, etc. The church must engage in a great variety of activities through which she is enabled both to witness verbally to the world about God's love and

19 For theological justification of the use of this obviously loaded word, see above, pp. 219ff. It is worth observing that in an early writing Paul Tillich characterized the proper stance of the church in much the same way: ". . . the 'church' in the essential meaning of the word . . . [is] a community which is determined explicitly and representatively by those transcendental norms, in which the renunciation of power is expressed. A church which really was what it essentially should be, would be the institution in which the structure of power in society and being would be transcended. It would be the visible conquest of the ontology of power. . . . A people can become the 'church' only if in an unexpected historical moment it is seized as a whole by the transcendental idea and for its sake renounces power. Such an event would be one of the great turning points of human history; it would perhaps create 'mankind'" (The Interpretation of History [New York: Scribners, 1936], pp. 199–200).

mercy and to express in concrete acts and institutions of service that same mercy and love. She needs to engage in prophetic criticism not only of the social and moral evils in society, but also of the methods which misguided worldly men too often use, in the supposition that they will bring good in their wake. She must continuously experiment with novel forms of ministry and service which can bring God's reconciling love and power into newly emerging patterns of life and institutional structures, as well as into hitherto untouched corners of society and culture. For such diverse tasks a variety of talents is necessary, and it should occasion no surprise that there is much difference of opinion as to what is proper and right. This is all to the good. But there cannot be disagreement about the church's stance in the world: she is to manifest the same "form of the servant" (Phil. 2:7) which was seen in her Lord's march to the cross. Only in this way is she indeed the "body" of which he is the "head" (Eph. 5:23,30), and thus the continuing agency of God's salvation of men.

If the church's basic character and stance in the world are as definitely prescribed by her historical foundation as I have argued here, she exists only when she consists of a body of committed believers. The church is called to work against the grain of ordinary human desire, to give herself even to her enemies, not seek to save or establish herself (Mk. 8:35). Only those who really believed history to be under the sovereignty of One who is himself self-sacrificial love could honestly and wholeheartedly take up such a task. The extreme demands of the Gospel of the cross are surely utter foolishness from the perspective of ordinary human understanding of what is going on in the world and what powers are actually determining the course of history (1 Cor. 1:18–25). Because (as noted above) the church necessarily has certain "religious" functions, she has often been considered simply the standard institution in Western society for those who happen to have "religious" needs or interests; and too often she has gathered her people on this basis rather than as believers committed to her historical mission. I will not argue here the question whether in our increasingly secular society the need for a merely "religious" institution is now past; that may or may not be so. Suffice it to say that it is not the church's primary business to be that institution. For the church has been given the special mission of historically mediating God's reconciling love in the world; that, and that alone, is her proper work. As the task force of the kingdom, she must be a well-disciplined body of committed believers, willing to give anything and everything for the cause.

In view of this, whatever values may have devolved from the practice of infant baptism in the past, little justification can be given for it today.[20] For the pedobaptist position presupposes that all members of the community will as a matter of course become Christians.[21] But that assumption is neither factually true nor a proper theological expectation. Christian faith goes counter to many ordinary beliefs and makes the most strenuous demands on its adherents. There is little reason to suppose more than a few will ever be seriously interested in it, not to say committed to it.[22] One would expect, therefore, that the rite initiating new members[23] into this community would be performed only upon those mature enough to understand, and willing voluntarily to accept, the heavy demands laid upon them by the work of the people of God in history. Moreover, if, after a period of

[20] It is significant that, especially in Europe, an increasing number of churchmen are coming to this position. Not only is it advocated by theologians of the stature of Karl Barth (see *The Teaching of the Church Regarding Baptism* [London: SCM Press, 1948]); one hears with increasing frequency of clergymen, and even bishops, who can no longer in good conscience baptize infants, though their church tradition has always prescribed this.

[21] I do not consider here the biblical arguments on this problem at all, since, for the position being developed in these pages, the question of how and where one draws the boundary lines of the church is primarily a tactical one, not to be resolved by appeal to biblical authority. Suffice it to note that New Testament practice and teaching appear to support the position of "believers' baptism" much more definitely and clearly than the other.

[22] "For the gate is narrow and the way is hard, that leads to life, and those who find it are few" (Mt. 7:14).

[23] The sacramental position developed earlier in this chapter clearly requires that greater weight be placed on the Lord's Supper than on baptism, since the supper's function is to relate the living community to the formative events of its past, and is thus very important to the continuing life of the community, while baptism has significance largely as an initiatory rite. That such a ceremony emphasizing the new situation of the individual when he enters the community is important, and that washing with water is a particularly appropriate way to symbolize the significance of this event, I would not dispute at all. But the form of the rite here is surely of less significance than the question whether the community is to be defined as consisting of mature and committed believers; accordingly it is on that issue that emphasis has been placed in the text. Baptism could be given theological significance commensurate with that of the Lord's Supper only on the basis of a heteronomously traditionalistic and/or quasi-magical sacramentalism.

life within the church, individuals were unwilling to continue giving themselves to her special work, the community should expect, and they should be willing, to sever their relationship with her. It is hardly possible for anything less than a disciplined body to be the historical agent of God's work in the world.[24]

Having stressed the church's historical task in the world, given her and defined for her by the salvation-history from which she came, it is necessary to conclude with a few qualifying remarks. The church must not be understood as simply and merely the continuation of a particular historical current. She has, as we have observed, a double foundation: the activity of God, and a particular history. It is just as necessary that her rootage in the transcendent One qualify her understanding of the import of her history, as that her concrete history interpret to her the purposes and nature of God. Thus, the church's history, like any other historical stream, must be understood as finite, limited, relative, subject to correction and qualification by other points of view and modes of life. To absolutize her history, or the understanding of herself, her world, and her task emergent from that history, would be obvious idolatry, confusing the created with the Creator. Moreover, it would be an especially dangerous idolatry, for it would tend to conceal its true character from its adherents by claiming the authority of the One High God, believed to have acted in and through this history and these traditions. All too often Christian churches have claimed for themselves and their beliefs or practices this ultimate authority and truth which belongs to God alone—and thus they have become merely another expression of human pride and sin rather than the community of faith.[25] From this self-idolatrous position fanaticism and the repres-

---

[24] I am not arguing for some kind of vindictive and legalistic order within the community's life, of course. That would hardly be likely on the very open theological basis herein developed. I am saying rather that the church, like any other group committed to a cause and with a specific job to perform, can do her work effectively only if her members are actually interested in and willing to work at the task. In a large proportion of contemporary churches that is scarcely the case.

[25] It is this self-idolatrous puffing-up, of course, that is at the root of many of the divisions within Christianity, each denomination claiming for itself a kind of absoluteness and truth that belongs properly to God alone. Claims that only certain types of ordination or ministry, or certain baptismal forms, or certain creedal formulations, or certain sorts of vocations, are right and proper and to be followed within the church, while

sion of diverse points of view easily develop; and not infrequently inhuman atrocities have been committed in the name of the God of love and mercy. The servant of man has become a tyrant.

There is no guarantee that such misinterpretation of the Christian faith will not continue. Since the Christian understanding of God is closely bound to a concrete history, there is always danger of confusion between historically relative custom or belief and God's requirements. The only protection is to remember that what this concrete history really means is, first, that it is *God* who is God, and men are only his creatures and children, and, hopefully, his loyal servants; and second, that this God is one who wins his way among men not by acts of compulsion but by bearing the burdens inflicted by others, out of love for them.

As was noted earlier in this chapter, it is the intention preeminently of the act of worship to reorient men's prevailing anthropocentrism and egocentrism into an existence centered in and on God. Worship, as the deliberate attempt to focus on and attend to the transcendent One, is a continuing necessity in the church. Those who would argue that "God is dead" and the church must now live out of her history alone are in effect asking the church to give up the possibility of radical self-criticism and be content simply to perpetuate tradition. But if the church has any distinctiveness at all among human institutions and communities, it arises precisely from her awareness that loyalty to her history and traditions is not sufficient, that her ultimate Lord must be the creator God who is working out his purposes in history and who even now may be demanding something new, of which no man in the past dreamed.[26] This kind of freedom from one's past and present, from all that one knows or believes in,[27] is possible only for a radically theocentric orientation. It is the purpose of the act of worship continually to re-create this possibility of openness to the God beyond all tradition. Worship is

others are proscribed or even anathematized, are all exemplary cases in point. All such questions should be considered tactical and strategic, and thus subject to revision and qualification when a new situation requires it.

[26] "From this time forth I make you hear new things, hidden things which you have not known. They are created now, not long ago; before today you have never heard of them, lest you should say, 'Behold, I knew them'" (Isa. 48:6–7).

[27] Cf. 1 Cor. 7:17–31.

thus an essential corrective to an unrelieved historicism, just as the serious appropriation of the foundational events of Christian faith is a necessary corrective to abstract devotionalism.

Even playing christocentrism off against theocentrism, and *vice versa*, and attempting serious theological evaluation and criticism of both, does not, of course, guarantee men's faithfulness to God. Nothing men can do could provide such a guarantee; if it could, they would be their own masters, not God, and all the Christian claims would be false. The Christian community lives in the confidence that, despite all her failures, the gracious Lord and merciful Father whom she worships as God will redeem her work and use it to the upbuilding of his kingdom. It is God who has created her; God will surely sustain and use her for his ends. Hence, though she can make no claims for herself, her work, or even her faith, she can continue to work at her tasks in confidence and hope. "For by grace you have been saved through faith; and this is not your own doing, it is the gift of God—not because of works, lest any man should boast. For we are his workmanship, created in Christ Jesus for good works, which God prepared beforehand, that we should walk in them" (Eph. 2:8–10).

32 / The Individual Disciple[1]

In a radically historical understanding of man consideration of the nature and meaning of individual existence cannot come until the end. This is not because the individual self is not deemed interesting or important; on the contrary, as we have seen, the birth and growth into maturity of free and creative selves is one of the major ends of the creation of man. However, because in certain respects individuality is the last and most delicate flower of the historical process, it is dependent at every point on sustenance from structures produced in prior and contemporary historical development. No one is a "self-made man," least of all those who have managed to find some modicum of success in highly complex societies like our own; if anyone qualified for this title, it would have to be some early predecessor of *homo sapiens,* who could at least provide for his own physical needs fairly well. A modern civilized man could not survive for any extended period without the continued work and help of unnumbered other human beings supplying his daily needs through the complex organization of society. The greatest genius, whether in music or mathematics or industrial management, can exercise and develop his special aptitudes and interests only in a society which has sufficient need for his particular talents to have already developed traditions in which he can be properly trained and institutions within which he can effectively mature and work. Moreover, the community must be willing to continue supporting him in, and rewarding him for, his special labors by making provision for his

[1] Chs. 4 and 5 of my *The Context of Decision* (New York: Abingdon, 1961) deal directly with certain aspects of the problem of the individual not discussed here; indeed, one might say the whole book is an attempt to sketch out the situation of the individual.

other needs. It took mankind many hundreds of generations to develop differentiated and mature cultural traditions and highly complex patterns of social organization which would make possible the emergence and sustenance of the sort of free individual we often take more or less for granted. In a similar way, as has been observed throughout these pages, it was only through a long and painful history that the awareness of who God is and what he requires of man could arise; and it was because of the appearance of a community responsive to that revelation, which became its bearer and propagator within history, that Christian faith became a historical possibility for individuals. However much one may wish to emphasize that faith is God's own gift to each person, it remains true that every individual Christian receives his faith historically through the Christian community and traditions that have (directly or indirectly) nurtured and educated him. Individual Christian existence, therefore, must always be understood as possible only within the matrix of communal Christian existence and history.[2]

This places in proper perspective the situation of the individual Christian: he should be understood first of all as member of this community and participant in this history which preceded and helped constitute him and which will continue its work long after he is gone. His work should be seen, then, as an expression of the life of this community and as a further contribution to this developing history: his individual life has its meaning and definition within this communal existence. This does not mean that the individual is called upon to give up his proper identity and destiny that the group might be enhanced, that, as in a totalitarian social order, a particular and parochial society becomes everything and the individual nothing.

[2] I am of course not arguing here that only those who are formally members of churches can be Christians; that thesis is too absurd to discuss. Nor am I meaning to deny that some men, either repelled or completely untouched by living Christian communities, may become believers through, say, simply reading the Bible. I am contending that Christian faith is a live option in our culture—with Bibles readily available in good translation, books and articles interpretive of Christian ideas accessible on every hand, and much of the terminology and conceptuality of Christian faith a part of the cultural atmosphere breathed by every Western man—only because there has been and continues to be a living Christian community which accepts the events of biblical history as the very acts of God. It is because of the continuing life and work of this community that Christian faith is historically available to us in a way that, for example, druid or orphic religion is not.

Such a conclusion would be false on two counts. (a) The church, though doubtless a particular historical community, is potentially and by intention the universal human community which includes within itself all nations, races, and peoples; only to the extent that she is in fact moving toward this end is her parochialism in process of being transcended and devotion to her justified. Only as the historical-community-becoming-the-kingdom-of-God can she rightfully claim that each member's life and work should be an expression of and contribution to her own historical task. (b) As the historical-community-becoming-the-kingdom-of-God the church is the community in which, above all, the various kinds of enslavement and destruction of men are being overcome through the provision of a historical context informed by God's love, within which free persons can emerge and find fulfilment. Defining one's life by and devoting one's self to the work of this community, therefore, does not really stultify or thwart one's individual potentialities; on the contrary, it provides precisely the proper context for finding genuine self-realization and meaning. ". . . seek ye first the kingdom of God, and his righteousness; and all these things shall be added unto you" (Mt. 6:33 KJ).

These implications of Christian faith are not often taken seriously in thinking through the ethic of individual discipleship. In protestantism the church has become a largely voluntary—which is to say, optional and nonessential—association of autonomous individuals. Though most might agree that the individual should take important problems and plans to God in prayer, few would consider such "personal" matters as a vocational decision or the choice of a marriage-partner, or even one's behavior in business or the world generally, as the proper concern of the Christian community; and most would strongly resist any suggestion that "individual freedom" should be in any way infringed at such points by the church: that is supposedly a matter between each individual and God. Such pietistic declarations are obviously very misleading if the mode of God's presence with and activity toward man is actually the *Heilsgeschichte* which has produced, and is borne in history by, the church. In such a case the more important the decision, the less could it be viewed a matter of only private interest; the community which is the very body of Christ in the world quite properly has an interest in, and should in some measure guide and even discipline its members in regard to, matters of moment. If Paul's strong metaphor interpreting the church as like a physical body (1 Cor. 12:12–27) is appropriate at all, then surely whatever is of considerable import to individual members is a proper concern for the entire community. Christians are not atomic individuals, but are so bound together in God's work transforming history that they can properly be described as "one body in Christ, and individually members one of another" (Rom. 12:5). The implications of this extraordinary unity of the community in its work in history, transcending the desires or decisions of individual members, were taken so seriously in at least some quarters of the early church that it was believed that particular judgments of the community might bind its members for all eternity.[3]

What, now, can this radical community-centeredness mean for individual discipleship in our own time? Clearly it makes some sense and has some justification only in a genuinely committed Christian community (see Chapter 31). To the degree that the congregation as a whole—and each member of it—appreciates and seeks to serve God's work on earth, the individual members can well afford to submit their personal problems and decisions to the common judgment of the group; to the extent that the church and its task in the world is viewed as a matter of peripheral interest and spare-time concern, in competition with Rotary Club and Sunday morning fishing—as it certainly is in much contemporary life—it would be meaningless or wrong to develop an individual ethic on this basis. It is clear, then, that a first concern of contemporary Christians should be the reconstruction of the church so she can function as this kind of unified and disciplined community.

Apart from concrete participation in the actual work of such a committed community, the life of the individual believer will necessarily be lonely and truncated. For he must supply in imagination

---

[3] In regard to disagreements between an individual member and the community as a whole, Matthew reports a word of Jesus as declaring: "whatever you [i.e., the church] bind on earth shall be bound in heaven, and whatever you loose on earth shall be loosed in heaven" (18:18; cf. 16:18–19).

the historical context for his life that is missing in actuality. There is a great danger here that faith will become abstract and otherworldly and lose its concrete historical relevance. Thus, he may create, perhaps, a conception of the "invisible" church or the "latent" church as the true "spiritual community" in contrast with the inadequate "visible" or "manifest" community of believers to which he belongs (Tillich), or faith may be seen as a "hidden" or "secret" gift of God to his elect, to which all empirical or experiential evidences are irrelevant (Bultmann); he may hold that the true "knight of faith" rides "incognito" through the world (Kierkegaard), or that this world has been completely redeemed or transformed by God though to the naked eye nothing seems changed (Barth); little wonder that at last he may conclude with Nietzsche that "God is dead" (e.g., Van Buren). With such maneuvers the whole concrete and historical meaning of Christian faith tends to evaporate into the irrelevancies and vague abstractions of an empty spiritualism and otherworldliness; and it is forgotten that the central prayer of Christian faith is that God's will be done and, indeed, that his kingdom come "on earth as . . . in heaven" (Mt. 6:10). If faith is to be relevant to actual concrete existence, one dare not substitute creations of the theological imagination, however interesting, for the real historical situation and movement in which he lives; and yet apprehension and understanding of this empirical world will have to be informed and interpreted by the theological imagination. That is, one will have to learn to see God's historical working and moving within the actual empirical communities and movements (including the church) in which he in fact participates, so that it becomes possible to act in response to and accord with God's own historical action.

With God's suffering love manifest on the cross one's only criterion of Christian—that is, genuinely redemptive—action, and the hoped-for kingdom of God's love discerned as the ultimate goal or end toward which all such action is tending, one must judge which movements and activities are the actual historical expression of God's redemptive work today, and find his proper place there. This may mean for some immersion in the civil rights movement; for others, actively working to prevent the outbreak of a third world war; for yet others, continuous service in the institutions of business, government, or education which sustain such community as we now have and are necessary vehicles for its further enhancement. All such work, of course, is highly ambiguous. Though it may often be redemptive and reconciling in its methods and effects, it is seldom explicitly and deliberately informed by God's reconciling love as revealed on the cross. Consequently, the institution or movement does not evaluate itself by that standard and does not understand itself as directly responsible to that God, though it may have been influenced in many ways by the values and traditions of Christian humanitarianism. Since precisely the cross must be the criterion for the Christian, his participation in such movements, however worthy they may be, can never be without reservation. His work within them must always be directed toward support of their constructive and reconciling activity, always critical of their tendencies to self-idolatry and the uses of this-worldly types of power which tend to perpetuate or even increase the chaos in human affairs. Doubtless it is not possible to keep oneself "unspotted from the world" (Jas. 1:27) when participating actively in frankly nonChristian institutions and movements with expressly secular objectives; but in a historical situation like our own, where redemptive and reconciling work is often carried on through channels outside the church, the Christian has little option but to contribute whatever he is able, however ambiguous the circumstances.

This diffusion of God's redemptive activity through many cultural vehicles, few of which acknowledge any explicitly Christian commitment, holds serious dangers for the Christian cause as a definite historical movement. It means Christians are scattered in most of their work instead of self-consciously cooperating in one body; it means they are engaged in a great variety of tasks and movements, many at cross-purposes with each other. In such situations it is easy for even the most thoughtful and devoted to begin too easily to identify the specific goals of the particular historical movement in which he is involved with the kingdom of God. The result is "the evil that good men do" in their too self-righteous supposition that the work they are doing is good not only in their own eyes, but in God's as well. Fanatical crusades for this or that finite objective lead only to an increase in the warring and chaos of human affairs, not to their amelioration. The way in which the often very worthy goals of a nation become easily corrupted into nationalism and imperialism and thus disruptive of the movement toward God's kingdom has become so clear to all as almost to be trite. Yet in the obviously growing sense of American destiny in the struggle with "communism" precisely the same appears to be happening once again. In such situations, however painful it be, the duty of the Christian may be to withdraw his support of and participation in the cause within which he has worked, and protest in the name of the God who does "not resist one who is evil" but turns "the other cheek" when struck (Mt. 5:39). For only in this way can one keep clear in his own mind, as well as in his witness to others, that a Christian's proper business here on earth is "the ministry of reconciliation" (2 Cor. 5:18), a ministry rather difficult to perform with bayonet or bomb.

The question here at issue ultimately comes to this: Has the nature and will and mode of reconciling action of the Lord of all history been revealed in the cross of Christ or not? Has the criterion and standard for the Christian stance in the world been given through these historical events or has it not? If it has, then it is clear that however difficult and ambiguous may be certain situations, and however socially or historically necessary certain policies or courses of action, a Christian will know these are not *his* particular task in history, for his task must always be construction and reconciliation, performed according to the model of God's own act in Christ. If the Christ-event cannot be taken as the proper criterion of one's stance here, then the whole basis of Christian faith and action is destroyed, for the ultimate reality with which men have to do is evidently no more decisively manifest in the cross than elsewhere; and men must govern their lives, therefore, simply through exercise of their best human judgment.

It would be a great help to each believer were he a member of a congregation committed to the ultimate authority of the cross for faith and life. Then he could bring the problems of his participation in the ambiguities of life to his fellows for counsel and help, and they could mutually strengthen each other. But in our time the church seldom if ever provides in this way a real "home" for those actively at work in an alien world; all too often the church herself is so much compromised by her involvement with the world that she is "neither cold nor hot" (Rev. 3:15) on any matters of real consequence. Even her attempts through word and sacrament to remind her members of the historical events through which God has definitively made himself known are so formal and pallid as to be of little effect. The individual believer, seriously concerned to do God's will, must therefore supply for himself much of the study of and reflection upon the salvation-history by which he is oriented and from which he lives. This means, of course, not only Bible reading and meditation, but grappling with the best historical and theological commentaries and reconstructions as well. But most of all it involves willingness, renewed again and again, to reorder his life according to the image of the man hanging on the cross, no matter what the cost.

There is little in the world round about us—whether in the church or out—to commend such radical faith in God. On every side we see the power of strictly human affairs; there seems little reason to believe our history is governed by a God of love. The summons of life appears to be to our own survival and achievement, not sacrifice of self for fellows. And the teaching of experience is that the spoils go to the victor. Even in the church one is counseled to be "realistic" and to recognize the role that sheer power plays, and must play, in human affairs. There is no disputing this worldly wisdom and realism. If life is to be based primarily in what man can learn through his experience and science, and the values of existence are to be defined by his best insight into the powers that govern nature and his own destiny, then man will, and should, follow some such course. The mark that distinguishes *homo sapiens* from lower forms of life is precisely a measure of freedom and power over himself and his world gained through gradually cumulating insight and wisdom; and in the last several hundred years he has managed to develop techniques for directly checking and increasing his knowledge. Surely the most reasonable life—and thus the right life for a rational being—is one ordered as far as possible by the fruit of man's pursuit of knowledge.

All this is true if man is alone in the world. If the only purposive activity is that wrought by man's deliberate decisions, and the only rational insight into and understanding of order and meaning is that accomplished through his intellect, then man must finally determine his own course, plot his own destiny, give life and history whatever order and meaning he can create. Under these circumstances human existence can be joyous and full, as well as tragic and chaotic, and always it will carry the reward of knowing that he himself has made it what it is. There is a proud and glorious vision of man in every great humanism, and it should be honored and respected, however tragic be the final outcome of man's course when he and all his works are finally obliterated as "omnipotent matter rolls on its relentless way."[4] But if man is not alone in the universe, this whole picture is misleading. If there is rational will behind all that is, and a purposive activity moving the course of cosmic and human history, then the ultimate realism for man will not necessarily coincide with what can be distilled from human experience and discerned by human intellect. Rather, it will be existence lived in accord with those ultimate structuring purposes which, however hidden to man's natural eye, actually undergird the world in which he lives, guaranteeing the future into which it, and he, are moving. If the world is all, men had best be humanists; if there is a God, the only rational and meaningful life will be fulfilment of his will.

Until the process has run its course, purposive activity cannot be discerned by mere external inspection; it will be discovered, as has been observed repeatedly in these pages, only if the agent chooses to disclose it. Whether there is a God at work in this world could not be known until the end of history (if then)—unless he should deliberately reveal himself and his purposes to man. The Christian claim, of course, is that in and through the history of the Hebrews the ultimate Agent in the world has been revealing to the finite agents he created that he is and who he is, and that at last he succeeded in

---

[4] Bertrand Russell, "A Free Man's Worship," in *Mysticism and Logic* (Garden City: Doubleday Anchor Books, 1917), p. 54.

making "known to us in all wisdom and insight the mystery of his will, according to his purpose which he set forth in Christ" (Eph. 1:9). There is no way of empirically confirming whether in fact God is ordering the history of the world so that "when the time should have fully come, . . . everything in heaven and on earth should be unified in Christ" (1:10 Goodspeed), the final order and power in the universe being that manifest on the cross. Indeed the evidence of experience and the conclusions of science seem to point to the contrary. One is faced then, finally, with a choice: whether to order one's life on the assumption that man is the only purposive agent in the world, or in the confidence that the universe is ultimately the expression of the will and work of God, who revealed himself and his purposes in the suffering and death of a man 2000 years ago.[5]

We are not concerned in these pages to examine the implications of the negative choice, that of unfaith; our interest here is in the positive meaning of the Christian claim that there is an ultimate purposive Agent at work in and through the world, and he has made himself and his purposes known through Jesus Christ. If one accepted this position, he would be foolish and irrational not to base his whole existence on that revelation, regardless of seeming empirical evidence to the contrary; for he would understand that all other evidence, however compelling it might be in man's eyes, must be measured and evaluated with reference to this disclosure of the ultimate reality with which man has to do. If there is a sovereign Creator of the world, the mere opinions of the creature can never determine what is authentic and meaningful created existence; that will already have been determined by the Creator. And if in his mercy he has made known his will, that men might appropriate it as the basis of their existence so far as that is self-created and self-ordered, it would be insane indeed to prefer man's superficial insights and opinions. "For the foolishness of God is wiser than men" (1 Cor. 1:25).

Were one genuinely to believe that through the ministry, and par-

---

[5] I do not mean arbitrarily to exclude the possibility of an ultimate Purposer who has either not made himself known at all or has revealed himself elsewhere in some other way; these of course are possibilities. But our concern here is with the *Christian* claim and its implications. If that claim is true, then the ultimate criteria for understanding God's will are found in the cross.

ticularly the death, of this Jesus from Nazareth God was rescuing mankind from the chaos into which it had fallen and definitively making himself known, then he would have no choice but to take up his cross and follow Jesus (Mk. 8:34), that is, to order his existence in the same mode as Jesus' was ordered in his suffering and death.[6] This may seem sheer simplemindedness or stupidity from the point of view of worldly knowledge. "The word of the cross" may be, as Paul declared, "folly to those who are perishing, but to us who are being saved it is the power of God" (1 Cor. 1:18)—that is, the very basis for all life, that on which one can depend absolutely. The transvaluating miracle which is so difficult for men to believe is that God's "power" is really "made perfect in [and through human] weakness" (2 Cor. 12:9), that it is really through what is weak and lowly and despised in the world that God overcomes the strong and powerful (1 Cor. 1:27–28), that it is when one is weak that he is really strong (2 Cor. 12:10). If such notions are true—and this is surely what it means to say that ultimate reality is manifest in that image of a helpless man dying on a cross—then man's contrary worldly wisdom is sheer foolishness (1 Cor. 1:20); and life should no longer be ordered by it. To be Christian one must bring whatever the world teaches, whether it call its teaching secular or garb it in the pious robes of the church, to the cross for evaluation. If this image of weakness and suffering and death requires one to reject as specious and misleading what even his churchly brethren say, then so be it! The ultimate standard of judgment and life is the historical event through which God has decisively manifested himself, and no traditions or interpretations of men must be allowed to displace it.[7]

---

6 "Therefore be imitators of God, as beloved children. And walk in love, as Christ loved us and gave himself up for us" (Eph. 5:1–2; cf. also 1 Cor. 11:1; Phil. 2:5–8; 1 Pet. 2:19–23).

7 By this stress on the "nonresistant" stance of the Christian in the world, I do not mean to imply either that one can avoid recognizing (and taking responsibility for) the great diversity of evils in human life or that he may propose a simpleminded single solution to all problems. Human life is much too complex for that, and Christian love is much too concerned to speak relevantly precisely to those complexities. But, however the detailed problems of Christian ethics are finally worked out, it is the ultimate normativeness of the cross which marks an ethic as distinctively "Christian," and theological ethics may not lose sight of that fact. (I have dealt briefly elsewhere with certain of the problems which the cross' radical inversion of values raises for ethics. See my *The*

One could live by this foolishness of the cross only if he were able to believe it really the "foolishness of God" himself, for only then is it "wiser than men" (1 Cor. 1:25). Only if this upsetting of man's natural instincts and valuations corresponds to the primary and thus the ultimate ordering power in the universe is it reasonable and meaningful. But "If God be for us, who can be against us?" (Rom. 8:31 KJ). Christian existence stakes everything on God, the God manifest in the cross of Jesus. Christian life is based on faith in him, and on what he will yet do to bring creation into accord with his will, not simply on the empirical evidence which is now visible to the eye of man.[8] Because God is believed to be the Lord of all history, he can be trusted finally to overcome completely the hostile powers that have turned history into chaotic warfare, concealing its true character and meaning; indeed, precisely in the cross he has shown how he is even now overcoming the most hostile and intractable of all these powers, the sinful human heart. In confidence that the forgiving love which has broken into their hearts will finally also overcome even the most disobedient, believers can offer themselves as agents of that redeeming love in the present historical situation.

Therefore, my brothers, I implore you by God's mercy to offer your very selves to him: a living sacrifice, dedicated and fit for his acceptance, for such is the worship which you, as rational creatures, should offer. Adapt yourselves no longer to the pattern of this present world, but let your minds be remade and your whole nature thus transformed. Then you will be able to discern the will of God, and to know what is good, acceptable, and perfect.

ROMANS 12:1–2, NEB footnote

In this context we can properly consider the difficult problem of personal prayer. In traditional discussions of this subject, where a

---

Context of Decision [New York: Abingdon, 1961], Ch. 5, and "Nonresistance and Responsibility," in *Concern*, A Pamphlet Series for Questions of Christian Renewal [Scottdale, Pennsylvania: Herald Press, November, 1958], 6:5–29).

[8] "Now faith is the substance of things hoped for, the evidence of things not seen" (Heb. 11:1 KJ; cf. 1 Cor. 2:9–10).

mythological view of the world was taken for granted, an almost magical conception of prayer was often presented on the basis of more or less literal interpretation of individual scriptural texts.[9] Thus, it was believed that God acted from time to time to give those faithful to him special gifts or to rescue them from difficult circumstances into which they had come, simply because they called on him for help. Devotion nourished on the Psalms, with their emphasis that God cares especially for the faithful and punishes the wicked,[10] served to strengthen such interpretations of prayer.

> *Because he cleaves to me in love, I will deliver him;*
> *I will protect him, because he knows my name.*
> *When he calls to me, I will answer him.*
>
> PSALM 91:14-15

Such views, however pious and sanctioned by tradition, must be subjected to serious theological criticism. In the first place, they presuppose far too simple a conception of the way God acts in the world. God is here seen as a more or less arbitrary agent who directly "causes" particular events to happen in history without regard to the natural and historical processes that have preceded or will follow upon them, rather than as the Lord of history in its entirety, whose purposes give history its peculiar structure and movement (and in this sense are causative, even though they are not the "efficient" causes of particular events).[11] Such a mythological view actually undercuts understanding history as unified and governed by God's purposive action, through picturing it as a series of essentially atomic and independent events, and through portraying God himself as arbitrary and thus unreliable. Interpretations of prayer which are premised on this picture of God as the great champion and leader of "our side," who comes to the aid of his friends whenever they need him, are surely more an expression of the desperate unbelief which is

---

9 E.g., "Ask, and it will be given you" (Mt. 7:7); "And whatever you ask in prayer, you will receive, if you have faith" (21:22); "Whatever you ask in my name, I will do it" (John 14:13; cf. 15:16).

10 Cf. Pss. 1, 5, 7, 9, 10, etc.

11 For further discussion, see the interpretation of "special" and "general" providence, above, Ch. 21.

always crying for a genie to accomplish its own will than of faith in the One who is Creator and Lord of all that is.

In the second place, such traditional interpretations of prayer too seldom remember that, for the Christian, God's definitive manifestation of himself was in Jesus' crucifixion, and, therefore, that whatever prayer might mean in general, for Christian faith it must be prayer to *this* God whose "power is made perfect in weakness" (2 Cor. 12:9). Prayer to such a God would hardly expect special manifestations of divine power in behalf of the faithful. Indeed, faithfulness to God would be precisely that stance which, when it discovered its wish to be powerful and dominating, would submit itself in weakness and humility to the powers of this world. And the only real "answer" to prayer to be expected from such a God might well be strength to be in this way "weak" in the world, and thus a vehicle of the divine reconciling will. It is worth remembering in this connection that Jesus' prayer that God "remove this cup from me" (Mk. 14:36) was not followed by the Father's sending legions of angels nor even by words of comfort from heaven; it was succeeded rather by a moment even blacker in its apparent lack of divine presence and power: "My God, my God, why hast thou forsaken me?" (15:34). And it is precisely this moment of greatest weakness and suffering, darkness and death, that Christian faith has taken to be the very paradigm of God's activity in the world.[12] Prayer based on such an understanding of God will hardly be a chatty and informal conversation with a "man upstairs" about our problems and plans.

This does not mean there is no place for prayer in Christian faith. On the contrary. If the Christian claim means anything, it surely means that God is personal: his definitive self-revelation was

---

[12] Cf. Bonhoeffer: "God allows himself to be edged out of the world and on to the cross. God is weak and powerless in the world, and that is exactly the way, the only way, in which he can be with us and help us. Matthew 8:17 makes it crystal clear that it is not by his omnipotence that Christ helps us, but by his weakness and suffering.

"This is the decisive difference between Christianity and all religions. Man's religiosity makes him look in his distress to the power of God in the world; he uses God as a *Deus ex machina*. The Bible however directs him to the powerlessness and suffering of God; only a suffering God can help. . . . The process . . . by which the world came of age was an abandonment of a false conception of God, and a clearing of the decks for the God of the Bible, who conquers power and space in the world by his weakness. This must be the starting point for our 'worldly' interpretation" (*Prisoner for God* [New York: Macmillan, 1953], p. 164).

in a personal life and death, and the most characteristic Christian appellation for God is "Father." (This entire volume is devoted to showing the appropriateness of conceiving God in personal terms.) In speech person confronts person directly and openly; language is the very stuff of interpersonal relationship. It is most appropriate, therefore, that men should use words when consciously and deliberately acknowledging and participating in the supreme interpersonal relationship which grounds and sustains their being. Prayer is just this personal stance toward the personal God. In distinction from theology, which is *reflection* on God and man's relation to him, prayer is consciously *living* in that relation. All the life of faith, so far as it is made verbal and conscious, is thus prayer. Speeches of confession and thanksgiving, cries for guidance and help, words of praise and words of resignation, are simply the moments that make overt and explicit the personal character of the grounding relationships in which one stands at all times. Doubtless, just as explicit worship is necessary on regular occasions to remind the community of faith repeatedly that its life must be oriented beyond everything finite, so also deliberate prayer helps protect the believer from forgetting that God is personal and purposive.[13] But also, just as the activity of worship must always be corrected and qualified by continuous reference to the concrete history of salvation, so Christian prayer must always be "in Jesus' name."[14] That is, the act of praying must always be corrected and qualified by remembering it is not just any God, but the God manifest in Christ, to whom the prayer is addressed; and this means in turn that not just any stance (or any prayer) will be appropriate, but only one in which the believer expresses the spirit of the crucified one.[15] When it is genuinely Christian, deliberate prayer may

[13] Jesus' own example of personal trust in and fellowship with God, as well as his words about prayer, have always been very meaningful to Christians in this respect. "Ask, and it will be given you; seek, and you will find; knock, and it will be opened to you. For every one who asks receives, and he who seeks finds, and to him who knocks it will be opened. Or what man of you, if his son asks him for a loaf, will give him a stone?" (Mt. 7:7-9).

[14] John 14:13-14; 15:16; 16:23-24.

[15] The theological inconsistency of much allegedly Christian prayer is expressed superbly in Mark Twain's ironical war prayer: "O Lord our Father, our young patriots, idols of our hearts, go forth to battle—be Thou near them! With them—in spirit—we also go forth from the sweet peace of our beloved firesides to smite the foe. O Lord our

help to bring the condition and task of the believer to an intense focus which frees him from bondage to his own desires that he may become the vehicle of God's purposes: "Father, all things are possible to thee; remove this cup from me; yet not what I will, but what thou wilt" (Mk. 14:36).

Christian life, existence under the lordship of Christ, is simply the creature living in fulfilment of the purposes of his Creator. Christian faith is that trust in God, the Father of Jesus Christ, which makes such life possible and truly desirable.

God, help us to tear their soldiers to bloody shreds with our shells; help us to cover their smiling fields with the pale forms of their patriot dead; help us to drown the thunder of the guns with the shrieks of their wounded, writhing in pain; help us to lay waste their humble homes with a hurricane of fire; help us to wring the hearts of their unoffending widows with unavailing grief; help us to turn them out roofless with their little children to wander unfriended the wastes of their desolated land in rags and hunger and thirst, sports of the sun flames of summer and the icy winds of winter, broken in spirit, worn with travail, imploring Thee for the refuge of the grave and denied it—for our sakes who adore Thee, Lord, blast their hopes, blight their lives, protract their bitter pilgrimage, make heavy their steps, water their way with their tears, stain the white snow with the blood of their wounded feet! We ask it, in the spirit of love, of Him Who is the Source of Love, and Who is the ever-faithful refuge and friend of all that are sore beset and seek His aid with humble and contrite hearts. Amen." (Reprinted in *Mark Twain at Your Fingertips*, ed. C. T. Harnsberger [New York: Beechhurst Press, Inc., 1948], pp. 502f.)

33 / Jesus Christ as Prophet, Priest, and King

Since Christian theology is essentially the attempt to grasp the meaning of Christ, it is appropriate that in concluding now we return once again to christology. We need not consider here the way in which Christ is the center of the Christian *Weltanschauung*, and how it is possible to define and interpret all else with reference to him: these themes have occupied us sufficiently in the body of this book. It remains to consider what existential content faith in Christ can have for the modern believer. Some might think that after all that has been said here about the false and misleading character of traditional interpretations—for example, of Jesus' resurrection, or of God's providential guidance, or of prayer—much of the warmth and meaning often engendered in traditional Christian faith by the sense of Christ's personal presence and God's loving care must by now be destroyed; though history and life are here viewed as governed by God's purposes, man may seem largely alone and on his own in the cosmic historical process. To some extent such conclusions are true, and this is, perhaps, a gain for realism at the expense of the sentimentality of much traditional piety. But it would be a serious misunderstanding of the implications of the historicistic perspective being sketched here if this criticism were not carefully qualified.

From biblical times onward Christian existence was believed permeated by the "mystical presence" of Christ among the faithful: "I am the vine, you are the branches" (John 15:5); "Christ is the head of the church, . . . we are members of his body" (Eph. 5:23, 30) ; ". . . where two or three are gathered in my name, there am I in the midst of them" (Mt. 18:20). There is an appropriate and meta-physically defensible sense in which it remains possible and indeed requisite to speak in some such ways as these of the continuing ac-tivity of Christ in his church. Doubtless many events disappear into a dead past and will be forgotten forever, but the genuinely signifi-cant happenings of the past live on as effective powers in the present. It would be strange indeed if that person-event, through which the living Lord of all history became supremely manifest and effective, and through which he continues to work within history, could be spoken of only as dead and gone. It is true, of course, that the flesh-and-blood man Jesus was crucified by his enemies and can no longer properly be said to be present; but Christian faith has always af-firmed this. Yet for faith his spirit is still alive and at work and his impact is felt. We can explore the sense in which Christ continues to be present in and to the church through a consideration of the mean-ing of three titles traditionally applied to him: "prophet," "priest," and "king."[1] I hope to show in these concluding interpretive remarks that the existential meaning of the present theological perspective, despite tremendous differences, does remain in significant continuity with the faith of that "great cloud of witnesses" (Heb. 12:1) who made such affirmations in the past.

The term "prophet" was one of the earliest titles applied to Jesus and was probably used by himself (cf., e.g., Mk. 6:4, Lk. 13:33). Jesus was God's prophet, his mouthpiece, the one who brings God's word to men and pronounces it in their midst. "The time is fulfilled, and the kingdom of God is at hand; repent, and believe in the gos-pel" (Mk. 1:15). God's sovereignty is now at last about to be fully established in rebellious human existence. Men therefore must re-pent their evil ways, turn radically about with love to God and neigh-

---

[1] The application of these Old Testament types to the interpretation of Christ's person apparently goes back to Eusebius of Caesarea but it became a common pattern only with the Reformation. "The origin of this threefold type is to be found in the literal meaning of the word Christ, it being regarded as legitimate to refer the anointing with the Holy Spirit not only to the anointing of a king, but also to that of a priest and of a prophet" (A. Ritschl, *Justification and Reconciliation* [Edinburgh: T. & T. Clark, 1900], p. 417).

bors (Mk. 12:28–34), loving even enemies as themselves (Mt. 5:43–47; Lk. 6:27–35). For it is with just this kind of radical love that God has come to us; and we are to "be perfect, as [our] heavenly Father is perfect" (Mt. 5:48).

We are not concerned at this point to examine these teachings for their ethical import, or to consider the question whether, after all, they are not so extreme as to be utterly impracticable. Our attention here is on another question: What concrete existential content does faith in Jesus Christ have? In what sense can it be said that he continues to be present and effective in the church and the lives of believers? The category "prophet" throws some light on this question. For it is evident that for many, though it is centuries since Jesus walked this earth, his words, nevertheless, impinge as prophetic pronouncements: they cut into men as the very demand of God. Jesus is thus for many twentieth-century men, as he was for the men of his own time, the mouthpiece of the Lord of heaven and earth.

"Thou shalt love thy neighbor as thyself!" We cannot help but apprehend this word as a real demand upon us, as a command to us. This is what we ought to do! We should serve our fellows as we now seek to serve ourselves. The sense of guilt which one feels as he considers how far he falls short of this standard is existential evidence that this word is experienced as a veritable command of the Creator. These words of Jesus, then, fall on one's ears as words of a prophet of God.

"Love thy enemies!" Here even more vividly the prophetic word of Jesus brings one into searing encounter with the Almighty. For however little we in fact love our neighbors, we can see it would be prudential so to do—at least to some extent—in order to create a good society. Mutual cooperation and service make sense from an enlightened human point of view and are commended in every ethic. But to love one's enemies?—that would be not only ridiculous and foolhardy but probably suicidal. Every man, we say, has a "natural right" to self-defense against those who seek to enslave or destroy him. Sacrificing oneself out of love for the evil and tyrannical who walk this earth is surely more than one need or can do. But we protest too much. For we know, somehow, that we would be better men did we love those who hate us; we cannot escape the essential rightness of this command either. Jesus' prophetic word confronts us with the command of God, with the ultimate purpose of our existence and the final destiny to which he is bringing us.

Hence, if we ask the question, How is the man Jesus effective in our lives now? one answer must be: through his prophecy. Let there be no mistake here: Jesus is not acknowledged as prophet because he is believed to be a superior being, the Son of God come down from heaven. His words burn into one's being as alive and prophetic, cutting with the fire of an absolute demand—whether one will or no, whether one is consciously Christian or not—and thus the living God himself continues to speak in and through this Jesus, and his spirit comes to life again in our midst.

Of course it is clear that Jesus' words do not have this effect on all; some laugh at his moral demands as foolish sentimentality. But that is not our concern here. We are considering the significance of these words' vitality for those whom they convict of guilt, for those whom God *does* confront through Jesus the prophet. Though Jesus of Nazareth has long been dead, his words preserved in the New Testament and transmitted and interpreted by the church continue to speak to many as God's living voice. And thus, not in some mysterious or mystical way, but in and through contemporary moral experience, Jesus the man remains the one through whom the almighty God is present and known.

However, the Christian community has never been satisfied to regard Jesus simply as prophet. For one thing, there are many other prophets through whom God is mediated in similar ways, and this title, therefore, hardly does justice to his uniqueness. For another, the confrontation with God of which the Christian is aware is not merely through Jesus' *words* (however important these may be); it penetrates to the deep strata of the self. So another title, "priest," has often been employed. A priest, in a much fuller sense than a prophet, is intentionally a mediator between God and man. The priest, as the official representative of the religious institution, is one whose person symbolizes man's estrangement from God, on the one hand, and the means of overcoming that estrangement, on the other.

The very separation in human existence between sacred and secular is evidence of an awareness that everyday life is not lived continuously under God's lordship but is filled with self-assertion and attempts at autonomy, with rebellion against the Creator. Hence, men set aside special times and special places and special kinds of activity through which to compensate, as it were, for this lack in ordinary existence. The real meaning of the religious institution in every culture, as one alongside others, is the symbolic pointing of its very existence to the fact that men are alienated from the ground of their being, are sinners before God, and hence need special procedures to reestablish the proper and necessary relationship.[2] The priest is thus one who symbolizes in his person both man's estrangement from God and his hesitant rededication to him.

Now in what sense is Jesus *priest* for contemporary men? How does this title suggest the living God's continuous presence through that man of twenty centuries ago? It is not enough to characterize Christians as those who are impressed and convicted by Jesus' prophetic words: if this were all to be said, Christians would be men with guilt heightened to despair, for their consciousness would be determined by awareness of failure to fulfill God's demands. The impact of Jesus is much deeper than the symbol "prophet" suggests. It has to do with the fundamental set or stance of the self, the very orientation of one's being. Somehow, however incredible it may seem—especially when their failures are considered—Christians apprehend themselves as no longer radically estranged from God, cut off from the ground of existence. On the contrary, they have been met with the healing efficacy of God's merciful love and know themselves to be forgiven.

Doubtless this is a great mystery. But the church has never been able to escape from the conviction that this penetration of her present existence with God's love and mercy is directly connected with the powerful historical drama of Calvary, the march to the cross of that man so devoted to God's will. His act of self-sacrifice, with all its blood and gore, has imprinted itself on her consciousness as the appropriate and thus the ultimate symbol mediating God's true char-

---

[2] Cf. Paul Tillich, *The Protestant Era* (Chicago: University of Chicago Press, 1948), p. 59.

acter and action. "God shows his love for us in that while we were yet sinners Christ died for us" (Rom. 5:8). Only in actions—and not mere words—does the self fully commit and thus unveil itself; and thus only an act—and no mere word—could properly symbolize, and thus be the historical vehicle of, God's love for man. Free submission to total destruction is the one act in which the self is given entirely: when such an act is appropriated, not only is consciousness affected (as it might be with a mere word) but the deepest recesses of selfhood may be impressed and transformed and recreated. Jesus' act of full self-giving thus becomes much more than a parable or example of the hidden God's disposition toward man; it is God's own act radically recreating us.[3] Christian faith apprehends the cross not only as a profound act of human self-sacrifice; the transformation it effects is so revolutionary that it is received as the true symbol—and thus the actual *channel* into human existence—of God's love making men into "new creations" (2 Cor. 5:17).

This new life is experienced in many ways within the Christian community. For some it comes in and through reenactment of the closing hours of Jesus' life in the sacrament of the church; for others through hearing the Gospel of God's forgiveness. For some the patience and forbearance and love of friend or stranger in an hour of need mediates the new relation to the love in which man's being is grounded; for others, meditation on the words and ministry of Jesus. Appropriated in such variant ways, the new life naturally is interpreted with similar diversity. Some speak of the inspiration of Jesus' moral example giving new strength to face their problems; others prefer the bolder image of the infusion of God's grace into the soul through the "medicine of immortality" (Ignatius), the Eucharist; still others find they must confess "the saving power of the blood of

[3] "For God simply to have told or shown the evil world how much He loved it would have been a most ineffectual thing. Something had to be *done*. . . . If God in Christ simply said the most powerful word about His goodwill, His placability, and His readiness to forgive, . . . God would be *saying* more than He *did*. . . . If Christ were simply an expression of God's love, then His cross would simply be what is called an object-lesson of God's love. . . . The work of Christ would be only something educational, or at most impressive [and] . . . as soon as the lesson had been learnt, the work of Christ might be left behind" (P. T. Forsyth, *The Work of Christ* [London: Independent Press, Ltd., 1910], pp. 57, 100–102).

the lamb." But the central point is this: however experienced and expressed, each is witness to the more abundant life found in relation to this Jesus Christ, through whom, all are convinced, their relationship to the ultimate reality with which men have to do has been transformed. Where before there had been alienation, there is now rapport; where there had been bondage and despair, there is freedom and hope; in place of death, life. Full human existence for the first time is a genuine possibility. In the community of love and self-giving which emerges in response to God's act on the cross one comes to sense something of the glorious freedom and creativity which is our proper destiny.

In this situation it is not enough to speak of Jesus merely as "prophet." And so he is called "priest." Moreover, as the writer of Hebrews says (Chapters 5, 7), he is the one high priest who does away with all other mediators as superfluous and distracting: here is God himself come into human existence to heal our estrangement.

If we now ask again, How is that Jesus of two thousand years ago still alive and present with us? our second answer may be: as our "priest," as the one through whose cross God's love and forgiveness become real, making possible new life within us and new love and forgiveness to our fellows. Of course, not everyone is prepared to make this confession; indeed, some will scoff at the claim that the foundation of the universe, the ground of all being, *loves*. But in the church God's love and forgiveness—supremely expressed in the cross of Jesus of Nazareth—is again and again appropriated as ultimate reality. Though Jesus himself died nearly two thousand years ago, this historically manifested love is present in no mysterious or mystical or superstitious sense. In the proclamation of the Gospel, in participation in the sacraments, in the devotion of personal lives of true self-sacrifice, the healing and saving power to become authentic persons—the "love of God"—is present and known. And thus the cross of Christ is no mere event in some dead past; it is a living reality and power in men's lives. In the life—and especially the death—of the man Jesus, God's mercy and forgiveness broke into human history; the vivid memory in our souls of the cross is thus the actual living power of God's love in our lives.

The conception of Jesus as prophet interprets one dimension of this living presence of the past: he is the one who brought—and continues to bring—the word of God, convicting us of sin and challenging us to live under God's sovereignty. A second dimension is emphasized through the conception of Jesus as priest, pointing to awareness that the transformation of our existence from its characteristic anthropocentrism to an actual beginning of life in God's kingdom is rooted in Jesus' self-giving on the cross and repeatedly renewed by reference to and reappropriation of that event. Those for whom in this way Jesus is prophet and priest, find themselves now in a drastically altered situation: they are living in anticipation of the historically coming kingdom of God and thus must always act in conscious and deliberate response to God's lordship, as mediated and made real, given meaning and content, by Jesus Christ. This fact calls for use of one more interpretive analogy, Jesus Christ as *King*. Christians know they must live as servants and disciples of Christ, as those who acknowledge him to be living Lord of their lives. Is it still possible or meaningful to make this traditional confession?

It is not necessary here to develop the symbol "king" with reference to the human situation from which it emerges; the idea is essentially the same as "lord" (discussed above, Chapter 9). The important thing to notice is that we are now saying not simply that *God* is lord and king but that *Jesus Christ* is king and lord. What is the meaning of this different formulation? The general answer to this question ought to be apparent. In the first place, there is no difference: by "Jesus Christ," as has been noted repeatedly, is meant *the presence of God to man in history;* this name refers to the specific concreteness and content which the word "God" has for Christians. Hence, to say that Jesus Christ is king is not to suggest that some being other than God be given ultimate loyalty, but rather that precisely this God made known in Jesus is acknowledged as Lord. In the second place, this formulation—Jesus Christ is king—emphasizes that to speak of God as Lord is not to say something abstract and empty. God's lordship is known in a very concrete and specific way: *in the demand we become disciples of Christ.*

This is a hard doctrine. For it involves the awareness that we must be willing to sacrifice natural and normal human wishes, desires, and needs for the sake of Jesus and the kingdom he is ushering in. Jesus himself is reported to have said:

> Do not think that I have come to bring peace on earth; I have not come to bring peace, but a sword. For I have come to set a man against his father, and a daughter against her mother, and a daughter-in-law against her mother-in-law; and a man's foes will be those of his own household. He who loves father or mother more than me is not worthy of me; and he who loves son or daughter more than me is not worthy of me; and he who does not take his cross and follow me is not worthy of me. He who finds his life will lose it, and he who loses his life for my sake will find it.
>
> MATTHEW 10:34–39

The last two chapters suggested something of what discipleship to Jesus involves, with its implications about loving neighbor and enemy even to the point of turning the other cheek and blessing those who curse us (Mt. 5:38ff.). For now, we will simply observe how radical and self-condemning is one's statement when he says, "God is Lord," "Christ is king." For these phrases imply one's relation to God through Christ consists not only of the unavoidable dimension of guilt, arising when the prophet's word is heard, nor the beneficial dimension of new at-one-ment with God through our high priest: it must also consist in *voluntary obedience*, the conscious and deliberate giving up of one's own desires and will to become freely (in Paul's word) a *slave* of Christ the king (cf. Rom. 1:1), taking "every thought captive to obey Christ, being ready to punish every disobedience" (2 Cor. 10:5–6) in oneself. To confess Christ as lord and king is to lay on oneself this obligation of complete subservience to him. "Worthy is the Lamb, the Lamb that was slain, to receive all power and wealth, wisdom and might, honour and glory and praise!" (Rev. 5:12   NEB).

Christ, then, is not only prophet and priest for Christian faith; he must also be king and lord of Christian lives. From the perspective now attained we may look again at the christological titles examined earlier (Chapter 13)—"servant," "word," and "son." Those symbols can be honestly and rightly employed only in that orientation which has been taken captive by Christ. That is, only from the perspective which finds the center and norm of existence in him—which knows him as prophet, priest, and king—is it meaningful and significant to call him servant, word, and son of God. But for those who discover themselves thus oriented—that is, for Christian believers—it is not possible to avoid employing some such titles, for they denote and interpret the metaphysical significance of Christian faith. To be oriented by and toward a historical person or event is to regard that event or person as the real source and basis and revelation of one's true being and meaning. The designation of Jesus Christ as servant of God, word of God, and finally son of God, expresses just this implication: he is the presence to man of God himself. No mere human being—though Jesus is certainly that as well—is man's king: the Creator of the heavens and the earth, the foundation of all reality, the living God, is present here. In Jesus of Nazareth—life, death, and resurrection—the ultimate limit of our being has definitively manifested himself as personal love. For faith, therefore, Christ is the veritable center of history: the culmination of all preceding *Heils-geschichte*, the breaking-in of God's eschatological kingdom, the final norm and criterion of all authentic value, meaning, and reality. He is "the Alpha and the Omega, the beginning and the end . . . , who is and who was and who is to come, the Almighty" (Rev. 21:6; 1:8).

Indexes

INDEX OF SUBJECTS

INDEX OF NAMES

INDEX OF SCRIPTURAL REFERENCES

Index of Subjects

Index of Names

Index of Scriptural References